Copyright N. Y. S. E.

The Façade of the New York Stock Exchange

THE WORK
OF THE
STOCK EXCHANGE

By

J. EDWARD MEEKER, M.A.
Economist to New York Stock Exchange

THE RONALD PRESS COMPANY
NEW YORK

PREFACE

During the past half-century the entire machinery of production, transportation, and distribution by which modern civilization is fundamentally sustained, has grown both in the volume of its transactions and in the complexity of its mechanism with a speed altogether unparalleled in history. Particularly in our own new and still unsettled country, so relentlessly swift an evolution in these respects has been experienced that public opinion and public knowledge have by no means kept pace with it. Thus, even if we do not quite misunderstand the financial institutions and methods of today, we are nevertheless only too prone to judge them by the standards of an economic America which already has largely ceased to exist. This dangerous tendency of public understanding to lag far behind the economic progress of the nation was, indeed, clearly stated some decades ago by W. G. Sumner in the following terms: "Our scientific knowledge of the laws which govern the life of man in society must keep pace with this development, or we shall find our social tasks grow faster than our knowledge of social science, and our society will break to pieces under the burden."

After the acute economic convulsions which have resulted from the war, it is more than ever important to make available to the entire reading public of the United States accurate and dependable information concerning all parts of the economic structure of the nation. To this gigantic educational task many published economic studies and many far-sighted institutions of learning have already bent their efforts. Such an educational movement should, of course, include a careful consideration of the present-day money and securities markets. Especially in the instance of the New York Stock Exchange a wider and more accurate knowledge on the part of the public is desirable. Indeed, this institution has in the past evoked a literature scanty out of all proportion to its importance—a natural result, it may be, of the average broker's strenuous preoccupation with the burdens of his business there. Because of the inclusion here of considerable material concerning the Stock Exchange never before published, the author is perhaps justified in the hope that the present study may place before the general public a more complete and correct picture of a great and often misunderstood American institution.

The task of describing simply and yet with some degree of thoroughness the actual operations of this vast market place in securities is not without its peculiar difficulties. Indeed, it is typical of the extreme complexity of our entire modern economic system that an adequate account even of one of its component parts cannot easily be compressed within the covers of a single book. As a matter of fact, many volumes as large as the present one would be needed for an exhaustive analysis of all the stock market's methods, functions, services, and relationships. It is to be hoped that in the near future such specialized economic studies in the more detailed and abstruse phases of the Stock Exchange may be made. In the meantime the present work, being intended merely as an introduction to this extensive and little understood subject, has been written with the aim of being readable rather than of being ponderously exhaustive or tediously subtle. Thus, lest it should dull the interest of the more general reader, considerable statistical, technical, and corollary material has been included in a series of appendices, where the closer student may refer to it. In addition, a bibliography, based upon the pioneer work of Professor S. S. Huebner, has been prepared as an aid to that further research into an interesting and relatively neglected economic field which the author cannot here pretend to undertake.

The attempt has been made to develop the general theme of the book cumulatively, from its simpler to its more complex aspects. Accordingly, Chapters I and II are introductory in character; Chapters III to XIII describe the contemporary machinery of the Stock Exchange; and Chapters XIV to XVIII deal in broader terms with the economic significance of the machinery thus described. Unfortunately the general subject matter provided by the Stock Exchange, even apart from its mere extensiveness, is exceedingly intricate, and so closely interwoven as stubbornly to resist this inevitable separation into successive chapters. For this reason, cross-references have been constantly employed to correlate material which, owing to this chapter structure, has been separated in the course of writing. In some cases these cross-references are by chapters only. In addition, a general index of names and topics has been prepared to enable ready reference to all subjects discussed in the book.

The writer's task has not been made any easier by the constant development now occurring within the Stock Exchange system itself—a development which naturally implies many changes in the details of its operation. The present volume has almost literally been written in the shadow of the mounting steel girders which will soon uphold an extensive addition to the Stock Exchange building. With the completion of this structure, its present securities market may be expected to undergo further change and expansion, the specific effects of which can be only feebly and uncertainly forecast in these pages. In consequence there is the likelihood that the present account of the Stock Exchange may by that time become somewhat obsolete in its details. Yet in this respect the present volume must risk the inevitable penalty to be paid by all such attempts to describe with any degree of permanency, living institutions pulsating with the changes of progress. Throughout its long history the New York Stock Exchange has constantly adapted its methods to suit the swiftly expanding economic conditions in the nation which it has served, and if a description of its operations must be delayed until no further possibility of change remains it would cease to be of value to any but the historian. Moreover, the fundamental economic principles upon which its business rests have not and will not change, however rapidly or considerably its detailed methods may. Meanwhile the readers of these pages can always inform themselves with respect to new features in the Stock Exchange by communicating with the secretary of the Committee on Library.

Finally, the many controversial questions with which the whole subject of financial economics abounds have wherever possible been avoided, for the writer claims no adherence to any particular school of economic thought, nor has he any desire, by producing either a panegyric or polemic, to enter into controversy for its own sake. Yet certain mooted problems have inevitably stood in his path, and they have been met with such fairness and practical knowledge of the subject as the author possesses. It is doubtless too much to think that all economists will agree with the views expressed in the present volume, for thus far no economic work of like nature has ever enjoyed so happy a fate. Enough will have been done if he has described and explained the machinery and the functions of the Exchange simply and clearly, without bandying abstractions, or employing the cloudy and impotent metaphysics into which economic controversy only too often degenerates.

The present study is in no sense an official publication of the Stock Exchange, nor does it bear any official indorsement by that body. Much of the information contained and opinions expressed herein have been derived from the personal experience of the author as economist to the New York Stock Exchange, and for these included statements and opinions he, of course, assumes complete and sole responsibility. Previous writers upon the Exchange and its economic functions have, however, been constantly cited, and many valuable and suggestive quotations from former students of securities markets purposely included. The chief source books of the present study may be found in the table of references, and much material of value has also been obtained from various other books, pamphlets, and articles included in the general bibliography. An even greater acknowledgment, however, must be made to many of the officials and members of the Stock Exchange, as well as to other men of long experience in the financial metropolis, who have with such unfailing generosity placed their valuable time and expert knowledge at the author's disposal in connection with the inevitably complex and technical problems which he has necessarily encountered. Specific acknowledgment would unfortunately prove entirely too lengthy to permit of inclusion here.

J. EDWARD MEEKER.

New York,
February 24, 1922

CONTENTS

LIST OF ILLUSTRATIONS

TABLE OF REFERENCES

The principal sources employed in the present volume are indicated in the footnotes and appendices by the following abbreviated titles:

CONSTITUTION — "Constitution of the New York Stock Exchange, and Resolutions adopted by the Governing Committee," 1921.

EMERY — "Ten Years' Regulation of the Stock Exchange in Germany," by Professor H. C. Emery. Included in "Regulation of the Stock Exchange" (*vide sub*), p. 822. Appeared originally in *Yale Review* for May, 1908.

HUGHES REPORT — "Report of the Governor's Committee on Speculation in Securities and Commodities," 1909. Included in "Van Antwerp," p. 415, and "Regulation of the Stock Exchange," p. 797.

MARTIN — "The New York Stock Exchange," by H. S. Martin, 1919.

MONEY TRUST INVESTIGATION — "Investigation of Financial and Monetary Conditions in the United States under Resolutions Nos. 429 and 504 before the Subcommittee of the Committee on Banking and Currency," 1912.

NOBLE — "The New York Stock Exchange in the Crisis of 1914," by ex-President H. G. S. Noble, 1915.

PRATT — "The Work of Wall Street," by S. S. Pratt, 3d ed., 1921.

REGULATION OF THE STOCK EXCHANGE — "Hearings before the Committee on Banking and Currency, United States Senate, on S. 3895 a bill to prevent the use of the mails and of the telegraph in furtherance of fraudulent and harmful transactions on Stock Exchanges," 1914.

STREIT "Term Settlements: a Study of Clearing and Settling Security Contracts on Foreign Stock Exchanges" (pamphlet), by S. F. Streit, President Stock Clearing Corporation. 1920.

VAN ANTWERP "The Stock Exchange from Within," by W. C. Van Antwerp, 1913.

THE WORK
OF THE
STOCK EXCHANGE

CHAPTER I

THE EVOLUTION OF SECURITIES

Two Main Classes of Securities

The many indispensable services performed for American business and society by the New York Stock Exchange cannot be adequately explained until the real nature of the securities which find their principal market on its floor is first understood.

Securities, in the Stock Exchange meaning of the term, may be broadly classified as either governmental or corporate, according to whether they are created by public and political, or private business organizations. In consequence, a brief preliminary sketch is called for here of the development of government financing on the one hand, and of the origin and present economic significance of the modern stock corporation on the other. Inasmuch as political stability has always been a necessary prerequisite to the higher organization and expression of business enterprise, it is only natural that as a rule the extensive issue of government securities should have occurred the earlier in point of historical evolution. To this topic of governmental financing by means of security issues, then, we should first give our attention.

The primary purpose of government, speaking generally, is and has from the earliest times been to protect the governed. The administrators of a governmental organization, which in the nature of things is not constructed so as to be run for a profit, must in the absence of earnings necessarily look to the levying of taxes upon the governed as its sole normal source of financial support.

Need of Government Financing

From the financial and economic standpoint the ideal and perfect government—which has never yet in human history been actually realized, and probably never will be—would be one whose income from taxation exactly equaled its expenditures. Constant attempts have been made to attain this ideal through budget systems and the like, and on certain rare occasions an approximate equilibrium between income and expense has temporarily been achieved. But, at least in the hazardous world of today, only a relative success in exactly balancing the government's books without a remaining surplus or debt seems practically possible; for both the expenses and the revenues of modern government are necessarily variables. Wars in particular may quite unexpectedly make necessary vast increases in governmental expenditure, while the actual sums to be realized through the various kinds of taxation in turn depend upon the veering course of economic development and business prosperity and other uncertain factors. In the absence, then, of an ability consistently to pay the current expenses of government out of its current taxation revenue, methods have naturally had to be devised for financing the sudden financial needs of government in excess of the amount of its current income.

Financing with the Printing Press

One age-old fallacy looking to this end—the printing of large quantities of irredeemable paper money—deserves passing comment here. To those innocently or wilfully ignorant of the intricate and delicate mechanism of modern currency such an inflation of the money system may seem a simple and obvious panacea. Their line of reasoning runs somewhat as follows: "The government needs money—money is produced by the printing press—therefore we should print what we need." While this is not the place to inquire into the complexities of modern currency sufficiently to explode this superficial but tremendously dangerous economic fallacy, it is enough to state that every government which has followed this primrose path of financing has in the end discovered it to be not only a highly dangerous but a completely futile expedient. A modern instance of the always disruptive effect of fiat money on the whole economic structure of civilization is afforded by the naive and lunatic policy of the Russian Bolsheviks in gleefully and deliberately printing more and more paper money until economic chaos resulted.

The truth is that there is no royal road to financing governments, simply because they are governments. No practical magic is available which will permit government officials to escape the same invariable economic laws that the individual constantly encounters in his check book. As with individuals, governments, when unable to obtain enough current revenue to pay current expenses, must contract debts, whose reduction can be effected only by a more favorable ratio between revenues and expenses in the future.

Former Methods of Government Borrowing

The exact methods employed by governments in borrowing money, along with the similar methods of business borrowing, have, of course, undergone great changes in the past two centuries. Governments were at first accustomed to borrow temporary funds from private lenders and pay off such loans by subsequent taxation. Thus, in the sixteenth and seventeenth centuries, the kings and queens of Europe constantly resorted to private money-lenders for accommodation. Such loans were frequently made on the pledged collateral of the royal jewels, or even on the assignment of a specified tax. The great but troublous reign of Elizabeth was financed through loans made by the Amsterdam money-lenders. Such transactions afford strong contrast with governmental financing as we know it today. The risks in such loans were large, for the proverbial honor of princes seemed only occasionally to extend to their debts. Interest rates had to be high enough to insure against the risk of royal repudiation. The element of patriotism in such loans was practically non-existent, nor was there yet any employment of them to promote international trade. Moreover the sums borrowed in this way were comparatively small, and could be made only for short periods, owing to the limited resources of private money-lenders. This type of government financing has not wholly passed away—witness the temporary advances still made to the French government by the Bank of France. Nevertheless today accommodation to governments from private lenders is an inconsiderable fraction of the indebtedness of the modern government.

The Increasing Expensiveness of Governments

However crude this system of private loans may seem today, it sufficed fairly well for the relatively small needs of sixteenth and seventeenth century governments. In those distant periods populations were smaller than at present, the standard of living was almost inconceivably lower, and the contemporary warfare with blunderbusses, swords, and sailing ships vastly cheaper. Many a modern city requires vastly more financial accommodation than did the whole kingdom of Elizabeth. Nevertheless the expenses of government were through this period steadily increasing, owing to such diverse factors as the Spanish discoveries of gold in America, the frequent and expensive amours of a Charles or a Louis, and the semi-religious, semipolitical wars in the low countries and elsewhere. Financial stringency helped to expel the last Stuart king from England in 1688, and to dampen the warlike ardor of his successor, William III.

During the reign of the latter, however, a financial discovery was made with profound consequences for the human race. The policy was adopted of issuing the interest-bearing government debt in the form of negotiable certificates and selling these to the recently created class of English investors who were earnestly seeking a safe way of investing their savings. In contrast to the private money-lending institutions of the day, such investors possessed a vastly larger aggregate of investable funds, and in addition they generally preferred to make long-term rather than short-term loans—so much so in fact that the principal portion of both the British and French funded national debts came subsequently to be issued in securities without a maturity date.

Modern Government Expenditure

Since about 1700, when this new and practical means of obtaining larger funds for government use by the sale of interest-bearing government certificates of indebtedness to private investors began, the expenditures of governments have continually grown. The increased economic complexity of civilization has necessitated a vast extension of the functions of government even in times of peace. Today the United States government, besides protecting Americans against external invasion or domestic violence, distributes the mail, builds roads, inspects food products, conserves natural resources, carries on scientific research in behalf of American agriculture, commerce, and industry, and performs for its citizens thousands of other distinct and often costly services which were undreamt of a century ago. In this expansion of its functions our government has been typical of other modern and progressive governments throughout the world.

But a still more significant need for governmental borrowing has arisen from the vastly increased cost of warfare. In the recent terrible conflict not merely specialized fighting men but entire populations had to be mobilized at an appalling expense. Although only about a quarter as long in duration as the Napoleonic Wars, the recent war proved in the case of England, roughly, ten times as expensive.[1] It is, of course, owing to the tremendous cost of modern scientific methods of warfare that every great government in the world today carries an unprecedented burden of debt, and that every important stock exchange in the world experiences a huge daily volume of purchases and sales of government securities. Figure 1

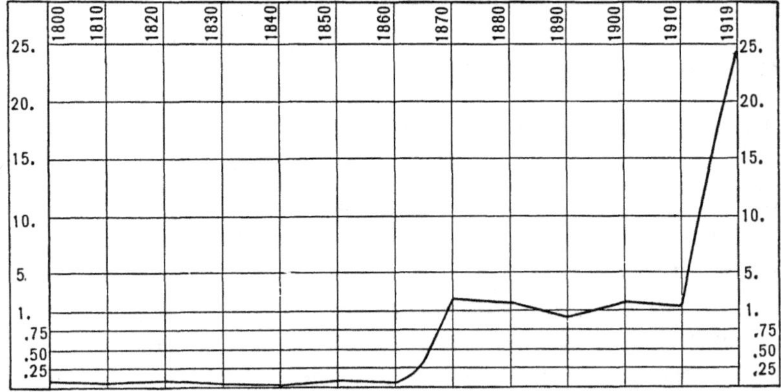

Figure 1. Chart of National Debt of the United States—1800–1919
In billions of dollars.

represents graphically the course of the national debt of the United States from 1800 to 1919.

Not only national governments but also their various subdivisions have likewise become accustomed to finance their needs through the issuance of securities. In this country, for example, our investors hold, in addition to the bonds of our national government, the interest-bearing obligations of our states, counties, and municipalities. In most respects these bonds of political subdivisions resemble national government bonds in their basic characteristics.

[1] See Appendix, Chapter I (a).

Government Securities

While sufficient space is lacking here for any adequate exposition of the technical features of government securities, nevertheless a few essential points may briefly be enumerated. There is considerable difference among present-day government securities as to the coin in which they are repayable. While in most cases the coin of the issuing nation is specified, with some "external loans" the standard coin of some other nation where the bonds have been mainly sold may be designated. Some government securities which have had an international distribution provide for repayment in the coins of any one of several different countries. Also the practice in respect to the redemption or maturity date varies widely—contrasting with some temporary government obligations extending only a few months, are the classic British consols or French *rentes* which, having no specified maturity date, are practically irredeemable. Also some government securities possess a sinking fund provision whereby a certain sum must be periodically set aside for retiring and paying off the issue at its maturity.

All government securities, however, are fundamentally based upon taxation and their value must therefore depend upon the honor and prospective financial future of their respective governmental organizations. In the abstract, the obligation of a government, whether a nation or only a city, may constitute a claim against all the wealth of its inhabitants, but practically no way is provided for the holder of a government bond in default to attempt to enforce any such claim.

Evolution of the Corporation

We now come to the other type of security-creating organization—the private business stock corporation. As in the case of governments, something of the historical background of the stock corporation must be known before its present-day economic significance can be adequately grasped.

Simple business partnerships, in which two or more men engage in an enterprise together, provide its capital, assume its debts, and divide its profits, are older than the Pyramids. But the great stock corporation of today, although its roots may extend back into history as far or even further than the *collegium* of the Romans, is nevertheless a comparatively new form of business organization. Nothing, in fact, more clearly indicates how very swiftly commerce, industry, and transportation have expanded during the past half-century than the recent dates at which so many of our greatest modern corporations have been organized. Indeed, many men who have yet to attain old age have lived through that whole marvelous economic period in American history which our historians are already calling "the age of big business."

With the constantly increasing amount of goods produced, transported, and consumed, there has been an inevitable corresponding increase in the size and capitalization of the business organizations which conduct this production and distribution. Profound economic forces in the modern world have for over a century been constantly calling for larger and larger operating units in almost all lines of business. And, as we shall presently see, experience has clearly shown that in most cases a large business enterprise can be more advantageously conducted as a corporation than as a partnership.

America's Debt to Corporations

It is peculiarly fitting that the fullest and most rapid development of the stock corporation as a mechanism for carrying on the "big business" of the modern world should have occurred in the United States. The stock corporation has entered more deeply into our history than into that of any other modern nation. From its earliest history North America has been explored by corporations, colonized by corporations, and developed by corporations. To be sure, Raleigh, Gilbert, and those other daring British sea-rovers who first attempted to establish colonies on our Atlantic seaboard, were financed through partnerships formed by a few wealthy London noblemen; but their repeated failures proved that a few men of wealth could not easily raise sufficient funds to insure the success of such colonizing enterprises.

Accordingly, the British effort to settle this continent was taken up in the early seventeenth century by crude joint-stock companies,[2] whose organization made it possible to attract more partners into these colonizing attempts and by so doing give them a larger financial backing. As a result the first permanent European settlement in this country at Jamestown in 1607, was established by the London Company. Financially speaking the Pilgrim fathers were holders of labor-shares in a subsidiary of the Plymouth Company, chartered in 1620. The expenses of the initial venture which resulted in our present New England states were borne by the stockholders of this corporation. One share was allotted to each of the Pilgrims and additional shares were sold to them for £10 apiece, so that even in the beginning some of its stock was held in America. Not all New Yorkers remember that it was from an employee of another ancient corporation, the Dutch East India Company, that the majestic Hudson River derived its name. Indeed, the venerable Hudson's Bay Company (or, to use its quaint legal title, "The Governor and Company of Adventurers of England trading into Hudson's Bay"), which was organized in 1670 and named after the same intrepid explorer, still exists after having played a huge part in the economic development of modern Canada.

Early British Companies

During the seventeenth and eighteenth centuries, however, the control of these early corporation settlements in what is

[2] See Chapter XV.

now the United States was soon taken over by the settlers themselves. These early British companies differed in important respects from the modern corporations of which they were the forerunners. Their shares were, of course, intensely speculative, and since there was then no organized stock market, were neither easily salable nor readily available to the average Englishman as investments.

Compared with our own times the business world of the seventeenth and eighteenth centuries was poor, slow-moving, risky, wasteful, and inefficient. Steam power had not yet been harnessed to industry and transportation, and large business organizations as we know them today were, if only for this reason, still impossible. The manufacturer of 1700 could produce his wares only by hand and in small quantities—consequently he made little effort to concentrate his manufacturing under a single factory roof, but let it out piecemeal to his employees to be performed in their cottages. From this last fact the term "cottage industry" is used to designate the manufacturing enterprises of this period.

Eighteenth Century Transportation

But even if such an inefficient system had permitted the manufacturer to produce large quantities of goods they could not have been distributed quickly, securely, or in considerable amounts by the clumsy stage coaches and canals of that period. Macaulay has drawn a graphic picture of English transportation conditions[3] in the latter decades of the seventeenth century:

> There were no railways, except a few made of timber from the mouths of the Northumbrian coal pits to the banks of the Tyne. There was very little internal communication by water. A few attempts had been made to deepen and embank the natural streams, but with slender success. Hardly a single navigable canal had been even projected.

[3] Macaulay, History of England, Chap. III.

> It was by the highways that both travellers and goods generally passed from place to place. . . . on the best lines of communication the ruts were deep, the descents precipitous, and the way often such as it was hardly possible to distinguish, in the dusk, from the unenclosed heath and fen which lay on both sides. . . . It was only in fine weather that the whole breadth of the road was available for wheeled vehicles. Often the mud lay deep on the right and the left, and only a narrow track of firm ground rose above the quagmire. . . . It happened almost every day, that coaches stuck fast, until a team of cattle could be procured from some neighboring farm to tug them out of the slough. . . .
>
> The markets were often inaccessible during several months. It is said that the fruits of the earth were sometimes suffered to rot in one place, while in another place, distant only a few miles, the supply fell far short of the demand. . . . On the best highways, heavy articles were, in the time of Charles the Second, generally conveyed from place to place by stage wagons. . . . The expense of transmitting heavy goods in this way was enormous. From London to Birmingham the charge was seven pounds a ton; from London to Exeter twelve pounds a ton. This was about fifteen pence a ton for everv mile . . . fifteen times what is now demanded by railway companies. The cost of conveyance amounted to a prohibitory tax on many useful articles. Coal in particular was never seen except in the districts where it was produced, or in the districts to which it could be carried by sea, and was indeed always known in the south of England by the name of sea coal.

What transportation was like in newly settled America, when the above conditions prevailed in the world's leading commercial nation, can best be left to the imagination.

Moreover, owing mainly to these primitive methods of producing and distributing goods, the buying or consumptive powers of the people were then exceedingly limited. Poverty was much more widespread than today, and not only were existing populations only a fraction of what they now are, but the per capita buying power was likewise very much lower. Neither had organized markets nor other parts of the modern machinery of credit yet been created. In consequence of these temporarily insuperable difficulties the eighteenth century was in the main a period of small business enterprises, which could be organized satisfactorily enough as partnerships, with, of course, no stocks or bonds to sell to the public.

The Utilization of Steam Power

It was principally the invention of the steam engine and its practical employment in steam railways and steam factories that at the opening of the nineteenth century wrought a profound and permanent change in business methods and business organization. Indeed, the so-called Industrial Revolution which resulted from this utilization of steam power was ultimately destined to raise standards of living, increase populations, modify laws, overthrow governments, upset almost immemorial business practices, transform finance and the stock exchanges, shift the routes of trade, create and destroy market places, and alter profoundly the morals, beliefs, and the very security of many nations.

The early inventors in this Industrial Revolution, however, at once encountered serious obstacles to the general adoption of their inventions, rising from the very structure of the small-scale business of that day. Unconsciously the industrial enterprise had grown beyond the point where a few wealthy partners could finance it. Thus the larger enterprises which steam locomotives and steam factories necessitated could not be financed until the stock corporation was developed to enable more partners to engage in them, and until stock exchanges grew up to stabilize and protect investment by the public in the new corporate bonds and shares.

Financing the First Railroads

A significant example of just how difficult it was for individuals to finance the great American business enterprises launched in the first decades of the nineteenth century is furnished by the early development of the steam locomotive. That this machine could successfully pull unheard of loads over rails at an unprecedented speed was demonstrated beyond the peradventure of a doubt. The public, too, had sufficient imagination to realize the new era in the history of transportation which was promised. But for all that, the locomotive was for some time considered only an impracticable inventor's dream. No American, nor partnership of Americans, it was publicly argued, was rich enough to finance the building of a railroad—therefore railroads could never be built.[4] This hasty syllogism was not exploded until the organization of some of our great railroad stock corporations revealed its fallacy. Not until the savings of thousands of individuals were successfully enlisted in railroad enterprises by the creation of the large stock corporation, did steam railroad transportation emerge from the inventor's shed to become the indispensable carrier upon which all modern industry and much of modern social life has since been builded.

Nor was the ability to handle a larger volume of business with a greater equipment the only advantage gained for the more secure and successful conduct of business by the development of the modern stock corporation. Many important advantages resulted to the benefit of the shareholder as an investor. For one thing the corporation became a deathless entity whose affairs would not have to be liquidated or reorganized whenever a partner died. It furthermore permitted a greater concentration of control in its management, which likewise made for greater safety and efficiency. It could attract capital in amounts varying from the small investor's mite to the fortune of the financier, and also made it easier for anyone to invest in a business without the need of directly sharing in its management as well. In addition, since almost

[4] See Appendix, Chapter I (b).

all stocks in time became non-assessable, the investing shareholder was freed from personal liability for the losses of the corporation.

The Stock Exchange and Corporate Development

In the distribution of corporate securities among American investors during the past century the New York Stock Exchange has played and is today playing a necessary part. Exactly how the constant market for securities maintained by the Exchange operates today to assist corporations in obtaining funds and the public to obtain the best investments at the fairest prices, will be related in subsequent chapters.[5] It is sufficient at present to point out that the Stock Exchange has been a vital factor in helping our railroad corporations to secure the funds which made it possible for them to span our great continent with their myriad tunnels and bridges and their thousands of miles of steel-shod roadways.

Still more recently our gigantic industrial corporations have been enabled through the assistance of the Stock Exchange to build those vast mills and factories which the whole world trend of modern production has necessitated. Without the creation of these huge companies and the safeguarding of their stockholders through the daily operations of the New York Stock Exchange the marvelously swift development of American transportation and industry would have been quite impossible.

Growth of the "Trusts"

Ever since our Civil War, powerful economic factors have caused our corporations to become larger and larger. A similar tendency has more recently been seen in Great Britain and Germany, particularly since the armistice. Despite the clamor over the "trusts" which was so prevalent with us a decade ago,

[5] See Chapters XIV and XVI.

experience has shown us that the mere bigness of a corporation does not as such constitute any offense to the public, nor any inherent danger to its welfare. The truth of the matter is that resistless economic forces have necessitated the large corporation today, and we cannot any more return to the small business organizations of even twenty-five years ago than we can turn backward the hands of the clock.

The shares of even our soundest corporations were, of course, highly speculative in the beginning. But the American public, believing in the future of this country, has always been willing to speculate in our new corporate shares. From the financial standpoint, indeed, this speculation is mainly responsible for our amazing growth in the past century—a growth which for swiftness and extent is without parallel in history.[6]

Variety of Listed Securities Today

The list of stocks which are traded in on the New York Stock Exchange today is a striking illustration both of the vast extent to which modern American business is carried on by stock corporations,[7] and the importance of our stock markets as distributing centers for their shares and obligations. Apart from the numerous steam railroad and electric traction company stocks, the group loosely designated as "industrials" includes shares in companies which operate in finance, retail selling, security-holding, telephones, telegraphs, gas, terminals, electric light and power, coke, rubber goods, tires, magnetos, carburetors, pleasure automobiles, fire engines, tractors, motor trucks, auto bodies, auto wheels, machine tools, plows, cane and beet sugar, cotton oil, ice, fisheries, fruits, candy, corn products, tea, biscuits, meats, and refrigerating service.

Other listed stocks represent companies interested in steel, iron, fertilizers, drugs, chemicals, harvesters and all kinds of agricultural machinery and implements, cans, brake shoes,

[6] See Chapter XV. [7] See Chapter XVII.

locomotives, steel springs, steel cars, pneumatic tools, fuels, scales, tankers, air brakes, elevators, cast iron pipe, enameled goods, the production, refining, and distribution of petroleum, zinc, lead, copper, silver, gold, coal, metal smelting and refining, shipping, foreign trading and foreign securities, land development, snuff, cigars, cigar stores, tobacco and its various products, temperance drinks, woolens, dry goods, linen collars, carpets, hosiery, shirts, underwear, hides, leather, shoes, bank notes, express service, safety razors, writing paper, magazines, graphophones, office appliances, docks, glass bottles, typewriters, real estate, and perfumery and toilet articles. And almost weekly the list grows with the addition of the securities of new and different enterprises. The bond issues listed on the Stock Exchange are even more numerous than the stocks, although they represent fewer different industries.

The foregoing list of stock companies indicates not only how necessary it has been for our corporations to sell partnerships to our investing public, but also how great is the number of present-day investors in corporate securities. In order to obtain this vast participation by American investors in American industry, a wide range of securities has been created to meet their varying needs and desires. Some investors wish to become the creditors of a corporation, while others prefer to buy a partnership in it. The most fundamental differences between such distinctive securities as mortgage or debenture bonds, and preferred or common stocks, are to be found in the degree of safety and the rate of income possessed by each type. How these various kinds of securities originate and what the salient features of each kind really are, is best related from the standpoint of the corporation which issues them.

Launching a Typical Corporation

Accordingly, let us for a moment imagine ourselves the promoters of a new railroad. We see that a splendid opportunity exists for the line which we propose to build, and we believe that, once established, it should pay handsome profits. But our engineers inform us that it will require almost $10,000,000 to build it. Between us we can raise, let us say, $6,000,000, or a little over half this sum. But before we can hope to carry the project through we must obtain the remaining $4,000,000 from someone else.

Now no one can afford to give us as large a sum as that simply to make us happy. If we are going to attract $4,000,000 into our enterprise, we must give the men who advance this money something in exchange for their funds. So many new partners would be needed to put up the required $4,000,000 that it would prove impracticable to organize our railroad company as a straight partnership. We accordingly form a corporation. Legally considered, this corporation is a separate entity by itself and apart from its owners—a sort of deathless, inanimate *person*. Since such an incorporated business can be divided into a large number of equal shares, we can obtain the $4,000,000 we need by selling two-fifths of the shares to an unlimited number of individuals who have no particular desire to help us in the active management of our railroad but who wish to find a profitable investment for their surplus funds.

Par Value of Stocks

Consequently we capitalize our railroad enterprise at $10,000,000 and divide it into 100,000 shares. A single share of stock will necessarily be worth only the fraction it represents of the value of the whole company. According to long-established custom we declare that each of these shares has a normal or par value of $100. Yet it must always be remembered that this par value will not be an accurate index to the market price of the stock, for this will depend, not so much upon the assets of the company as upon its earning power and the dividends it can pay to its stockholders. For this reason the term "par value" as it applies to common stock is apt to be quite misleading and in consequence many companies have recently issued stocks with "no par value," which have been listed on the Stock Exchange. But most listed stocks still have a par value, although it is a purely nominal figure.

For the $6,000,000 which we put into the railroad we receive 60,000 shares, leaving 40,000 shares to be sold to the investing and speculating public. As a later chapter will more fully explain,[8] we probably will have some banking house underwrite this $4,000,000 of stock. With the $4,000,000 (less, of course, underwriting and other selling expenses) which we receive from the sale of our surplus 40,000 shares, we now have the needed funds and we proceed to build our railroad.

Privileges of Shareholders

Our stockholders are just as truly partners in our railroad as ourselves, although, of course, to a lesser extent. In fact, anyone who can get together roughly $100 can buy a share of our stock through the Stock Exchange, can attend our stockholders' meetings, and can cast one vote in any of its proceedings. Furthermore, as part owner of the corporation, such a shareholder is entitled to a dividend, or his proportionate share of the company's profits each year, provided, of course, the company finds it possible to pay dividends. The amount of this dividend is usually determined by the directors of our company, subject to ratification by a majority of our stockholders. This first year or two, perhaps, we find it difficult to pay even small dividends, and our stock may sell at low figures in consequence, but afterward, when we shall have thoroughly established our business, the profits of our railroad will increase and we can pay larger and larger dividends.

---

[8] See Chapter XVI.

Issuance of "Rights"

But after we have operated our railroad for a few years and have placed it on a dividend-paying basis we may discover that with an additional $1,000,000 we could build some new lines which would largely increase our profits. The most natural way of raising this new money would be to increase our capitalization from $10,000,000 to $11,000,000 and sell 10,000 additional shares of common stock at par. This is usually done by giving to all existing stockholders a "right" to subscribe to the new stock issued in the same proportion as his present holdings of stock stand to the previous stock issue. If, for example, a stockholder already owned $200,000, or one-fiftieth of the original $10,000,000 of stock, he would be given engraved certificates of the company certifying his right to buy one-fiftieth, or 200 shares, of the new stock issue.

The price at which old stockholders can purchase new stock in this way must, of course, be fixed. Often the market price of the old stock on the Stock Exchange will be considerably higher than the subscription price to the new stock stated on the "right" certificate—in such a case this right will have a market value.[9] Accordingly, certificates which give their holder the right to subscribe to new stock on such profitable terms are occasionally listed on the New York Stock Exchange and traded in until the subscription period covered by the right expires.

Characteristics of Bonds

But, returning to our railroad, we may decide that it would be impracticable to obtain the $1,000,000 which we need by selling new common stock. Perhaps investors for the moment do not look with any eagerness at such issues, or perhaps this issuing of more common stock would in some way disarrange the voting power in our corporation. Hence our directors

[9] See Appendix, Chapter I (c).

might decide to raise the money by selling mortgage bonds instead.

A bond is completely different from a stock in many ways. A bond does not represent any degree of partnership in a corporation, as does a share of stock. Instead, it is simply an obligation or I O U of a corporation. The bond certificate states that the corporation owes its holder a given sum of money which it agrees to pay back by a certain maturity date and upon which it agrees meanwhile to pay a fixed rate of interest. Such a bond may be a debenture—that is, simply an unsecured promise to pay—or it may be a mortgage bond, secured by some sort of mortgage upon the corporation's property, which the bondholders can seize if they do not receive their interest, or, at the bond's maturity, its face value.

The bondholder is consequently not a partner in the company, but simply one of its creditors. Under normal circumstances he naturally has no voice in the councils of the corporation, nor does he own any part of the business. On the other hand his interest must be paid to him out of the annual earnings of the company before the stockholder can get any dividends, for dividends result from the company's net profit, which remains only after its current expenses and the interest on its bonded indebtedness have been paid. Moreover, if at the maturity of a mortgage bond issue the corporation fails to repay the principal sum of the bonds to their holders, the latter can seize the property covered by the mortgage securing the bonds, leaving the stockholders what may remain of the company's assets. In this connection it is important to notice that while the company owes the face value of its outstanding bonds to their holders, it does not owe its stockholders the face or par value of their shares. In case of liquidation, or a winding up of a corporation's business, each shareholder will receive that fraction of the clear assets of the company, after all its debts, bonds, etc., have been paid off, which is represented by the ratio of his shares to all the outstanding shares in the company.

Preferred Stock

But we must again get back to our railroad. We have thus far issued $10,000,000 of common stock, and (since increasing our stock issue to $11,000,000 by issuing rights seemed inadvisable) we have sold $1,000,000 of, let us say, 5 per cent first mortgage bonds of the company. Now it may be that in a few years more we again see a splendid opportunity to increase the company's profits by building additional tracks, which will cost about $2,000,000. We may have the same reasons as previously for not wishing to sell that much more common stock. On the other hand, we may not wish to have a bonded indebtedness to the extent of $3,000,000, and perhaps by this time the investing public, which has its moods and fancies, cannot be attracted by mortgage bonds. Under such circumstances a third alternative is still open to us—to obtain the $2,000,000 we need by selling that amount to preferred stock paying, let us suppose, 7 per cent. Preferred stocks resemble bonds in that the dividends on a preferred stock are fixed at a certain rate of interest. But unlike bonds and like common stocks, dividends on preferred stocks can, in an emergency, be omitted or "passed" if conditions do not warrant their payment. With "cumulative" preferred stocks, however, such passed dividends accumulate on the stock, and its holder must be paid all such back dividends to date before the common stockholder can receive any dividends on his stock at all. The title of "preferred stock" is given this class of security because its holder usually has a preferred or prior claim over the common stockholder to the earnings and assets of the company, both for the payment of its dividends and the payment of its value in the event of a winding up of the business. Usually, however, the preferred stock does not entitle its holder to voting power, except in cases where its dividends may be endangered or suspended.

Disposition of Earnings

With the issuing of $2,000,000 of 7 per cent preferred stock our railroad now has a bonded indebtedness of $1,000,000 and $12,000,000 of capital stock, consisting of 20,000 shares of preferred and 100,000 shares of common stock. In paying all these investors their interest or dividends each year, the earnings of the company over its operating expenses are first determined. Then $50,000 (or the 5 per cent interest on its $1,000,000 bonds) is paid to its bondholders. Next $140,000 (or the 7 per cent dividend on its $2,000,000 of preferred stock) is paid out in dividends to the preferred stockholders. Meanwhile the holders of the 100,000 common shares wait hungrily. In case the railroad only earned $200,000 that year, they probably will receive no dividend at all, thus not faring as well as the holders of either the bonds or the preferred stock. But in case it proved a very prosperous year, and after operating expenses were paid $1,200,000 remained, the company might decide to declare a 10 per cent dividend on its common stock, in which event the common stockholders would come off better than either the bondholders or the preferred stockholders.

Claims to Assets

But should the worst happen and our railroad prove so unprofitable financially that everyone concerned should agree to wind up its business, the first $1,000,000 obtained from the sale of its assets would go toward paying off the bondholders. The next $2,000,000 would probably be used to compensate preferred stockholders, although this would depend somewhat upon the exact provisions under which preferred stock was issued. Last would come the holders of the 100,000 shares of common stock; whatever was left over the $3,000,000 already repaid, would be paid back pro rata to holders of this common stock. From the above it is obvious that to the investor common stock offers the greatest risk but the greatest possible profits, while mortgage bonds are least risky, but also often yield the smallest income return. As an investment preferred stock represents a compromise between the two, being more secure than common stock but less so than bonds, and yielding more than bonds but less than is possible in the case of common stock.

Twain Roots of Modern Stock Exchange

The above brief outline of the modern corporation and its typical securities, of course, omits or slurs over many considerations which, while in the main irrelevant to our present purpose, are nevertheless highly important from the practical standpoint. But a more elaborate consideration of the corporation must be sought for in separate volumes upon that subject, rather than in the present volume, which relates as exclusively as possible to security markets. It is sufficient if those principal features of corporate activity which immediately relate to corporate securities and their varying attractiveness to the different classes of investors, have been suggested. Such corporations as the imaginary one whose creation and progress we have just traced, have during the past century been developed in all civilized countries to exploit the natural resources, manufacture new articles, and provide speedier and cheaper methods of transportation and distribution.

In our brief review of the evolution of government and corporate securities we have bared the twain roots of the modern stock exchange. For as soon as these new forms of property began to be extensively created and widely distributed, it was inevitable that the buying and selling of them should in turn gravitate from scattered and sporadic bargainings into regular market places especially devoted to this purpose. The account of this development from humble beginnings of the great securities markets of today, and in particular of the rise of the New York Stock Exchange as the principal security market in this country, will be related in the next chapter.

CHAPTER II

THE RISE OF THE NEW YORK STOCK EXCHANGE

Swift Evolution of the Stock Exchange

Many a well-educated American business man asks each day in perplexity, "What *is* the Stock Exchange? What useful purpose does it serve?" The difficulty of framing a clear and comprehensive reply to these fair and natural questions may be realized the better when it is stated that the present by no means slender volume has resulted from an attempt to answer them with only a moderate degree of completeness. But before plunging into the mass of detail which is essential to an understanding of the Stock Exchange of today, some preliminary ideas of value can be gained by reviewing quite briefly a few of the leading historical events and economic forces which created it and impelled it toward its present significant position.

Indeed, the history of the New York Stock Exchange's swift evolution is one of the greatest romances in the economic development of America. One of the very oldest wheels in our modern financial machinery, it has evolved within the past century from the simplest beginnings to a great national organization, housed in a splendid marble edifice in Wall Street, and equipped with every appliance for facilitating its business that science as yet has made available.

Earliest New York Markets

Owing to its splendid natural port facilities, New York had early in the eighteenth century become a commercial and trading center of no small importance. Its merchants seem from the first to have possessed both energy and vision. As early as 1752, in fact, they had established a general meeting place for merchants, or "Exchange" as they called it, at the foot of Broad Street, for dealings in meal and slaves. Shortly afterward, in 1768, the present Chamber of Commerce was organized in the long room of the historic Fraunces' Tavern, which still remains as a landmark of pre-Revolutionary Manhattan.

The financial effect of the Revolution was to create a heavy national debt. The first Congress, which assembled in Federal Hall (on the site of the historic Sub-Treasury building at Wall and Nassau Streets), authorized the issue of $80,000,000 in bonds (or, as they were then called, "stock") to refund the public debt arising from the war. Sufficient investment demand apparently existed, either here or abroad, to absorb this issue—a tremendous one for those early times. Meanwhile, the financial necessities of the new republic were leading to the creation of a new financial machinery. In 1781 the Bank of North America was incorporated in Philadelphia. Not to be outdone even by what was then the commercial and financial center of the country, the merchants of Manhattan organized the Bank of New York in 1784. But a still more significant step was yet to be taken. In 1791 Alexander Hamilton, the first and perhaps the most brilliant of American Secretaries of the Treasury, prevailed upon Washington and Congress to establish the first United States Bank.

Origin of the New York Securities Market

The scrip stock of this new institution, when it was offered to the public, inaugurated the first wave of security speculation in this country, in which the 6 per cent United States government stock and the shares of the new United States Bank and the Bank of North America were favorites. The frequent purchases and sales of these early American securities created the need of some regular market where they could be more readily and efficiently conducted, for investors were naturally averse to exchanging their savings for securities which could not be easily sold again. As a result about ten individuals were attracted into the new profession of acting as agents and brokers for investors interested in these securities. These earliest stock-brokers formed the custom of meeting for this purpose under an old buttonwood tree that stood at 68 Wall Street, except when inclement weather drove them to shelter in the coffee houses nearby. Here they became accustomed to transact their business, and so far as they could, provide the ready security market for which the times called with increasing insistence. And thus, for all its present marble magnificence, the New York securities market began very humbly indeed in the heat and rain and dust of a village street.

First Brokers' Agreement

The first sign of an organization in this original open-air market was manifested on May 17, 1792, when the following agreement, still preserved in the archives of the Stock Exchange, was signed by these early brokers:

> We, the Subscribers, Brokers for the Purchase and Sale of Public Stock, do hereby solemnly promise and pledge ourselves to each other that we will not buy or sell, from this day, for any person whatsoever, any kind of public stock at a less rate than one-quarter per cent commission on the special value, and that we will give preference to each other in our negotiations.

There are twenty-four signatures to this interesting document, which is the first stock exchange agreement of any kind in this country.

The stock market thus inaugurated grew rapidly.[1] After playing a vital part in the creation of our earliest banks, the fire and marine insurance companies were likewise presently enabled through its agency to obtain the capital needed to engage in that business. State and municipal obligations were

[1] See Appendix, Chapter II (a).

also added. The war of 1812 resulted in heavier government debt, more government bonds, and a heavy increase in their purchase and sale in the New York securities market. So rapidly did the security brokerage business increase that steps soon had to be taken not merely to provide for the greater dignity and comfort of the stock-brokers themselves, but also to protect their contracts more completely by restricting memberships in the market. To this end the original street brokers went under a roof for the first time in 1817, and as a part of the further organization which this move necessitated, took for themselves the collective name of the "New York Stock and Exchange Board." The first constitution of this new organization bears the date of March 8, 1817, and among other matters provides that "any members making a fictitious sale or contract shall, upon conviction thereof, be expelled from the board." At this time trading was permitted in only about thirty stocks, and the new association was formed by only seven firms and thirteen individual brokers.

Original Stock Exchange Equipment

The Stock Exchange, however, was still a temporary lodger rather than an established inhabitant of Wall Street, for all the valiant national service which it was performing in stabilizing America's national and local public credit and in helping to organize our early banking system. On April 8, 1817, it was "Resolved, that we pay Mr. George F. Vaupell for the use of his front room in the second story of house No. 40 Wall Street, two hundred dollars ($200) per annum, he to furnish fire and chairs, when required, and to keep the room in order."[2] Further evidence of the makeshift equipment and leisurely transactions on the "Board" of this period is furnished by articles 2 and 3 of the contemporary constitution:[3]

---

[2] E. C. Stedman (Editor), The New York Stock Exchange, p. 65.
[3] *Ibid.*, p. 64.

2. It shall be the duty of the President to call the stocks at the hour that may be fixed upon by the Board, from time to time, as the season may require. . . .

3. It shall be the duty of the Secretary to keep the minutes of the Board in a book for the purpose, an account of all fines, and to collect the same, and also a register of all actual sales of stocks made at the Board. . . .

From the meager records which survive from these early days, it does not appear that the Exchange had any even comparatively permanent home until 1827, when it rented a room in the Merchants' Exchange Building at Wall and Hanover Streets. From this shelter the stock market was, however, rudely evicted by the great fire of 1835. But after several further wanderings, including the temporary occupation of a hay-loft, the Board at length reoccupied in 1842 a large hall in the new Merchants' Exchange Building on the present site of the National City Bank. Here it remained until 1854.

Beginnings of Railroad Development

Meanwhile, no sooner had our government established itself politically and financially, than the great task of opening up and settling the vast western areas of the country began. The keynote of this westward colonizing movement was, of course, transportation. At first carriage roads and then canals were constructed from the Atlantic seaboard over the mountains into the fertile hinterland of the Mississippi Valley. In 1825 the completion of the Erie Canal opened up a water route from New York into the Great West and definitely transferred the financial supremacy of the United States from Philadelphia to Manhattan. Nevertheless, it was not until the advent of the steam railroad that anything like transportation in the modern sense of the term became possible. The year 1829 saw the first train moved by an American steam locomotive in this country, an experiment fraught with the utmost consequence to the

United States, but still, for the nonce, nothing more than an experiment.

Something has already been said in the previous chapter concerning the initial difficulty experienced in raising the large sums of money needed to establish railroad systems. A way out of the difficulty was ultimately found by creating large stock corporations, whose bonds and shares were soon listed on the Stock Exchange. Largely through its efforts they were sold to the investing public, which in this way became creditors and partners in the new companies and provided much of the capital which was required. Accordingly, we find in 1830 the first railroad stock—that of the Mohawk and Hudson Railroad—listed on the New York Stock Exchange. Almost simultaneously the older London Stock Exchange began to quote nineteen American railroad stocks—the beginning of the famous "Yankee rail market" there, which did so much to make our present system of railroad transportation in this country possible.

The Stock Exchange During the Civil War Period

Through the fifties the Exchange continued to grow along with the rest of the country. On a single day in 1857 some forgotten chronicler proudly remarked that fully 70,000 shares changed hands in its market. The perennial problem of the Exchange to obtain large enough quarters was also already upon it.[4] In 1863 the New York Stock Exchange Building Company was organized, and it set about to provide a permanent and commodious home for the Exchange, which in the same year adopted its present title of "The New York Stock Exchange." Owing to its efforts, the Board in 1865 moved into its present building on Broad Street—then, of course, not so large as today.

But all the new space thus made available, and more too,

[4] See Appendix, Chapter II (b).

was needed at once. The enormous issues of irredeemable paper currency put out by the government during and after the Civil War had the immediate effect of inflating and temporarily stimulating American business. New enterprises were started, promoters flourished, and stock speculation overflowed the Stock Exchange into three additional and newly organized minor exchanges: an open-air exchange, the forerunner of the present curb market and in some ways like the original market of 1792 under the buttonwood tree; another unique body, which hired the room which adjoined the Stock Exchange and based its transactions on such quotations as it could overhear from the "Big Board"; and lastly, the "Coal Hole Exchange," which derived its name from its subterranean quarters at 23 William Street, where a securities market possessing little formality or decorum but a large turnover was for a time conducted.

It is significant of the growth of Stock Exchange transactions at this period that the present "continuous market" in securities dates from shortly after the Civil War. Prior to that war stocks and bonds were "called" at intervals during the day, and such trading as resulted in them were supposed to occur, and usually did occur, only after the "call" in each instance. This whole postwar period was from an economic standpoint an unhealthy one, with inflated currency a fundamental cause of distraction and unsettlement. This evil was for the most part corrected when specie payments were resumed in January, 1879. In the interim, however, the overstrained conditions of credit precipitated a panic in 1873 which proved so severe that for ten days the Stock Exchange was compelled to close its doors for the first time in its history.

Railroad Securities on the Exchange

None the less, the period of 1850-1880, for all its economic alarms and excursions, also witnessed a tremendous increase of railroad construction in this country, which was alternately stimulated and depressed by the tides of economic circumstance. Even before the first railroad train crossed the continent in 1869 and doomed to extinction the Conestoga wagons, prairie schooners, and overland stages, the deluge of railroad bonds and stocks had already swept into the Stock Exchange. To the Stock Exchange the organizers of our railroads came to obtain the capital needed in laying the vast and permanent steel highways of our inland transportation system. To the Stock Exchange, investors looked to give their newly acquired railroad securities an instant negotiability. It is little wonder, then, that until very recently both the stock and bond markets on the Board have been pre-eminently markets for railroad securities.

Improvement and Expansion of the Exchange System

That the Stock Exchange kept pace with the latest scientific discoveries to facilitate its business is attested to by its adoption of the stock ticker as early as 1867 to give widespread publicity to its transactions. The opening of the Atlantic cables in the preceding year also tended to broaden the market for the Board's listed securities, and make easier the flow of European capital into American business enterprises. In 1878 telephones were installed on the Exchange floor—a mechanical improvement which also tended to make possible a greater turnover in the market. The number of Exchange members was greatly increased in 1869, when the Old Board consolidated with the Open Board of Brokers, a competitive organization formed in 1864, and the Government Bond Department, an organization devoted to trading in United States government securities. At the time of this merger there were 533 members of the Stock Exchange, 354 members of the Open Board, and 173 members of the Government Bond Department—or 1,060 altogether. The membership was brought up to its present figure of 1,100 by the sale of 40 "seats" in 1881, to defray the expenses incurred by an expansion of the Board southward along Broad Street, which its steadily increasing business made necessary.

Public Utility and Industrial Securities

As we approach modern times through the prosperous eighties, another tendency becomes apparent in the stock market. In the wake of the great railroad lines which earlier decades had established, cities had rapidly sprung up—cities which needed gas and then electric lighting, local traction facilities, and telephone service. Accordingly the thin trickle of public utility securities into the New York securities market broadened into a steady and heavy current. Mining and oil stocks, although looked at askance in the beginning by the Exchange, nevertheless became common in the financial district as the industrial exploitation of America's national resources gained momentum, and a few of the best companies were able to list their stocks and bonds on the Exchange. Furthermore, powerful manufacturing industries were being organized, both in our older eastern cities and in the new western centers which the railroads had created and nourished into prosperity. Particularly after the Spanish War, these new industrial companies experienced a rapid growth and tended to evolve into large-scale corporate units with a huge capitalization, and in consequence shares and bonds to sell to the public through the indispensable market provided by the Stock Exchange.[5]

The Rôle of the European Investor

As was inevitable in a country so new and for the time being so economically immature, this amazingly vast and swift development of American transportation, American cities, and American industry from 1850 to 1900, completely outran the ability of American speculators and investors to finance it.

[5] See Appendix, Chapter II (c).

Accordingly, great blocks of our railroad, utility, and industrial stocks and bonds were absorbed by the wealthier investors of Europe and were listed on the stock exchanges of London, Paris, and other foreign financial centers, as well as on the New York Stock Exchange.

Even prior to the panic of 1837 the British had absorbed many of our early and sometimes quite unreliable state bonds and later even larger amounts of the securities of our leading railroad corporations. After the Civil War, too, the rising financial nation of Germany purchased heavily into our far western railroads, particularly the Atchison, Northern Pacific, and Union Pacific railroads. It is well known that the ultimate prosperity of the northwestern "Hill roads" was largely founded upon large buying of the shares and obligations of the original companies by Dutch investors. Many examples might likewise be cited of American utility and industrial securities which had similarly found their way into the coffers of European investors. Thus the almost incredible swiftness with which this country was built up involved a debt of our corporations to European security-holders of several billions of dollars —a debt whose interest and dividends amounted to several hundred millions of dollars annually.

Speculative Beginnings of the Industrials

Both because the New York Stock Exchange was at that time mainly a railroad market and also because even the best of our new industrial companies were in the beginning intensely risky and speculative enterprises, the Exchange first created an Unlisted Department in 1885, where the new industrial shares which could not altogether meet the increasingly strict requirements of the Committee on Stock List could nevertheless be admitted for trading purposes. Many of the soundest industrial investment securities of today began here as highly speculative and, to the older Exchange members, rather dubious propositions.

One of the striking changes, in fact, which the last quarter-century has witnessed in the stock market is the growing repute of industrial securities and the waning glory of the rails.

How and why the growing market organized its clearing house, on May 17, 1892—the centenary of the signing of the original brokers' agreement—will be told in a later chapter.[6] The next to the last step in architectural expansion was taken in 1903, when the present Stock Exchange building (see frontispiece) was erected. From 1901-1903, while the new building was under construction, the Stock Exchange conducted its securities market in the Produce Exchange. The twentieth century has seen two panics on the Exchange, in 1901 and 1907, as well as serious periods of liquidation in 1903, 1914, and 1920. It is significant of the growing soundness and popularity of the new industrial stocks that on the recommendation of the Hughes Commission the Exchange in 1910 abolished its Unlisted Department and admitted its industrials to the regular stock list. The stock market, in common with all American business, has since that time greatly benefited by the increased stability of American credit brought about by the enactment of the Federal Reserve Act in 1913.

Effects of the World War

The immediate effect of the outbreak of war in 1914 upon the Stock Exchange has been related in a vivid manner by a former president of the Exchange.[7] In addition to the unprecedented breakdown of the international credit structure, so tremendous a wave of liquidation by Europeans of their American securities in our market set in, that, after maintaining itself as the last liquid security market in the world, the New York Stock Exchange was compelled for the second time in its history to close its doors on July 31, 1914. Trading in

---

6 See Chapter IX.

7 H. G. S. Noble, The New York Stock Exchange in the Crisis of 1914.

carefully restricted securities began again late that fall and by skilful graduations the whole market was finally reopened by December 15, 1914. The subsequent history of the Exchange is, for the most part, still fresh enough in the popular mind to need no further comment here.[8]

The late World War will undoubtedly prove a landmark in the annals of the Stock Exchange. The period from 1913 to 1919 witnessed a vast expansion of America's whole industrial establishment and a mighty increase in our national wealth. Another distinctive development which profoundly affected the tendencies of the Stock Exchange market was the operation of our entire railroad system by the United States government during 1917-1919.

The most obvious result of the war on the stock market—as in the instances above cited of the Revolution, the War of 1812, and the Civil War—was a tremendous increase in our national debt, largely represented by the issuance of over twenty billion dollars in Liberty and Victory bonds, which were, of course, listed and marketed upon the Exchange. But another less obvious but even more significant development has been the gradual but very extensive liquidation on the Exchange of billions of dollars' worth of our best securities by European holders during 1915-1920, and their subsequent distribution among our own constantly widening investing public.

By this and similar processes America for the first time in her history became a creditor nation internationally.[9] A further unique sign of this new era in American financial history has been the appearance on the Board of the obligations of foreign national and municipal governments. The simultaneous pressure which from these various sources has fallen upon the Exchange is responsible for the acquisition of more land and another effort to provide adequate space for the ever-growing market.

---

[8] See Chapter XVIII.

[9] *Ibid.*

Origin of Seats on the Exchange

And now a word regarding the specific machinery of the Stock Exchange. Beginning as we have seen without equipment of any kind, the Board has evolved into a highly complex and scientific mechanism. Some of the intermediate stages of this evolution have been preserved in the language of the Exchange, even after they have vanished completely and forever. The phrase "a seat on the Exchange," so often employed today as a synonym for membership, means nothing now, for the modern Exchange member has little time or opportunity to sit down. Yet in the far-distant and more formal past Exchange members sat in their seats during trading hours like a financial senate. We are not told whether one of the chairs which "George F. Vaupell" had to furnish along with "fire" for "$200 per annum," or some more ostentatious piece of furniture, was originally responsible for this term. A rich field awaits the antiquarian in Wall Street, which for all its absorbing interest in the present and future cherishes here and there queer phrases and quaint customs with the utmost conservatism.

Parts of Present Stock Exchange System

The modern organized security market system which centers in the New York Stock Exchange can for purposes of study be divided into three principal parts: (1) the floor of the Exchange itself, where contracts for the purchase and sale of securities and for the borrowing and lending of both stocks and money are made; (2) the clearance system (embodied in the Stock Clearing Corporation), whereby the contracts made on the floor of the Exchange are cleared and settled; and (3) the commission houses, including their branch and correspondents' offices in all parts of the nation and even abroad, through which the American public has access to the security market upon the floor. Inasmuch as transactions on the Exchange itself are the basis and necessary background for the work performed by the clearance system and the commission houses, the whole subject of the Stock Exchange system can best be approached from the standpoint of the floor. Accordingly the remaining portion of the present chapter as well as six chapters immediately succeeding will be devoted to this part of the subject; the clearance system will then be described in three chapters; after which the commission house may be discussed with some understanding of its background and its contacts.

The Present-Day Quarters of the Stock Exchange

The present Stock Exchange building contains the large board room (Figure 2), where the actual trading in securities is done, and many smaller offices and committee rooms as well as a spacious Luncheon Club in its upper stories. In the basement are the offices of the Stock Clearing Corporation (of which more anon) and the massive vaults of the Stock Exchange Safe Deposit Company,[10] probably the largest and best protected safe deposit vaults in the world. As one stands in the visitors' gallery of the huge square lofty-ceilinged board room twenty posts range themselves beneath him on the floor, to which only members and employees of the Exchange are admitted. At each of these posts certain stocks are traded in. Fringing the floor are stalls lined with the 650 odd telephones which form the connecting links between the brokers on the floor and their outside offices. From the Wall Street commission houses, in turn, private telegraph wires spread out like a fan to all parts of the country.[11] Through these telephones, therefore, the buying and selling orders of the nation from its farthest corners swiftly converge upon the Exchange floor.

Machinery of the Floor

Two of the high walls of the board room contain enormous windows, beneath which the visitors' galleries run. On the

[10] See Chapter XII.

[11] See Chapter XIV, Figure 55.

Figure 2

The Floor of the New York Stock Exchange

Taken from the Broad Street gallery, showing both annunciator boards, stock posts, telephone booths, etc.

other two walls are the large black annunciator or signal boards upon which white numbers are constantly appearing and disappearing. Each broker on the floor below has his own number, and by flashing it on the signal boards his telephone clerk can quickly call him to his telephone out of the dense crowds about the posts. Below one of these annunciator boards is a small rostrum, about as far above the floor as are the visitors' galleries; it is from here that the opening and closing of the market is announced each day at 10 A.M. and 3 P.M. respectively by striking on a brazen gong. In the northeast corner of the floor three booths are partitioned off for trading in the United States government, foreign, and American railroad and industrial bonds respectively. On the floor between the stock posts four telegraph stations are also to be noticed. It is from these stations that the sales made on the Exchange floor are reported to the headquarters of the ticker company in the upper stories of the building, whence they are put on stock tickers all over the land.

Restricted Admittance to the Floor

The most stringent rules are and have always been in effect concerning admission to the floor of the Exchange. Only members of the Stock Exchange, as well as such employees of the Exchange as the bond clerks,[12] reporters and telegraphers, pages and tube attendants,[13] etc., are allowed on the floor.[14] The telephone clerks, who are employees of members, are forbidden to go on the floor beyond the telephone booths. Even partners of members, in case of the illness of a member, are forbidden the floor. This rule is made to prevent the possibility of inexperienced persons standing about the posts and

[12] See Chapter VII, page 161.

[13] See Chapter VI, page 135.

[14] Recently, for educational purposes, partners of Stock Exchange members were admitted on special occasions on the floor of the Exchange during business hours. Also on rare occasions eminent foreign visitors have been similarly admitted, as, for example, the King of Belgium and the Prince of Wales in 1920.

crying out bids or offers for securities or in any other way interfering with the trading occurring between members. Without such restrictions on admittance to the floor the complete present inviolacy of contracts between members made there could not well be maintained. A gallery is, however, provided for visitors to the Exchange and any responsible person, after being properly introduced, can from this vantage point watch the activities on the floor.

Of the 1,100 members of the Exchange, not more than 600 are generally present on the floor, and often not more than 400. In addition, there are about 225 pages of different sorts,[15] about 50 reporters and telegraphers, about 10 bond clerks, and about 550 telephone clerks.

Description of an Opening

The opening of the market at 10 A.M. provides one of the most picturesque moments in the day on the Exchange. Shortly before 10 A.M. the employee of the Exchange whose business it is to open and close the stock market, enters the rostrum and takes his seat. On the floor below are, roughly, a thousand people, all members or employees of the Exchange. The brokers and traders gather about the posts—waiting. In the telephone booths along the side walls the telephone clerks are busy with orders for purchases and sales. The black signal boards are flashing one white number after another as the clerks summon the brokers to the telephones. A low hum of conversation fills the board room. There is a tension in the air, for orders have accumulated in the brokerage houses overnight from all over the country and the opening is therefore usually energetic.

[15] A highly efficient employment department, under the Committee of Arrangements, supervises the work of the younger employees of the Exchange, and co-operates to assist them in continuing their education and improving their business status. The intensely human and progressive policy carried out by the employment department, which in any but an economic study of the Stock Exchange would deserve extensive comment, has brought commendation to the Exchange from official representatives of the Board of Education of New York City, principals of high schools, and leaders of well-known institutions of higher learning.

Suddenly, exactly on the hour of 10 A.M., the employee of the Exchange in the rostrum strikes a brass gong. The market has opened! Instantly a roar of voices rises as the brokers rush into the "crowds" around the various posts and back to their telephone stalls. Hundreds of men swarm about the posts shouting bids and offers and waving their hands in the air.

Although at first the spectator may think that bedlam has veritably broken loose, if he will follow closely the movements of almost any one of the brokers on the floor he will suddenly realize that the noisy chaos below him is in reality made up of hundreds of orderly but very energetic individuals performing their work systematically and efficiently. In spite of the clamor and excitement on the floor, hundreds of thousands of shares valued at many millions of dollars are bought and sold there daily with a negligible number of errors or misunderstandings.

Continual Expansion of the Stock Exchange

Yet extensive and efficient as the present facilities of the Stock Exchange are generally admitted to be, they have been taxed to the limit in the great market activity during and since the period of the Great War. A host of new corporate enterprises have sprung up with securities to list upon the Exchange. Moreover the year of 1919 established the record figure of 307,889,450 shares of stock and $3,763,217,764 par value of bonds sold on the Exchange floor.[16] Once again it has become necessary for the New York Stock Exchange to expand its physical equipment, to meet more easily this increased pressure upon it by our expanding industrial establishment and our new national position as a creditor nation.

Accordingly, the corner properties on Wall and Broad, and on Wall and New Streets, have been acquired by the Stock

[16] See Appendix, Chapter II (d).

Exchange, the buildings on these sites have been demolished, and the erection of a larger Stock Exchange building, which will occupy the whole block on Wall Street from Broad to New, has been commenced. This addition to the present Exchange building will extend upwards twenty-two stories and will be erected on a cofferdam resting on the solid rock some sixty feet below the level of the street. The Stock Exchange will occupy the three basement floors of the new building and several floors in the superstructure. The remaining space, particularly in the upper stories of the building, will be rented.

By this extensive addition the floor of the Exchange will be considerably enlarged, thus permitting the erection of new stock posts and bond counters, and the listing of new securities, some perhaps of foreign nations or arising from foreign financing. The equipment of the new building will be perfected to the utmost degree, particularly the elaborate apparatus which "washes" the air in the board room, the complicated pneumatic tubes which run underneath the floor, and the electric signal and intercommunicating telephone systems. Needless to say the partial demolition of the present Stock Exchange building and the erection of the new structure have been and will be so timed that the daily work of the security market can continue without interruption and with only slight inconvenience.

Brokers and Dealers

Before passing on to another chapter a brief analysis of the human mechanism of the stock market must also be given, for the market is able to function only through the highly specialized work of the several different types of brokers, dealers, and traders who go to compose it.

The Exchange members fall into two main classes—the brokers, and the dealers and traders. The broker executes orders to purchase or sell securities simply as the agent for someone else, on a fixed commission. The dealer or trader, on the other hand, has no customers and acts as nobody's agent but his own—that is to say, he buys or sells stocks entirely for himself and "on his own account," as it is usually phrased in Wall Street. Dealers and traders on the Exchange consequently make their livelihood out of selling securities for more than they pay for them, not out of commissions. In a general way the dealer in the New York Stock Exchange resembles the "jobber" in the London Stock Exchange, except that the dividing line between the jobber and the broker in the London market is drawn more distinctly than between the dealer and the broker in the New York market.

Brokers can be subdivided into several classes, the most important of which is perhaps the commission broker.[17] The latter usually represents a partnership of two or more men one of whom is a member of the Exchange and executes the orders of his "house" on its floor. The different "commission houses," [18] as they are commonly called, differ considerably in the clientele they serve and the type of business they do. Some have a few wealthy customers, while others through their branch offices and out-of-town correspondents handle the smaller orders of thousands and thousands of average investors all over the country. Certain houses also specialize in some special group of securities and gain a reputation in—say—railroad, or sugar, or motor stocks.

"Two-Dollar" Broker

Then there is the "two-dollar broker," who is attached to no one commission house but who makes use of his Exchange membership to assist the commission houses in executing their orders, particularly in heavy markets when the work is too great for the regular commission broker to handle it all on the floor. The two-dollar broker is therefore a free lance whose customers are other brokers. His name arises from the fact

[17] See Chapter III.

[18] See Chapter XII.

that his compensation for purchasing or selling 100 shares of stock used to be $2 out of the $12.50 which the commission broker formerly charged his customer. Although his commission rate has recently been changed to $2.50 out of $15, nevertheless the two-dollar broker's old title has persisted. The practical value of the two-dollar broker is that his work imparts a flexibility and a reserve power to the machinery of the Exchange which it would not otherwise have, and enables the violently fluctuating number of sales made from day to day to be handled smoothly and efficiently, whether they are many or few.

The Odd-Lot Dealer and the Floor Trader

As for the dealers, the odd-lot dealer buys and sells less than the trading unit of 100 shares of stock. So complex is his work that consideration of it must be deferred to a later chapter.[19] Then there is the floor trader,[20] who is a free-lance dealer in all stocks listed on the Exchange and who will buy or sell any of them on his own account whenever he sees the likelihood of a profit in the transaction. The floor trader is an indispensable factor in the essential work of the Exchange in constantly helping to create close prices for stocks and thus enhance their negotiability. Both the odd-lot dealer and the floor trader act for themselves rather than as agents for other principals, and their earnings depend in consequence upon obtaining a profitable difference between the buying and selling prices of their transactions rather than upon any commission such as the brokers obtain.

The Specialist

Lastly, and most difficult of all to define, is the "specialist."[21] Usually the specialist, as indeed his name would imply

---

[19] See Chapter VI. [20] See Chapter V. [21] *Ibid.*

specializes as a dealer or broker in a particular security or the particular securities located at a single post. He is not allowed to act as both dealer and broker in any single transaction, and he cannot charge a commission while he profits by the sale of a security at a higher price than that at which it was purchased.[22]

Commission brokers often turn over their orders for the specialist to execute, as a broker and their agent, on the same basis as with the two-dollar broker. Some specialists act as dealers in 100-share orders, and occasionally in odd-lot orders as well. In the former case their work resembles that of a floor trader, except that it is concentrated on one stock or group of stocks; in the latter case, of odd-lot orders, they do in their few special stocks what the odd-lot house does in all stocks.

In addition to the above brokers, dealers, and traders in stocks, there is also a class of dealers and brokers who specialize in bonds. These must likewise be allotted a chapter by themselves.[23]

Ethics of Yesterday and Today

It was inevitable that in the earlier history of the New York Stock Exchange, as well as of every other organized securities market in the world, methods were looked upon as legitimate which would not be tolerated for a moment today. In its long evolution into its present form, ethical as well as economic factors have entered. This fact is attested to in the former case by the continual growth of the Stock Exchange Constitution and the steadily increasing complexity and scope of its rules and regulations. Banking, corporate organization, commercial practice, and the very methods of government itself have likewise, during their incipient periods, experienced abuses which in their maturity have been minimized or wholly eliminated. This is only a corollary of progress itself, for if

[22] See Chapter V, page 108.

[23] See Chapter VII.

all our institutions were perfect in the beginning, progress and improvement would be impossible.

The Stock Exchange makes no claims to perfection. It is still deeply concerned with improving many of its methods and still struggling with the stubborn vestiges of ancient abuses. Yet in its integrity of purpose, in its efficiency of operation, and in its broad economic usefulness, it can today invite comparison with any other business institution in this country.[24] Indeed, in these respects it has always compared favorably with contemporary conditions in America, from the slave-holding days of the old brokers under the buttonwood tree down to the present time.

Omnipresence of Stock Exchanges

To summarize and conclude a somewhat rambling chapter, the stock exchanges have owed their origin and subsequent growth to the increasing government debts entailed by wars, and the tendency of modern business ever since the utilization of steam power to organize itself in larger corporate units for the more efficient production of goods and services. Owing to these two chief factors stock exchanges during the last century and a half have sprung up and flourished all over the world. The mighty London Stock Exchange was founded in 1773. The leading financial centers on the Continent all have their bourses. The United States possesses over twenty separate stock exchanges in its leading cities, while distant Japan has organized security markets in Tokio, Osaka, and other centers. Even immemorial China has organized a stock exchange at Shanghai in response to the awakening of corporate industry and transportation in her ancient regions. Stock exchanges are therefore everywhere recognized as a necessary part of the

[24] "There are 1,100 members of the Exchange, and the average of business failures among them during the past ten years is less than ½ of 1% per annum—of these, half settled with their creditors and were reinstated, reducing the absolute failures to ¼ of 1%." (H. S. Martin, New York Stock Exchange, p. 51.)

credit machinery demanded by modern civilization. It is through no accident that the most prosperous and cultured nations are in every instance those having the most and the largest stock exchanges.

CHAPTER III

A TYPICAL INVESTMENT TRANSACTION

Bidding and Asking

Before plunging directly into a detailed account of how securities are purchased and sold on the Stock Exchange, it is necessary to consider in a general way what sales are and how they are made. Every sale on the Stock Exchange, or anywhere else for that matter, naturally involves two separate parties—a buyer and a seller. The buyer, who expresses the demand for the commodity to be purchased, wishes, of course, to obtain it as cheaply as possible, while the seller, who expresses the supply side of the market, is equally desirous of getting the highest possible price for his goods. The interests of the buyer and the seller are, therefore, in direct opposition to each other. Hence, the seller almost invariably "asks" more for his goods than the buyer willingly "bids," and usually it is only after considerable higgling that a compromise is reached and a sale is effected at some intermediate point in the "spread" or difference between these bid and asked prices. When, for example, A tries to sell his automobile for $500 to B, who only wants to pay $400 for it, the situation might be described in financial language as "$500 asked—$400 bid." If A was only as anxious to sell as B was to buy, they would probably split the difference or spread of $100 and close the deal at $450. But if A was more eager to sell than B to purchase, he might have to take $425 or less for his car; while if B was more eager to purchase than A to sell, he might have to pay $475 or more.

Market Price Fluctuations

It is obvious that the stability of any selling price depends largely upon how great or how small the difference is between the bid and the asked prices previously quoted. When it amounts to 100 points out of 500, as in the case of A's automobile, the selling price might fluctuate anywhere along that wide range. But when, as is usually the case with an active listed stock like United States Steel common, the spread amounts to only 1/8 per cent, it is obvious that selling prices are apt for the time being to flutter closely about a relatively fixed point.

The market for securities provided by the New York Stock Exchange is the largest and most highly organized in America. Through a vast network of private brokerage wires the buying and selling orders of the entire nation converge upon the floor of the Stock Exchange. By the severe competition in establishing prices for stocks and bonds thus made possible, any buyer or any seller can be sure of immediately obtaining or disposing of securities there, at the closest prices which a national demand and a national supply for such securities can effect.

Work of the Commission Broker

With this general philosophy of prices the average broker is, of course, perfectly acquainted, although his mind is too fully occupied between the trading hours of 10 A.M. and 3 P.M. with specific orders to spend overmuch time pondering upon it. His business consists not of theorizing about the forces of supply and demand, but of executing the buying and selling orders caused by those forces, amid the posts, tickers, telephones, and signal boards on the Exchange floor. If we are to comprehend his every-day work, as well as the Stock Exchange machinery whereby he is enabled to carry it on, we must follow a typical "investment transaction" [1]—that is, an

[1] See Chapter XV.

outright purchase and outright sale of a given security—through all its various stages from beginning to end.

Origin of a Selling Order

To commence with the supply or selling side of the transaction, we find Mr. Jones of Baltimore one fine morning reading the stock ticker with evident interest. Some months before Jones had bought 100 shares of United States Steel common stock as an investment. Since that time the dry goods business which he conducts in Baltimore has grown so rapidly that funds for its expansion are now urgently needed. Jones had noticed that his Steel common was selling at about 95—that is, at $95 a share—and has decided to sell his shares and put the money into his business. Accordingly, he went to his bank, obtained his stock certificate from his safe deposit box, and took it over to the office of Jenkins and Company, his brokers, where he now stands over the ticker. After again satisfying himself by glancing at the tape that United States Steel is selling at 95 or better, Jones decides to sell at once and prepares a selling ticket.

There are several different ways in which he can make his order out, depending, of course, upon his exact wishes regarding the sale of his stock. If Jones indicates a definite price at which he will sell his stock, the order is called a "limited" order, and can be executed only at or above the price designated; but if no price limit is set it is called a "market" order, and is executed at the most advantageous price obtainable in the market at that particular time.

Usefulness of the Stop-Loss Order

Jones may also wish to place a stop-loss order, so as to limit any losses which he might encounter in the stock he purchases. He may, for example, at the time he gives his order to purchase 100 American Sugar at 85, also order his broker to sell that amount "on stop" at 80, in order to limit his loss to around 5 points on the stock so purchased. A stop-loss order is a limited order until the limit is reached, when it becomes a market order. For example, until Sugar sells down to 80 it is not executed, but once this stock has descended to this price, the order becomes an active market order calling for immediate execution.

The exact figure at which a stop-loss order is executed, therefore, depends entirely upon the exact conditions in the market at that time. If Sugar falls to 80 but rebounds to 82 on the next sale, the customer may sell out his stock on his stop-loss order at that price. But if Sugar, after reaching 80, should sink further to 78, it is around that price that the stop-loss order will be executed.

Simply because the limit on a stop-loss order is set at 80, therefore, is no reason that the customer should expect to make his sale at just that price.

Of course stop-loss orders placed above the market to protect the short seller from a swift rise in prices are just as permissible and common as similar orders placed below the market to protect the purchaser from a drop in prices. Since so many stop-loss orders are in practice handled by the specialists, some further points concerning their execution will be treated in the chapter which outlines the specialist's work.[2]

Forms of Limited Orders

Orders also differ as to the time for which they remain good. If Jones marks "G.T.W." on his order it means that it is "good this week" and that after the next Saturday it will become automatically void. Similarly, an order marked "G.T.M." is "good this month." But an order marked "G.T.C." is by that fact "good till countermanded," and remains in force indefinitely. Of course only limited orders

[2] See Chapter V.

ever bear these symbols—market orders are for immediate execution without any limit as to price, and hence do not involve the element of time.

Transmission of the Order

To return to Jones as he is making out his selling order, he decides, after a moment's reflection, to "put a limit" of 95 on his stock, and accordingly places this limit as well as the letters "G.T.C." on the slip.

He then gives the slip to the customer's man in Jenkins and Company's office, who at once turns it over to the order clerk. It is the business of this order clerk to record and supervise the transmission of orders to the main office of Jenkins and Company in New York, over the company's private telegraph wire.[3] In the present instance he sends Mr. Jones's order to the wire room, where the wire operator telegraphs the order over the firm's private wire to its New York office. The moment Jones hands his order slip to the customer's man he thus sets in motion the whole machinery of the Stock Exchange for executing orders and for the clearance and delivery of stock—a machinery concerning the complexity of which Mr. Jones has probably only the vaguest notion. And so while Jones lingers in the Baltimore brokerage office to watch for the record of his sale on the tape, the scene shifts to New York.

In the Wall Street Office

Meanwhile, in the main office of Jenkins and Company at 500 Wall Street a wire operator sits waiting for just such out-of-town orders as Jones's to come in over the firm's private long-distance wires. He receives the message from Baltimore to "sell 100 Steel at 95," and turns it over to the order clerk, who makes a record of it for filing purposes and transmits the order at once to the Exchange floor over the private telephone

---

[3] See Chapter XII.

Figure 3 Copyright N. Y. S. E.

Telephone Booths on the Floor

Showing a tube station and tube attendants.

maintained by Jenkins and Company for this very purpose. The telephone of Jenkins and Company is situated in one of the many telephone booths which fringe the Stock Exchange floor. (See Figure 3.) The firm's telephone clerk immediately takes down the order on a specially prepared selling slip (Figure 4), containing Jenkins and Company's name and a letter and number which indicate the location of their floor telephone.

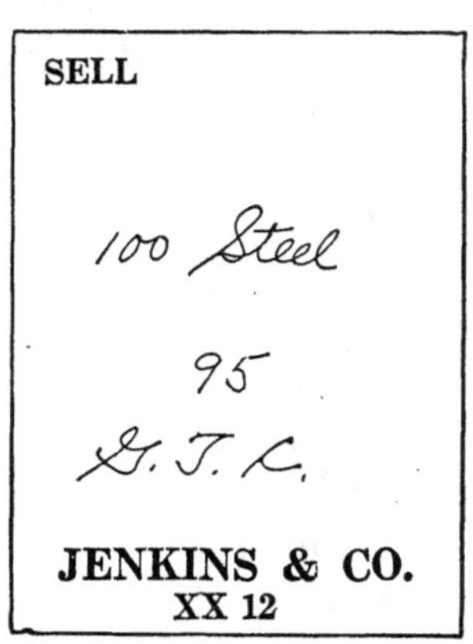

Figure 4. Floor "Sell Slip." (Size 3 x 4.)

Signaling the Exchange Broker

The next step is, of course, for the phone clerk to get this order into the hands of Mr. Jenkins, who is the floor member of Jenkins and Company and who personally executes on the Exchange the orders received by that firm. If the order were for an odd lot—that is, for less than 100 shares—the phone clerk would probably hand the written order to the tube attendant stationed near his telephone booth, who would enclose it in a container and send it through a pneumatic tube to the "Steel post," where another tube attendant would receive it and hand it over to an odd-lot dealer for execution.[4] If the order were for 100 shares, but limited at a price far away from current prices, it would perhaps be advisable to send it to the specialist in Steel,[5] and since the latter is always stationed at the Steel post, it would be sent to him through the tube in the same manner as an odd-lot order is to the odd-lot dealer. Also in certain exceptional instances Jenkins' phone clerk might give the order to a page with instructions to find Mr. Jenkins and give it to him.

[4] See Chapter VI, page 135.

[5] See Chapter V, page 110.

But, as is usually the case, the telephone clerk does not know where on the crowded Exchange floor Mr. Jenkins is, and he therefore signals for him on the two great annunciator boards which stand on opposite walls of the Exchange board room. Each broker has his own number and as he moves from one post to another on the floor he constantly watches for it to appear. Consequently, when Jenkins' telephone clerk presses a button beside his telephone, Jenkins' number, 371, suddenly appears in white on the great black signal boards. This at once attracts Jenkins' attention; he hastens over to his telephone booth and takes the order from the telephone clerk. In case Jenkins had been forced to absent himself from the floor at this time he would have probably instructed his clerk to give such orders as come in for him to one of the two-dollar brokers in order that there might be no delay in their execution.

Composition of a "Crowd"

Every stock listed for trading on the Exchange is assigned to some one of the twenty posts on the floor. Naturally there are many stocks traded in at each post. Jenkins quickly finds his way to the Steel post, where United States Steel stock is bought and sold. The so-called "Steel crowd" about this post is composed not only of commission brokers like Jenkins, who are buying and selling the stock as agents for other Exchange members or outside principals, but also of the floor traders, who trade entirely on their own account and who often provide a backbone for the whole market, of the odd-lot dealers, who stand ready to buy or sell any number of shares less than the ordinary trading unit of 100 shares, and of the specialists who confine their dealings entirely to the few stocks located at this post. This constantly shifting group of brokers and dealers represents the whole world demand and world supply of Steel stock at that particular moment.

The stock post itself (Figure 5) is about ten feet high, and its upper portion has twelve faces, each devoted to several different stocks. For each stock there is a metal plate bearing the name of the stock, and movable figures which record its price on the latest sale. Beneath this hang paper slips, one for every day over a course of the last few weeks, upon which are written the stock's daily opening, highest, lowest, and last price quotations. The purpose of these price records is to enable the broker or dealer to learn quickly and accurately recent selling prices for the security in question. On one side of each post are located the pneumatic tubes by which orders are sent to the specialists and odd-lot dealers who station themselves at that particular post and are often to be found seated on the circular cushion surrounding the base of the stock post.

"What's the Market for Steel?"

Prices for stocks on the New York Stock Exchange are quoted at a minimum difference of ⅛ per cent.[6] When Jenkins first arrives at the Steel post he learns from the indicator and slip attached to the post that Steel common opened that day at 94¾ and that its last recorded sale was at 95⅛. But in order to obtain the absolutely latest information on the "market" for Steel, Jenkins thrusts his way into the Steel crowd, which is crying out bid and offer prices at which they will buy or sell the stock, and inquires, "What's the market for Steel?" The specialist, who concentrates all his attention on this particular stock and consequently is thoroughly familiar with the subject, tells him, "95 bid, offered at ⅛," or perhaps replies simply "95 to ⅛," a shorter way of saying the same thing. In other words, the most any buyer at that particular moment is willing to pay for the stock is 95 (or $95 per share), while the least any seller will take for it is 95⅛ (or $95.125 per share).

[6] See Appendix, Chapter III (a).

Jenkins' order is limited at 95—that is, he must sell his customer's stock for 95 or more. If this limit were far away from the market—say, at 100—the chances are that considerable time must elapse (perhaps indeed a number of years) before market conditions would make it possible for him to sell the stock at that price. In such a case Jenkins would probably leave the order with the specialist in Steel, who would inscribe the offer of 100 in his book.[7] Since the specialist remains at a single post and confines his trading to a few of the stocks assigned to it, he will be in a position to take advantage of any sudden change in market conditions by which Steel can be sold at the limit price of 100.

Effecting a Sale

But in the present case the market is very close indeed to the limit of 95 on Jenkins' order. Jenkins is, of course, anxious to sell his customer's stock for the highest possible price. In an attempt to get for the latter an additional 1/8 over his price limit of 95, Jenkins accordingly joins in the chorus of voices and offers it at 95 1/8. But since no one seems willing to buy Steel stock at 95 1/8, the lowest price so far quoted by sellers, he next shouts, "I'll sell 100 Steel at 95." Scarcely has he uttered this offer than Wilkins, another commission broker in the Steel crowd, promptly shouts, "Take it," thus indicating that he will buy Jenkins' stock at the price the latter has named. If Wilkins had not been swift in buying the 100 Steel, some floor trader or specialist in the crowd might have forestalled him by purchasing it. Sometimes, indeed, two Exchange members will cry, "Take it" (or in case both are attempting to sell, "Sold!") at exactly the same instant. But they settle such a difficulty instantly and impartially by producing coins and "matching" one another to see which shall "get the sale." The winner thereupon enters the transac-

[7] See Chapter V, page 115.

Figure 5

Copyright N. Y. S. E.

Stock Post on the Floor

Showing attached tube station and attendants.

tion on his records as a sale, while the loser remains at the post to buy the stock he is after from someone else.[8]

Reporting the Sale

The magic words "Take it" mark the real point at which Jenkins' order is "executed," although to obviate the possibility of any misunderstanding Jenkins takes the precaution to cry to Wilkins, "Sold to you 100 Steel at 95." Jenkins next writes out a ticket known as a "report" (Figure 6), recording the details of the sale which he has just made, including the name and amount of the stock, the price, and the name of the buyer, and gives it to his telephone clerk, who phones it back to his office. This main office of Jenkins and Company on receipt of the report wires it in turn to the Baltimore branch, where Jones is informed of the transaction. It is, of course, to be noticed that Wilkins and Jenkins do not exchange securities or money at the post, but simply make a sales contract. The actual delivery of the stock and payment for it, as will be explained in subsequent chapters, are effected through the

Aug. 2 1920
WE HAVE THIS DAY Sold
FOR YOUR ACCOUNT AND RISK.

100 Steel
95
Wilkins & Co.

JENKINS & CO.
BOOTH XX

Figure 6. Floor Sale Report Slip. (Size 3 ¼ x 5.)
Recording sale of 100 Steel by Jenkins and Company to Wilkins and Company.

[8] See Appendix, Chapter III (b).

complex and important agency of the Stock Clearing Corporation.

Inviolability of Stock Exchange Contracts

The thorough insistence of the Stock Exchange upon the inviolability of contracts made on its floor is attested to by the readiness with which such contracts are effected.[9] We have seen in the typical transaction cited that Jenkins and Wilkins do not exchange any written agreement, but that a single word, or even a nod of the head, is sufficient to close a contract for the purchase and sale of stock valued at $9,500. Indeed, millions of dollars' worth of securities change hands in the Exchange each day in just this way without signed agreements, and with less danger of loss through cancellation, per dollar involved, than in any other kind of modern business.[10] There is no "welching on a trade" afterwards; no evasion of a contract is sought or allowed. The wave of cancellations which swept commercial America in the winter of 1920-1921 did not pass the threshold of the Exchange.

If statistics instead of prejudices were to be consulted, it is indeed doubtful if any institution or any group of men in this country is as entitled to boast of as high commercial ideals, or of as strict adherence to what its Constitution calls the "just and equitable principles of trade," as the New York Stock Exchange. Certainly, the Stock Exchange need not suffer by comparison in this respect with any department or aspect of the modern American business world.

Origin of Demand

An inquiry into the demand or buying side of this sale—that is, into what impelled Wilkins, the broker, to enter the Steel crowd and bid for stock, will lead us to San Francisco, three thousand miles from Wall Street. At almost the same

[9] See Chapter XIII.

[10] See Appendix, Chapter III (c).

moment that Jones was reflectively fingering his 100-share Steel certificate in the Baltimore brokerage office, a Mr. Smith was pondering over the ticker tape in a similar branch office of Wilkins and Company in San Francisco. Smith has prospered in the oriental exporting business and finds himself with a surplus of $10,000, which he desires to invest. He at length selects United States Steel common stock as the security best

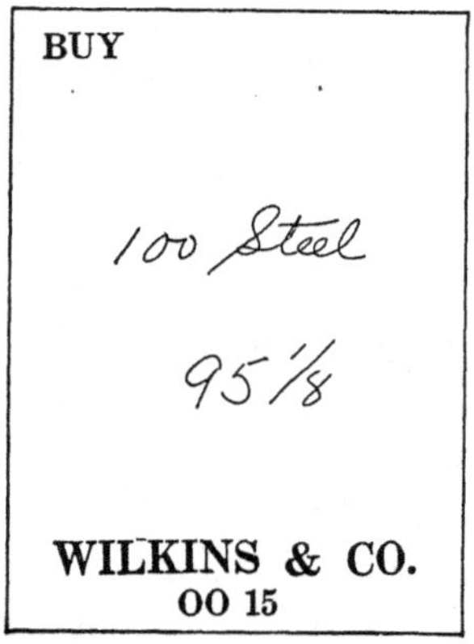

BUY

100 Steel

95⅛

WILKINS & CO.
OO 15

Figure 7. Floor "Buy Slip." (Size 3 x 4.)

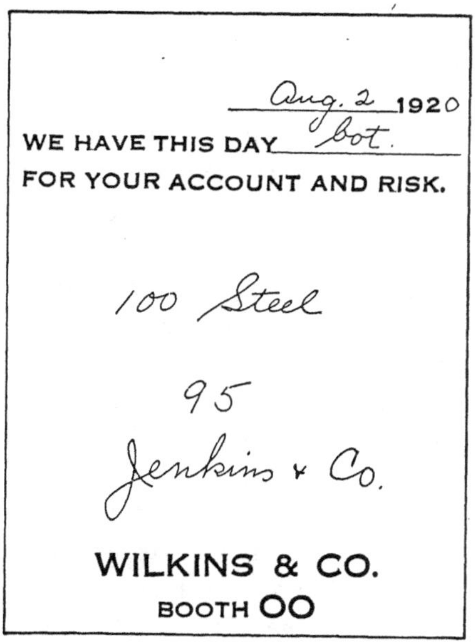

Aug. 2 1920
WE HAVE THIS DAY bot.
FOR YOUR ACCOUNT AND RISK.

100 Steel

95

Jenkins & Co.

WILKINS & CO.
BOOTH OO

Figure 8. Floor Purchase Report Slip. (Size 3¼ x 5.)

Recording purchase of 100 Steel by Wilkins and Company from Jenkins and Company.

fitted to his needs. Accordingly, he deposits his $10,000 with the San Francisco branch of Wilkins and Company and makes out a "buy" ticket for 100 shares of Steel, limiting the order to a price of 95⅛ or less. In due course this order speeds through channels similar to those observed in the case of Mr

Jones's order to sell. The order clerk in San Francisco sends the order over a private telegraph wire to the New York office of Wilkins and Company; thence it is relayed by private phone to the Stock Exchange floor, where a clerk takes it down on a buying slip (Figure 7); then Wilkins obtains and executes it. And, like the capable broker that he is, Wilkins obtained the stock ⅛ under the price limit set for its purchase by his far-away customer, by observing conditions and waiting at the post for just the right moment to buy the stock. He reports the purchase to his telephone clerk on a slip shown in Figure 8.

Machinery of the Ticker System

Meanwhile, the extensive and efficient machinery by which the daily transactions on the floor of the Stock Exchange are made public has not been idle. No sooner had Wilkins cried "Take it" to Jenkins' offer of stock at the Steel post than one of the quotation reporters who are stationed all over the trading floor notes the sale—the amount of stock sold and the selling price. He speedily turns this information over to the telegraph operator at the nearest of the four telegraph stations in the stock market. This operator in turn promptly telegraphs the news in Morse code to the headquarters of the New York Quotation Company, situated in an upper story of the Stock Exchange building. Here the message is put on the ticker machines of the New York Quotation Company, whose distribution is confined to Manhattan Island below Chambers Street. From one of these tickers in the head office of the Western Union Telegraph Company another operator copies off the quotations as they appear and transmits them to the Western Union Company's tickers, which are located all over the nation.

By this process, which takes longer to explain than to operate, the significant symbols "X 95" are almost at once stamped on the ticker tape all over the country. ("X" is the ticker symbol for United States Steel common stock, while the numeral shows that this sale has been made at 95. In the absence of any figure the sale of 100 shares of stock is presupposed. But the sale of 200 shares of Steel at 95 would be indicated on the ticker by "X 2.95," the sale of 300 shares by "X 3.95," etc.) Thus it comes about that Jones, waiting in the Baltimore brokerage office, presently sees the quotation and has reason to think that his stock may have been sold at its limit of 95, while about the same time Smith in San Francisco sees the same quotation and knows that at prices then prevailing, his buying order limited at 95⅛ or less should have been executed.

Limitations of the Stock Ticker

Of course, the customer in an out-of-town brokerage office must not be too hasty in concluding that the first quotation which appears on the tape following the placing of his order of necessity represents the sale of his own stock. Both from the many physical steps outlined above which must be gone through to transmit and execute orders for stocks and to report their prices over the ticker, and from the mechanical limitations of the ticker system itself, it is obvious that considerable delays may often arise between the placing of the order in the commission house and the appearance of the quotation on the tape. In fairly active markets it has been estimated that the ticker machine must print as many as 225 characters per minute, and 65,000 characters per five-hour Stock Exchange trading day.[11] The ticker may, therefore, if its physical limitations are surpassed by the volume of trading, lag fifteen or more minutes behind the market. Furthermore, it is often good brokerage for the broker to wait, as Wilkins did, before executing the customer's orders. Smith was saved ⅛ per cent on his stock through just such a delay. Yet if Smith, after placing his order, had begun at once to watch the

[11] Martin, p. 213.

ticker he might have thought that the very first subsequent quotation really represented the purchase of his own stock. While his order was en route to the floor Steel might have sold at 94¾ or 94⅞, and when he received confirmation of his own transaction at 95 he might have leaped to the natural but erroneous conclusion that he had suffered an injustice.

Complete Publicity of Stock Exchange Transactions

But not only Jones and Smith are informed of their transactions in Steel; everyone in the country from Duluth to New Orleans, or from Portland, Maine, to Portland, Oregon, who is in any way interested in the market value of this stock, whether because he is a stockholder or thinking of becoming a stockholder in the United States Steel Corporation, or because of the economic conditions in industry and trade which the price of its shares may reflect or even forecast, can gain almost instant information of the transaction in which Jones and Smith have figured, as well as every similar transaction that takes place that day and every other day on the Stock Exchange. The ticker service is of especial value to banks and other financial institutions.

The uncanny swiftness and accuracy of the American stock ticker system invariably astonishes foreign visitors to America. Indeed, as eminent an economist as Paul Leroy-Beaulieu has strongly urged its adoption by the Bourse, the great stock market of Paris.[12] It is safe to say that there is no other market in the world whose transactions are given as complete, as immediate, and as reliable publicity, as the New York Stock Exchange.

Value of a Ready Market

There is still another aspect of this sale of 100 shares of Steel, which through the operations of the two commission

---

[12] See Appendix, Chapter III (d).

brokerage houses Jones of Baltimore has been able to make so quickly and satisfactorily to Smith of San Francisco, that deserves emphasis at this point. In all probability Jones never heard of Smith or Wilkins. He may not even know that such men exist, and, granted the Stock Exchange system, he does not need to. But were there no Stock Exchange, no out-of-town brokerage houses, no thousands of miles of brokerage wires spreading like a vast network over the whole country, Jones could not effect his sale so easily and at so fair a price. Lacking all this machinery, he would be forced to go to considerable personal exertion and expense to sell his stock. He would have to talk to his friends and hunt out his friends' friends and perhaps to advertise in the newspapers. It might be months (instead of minutes) before he would happen upon such a buyer as he can find almost at once through the Stock Exchange, and even then he might have to sell his stock at a heavy discount. Without the work of the stock exchanges the public would indeed hesitate before investing its money in securities which would be so difficult to dispose of afterwards.[13]

Scope of the Stock Market

Contemporary fiction to the contrary notwithstanding, there is nothing particularly mysterious about the operation of the Stock Exchange. In its fundamentals it is like any other market, except that it is more completely organized and handles a larger turnover of sales. So huge is the field covered by this market, so numerous are the buyers and the sellers dealing in it, so widespread and efficient are the commission brokerage houses, and so ready are the dealers on its floor, that investors can at any time purchase the prime American investment securities there, or in case of need turn their securities into cash almost immediately. American investors and business men are so accustomed to this instant ability to sell or purchase

[13] See Chapter XIV.

securities that they sometimes forget the very real and very essential services which the stock exchanges render them.

True Nature of the Stock Market

The average American, of course, has not been, is not, and never will be, a member of the New York Stock Exchange. If he sees the operation of this great market at all, necessarily it is not at close hand from the Exchange floor but even at best from a distance in the visitors' gallery. And owing alike to the surf-like roar of many voices which its open-market system makes inevitable, to the swift movements of the many men on its floor, to its many unique mechanical devices, and perhaps to his initial suspicion that wickedness is somehow afoot there, the impression of the Stock Exchange which he forms from looking down upon it for a few minutes from the gallery is as likely to deepen his doubts and confuse his understanding of its real nature as to inform him of its actual methods and economic services.

Yet, however confused the spectator's mind might become at it all, the members of the Stock Exchange are so accustomed to the clamor of the market place that they are as a rule neither excited nor confused. As subsequent chapters may partially succeed in establishing, it would require years of patient study and observation, as well as no slight degree of imagination and intelligence, before an observer in the gallery could perceive the stock market below him with adequate knowledge and comprehension. But, as has been once stated,[14] if the onlooker from this vantage point possessed these several and difficult qualifications:

> He would see purchases for investments; he would see sales on behalf of persons wishing to convert their securities for one reason or another; he would see purchases and sales for the dealers in odd lots to meet the needs of the small investor;

[14] See Regulation of the Stock Exchange, pp. 531–532.

he would see purchases and sales with a purely speculative purpose; he would see the floor trader buying and selling for the profit of the hour; he would see the arbitrageur selling securities that he has bought in London, or Paris, or Amsterdam, or Berlin the same day, or buying here the securities he has sold on a foreign exchange the same day. Every transaction is recorded, and the quotations that go out are the result of all these manifold operations. They are the product of the judgments, temperaments, hopes, fears and doubts of the vast multitude that participate in them. It is a scene of competition; the conservatism of investment face to face with the enterprise of speculation; speculation in the expectation of a rise in prices with speculation in the expectation of a fall; optimism with pessimism; and the resultant of this play of forces is the market price of the securities dealt in moment by moment, hour by hour. The exchange is the crucible in which all these various elements are, as it were, chemically combined and concentrated to produce what we call market values. All these elements are indispensable as supplements and correctives of each other. Eliminate speculation and the conservatism of investment would arrest the development of the country. Eliminate speculation in the expectation of a fall in prices and the danger of inflation of prices would be constant. Without the free interplay of all these forces a market would not perform its function of fixing prices for the purposes of trade and commerce.

CHAPTER IV

CREDIT TRANSACTIONS IN SECURITIES

Need of Understanding Credit Operations

In the preceding chapter an account was given of the machinery of the Stock Exchange and how it enabled an investor in Baltimore to sell his stock to another investor in San Francisco. This imaginary but quite typical case was, in the instance of both buyer and seller, what is known as an "investment transaction"—a phrase which refers not to the character of the particular security bought and sold, but to the terms between broker and customer under which the sale was made.[1] It is to be noticed that in the case cited Jones of Baltimore simply took his stock to his broker and employed the latter to exchange it for money, while Smith of San Francisco took his money to his broker and employed him to exchange it for stock. The element of credit did not enter into either the purchase or sale of the stock in any vital way.

Such outright sales and purchases of stock occur in the Stock Exchange less frequently than purchases and sales of stock which employ credit, just as cash payments and immediate deliveries are the exception rather than the rule in ordinary wholesale commercial practice. Most of the significant economic forces in modern America find a natural and immediate expression in the credit transactions in securities which occur daily upon the floor of the Stock Exchange. At a time like the present, when even the existence of these eternal and unchanging economic laws is denied by reckless and misinformed writers on financial topics, a wider understanding by

[1] See Chapter XV.

the average American of these credit transactions in securities is more than ever imperative.

To understand thoroughly the more complex aspects of the selling or purchasing of securities in our stock markets, it is first necessary to consider briefly what a sale really is. Every sale, not merely of stocks and bonds but of any commodity whatsoever, is simply an exchange of money and goods. For this reason, strange though it may sound, it would from a purely economic standpoint be quite correct to speak of buying $75 with a ton of steel, or selling $60 for a suit of clothes. Owing to our constant use of money as the measure for all values, however, we habitually think of every sale in terms of money rather than in terms of goods.

Sales for Cash and on Credit

Sales can be divided into two general classes, depending on whether or not they involve the element of credit. In an outright or cash sale the buyer immediately pays his money and the seller at once delivers his goods. Since there is no delay on either side of the transaction, credit—which is simply a substitute for money or goods in the form of a promise either to pay the one or to deliver the other at some future time—is in no way involved. Yet cash sales undoubtedly furnish a smaller part of our daily business turnover today than do sales on credit. Indeed, the use of credit had come to constitute a vital factor in business even before the creation of the modern check and deposit banking system. If by some economic miracle credit transactions could be wholly abolished, our whole modern banking system would at once degenerate into the crude business of money-changing from which it rose centuries ago. All modern governments by their issuance of both bonds and fiduciary paper currency show how completely dependent they are upon the use of credit. As for commerce and industry, neither has been wholly upon a basis of cash payment and immediate delivery since the economic stagnation of the Middle Ages—if, indeed, they were even then. It is consequently no exaggeration to say that without the invention of the credit machinery which in modern times permits the deferred payment of money and the deferred delivery of goods, the vast material and spiritual progress of the human race since the twelfth century would have been utterly impossible.[2]

Fallacies Regarding Credit

In spite of the extensive and time-honored employment of credit in business, comparatively few men ever stop to analyze in detail exactly what credit is. In consequence, the average business man is only too apt to be puzzled when he is asked, "How can a man buy something when he doesn't want to keep it and hasn't enough money to pay for it?" or "How can a man sell something which he doesn't own?" Superficially considered, both of these questions would seem to imply a lack of business morality. And yet the simple answer to both these questions obviously is, "By using credit." Thanks to the vast extension of our credit machinery during the past century, the deferred payment of money and the deferred delivery of goods have both become a daily commonplace, not merely in Stock Exchange transactions but in every conceivable kind of modern business.

One phase of this universal use of credit deserves consideration at this point. Although a sale is really an exchange of money and goods, our inevitable habit of thinking only on the money side of what is necessarily a two-sided transaction makes it easier for the average man to understand a deferred payment of money than a deferred delivery of goods. Owing someone money is an experience with which, fortunately or unfortunately, most of the human race is only too well acquainted, whereas owing someone goods—whether it be an overcoat, a

[2] See Appendix, Chapter IV (a).

barrel of molasses, or a share of stock—is apt to seem a novel and highly perplexing situation.

Debts in Terms of Goods

Yet a moment's thought will show that it is no more unnatural to owe goods than to owe money. In ancient times, long before money had been invented, all trading was necessarily conducted entirely by barter, which consists of an exchange of goods for goods. Thus an ancient Roman would exchange his cattle for someone's bronze implements, or an American Indian would barter his furs for another Indian's corn. In point of historical evolution, therefore, it is altogether probable that credit was used to defer a delivery of goods, long before it was employed in the deferred payment of money. It is consequently apparent that owing someone goods rather than money is not at all a new device of what a perpetually indignant section of our press likes to refer to as "high finance," but an inevitable and immemorial practice arising from the fundamental nature of trade.[3]

Purchasing a House on Credit

Keeping it constantly in mind, then, that every sale is necessarily a two-sided transaction, involving goods as well as money, let us examine in more detail a typical purchase on credit. Mr. Jones, with a bank account of $8,000, a salary of $6,000, and an ability to save about $2,000 each year, is attracted by a $10,000 house. Obviously, he has not money enough at present to buy it, nor does he wish to tie up all his savings in it, yet he has every reason to believe that, counting in part of his bank balance, he can comfortably pay the necessary amount in four years. He therefore decides to purchase the house on credit. He puts up $2,500 of the money he has in the bank, and gives his note for $7,500 to the seller.

[3] See Appendix, Chapter IV (b).

This note is a promise to make a deferred payment of money, and is secured by a mortgage upon the house. If Jones cannot keep up the interest on the note or make the deferred payment on its principal at maturity, the holder of the note can seize the house to recover the $7,500 involved. But subject to these conditions Jones has the house, and can live in it and enjoy it while he is saving the money needed to complete payment for it. Or, if houses become more expensive and someone offers Jones $12,000 for his house, he can sell it, and after paying off his note have a profit of $2,000 on the transaction. The credit element in Jones's purchase of his house is involved on the money side of the transaction. Jones obtains the house when he "hasn't enough money to pay for it" by employing credit to defer the payment of 75 per cent of its price. But there is no deferred delivery of the house, which is handed over to him as soon as he signs his note.

Credit Sale of a Crop

Let us now consider a case where credit is used to defer the delivery of goods instead of the payment of money. Smith owns a fertile farm, where in the past he has grown wheat both successfully and profitably. But early one spring he finds himself without money enough to buy seed and pay for plowing, sowing, and harvesting the next year's crop. It seems a hopeless situation to Smith, as he murmurs to himself those ancient and tragic words, "If I only had the money. . . ." But the affair is not so impossible after all. The fundamental earning power in his dark rich soil is undoubtedly there. And so, perhaps just when Smith is most discouraged, a commission grain merchant who has heard of his dilemma, visits him and offers to buy the crop that Smith is so confident he can raise, before it is even planted.

If this is the first time that Smith ever made such an arrangement he is perhaps inclined to think the whole transaction fantastic and impracticable. Yet the modern machinery for handling such credit operations has rendered them a universally beneficial commonplace in American agriculture. With the money advanced by the merchant, Smith proceeds to purchase seed and do his plowing, sowing, and harvesting. Of course, the transaction has its risks. Smith has sold a wheat crop which as yet he does not possess. Winds, rains, and insects may prevent him from making the deferred delivery of wheat in return for the money advanced him by its purchaser. Nevertheless, without this sale for future delivery Smith would not have been able to raise a crop at all. In the majority of cases both Smith and the commission merchant will find their bargain a profitable one. Other familar examples both of purchases or sales made on credit could be cited almost indefinitely.

Use of Credit in Security Transactions

Buying and selling securities on credit is no different in principle from buying or selling houses or wheat on credit; neither does one have to go to the Stock Exchange to meet with such transactions. In floating the Liberty Loans our government employed the buying and selling of securities on credit to a vast extent. In order to obtain the enormous sums needed for the prosecution of the war, our Treasury Department urged Americans to purchase their bonds on credit by making an initial payment themselves and allowing the banks to furnish them credit for the balance of the price of the bonds. In this way subscribers were able to buy more bonds than they would otherwise have been able, and by gradually paying off with their savings the credit furnished by the banks, they were finally able to obtain complete ownership of their bonds.

The government also made a deferred delivery of most of the bonds which it sold. When the subscriber for cash deposited his check at his bank he was told that the bonds which he was buying were not yet ready to deliver—that they had not yet even been printed. Minus his money and at the same time without his bonds he walked out of the bank, perhaps in that puzzled state of mind which many of the new investors created by the Liberty Loans will still recall. The delayed delivery of the bonds was of course necessitated by the enormous task of engraving and printing them. The government consequently employed its credit in agreeing to deliver the bonds at some convenient future time in exchange for the subscriber's cash. And when the subscriber received his bonds he no doubt proceeded to forget—if indeed he had ever completely realized it—that the government had sold its securities to him on credit and for future delivery.

Financial Terminology

Now every profession has its own technical "lingo" which, however necessary, usually leads to considerable confusion in the public mind. Many simple incidents in business when paraphrased by the lawyer suddenly become mighty and perilous affairs indeed. Common ailments described with the lengthy Greek derivatives of the doctor grow into mysterious and fearsome diseases. Much the same thing occurs when such ordinary business operations as selling or buying on credit are referred to by the banker or broker in their financial argot as "buying on margin" or "selling short." The needless mystery which these mere words create about our stock markets largely explains why it is that the very newspapers and magazines which year in and year out accept the yearly subscription price for their journals in exchange for their promise to complete the deferred delivery of them to the subscribers a whole year afterwards, will so often express horror at "short sales" on the Stock Exchange, because, forsooth, they involve "selling what one doesn't own."

Purchasing Securities on Credit

In actual fact then, buying on margin is simply the financial phrase for buying stocks or bonds by employing credit to defer a payment of money; the same basic operation is known as "purchasing on credit" in some branches of commercial business. "Selling short," on the other hand, is simply the phrase used in finance to designate a sale of securities in which credit is used to defer their delivery; in its economic essentials this operation corresponds to what merchants and manufacturers usually call selling "for forward" or "future delivery." An investor or speculator who has bought stocks on margin is said to be "long" of stocks; whereas if he has sold them but has not yet delivered them, he is said to be "short" of stocks. Furthermore, the speculator who buys stock on margin in the expectation of seeing a rise in its price which will subsequently enable him to sell it at a profit, is called a "bull," while the name of "bear" is given to anyone who sells a stock short in the anticipation that its price will shortly decline so that he can buy it to "cover" his sale (i.e., make his deferred delivery of the stock) at a lower price and obtain a profit.

Thus Stock Exchange transactions when stripped of the hectic and unfamiliar verbiage with which the financial scribe so often invests them resolve themselves into a few commonplace and immemorial practices of trade which exist just as extensively, although unhonored and unsung, in every grocery store and newsstand in the nation.

Margin Purchase of 100 Steel

That the principles involved in purchasing securities on credit are fundamentally identical with those involved in the purchasing on credit of any commodity, is at once apparent when we examine in detail a typical purchase of securities on margin as it is carried out through the machinery provided by the Stock Exchange.

Let us suppose that just as Mr. Jones was about to purchase his house on credit a relative had died and left him a house and that he had therefore resolved to invest the same amount of money, present and prospective, in securities instead. After some deliberation Jones selects United States Steel common stock as a security yielding satisfactory dividends and likely to advance in price. Having thus become a "bull" on Steel, he goes to his broker, a member of the New York Stock Exchange, and requests his assistance in purchasing 100 shares of Steel on credit. Steel is selling at 100, and consequently the cost of 100 shares will be $10,000. Jones puts up $2,500 in cash as a part payment (or, as the financial phrase runs, a "25-point margin"), while his broker agrees to obtain credit for Jones for the remaining $7,500 needed to purchase the stock. The broker may loan Jones the $7,500 out of the funds of his own firm, or he may obtain that sum from a bank as a loan negotiated for and contracted in the name of his brokerage firm.

In order to secure the loan the broker will demand the right to hold Jones's certificate for 100 shares of Steel when it is purchased.[4] In case the loan has been obtained from a bank, he is in turn obliged to allow the bank to hold the certificate until the loan has been paid off.[5] Jones must, of course, pay interest on this $7,500 which he has borrowed. Meanwhile Jones is the owner of the 100 shares of Steel and is entitled to all dividends declared on it, which in normal times should roughly cover the interest charges on the borrowed funds involved by the transaction. Furthermore, should the price of Steel climb upwards to, say, 120, he can instantly sell his 100 shares for $12,000 and, after paying off his loan of $7,500 and recovering his "margin" of $2,500, obtain a profit on the transaction of about $2,000.

---

[4] See Chapter VIII.

[5] See Chapter XII and Appendix, Chapter IV (c).

Duties of the Broker

In stock purchases of this kind the broker, of course, demands and deserves ample protection. The actual purchase of stock on the floor of the Exchange, as well as any loan which he may subsequently obtain upon it at the bank, are both contracted for in the broker's name. Consequently, in case of the unwillingness or inability of the customer to "carry" the stock, as well as the loan and the interest upon it, his broker must do so. The broker's only profits in a 100-share transaction in a stock selling around $100 a share consist of his commission of $15 for buying the stock and $15 for selling it (or, for both transactions, about 1/3 per cent of the value of the stock), plus the interest on $7,500, in case the broker advanced this money to Jones to make the purchase. In case the broker obtained the $7,500 for Jones from a bank, he will charge a slight addition to the rate of interest demanded by the bank to compensate him for the trouble, expense, and responsibility he assumes in obtaining the money. The broker is acting simply as Jones's agent. He did not select the stock to be purchased, and since he will not share in any speculative profits which Jones may make in the transaction he cannot be expected to share any more of the speculative risks involved than he can help.[6]

The principal risk taken by a broker when his customer purchases stock on margin is that the cash value of the stock on the market may decline below the amount of money originally borrowed to purchase it. If, for example, Jones's 100 shares of Steel should suddenly decline from 100 to 70, their value would shrink from $10,000 to $7,000, or $500 less than the $7,500 loan originally made to purchase them. If meanwhile, the broker was so foolish as not to call upon Jones for more margin, he would find himself liable for the $7,500 loan, with only $7,000 worth of stock to secure it. To protect him-

[6] See Chapter XII.

self against possible losses of this kind the broker will therefore demand that his customer put up more margin whenever the market value of the latter's stock declines, so that there will constantly be a surplus of $2,500 when the purchase price of the stock is subtracted from its market value plus the customer's margin. Since the purchase price of the stock is fixed at $10,000, it is obvious that the less the stock is worth on the market the more margin the customer must put up to maintain this surplus of $2,500.[7]

There is no uniform rule regarding the exact percentage of margin initially required, or the extent to which a broker will carry his margin customer in a declining market before calling upon him for additional margin. The credit of individuals varies so widely that brokerage houses, just as banks, must decide each case involving an extension of credit on its own separate merits. It is, however, a well-recognized fact that it is to the advantage of both broker and customer to establish and maintain considerable margins, and that the most successful brokerage houses are apt to be those which are most conservative about margin requirements.

"Margin Calls" and Profit-Taking

But to return to our example: If the price of Steel declines to 90 the broker may demand that Jones put up an additional $1,000 of margin, since the 10-point decline has reduced the surplus of the value of the stock plus the margin over the purchase price to only $1,500. In case the stock continues to decline and Jones, after being notified by the broker, refuses to put up the amount of margin previously agreed upon, the broker will then sell his 100 shares of Steel at—say—85. Out of the $8,500 resulting from the sale he will then pay off the $7,500 loan and return $1,000 to Jones, minus interest charges, brokerage commissions, and stamp taxes.

[7] See Chapter XII.

If, however, the expected rise in the price of Steel occurs and the stock sells at 115 on the market, Jones's margin has increased by $1,500. But perhaps Jones decides to conclude the transaction and "take his profit." The broker, on Jones's instructions, then sells the 100 shares of stock for $11,500 and, after paying off the loan of $7,500, returns to Jones $4,000 minus brokerage commissions, interest charges, and stamp taxes. Thus Jones, in addition to recovering his original margin of $2,500, obtains a profit of almost $1,500 in the transaction.

Selling for Deferred Delivery

Since every sale is simply an exchange of money and goods it is obvious that the factor of credit can become involved in a sale in two different ways—either through a postponement in the payment of money or in the delivery of goods. Respecting transactions in the stock market, we have briefly considered the practice of deferring the payment of money known as "buying on margin." We must next examine "short selling," which involves the deferred delivery of stock.

The position of the man who sells stock short is fundamentally identical with that of the farmer who sells his crop before it is planted, or of the publisher who sells his newspapers months before the events which they will chronicle have even occurred. All these three sellers, by employing their credit and deferring the delivery of their goods, sell something which for the time being they do not own, but which they feel confident they can obtain. All three owe goods instead of money, and all three must depend, to conclude their sales on credit, upon obtaining later the articles which they have sold—a task which may be either harder or easier than to obtain an equivalent sum of money.

Attention has already been called to the fact that because of our almost universal habit of thinking of sales in terms of money rather than in terms of goods, owing goods is apt to seem to the average man much more dangerous than owing money. Let us follow through its various stages, a typical short sale of stock occurring on the New York Stock Exchange, and see if this practice is the evil and nefarious thing which many sincere but superficial critics of the stock markets would have us believe.

Selling 100 Locomotive Short

Thompson, who is a "bear" and anticipates declining prices, instructs his brokers, White and Company, to sell 100 shares of American Locomotive stock short for him at 100. Thompson does not possess this stock, but can, of course, buy or borrow it whenever he so desires. Before proceeding to execute this order the brokers must not only have confidence in Thompson's financial responsibility but will probably insist on possessing tangible evidence of it in the form of a margin of—say—25 points, or $2,500, to protect themselves against the unwelcome possibility of a rise in the price of the stock to be sold. It is also understood between Thompson and White and Company that in case American Locomotive stock should advance in price Thompson will maintain this 25-point margin by putting up more margin, so that a surplus of $2,500 shall always remain after the current purchasing price of the stock has been subtracted from the price of $10,000 at which it was sold plus the customer's margin. As in the case of a margin purchase, the broker in the event of an adverse movement in the value of the stock will demand that Thompson put up a proportionate amount of additional margin, while if the price of the stock moves favorably Thompson's margin will be increased to that extent. Also, in case Thompson does not furnish the additional margin agreed upon when notified of an advance in the price of the stock by his broker, the latter will proceed to buy 100 shares to conclude the transaction and return to his customer what remains of his margin. In a short sale the customer is not usually called upon to pay any interest charges, since he is not borrowing any money. But, as we shall see, he must expect to pay such dividends as may be declared upon stock of which he is short and which he has to borrow.

The Purchaser's Attitude

With these preliminaries arranged, White and Company proceed to sell for Thompson 100 shares of American Locomotive on the floor of the Stock Exchange to Brown, another broker, at 100. Brown, the buyer, does not know or care whether White's customer is selling outright or on credit. He has made an agreement on the floor of the Exchange to pay $10,000 for 100 shares of American Locomotive. Unless he settles for the stock by the next day he will be subject to the severe penalties imposed by the Stock Exchange when a broker fails to meet his obligations. Furthermore, he knows that White and Company are under the same compulsion to deliver to him the 100 shares of American Locomotive by the same time. Where White and Company will get this stock is no concern of his.

Meanwhile White and Company have assumed the responsibility of delivering by 2:15 P.M. of the next day stock which they do not possess.[8] It may happen that American Locomotive declines to 95 that same day, thus permitting Thompson to buy 100 shares at this price and make a profit of 5 points—or $500—on the whole transaction. If this is done, White and Company can deliver to Brown by the next day, the stock thus purchased and so obviate any further difficulty in the transaction. Yet in a majority of cases stock which has been sold short will not decline quite so conveniently. Probably, then, Thompson will wish to remain short of the stock for some time.

[8] See Chapter IX.

Function of the "Loan Crowd"

To avoid just this dilemma which brokerage houses would otherwise experience in making deliveries of stock which had been sold short by their customers, a system of borrowing and loaning stocks has developed on the floor of the Stock Exchange which is a counterpart of the system also developed there for borrowing the "call money" with which the margin purchases of brokers' customers are regularly financed. Every morning about 9:45 A.M. the "loan crowd" assembles at a certain post, and within it the loaning and borrowing of stocks go on intermittently till 1:30 P.M.; it then ceases entirely until between 3 and 3:30 P.M., when most of the day's loans are made.

This loan crowd is composed of Exchange members who wish to borrow or loan stocks. White and Company's Board member—i.e., the particular partner in the firm who is a member of the Exchange and who handles its business on the floor —therefore seeks out Green, a broker with 100 shares of American Locomotive to lend. To obtain the loan of Green's stock, White and Company usually have to agree to lend Green a sum of money equal to its market value. If, for example, American Locomotive closed that day at 100, Green will obtain a loan of $10,000 in return for the loan of the stock which he makes to White and Company. It is understood between such lenders and borrowers of stock that the amount of this money loan must be kept at a figure equivalent to the market value of the stock in question. Should American Locomotive rise from 100 to 105, White and Company would have to loan to Green an additional $500 upon it; while if the stock should decline from 100 to 95, Green would have to return to White and Company $500 of the original loan of $10,000.

Thus Green borrows White and Company's money and White and Company borrows Green's stock. But the money still belongs to White and Company, and the stock to Green.

For this reason Green must normally pay interest on the money borrowed from White and Company. On the other hand, White and Company must pay to Green such dividends as may be declared upon the stock borrowed from him.[9] Of course, Thompson, as a principal, must in turn repay these dividends to his agents, White and Company. This necessity of the short seller to pay for dividends in this way, which often puzzles inexperienced traders and investors, has been likened to the case of farmer X who loans his cow to farmer Y. If in the course of this loan the cow has a calf, it naturally belongs to X, the owner of the cow, and not to Y, who is simply the borrower of the cow.

Loans Made "Flat" or "at a Premium"

While the above arrangement between the borrower and the lender of stock is typical, its details may vary considerably because of conditions connected with the supply of and demand for the stock in question. If American Locomotive shares grow scarce, Green will demand and obtain a low rate of interest on his loan of money or he may get the loan of money "flat"—that is, without having to pay any interest on it at all. In cases of extreme scarcity of stock he may even obtain, in addition to his loan of money without interest, a cash premium from the borrower of his stock. Of course, this premium is in turn charged by the borrowing broker to his customer who has gone short of the stock in question.[10]

Returning to our example, White and Company deliver the 100 shares of American Locomotive borrowed from Green to their purchaser, Brown. The latter in turn sends to White and Company his check for their selling price of $10,000. Brown, therefore, having paid his money and received his stock, is now out of the transaction. There remain involved in it Thompson (who owes White and Company, his brokers, the 100 shares of

---

[9] See Chapter XII.

[10] *Ibid.*

stock), White and Company (who owe Thompson his margin of $2,500 and $10,000—the selling price of the stock—and who owe Green the 100 shares of stock), and Green (who owes White and Company $10,000, and who is owed the 100 shares of stock by White and Company). Green is protected for his loan of stock by the money he borrows from White and Company; White and Company are protected in their debt of stock owed to Green by Thompson's debt of stock to them and his margin. Thus, since Thompson alone can make any speculative profit in the transaction, its speculative risks are placed squarely up to him.

"Short Covering"

Sooner or later Thompson will wish to conclude the transaction, which from his standpoint may or may not have been successful. If unsuccessful, he will lose a part or perhaps the whole of his margin. Let us, however, suppose that the price of American Locomotive has sunk from 100 to 90. Thompson, in order to take his profit, instructs White and Company to buy 100 shares of the stock to cover his short sale (i.e., make his deferred delivery of stock). White and Company buys the 100 shares at 90 and turns them over to Green, who promptly returns the money he has borrowed (then probably amounting to about $9,000) to White and Company. Thus Green, having recovered the stock he loaned and paid back the money he borrowed, is eliminated from the transaction, leaving only White and Company and their customer, Thompson, still involved in it. The debt of stock which Thompson owed White and Company and which the latter owed Green, has, as we have seen, been all wiped out by the delivery made to Green. Thompson, apart from his original margin of $2,500, had a credit on White and Company's books for $10,000 (the original price of the stock), and after paying out $9,000 to purchase the 100 Locomotive has, in consequence, in addition to the original

$2,500 margin, a profit of $1,000 minus brokerage commissions, dividends paid while the short sale was still unconcluded, and stamp taxes. And thus Thompson's whole short sale terminates.

Reciprocal Nature of Short Sales and Margin Purchases

Some critics of stock market transactions, while conceding the necessity for purchasing stocks on margin, still believe that short sales should be forbidden. This attitude of mind is the more remarkable when it is realized that every purchase of stock on margin simultaneously causes a short sale of money, and, conversely, that every short sale of stock inevitably causes a margin purchase of money.

We have seen how Jones bought his Steel stock on a 25-point margin. In obtaining more stock than he paid for, he employed $7,500 which he did not own. Since in effect he obtained value in stock for money he did not own, exchanging it for 100 shares of Steel, he thus sold money short and became long of stock.

Also, when Thompson sold 100 shares of American Locomotive short, he received a credit on his broker's books for $10,000, in addition to his margin of $2,500, to balance the debit of the 100 shares of stock. Consequently, although perhaps he did not think of it in just this way, he really bought money on margin at the same time that he went short of the stock.

Fluctuating Values in Goods and in Money

Since the value of goods is so invariably expressed in terms of money, it is difficult to realize that the value of money itself, like any commodity, constantly fluctuates.[11] Some economists, indeed, have attributed the soaring commodity prices of recent years mainly to an increased supply of currency, while others

[11] See Appendix, Chapter IV (d).

have insisted that an increased demand for and a decreased supply of goods was chiefly responsible. Actually, both of these forces undoubtedly operate to produce rising prices.

Since a margin purchase of goods inevitably produces a short sale of money, the margin purchase and the short sale are inseparable operations in any market in which credit transactions occur. If it is an evil deed to sell stocks short, then it must be equally wicked to sell money short. And, if we cannot purchase any commodity on margin without selling money short, then all credit transactions must be wicked. Thus the logical outcome of driving the wild asses of mistaken ethics into the field of financial economics, is a return to the dark ages, when there were not only no wicked credit transactions but no business, law, order, or civilization either.

Twofold Aspects of Margin Purchases

The somewhat complicated results arising from this double nature of credit transactions may be summarized by saying that whoever purchases stocks on margin has a double chance for profit and a double chance for loss in the transaction. As we have seen in the instance of Jones and his 100 shares of Steel, if the price of Steel rises he obtains a profit, and if it declines he takes a loss. But in becoming long of stock he has also gone short of money. Consequently, if the value of money advances he will tend to suffer a loss; while if it declines he will tend to profit. In the first case the rising interest rate on call and time loans will make Jones's transaction too expensive to be profitable, and he will probably "liquidate," as it is called, by selling out his stock for what it will bring. Usually, the result of such liquidation by many margin purchasers will be to force down in turn the price of the stock itself.

On the other hand, if the interest rate declines, it will assist the margin purchaser to obtain a profit, since he will be directly responsible for smaller interest charges on his loan (which often may be offset by dividends paid on his stock) and since a lower "call rate" will often induce greater margin buying by others, which in turn tends to raise the price of the stocks he has purchased.

Twofold Aspects of Short Sales

Short sales of securities are in the same way subject to a loss or a profit, both on the money and the stock side of the transaction. We have seen that Thompson obtained a profit if American Locomotive declined in price, and stood to lose if it advanced. But conditions in the money market may also mean a profit or a loss to him, since in going short of stock he has also gone long of money. An advance in the call rate of money is therefore favorable to him, since his broker, White, can often obtain from Green a higher interest rate on the money loaned to the latter in return for the loan of his stock. Also, as has been pointed out, a rising rate in call loans is apt, through forcing liquidation by margin purchasers, to depress the price of stocks, by which development Thompson, of course, profits. On the other hand, a declining interest rate may result in the interest on White's loan of money to Green becoming smaller than the dividends which Thompson must pay on the stock Green loaned to White, and since a declining call rate is also apt to result in rising stock prices by encouraging margin purchasers, the chances are that American Locomotive will rise rather than decline in price.

Stock Prices and the Money Rate

So many factors enter vitally into the establishing of stock prices that the influence of the call rate upon them is frequently offset by some counter-force. In some of the duller periods in stock market history, although call funds were ruling as low as 2 per cent, nevertheless dividends on stocks had been proportionally reduced with the consequence that, despite the prevalence of "cheap money," stock prices also remained very low. Yet, other factors being equal, the result of changes in the call rate on stock prices will be as stated above, and thus forcibly demonstrate that every margin purchase of stock presupposes a short sale of money, and that every short sale of stock presupposes a margin purchase of money.

As methods of purchase and sale the margin purchase and the short sale are therefore inseparably and reciprocally connected, like the two sides of a coin, owing to the fundamental fact that every sale is and must be a twofold operation involving both money and goods. The folly of attempting to restrict short selling, and at the same time to permit margin purchasing, is thus apparent.

Shortages of Money

Since every margin purchaser of stock assumes a debt of money and every short seller a debt of stock, it is obvious that a shortage of money may seriously hinder the former from making his deferred payment, while a shortage of stock may similarly embarrass the latter in making his deferred delivery. These shortages of money and stock are risks inevitably involved by credit transactions in the stock market.

While an examination of the "call loan" system employed to finance margin purchasers of stock must be deferred to a later chapter,[12] some few of its features deserve comment here. The Stock Exchange has no control over the shortages which occasionally develop in the money market, for, as we have already seen, its members usually go to the banks when they need funds, just as any other customers of the banks do. The banks, in turn, can only minimize, without being able to prevent, these shortages of money, which are produced by far-reaching and profound economic causes, not merely in all parts

[12] See Chapter VIII.

of our own extensive country but all over the world. The Stock Exchange, however, has for a long time made every effort to prevent violent fluctuations in call loan interest rates which result from a surplus or a shortage of funds in the money market.

Efforts to Prevent "Corners"

The Stock Exchange is equally anxious to prevent any shortage of stock resulting from a "corner." Its Committee on Stock List, to begin with, makes a thorough examination of the distribution of the stock of every company that applies to list its securities on the Exchange, in order to prevent trading in any stock which is largely held by a single individual or interest.[13] Its Committee on Quotations, through the extensive ticker service under its supervision, sees that almost instant and nation-wide publicity is given to transactions in all securities listed on the Exchange. Furthermore, once it is clear that a corner has developed in any listed stock, the Governing Committee of the Exchange promptly prevents further trading in it on the Exchange by striking it from the list.[14] In every such case the interest of the Stock Exchange is identical with that of the public in maintaining on its floor a market for securities which shall at all times be free and open.[15] In spite of such recent exceptions as the rise of call money to 32 per cent in November, 1919, or the corner in Stutz stock in March, 1920, it is rare that an acute shortage of either money or stock really occurs on the Stock Exchange.

Thus we see that, as operations, margins purchases and short sales are identical with the purchases or sales on credit which are of universal occurrence in every line of modern business, which have on the economic side powerfully and profoundly furthered human progress in the past few centuries, and without which (as even the Bolsheviki in Russia discov-

[13] See Chapter XVI. [14] *Ibid.* [15] See Chapter XIV.

ered) not merely the luxuries, conveniences, and comforts, but even the barest necessities of life cannot be daily afforded to mankind. It has furthermore been shown that margin purchases and short sales are reciprocal and presuppose each other, for if we cannot sell (or exchange) what we do not possess, we can never buy more of anything than we are able to pay for.

The question then arises whether the economic results flowing from the employment of these methods of purchasing or selling on credit, however legitimate they may be as mere methods, are beneficial or desirable.

Use of Credit for Investment Transactions

In this connection one fact infrequently recognized is that neither margin purchases nor short sales of stocks are necessarily undertaken for speculative purchases. In many cases, where the investor wishes to purchase stocks outright for cash, the broker, who, of course, cannot tell at exactly what price the required shares can be purchased, will probably instruct him to deposit 50 per cent of their latest price and pay the balance after they have been purchased. Such a practice is essentially a purchase on credit, even if it is not commonly called a "margin purchase" in Wall Street. Similarly, the owner of 100 shares of Steel may desire to sell them at a time when he is in London or San Francisco and his shares are securely locked up in his New York safe deposit box. Under such circumstances he will probably instruct his broker to sell 100 shares of Steel short, and cover the short sale on his return to New York by getting his stock from his box and delivering it to his broker. Thus margin purchasing and short selling may be and often are employed as conveniences in what are essentially outright purchases and sales.

Furthermore, were it impossible to buy and sell stocks on credit, the odd-lot dealer, whose business consists of purchasing or selling from 1 to 99 shares of all listed stocks, could not carry on his useful work.[16] The odd-lot dealer is constantly forced to take a long position of stocks in 100's, by purchasing the various odd lots which customers may sell to him at all times, and to take a short position in 100's by selling customers any number of shares they may wish. Of course the odd-lot dealer ultimately sells in 100-share lots the stock which he has accumulated by his odd-lot purchases, and he ultimately covers his short sale of odd lots by purchasing in 100-share lots. Yet it is obvious that if purchases on credit or short sales were forbidden, the odd-lot dealer could not successfully carry on his considerable and essential business in enabling small investors to sell or purchase readily.

Speculative Nature of Margin Purchases and Short Sales

For all the above instances, however, and many others of a similar nature, it is, of course, undoubtedly true that the vast majority of both margin purchases and short sales are made purely for the sake of obtaining a speculative profit through buying at a lower and selling at a higher price. The broader aspects of speculation as an economic phenomenon must be reserved for a later chapter.[17] Speculation will therefore be considered here only in so far as it finds a practical every-day expression through the margin purchase and the short sale.

Every so often some native Solon will obtain a half-column in the papers to declare that stock speculation, particularly that of bears who sell short in the anticipation of declining stock prices, is injuring the intrinsic value of our railroad and industrial companies. Some indignant critics, indeed, openly state that short selling destroys the companies' property, and picture the bear raider as a sinister villain who delights in the ruin of other men's goods by some mysterious means in the stock market. The sheer nonsense of such statements is, of course, apparent to anyone who knows anything at all about stock

[16] See Chapter VI, page 136.

[17] See Chapter XV.

market transactions—a knowledge which, paradoxically enough, these critics of stock exchange speculation often hasten to disclaim at the outset.

Effect of Short Sales on Values and on Prices

A share of stock is simply a certificate of fractional ownership in the assets and earning power of some corporation.[18] Let us suppose that some bear trader, believing that the shares of a copper company are selling higher than they should, sells enough of these shares short to depress their price temporarily 2 points. By this operation he has not decreased the amount of copper in the company's mines, nor injured its mining or smelting machinery. Neither has he affected in any way the industrial demand for the company's products, nor its earning power. The effect of his short sale has been to decrease for the time being, not the inherent equities of the company but merely the price of its shares, which are only the warehouse certificates to these assets and earning power.

Thus it is apparent that the fundamental and intrinsic value of a given share of stock may be a wholly different thing from the price at which it can be bought and sold in the market at any given time. If it were easy to determine exactly what the present and prospective value of a given stock was, there would be as little speculation in stocks as there is in bonds. But the prospective earning power of any corporation depends upon so many constantly changing economic circumstances, and the value of its present assets depends upon the steady price fluctuations of so many commodities, that the inherent value of its shares cannot be infallibly determined. The market price of such shares, therefore, is simply a composite estimate reflecting the opinions of the keenest students of industry and finance all over the country.[19] The "bear raider," as he is sometimes picturesquely but rather inaccurately called, may by his short

[18] See Chapter I, page 19.

[19] See Chapter XIV.

sales depress prices for a time, but he can no more destroy intrinsic values than he can lower the temperature by putting ice on the thermometer bulb.

Effect of Purchases and Sales on Prices

Every purchaser of a commodity, whether of stocks or of "shoes and ships and sealing-wax," tends to raise the price of that commodity, since he tends to increase the demand for it and decrease the supply of it. Conversely, every seller tends to lower prices by increasing supply and decreasing demand. These laws operate in the establishing of prices utterly irrespective of whether purchases or sales are made outright or on credit. The outright purchaser of 100 shares of Reading tends to raise the price of this stock just as much as a margin purchaser of the same amount, and an outright seller tends to depress its price just as much as a short seller, if they sell the same amount of stock.

But there is this difference, as regards their effect upon prices, between purchases and sales made outright and those made on credit. The outright purchaser tends more *permanently* to increase the price of the stock he purchases, since he usually withdraws for a long period a number of shares from the supply. Also, the outright seller tends more *permanently* to depress stock prices, since in most cases he does not soon buy back his stock. Credit transactions in stocks, however, almost always involve both a purchase and a sale. The buyer on margin must ultimately prove a seller before he can obtain his profit, and for the same reason the short seller in the end must buy stock. Moreover, both margin purchases and short sales must usually be terminated within a reasonably short period lest interest charges and dividends eat up all hope of profits. In consequence, it is obvious that the buyer on margin at first tends to raise prices and later to lower them; and that similarly, the short seller for the time being tends to lower prices, but later to raise them again. Thus a double check is created against the undue inflation of the price above, or the undue depression of prices below, the actual value of any security in which active speculation occurs on the Stock Exchange.[20]

Automatic Checks Against Inaccurate Prices

Let us suppose that the actual inherent value of 1 share of United States Steel common stock is really $100. Should the price of this stock rise to 105—or higher than its value warranted—the margin buyers who had originally bought their stock at lower prices would begin to take their profit by selling at this price. Also, speculators who believed that 105 was more than Steel common was really worth, would sell the stock short. Selling from this double source would soon tend to depress the price of the stock toward its real value of 100.

If, however, Steel common should be selling at 95, these corrective forces set in motion by speculation would also tend to bring up the price nearer to the real value of 100. Previous short sellers would begin to purchase at the low figure of 95 to cover their short sales and obtain their profit, while buyers on margin, encouraged by the belief that the stock was selling under its real value, would begin buying it "for the rise." And this buying, both from the optimistic bulls and the previously pessimistic bears would, of course, tend to lift the price back toward its real value of 100. Thus speculation through margin purchases and short sales normally prevents the wide and violent price fluctuations which would inevitably result if stocks were removed from the price-registering machinery of the stock exchanges.

Economic Value of Short Covering

Particularly in times when panic is threatening does the "short interest"—i.e., the speculators who have sold short and

[20] See Chapter XV.

who are waiting to purchase and cover—perform a valuable service to investors by supporting the falling market with their buying orders and thus helping to hold prices up even in the face of disaster. For at such times the investor and margin purchaser become extremely timid and thus the previous short seller, who is under compulsion to purchase and cover his sales, alone enables the investor who must liquidate, to sell his securities.

Writing of conditions prevailing on the New York Stock Exchange at the outbreak of the Great War in 1914,[21] the president of the Exchange at that time made the following statement:

> The conditions on the Stock Exchange when the storm burst, were in some respects very hopeful . . . the unsettled business outlook due to new and untried legislation had fostered a heavy short interest in the market, thereby furnishing the best safeguard against a sudden and disastrous drop. This short interest was a leading factor in producing the extraordinary resistance of prices in New York which caused so much favorable comment during the few days before the closing (of the Stock Exchange). It were well if ill-informed people who deprecate short selling would note this fact.

In the violent price declines which occurred in 1920 in such staple commodities as leather and wool, the lack of just this buying support which short covering provides in the more speculative stock markets, has been forcefully illustrated. Since there was nothing to halt the downward crash of prices for wool and leather, the decline came the more suddenly and violently. In consequence, the fact that there was no short interest in these two commodities resulted in placing in serious difficulties not merely the leather and wool trade, but also those banks which had discounted bills secured by high-priced stocks of these commodities.[22]

[21] Noble, pp. 5–6.

[22] See Chapter XIV.

Stabilization of Security Prices

In conclusion, therefore, it may be said that the effect of margin purchases and short sales is really to stabilize prices, that this result is beneficial to both buyers and sellers, and that in an economic sense the undue inflation of prices above values is just as dangerous to everyone concerned as their undue depression below values.[23] If, therefore, short selling were prevented, an effective check would be removed from an upward trend of prices which in the long run would be bound to fall again with a crash, while the support to prices which a short interest provides in just such a declining market would also be removed.

Legislation Against the Short Sale

The popular misunderstanding and prejudice against short selling of securities is not new. As long as the stock exchanges of the world have existed the short sale has been bitterly condemned, but invariably indorsed, after thorough investigation or painful experience, as a vital and indispensable factor in the maintenance of free securities markets everywhere. As a necessary operation to organized speculative markets it has, therefore, stood that hardest of all tests—the test of time. Short selling was forbidden in England by Sir John Bernard's Act in 1733; yet this law failed to halt the practice, and in 1860 it was repealed. Similar English legislation later adopted to prevent short selling of bank stocks has also been more honored in the breach than in the observance.

Such, too, has been the experience of France. Napoleon I was dissuaded from forbidding it only by his Finance Minister; later on, the French did legislate against the practice only to repeal the law after its futility and harmfulness were clearly shown. The state of New York has tried the same experiment and with the same result; it prohibited short sales

[23] See Chapter XIV.

early in 1812, only to remove the ban against them in 1858.[24] Last but not least is the example of Germany. In 1896 a stringent regulation of the Berlin Bourse (or Stock Exchange) was undertaken by the government and again short selling was forbidden, to be reinstated by the repeal of this legislation in 1909. But a famous American economist has stated:[25]

> Finally, the effect of interference, increased cost, and legal uncertainty (entailed by this restriction of stock transactions) was to drive business to foreign exchanges and diminish the power of the Berlin Exchange in the field of international finance. The number of agencies of foreign houses increased four or fivefold, and much German capital flowed to other centers, especially London, for investment and speculation. This in turn weakened the power of the Berlin money market, so that even the Reichsbank has at times felt its serious effects.

Indeed, it is far from fanciful to say that to Germany's uneconomic legislation concerning her stock and produce markets can in large measure be attributed the economic collapse of Germany during the war, and the profound financial difficulties in which she subsequently found herself.

So long as optimists are more popular than pessimists, buying on margin will doubtless seem to many people a more beneficial operation than short selling. So long as men think on the money rather than the goods side of sales, short selling will doubtless remain more mysterious to the public than margin purchasing. So long as the fallacious benefits of inflation can claim a popular following, while deflation remains an unpopular and misunderstood process, whatever tends to lift prices above values will continue to be generally judged preferable to whatever may depress them below values. And thus, while perhaps human nature will always condemn the short sale, the changeless and unswerving laws of economics will invariably necessitate its employment.

---

[24] See Appendix, Chapter IV (e).

[25] See Emery, p. 828.

CHAPTER V

THE FLOOR TRADER AND THE SPECIALIST

Function of Dealer in Maintaining Continuous Market

In Chapter III we saw two commission brokers, Jenkins and Wilkins, meet at the Steel post and conclude a sale of 100 shares of United States Steel common stock. This stock was purposely selected in that imaginary transaction, since its comparatively broad and continuous market often permits of just such transactions between commission brokers. In less active and steady stocks, however, it might be impossible for one commission broker to effect a trade with another. Commission broker Jenkins might obtain his order in such a stock and proceed to the post where it was listed; but the chances are he would not happen to find another broker like Wilkins waiting there to buy his customer's stock at just that time, or at a mutually satisfactory price. Of course, it takes two to make a bargain in the Stock Exchange as elsewhere, and if Jenkins cannot find a buyer he cannot sell his customer's stock. As a matter of fact, if Exchange commission brokers could sell only to other commission brokers, cases would constantly arise where sales could not be effected for very considerable periods of time, with the result that listed securities on the Exchange could not possibly possess their present negotiability and comparatively small daily fluctuations in price.

In the process of obviating such inability on the part of commission brokers to sell or to buy immediately at a price, several classes of dealers have arisen on the floor of the Exchange, who, in the absence of a broker with just the right sort of order, stand ready to intervene in such transactions, and at their own risk "make a market" for the stock in question. In the main, the work of these dealers is speculative—as indeed the work of a dealer of any sort is bound to be. They will buy stock from a broker at a slight concession, or sell it to him at a slight advance, on their own responsibility and in the hope of obtaining a profit later through the sale or purchase of the stock as the case may be. When, for example, Jenkins goes to the post where United States Rubber stock is traded in with a customer's order to sell 100 Rubber at 75 and finds no broker ready to purchase from him, a dealer may buy his stock, and a little later, if fortune favors, sell it for 75⅛. Dealers are fundamental to all markets in the world, and it would indeed be most surprising if we did not find them equally necessary to the continuous market made for securities on the floor of the Stock Exchange.[1]

The Floor Trader

One of the most important types of dealers on the Stock Exchange is the so-called "floor trader." He is a professional speculator who trades in stocks for very small quick profits. As a member of the Stock Exchange he executes only his own orders and thus escapes paying commissions, which the speculating non-member customer in a broker's office must pay. Formerly there were many of these floor traders in the stock market, but, for reasons presently to be explained, there are only about 50 of them left at the present time.

A graphic sketch of the typical floor trader has been given by a former governor of the Stock Exchange:[2]

> These gentlemen afford an interesting study. They do not accept orders; each man is in business for himself. They entertain no illusions, and they recognize no alliances with each other. Each one follows his own inclinations, and does not permit himself to be moved by tips, or rumors, or gossip, or sentiment. He scoffs brazenly at all forms of "inside in-

[1] See Chapter XIV.

[2] Van Antwerp, p. 285.

> formation." His power of observation is keen, and his habit of analysis and deduction is wonderfully developed. In the surging crowd around an active stock he sees things with miscroscopic eye, and acts with surprising promptness; once his conclusions are reached, speed and agility are relied upon to do the rest. Age cannot wither, nor custom stale, his infinite variety. He is a bull one minute, and a bear the next. He is intent, resourceful, suspicious, vigilant, and ubiquitous. He asks no quarter, and gives none. Now he is sphinx-like, deaf, inscrutable and impenetrable; now exploding with the frenzy of battle. You may stand and chat with him, and he may seem to listen to you. In reality he does not hear you at all. His roving eye is elsewhere, his mind is intent on other things. In the middle of a sentence he may leave you abruptly and go tearing from crowd to crowd like a thing possessed, the incarnation of energy.

From the nature of his business the floor trader does not usually need to maintain an elaborate office. Often, indeed, the floor trader simply hires desk room in some commission office. For the same reason he usually clears his transactions through some commission house instead of attempting to handle the work of clearance through an office and with employees of his own. In such an event his purchases and sales of stock are consequently entered on the clearance sheet of that commission broker, along with the latter's transactions.[3] Usually, therefore, in making contracts for the delivery or receipt of stock on the floor, the floor trader "gives up" the name of this clearing member rather than his own. In return for the responsibility and labor assumed by the clearing member, the floor trader pays him a clearance fee of $1 or upwards per 100 shares of stock cleared.

The Floor Trader's Economic Services

The floor trader regularly performs two important economic services. For one thing, his speculative purchases

---

3 See Chapter IX.

and sales are of great assistance in maintaining a continuous market. As we have seen, they fill gaps which would inevitably occur in a purely broker's market. The floor trader's operations consequently serve as one of the means of imparting instant negotiability to all the Exchange's listed securities.

In the second place, he is of an even greater significance in stabilizing prices. As a matter of fact, the floor trader's best opportunity for a profit exists when prices are for the time being out of line with true values.[4] Since as a rule he quickly sells out purchased stock, and quickly covers his short sales, his transactions are self-nullifying so far as any permanent effect on security prices are concerned. Nevertheless, his swift purchases and sales tend temporarily to restrain rising and to cushion falling prices, and, since they are normally undertaken for only fractional profits, they help to create a close market. It is mainly owing to the work of the floor trader that momentary inequalities in the market arising from the mechanical methods of executing the round-share orders of commission houses and odd-lot dealers are instantly smoothed out and eliminated. In the maintenance of a stock market, therefore, whose prices are constantly sensitive to supply and demand without erratically responding to mechanical and temporary limitations and conditions, a quick dealer for small speculative profits like the floor trader constitutes an indispensable factor.

Uninformed Prejudice Against the Floor Trader

The floor trader could not afford to do business at such slight profits in a less highly organized market than the Stock Exchange, since he could not then be certain of buying or selling at will. Hence, as a quick "in-and-out" dealer in securities, he is essentially a product of the modern continuous market which by a process of evolution has been established

[4] Chapter XV.

on the exchanges in the past few decades. The popular prejudice against him is basically due to the fact that public knowledge has not kept up with the recent swift development of organized markets. Because the floor trader's operations differ from the operations of dealers in more primitive and sluggish types of market places, in details imposed by the recently created organized markets, they are apt to be regarded as illegitimate gambling transactions. Critics of the floor trader, lacking usually anything but an uninformed prejudice concerning his indispensable work in the market, fall back upon the clearance system as proof of his villainy. The fact that he often buys and sells the same day, and, in consequence, does not usually need to receive or deliver securities but employs the Stock Clearing Corporation as his agent to look after these matters for him, is made much of by critics of the Exchange. Absurd as such charges are, it is nevertheless worth while to point out a few real facts on this very subject.

First, with respect to stocks listed on the Exchange but not cleared through the Stock Clearing Corporation, the floor trader like everyone else is compelled to employ his time, labor, and capital in the former archaic methods of direct clearance.[5] But in the "cleared" stocks the Stock Clearing Corporation as agent performs this work for him in the same way and with the same splendid economy of time, labor, and capital as it does for the other classes of Stock Exchange members. The contracts he makes are precisely similar to the contracts made on the floor by any other member of the Exchange, and are settled and cleared in just the same way. Far from allowing him to escape responsibility for his contracts in any way, the Stock Clearing Corporation is in reality the main agent for their punctual and absolute enforcement.[6]

Hence, so long as the floor trader is, by virtue of having made a contract to buy, long of any stock, he is just as certainly

[5] Chapter IX.

[6] *Ibid.*

assuming the risk of owning that stock as if he already held the certificate itself in his box. The legitimacy of the floor trader's transactions in consequence cannot be questioned nor through a misunderstanding of the clearance system termed "gambling," without questioning the legitimacy not only of the whole system of clearing stocks and bank credit operated by the Stock Clearing Corporation, but of every bank clearing house in this or any other nation. A wider knowledge of clearance as it is employed in the vast credit, security, and commodity markets of today will quickly remove any such unfounded prejudice against the floor trader.

The Floor Trader's Profits

An adequate notion of the floor trader's business can be gained only after some reference to its dollar-and-cents side. When his operations are normal and most useful economically, he is trading at his own risk for a profit on each transaction of 1/8 of a point, which amounts to $12.50 on 100 shares of $100 par stock. It must be remembered that the floor trader's calling involves large risks and necessitates the constant taking of losses. There is no magic and infallible formula available to the floor trader as he stands about the posts on the Exchange floor and makes his trades. Years of experience and the highest degree of natural aptitude and ability in the business do not prevent him from incurring heavy losses. His aim must be, therefore, not so much to avoid losses absolutely—for this would be utterly impossible—as to overbalance his losses with his profits.

But even if he is successful in three out of four trades, his net profit is not $25, or anything like it. To begin with, as we have seen, he usually is forced to pay some commission house $1 or more on each 100 shares to clear his trades, or else assume the considerable overhead expense of becoming a clearing member himself and providing the office machinery required to perform his own clearance. In either case the clearance expense is just as great on an unprofitable as upon a profitable transaction. Thus, on account of this expense alone, his net profits on a successful trade can be only $11.50, and his total loss on an unsuccessful trade will be $13.50.

State and Federal Stamp Taxes

But this is not all. On every sale of 100 shares of stock of $100 par value he must pay $2 for the state tax stamp and $2 for the federal tax stamp. These tax levies in themselves seem small enough, for both amount to only 1/25 per cent of the par value of the shares. But when the small profits for which the floor trader deals are remembered, the matter assumes a very different aspect. Moreover, he is taxed just as heavily on his losses as upon his profits. Counting in these taxes, when he makes ⅛ on a trade his cash profit is only $7.50, while when he loses ⅛ on a trade his actual cash loss is $17.50. In consequence, if three out of four of his trades are successful, he makes a net profit of only $5. And to be 75 per cent successful in this business, with its stern demands of swiftness and accuracy and with its constant risks, is, as any floor trader will testify, no slight achievement.

Thus, the imposition of these state and federal taxes upon sales of stock has placed a crushing burden upon the dealer in stocks who operates for small profits, and has led to abnormal and undesirable changes in the market's structure and methods of operation. To begin with, the number of floor traders has been reduced from over 200 to only about 50. Former floor traders have either sold their seats and retired from the Exchange entirely, or else have abandoned this particular work for some other more lucrative activity on the Exchange floor.

Moreover, the floor traders who still remain have been forced to trade more intermittently and for larger fractions than 1/8. Many have tended to become "long-pull" speculators, and to take a position in the market, thus being warped by heavy taxation out of their true function and greatest economic usefulness. For it is the customer in the brokerage office who, from the economic standpoint, can most usefully engage in security trades involving considerable intervals of time. Furthermore, the present-day floor trader has to some extent been forced to confine his operations to low-priced stocks. When he does deal in stocks selling over $100 per share he is likewise impelled to avoid any except those with a small turnover and considerably greater fluctuations between sales than 1/8, in order to realize a higher fractional profit on each trade.

Economic Effects of Stamp Taxes

As a result of this reduction and metamorphosis of the floor trader's normal activities, the whole stock market has to a considerable extent been rendered less stable than formerly. It has been subject to slightly wider fluctuations, and as it has been largely deprived of the floor trader's intermediary bids and offers, the execution at close prices of the commission broker's orders, in both round and odd lots, has become more difficult.

When the state tax of $2 was first laid, no very perceptible difference was felt in the market. Of course, the floor trader's risks were increased and his profits lessened, but no particular economic harm was done. But when the tax was doubled by the addition of the federal tax the differential was sufficient to be of considerable importance. The Stock Exchange authorities, however, did not appear before any Committee of Congress to "protest." They considered the tax a war measure and felt that even though the stock market suffered by it they must patriotically do their share in bearing the burden of the war.

But the continuation of these taxes into peace times, and particularly into an era when the stock market is burdened with the vast problems and risks of reconstruction, would seem from the economic standpoint to be of very doubtful wisdom indeed.[7] For the imposition of a heavy tax on the sale of securities, which are really credit instruments, amounts to and results in placing a dangerous burden upon credit itself. The untoward results of the tax are not dramatic nor vivid; nevertheless the tax constitutes an unseen drag and brake upon all large-scale American commercial and industrial enterprises. It remains to be seen whether the United States, today recognized everywhere as the financial bulwark of the world, can really function as a creditor nation and at the same time levy excessive and burdensome taxes upon the security markets upon which her own economic restoration, along with that of the rest of the world, must inevitably depend.[8]

This whole question of the national advisability of overtaxing sales of stocks is intimately related, not simply to the livelihood of the various classes of security brokers and dealers in and out of the Stock Exchange, but to the broader and more fundamental financial and economic problems now confronting the whole field of American business.[9] The tax has been discussed in connection with the floor trader because its uneconomic and harmful effects have in his particular case been most clearly and directly manifested.

The Specialist

Returning again to the subject of dealers in the Exchange, we must next consider the specialist, a most important factor both as a dealer and a broker in the market place of today. For, as we will shortly observe, the specialist may execute orders in stocks either for himself or as an agent for other brokers. The name "specialist" is derived from the fact that

[7] See Appendix, Chapter V (a).

[8] See Chapter XVIII.

[9] See pamphlets entitled "The Effect of Taxing Stock and Bond Sales" (publication of Committee on Library, New York Stock Exchange), and "In re H.R. 14157" (brief by counsel for the Exchange).

he specializes in the execution of orders in stocks located at the same post on the floor. Sometimes, indeed, in an unusually active stock with a heavy turnover, he will confine his entire attention to dealing in the stock issue of a single corporation.

Tradition has it that the first specialist on the Exchange was a member who had been prevented from pursuing an active career in the commission business through breaking his leg. As a temporary experiment, therefore, he took his seat in the midst of the crowd trading in Western Union, then a very active stock, and executed orders only in it. Much to his own surprise, as well as to that of his associates, he soon found his new occupation more profitable than his former one, and even after his leg had mended, he continued in it. Other brokers followed his example and became specialists—a shift which the steadily growing volume of business on the Exchange favored—until today about 150 Exchange members can be found constantly stationed at the various posts, and constituting a vital and integral factor in the present-day stock market. Since there is probably no class of dealers or brokers within the membership of the Stock Exchange concerning which more misunderstanding exists, it is of importance that the methods and significance of the specialist be described at some length here.

Clearance and Speculation of Specialist

Often, as in the case of the average floor trader, the specialist clears his own purchases and sales of stocks through some commission house. For such service he pays the same sort of fee as the floor trader does. On the other hand, the specialist sometimes not only performs his own clearance, but also clears for other members in return for a clearance fee. On the 100-share orders of stock which he purchases or sells as a broker for other members, the specialist, as in the case of the two-dollar broker,[10] receives $2.50 out of the $15 which the commission broker charges his customer.

The majority of specialists act as dealers in much the same way as the floor traders do, and speculate for small, quick profits. In this buying and selling of securities with other exchange members for their own account, the specialists perform many of the functions of the "jobbers" in the London Stock Exchange. Far from there being any reasonable ground to object to this speculation by specialists, in reality the practice constitutes one of his necessary functions in the Exchange and renders the same general economic service that the more scattered transactions of the floor trader do. For, if the specialist refused to engage in speculative dealings on his own account, there would not be sufficient orders for inactive stocks, either in his book or with other members of the crowd, to make a close market for them. The Exchange insists, however, that when the specialist does trade for himself, he must not pretend to be executing orders as a broker.[11] The specialist is, of course, forbidden in any transaction to charge a commission as a broker and at the same time make a profit as a dealer.

Precedence of Customers' Orders

Furthermore, the specialist is compelled to give precedence to his customers' orders for the purchase or sale of securities, over the orders which originate with himself as a dealer, granting always that both his and his customers' orders are either market orders or else limited at the same price. If, for example, a specialist has a customer's order to buy 100 Reading at 75, and at the same time wishes to purchase the same amount of the same stock at the same price, he must execute the customer's order before buying his own stock. But if the special-

[10] See Chapter II, page 45.

[11] "A member, acting as a broker, is permitted to report to his principal a transaction as made with himself, only when he has orders both to buy and to sell and not to give up, and then he must add to his name on the report, 'on order,' or words to that effect." (Constitution, p. 85.)

ist is willing to pay 75⅛ or 75¼ for the 100 Reading, he can, of course, do so first. Similarly, if the customer's order is for the sale of 100 Union Pacific at 80, the specialist can sell 100 Union at 79⅞ or 79¾ for himself, but cannot sell his own stock at 80 till he has executed his customer's order. With market orders the customer's order always has precedence.[12]

This rule with regard to the execution of orders by the specialist is strictly enforced and violations of it, which would, of course, amount to "trading on his customer's orders," have long been severely punished. Years ago a certain specialist sold 500 shares for his own account when he had orders for that amount to sell, and made about a point, or $500, on his illegitimate transaction. But he was caught within three days, and, facing the loss of a good business reputation acquired over the course of thirty years, died of heart failure before he ever came to trial. Indeed, attempted breaches of this regulation are in practice quite easy to detect, both from the action of prices on the ticker tape and from the keen and experienced observation of other members about the post.

Specialist as Broker

As in the case of the floor trader, the present tax upon sales of securities has proved very burdensome to the specialist as a dealer, and by artificially deterring him from entering into transactions for close profits, has extended a similar disruptive and weakening influence upon the machinery of the stock market. Nevertheless, unlike the less fortunate floor trader, the specialist has his brokerage business to fall back upon. Indeed, his principal business has always consisted in serving as a broker for other brokers in his few particular stocks.

Since he is always stationed at a single post, he is able to handle customers' orders which other brokers are unwilling

[12] See Appendix, Chapter V (b), and Chapter XIII.

or unable to execute. If the commission broker were forced himself to execute for his customers, stop orders or other orders limited to prices far from the current market price, he might be compelled to remain at the given post with a single order for an indefinite period of time, lest he should "miss his market." Such a course would be unprofitable and impossible. Consequently such orders, as well as orders that are difficult of execution because of the inactivity or the intense activity of the stocks in question, the commission broker usually turns over to the appropriate specialist to watch and to execute, when the right moment arrives.

From the specialist's standpoint, therefore, he is entrusted as a rule only with those orders which no one else wants to try to execute. For, when the order first comes to the Exchange floor the commission broker gets it at his telephone; if unwilling to try to execute it he may turn it over to a two-dollar broker, and not until the former or both have abandoned it does the specialist get it. Thus, the specialist's business has its drawbacks, like everyone else's—otherwise everyone on the Exchange would want to be a specialist and nobody would be left to fill any other function.

Odd-Lot Business of Specialist

Formerly, before the present extensive odd-lot houses [13] had evolved, the specialist used to execute in his few particular stocks fractional orders from 1 to 99 shares as a broker for the odd-lot dealers of that time. This commission business in odd lots materially assisted the specialist during the earlier and financially leaner years of his existence, when the turnover in the market was small and his business was scanty. But with the growth of Exchange transactions and the increasing 100-share business undertaken by the specialist, his odd-lot business became less welcome and in the end suffered from unavoidable

[13] See Chapter VI.

and natural discrimination. In consequence, as will be related in the next chapter, the present odd-lot houses naturally evolved.

Some few specialists, however, still execute orders for odd lots in the same way as the present-day odd-lot dealer. Although the aggregate bulk of odd-lot orders thus executed is not a large factor today, nevertheless the specialist, among his other functions, is always a potential if not an actual competitor to the odd-lot dealer, and as such exerts a salutary even if a somewhat negative effect on the odd-lot business of the present time. This fact perhaps accounts for a common tendency on the part of the public to confuse the specialist with the odd-lot dealer.

"Crossing" Orders

There is still another constitutional restriction [14] upon the specialist as a broker which deserves attention. Even more frequently than is the case with the commission broker, he will find on his book (of which more anon) orders to buy and to sell the same amount of the same stock at the same price. He might, for example, discover that he had 200 shares of Union Pacific to buy, and 200 shares to sell, at 90. Before he can "cross" these orders, as it is called, he must publicly offer the 200 to sell at 1/8 higher than the 200 to buy. Thus, if anyone in the crowd is willing to pay 90 1/8 for the stock to be sold, its seller gets the advantage of the 1/8. But if no one accepts the offer, he may then cross the orders without the possibility of doing the seller any injustice.

Occasions for Specialist's Services

Before a clear notion of the specialist's work can be acquired, reference must be made to the actual methods by which it is conducted. If our friend Jenkins, the commission broker,

[14] See Chapter XIII.

is called to his telephone and given an order to buy 100 shares of Sinclair Oil at 15 when the stock is selling around 25, Jenkins knows it would be a waste of his time to take the order to the post where this stock is dealt in and attempt its execution. Accordingly, he instructs his phone clerk to dispatch the

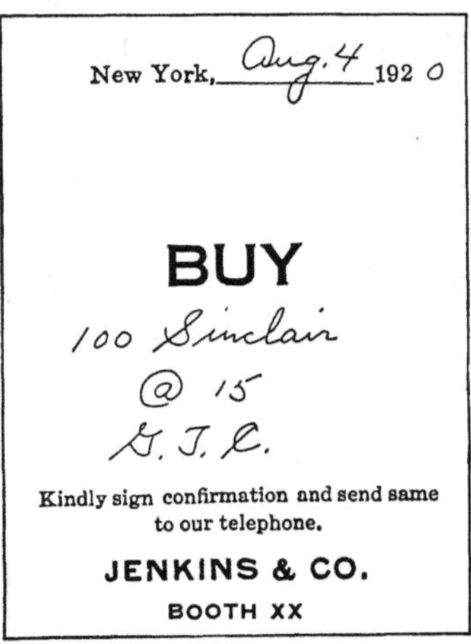
New York, Aug. 4 1920

BUY

100 Sinclair
@ 15
G. T. C.

Kindly sign confirmation and send same to our telephone.

JENKINS & CO.
BOOTH XX

Figure 9. (a) Buy Slip for a "Give-Out" Order. (Size 3¼ x 4½.)

Employed when one member instructs another member to execute an order in his behalf.

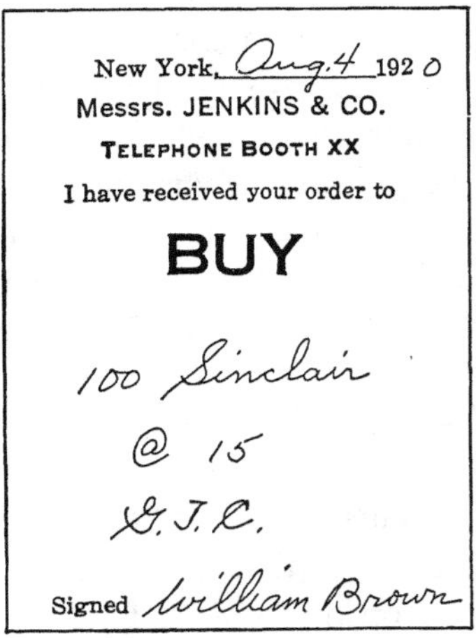
New York, Aug. 4 1920
Messrs. JENKINS & CO.
TELEPHONE BOOTH XX
I have received your order to

BUY

100 Sinclair
@ 15
G. T. C.

Signed William Brown

Figure 9. (b) Carbon of Figure 9a.

Showing confirmation signed by specialist.

order to William Brown, the specialist in Sinclair Oil, through the tubes. This pneumatic tube system, which is one of the mechanical accessories of the Stock Exchange floor, will be described in more detail in the next chapter. When the specialist in Sinclair Oil gets Jenkins' order for 100 shares at 15 from the tube attendant at his post, he inscribes the order in his book, and there it stays (unless it is canceled in the interim) until the stock declines sufficiently to permit of its execution at the limit of 15 set. The order to the specialist is sent on a slip shown in Figure 9a. Attached to this slip is a carbon copy (Figure 9b) which the specialist signs and returns to

Jenkins' phone clerk by way of confirming the receipt of the order.

A somewhat different case might call for a slight departure from the above routine. If Jenkins receives an order to buy 100 American Sugar Refining at par, at a time when it is selling at about 101, he will probably go to the Sugar post with it himself. He will not give the order to a specialist to execute if he can avoid it, since if he makes the purchase himself he will get the full commission of $15 upon it, whereas if he turns the order over to a specialist to execute he must pay the specialist $2.50 out of the $15 he receives from the customer for executing the order. After watching Sugar sell at 101, 100¾, 100⅞, and 100½, Jenkins sees his number appear on the annunciator board, and knows he is wanted at his phone. On the other hand, he does not dare take the order with him, while the stock is breaking toward par lest he miss his market. Hence, he gives the order to the specialist in American Sugar. Even while he is at his phone getting another order, the specialist may have executed the order in Sugar. If he has, he makes out a report of the purchase [15] and sends it back to Jenkins' telephone clerk through the tube system.

Method of Operating

Let us look for a moment at the physical conditions surrounding the work of the specialist. All day long he stands beside a single post on the floor, or sits on the circular seat at its base. Around him gather the crowds in the particular stocks in which he deals, composed of eager commission brokers, two-dollar brokers, busy odd-lot dealers, and swift floor traders. In a moment of activity, especially at the opening at 10 A.M the crowd may number forty or more. The specialist is receiving new orders and canceling old ones, quoting bids and offers and effecting sales, making out binding reports, constantly revising

[15] See Chapter III, page 59.

the orders inscribed in his book, and perhaps attempting to deal on his own account, in competition with the lightning-like floor traders. The specialist must not only watch the market, and everyone in the crowd likely to do business in it, but he must also, as a broker, represent both buyers and sellers at once, and favor neither unduly. Meanwhile, since he is apt to be the core of the market himself, everyone is watching him intently, ready to cry "Sold" to his bids or "Take them" to his offers. As a prominent specialist [16] has stated:

> You must remember that the specialist is not over in a closet or up on a pillar where nobody can see what he is doing, but is standing down on the floor; and in an active market, twenty, thirty or forty men see him; they see him get the orders and see him execute these orders, so that there is almost, you might say, a check-up on him, every single minute.

"Stopping Stock"

The practice of "stopping stock," which is employed by brokers on the floor, should be mentioned in especial connection with the specialist, since the responsibility for the occasional misunderstandings to which it gives rise are so often placed at his door.[17] This class of orders must not be confused with stop orders. A broker with 100 shares of United States Rubber to sell may make a private agreement with the specialist or some other broker, to "stop" them with him—that is, to sell them to him either at the price of the next sale, or at a subsequent sale at a stated price. The principal purpose in "stopping stock," as it is called, is, of course, to insure both parties against the danger of missing a market and the practice tends to stabilize the market and to reduce the number of separate fractional fluctuations. Since such an agreement is essentially a private transaction, although based upon the public

[16] Address of Erastus T. Tefft before the Convention of Out-of-Town Stock Exchange Members, April 15, 1921.

[17] See Appendix, Chapter V (c).

market, a sale of stopped stock is not reported on the stock ticker, although, of course, the simultaneous sale in the open market upon which it depends is printed there. If, for instance, A as a seller stops 100 Rubber with B at 75, and if B, who is buying 200 shares, later purchases 100 Rubber from C in the open market at 75, the quotation in the ticker states the price at which both sales were made, but only the amount of stock publicly sold—or in this instance, the 100 Rubber which B bought from C. Incidentally, this fact is often overlooked by statisticians in computing total sales of stock on the Stock Exchange.

Stock which is stopped at the opening must be offered without reference to any definite price, for the Constitution of the Exchange[18] forbids the making of any bid, offer, or transaction before 10 A.M. or after 3 P.M. (Saturdays, after 12 M.). On a wide opening such agreements to stop stock are made "fair opening"—that is, at a fair mean between the high and low opening prices. If a stock simultaneously opened at 60 and 61, a fair opening would usually be 60½.

Specialist's Book

But it is high time that we examine in more detail the specialist's "book" so frequently referred to above, in which orders entrusted to him as a broker are kept. This book is, on the average, some 8 inches long by 3½ inches wide. At the top of each page (see Figure 10, page 118) in the middle is printed a figure—say 95—and all the specialist's orders for the given stock, limited at that price, are inscribed below it in two parallel columns, buying orders being placed in the left-hand column and selling orders in the right-hand column. At appropriate distances down the middle, and directly beneath the "95," are increasingly higher figures, such as 95⅛, 95¼, etc. Below these, orders limited to these higher prices are

[18] See Constitution, Art. XX, Sec. 3.

similarly inscribed. The range of prices on a page depends upon the number of orders to be entered beside them, which in turn depends upon the relative activity or inactivity of the stock in question. The way in which an order is usually entered in the specialist's book also requires explanation. First, the number of shares involved is recorded in terms of hundreds (i.e., 1=100, 2=200, etc.); next is inscribed the name of the firm or individual who has given the order to the specialist, and after this name the period during which the order is effective. "G.T.C." indicates orders "good until countermanded"; "M.," "orders for the month"; "Wk.," "orders for the week"; if no sign at all is added, an order good for the day only is indicated.[19] Stop orders are denoted by "Stop." It will be recalled that stop orders are not limited at the price set, but simply become market orders when that price is reached.[20] In addition to his book, market orders are handed to the specialist on slips made out by the brokers' telephone clerks, and are not inscribed in his book but handled separately. The specialist's book is, of course, not shown by him to others, except in case he is compelled to leave the floor, when he temporarily entrusts it to some one person—either another specialist at the same post or some other member.

The specialist, with his book and his market orders, is a factor of constantly varying importance in the market for each stock. Sometimes, especially in the more inactive stocks, he will have almost all the orders for a given stock, and will consequently make the market for it. But, of course, anyone at any time can take the market away from the specialist by quoting closer prices. Furthermore, there are often several different specialists in a given stock, competing with each other. Moreover, the floor trader will, under normal circumstances, compete with him to render prices closer, if there is a prospective profit of only ⅛ per cent to be gained thereby.

---

[19] See Chapter III, page 53.

[20] *Ibid.*, page 52.

On the other hand, a majority of orders in the stock may drift into the hands of brokers in the crowd—in which case the specialist ceases to be a dominant factor in the market for the stock.

Before the Opening of the Market

We are now prepared to follow with readier comprehension a detailed and typical cross-section of the specialist's daily work.[21] For this purpose an active opening had best be selected, since this point in the day constitutes the weakness of the present system and creates the most serious problems and misunderstandings. In order that the opening may be sufficiently active, let us suppose that the stock selected closed the previous day at 93, and that overnight announcement has been made that its dividend would be increased.

Knowing in advance that the opening will be active, the specialist arrives at his post that morning at 9:30, and begins to enter in his book the orders which are given him. It has been estimated that the tubes and the boys on the floor handle over 20,000 separate slips of paper between 9:30 and 9:45 A.M. Every one has to be opened and examined, and if the man who reads them makes any mistake, he is, of course, held responsible for it. In this connection it may be said that out-of-town branches can greatly assist the specialist by not sending in, just before the opening, orders with limits 30 points away from the market, as the congestion at this time is at its height.

The specialist finds at 9:59 (see Figure 10) that, counting both his old orders and those received that morning, he has stop orders at 95 to buy 300 shares for West and 100 for Lee; at 95¼, 100 for Lamb; at 95½, 200 for Ross; at 95⅝, 200 for Long; and at 95¾, 200 for Parlos. On the other hand, he has to sell at 95, 200 for Lewis, 500 for Park, 1,000

[21] For the subsequent practical examples of the specialist's work, the author acknowledges his indebtedness to the address of Mr. Erastus T. Tefft previously cited.

BUY		95	SELL
E. West	3 Stop M.	2 G.T.C.	H. Lewis
Lee & Co.	1 Stop M.	5 G.T.C.	F. Park
		10 M.	Fisk & Co.
		7 M.	Stan & Co.
		1 M.	E. Lorin
		2 M.	May Bros.
		4 M.	F. Dean & Co.
	1/8		
		2 M.	F. Hill
	1/4		
R. Lamb	1 Stop Wk.	2 M.	F. Mason
		1 Wk.	B. Allen
		1	Rolls Co.
	3/8		
	1/2		
E. Ross	2 Stop M.	5 M.	M. Craig
		4 Wks.	L. Wilcox
		1 Wk.	Munroe & Co.
		1 Wk.	R. Gibbs
	5/8		
Long & Co.	2 Stop M.		
	3/4		
E. Parlos	2 Stops M.	1 M.	E. Store
		1 M.	R. Lard
		2 M.	Butt & Co.
		1 Wk	W. Austin

Figure 10. Specimen Page of Specialist's Book. (Size $3\frac{1}{2} \times 8\frac{1}{2}$.)

for Fisk, 700 for Starr, 100 for Lorin, 200 for May, and 400 for Dean. In addition, there are the selling orders at 95⅛, 95¼, etc., which are indicated in the illustration.

Before 10 A.M. the crowd begins to gather about the post, ready to execute orders in this stock as soon as the gong sounds. On a day like this there are naturally many more buying than selling orders, since the dividend has been increased. Consequently, it is easier for sellers to find buyers than for buyers to find sellers. Each seller who comes into the crowd says, "I will sell a hundred." At once he is pounced upon by a buyer and he stops his stock with him at a fair opening. That is, the seller agrees to sell his stock to the buyer at a fair opening price; for reasons already given, no price can be named in such transactions. Such an arrangement is, of course, beneficial to both buyer and seller, and insures both against executing their orders at a price other than the actual opening price, which it is doubtful if they could otherwise exactly secure. But this process of stopping stock leaves many buyers in excess, who, lest they miss their market, hand their orders at about 9:57 A.M. to the specialist to execute for them. At 9:59, therefore, the specialist discovers that these order slips which have been handed to him will force him to buy 2,200 shares at the market on the opening. On the other hand, he has 3,100 shares to sell at 95. Meanwhile, about thirty brokers and traders have gathered in the crowd around him. With all these orders both to buy and to sell, he must, of course, make both bids and offers for the stock on the opening. He cannot guess exactly at what price the first sale will be made, but tries to approximate it as nearly as he can on the basis of the orders he has received.

Trading at the Opening

Hardly has the gong sounded at just 10 A.M. when the specialist cries "1,000 at 95, 94¾ for a thousand," meaning that he will sell 1,000 shares at the former price, and buy 1,000 at the latter. Simultaneously, some other broker bids "95¼ for 500" and another cries "Sold"; another man offers "500 at 94¾" and someone else says "Take them"; while (as the specialist learns a moment later) another pair on the edge of the crowd make a sale of 200 shares at the higher figure of 95¾. All three transactions happen at the same instant. A fraction of a second later the specialist cries "⅞ for a thousand, a thousand at 5—take a thousand at 5—2!" These cryptic and tremendously abbreviated words mean that the specialist bids for 1,000 shares at 94⅞, and offers 1,000 at 95, and then buys first 1,000 shares from his selling customers for his buying customers at 95, and then another 1,000 shares.

The next problem is to determine what the opening price was. As we have seen, it has really been a "split opening," for 500 shares have been sold at 94¾, 2,000 shares at 95, 500 shares at 95¼, and 200 at 95¾. The last-mentioned sale has not been skilfully made, and, considering the few shares sold at this price, it would not be fair to quote the split opening 94¾—95¾. Thus the opening is printed on the tape as "3,000 shares from 94¾ to 95¼." But the 200-share sale cannot simply be disregarded, so "200 sold at 95¾" is also put on the tape. Meanwhile, orders which were stopped have been executed at 95 as a fair opening price, but these, as previously explained, are not put on the tape.

Returning to the specialist, we find that in addition to the 2,000 shares he has crossed 200 more, and has sold 500 besides in the open market. Thus far, after doing everything humanly possible, he has executed all his market orders, and 2,700 out of his 3,100 original selling orders, leaving him 400 more to sell at 95. Meanwhile the ticker reports the opening price as "3,000 at 94¾ to 95¼," and every customer who has placed an order within those limits at once concludes that his stock has been sold. The specialist may yet sell out his 400 at 95, his

200 at 95⅛, and his 400 at 95¼, if the market moves in just the right way. But if it grows somewhat dull and prices do not rise again above 95, all the ⅛ and ¼ stock customers, whose orders, of course, cannot be executed under these circumstances, are going to blame the specialist for not being able to sell their stock, and quote the split opening of 94¾—95¼ as conclusive proof that they have been done an injustice. And usually it is the specialist upon whom they ultimately saddle the blame. Split openings also sometimes create a supicion that somehow the specialist has bought at the lesser and sold at the greater price on his own account. Indeed, years ago, one specialist in an opening of 61—61¾ did attempt to buy for himself all the stock he had to sell at 61, and to sell for himself all the stock he had to buy at 61¾. He lasted just four days.

Overworked Specialist

The opening is obviously, from a mechanical standpoint, the weak point in present business methods and routine on the Exchange. The specialist in particular is often subject to tremendous pressure and is hugely overworked. In addition to his sufficiently difficult and extensive tasks outlined above, he must watch everyone in the crowd to see that someone does not sell stock above the limit at which he must buy it, or below the limit at which he has to sell it; he must see just what the fair opening is, and just how the telegraph operator is printing the split opening on the ticker; and he must constantly make changes on orders in his book as indicated by messages which pour in upon him. Sometimes a single order will be changed half a dozen times in ten minutes. (Figure 11 shows the slip on which the broker cancels an order previously given to the specialist) Furthermore, he must make out a written binding report on every sale he has made. He must check each report before it goes out, lest in his haste he write ⅜ instead of ¾ and either make enemies or incur losses. This is the reason why reports from transactions by specialists take ten or fifteen minutes to make. The authorities of the Stock Exchange have long realized the difficulties involved by the present system of opening the market, particularly as they relate to the specialist's work. The problem has been worked upon and thought about for years, but thus far at least, no practical method of improving it has been arrived at.

JENKINS & CO.
XX 12
CANCEL:
Buy 100 Rubber
70
G. T. R.

Figure 11. Cancel Slip. (Size 3 x 4.)

Execution of Stop Orders

Another source of difficulty and misunderstanding arises from the execution of stop orders. As has already been explained, a stop order becomes a market order when its limit price is reached. It sometimes happens that as stock prices decline on the Exchange, a figure will be reached at which several stop orders will suddenly become market orders to sell. In consequence of the large amount of stock thus thrown on the market for instant sale, a violent and sudden drop in the price of the stock may ensue. Since such stop orders are almost entirely handled by the specialist, the subject is especially germane to this exposition of his activities.

For purposes of illustration, let us take another imaginary opening, when the problems presented by the execution of stop orders are usually most acute and difficult. Figure 12 shows the specialist's book in a very inactive stock just before the opening. The considerable number of stop orders to sell from 70 to 65 is here the source of the inevitable violent price fluctuation. We may also presuppose that a severe decline has

BUY				SELL
		73		
			1 G.T.C.	F. West
		70		
Macy & Co.	2		1 Stop M.	Doe & Co.
		69½		
			1 Stop M.	J. Nash
		69		
Wells & Co.	1 G.T.C.		2 Stop G.T.C.	R. Roe
		68½		
S. Cooper	1 M.			
		68		
E. Dunn	1 wk.		4 Stop	E. Smith
		67		
Doe & Co	2 wk.			
		66		
L. Ray	2 G.T.C		2 Stop G.T.C	E. King
		65		
Field & Co	1		1 Stop	G. Platt
		64		
H. Cole	6 G.T.C.			

Figure 12. Another Specimen Page of Specialist's Book. (Size 3½ x 8½.)

taken place in this stock the day before and that overnight the dividend has been reduced 1 per cent. At the close the day before, 70 was bid for 200 shares, and 100 were offered at 73.

At 9:55 the next morning the specialist finds that in addition to the orders in his book, as shown in Figure 12, he has five 100-share lots to sell at the market. And now comes the crucial question—at what price will the market open? No matter what price between 69 and 65 this stock sells at, the specialist's shares to sell at the market will be increased by the many stop orders to sell. Under such circumstances stock to be sold is bound greatly to overbalance stock to be bought, and hence a severe decline is unavoidable. In this instance the specialist happens to have the market all to himself, and opens the stock "1,600 shares sold at 64." By so doing all selling and buying orders, except the 100 to sell at 73, are executed at this single price. The disadvantage of this method of opening the stock is, of course, that the 500 shares to sell at the market are sold at a very low price. But it must be remembered that the specialist as an agent and broker stands in the same relationship to his buying customers as to his selling customers. In the light of the obvious conditions of supply and demand in this stock, prices are bound to decline. What is fair to pay for the seller's stock when the specialist knows these conditions? Why should he pay more for that stock than the price at which all the orders can be crossed? So it is undoubtedly better that the stock should open 1,600 shares at 64. Since this is the first and only sale, customers could not declare that they had been discriminated against and would probably be inclined to take such an occurrence as the fortunes of war.

Advantage of Present System of Opening

The advantage and fairness of opening the stock in this way becomes more apparent when some other way is attempted. Let us suppose that in the above instance the specialist proceeded as follows: He opens the stock, 400 shares at 68½, by selling 200 shares of his stock to be sold at the market to Macy, 100 shares more of it to Wells, and still another 100 of it to Cooper. In addition to the remaining 100 shares to sell at the market, he now has 400 additional market orders to sell, owing to the fact that the first sale at 68½ made active the stop orders of Doe for 100, Nash for 100, and Roe for 200. He next sells his last 100 shares of original market stock to Dunn at 68, thereby increasing his market selling orders to 800 shares by making active Smith's stop order at 68 to sell 400 shares. All his original market orders to sell have, however, now been executed. He next sells Doe's 100 and Nash's 100 to Doe at 67, and then 200 of Smith's stock to Ray at 66. But this latter sale "touches off" King's 200-share stop order at 66, and thus the specialist still has 600 shares to sell at the market. The third 100 of Smith's stock is next sold to Field at 65, thereby making Platt's 100-share stop order at that price a market order. The specialist still has 600 shares to sell at the market, namely, Smith's last 100 shares, Roe's 200, King's 200, and Platt's 100. These are all sold to Cole at 64, thus cleaning up all the orders on the book except West's 100 to sell at 73, which cannot under the circumstances be executed at all. Soon the tape gives the report of these transactions: 400 at 68½. . . . 100 at 68. . . . 200 at 67. . . . 200 at 66. . . . 100 at 65. . . . 600 at 64. The last sale, of course, includes 100, 200, 200, and 100 shares to sell.

But what does Doe, with the stop order at 70, say when he is told that his stock brought only 67, after seeing 400 sell at 68½ and 100 at 68? What does Roe say when he learns that his 200 shares went for only 64? Neither is Smith pleased to receive the reports from his 400-share stop order at 68, which show sales at 66, 65, and 64. Such executions could not be explained, and apart from the endless quarrels and dissatisfaction they would cause to sellers, the buyers would meanwhile be treated unfairly. The fairest way to both buyers and sellers is, therefore, to open the stock 1,600 shares at 64. And this is one of the chief reasons why in such inactive stocks occasional bad breaks in price of this kind occur.

Unfounded Complaint

A common complaint against the Stock Exchange is that traders there make it a practice to "gun for stop orders." In other words, if a trader knew that by selling a few shares short he could sufficiently exhaust the demand for it at higher prices, and cause its price to decline to a point where several stop orders would automatically be converted into market selling orders and cause a further price decline, he could cover his short sale at the lower price thus reached and thus obtain a profit for himself. In point of fact, this sequence of events occurs now and then but more by accident than by design. For it must be remembered that the short seller cannot possibly know all the factors of supply and demand existing in the market. Such an attempt might involve sales of a large number of shares, and the consequent danger of heavy losses. Moreover, the depression of a price by such selling might equally well uncover large buying orders, which would either halt the decline, or in certain circumstances (as with stop orders to buy) drive prices back to higher levels.

Of course, if the specialist attempted to take advantage of his knowledge of his orders, he would by no means be certain of success, since, as we have seen, the dominant influence of supply and demand may really exist at a given time in the crowd rather than in his book. Moreover, such an attempt by the specialist would be practically certain of detection by the crowd, and, owing to the concentration of orders in his hands, he would be certain of conviction. The price of such an attempt on his part would, of course, be expulsion from the Exchange, permanent disgrace, and the end of his career as a security dealer.

Violent declines due to stop orders being accidentally "touched off" will always occur now and then in the Stock Exchange. An example of much the same thing has, indeed, been given above. The newspaper man, bending over his typewriter and hurrying his daily column of market news to press, will no doubt continue to find in this alleged "gunning for stops" a spirited human-interest motif with which to enliven the inevitably bleak mathematics of his items. The customer whose market order to sell has been executed for a smaller price than he could wish, will accept this, as other Wall Street legends, with conviction. But the practical broker, trader, or specialist on the floor will tell a very different story concerning it.

Specialist's Economic Services

A concluding paragraph is called for, to relate the more obvious economic services rendered by the specialist directly to the stock market on the Exchange, and indirectly to all those having contact with and being dependent upon it. In so far as he acts as a dealer his function resembles that of the floor trader, in that he greatly assists in maintaining at his own risk a continuous market in securities. Hence, like the floor trader, he is a necessary instrument in the task of rendering securities listed on the Exchange instantly negotiable. Also, because of the close prices at which his own trades are carried out, the specialist performs a similar service in stabilizing price movements.

But apart from these considerations, the slow and natural evolution of the specialist as a broker's broker has been due to the mechanical impossibility of executing difficult brokerage orders in any other way. Without his services, therefore, the acceptance and execution of many orders of vital moment to customers all over the country would be impossible. As we have seen, the stop orders whereby purchasers of stock are enabled to insure themselves against anything but minimum losses could not be handled except for the specialist. In the universal process of specialization through which all modern business is passing, the specialist, as indeed his very name would imply, has been created by natural economic and practical causes to support weak markets, restrain soaring markets, stabilize prices, and in addition to prove at all times an indispensable medium through which a vast number of the buying and selling orders of the nation must inevitably flow.

CHAPTER VI

THE ODD-LOT BUSINESS

Odd Lot vs. Round Lot

Thus far in the present volume the description of transactions in stocks occurring on the New York Stock Exchange has invariably presupposed a purchase or sale of 100 shares, or some multiple of 100 shares. The reader, however, must not conclude on this account that no smaller number of shares than 100 can be bought or sold on the Exchange. As a matter of fact, a customer can through the agency of almost any ordinary Stock Exchange commission house buy or sell any number of shares from 1 to 99 with perfect readiness. But in the case of such orders for "odd lots" of stock (as orders involving less than 100 shares are called), resort must be had to special machinery which is unnecessary with orders for "round lots" or "full lots" of 100 shares, or multiples thereof, and which in consequence was not touched upon in the typical investment transaction described in Chapter III. So considerable is the proportionate volume of these odd-lot orders today that the matter of their handling on the Stock Exchange deserves a separate chapter.

Basis for the 100-Share Unit of Trading

First of all a word is necessary concerning this 100-share unit of trading which prevails in the Exchange. Under ideal conditions the unit number of shares in which trading normally takes place would be the single share of stock. But the New York Stock Exchange is the principal security market in the United States—now the wealthiest nation in the world—and because of the vast extent and enormous cash value of the transactions which occur under its auspices it was long ago compelled to adopt wholesale as distinguished from retail methods of operation in order to carry on its work efficiently and successfully. One instance of this fact has been the fixing of 100 shares of stock as the unit for ordinary trading on its floor.

Difficulties with Smaller Trading Unit

Many practical considerations have combined to establish this 100-share unit as a necessity today. The flood of small orders which would result from the adoption of a smaller unit of trading would make it both impracticable and unprofitable for the commission broker or the specialist to give that conscientious attention to each individual order which is now a vital factor in establishing prices fairest to both buyers and sellers. A smaller trading unit would furthermore exaggerate the difficulty of making large purchases or sales of stock almost past the possibility of satisfactory performance. A broker, for example, with an order to purchase 10,000 shares—a delicate and laborious task even with the present 100-share unit—would find it practically impossible to execute it quickly and efficiently were he forced to accumulate it by 10-share or even 25-share purchases.

Other obstacles would also arise from trading in such a small unit. The banker loaning funds on security collateral would be forced to receive huge bundles of securities which would be hard to safeguard and inspect. Moreover, the full burden of the greatly increased number of separate transactions in less than 100 shares would at once descend upon the indispensable stock ticker and largely destroy its usefulness; the tape would be clogged and delayed with the records of thousands of small and relatively unimportant transactions. So often would its quotations be based on a negligible number of shares that a recorded price would lose the significance possessed by present prices, which represent transactions in

100 shares. The adoption of the 100-share trading unit on the New York Stock Exchange today is in consequence not a matter of theoretical preference but of practical and unavoidable necessity.

But at a market value of $100 per share, $10,000 would be needed to purchase 100 shares of stock outright, or $2,000, say, for their purchase on credit. It is apparent that the present 100-share trading unit, were it not supplemented by other arrangements suited to the needs and requirements of the small investor, would deprive him of many facilities and services which the Stock Exchange daily renders the larger investor.

The Odd-Lot System

Accordingly, a system has grown up in the Exchange whereby certain of its members will purchase odd lots of stock and later sell them out in 100-share lots, or sell odd lots which they obtain by purchasing 100-share lots and splitting them up into the smaller desired denominations. Sometimes, instead of buying 100 shares it proves more desirable to borrow that amount in the manner previously described in the instance of short sales;[1] but this practice amounts to about the same thing. Any member of the Stock Exchange is, of course, entirely at liberty to take up this work of dealing in odd lots, as well as any other particular sort of business transacted on the floor. But in practice such work has become to a large degree specialized. As a result this business of dealing in less than 100 shares, although done to some extent by the specialist in his few particular stocks, is almost all carried on by what are known as the "odd-lot houses."

Evolution of the Odd-Lot House

These odd-lot houses have developed during the past half-century. When in the Civil War period a continuous market

[1] See Chapter IV, page 82.

was established on the Exchange it had already adopted the 100-share unit, and a single dealer on the floor, named Munroe, was able to attend to all the odd-lot orders received. After the panic of 1873 other Exchange members took up this branch of the work, which gradually increased in volume as time went on. After the appearance of the specialist[2] as a dealer and broker in the growing stock market, it came to be the custom for the few odd-lot dealers to have the specialist trade for them on commission. But with the further passage of time and the continued increase in the turnover of sales on the Exchange, the specialist's increasing work in 100-share lots prevented his handling these odd-lot orders with sufficient attention and care. The growing difficulty of finding a market for odd lots of stock which resulted was thus the immediate cause for the organization of the present odd-lot houses, which depend entirely on their own dealers for making their sales or purchases.

Nature of the Odd-Lot Business

In consequence, the odd-lot dealers today stand always ready to deal in any number of shares from 1 to 99 and thus make it possible for the small investor to purchase or sell odd lots of listed stocks at all times. Their only customers are the commission brokers who, as middlemen, bring to them the orders for small lots which originate from small investors and traders all over the country. The odd-lot houses, as we shall presently see, not only maintain extensive offices and large clerical forces, but also must possess many partners or representatives who are Stock Exchange members. Several odd-lot houses require the services of twenty or more members of the Exchange, and have a partner or associate stationed at each of the twenty stock posts on the floor.

The odd-lot dealer is able to perform his useful function by purchasing shares wholesale in 100-share lots from commis-

[2] See Chapter V, page 107.

sion brokers and traders, and then splitting up the 100-share certificates into certificates of lesser denomination and selling them to commission brokers to fill such odd-lot buying orders as may have come into the market through the latter from the general public. On the other hand, the odd-lot dealer stands equally ready to purchase at any time such odd lots of stock as may be offered by customers through their brokers. When his odd-lot purchases have aggregated 100 shares he can readily sell them out as a round lot to some broker or floor trader. Thus the odd-lot dealers act as jobbers for the execution of buying and selling orders involving less than 100 shares which commission brokers receive from the public. Owing to the extensive equipment and efficient operation of the odd-lot houses, these small orders, whether for a purchase or a sale, can be placed by a customer in a commission broker's office, and then be executed almost instantly on the Exchange floor.

A Typical Odd-Lot Transaction

Perhaps the best method of explaining the exact nature and methods of the odd-lot business is to describe a typical transaction from beginning to end. When a customer gives his order for the purchase of 30 shares of United States Rubber common stock to his commission broker, the latter at once transmits it to his telephone clerk on the floor of the Exchange. Some commission houses, either because of the large volume of their total transactions, or because of a tendency to specialize in just this odd-lot brokerage business, maintain on the Exchange a separate telephone booth for their odd-lot orders. With other commission firms the order will be sent over the same telephone by which orders for 100 shares are transmitted. In either case the odd-lot order is speeded from the commission office to the board room by precisely the same methods described in Chapter III in the instance of a 100-share order.

Transmission of Odd-Lot Orders

The telephone clerk might, of course, signal for the floor member of his firm on the annunciator boards, and turn the order over to him to execute at the Rubber post, as in the case of a round-lot order. But a more satisfactory method than this has been devised in the special case of odd-lot orders. The telephone clerk has probably been previously instructed to turn such orders over to some one of the several odd-lot firms direct. He therefore writes out the order on an order blank containing the printed name of the odd-lot house in question, and hands it to one of the tube attendants stationed nearby. The attendant at once places it in a small cylindrical container and slips it into the appropriate hole in the nearest pneumatic tube station.

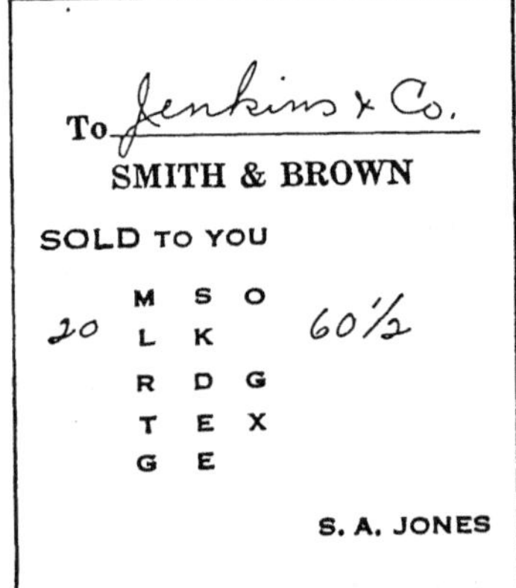

To Jenkins & Co.
SMITH & BROWN
SOLD TO YOU
20 M S O L K R D G T E X G E 60½
S. A. JONES

Figure 13. (a) Odd-Lot Dealer's Sale Report Slip.
(Size 2¾ x 3¼.)
Sale of 20 shares of Lackawanna Steel at 60½.

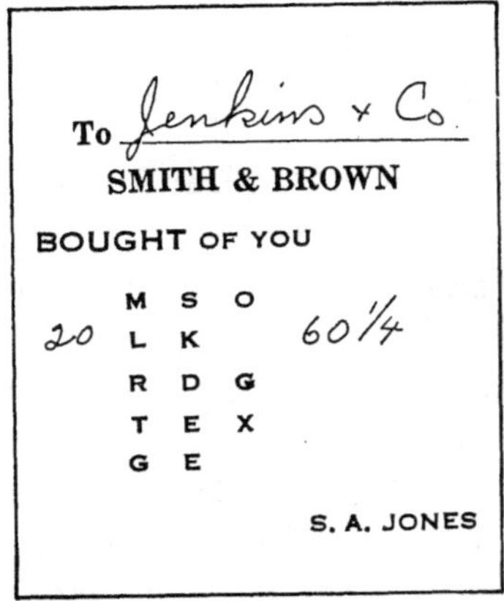

To Jenkins & Co.
SMITH & BROWN
BOUGHT OF YOU
20 M S O L K R D G T E X G E 60¼
S. A. JONES

Figure 13. (b) Odd-Lot Dealer's Purchase Report Slip.
(Size 2¾ x 3¼.)
Purchase of 20 shares of Lackawanna Steel at 60¼.

These tube stations are located on the Exchange floor at the end of the stalls containing the members' telephones, and each contains the entrances to pneumatic tubes running to the twenty stock posts. There are some twenty miles of pneumatic tubing altogether under the floor of the board room. The containers with odd-lot orders shoot through these tubes and almost instantly emerge at the various receiving stations of the tube system, which are attached to every stock post. Thus the order for the 30 Rubber very quickly arrives at the particular post where that stock is traded in. A tube attendant there at once takes the order from its container and turns it over to the odd-lot dealer for whom it is intended and who proceeds to make a sale as quickly as possible. If it is a limited order away from the market of that moment, he may have to enter it in his book and sell the customer the 30 Rubber desired as soon as conditions will permit.

As soon as possible after the sale or purchase of an odd lot has been made, the odd-lot dealer makes out a report slip (Figures 13a and b) which records the price at which the transaction was made, and sends it back via the tubes to the telephone clerk from whom the order came. The phone clerk in turn reports it to the commission office.

Methods of the Odd-Lot Dealer

Let us now consider the transaction a moment from the viewpoint of the odd-lot dealer. He stands at or near a given post all day, prepared to buy or sell such odd lots of stock as are offered to him or sought from him. The price at which he makes the sale of 30 Rubber depends upon special conditions presently to be treated. But he learns from his notebook whether or not his firm already owns any United States Rubber common stock. In case, to use his own phrase, his house is "long" of 54 shares, he can, of course, sell 30 of them without needing to buy any of them. But if, on the contrary, his firm has less than the 30 shares required, it will be necessary for him to sell this amount short to the purchasing broker for the time being, and cover the transaction afterwards by purchasing a 100-share lot of the stock from some commission broker or floor trader.

Sometimes odd-lot houses may be temporarily long of thousands of shares of a stock, and at other times carry very little. But in general, of course, the odd-lot houses do not conduct their business like a retail grocery shop and keep "stocked up" with a variety of shares as the latter does with different kinds of provisions. There is no need of such a cumbrous method of doing business, since the odd-lot dealer is standing in the very center of the world market for Rubber common, and he can purchase as much as he needs of it in 100-share lots at any time, simply by making a bid for it.

Usefulness of the Short Sale

The fact that the odd-lot dealer, if he is to do his work efficiently and quickly, must constantly take a short as well as a long position in the market, furnishes one of the clearest examples of how very necessary the short sale is to a well-balanced and highly organized market. For if the odd-lot dealer could not become short of a stock just as readily as he can accumulate and become long of it, the odd-lot machinery of the Exchange would be thrown out of balance and prevented from rendering its present vast service to thousands of small investors all over the nation. As in the case of any other short seller, of course, the odd-lot dealer incurs the risk of loss if the stock advances, and a chance for profit if it declines, between the time of the sale and that of the subsequent purchase. But, unlike the ordinary speculator, the odd-lot dealer is often forced by the nature of his business to go short of stock, not when he wants to but at times when his customer-broker desires to purchase from him.

The 30-share certificate, after it is obtained from the transfer office, is sent to the purchasing broker in return for his check covering the purchase. The broker then delivers the certificate to his customer, obtains payment for it from him, and the transaction is concluded.

A Sale of an Odd Lot

When the customer wishes to sell his 30 shares of Rubber, the above process for purchasing is simply reversed. The selling order is sent over the telephone and through the tubes to the odd-lot dealer, who buys the shares in accordance with instructions accompanying the order. When by such purchasing of many small lots the odd-lot dealer becomes long of, or accumulates, 100 shares of Rubber common, he can, of course, either hold them temporarily, or else sell a round lot of 100 shares of the stock to someone in the Rubber crowd. In this operation, of course, the odd-lot dealer is compelled to stay long of the given stock in varying amounts and for varying periods of time, with the danger of loss if its price declines and a chance for profit if its price rises in the meantime.

Work of the Transfer Office

The methods employed in exchanging odd-lot certificates for 100-share certificates also deserve a word in passing. This exchange is, of course, effected at the transfer office of the corporation in question. Every corporation whose shares are listed on the Stock Exchange must either have its own transfer office in the Borough of Manhattan, or else must appoint some responsible party with an office in the borough to act as its transfer agent.[3] This transfer business is largely performed for corporations with Stock Exchange listings by the various trust companies in the Wall Street district. Every listed company also has two different kinds of share certificates—one for even 100 shares, and the other for less than 100 shares.

When, for example, the odd-lot dealer has accumulated by purchase 100 shares of Pennsylvania Railroad, in four lots—

[3] See Chapter XVI.

let us say—of 17, 13, 20, and 50 shares, he can send these four odd-lot certificates to the transfer office of the Pennsylvania Railroad; and this office, after destroying the certificates, will issue to the odd-lot dealer a single 100-share certificate. The reverse process takes place when the odd-lot dealer wishes to obtain odd-lot certificates to make deliveries of odd lots which he has sold. If, for instance, he has sold odd lots of 3, 14, 8, 20, 25, and 30 shares of United States Steel preferred, he sends to the transfer office a 100-share certificate of that stock, which is then canceled, and receives in exchange six odd-lot certificates, each for the stated number of shares.

This process of exchanging odd-lot certificates for 100-share certificates is not always necessary, and consequently by no means invariably employed. Odd-lot certificates aggregating 100 shares are considered a "good delivery" for a 100-share sale of stock, and frequently odd-lot houses will deliver to a purchasing commission broker odd-lot certificates to the total amount of 100 shares, instead of a 100-share certificate. Nevertheless, the latter has the right to demand that the stock be delivered to him by transfer—in which case he would, of course, get a 100-share certificate.

Deliveries, Commissions, and Profits

Finally, it should be noted that the odd-lot house never comes directly into contact with the public, but deals with it only through the commission brokers, who in odd-lot transactions act as middlemen. In consequence, the odd-lot dealer delivers the certificates of the odd lots of stock which he has sold to the commission broker, who in turn delivers them to his customers. Similarly, the odd-lot certificates which the customers sell, come to the odd-lot dealer only through the commission broker. The commission broker charges a commission for his services to the odd-lot customer exactly as in the case of the purchase and sale of round lots of stock. The exact amount of this commission varies among the different brokerage houses and according to the number of shares bought or sold; usually, in any case, the minimum commission charge is $1. The broker cannot make any other profit from an odd-lot transaction, however, since he is not a dealer, but merely his customer's agent. The odd-lot dealer, on the other hand, being a dealer and not a broker, cannot charge any commission for his services but must rely for his profits on the difference between the prices of his sales and his purchases.

Determining the Price

With this background of the mechanical side of the odd-lot business, we are now in a position to consider how the prices at which such typical purchases and sales as those discussed above are determined. The price at which odd-lot houses can profitably and regularly afford to deal in odd lots of stock depends fundamentally upon the current market prices for the sales of the same stocks in 100-share lots, as well as upon such limitations as may be placed upon the buying or selling orders of the customers. The activity of the particular stock is also an essential factor in this question of price, as we shall see.

In the case of the most active stocks it is customary for odd-lot dealers to sell odd lots at ⅛ above, or buy them at ⅛ below the next sale of 100 shares. Thus, an odd-lot dealer in receipt of an order to make a purchase or sale of 20 shares of United States Steel common will wait about the post where United States Steel stock is traded in until the next 100-share transaction occurs. If 100 shares of Steel should be sold—let us say—at 95, the odd-lot dealer would under the circumstances sell 20 shares of Steel for 95⅛, or buy them for 94⅞.

Transactions Made at Bid and Offer Prices

Since on this basis odd-lot trading involves waiting for a sale of 100 shares, another method is sometimes resorted to, which avoids the delay. In most active stocks the odd-lot dealer will buy or sell at once, if he is allowed to buy the odd number of shares from his customer at the bid price, or sell them to his customer at the asked price. If, for instance, the odd-lot dealer receives an order to buy or to sell 20 shares of Delaware and Hudson Company *at once,* he hastens to the appropriate post and finds that the stock is offered at 95½, and that 94⅞ is bid for it. Without waiting for the brokers who are bidding for or offering the stock to effect a compromise and make a sale at some price between these two figures, the odd-lot dealer will buy 20 shares of Delaware and Hudson Company from the commission broker at the bid price of 94⅞, or will sell them to him at the asked price of 95½. Unless, however, the odd-lot dealer is directed to obtain an instant execution based on these bid and asked prices, it is usually understood that an order for odd lots should be executed ⅛ from the price established by the next 100-share sale.

Quarter Stocks

It is, of course, true that the more infrequently a stock is traded in, or the more violently its price fluctuates, the greater is the danger that the odd-lot dealer in the purchases he makes will accumulate shares which it may prove difficult to dispose of later in 100-share lots. In the case of his sales of odd lots, inactive or violently fluctuating stocks of which he is forced to "go short" are also more difficult to purchase satisfactorily in 100's to cover the previous short sales. In the stocks which impose this greater risk upon the odd-lot dealer, it is only fair that he should trade on terms slightly more favorable to himself. This he does by selling odd lots of such stocks to his customers at ¼ over, and buying them from him at ¼ under, the next 100-share sale. An alternative sometimes preferred by customers for odd lots of these stocks is to purchase them at ⅛ over the asked price, or sell them ⅛ under the bid price.

Odd-Lot Transactions "at the Opening"

In determining prices for odd-lot transactions confusion occasionally arises because of the 100-share quotations themselves. When a market order—that is, an order which does not fix any specific price at which the odd lot will be sold or bought—is given for an odd lot by a customer before the opening of the market, it is executed by the odd-lot dealer at ⅛ (or with special securities, ¼) from the first 100-share sale that day—or, as it is commonly called, the "opening" sale. It sometimes happens, however, that this opening sale of 100 shares, upon which the price for the odd lot is based, is difficult to determine. In active markets many orders accumulate in the commission brokers' offices overnight for execution at the opening. The crowd waiting around the post of an active stock like Steel common, for example, may be large at 10 A.M. when the gong announcing the opening is rung. In the immediate roar of bids and offers two or more simultaneous first sales sometimes occur, at slightly different prices.[4] If no one can tell exactly what the opening price for 100-share lots is, naturally the odd-lot dealer cannot tell what price he should charge or pay his customers. In such cases, however, the representatives of the various odd-lot houses about the Steel post quickly determine a fair opening price for Steel by averaging the various simultaneous quotations. If two opening sales for 100 shares of Steel common, for example, should occur simultaneously at 95 and 95¼, in all probability the opening price would be declared to be 95⅛, and on this price odd-lot purchases or sales of Steel common would be based.

Often, too, orders come to the odd-lot dealers to buy or sell an odd lot of stock "at the close." Such orders are always

[4] See Chapter V, page 120.

executed on the final bid and asked quotations of the day. It would, of course, be impracticable to execute odd-lot orders at ⅛ from the last sale of 100 shares of the given stock that day, since with inactive stocks the last sale may occur early in the morning. Furthermore, the last sale of a stock might be made at 50, while the closing bid and offer for it might be 48–49. The only practice which is just to everyone is, therefore, to execute orders at the close on the final bid and asked quotations.

Limited Orders in Odd Lots

Another set of misunderstandings is occasioned by limited orders for odd-lot purchases or sales. A limited order, as we have previously noticed, is one which fixes a certain price at which a customer will buy or sell a stock. A buyer may stipulate, for example, that he will not pay more than 45 for the 25 shares of Pennsylvania Railroad he wishes to purchase. Similarly, an investor who has 30 shares of Standard Oil of New Jersey preferred, may instruct his broker to sell it if he can get 105. Such limited orders are always executed at the price limits set, and as soon as the appropriate price for 100-share lots is reached, that is, as soon as 100 shares of Pennsylvania sell as low as 44⅞, or 100 shares of Standard Oil of New Jersey preferred sell as high as 105¼, the execution of these orders—one at ⅛ and the other at ¼ from the 100-share sales—is automatically effected.

Yet even this uniform rule occasionally leads to misunderstandings. For example, a customer might give his order to purchase 20 shares of Union Pacific Railroad at 110. After selling at 111, Union Pacific might drop on the next 100-share sale to 109, thus moving through 110 without actually recording a sale at that price. In such a case the odd-lot dealer would sell the 20 shares to the customer's broker at 110. The customer might object that the next sale had really been made at 109, and that therefore he should get his 20 shares at 109⅛.

Yet he has purchased the stock and received it at the price he himself has named. Had he been willing to take the somewhat greater risk of putting in a market order instead of an order limited in this way, he might, of course, have obtained his stock for 109⅛.

Furthermore, if his order limited at 110 were permitted to be executed at 109⅛, he might in many cases be obtaining better treatment on his 20 shares than if he had ordered 100 shares. For had he ordered 100 shares at this particular time, his order would have most likely been executed at 110, particularly if it had been given to a specialist to execute. Such practice would work an obvious injustice to buyers of 100 shares as compared with buyers of odd lots. And if it generally proved more advantageous to buy or sell stocks in odd lots rather than in 100-share lots, it would be impossible to maintain the trading unit of 100 shares, the necessity for which has already been pointed out.

In case, however, the price of Union stays above 110 throughout the day on which the order is given, but opens the next morning at 109½, or below the limit of 110 set by the customer, the latter would then get his 20 shares of stock for 109⅝, or ⅛ above this first sale; for this price, although less than his limit of 110, is nevertheless slightly higher than the price the 100-share customer at that moment would have to pay.

Stop-loss orders are executed ⅛ (or ¼, in case of a less active stock) from the first 100-share sale which puts the stop order in force. To take the case of a customer who puts in a stop-loss order to sell 50 shares of Steel at 100, if Steel sells first at 100¼ and then at 99½, the order is executed at 99⅜.

Mechanical Limitations of the Ticker Service

Many customers after placing orders with their brokers to purchase or sell odd lots of stock linger in the offices to watch the ticker's record of 100-shares sales (Figure 14) upon which, as we have seen, the prices they must pay or take for

BSB ..COS ASP ..AIC ..MV .C .
56 5/8 10.33 61 1/2 39 1/4 2.30.2.1/4 48 3/8

STU ATT ..STU .ASP .FY LK ABS JWPF
81 1/4 115 81 4.61 3/8 32 1/2 46 3/4 35 39 3/4

FMPF .ST ..MV PA JW CEN BLPF .CRU
95 18 1/2.2.3/8 30 1/8 3.33 7/8 10 1/2 73 1/2 104 65

.AF SHARES .ASP GM .HMO VCPF .ATT
10 995 2.61 1/2 2.8 3/8 5.11 68 1/2 115

Figure 14. Specimen Sections of Stock Ticker Tape. (Width of tape, 5/8 in.)

Recording sales (top row) of 100 Bethlehem Steel Class B at 56 5/8, 1000 Cosden Oil at 33, 100 General Asphalt at 61 1/2, 100 American International at 39 1/4, 200 Midvale Steel at 30, 200 more at 30 1/4, 100 Anaconda Copper at 48 3/8; (second row) 100 Studebaker at 81 1/4, 100 American Telephone and Telegraph at 115, 100 Studebaker at 81, 400 General Asphalt at 61 3/8, 100 American Steel Foundries at 32 1/2, 100 Lackawanna Steel at 46 3/4, 100 American Beet Sugar at 35, and 100 Jewel Tea preferred at 39 3/4; (third row) 100 Famous Players preferred at 95, 100 Chicago, Milwaukee and St. Paul at 18 1/2, 200 more at 18 3/8, 100 Midvale Steel at 30 1/8, 300 Pennsylvania at 33 7/8, 100 Jewel Tea at 10 1/2, 100 New York Central at 73 1/2, 100 Baldwin Locomotive preferred at 104, and 100 Crucible Steel at 65; (bottom row) 10 Atlantic Refining at 995, 200 General Asphalt at 61 1/2, 200 General Motors at 8 3/8, 500 Hupp Motor at 11, 100 Virginia-Carolina Chemical preferred at 68 1/2, and 100 American Telephone and Telegraph at 115.

their odd lots is based. It is well for these customers to bear in mind a few of the mechanical limitations of the stock ticker.[5]

Sometimes a large volume of sales will make it physically impossible for the machine to keep abreast of the market, and consequently the closing prices may not appear on the tape until 3:15 P.M.—fifteen minutes after the closing of the market. Owing to such occasional delays the customer who has just sent in a market order for 10 shares of Bethlehem Steel may

[5] See Chapter III, page 62.

see on the tape some minutes later a record of the sale of 100 shares of Bethlehem at 93. He will naturally suppose that he must pay 93⅛ for his stock, yet because of the slowness of the ticker the 100-share transaction at 93 may have occurred long before the odd-lot dealer on the Exchange has even received the customer's order. Thus, while the dealer is waiting for the next sale the customer imagines that the whole transaction has been concluded. If the next sale should be at 93½, the customer must, of course, pay 93⅝ for his stock, and unless he realizes that the ticker was behind the sales, he will be apt to conclude hastily that he is paying ½ too much. If, on the other hand, the next sale is at 92½ and he gets his stock for 92⅝—½ less than he had anticipated—he may wonder whether a mistake has been made, but—at least according to the general run of human nature—he probably will say nothing about it.

It is, of course, unfair to blame the ticker for all delays between the giving of an odd-lot order and the appearance on the tape of the next 100-share sale on which its execution is based. From the account given above of the actual methods used in handling an odd-lot order it is apparent that slight and unavoidable delays may occur in the execution of the order itself by the pressure sometimes put upon the phone clerks and tube attendants.

Misunderstandings Regarding "Bunched Sales"

Sometimes, too, a number of sales of one security are run off on the tape together, when in reality sales of other stocks have occurred between them. This occasional "bunching" of the sales of one stock on the tape arises from the fact that sales are reported to the keyboard operator who puts them on the ticker, from four different stations on the floor, and it is often physically impossible for him to do otherwise than to run the reports on the tape from each station in succession. This practice, unavoidable under present conditions, occasionally misleads an odd-lot customer as to the precise time at which a 100-share order is reported, just as in cases where the ticker is behind the market in its recording of sales. Sometimes, too, the purchasing customer is under the impression that the odd-lot dealer has watched all these apparently simultaneous sales and has picked out the highest one on which to base the execution of his odd-lot order. To anyone who realizes exactly how quotations are reported, the fallacy of such a belief is apparent. From these brief examples of the physical limitations of the ticker service it is plain that the odd-lot customer, in scanning the tape for the quotation on which the price of his own transaction has been presumably based, must make due allowance for these limitations.

The New York Stock Exchange has never spared either pains or expense to render the ticker service as perfect as science will permit. Although its present ticker system is universally conceded to be by far the most efficient in the world, the Exchange has by no means ceased its efforts to improve it still further. At the present writing, plans for a new semiautomatic system of transmission are under consideration, which should considerably increase the speed of the service without sacrificing any of its proverbial accuracy.

Adjustment of Errors in Odd Lots

If at any time a customer has any reason to question the price on the purchase or sale of an odd lot, he will find the odd-lot house always willing to meet him more than half-way. Indeed, each of the large odd-lot houses maintains an extensive department of adjustments, which thoroughly investigates any disputed bargain, and on the basis of the conditions existing at the time of the complaint makes such adjustment as is fair to all parties to the transaction. This department has a ticker with a stamping clock attached which stamps the current time on the tape, minute by minute, all day long. Thus, the exact time at which every transaction was reported on the tape can be easily ascertained. Moreover, the odd-lot order, immediately on its receipt by the commission broker's telephone clerk on the Exchange, is stamped with a time clock. Thus, between these two records it is possible to determine with some degree of accuracy the actual time at which the given 100-share sale took place, and thus discover if there has been any error made in establishing the price of the odd-lot transaction based upon it. If for no other reason, the keen competition for business between the various odd-lot dealers on the Stock Exchange insures a painstaking and adequate effort to give their customers the greatest possible satisfaction.

Risks of Loss to the Odd-Lot Dealer

It has been pointed out that the odd-lot dealer must temporarily go short of stock when his customer buys, and go long of it when he sells. One inevitable disadvantage under which the odd-lot dealer must labor is the constant risk of suffering actual losses by sudden rises or declines in the prices of these stock commitments, whether long or short.

The odd-lot dealer has to take these losses constantly, and frequently they benefit his customer. To illustrate, in a recent instance a customer ordered, with instructions to "wait for sale," 50 shares of a stock, for which at the time 13 was bid and 18 asked. Since the next sale occurred at 14 he got his stock for 14⅛. But on the sale following that, the price had risen to 18. Had the customer ordered 100 shares instead of 50 he might have had to pay 18 for it. Furthermore, the odd-lot dealer was faced with a loss of 3⅞ in covering the short sale which he had made to obtain the 50 shares for the customer. Such cases where the odd-lot customer gets off much better than either the 100-share customer or the odd-lot dealer are by no means rare. Conversely, in the event of a rapidly sinking market, the seller of odd lots may often have a similar advantage over both a seller of 100-share lots or the odd-lot dealer.

In this connection it must be remembered that the odd-lot dealer is always willing to sell or buy odd lots of stock. In less than 100-share orders his function is akin to that of the "jobber" in the London Stock Exchange; he is the core of the whole market, in which the commission broker is a middleman. There is keen competition between the odd-lot houses on the Exchange, and to hold his business the odd-lot dealer must constantly take the risks of his calling.

Expenses of the Odd-Lot Business

Apart from the risks which must be taken, the odd-lot dealer is in some respects under greater expense in conducting his business than is the average commission broker. The successful execution of odd-lot orders, to begin with, calls for a large force on the floor of the Exchange. Two odd-lot houses employ from twenty to thirty Exchange members apiece to transact their business and with Exchange seats selling around $100,000, this alone represents an investment of from $2,000,000 to $3,000,000 each. Moreover, since the odd-lot dealer is a principal and not an agent, he must himself pay the federal and state transfer tax of 4 cents on every share he sells, instead of passing this charge on to the customer, as the commission broker can do and does.[6]

In addition to this, the odd-lot house must bear office expense in some respects far heavier than the average commission broker. The larger odd-lot houses are from the nature of their business compelled to maintain three hundred or more clerks in offices that sometimes cover three or four entire floors in the large and expensive office buildings of the Wall Street district. The necessity for constantly splitting 100-share cer-

[6] See Chapter V, page 104.

tificates into odd-lot certificates, and vice versa, alone demands a large and competent clerical force. Furthermore, since only 100-share certificates can be cleared through the Stock Clearing Corporation the odd-lot house must handle all its own clearances itself—an even greater task.[7] The bookkeeping in odd-lot houses, too, must cover thousands of small items and must be kept rigorously up to the minute.

When these items of risk and heavy overhead expense are remembered, it is obvious that only a firm with considerable financial resources, efficient management, well-trained help, and a large volume of the small orders in which it specializes, can hope to engage successfully in the odd-lot business. In the forty-five odd years in which the odd-lot houses have been an important factor on the floor of the New York Stock Exchange, no odd-lot house has ever yet failed.

Economic Significance of the Odd-Lot Business

In conclusion, something of a more general nature should be added concerning the broader economic significance of this machinery for the execution of odd-lot orders on the New York Stock Exchange. Small and individually inconsiderable as many odd-lot sales and purchases are, their aggregate amount is very large. It was recently estimated that, on the average, 25 per cent of the total sales made on the floor of the Exchange arose from odd-lot transactions. To the small investor particularly, the Exchange is able through its odd-lot machinery to render a very real and far-reaching service. Its present odd-lot system has placed the retail buyer and seller more nearly upon a plane with the wholesaler in security dealings than is the case in almost any other line of modern business. The retail or odd-lot prices are founded directly upon wholesale or 100-share prices, and are, as we have seen, for the most part only 1/8 or 1/4 per cent away from the wholesale

[7] See Chapter IX.

prices. To the best of their long experience and seasoned judgment, the ablest minds in the Stock Exchange have worked and are working to give the small investor and trader in odd lots every protection and benefit which is afforded the buyer or seller of 100-share lots. A later chapter [8] will summarize the chief among these benefits.

The Odd-Lot Dealer as a Factor in Distribution

The odd-lot machinery of the Stock Exchange also renders no small assistance to the large listed stock corporations, in enabling them to achieve a broad and stable distribution of their shares among the investing public. Corporations have long realized that it was to their decided advantage to distribute their shares evenly in small amounts among many stockholders, rather than simply in large amounts among a comparatively few holders. Such indeed has been the general trend in the recent distribution of the shares of some old and conservative corporations.[9] The effectiveness of the Exchange odd-lot system to this end is sufficiently obvious to need no further comment. According to one recent financial writer, "The steady increase in the odd-lot business shows the growth of the investment class in this country, and is to be regarded as one of the healthiest of economic indications of our financial endurance and stability." [10]

A further benefit rendered by the odd-lot system arises from the fact that it broadens, steadies, and strengthens the whole stock market. We have seen that if many small investors buy odd lots from the odd-lot dealer, he is in turn led to buy round lots in the 100-share wholesale market. Similarly, extensive selling of odd lots soon exerts pressure on the wholesale market, as the odd-lot dealer liquidates there in 100-share

[8] See Chapter XIV.
[9] See Chapter XVI and Appendix, Chapter XVI (h).
[10] Article by Willard T. Ingalls in *The Street*, Sept. 24, 1919, p. 25.

lots the smaller lots sold to him by the public. Thus the force of odd-lot purchases and sales is quickly imparted to the general 100-share market. And it is a general truth that the broader the market can be made, the more satisfactory its prices will be to everyone.[11]

Odd-Lot Purchases in Declining or Rising Markets

The economic advantage of the large odd-lot interest in the market is particularly manifest in declining markets, which are usually characterized and sometimes stabilized by heavy odd-lot buying. There is no more confirmed bargain-hunter in the financial field than the odd-lot purchaser. During the slump in the market which occurred in November, 1919, over 1,400 separate odd-lot transactions were reported in a single day by one Wall Street commission house alone, the majority of which arose from the public's purchasing orders. Thus, odd-lot buying on declines in the market is one of the principal factors which steadies falling prices and restores equilibrium, and with it public confidence in American business and American enterprise. A large proportion of odd-lot buying represents purchases of stocks in small amounts for permanent investment. The odd-lot certificates thus find their way into the strong boxes of a vast number of only moderately wealthy but thrifty and ambitious people in all parts of the country.

Similarly, in a wild bull market when the price structure is becoming top-heavy and dangerous, the odd-lot investor tends to liquidate his small lots of stock and take his profit. The aggregate effect of this tendency is to restrain the rising tendency of the market at times when such restraint is most salutary from the economic standpoint.

In a subsequent chapter,[12] the economic functions of the Stock Exchange as they affect the average 100-share customer will be discussed. But owing to the odd-lot system the services

[11] See Chapter XIV. [12] *Ibid.*

of the Exchange are likewise extended to thousands upon thousands of smaller investors also. By extending the scope of the Stock Exchange in this way the odd-lot dealer not only makes it a better wholesale market than it could otherwise be, but also enables it to render a very important service even to the humblest and poorest of our people.

CHAPTER VII

THE BOND MARKET

Partners and Creditors

Thus far in our survey of the machinery and services of the Stock Exchange nothing has been said concerning the extensive market maintained for bonds on its floor. In its general and fundamental features the Stock Exchange's bond market closely resembles its stock market, described in previous chapters. But before discussing this Exchange bond market, or "Bond Department," as it is often called, it is necessary briefly to summarize the basic differences between bonds and stocks here, even at the risk of wearying with seeming platitudes the more experienced reader of these pages.

By referring to the imaginary railroad corporation whose creation was described in Chapter I [1] the distinction between stocks as shares in a business, and bonds as the debts of a business, will be recalled. This fact—that the stockholder is a partner, while the bondholder is a creditor—is fundamental both to the different investment and speculative qualities and to the varying price movements of the two types of securities. On the one hand, shares, not being obligations, do not involve any necessary return to their holder. On the other hand, a bond is a hard and fast obligation of the given corporation. Its interest rate is fixed at a certain percentage and no more or no less is paid upon it, but that much *must* be paid, since the bond is an interest-bearing debt of the company.

Still another important distinction between these two kinds of securities should be noted. Stocks have no provision as to the repayment of the capital invested in them. A corporation

[1] Page 19.

is theoretically supposed to be deathless, and shares in its business, while indefinitely transferable between shareholders, naturally bear no pledge of redemption by the company. Indeed, a company could not well redeem its entire stock without committing suicide in the process. But bonds, being a debt, specify some date at which the borrowed capital, of which they are the acknowledgment, will be repaid. And lastly, bonds have a prior and more definite claim than stocks to the assets of the issuing corporation. In the case of mortgage bonds, indeed, some definite physical asset is pledged to secure them. Consequently, when mortgage bonds are not paid at maturity the bondholders may foreclose. But the stockholder is less certain with regard to the assets to which he is entitled. Shares may pay no dividends for years and years, and yet the company's business may not be wound up and its assets distributed among its shareholders. Thus the book value of a stock is only one of a number of factors which in a practical way go to determine its current market price.

Classes of Bonds

In a general way bonds can be divided into two principal classes—mortgage bonds, which are secured by a mortgage upon some physical asset of the issuing company, and debenture bonds, which are unsecured.

There are practically as many kinds of mortgage bonds as there are different varieties of mortgages. Oftentimes the order of precedence among these different types of mortgage bonds as claims against the assets and earnings of the issuing company is difficult to determine. Mortgage bonds are also often classified according to the nature of the assets which are mortgaged to secure them, and this in turn has led to the creation of almost as many different types of mortgage bonds as there are different kinds of assets possessed by the modern corporation. Railroad equipment bonds, for example, are generally secured by a mortgage upon the locomotives and cars of a given railroad company. Similarly, land grant bonds involve a mortgage upon the extensive grants of land made during the last century by our government to different railroad companies, in order to encourage new railroad construction in the West. Oftentimes, too, a railroad will place a mortgage upon its all-important terminals to secure what are known as "terminal" bonds. In addition, there is the collateral bond, which is usually based upon the pledge of the stocks or bonds of other, including subsidiary, companies which are held as assets of the issuing company. It was frequently through the sale of their collateral bonds that our present major railroad systems were able during the past half-century to acquire the funds needed to purchase and absorb many smaller and originally independent railroad lines.

Debentures and Convertibles

Debentures, the other principal class of bonds, are not secured by any mortgage. Corporation debentures, of course, rank ahead of preferred or common stocks as claims against the assets and earnings of the company. Almost all government bonds represent simply an unsecured claim against the issuing government's future taxing power. Income bonds—another and usually riskier type of debenture—pay their interest only when the earnings of their issuing corporation are sufficient to permit it, somewhat according to the manner of a preferred stock.

To this already overextended list of what are after all only the principal types of bonds, one more kind—the convertible bond—must be added. Convertible bonds, as their name implies, can under certain specified conditions be converted at the option of their holders into the stock of the issuing company. In case the stock for which such bonds can be exchanged experiences a marked rise in price, this conversion privilege may prove of considerable value to the bondholder, even if he does not turn in his bonds and get stock in exchange for them, for past a certain point the price of his bonds will usually fluctuate in close accord with the price of the stock into which they are convertible.

Since it is usually easier to estimate the income to be derived from bonds than from stocks, and consequently easier to determine the price at which the former should sell, there is as a rule less speculation in the bond market than in the stock market, for changing values, as well as uncertainty and differences of opinion concerning values, are necessary causal prerequisites to extensive speculation.[2]

Speculative Aspects of Bonds

Under certain conditions, however, bonds, like almost any commodity, may become distinctively speculative. When the bonds of a weak government or of an embarrassed corporation either omit the payment of their interest or seem on the verge of doing so, their price will tend to fluctuate in accordance with speculative factors. Conservative investors will "get out of them," and more and more they will shift into the hands of speculators or speculative investors, who assume the greater risks which the selling investors wish to avoid for the sake of possible profits greater than those which the latter could expect. Then, too, when the price of a stock for which a convertible bond can be exchanged rises to a point where such an exchange becomes profitable, the price of the convertible bond will fluctuate in sympathy with the speculative common stock for which it is exchangeable.

A speculative factor will also be imparted to bonds of foreign governments or foreign companies, which are issued in terms of foreign currencies, during periods when the foreign exchange rates are subject to considerable fluctuations. More-

[2] See Chapter XV.

over, new issues of even the soundest and most conservative bonds are also likely to possess some speculative features during their first few weeks on the market, until a definite price level has been established for them.[3] In addition, very large issues of bonds, both because of their size and their tendency to pass from weaker to stronger holders, sometimes experience heavy trading on the Exchange, attended with large enough fluctuations in price to interest the speculator. At certain periods of declining prices during recent years, for example, speculators, by purchasing Liberty bonds "for the rise," either outright or on margin, have done much to maintain consistent price levels for those large but pre-eminently conservative issues. We must not, therefore, conclude that speculation is absent from the bond market, but only that it is not present there nearly as frequently or as extensively as in the market for stocks.

In January, 1921, there were 1,111 separate bond issues listed on the New York Stock Exchange;[4] of this total 700 (or 63 per cent) were steam railroad bonds, 74 (or 6 per cent) city bonds, 23 (or 2 per cent) state bonds, 27 (or 2 per cent) United States government bonds, 37 (or 3 per cent) foreign government bonds, and 250 (or 22 per cent) public utility and industrial bonds. The railroad issues have decreased in number since 1910. City bonds have almost doubled since 1915. The miscellaneous group has almost tripled since 1900, reflecting America's vast industrial growth during the past two decades. But the greatest proportional increase has taken place in foreign government bonds, from 1 in 1900 to 37 in 1921.

Evolution of the Stock Exchange Bond Market

With this preliminary survey of the evolution of American bonds, we are now provided with sufficient perspective to consider the Stock Exchange bond market in a more detailed way.

3 See Chapter XVI.

4 See Appendix, Chapter II (c).

And first of all a word is necessary concerning that market's internal evolution. Naturally, the machinery of the Exchange bond market has experienced considerable changes during the last half-century. Not so many decades ago its listings were so few in number that an active broker or dealer could easily keep them all in his head. Originally, too, it was the custom to have calls in the bond market, similar to those employed today on certain commodity exchanges, or at auction sales. Beginning at 11 A.M. the chairman of the Board (a former official of the Exchange who used to open and close trading on the Exchange) would call the names of all the different listed bond issues in succession. As each bond was called, brokers and dealers would quote their bids and offers, and sales were made in the bond. But so rapidly did the number of listed bond issues increase that this system of calls in the bond market became tedious and impractical. In time, therefore, it was discontinued, and in its place the present continuous market, with its bond crowd and market ledgers, has gradually evolved.

The "Bond Corner"

The three not overlarge booths where trading in listed bonds now takes place are located in the northeast corner of the Stock Exchange floor (Figure 15). In the two smaller booths trading in foreign and United States Liberty bonds is conducted; while in the largest all other listed bonds have their market. This compact "bond corner" is fringed with the telephone booths of Exchange houses specializing in the bond business, and contains several double stock and bond tickers on its floor. For, although the bond market is for the most part separate from the stock market, nevertheless on special occasions and in such special securities as convertible bonds it is imperative for the bond men to keep their fingers on the pulse of the stock market also.

Figure 15

The New York Stock Exchange Bond Market

Copyright N. Y. S. E.

Liberty bond booth at left, main bond market to right, ticker dispatch station between them.

Between the booths is the telegraphic transmitter by which all bond sales are reported from the bond market to the office of the New York Quotation Company in the upper stories of the Stock Exchange building. Thence the quotations are dispatched all over the country on the same Western Union tickers that carry stock quotations. At 1 P.M. each day sales prices or quotations of bids and offers for practically all the bonds in which trading occurs on the Stock Exchange are printed and distributed on sheets. In this way not only investors but brokerage houses, banks, and other financial institutions are enabled to ascertain the market value of a large number of the principal American bond issues.

The Liberty Bond Market

In spite of the fact that the total amount of Liberty bonds sold sometimes exceeds the total of all other listed bonds, the Liberty bond market is not an especially impressive sight to the visitor of the Exchange. Many Exchange bond houses maintain a separate private telephone in all three sections of the bond market; thus, on the sides of the Liberty bond booth are telephones employed exclusively for orders in "Liberties." On the back wall of the Liberty bond market, the daily opening, highest, lowest, and last quotations for the ten United States war issues are marked on paper slips, while their latest quotations during the day are instantly registered on metal indicators by an attendant. In general, therefore, the same devices are employed here to keep Exchange members informed as to prevailing prices as are used for stocks on the stock posts. Because only ten issues are marketed here, a few brokers and dealers are able to maintain with ease and swiftness, in a comparatively small space and at very close prices, the leading market for over twenty billion dollars of our interest-bearing national debt. This separate market for Liberty bonds is, of course, a comparatively recent institution.

The Foreign Bond Market

The second booth, devoted to foreign bonds, has been constructed very recently, for these issues were formerly handled in the general bond market presently to be described. In appearance the foreign bond booth mainly duplicates the Liberty bond booth, except that slips for many more issues decorate its back wall. This foreign bond booth symbolizes America's present international creditor position.[5] Back in 1900 the only foreign security listed on the Exchange was a municipal bond of the City of Quebec—practically an American municipal issue so far as investors in the United States were concerned. Now there are about 40 foreign issues listed, and the number is constantly growing. Present foreign bond listings represent a total of about two billion dollars.

The Corporation Bond Market

The third and largest Exchange bond booth, however, is vastly more complicated and confusing than these two smaller sections of the Bond Department, for instead of only a few bond issues, over a thousand are marketed there—more separate security issues, indeed, than are possessed by the entire Exchange stock market. But so many of these listed bond issues are inactive and infrequently traded in, that instead of stock posts a number of ledgers are used to localize in one definite place the closest bid and asked quotations for each issue.

The most striking feature of the bond market is the large oak quotation board on its back wall. This board, which in some respects resembles the ordinary commission house's quotation board, is divided vertically into two sections. On the smaller part to the right are posted the latest sales prices of the most active bonds, for which no ledgers of bid and asked quotations are kept, while on the larger side to the left are posted those of some of the less active bonds, for which

[5] See Chapter XVIII.

ledgers are also maintained. On the left side of each bond symbol on the board is placed its closing sales price for the preceding day; on its right side are posted its price fluctuations by ⅛'s during the current day. Cardboard tickets are inserted to indicate sales of $1,000 bonds. The usefulness of this quotation board to the busy bond men below is apparent. A single glance at such a record as "55¼ INTBO, R. T. rfg. 5's 55½, ¾, ¼, ½, ¾, ⅞, ¾," informs the broker that on the previous day the closing price of the 5 per cent refunding bonds of the Interborough Rapid Transit Company was 55¼ (or $552.50 for a $1,000 par value bond), and thus far during the day the issue has sold successively at 55 plus the varying fractions.

The Reporting System for Bond Prices

Reporters obtain the prices of sales as they occur in the bond crowd, make out slips, and pass them to the board boys, who at once post the prices on the board—if the bond is one which is recorded there. Simultaneously they inform the telegraph operator, and very shortly afterward the quotations appear on the bond tickers throughout the country. The machinery of this bond ticker service (Figure 16) resembles that of the stock ticker system previously described.[6] Usually the board boys can record these quotations a trifle sooner than they appear on the ticker tape. Sales prices for bonds not posted on the board appear only on the bond ticker.

Since most bonds are relatively inactive, the bid and asked quotations for them are kept only on the bond ledgers. These ledgers, ten in number, are kept by Exchange clerks behind the writing stands in front of the quotation board. Each ledger contains bid and asked quotations for upward of 100 different bonds. Under the name of a given bond issue the clerk inscribes the various bid and ask quotations for it, as well as the amount of the bonds to be purchased or sold and the initials

[6] See Chapter III, page 62.

of the various bond-brokers and dealers from whom he received this information. When these bid and asked quotations are for any reason withdrawn by the bond men, they are erased

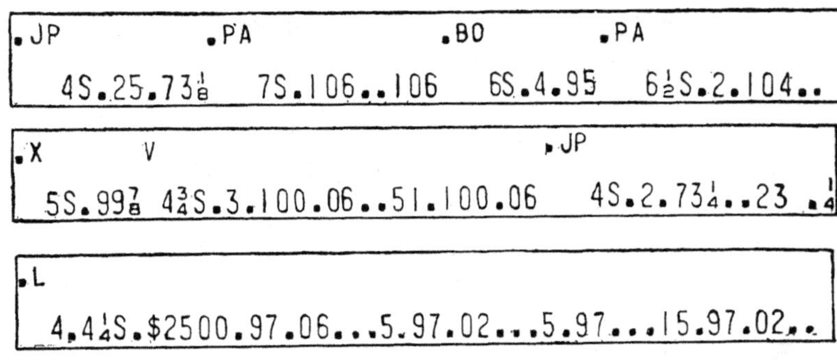

Figure 16. Specimen Sections of Bond Ticker Tape. (Width of tape, 5/8 in.)
Recording sales (top row) of $25,000 Japanese government 4's at 73 1/8, $1,000 Pennsylvania Railroad 7's at 106, $1,000 more at 106, $4,000 Baltimore and Ohio Railroad 6's at 95, and $2,000 Pennsylvania Railroad 6 1/2's at 104; (second row) $1,000 United States Steel 5's at 99 7/8, $3,000 United States government Victory 4 3/4's at 100.06, $51,000 more at 100.06, $2,000 Japanese government 4's at 73 1/4, and $23,000 more at 73 1/4; (third row) $2,500 United States government Fourth 4 1/4's at 97.06, $5,000 more at 97.02, $5,000 more at 97.00, and $15,000 more at 97.02; (bottom row) $1,000 United States government Liberty 3 1/2's at 95.26, $3,000 United Kingdom of Great Britain and Ireland 1929's at 99, $2,000 Grand Trunk Railway 6's (receipts) at 100, and $5,000 Manhattan Elevated Railway 4's at 57 3/4.

from the ledger. A bond man can thus learn the market for any inactive bond which he may desire to purchase or to sell, by asking the ledger clerk. Thus this system of ledgers and ledger clerks corresponds in a general way with the posts and specialists' books [7] in the stock market.

Composition of the Bond Crowd

Each morning, at the opening of the market at 10 A.M., what is known as the "bond crowd" takes its stand within the

[7] See Chapter V, page 115.

large bond booth and remains there, buying and selling bonds until the market closes at 3 P.M. The bond crowd is composed on the average of some thirty members of the Stock Exchange, most of whom specialize in bonds either as brokers or dealers. As in the case of the stock market, the bond market contains brokers who execute orders on commission and dealers who buy and sell for their own account. The latter, as in the instance of the stock market, constantly impart negotiability to the bonds listed there by their purchases and sales. In order to obtain the best possible prices for their clients, stock-brokers, who are often unacquainted with the peculiar technique of the bond crowd, frequently leave the bond orders they receive from their firms with some bond-broker to execute, in much the same way as they have the specialists or two-dollar brokers execute in the stock market orders which they cannot handle themselves.

Methods of Executing Bond Orders

The exact method of executing a bond order depends, as in the case of an order for stocks, upon the market activity of the bond issue in question, as well as upon the limits, if any, which accompany the order. In the case of market orders in the active bonds, whose prices are reported on the right side of the quotation board, the broker, after noting the latest price on the board, goes directly into the bond crowd and effects a sale at the most favorable bid or asked price which he can obtain. But in less active bonds, which must be "referred to the books" (i.e., for which bond ledger accounts of bids and offers are kept), the broker with a market order to execute will first learn from the appropriate bond ledger what is the best bid or offer as inscribed there and what broker or dealer has made it. The latter individual he then locates in the bond crowd, and perhaps concludes a sale or purchase.

In the case of limited orders it is, of course, not always possible to effect sales as easily and promptly as this. Orders whose limits are very close to the bid and asked prices quoted in the bond crowd or on the bond ledgers can be executed, perhaps after a slight delay, in much the same way as a limited order for stocks. But if the price limit on an order to sell is much higher than the offer quotations on the ledger (or, in the case of an order to buy, lower than the bid quotations there), the broker will instruct the appropriate clerk to enter his offer or bid price in the bond ledger with his initials, and wait until informed by this clerk of some other broker who wishes to make a sale at the price he has named. An exception to this procedure occurs when a limited order is given for an active bond, which is posted on the right side of the quotation board and is not referred to the books. Such an order is usually "kept in the market" as a bid or offer on the book of some broker in the bond crowd in much the same way as in the stock market limited orders for stocks are constantly kept in the specialist's book.

On the last Saturday of each month all bids and offers on the bond ledgers are considered void, and must be renewed if the Exchange houses which made them wish them to stand for the next month. Consequently, so far as the bond ledgers are concerned, G. T. C. orders for bonds run only until the end of the month.

Bids and offers for most bonds are made at a variation of not less than 1/8 per cent of their par value, or $12.50 per $10,000, very much as in the case of stocks. Because of the tendency toward close markets in rapidly maturing obligations, however, as well as for other reasons, fractional bids and offers of less than 1/8 per cent—for instance, 1/16 per cent—are allowed in certain short-term bonds and notes.[8] Bids and offers for Liberty bonds, as an especial exception, are made in fractions of 1/50 per cent, or $2 per $10,000 par value. Accordingly, Liberty bonds are quoted decimally, as, "Liberty 4th

[8] See Appendix, Chapter III (a).

4¼'s, 1933-1938, 85.34," whereas almost all other bonds are quoted fractionally, as, "Union Pacific 1st 4's, 1947, 85⅜."

Coupon and Registered Bonds

When a broker or dealer effects a sale in the bond market, it is understood that the bargain is for a coupon, not a registered bond. A coupon bond is a readily negotiable bond certificate to which are attached interest coupons. The holder can cut off the coupons and cash them as they mature. A registered bond, on the other hand, has no such coupons, but instead the issuing organization periodically remits interest to the bondholders registered on its books. The holder of a registered bond must at its maturity present the bond properly transferred to bearer before its principal amount can be paid to him by the issuing company. In consequence, a registered bond, like a stock certificate, must have a power-of-attorney form printed upon its back, so that the holder can assign it in blank.

Coupon bonds may also be registered as to principal, thus insuring for the time being their non-negotiability in case they should be stolen. Recently there has been a tendency to make registered bonds exchangeable for coupon bonds and vice versa, but in many of the older issues they are not thus interchangeable. In consequence, separate quotations are made for the two forms of bond, as one is not a good delivery for another—that is, a broker cannot make a contract to sell a coupon bond and deliver to the buyer a registered bond, or vice versa. If one desires to purchase or sell a registered bond, he must so state at the time of sale; otherwise it is presumed that he is dealing in coupon bonds.

The Bond Unit of Trading

Formerly the majority of bonds issued by corporations had a minimum denomination of $1,000, but in recent years the vast growth of small-scale investing in this country, particularly after the wide educational results of our gigantic Liberty Loans, has induced many issuing governments and corporations to lower the minimum denomination of their bonds to $500 and even to $100, in order to place their obligations within the financial reach of the small investor. This tendency has in turn gradually affected the regulations of the Exchange bond market with regard to its unit of trading, which has recently been reduced from $10,000 to $1,000. One thousand dollars in two $500 bonds is considered a good delivery, although $1,000 made up of smaller bond denominations than $500 is not.

Of course, sales of $500, $100, or even $50 bonds are readily made on the Exchange, but since they are below the unit of trading, dealers in the market will purchase or sell only at a slight price concession to themselves. In the case of Liberty bonds the proper number of the smaller "pieces" of $50, $100, or $500, are readily exchangeable at the Federal Reserve Bank for the larger pieces of $1,000 or $10,000, or vice versa, on the same day. Consequently, the adverse difference in the dealer's price on the smaller, as compared with the larger Liberty bonds, amounts to only 1/10 per cent or less—perhaps 10 cents on the $100 bond. In other bonds, where it is a more difficult and lengthy operation to make this exchange of the larger for the smaller, or the smaller for the larger pieces, the adverse price difference in the smaller as compared with the larger bonds is naturally much greater than in the case of Liberty bonds. Except for this latter custom in the case of small bonds under $1,000 denomination, there is no machinery in the bond market corresponding to that provided by odd-lot dealers in the stock market.

Bonds Selling "And Interest" and "Flat"

A further point concerning bond prices should also be noted. All bonds sell "and interest" except bonds in default, and income and adjustment bonds, where uncertainty exists regarding the payment of interest. Thus, when an investor purchases at 80 a $1,000 4 per cent bond, interest payable semi-annually, three months after the last interest day, he will actually pay $810 instead of $800 for it, because of the three months' interest accrued on the bond. Both buyers and sellers must with such a bond add to its market price the amount of the interest accrued upon it to ascertain the actual price at which it will be sold. In such cases interest is calculated not to the day on which the sales contract is made but to the day on which the seller delivers the bond to the buyer, and from the date of the last interest payment. But if a buyer agrees to purchase a $1,000 bond in default, or an income or adjustment bond, at—say—45, it will be sold "flat," that is, without any addition of interest to the market price; and he accordingly will pay $450 for the bond.

In a succeeding chapter, dealing with the Night Clearing Branch, it will be pointed out that only transactions in Liberty bonds are regularly cleared,[9] although very active and speculative bonds in which large trading is occurring may likewise be cleared on special occasions, when circumstances warrant. When the Stock Clearing Corporation is in full operation, however, some of the regularly active bonds may also be regularly cleared.[10]

One admirable feature of the Exchange bond market is the instant and complete publicity given to all its transactions by the bond ticker. With the more inactive bonds bids or offers will occasionally be put on the bond tape along with the regular report of sales, in order to extend the market to all points reached by the ticker. This same thing is done on the stock ticker in the very inactive stocks, only very much more infrequently, because of the greater number of sales quotations appearing on the latter instrument.

---

9 See Chapter IX.

10 See Chapter X.

Necessity for Expanded Facilities

The continual difficulty of the Stock Exchange in providing sufficient physical room for the ceaseless growth of its market has nowhere been more acute than in its Bond Department. Indeed, the large number of listed bond issues is quite out of proportion to the floor space at present available for bond trading. The creation of separate headquarters for trading in Liberty bonds and foreign bonds has prevented an impossibly crowded condition in the old bond market, without relieving the already serious congestion of the bond crowd and its equipment. But the additional floor space provided in the new Stock Exchange building will shortly relieve this congestion; the space at present available for the bond market will be expanded, and every facility afforded for its maintenance and continued growth.

Economic Functions of the Bond Department

Since in general the Bond Department performs in bonds much the same economic functions as the stock market does in stocks, the broad question of the economic services rendered by the Bond Department can be deferred to a later chapter [11] where both these markets can be considered together. Nevertheless, a few features peculiar to the Stock Exchange bond market deserve some consideration here.

As is the case with any highly organized market,[12] the Bond Department of the Stock Exchange tends to bring about a readier market and closer prices than would otherwise be the case. The important quality of negotiability is imparted to bonds listed on the Stock Exchange not only through the machinery already described on the Board itself, but also through the machinery maintained by the many Exchange firms which engage in the investment business. Such houses keep in close connection with institutional and individual buyers, as well as

---

[11] See Chapter XIV.

[12] *Ibid.*

with dealers in securities generally. The investment broker knows the particular wants of each and constantly communicates to them the latest bids and offers on the Board (Figure 17), thus vastly facilitating the ability of sellers to sell and buyers to buy in the Bond Department. Furthermore, the Exchange bond market, by its policy of complete and widespread ticker publicity, clearly reveals the general current conditions of supply and demand for all investment securities and thus serves as a criterion for the price movements of bonds not listed on the Board.

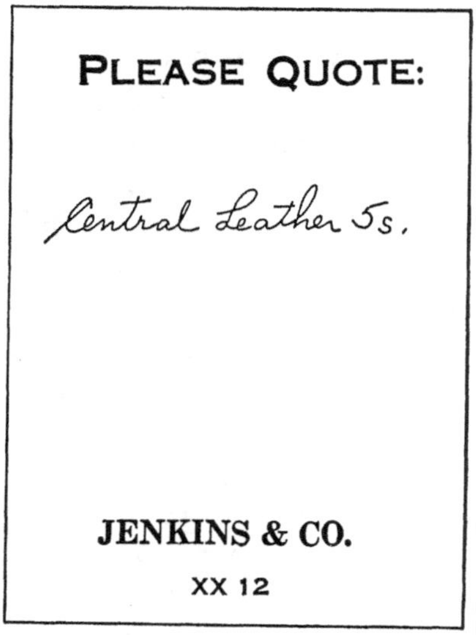

PLEASE QUOTE:

Central Leather 5s.

JENKINS & CO.

XX 12

Figure 17. Quote Slip. (Size 3 x 4.)
Indicating request for quotations on Central Leather 5 per cent bonds.

The Bond Department of the Stock Exchange performs a nationally beneficial economic service in that it provides at all times a ready market for speculative bond issues. We have seen that, in comparison with the stock market, the Exchange bond market is non-speculative and sluggish. But numerous circumstances have also been cited under which investment bonds may suddenly become speculative. In such cases the complete facilities which the Bond Department provides for speculative dealings are at once made available. Particularly for previously sound bonds, which have suddenly become hazardous and speculative, the Bond Department acts as a "shock-absorber," since it enables the investor to sell his bonds and the speculator, by purchasing them, to assume the risk they now involve. For such speculative transactions the

Bond Department provides equal facilities for all in its free and open market. In the closing months of 1920 the Stock Exchange served in this way as a shock-absorber for America's entire credit system, and much of the vast liquidation of securities which then took place occurred in its bond market.

Services to Investors

Since the economic functions of speculation are almost always less understood than those of investment, the speculative services of the Bond Department have in the present study been purposely stressed—perhaps out of due proportion to their real comparative importance. For the primary function of the Bond Department is undoubtedly in the field of investment rather than in that of speculation. As will be later demonstrated,[13] speculation in reality represents only an intermediary, although often a protracted stage in the distribution of securities. But the substratum of the processes of speculation are necessarily the processes of investment, and each is the complement of the other. The economic importance of the Stock Exchange Bond Department as essentially an investment market is revealed more by the large number and huge aggregate capital of its listed issues than by the volume of its turnover—large though the latter is. The broader economic features of investment will be discussed in a subsequent chapter,[14] and here merely the function of the Bond Department as the ultimate investment market of the nation can be outlined.

It is worthy of notice that the Bond Department of the Stock Exchange particularly benefits the small investor, since he can for a slight commission obtain the services of an expert broker to handle his orders in small amounts, in a market whose transactions are immediately subject to supply and demand conditions and whose prices are at once publicly re-

[13] See Chapter XVI. [14] *Ibid.*

ported all over the country on the ticker. Moreover, the Exchange bond market places at the disposal of the small investor a great variety of old and seasoned investment securities which can be readily purchased or sold at all times. The small American investor is becoming to a rapidly increasing extent a powerful and helpful factor in our whole financial scheme of things, as even to a greater degree he has so often proved in France and other countries. Without the Bond Department, which the countless branch offices of Exchange commission houses all over the country place immediately and fully at his service, the small investor would find it vastly more difficult and hazardous to transform readily his savings into small but high-grade and conservative bonds.

The ever-present risks and lightning changes of the stock market, its thrills of optimism, and its fits of utter dejection, penetrate the bond crowd only slowly and temperately. The Bond Department of the Exchange will, therefore, always be less animated and picturesque than the larger adjoining market for shares. Nevertheless, in the more conservative field of investment the Bond Department is also a very vital factor in the general machinery of American finance, and a necessary and integral part of the great market for American securities maintained by the New York Stock Exchange.

CHAPTER VIII

THE SECURITY COLLATERAL LOAN MARKET

Lack of Rediscount Facilities

In a preceding chapter[1] the instance was cited of a customer who purchased 100 shares of United States Steel at 100 on a 25-point margin. It was pointed out that the broker in this transaction was able to furnish $7,500 credit to his customer by turning over the 100-share Steel certificate to a bank as part of the collateral for a loan of the necessary amount of money (or, to speak more accurately, of bank credit). We must now examine in more detail the methods employed in obtaining these loans by means of which so large a majority of transactions on the Stock Exchange are financed each day.

From the standpoint of American banking, loans made on security collateral differ considerably from ordinary commercial loans, which if they are secured at all, generally have commodities for the collateral. This sharp differentiation between collateral security and other loans is due in part to the inability of the federal reserve banks under the present law to rediscount for their member banks loans secured by any securities other than United States government obligations.[2] The American practice in this respect is quite at variance with the prevailing custom in London, Paris, and other European financial centers, where loans on securities are rediscounted by the central banks.[3]

Because of the impossibility of rediscounting loans based on our railroad or industrial securities, as well as for reasons arising from the peculiarly American methods of settlement

[1] See Chapter IV, page 76.
[2] See Appendix, Chapter VIII (a).
[3] See Appendix, Chapter VIII (b).

in vogue on the New York Stock Exchange, such collateral security loans constitute a separate market quite apart from that for commercial loans—a market with its own interest rates, and to a certain temporary extent with its own conditions of supply and demand.[4] This special security loan market, through which the New York stock market is financed, is the only money market of its kind in the world. Owing to the fact that so many loans are made in it for only a single day, its turnover is large, varying in recent years between a maximum of $40,000,000 and a minimum of less than $10,000,000 per day.[5]

The Time Loan

There are two distinct types of loans made upon security collateral—time and call loans. The time loan, as its name implies, is made for a definite period of time—three, six, nine, or twelve months—at a fixed rate of interest which does not change during the life of the loan. To secure the loans there are deposited as collateral with the lender, securities whose value exceeds the amount of the loan by a minimum of 20 to 30 per cent. The lender is also protected by the agreement (Figure 18) that if the market price of the security collateral declines, the borrower must put up additional securities as collateral. For if during a falling market the borrower allows the value of his collateral securing a time loan to decline below the margin agreed upon, then by the terms of the time loan agreement the loan immediately becomes due, irrespective of its maturity date, and the lender can at once demand payment. This being refused, he can at once sell the collateral securities to recover the principal and interest of his loan. In practice the borrower always hastens to put up more collateral on his time loans, whenever such a course is necessary.

Time loans are never negotiated on the floor of the Stock

[4] See Appendix, Chapter VIII (c).

[5] See Senate Document 262, 66th Congress, 2nd Session, p. 8.

$100,000 00/x NEW YORK, May 8 1920

Jenkins & Co for value received

the undersigned promise to pay to The Blank Trust Co

or order, at the banking office of The Blank Trust Co. New York, on August 8, 1920

One hundred thousand dollars, with interest

from date until payment hereof at the rate of 5 per cent. per annum,

having assigned and transferred, and hereby assigning and transferring, to the holder hereof for the time being, as collateral security for payment hereof,—as well as for the payment of any and every debt or liability of every name and nature, whenever contracted and whenever due, from the undersigned to such holder hereof existing while such holder,—the following property, hereby and herewith pledged and delivered to such holder for the time being as collateral security for this and for every other such indebtedness, viz.:

400 Atchison, Topeka and Santa Fe	@ 88	35,200.00
200 Union Pacific	@ 126	25,200.00
200 Pennsylvania	@ 43	8,600.00
300 Baltimore & Ohio	@ 47	14,100.00
300 Consolidated Gas	@ 89	26,700.00
200 Republic Iron & Steel	@ 77	15,400.00

of which the present market value is now estimated by the undersigned to be $125,000, and also, any and all property, claims and demands of every name or nature belonging to the undersigned and either directly or indirectly or for any purpose in possession or under control of such holder hereof, while such holder, including a lien upon any balance of any deposit account of the undersigned with such holder hereof, while such holder; and the undersigned hereby agrees from time to time, and at any time, similarly and forthwith upon demand therefor by any such holder, to pledge and to deliver hereunder any and all such additions or substitutions of collateral security as may be indicated in a notice addressed to the undersigned and left at 500 Wall St, New York City.

On the non-performance of this promise, in whole or in part, or upon the non-payment of any liability above mentioned, or upon failure to furnish other satisfactory securities, as and when so called for, then, and in every such case, at the option of such holder, this note forthwith shall become and shall be due and payable, without other demand or notice, and full power and authority are hereby given to such holder to demand payment of and to collect any promises to pay forming part of the said securities, and also full power and authority to sell, assign and deliver the whole of the said securities, or any part thereof, or any substitutes therefor, or any additions thereto, or any other securities or property either directly or indirectly given to or left in the possession of such holder by the undersigned, at any Brokers' Board or at public or private sale, at the option of such holder, without either demand, advertisement or notice of any kind, all of which are hereby expressly waived. At any such sale at any Brokers' Board, or at any public sale, such holder, on his or its own account, and without further accountability except for the purchase price thereof, may purchase the whole or any part of the property sold, free from any right of redemption on the part of the undersigned, which right is hereby waived and released. In case of sale for any cause, after deducting all costs or expenses of every kind for collection, sale or delivery, the holder for the time being, without any marshalling of securities, and in such manner or order as he or it may deem proper, may apply the residue of the proceeds of the sale or sales so made, in payment or in reduction of any one or more of such liabilities to such holder then unpaid, whether then due or not due, making proper rebate for interest on liabilities not then due, and returning the overplus, if any, to the undersigned who, notwithstanding any transfer, shall continue liable to the holder hereof for the time being for any deficiency arising upon such sale or sales.

Jenkins & Co.

Figure 18. Time Loan Agreement. (Size 9 x 12.)

Exchange but are made either directly between the borrowing broker and the lender, or through a money broker, who charges the borrower on the average 1/32 per cent for his services in obtaining the funds. Most of the time money employed in the stock market is loaned by New York banks and other financial institutions, and occasionally out-of-town banks will also make such loans directly. Out-of-town institutions are heavy lenders of money through the New York banks. Generally speaking, the interest rate charged for time money is based upon the prevailing and the anticipated movement in the rates for the demand or call loans.

Formerly about 40 per cent of the money loaned on securities in New York was in time loans and the remaining 60 per cent in call loans. During the war period, however, owing to the huge demand for funds for commercial and industrial purposes, the proportion of time funds dwindled to only 25 per cent or less of total stock market loans,[6] and consequently produced a heavy strain on the call loan market, some of the effects of which will be presently discussed.

The Call or Demand Loan

We now come to the call or demand loans and the machinery in and out of the Stock Exchange for handling them. Most of the sales of securities made on the Exchange are made "regular way"—that is, for delivery and payment on the following full business day.[7] The New York Stock Exchange in this respect presents a strong contrast to the exchanges of London, Paris, and other leading financial centers abroad, where sales are normally made chiefly "for the account"—that is, for delivery or payment at weekly, fortnightly, or even monthly settlement periods. This daily settlement prevailing in New York has necessitated the employment there of funds

---

[6] See Senate Document 262, 66th Congress, 2nd Session, p. 8.

[7] See Chapter IX, page 203.

by the day only, and consequently the creation of a form of loan which can be terminated by either lender or borrower the day after it is made. Legally, indeed, the call loan, the logical outcome of the unique conditions in New York, can be terminated at any time by either borrower or lender, although in practice no such loans are called after 12:15 P.M. The call loan is renewed each day, often at a different rate of interest, either higher or lower than the rate on the original loan. Call funds are loaned at the "money desk" on the floor of the New York Stock Exchange, or, as in the case of time loans, through money brokers, or through direct negotiation between the borrowers and lenders.

The Demand for Security Collateral Loans

Before describing the machinery of this Exchange money market, let us first consider how the demand for funds comes into the market. We have seen that the broker must frequently obtain credit for his customer by depositing with a lender of money as collateral for a loan the securities which the customer has purchased on margin. Frequently between 10 A.M. and 2:30 P.M. the various brokerage firms in the financial district telephone their floor members on the Stock Exchange to obtain loans for the various aggregate amounts needed on the day's transactions, or on account of loans made previously being called or paid off, or for other purposes. The floor member, after receiving such a telephone message from his office, goes to the money desk and fills out a memorandum which states how much money he requires. These memoranda of brokers who wish to borrow money are for the time being filed at the money desk. Of course, the greater the total sum of money required by all borrowers, the higher the rate of interest on call loans is apt to be. Nothing could therefore be simpler than the manner in which the demand for call funds obtains practical expression at the money desk.

The Supply of Call Money

Let us now consider for a moment the somewhat more complicated supply side of the call loan market, in order to determine whence the funds come that are loaned each day on Stock Exchange securities.

As has already been noted, loans made on securities other than United States government bonds cannot, like commercial loans, be rediscounted by member banks at the federal reserve banks. For this and other reasons, the average banker in the regular course of his business will necessarily prefer to make commercial loans rather than either time or call loans based upon security collateral. The natural result of this inevitable preference is that only the excess funds of bankers—the surplus money, such as funds accumulated for special purposes, or the reserves of non-members of the federal reserve system, which cannot be safely and profitably placed in commercial loans or other investments—are available for call loans.[8]

Such excess funds of banks all over the nation, and even beyond our borders, are therefore collected in New York to loan in the stock market. The larger banks in such local financial centers as Chicago, Philadelphia, Boston, Cleveland, Detroit, St. Louis, Richmond, Baltimore, San Francisco, or Montreal will carry accounts of the smaller banks of the immediate vicinity and constantly absorb their surplus funds at a low rate of interest. But these large banks in turn carry accounts with the still larger banking institutions in New York, to which they transmit the surplus funds they have gathered in their immediate vicinity, to be employed in stock market loans and other investments. The result is that a large part of the excess funds of the nation's banks, instead of being allowed to remain idle, is mobilized in New York banks and profitably placed in loans on security collateral. The advantage of this

[8] See Appendix, Chapter VIII (d).

system to the country banker is that a market is provided for him in which he can invest funds at any time and to any extent he wishes, and from which he can withdraw his funds with equal speed.

The Machinery Behind Supply

The machinery by which this national reservoir of surplus capital is accumulated for loaning on call in the stock market operates to produce the supply side of the call loan market, which is just as simple as the demand side already outlined. The New York banker usually waits each morning until his returns from the bank clearing house are received. From these reports he learns his exact financial position at that time, and he can estimate just how much of the funds of his institution he can surely loan out on call. Later in the day, through the shifting of accounts either from local or out-of-town depositors, the banker's position may be changed, and the amount of his funds available for call loans may either be increased or decreased. In the former case he may offer additional sums of money for loaning on call, while in the latter he may be obliged to call loans already outstanding.

When the banker finds that he has—say—$2,000,000 surplus funds to loan in the stock market, his first move is to call up the office of a New York Stock Exchange member and request him to make a loan for him at a stated rate or at the market rate. The brokerage office at once telephones over its private wire to the floor of the Stock Exchange and informs the floor member of the firm what funds the bank wishes to lend. The same machinery is therefore used in directing the loaning of money as is employed in buying or selling a security. When the broker on the floor has received his instructions, he enters the offering with the clerk at the money desk. No commission is received by the broker for this service of effecting call loans.

Changeability of Supply and Demand

The extreme liquidity of the call loan market, as well as the restrictions placed for one reason or another on its supply side, permits of swift changes in the supply as well as in the demand for call funds all day, and this accounts for the rapid changes that sometimes occur in the call rate of interest. For many of the changing conditions in the supply of call funds American geography rather than American financiers is to blame. It is a frequently forgotten fact that in point of time Chicago and New Orleans are one hour, Denver and Omaha two hours, and San Francisco three hours behind New York. In consequence of these unavoidable conditions imposed by the laws of longitude, it frequently happens that late in the day funds suddenly pour into the call loan market from out-of-town financial centers—sometimes barely satisfying the demand for call funds there, but sometimes swamping it with funds and driving down the interest rate on call loans.

Owing to the more conservative margin requirements in the present-day brokerage business, the average amount of money out on call in stock market loans has not increased in proportion either to the increase of capital issues listed on the Stock Exchange or to the increased turnover of shares in recent markets. The general shortage of credit in this country since the United States entered the Great War has been fundamentally responsible for the high level of call interest rates reached since that time. For, as in any other market, prices inevitably rise when the demand tends to outrun the supply.

The Money Desk

We have seen that the demand for call loans finds expression in some brokers filing their requirements at the money desk, while the supply of loanable funds results in other brokers going to the desk with funds offered by lenders. This money desk, where the forces of supply and demand meet, is a prosaic piece of furniture located on the floor of the Stock Exchange. Before the present system of allotting call funds at the money table was devised, the call loan market closely resembled the market in any active stock about a post on the floor.[9] The lending brokers and the borrowing brokers assembled to form what was commonly known as the "money crowd," and bids and offers were made there for call funds just as they are made for—say—United States Steel in the Steel crowd.

But this system of loaning and borrowing call funds became impossible under the conditions which the war imposed on the market for credit.[10] In this connection, the report of the federal reserve agent in New York, made on the request of the Governor of the Federal Reserve Board to the President of the United States Senate (designated in the footnotes of the present chapter as "Senate Document 262, 66th Congress, 2nd Session") deserves careful consideration:

> Prior to the armistice, agencies of Government were employed to restrict the issue of new securities for purposes other than those which were deemed essential for carrying on the war. At the same time, as the Treasury undertook to sell large amounts of certificates of indebtedness and Liberty Bonds bearing low rates of interest, the question arose as to whether the competition of the general investment market might not prejudice the success of the Government issues. In these circumstances, with full understanding on the part of the Treasury Department, the officers and members of the New York Stock Exchange undertook to limit transactions which would involve the increased use of money for other purposes, in consideration of which the principal banks of New York City endeavored to provide a stable amount of money for the requirements of the security market.
>
> After the armistice these restrictions were removed and

[9] For details of the pre-war methods of loaning money on the Stock Exchange floor, see testimony of J. H. Griesel. (Money Trust Investigation, Vol. I, p. 742 *et seq.*)

[10] For a detailed description of the purpose ,actions, and achievements of the war time "money committee," with special reference to the collateral loan market for Stock Exchange securities, consult "Agricultural Inquiry" (Washington, Aug., 1921), statement and testimony of Governor Benjamin Strong, pp. 543–546, 665–684.

ordinary market forces reasserted themselves. The issuance of new securities was resumed in unprecedented volume and consumed a vast amount of capital and credit when bank credit was already extended by the necessity of carrying large amounts of Government securities which the investment market was not prepared to absorb. Thus, arose a further cause for the increased cost at times of accommodation on collateral loans.

The extremely capricious nature of the supply of available call funds, due alike to the lack of rediscount facilities for such loans at federal reserve banks and to the competitive popularity of rediscountable acceptances and other liquid forms of investment for excess banking funds, made it imperative, both during and following the war period, to stabilize the extreme fluctuations of call interest rates and keep them roughly in harmony with rates on other classes of loans, without attempting to set arbitrary rates in defiance of the laws of supply and demand. In a time of world-wide credit shortage it was imperative that a market, the freedom of whose supply was discriminated against by law, should be attended with more than usual vigilance, if it was to perform its indispensable functions for American business. Accordingly, the present impersonal and largely automatic system of allotting loanable funds to the borrowing brokers was adopted. In the obtaining of funds no favorites are played, and the rule of "first come, first served" is strictly observed.

Diversification of Risk

In order to diversify its risks, the lending institution usually prefers to loan its funds to several different brokerage firms rather than simply to one house. Also, the broker is equally anxious to borrow what money he needs from several different banks, in order to diversify the risk that all his loans be called by lenders on the morrow. For this twofold reason, therefore, a bank with—say—$2,000,000 to lend will usually lend it to several houses in units of from $100,000 to $500,000, while a broker with $500,000 to borrow will often attempt to obtain it from more than one bank. The course followed in any given case depends naturally upon the lenders' and borrowers' circumstances at the time.

After the loan has been made, the lending broker informs the lending institution to whom its funds have been loaned, and then steps out of the transaction completely. But, just as in the case of a sale of stock, the lending broker sends a report to the lending institution which he represents, stating the terms under which its funds have been loaned, while the borrowing broker sends a similar report of the loan to his office. These reports are, of course, only memoranda, and are unsigned. It remains for the borrowing broker to deliver his security collateral to the lender and obtain the funds.

War Measures in the Call Money Market

In recent years, there has never occurred an instance when brokers with good collateral were actually unable to obtain the funds they needed. Even in 1907, although call rates soared and the historic intervention of Mr. J. P. Morgan was finally necessitated, nevertheless the brokers in the end got their loans. In fact, no brokerage house in Wall Street with good security collateral has ever failed for lack of banking accommodation. During the unprecedented shortage of funds in the recent war period, a "money pool" composed of prominent New York bankers was organized at the instance of the United States Treasury Department to "ration" the stock market. Under this arrangement, when the demand for loans at the money desk outran the supply, the Exchange authorities communicated with the chairman of the bankers' committee, who then proceeded to obtain the needed funds from various banks. Now that the strain imposed upon our credit markets during the war can be seen in perspective, it is becoming more and more apparent that this wise co-operation between the Stock Exchange and the banks during the war period prevented conditions which might have resulted in a panic. But, although the banks in self-protection as well as in fulfilment of their duty to American finance, industry, and commerce, must finance the legitimate needs of the stock market, it is not equally true that the market can invariably absorb all their surplus funds. In quiet markets there is sometimes a surplus of money offered by the banks at the money desk, which cannot find borrowers. Nevertheless, while credit is abnormally scarce, the money desk system makes possible a far more accurate knowledge of the real conditions of supply and demand than could otherwise be obtained, and produces more stable interest rates and greater public confidence than would be possible under the old system of indiscriminate bidding for and offering of call funds in the money crowd.

Settlement of Loan Contracts

Thus far only contracts made for lending call money on the Exchange have been described. We must now consider how these contracts are carried out. After the loan has been negotiated at the money desk, the lending bank is informed to what firms its funds have been loaned, and the borrowing firms are notified from what bank or banks their loans have been obtained.

Ordinarily a loan thus contracted for on the floor of the Stock Exchange will be settled through the Stock Clearing Corporation under the rules and regulations of that organization presently to be described.[11] But, owing to the lack of sufficient space in the present offices of the Stock Clearing Corporation to accommodate all lending institutions, there are lenders, technically known as "non-clearing lenders," who do

[11] See Chapter XI.

not make use of the Stock Clearing Corporation. When, therefore, a loan is contracted with such a lender it is said to be an "ex-clearing house" loan (or, perhaps, a "loan made ex"), and the delivery of the collateral and payment of the loan is brought about independently of the Stock Clearing Corporation in the manner described in the present chapter.

The Loan Envelope

The next step for the borrowing broker is to prepare his loan envelope (Figure 19). So large a proportion of the work of the Stock Exchange is based upon these loan envelopes that they deserve more than passing comment here. In this envelope are placed security certificates belonging to the brokerage house and to those of its customers who have purchased securities on margin and agreed to this hypothecation of their stocks or bonds by the broker.[12] The outside face of the envelope contains the name of the borrowing brokerage house and the lending institution, as well as the date, the amount of the loan obtained, and the rate of interest at which the loan has been made. In addition, there is an itemized list of the particular securities used as collateral for the loan, together with the number of shares of each and their market value in even figures. The face of this call loan envelope, as we shall presently see, in most cases constitutes a loan contract between borrower and lender.

Desirability of Various Security Collateral

It is obvious that all stocks thus pledged against loans are not equally desirable to bankers. There exists, in fact, a considerable body of technical practice in this respect which vitally affects the seeking and granting of call loans. Before the war the most desirable selection of collateral securities was known as a "regular" loan, and consisted of "mixed" collateral—that

[12] See Chapter IV, page 76.

No. 234

Fiftieth National Bank

DEMAND LOAN

JENKINS & CO.

$ 100,000.00

Date August 16, 1920 Rate 6%

Shares	SECURITIES	Price	Amount	
400	Southern Pacific	97	38	800
200	Canadian Pacific	121	24	200
200	U.S. Steel	86	17	200
200	U.S. Rubber	73	14	600
300	American Sugar Refining	103	30	900
1,300			125	700

Figure 19. Face of Call Loan Envelope. (Size 5 x 11.)
Recording a loan of $100,000 by the Fiftieth National Bank to Jenkins and Company on $125,700 of collateral.

is, of both railroad and industrial securities—in the rough proportion of two-thirds of the former and one-third of the latter. But the war period, which changed so many financial methods and customs, likewise made its peculiar exigencies felt inside the loan envelope, and the regular loan came to mean railroad and industrial securities in about equal proportions. This change was an interesting result of the uncertainties of most railroad securities during 1917—1919, and the strongly contrasting strength of industrial securities during the era of enormous production inaugurated by the war. If future changes in the relative values of railroad and industrial securities occur, a corresponding change in the proportions in which they are accepted as mixed collateral for regular loans will no doubt also result.

Loans on all railroad stocks have in recent years grown comparatively rare, while loans based on all-industrial stocks have become common, and have sometimes proved even more desirable than the regular loans on mixed collateral already mentioned. As typical of the foregoing different combinations of stock collateral employed to secure call loans, the following examples are appended. In order to avoid complications, only stocks have been included in these imaginary loans, although in actual practice probably 75 per cent of security loans contain bonds.

Old Regular Loan of $100,000

Based on mixed collateral, ⅔ rails and ⅓ industrials. Margin about 25 per cent.

400	Atchison, Topeka and Santa Fé R. R. at 88	$ 35,200.00
200	Union Pacific R. R. at 126	25,200.00
200	Pennsylvania R. R. at 43	8,600.00
300	Baltimore and Ohio R. R. at 47	14,100.00
300	Consolidated Gas at 89	26,700.00
200	Republic Iron and Steel at 77	15,400.00
1,600		$125,200.00

NEW REGULAR LOAN OF $100,000

Based on mixed collateral, ½ rails and ½ industrials. Margin about 25 per cent.

400	Southern Pacific R. R. at 97	$ 38,800.00
200	Canadian Pacific R. R. at 121	24,200.00
200	United States Steel at 86	17,200.00
200	United States Rubber at 73	14,600.00
300	American Sugar Refining at 103	30,900.00
1,300		$125,700.00

ALL-RAIL LOAN OF $100,000

Based entirely on railroad stocks. Margin about 25 per cent.

200	Delaware and Hudson R. R. at 105	$ 21,000.00
300	New York Central R. R. at 82	24,600.00
300	Reading R. R. at 96	28,800.00
400	Northern Pacific R. R. at 83	33,200.00
200	Illinois Central R. R. at 90	18,000.00
1,400		$125,600.00

ALL-INDUSTRIAL LOAN OF $100,000

Based entirely on industrial stocks. Margin about 30 per cent.

600	General Motors at 17	$ 10,200.00
200	Pan American Petroleum at 89	17,800.00
300	American Sumatra Tobacco at 87	26,100.00
200	Crucible Steel at 95	19,000.00
300	Sears-Roebuck at 111	33,300.00
200	American Telephone and Telegraph at 100	20,000.00
100	International Mercantile Marine, pfd. at 54	5,400.00
1,900		$131,800.00

The banker naturally prefers to see in his loan envelopes stocks with a ready market, whose prices do not fluctuate very much. He is wary of stocks with very high prices, such as the old stock of Bethlehem Steel or Standard Oil of New Jersey, when these issues stood at 600 and 650 respectively. He dislikes odd lots of from 1 to 99 shares of any stock, since these involve a more complicated process in marketing [13] than

[13] See Chapter VI.

round lots of 100 shares. And when unlisted stocks are presented to him in the loan envelope, if he is willing to make the loan at all, he will demand a very high interest rate and a relatively large margin. The lender's requirements are so well understood by borrowers that in the ordinary loans made on the Exchange such exceptional features as have been mentioned above are eliminated by the borrower at the outset. Loans possessing these especial features are therefore usually negotiated directly between lenders and borrowers instead of through the Exchange.

Acceptance of Collateral

The loan envelope having been prepared in accordance with the verbal contract for the loan made on the Exchange, the broker's messenger takes it to the loan department of the lending institution. The officer in charge of this department may find the securities which it contains unacceptable for some of the reasons suggested above, in which case the brokerage firm may be forced to make up a new collateral envelope containing a greater number of securities or more desirable securities. But if the collateral is satisfactory to the lending institution, it places the loan envelope in its safe and gives the borrowing brokerage house a check for the amount of the loan.

In the case of call loans the borrower does not sign a separate agreement with the lender every time he obtains a new loan. Instead he files with the lending institution a general agreement (Figure 20) governing all the loans to be contracted with it, on the occasion of the first loan he obtains from it. So far as there is any contract for each individual loan, it consists simply of the face of the loan envelope, on which in some cases the lender requires the signature of the borrower. But even if the borrower's signature is not affixed to the loan envelope, the terms under which the loan is granted are sufficiently covered by the above-mentioned initial and general

STAMP.

Know all Men by these Presents, That the undersigned, in consideration of financial accommodations given, or to be given, or continued to the undersigned by The Blank Trust Co. of the City of New York. hereby agree with the said firm that whenever the undersigned shall become or remain, directly or indirectly, indebted to the said firm for money lent, or for money paid for the use or account of the undersigned, or for any overdraft or upon any endorsement, draft, guarantee or in any other manner whatsoever, or upon any other claim, the said firm shall then and thereafter have the following rights, in addition to those created by the circumstances from which such indebtedness may arise against the undersigned, or his or their executors, administrators or assigns, namely:

1. All securities deposited by the undersigned with said firm, as collateral to any such loan or indebtedness of the undersigned to said firm, shall also be held by said firm as security for any other liability of the undersigned to said firm, whether then existing or thereafter contracted; and said firm shall also have a lien upon any balance of the deposit account of the undersigned with said firm existing from time to time, and upon all property of the undersigned of every description left with said firm for safe keeping or otherwise, or coming to the hands of said firm in any way, as security for any liability of the undersigned to said firm now existing or hereafter contracted.

2. Said firm shall at all times have the right to require from the undersigned that there shall be lodged with said firm as security for all existing liabilities of the undersigned to said firm approved collateral securities to an amount satisfactory to said firm; and upon the failure of the undersigned at all times to keep a margin of securities with said firm for such liabilities of the undersigned, satisfactory to said firm, or upon any failure in business or making of an insolvent assignment by the undersigned, then and in either event all liabilities of the undersigned to said firm shall at the option of said firm become immediately due and payable, notwithstanding any credit or time allowed to the undersigned by any instrument evidencing any of the said liabilities.

3. Upon failure of the undersigned either to pay any indebtedness to said firm, when becoming or made due, or to keep up the margin of collateral securities above provided for, then, and in either event, said firm may immediately, without advertisement and without notice to the undersigned, sell any of the securities held by it as against any or all of the liabilities of the undersigned, at private sale or Brokers' Board or otherwise, and apply the proceeds of such sale, as far as needed, toward the payment of any or all of such liabilities, together with interest and expenses of sale, holding the undersigned responsible for any deficiency remaining unpaid after such application. If any such sale be at Brokers' Board or at public auction said firm may itself be a purchaser at such sale free from any right or equity of redemption of the undersigned, such right and equity being hereby expressly waived and released. Upon default as aforesaid said firm may also apply, toward the payment of the said liabilities, all balances of any deposit account of the undersigned with said firm then existing.

It is further agreed that these presents constitute a continuing agreement, applying to any and all future, as well as to existing, transactions between the undersigned and said firm.

Dated New York, the 22 day of April 1917 Jenkins & Co.

Figure 20. General Loan Agreement. (Size 8¼ x 6½.)

Employed to cover call loans.

agreement between borrower and lender. In the case of time loans, however, usually a separate agreement or note is drawn for each individual time loan made.

Obligations and Privileges of the Borrower

Yet the financial operations brought into being by the call loan envelope do not cease when the loan is made. In the general agreement between the lender and the borrowing broker under which the call loans are granted, it is expressly stipulated that at all times collateral securities satisfactory to the lender shall be deposited there to protect his loan. In case the ticker reports a violent fall in stock prices, the lender will demand that the borrowing broker put more securities in his loan envelope, or else substitute stronger for weaker securities in it, to maintain his margin of collateral. The broker is quite aware that his collateral securities will be "marked to the market" in this way, and frequently delivers additional securities to the lender even before the latter has demanded them. It often happens, too, that the broker will wish to recover some stock certificate which has been included in his loan envelope, either to deliver to one of his customers or to some other broker under instructions from the Stock Clearing Corporation, or for some other reason.[14] In such a case he may withdraw the needed certificate and substitute some other security satisfactory to the lender. Such substitutions are constantly taking place, thus complicating the duties of the loan officer but rendering the operations of the whole Stock Exchange more flexible.

The Termination of Call Loans

Call loans may be terminated either by the lender "calling the loan" or the borrower paying it off. In either case, provided the matter is handled "ex" and not through the Stock

[14] See Chapter XI.

Clearing Corporation, the borrower is under the necessity of turning in a certified check for the principal and interest on the loan to the lending institution, whereupon the latter returns to him his security collateral. The methods employed by the Stock Clearing Corporation in handling paid-off loans will be reserved for a later chapter to describe.[15]

Factors of Supply and Demand

The interest rates which are made upon call loans at the money desk result from the conditions of supply and demand for funds then prevailing. If the supply of funds diminishes or the demand increases, higher rates result; while if the supply increases and the demand lessens, lower rates are made. As is well known, the call rate at any given time is exceptionally sensitive to temporary shifts in the money market arising from such causes as lowered bank ratios, withdrawal of government funds, maturity or interest dates for large security issues, or the degree of distribution new security issues have attained.

The machinery by which the forces of supply and demand express themselves in the call loan market is extremely simple. As we have seen, the various lending brokers file their offerings of call money at the money desk. Also, the borrowing brokers file at the same desk the loans they need. Thus, the supply and the demand for funds can be fairly well ascertained. Then, too, the closing and majority call rate of the previous day, and the amount, if any, of funds offered but left unloaned on the previous day are known and can be taken into due consideration. On the basis of these several factors, therefore, an estimate of the fair value of money at that time is made.

This "renewal rate," which in reality is only an expression of opinion, is, of course, not binding either upon lenders or borrowers—it would, indeed, be a preposterous situation for either party to a loan to allow the interest rate upon it to be

[15] *Ibid.*

fixed by anyone but themselves. In consequence, it often happens that a lender will refuse to loan his funds at what may seem to him too low a rate, in which case he will fix a rate higher than the renewal rate established on the Exchange, which borrowers are, of course, at perfect liberty to accept or not as they see fit. But so delicately and expertly is the suggested renewal rate made on the Exchange that it is usually recognized as a very accurate indication of the existing fundamental conditions of supply and demand, and it is, therefore, generally adopted by both lenders and borrowers as a satisfactory basis upon which to renew old loans or make new ones.

Significance of the Renewal Rate

The true economic nature and significance of the renewal rate is frequently misunderstood. Again, reference must be had to the excellent and thoroughgoing analysis of the call loan market previously quoted:[16]

> The underlying cause of fluctuations and especially of increases in call money rates is the operation of the law of supply and demand. In other words, as the supply of loanable funds diminishes in proportion to the volume of the demand, the rate for collateral demand loans advances. However, in the case of daily borrowings of call money—to which the abnormal high and low rates apply and which represent but a comparatively small proportion of the total outstanding loans—other factors, incidental to the temporary circumstances and conditions of the market, tend in times of stress to greater fluctuations in rates than result from the more normal operation of the law which is reflected in the renewal rate for the greater volume of the outstanding call loans. The renewal rate is regarded as the real barometer of market conditions and its fluctuations throughout the longer periods more nearly reflect the relation between the amount of the loanable funds and the amount of the demand. In other words, high renewal rates are mainly due to other demands for credit, resulting in part from other

[16] See Senate Document 262, 66th Congress, 2nd Session, p. 9.

temporary factors, such as depletion of bank reserves resulting either or both from credit expansion or loss of reserves through gold export, speculation in commodities and real estate, and congestion of commercial transactions incidental to slow or interrupted transportation.

After the renewal rate has been posted, the rate for call funds may fluctuate upwards or downwards, either because the rate has proved to be unsatisfactory to lenders or borrowers, or because of the constantly changing conditions of supply and demand themselves. The well-known tendency of the call rate to fluctuate more widely and more rapidly than any other money rate in the world is, as has already been pointed out, fundamentally due to the fact that, of all the leading financial nations, America alone does not permit loans based upon security collateral to be rediscounted and employs a daily settlement system in her leading security market. So long as these conditioning factors exist, the comparatively violent fluctuations of our call rate must frequently recur. But the extreme fluctuations which would otherwise have occurred during the recent acute credit stringency, have been minimized by the co-operation between bankers and brokers obtained through the intelligent estimation of the forces of supply and demand at the money desk.

Reasons for High Call Rate in Recent Years

In this connection, too, it must be remarked that the war created an unprecedented demand for capital in reconstruction work of a thousand kinds all over the world, and also destroyed vast amounts of wealth during the unparalleled destruction which it wrought. Since the supply of the world's capital has decreased and the demand for it increased, it was inevitable that all over the world high rates of interest should universally prevail.[17] While the United States government was compelled

[17] See Appendix, Chapter VIII (e).

to pay 6 per cent on its Treasury certificates, while commercial paper rose to 8 per cent, the federal reserve rediscount rate to 7 per cent, and our strongest industrial corporations paid 7 to 8 per cent on their new gold sinking fund mortgage bonds, it is little wonder that call money soared to still higher rates.[18] Indeed, during the critical winter of 1919 the call money interest rate rose at one time to 30 per cent, owing to the bidding of necessitous borrowers for the scanty supply of funds available for lending on sale.[19]

It must, of course, be remembered that such extreme rates were applicable to only a few individual loans, and therefore affected an inconsiderable proportion of the total call loans outstanding. Moreover, unlike other interest rates, these high call rates remain in force for a single day only, the loans to which they apply being either paid off the next day or else renewed at the lower renewal rate. When such high rates are averaged in with lower renewal rates on succeeding days on a yearly basis, their effect upon borrowers is consequently unimportant. Sensational as a 30 per cent rate may appear, therefore, its real significance either to lenders or borrowers has been vastly exaggerated in the minds of those who are unacquainted with the practical workings of the American call money system.

Until this credit strain resulting from the war has abated and the normal proportion of the supply to the demand for capital has been restored, call money, along with time money, commercial loans, and investment securities, will continue to bear abnormally high interest rates all over the world. And our future experience with these high interest charges will undoubtedly prove that hard work and steady thrift on the part of all of us, rather than mistakenly assailing the banks or the brokers as the cause of it all, will alone tend to bring interest rates down to more normal levels.

---

[18] See Appendix, Chapter VIII (*f*). [19] See Appendix, Chapter VIII (*g*).

Renewal of Call Loans

So much, then, for the high rates recently borne by call loans. A few details of the present system by which they are handled remain to be mentioned. Since call loans are made for the day only, every loan must be either called or renewed the next morning between 10 A.M. and 12:15 P.M. If the Exchange renewal rate is unchanged from the previous day and is still satisfactory to the lender, the latter usually does not trouble to send to the borrower a formal notice of the renewal of his loan, for in the absence of notice this is understood. But if the Exchange renewal rate is changed from the previous day's rate, or if the lender finds the earlier rate now unsatisfactory, he notifies the borrower between 10 A.M. and 12:15 P.M. either to pay off his loan or else at what rate he is willing to renew it—whether at the new Exchange renewal rate, or at some other rate which may be more satisfactory to the lender.

The borrower is left equally free. Whenever he thinks that any rate is too high he is always perfectly at liberty to pay off his loan, recover his certificates, and borrow on them for a similar amount later in the day at a lower rate of interest —if he can get it. But in most cases the fairness of the renewal rate is recognized and the interest on renewed loans is mechanically marked up or marked down, as the case may be. Of the total call loans outstanding at any given time the great majority are renewed in this way and the loans which are called constitute only a small fraction of the total. It has been recently stated on the highest authority that of the $600,000,000 of call money steadily employed on the average over a period of years in the stock market, between 25 and 40 millions in the active markets of 1919, and between 15 and 30 millions in the duller markets of the early months of 1920, represented new loans made and old loans called and reborrowed.[20]

[20] Senate Document 262, p. 8.

Economic Functions of Security Collateral Loans

At this point it would be well to consider some of the broader economic aspects of money invested in call loans. To some superficial yet opinionated critics of finance and financial institutions generally, the employment of money in this way has seemed utterly wrong. "When all commerce and industry is so keenly in need of fresh capital," they ask, "why should such large sums be employed in financing the wicked speculator in the equally iniquitous stock market?" Something of this same prejudice is perhaps responsible for the fact that America is the only considerable nation on earth which will not allow loans based on absolutely liquid security collateral to be rediscounted by its central banking system. Indeed, if these loans are wastefully used and if their present employment serves no sound economic purpose, then every sensible person, either in Wall Street or out of it, will wish to abolish the present system.

One of the first facts which the impartial student of finance will discover with regard to funds loaned on call is that they do not compete with commercial loans for the available capital of the nation.[21] This may appear somewhat surprising to the layman, who has no doubt been informed that funds were regularly "wasted in the stock market" which were most desperately needed in our fields and factories. Yet the refusal of our federal reserve banks to rediscount loans based on security collateral has undoubtedly rendered commercial loans much more desirable to the average banker. But even apart from this, the banker must do his best to accommodate his regular depositors with commercial loans, unless he wishes to lose their deposits. As a result bankers will loan on call only that excess amount of their funds which they cannot for the time being profitably or safely employ in commercial loans. The violent fluctuations in call money, particularly in these recent years

[21] See Appendix, Chapter VIII (h).

when capital has been out of supply all over the world, are in themselves sufficient indication of the extreme shifts to which the stock market has been put to obtain the funds necessary to perform its vitally important services to the whole nation.

Relation Between Call and Other Money Rates

Then there is that other equally venerable fallacy about call rates—that their fluctuation causes similar fluctuations in the current rates for commercial loans and in the current yields of investment securities.

In a communication [22] to the United States Senate, dated March 27, 1920, from the Governor of the Federal Reserve Board, it was stated:

> The operation of the law of supply and demand is equally effective in determining the rate for commercial loans and all other borrowings. In fact, rates for commercial loans and rates for collateral call loans have a common root in the law of supply and demand, and the conditions which affect one in the main affect the other, although not in like degree, as is demonstrated by the far wider fluctuation of call rates and the higher points to which they go. The rates of call money do not determine and have not exerted an important influence on the rates for commercial borrowings.

It often happens that an upward or downward movement of all money rates will first be seen in the call money rate. This is natural enough, for the fact that call money represents excess or surplus funds only, makes the call loan market the most sensitive to the fundamental factors of supply and demand underlying all money markets. In reality, therefore, the call loan rate often serves as a barometer for other money rates. But it no more causes later disturbances in these markets by its own fluctuations than the changes inside the barometer cause storms or calms at sea. In the long run all money rates

[22] See Senate Document 262, pp. 9–10.

tend to move in unison, and like water to seek their own level. When there is a general shortage of money, all money rates are high. When there is a plethora of funds, all money rates are low. The first upward or downward trend in all money rates will usually become apparent in the movement of the call loan rate. But in the vast, slow, and profound world processes and conditions which create a general shortage or surplus of money, and hence create high or low interest rates, the demand for and supply of funds in our call loan market are inconsiderable factors.

Services of the Call Loan Market to Investors

Apart from these supposed transgressions of which the call loan market is so often falsely accused, there are many positive benefits which its funds render the whole country. It is a fact that no market can exist either in America or in any other country in which the "simon pure" investor can at all times purchase or sell securities at a fair price, which at the same time lacks the hearty support of the speculator. It is after all speculation which gives every market what is known as "firmness." If all the speculative credit transactions in the stock market, either for long or short account, should be suddenly abolished, the investor would find only a crippled and spasmodic market in which either to buy or to sell.

The truth of the matter is that it is chiefly the speculator who assumes the risks of industry—risks which someone must assume if industry is to obtain the funds and maintain the confidence which are essential to its very existence.[23] For speculation is an inevitable stage in the process of distributing securities, as for that matter in the distribution of almost every known kind of goods. The call loans by which the speculator is able profitably to assume these inevitable risks of business, therefore, serve a very vital economic purpose. Although this

[23] See Chapter XV.

service which the employment of the call loan in the stock market renders to American business is indirect, it is nevertheless both imperative and profound.

Advantages of the Call Loan Market to Lenders

The call loan market, too, is not without genuine usefulness to the banker. The mere hoarding of capital has long been recognized as an economic waste, and nowhere is this truer than in the banking business. Idle funds furnish a constant problem to every banker and a serious reflection upon his professional skill, unless he can quickly set them to earning interest by helping to carry on the world's work in some way. The call loan market has long afforded the banker a constant opportunity to invest safely and profitably money that would otherwise be idle. To the country banker in particular, whose business is subject to such wide seasonal fluctuations between a shortage and a surplus of good available investments, the call loan market has proved a safe and convenient way to increase his earnings. The word "safe" is used advisedly, for granted intelligent oversight, there is no safer type of loan in existence than the call loan. On such loans, as we have seen, the banker is secured against loss by actually holding in his possession the securities used as collateral, by the initial margin of their value over the amount of the loan, by the privilege of demanding the maintenance of this margin, and, if need be, by the substitution of better for weaker stocks, and finally by the ability to sell the collateral if these previous conditions are not satisfactorily met.

Except for the unprecedented conditions in the fall of 1914 occasioned by the outbreak of the Great War, when for the first time in its history the New York Stock Exchange, along with every other major stock exchange in the world, was closed for several months, the security of call loans has never been seriously endangered. And that such a condition, when the closing of the Exchange would be necessary, is quite unlikely to recur, is shown by America's present creditor position as contrasted with her debtor's status in 1914.[24] This record is in sharp contrast with the graver difficulties encountered during the sharp price declines of 1920 by banks who had loaned billions of dollars on warehouse receipts for leather, wool, silk, and similar commodities while these commodities sold at very high prices, only to see the cash value of their collateral melt away below the amounts of the loans made upon them and the commodity collateral itself become for the time being unsalable at any price.

Services of the Call Loan Market in 1920

As a matter of fact, in the critical period of 1920 the Stock Exchange loan market, although deprived by law of the privilege of rediscount at federal reserve banks enjoyed by commercial loans, nevertheless came powerfully to the aid of the latter when its theoretical ability of "self-liquidation" had badly broken down in practice. Many large American corporations, being unable to sell their inventories, were consequently unable to pay off their commercial borrowings, which soon became "frozen" in the portfolios of federal reserve and member banks. These frozen commercial loans were finally liquidated and paid off with funds which the corporations obtained by issuing their stocks and bonds, and listing and distributing them with the aid of the Stock Exchange and the security collateral loan market. Thus the liquidity of many supposedly self-liquidating commercial loans was shown to depend upon the liquidity imparted to its listed securities by the Stock Exchange.

Moreover, during the credit strain in the autumn of 1920 the commercial bankers were frequently assisted in the difficult task of readjusting and strengthening their position by being able to call in their outstanding security collateral loans

[24] See Chapter XVIII.

and thus protect their frequently illiquid commercial loans.[25] In this connection prominent banking authorities have recently declared:[26]

> The crisis of 1920 demonstrated the fact that loans to the stock market were the most liquid resources which the New York banks possessed. . . . Loans to the stock market proved to be an extremely valuable liquid resource, and the ability of the stock market to absorb securities, supplying the banks with new cash to lend for other purposes, eased the situation greatly.

The fact that the rules of the Federal Reserve Bank Act governing rediscounts thus tend to separate the security collateral loan market from the commercial loan market, is a fundamental defect in the American banking system. This isolation of the security collateral loan market and its dependence upon only excess banking funds make it supersensitive and liable to extreme fluctuations. They finance their stock exchanges more wisely and more liberally in Europe.

The Problem of Term Settlements

But the European system also involves the term settlement —that is, the weekly, fortnightly, or monthly delivery of and payment for stocks, instead of the American system of daily settlements. In addition, European methods presuppose the existence of a strong discount market, based upon the extensive use of bankers' and trade acceptances. Our present and admittedly defective loan and discount system is not the fault of American bankers, the New York Stock Exchange, or the United States government, but is rather due to the amazingly hasty rise of this country to its present financial pre-eminence. It seems probable that our Stock Exchange, like the European bourses, may sooner or later adopt the term settlement system

---

[25] See Appendix, Chapter VIII (i).

[26] A. Barton Hepburn and Benjamin M. Anderson, "The Gold and Rediscount Policy of the Federal Reserve Banks," *The Chase Economic Bulletin*, Vol. I, No. 5.

in one form or another.[27] Yet so thoroughgoing a change in our whole financial system involves a host of practical problems, and if the transition is to be made securely it must come about through a slow evolution along many apparently unrelated lines.

---

[27] See Appendix, Chapter VIII (j).

CHAPTER IX

THE NIGHT CLEARING BRANCH

Only Negotiation of Contracts on the Exchange

In Chapter III we watched Jenkins and Wilkins, two typical commission brokers, effect a sale of 100 shares of Steel common at 95 on the floor of the Stock Exchange. It is highly important to notice that they exchanged no stock or money there, but simply made a contract to deliver stock and pay money later. Since every sale is in reality an exchange of money and goods, the seller, Jenkins, contracted to receive $9,500 as well as to deliver the 100 shares of Steel, while the buyer, Wilkins, contracted to deliver $9,500 as well as to receive the 100 shares of stock. As we saw, each broker made a report of the transaction, which was sent to his office by his telephone clerk. It was left for the offices of the two firms, and not for Jenkins and Wilkins personally, to see that the stock and the money involved by this contract should be properly received and delivered. Our next task must, therefore, be to investigate the methods and machinery by which this settlement of Exchange contracts is brought about, and in particular the function of the Stock Clearing Corporation in effecting it.

In the vast majority of cases, and always unless otherwise stated at the time, sales effected on the Exchange are made regular way, for delivery by 2:15 P.M. upon the next full business day following the date of contract. Transactions occurring on Fridays and on Saturdays (on the latter day the Exchange closes at 12 P.M.) are cleared and settled the following Monday. In consequence of this, the New York Stock Exchange is said to have a system of "daily settlements," in contrast to most European stock exchanges which are said to have "term settlements," since their contracts need not be settled for periods from a week to a month after they are made.

Different Deliveries on Exchange Contracts

The time which may elapse between the making of a sales contract on the New York Stock Exchange and the final settling of the contract may, however, in special cases and within certain limits,[1] be determined by a special agreement between buyer and seller when the contract is made. Jenkins and Wilkins, for example, may agree on a "cash" delivery, in which case Jenkins must receive the $9,500 and Wilkins the 100 Steel on the same day on which the contract is made. Delivery may also be fixed "at three days"—that is, for the third day following the date of the contract. Again, the delivery may be arranged according to "buyer's" or "seller's" options for not less than four days nor more than sixty days. Under a seller's option the seller can deliver the stock and demand payment for it on any day within the period of the option, provided he notifies the buyer by 2:15 P.M. the previous day, while the buyer during the life of a buyer's option can at any time similarly pay his money and call for his stock.

In the Pre-Clearing House Days

In order to understand how contracts made on the New York Stock Exchange are settled at the present time, we must first consider how settlements were originally effected before the establishment of the present clearance system, both because such an understanding is necessary before we can appreciate just what service the latter renders, and because even today the original method is still followed to a limited extent.

First of all, under the old system a "comparison" was made

[1] See Constitution, Art. XXIII, Sec. 3.

on each contract to be settled between the buying and selling firms concerned, in order to avoid the possibility of misunderstanding concerning it. The selling firm sent its messenger to the office of the buyer with an original and a duplicate comparison ticket which recorded the amount and name of the stock sold, as well as the price at which the sale had been made. If the ticket was correct, the buyer retained the original and at once returned the duplicate duly stamped. In this connection, a provision [2] of the Stock Exchange Constitution should be noted:

> No comparison or failure to compare, and no notification or acceptance of notification, shall have the effect of creating or of cancelling a contract, or of changing the terms thereof, or releasing the original parties from liability.

Thus the absolute inviolability of contracts made on the Stock Exchange floor was and is maintained throughout the process of comparison and thereafter. According to the Constitution,[3] it is the duty of the seller to compare each transaction he has made on the Exchange with the buyer, at the office of the latter, not later than one hour after the closing of the Exchange. Neglect of a member in this regard is punishable by fine. (An exchange of exchange tickets, as defined in the Rules of the Stock Clearing Corporation and subsequently described, constitutes a comparison, and the failure to exchange such exchange tickets constitutes a default.)

The terms of each contract being thus mutually agreed upon, and any difference promptly eliminated by purchase, sale, or mutual agreement, the task of settling the contracts by actually delivering purchased securities and paying for them began at 10 A.M. the following day and continued until 2:15 that afternoon. In the absence of any clearance system,

---

[2] See Constitution, Art. XXIV, Sec. 8.

[3] *Ibid.*, Secs. 2, 4, and 5.

the messenger of the selling firm was compelled to make a separate trip to each firm which had purchased securities of his employers the proceding day, and deliver the certificates purchased, to which a double delivery ticket was pinned. The receiver stamped one of these tickets and gave it back to the deliverer as an evidence of delivery, together with a check for the amount which the buyer had agreed to pay for the security. The messenger next took this check to the bank upon which it was drawn to be certified, and then conveyed it to the office of the selling firm, which recorded it and deposited it in its own bank.

Inadequacies of the Early System

Although this method of making delivery on Exchange contracts proved well enough in the relatively small stock markets up to thirty years ago, nevertheless the continually increasing volume of sales on the Stock Exchange rendered it more and more irksome and impracticable during the later eighties. The brokers' messengers and clerks, and sometimes the firm partners themselves, were compelled to rush from office to office and from bank to bank between 10 A.M. and 2:15 P.M. each day. Often, after particularly active days on the Exchange, the innumerable delays at buyers' offices and at the certifying banks rendered it physically impossible to complete by 2:15 P.M. all the separate trips necessitated from the single day's transactions on the Exchange. In such cases the seller was compelled to "fail to deliver" the stock he was trying to deliver and, in carrying it overnight, to pay the interest on it himself.

Financing the Stock Market Turnover

A still graver difficulty arose from the increasing strain put upon the banks in financing the daily turnover of the stock market. In the preceding chapter the system of collateral loans was explained, through which the broker obtains the credit needed for his customers by depositing the securities purchased on margin as collateral with the lending institution. But the broker cannot, of course, obtain the loan until he has the stocks and bonds to secure it, and these latter he cannot get from the seller until he has made payment for them to him. Thus the broker, who cannot get money till he gets stocks, nor stocks till he gets money, is compelled to seek temporary banking accommodation for a few hours each day to enable him to make payment to the deliverer of the stock.

Accordingly, the broker obtains a loan at his bank each morning based on his single-name paper. On receipt of this unsecured note of the broker the bank credits his account with its amount, thus enabling him to draw against it later in the day such checks as he wishes to pay out for stock he must receive. Often, as a matter of fact, the broker does not need to employ all the credit thus placed at his disposal, for while he is paying out checks during the day against stocks delivered to him, he is just as steadily taking in checks from other brokers for stocks which he has himself delivered to them. These checks he deposits with his bank as speedily as possible, to cover the day loan he has contracted there. Furthermore, as soon as he receives the securities for which, by means of this temporary accommodation, he has been able to make payment, he can at once arrange a collateral loan based upon them, with the proceeds of which he can pay off the day loan and redeem his note.

Day Loans from the Bank's Standpoint

The bank on its part stipulates that the broker who wishes to obtain such unsecured day loans from it, must keep a certain amount of cash always on deposit in the bank. While the amount of this standing deposit generally determines the amount of accommodation which the bank will extend to the broker, nevertheless a moral element is likewise involved.

Superior personal character and status, of course, favor greater extension of accommodation among brokers, just as they do among commercial borrowers. The only direct profit obtained by the bank on these day loans is the interest earned on the broker's standing deposit. Nevertheless this branch of the bank's business is also related to other branches, such as the collateral loans, described in the preceding chapter. In some instances there is, consequently, an indirect profit accruing to the banker from making day loans, apart from the interest made on the broker's deposit.

This type of accommodation must have been considered safe, or else banks would hardly have practiced it over so long a period of years. Indeed, a vastly smaller loss has been occasioned to banks in brokers' day loans per dollar extended than in any other class of loans, with the possible exception of security collateral loans. Compared with the losses to banks on commercial paper, their losses on day loans to brokers is infinitesimal.[4]

Opportunities for Increased Efficiency

Nevertheless, with the ceaseless growth of transactions on the New York Stock Exchange, the time and labor consumed in making deliveries and payments in the manner outlined above became both impracticable and expensive, and the accommodation demanded of the banks became increasingly inconvenient and burdensome. Accordingly it became more and more necessary to devise some method of effecting stock deliveries and money payments between Stock Exchange firms which could bring about economies in these several respects, without in any way endangering the complete inviolability of any sales contract made on the Exchange or changing in the slightest degree the original liability assumed by the two parties to the contract.

4 See Appendix, Chapter IX (a).

Many opportunities for bringing about such economies of effort and of the use of bank credit were discovered. In a case where A sold 100 shares of stock to B, who then sold them to C, who proceeded to sell them to D, who in turn sold them to E, under the old method, or lack of method, in effecting deliveries, 400 shares of stock, four separate trips to buyers' offices, four trips to certifying banks, and if the stock in question were selling around 100, about $40,000 of bank accommodation were involved. Yet it is obvious that if some central and supervisory agency could have known of this situation, it could have satisfied all four parties concerned simply by directing A to deliver his stock to E and to obtain payment from him.

Thus only 100 shares, one trip to the ultimate buyer's office and the certifying bank, and only about $10,000 of bank accommodation would have been needed. The contracts for both the purchase and sale of this stock by B, C, and D were intermediate contracts. It is obvious that if some agency could be devised to settle these intermediate contracts on their behalf, B would be saved the trouble of paying A for the stock, and then rushing off to C's office to deliver it and get C's money; a similar saving would also be effected in the cases of C and D.

Also, in case A had purchased 400 shares of stock from B and had on the same day sold him 500 shares of the same stock, under the original system of settlement these two contracts would have involved 900 shares of the stock, roughly $90,000 of bank credit, and trips to both brokerage offices and to their banks. But if A's intermediate contract for the purchase and sale of 400 shares of the stock could be settled by some agency, in the same manner as suggested above, A would have to deliver only the balance of 100 shares to B, thus involving only $10,000 of bank credit and a trip to a single bank and to a single brokerage office.

The Development of Stock Clearance Systems

To bring about economies based upon these and similar principles, every great stock exchange in the world has in the course of the past half-century developed a stock clearing house of one kind or another, as a central agency to effect the settlement of intermediate contracts and to direct the deliveries of securities on balance and the payment of money due upon them.

The first complete system of stock clearance—as this work is called—was inaugurated at Frankfurt in 1867, and its success soon led to the development of similar systems in London, Paris, Vienna, Hamburg, and Berlin. The first attempt in America to clear stocks was made by the Philadelphia Stock Exchange. The New York Stock Exchange was comparatively slow in developing its clearance system, and its original Clearing House of the New York Stock Exchange was not established until May 17, 1892, the centennial of the first broker's agreement from which the Exchange had developed.[5]

Yet, from the ease with which the huge and varying total sales made on the New York Stock Exchange have since that date been cleared each day, the efficiency of its clearance system has obviously been second to none in the world, if, indeed, it has anywhere been equaled. Next only to the highly developed American ticker system, nothing in Wall Street so astonishes the foreign financier, accustomed as he is to the fortnightly or monthly settlements on the European stock exchanges, as the fact that practically all transactions made each day on the Exchange result in a complete delivery of stock and payment of money by the following day. The editor of the *London Economist* says in his valuable little study of stock exchanges:[6]

> . . . it is almost incredible to an English broker that the day's transactions can be settled, as New York settles them, by the day. On one record occasion the Clearing House set-

[5] See Chapter II. page 29.

[6] F. W. Hirst, The Stock Exchange, p. 113.

tled and balanced transactions in about 3,200,000 shares, of an approximate value of 50 millions sterling. This test proved conclusively the perfection of New York's financial machinery for settling Stock Exchange transactions.

Scope of New York Stock Exchange Clearance

The machinery of the Clearing House of the New York Stock Exchange (which is now known as the Night Clearing Branch of the Stock Clearing Corporation) presents certain analogies to that of a bank clearing house. Yet, where the latter clears only money (or rather bank credit, which is, of course, an acceptable substitute for money), the former must clear not only money but also more than two hundred different kinds of stocks. By no means all the stocks listed on the Stock Exchange are cleared, the list of cleared stocks at present numbering about two hundred and twenty. At the present writing no bonds except the Liberty Loan issues are regularly cleared, although in the near future transactions in other active bond issues may be similarly settled. Also, except on special occasions, the present clearance system does not clear odd-lot transactions in from 1 to 99 shares, but confines itself to round lots of 100 shares and multiples thereof.[7]

The work of clearance is at present consequently confined to the most active stocks in which the greatest number of intermediate contracts occur, and to some of the high-priced though less active stocks, wherein, as we shall see, the Day Clearing Branch can effect economies in the use of banking accommodation. Furthermore, by a special provision in its By-laws and Rules the Stock Clearing Corporation may on occasion act for two of its members in making and receiving payment for transactions in securities not regularly cleared.[8] There is at present a strong tendency for more and more different security issues to be cleared.

---

[7] See Chapter VI, page 149.

[8] By-laws and Rules of the Stock Clearing Corporation, Rule 7, p. 20.

Stock Clearance a Twofold Process

Before describing the machinery of the original clearing house, now consolidated in the recently organized Stock Clearing Corporation as its Night Clearing Branch, a further example is necessary to show just why both money and stocks must be cleared. Broker A, let us say, sells 100 shares of Reading to broker B at 79; B in turn sells them to broker C at 81. In all human probability A knows nothing at all about this subsequent transaction between B and C. Yet the Night Clearing Branch, as agent for all three brokers, settles B's intermediate contracts by directing A to deliver his 100 Reading to C. Thus B is saved bother and needless banking accommodation, which would be necessitated if he had to receive and deliver the shares himself.

But this delivery of the stock is only half the story, for there is a clearance of money still to be made. Since B has sold the 100 Reading for 2 points more than he has paid for them, he is entitled to a profit of $200. Also, A has sold them for $7,900 and C has purchased them for $8,100. Consequently, when A delivers the shares to C, if C makes payment to him A will receive $200 more than he is entitled to. To settle these cash balances is simplicity itself. B draws a draft against the Stock Clearing Corporation for $200 to obtain the balance due him, while A makes out his check for the $200 he receives in excess of his due. The Night Clearing Branch has only to pay B's draft with A's check. Of necessity, then, the checks received by the Stock Clearing Corporation will always exactly equal the drafts drawn against it.

Establishment of the Delivery Price

In one detail, however, the above transaction has been incorrectly described. The payment for stock balances delivered, such as the 100 Reading which A delivers to C, is really based, in the case of each cleared stock, not upon the actual prices at which various brokers may have sold the stock, but upon one delivery or clearing house price which is arbitrarily set by the Night Clearing Branch for each day's transactions immediately after the close of the market, in order to simplify its operations. This delivery price for each stock cleared is usually arrived at by selecting the nearest even price (excluding fractions) to the closing bid price for the day. The delivery price on a closing bid of 79⅛ would consequently be 79; and on a closing bid of 79⅝ it would be 80. Sometimes, in the less active stocks, when this closing bid price is too weak to furnish a satisfactory basis, the price of the last sale is similarly used. For example, when the last sale of such a stock has been made at 86 and its closing bid and asked prices are 82-87, the delivery price might be made 86.

Daily Adjustment by Check or Draft

Such inequalities as arise between the delivery price for a particular stock and the various actual prices at which different firms have bought and sold the stock are adjusted in the checks and drafts made out by the clearing members. In the example above, if the closing bid price for Reading is 79¾, the delivery price is fixed at 80. Therefore, when A delivers his 100 Reading to C, the latter pays him $8,000. A, who has sold the shares for $7,900 but actually gets $8,000, makes out his check to the Stock Clearing Corporation for the excess amount of $100. C, who has bought the shares for $8,100 but pays only $8,000, on receiving them makes out a similar check for the $100 he still owes. B, who has bought the stock for $7,900 and has sold it for $8,100, draws a draft against the Stock Clearing Corporation for his profit of $200. This draft the corporation pays with the two checks, for $100 each, received from A and C.

Thus the Night Clearing Branch, as an agent for the various members of the Stock Exchange which employ it, settles their intermediate contracts in the stocks which it clears, without the need of direct physical delivery between them of the stocks involved or payment of their money value. Furthermore, as we shall subsequently discover, it supervises the delivery of cleared stocks on balance and the payment made for them.

Settlement of Ex-Clearing House Contracts

It is constantly necessary to distinguish between stocks which are and stocks which are not cleared, or, as they are generally designated, between "clearing house" and "ex-clearing" stocks, because contracts in those securities which are not handled through the Stock Clearing Corporation are settled today in just the same way as contracts in all stocks were settled before the institution of the clearing house. This method of direct delivery and payment has already been described and needs no further comment here. Ex-clearing house transactions constitute only about 10 per cent of the total transactions which take place on the New York Stock Exchange today.

Use of Comparison Tickets and Exchange Tickets

With this preliminary sketch of the historic background of the present-day Stock Exchange clearance system, as well as of the chief principles upon which it operates, we are now ready to follow a typical present-day case of stock clearance through its various stages from beginning to end. For this purpose we shall again hark back to the sale of 100 shares of Steel common at 95 which Jenkins made to Wilkins.[9] We have seen that when this sales contract was made at the Steel post, both brokers made a report of it. Jenkins wrote on his pad, "Sold 100 Steel 95 Wilkins and Company," thus indicating the amount and name of the stock sold, the price, and the

---

[9] See Chapter III, page 58.

name of the buyer. Similarly, Wilkins made out his report, "Bought 100 Steel 95 Jenkins and Company." Each broker gave his report to his telephone clerk on the floor, who reported the transaction to their respective offices in the Wall Street district.

Before any further steps can be taken by the two brokerage firms to exchange the 100-share Steel certificate and the $9,500

COMPARISON

ORIGINAL

JENKINS & CO.
500 WALL STREET
NEW YORK, August 2 1920

SOLD TO Thompson & Co.

ACCOUNT OF

100 National Biscuit pfd @ 102

Figure 21. (a) Comparison Sale Ticket. (Size 5½ x 3½.)

Employed by Jenkins and Company after a sale to Thompson and Company of a non-cleared security. When Jenkins and Company "gives up" some other house, the name of the latter is inscribed after "Account of ——."

called for by the terms of their contract, both must make sure that its terms have been accurately reported from the floor of the Exchange and are mutually agreed upon. If the transaction had occurred in a stock not cleared by the Stock Clearing Corporation, it would be handled "ex-clearing house," as the phrase goes, and Jenkins and Company as the seller would exchange double comparison tickets (Figures 21 a and b) with Wilkins and Company, the buyer, in the manner previously described.[10] With a cleared stock like Steel, however, the procedure is somewhat different. Jenkins and Company, as the seller, makes out a deliver ticket, printed in red on white paper (Figure 22).

Meanwhile, in the office of Wilkins and Company, the

COMPARISON

ORIGINAL

JENKINS & CO.
500 WALL STREET
NEW YORK, August 2 1920

BOUGHT FROM Green & Co

ACCOUNT OF

100 Otis Elevator @ 50

Figure 21. (b) Comparison Purchase Ticket. (Size 5½ x 3½.)
Employed by Jenkins and Company after its purchase from Green and Company of a non-cleared security. When Jenkins and Company "gives up" some other house, the name of the latter is inscribed after "Account of ———."

buyer, a receive ticket printed in black ink on yellow paper is being prepared (Figure 23).

The above exchange tickets, unlike the comparison tickets previously noted, are more than simply a record of the sale which has been contracted on the floor. They are orders, stamped with the firm's name, upon the Stock Clearing Corporation to deliver and to receive the specified stock to and from the indicated firms, and as positive orders are legally binding. Thus the Stock Clearing Corporation is constituted

[10] See pages 204–206.

the agent of both firms, to settle their intermediate contracts, and to direct their deliveries of stocks on balance. According

No. 400 Our Line Number 51 New York Aug. 3, 1920

STOCK CLEARING CORPORATION (NIGHT CLEARING BRANCH)

DELIVER TO Wilkins & Co.

100 shares U.S. Steel common @ 95 $ 9500.00

for account of the undersigned.

Their Line Number 7 Jenkins & Co.

Figure 22. (a) Deliver Ticket. (Size 7¼ x 2¾.)

No. 400 Our Line Number 51 New York Aug 3 1920

SOLD TO Wilkins & Co.

100 shares U.S. Steel common @ 95 $ 9,500.00

Their Line Number 7 Jenkins & Co.

Figure 22. (b) Memorandum of Sale Attached to Deliver Ticket. (Size 7¼ x 4.)

To this form tax stamps are attached.

to the Stock Exchange Constitution,[11] "an exchange of exchange tickets, as defined in the Rules of the Stock Clearing Corporation, shall constitute a comparison." The seller's deliver ticket is provided with a detachable sales ticket, upon which are placed the federal and state tax stamps.[12] This sales ticket is then torn off by the delivering member, and sent to the Stock Clearing Corporation by 11 o'clock the next day.

[11] See Constitution, Art. XXIV, Sec. 5.

[12] See Chapters V, page 104.

No. 410 Our Line Number 7 New York August 3 1920

STOCK CLEARING CORPORATION (NIGHT CLEARING BRANCH)

RECEIVE FROM Jenkins & Co.

100 shares U. S. Steel common @ 95 $ 9500.00

for account of the undersigned.

Their Line Number 51 Wilkins & Co.

Figure 23. Receive Ticket. (Size 7¼ x 2¾.)

Distributing Department of the Night Clearing Branch

The actual exchange of these exchange tickets is not effected directly between houses, as formerly, but through the distributing department of the Night Clearing Branch. This department is housed in a long room attached to the headquarters of the Night Clearing Branch at 55 New Street and divided by a partition into an outer and inner office. Every day after 10 A.M. the messengers from Exchange houses enter the outer office and deliver both the deliver and receive exchange tickets of their firms, for that day's trading, through a slot in the partition to the clerks in the inner office. This inner office is equipped, like a post-office, with pigeonholes for all of the firms who employ the Stock Clearing Corporation. The clerks sort the deliver and receive tickets as they come in, and place them in the box of the firm to whom they are directed. When, for example, Jenkins' messenger thrusts his deliver ticket through the slot, it is placed in Wilkins' box, and in a like manner, Wilkins' receive ticket is placed in Jenkins' box.

After delivering his firm's tickets to the distributing department, the messenger then goes to a window in the partition and obtains all the deliver and receive tickets which have been made out and delivered there by other firms and placed in Jenkins and Company's box, because they involve that firm as a buyer and seller respectively. Thus a single trip to the distributing department obviates the need of making many trips to many offices, as is necessary in the case of comparison tickets for ex-clearing house contracts. A buying firm does not, therefore, wait to receive a deliver ticket, but every firm sends both its deliver and receive tickets to the distributing department simultaneously. All these exchange tickets are usually turned in at this department by 4 P.M., and even in heavy markets they must all be in by 4:20 P.M.

Effecting a Comparison

By these methods, Jenkins and Company soon gets Wilkins and Company's receive ticket for the 100 Steel and can compare the data it contains with its office records. Likewise, Wilkins and Company obtains Jenkins and Company's deliver ticket and can check it against its own records. Thus a double comparison is indirectly effected, instead of a single direct comparison in the buyer's office, as on ex-clearing house contracts, and with greater speed and economy than in the case of the latter. Any differences arising from this mutual checking up, as in the comparison on ex-clearing house contracts, is speedily settled "by purchase, sale, or mutual agreement." [13] It is to be noticed that after this exchange of tickets has taken place, Wilkins and Company retains Jenkins and Company's deliver ticket and Jenkins and Company retains Wilkins and Company's receive ticket.

All day long, as transactions in cleared stocks are entered into by a Stock Exchange firm, they are recorded on its clearance sheet and checked against the receipt of the receive and deliver exchange tickets of the corresponding firm in each case. This clearance sheet, which is thus in process of preparation all day, is completed shortly after the close of the market at

[13] See Chapter XIII.

STOCK CLEARING CORPORATION (NIGHT CLEARING BRANCH)

EXD J. P. R. — No. 400
CKD L. W. S.
NEW YORK, August 3 1920 OFFICE ADDRESS 500 Wall St. CLEARING SHEET OF Jenkins & Co.

	RECEIVE FROM	SHARES	SECURITY Print N.Y.S.E. Abbreviations in CAPITALS	PRICE	√	VALUE			DELIVER TO	SHARES	SECURITY Print N.Y.S.E. Abbreviations in CAPITALS	PRICE	√	VALUE	
1	Jefferson & Co.	100	Reading Com	93 5/8		9362	50	51	Wilkins & Co.	100	Steel Com	95		9500	
2	L. S. Jones & Co.	400	" "	93 3/4		37500		52	O. S. Harkness & Co	500	" "	94 7/8		47437	50
3	Harrison & Co.	300	" "	93 5/8		28087	50	53	Earle Wright & Co.	200	" "	94 1/2		18900	
4	R. P. Hodge & Co.	100	" "	93 3/4		9375		54	A. J. Brothers & Co	200	Reading Com	93 3/4		18750	
5	J. Long & Co.	100	" "	93 7/8		9387	50	55	Peck, Lamb & Co.	500	" "	94		47000	
6	Byron & Co.	200	Steel Com	94 1/4		18850		56	P. W. Lane & Co.	100	" "	93 7/8		9387	50
7	Smith, Reed & Co.	100	" "	94 5/8		9462	50	57	Murphy, Campbell & Co	400	Rubber Com	84 7/8		33950	
8	J. E. Halpin & Co.	200	" "	94 1/2		18900		58	C. E. Bowman & Co	200	" "	84 3/4		16950	
9	Tompkins & Co.	200	Rubber Com	84 1/2		16900		59							
10	Judson, Fitch & Co	300	" "	84 3/4		25425		60							
11	Barker & Co.	100	" "	84 5/8		8462	50	61							
12								62							
13	Balance to Deliver	300	Steel Com	95		28500		63	Balance to Receive	200	Reading Com	94		18800	
14								64							
15		Draft				462	50	65							
16								66							
17								67							
18		2400				220675		68		2400				220675	
19								69							
24								74							
25								75							

ENTER ON THIS SHEET ONLY THOSE TRANSACTIONS FOR WHICH TICKETS HAVE BEEN EXCHANGED — THE TICKETS MUST AGREE OR BOTH PARTIES WILL BE FINED.

Figure 24. Clearance Sheet. (Size 14 x 10.)

3 P.M. and is a full record of all purchases and sales of cleared stocks made on that day by the firm. In addition, as will later be explained in more detail, borrowed and loaned stocks also may appear upon it, as well as the purchases and sales of some Exchange member who is not a clearing member but who clears his transactions through the given firm.[14]

A Typical Day's Business

Suppose Jenkins and Company on August 2, 1920, has purchased 1,000 shares of Reading, 500 shares of Steel, 600 shares of United States Rubber; and 100 shares of Otis Elevator, and has in addition, sold 800 Reading, 800 Steel, 600 Rubber, and 100 National Biscuit preferred. If Jenkins and Company had had any transactions in Liberty bonds, they would have been recorded on a separate sheet, which is designed on the same principles as the stock clearance sheet we are about to consider and therefore needs no special explanation here. National Biscuit preferred and Otis Elevator are ex-clearing house stocks—that is to say, these stocks are not regularly cleared through the Stock Clearing Corporation. For this reason, after comparisons have been made, Jenkins and Company must on the morrow deliver 100 shares of National Biscuit preferred direct to its purchaser and get a check for their selling price, and must receive 100 shares of Otis Elevator from the firm from which they were purchased, and give a check for their purchase price. In other words, with these two ex-clearing house stocks the original method of direct delivery, described early in the present chapter, is followed. But with the rest, which are cleared stocks, the first step is the preparation of the clearance sheet. Jenkins and Company's completed clearance sheet (one of whose items is the sale of 100 Steel to Wilkins and Company described in an earlier chapter) is shown in Figure 24.

[14] See Chapter V, page 103.

The Clearance Sheet in Detail

Even at the expense of a somewhat tedious and perhaps puzzling foray into the dreary realm of bookkeeping, this clearance sheet will repay careful study, as it is fundamental to the whole system of stock clearance. In the upper right-hand corner there is a line on which the clearing number of the firm whose transactions the sheet records is placed. As we shall presently see, firms are known by these numbers rather than by their names in the Stock Clearing Corporation. In the upper left-hand corner the letters "EXD" and "CKD" will be noticed. These are abbreviations of "Examined" and "Checked," and refer to operations in the process of clearance which will presently be explained.

The sheet is divided down its center into two parts. On the left-hand side are recorded the stocks which Jenkins and Company has bought and will receive when the clearance is finished, together with the name, number, and price of the stocks, and their cash extensions, or the amount of money they represent. The right-hand side of the sheet contains a similar record of the stocks which Jenkins and Company has sold during the day and must deliver before the clearance is completed. Prominent among these selling transactions will be found the 100 shares of Steel sold to Wilkins. In addition, as we shall presently note, loaned stock is included as stock to deliver, and borrowed stock as stock to receive, in the same manner as sold or purchased stock respectively.

Stock Balances "To Receive" and "To Deliver"

The clerk who prepares this clearance sheet next ascertains the stock balances of clearing house stocks which his firm has to receive and deliver. Jenkins and Company has during this particular day bought 1,000 shares of Reading, 500 of Steel, and 600 of Rubber; and has sold 800 shares of Reading, 800 of Steel, and 600 of Rubber. In the case of Rubber there is no stock balance, since the firm has sold the same amount as it has bought. But it has sold 300 shares more Steel than it has bought, and has bought 200 shares more Reading than it has sold. Consequently, it has a stock balance of 300 Steel to deliver and of 200 Reading to receive. In order to strike a balance on the clearance sheet, the stock balances to deliver are entered under the stocks to receive, and the stock balances to receive under the stocks to deliver. The accuracy of this much of the record is proved by the total of 2,400 shares of stock appearing on both sides of the sheet. It should be noticed that this total figure for stocks by no means represents simply total sales or purchases, but in addition includes stock balances to deliver or receive, and perhaps also, as will be explained presently, stocks which have been borrowed or loaned.

The Cash Extensions

Besides the entry for the stocks is a column for the prices at which they were bought and sold. Ordinarily this column is not filled, since the amount of the cash extension next to it gives this information. To make the sheet more intelligible to the layman, however, the prices have been entered in the typical sheet in question. The cash extension represented by each stock item is, of course, determined by multiplying the price by the number of shares; 100 shares of Reading at 93⅝ are worth $9,362.50; 100 shares of Steel at 95 are worth $9,500; etc.

We have seen that the Stock Clearing Corporation will direct Jenkins and Company to receive and deliver, not all the stocks it has bought or sold but only the stock balances. Thus, Jenkins and Company will have only 300 instead of 2,200 shares to deliver and obtain payment for, and only 200 instead of 2,100 shares to receive and pay for. But Jenkins and Company cannot tell to what firm the Stock Clearing Corporation may direct it to deliver its balance of 300 Steel, or from whom to receive its balance of 200 Reading. Consequently, it would be at a loss to know what price to put upon these stock balances, were it not for the use of the delivery prices already mentioned. On this particular day the delivery price is 95 for Steel, and 94 for Reading. Consequently, Jenkins and Company puts down on its sheet $28,500 as the value of the stock balance of 300 Steel it has to deliver, and when it delivers this stock to the firm indicated by the Stock Clearing Corporation it will expect this sum in return for its stock. Also, Jenkins and Company will pay $18,800 for the 200 shares of Reading which it has to receive.

Inclusion of Loaned and Borrowed Stocks

In an earlier chapter [15] it was pointed out that a broker is able to deliver to the purchaser stock which he has sold short by borrowing it from some other broker in exchange for a loan of money equivalent to the market value of the stock borrowed. Such loans and borrowings of stock and their money equivalents are included in the clearance sheet, exactly as if they were sales and purchases. If, for example, Jenkins and Company had borrowed 200 shares of Crucible Steel from some broker and loaned 100 shares of Mexican Petroleum to another broker, the 200 Crucible would appear with stocks to receive on the left side of the clearance sheet, and the 100 Mexican Petroleum on its right side, with stocks to deliver. The money equivalents or cash extensions of these items would appear after them on the sheet, just as with stocks bought or sold.

Tickets are exchanged for such loans of stock just as in the case of sales of stock. Even though such loaned or borrowed stocks create a stock balance to receive or to deliver which are settled at clearing house prices, the broker's check or draft automatically adjusts any inequalities in money arising between

[15] See Chapter IV.

the actual price at which the money loan was made, and the delivery price. Indeed, for all we can tell, some of the stocks to deliver on Jenkins and Company's sheet may really be loans of stock and some of its stocks to receive may be borrowings of stock.

Economies Obtained by the System

The tremendous saving in time, labor, and money effected by the clearance of stocks can be illustrated in no more concrete way than by reference to just such a clearance sheet as the above. On the given day the firm has bought 2,100 shares for $191,712.50 from eleven different firms, and sold 2,200 shares for $201,875.00 to eight other firms. Before the institution of the clearance system it would have required trips to nine separate offices, the receiving of eleven deliveries, the handling of 4,300 shares of stock, and the employment of $393,587.50 of credit to settle these contracts. But under the system of which the clearance sheet is the record (and even before the recent establishment of the Day Clearing Branch of the Stock Clearing Corporation), Jenkins and Company can settle the day's business by giving a check for $18,800 and getting 200 Reading, by receiving a check for $28,500 and delivering 300 Steel, and by drawing a draft against the clearing house for $462.50.

Delivery of the Clearance Sheet

Let us see by what operations the Night Clearing Branch is able to bring about these huge economies. Jenkins and Company preserves a record of the various items on its clearance sheet on what is known as its "clearing house blotter," [16] along with interest charges and other items of value to the firm but not to the Stock Clearing Corporation. The clearance sheet itself, which constitutes legal proof of delivery, is sent to the

[16] See Chapter XII.

corporation that evening. Formerly, in order to conserve valuable space, the old clearing house did not preserve these sheets, but the present Stock Clearing Corporation, partly as a result of a recommendation of the Hughes Commission,[17]

Stock Clearing Corporation Night Clearing Branch (Clearing Account) Approved Peter Brown Manager

No. 400 New York, August 3, 1920

Manhattan Company

Payable only through N. Y. Clearing House

Pay to the order of the undersigned Four Hundred Sixty Two and 50/x Dollars as advised this day by the Stock Clearing Corporation (Night Clearing Branch)

$462.50 Jenkins & Co.

Figure 25. Night Clearing Branch Draft. (Size 8½ x 3.)
Settling Jenkins and Company's account with that branch.

now retains these clearance sheets for a period of about six years. The rule is that before 7 P.M. on the day when the above transactions are made, Jenkins and Company must deliver its clearance sheet to the Night Clearing Branch of the corporation. With it is sent the firm's draft for $462.50 (Figure 25) which, as we have seen, is needed to balance the cash side of the day's business.

As shown in the illustration, this draft is drawn by Jenkins and Company against the account of the Stock Clearing Corporation in the Bank of the Manhattan Company. After all the items on the firm's clearance sheet have been audited and found correct, the manager of the corporation will sign his name under the word "Approved" in the left-hand lower corner of the draft. Jenkins and Company will get the draft back the next morning and deposit it in its own bank to its account. Later on, in the regular course of events, the proceeds of the drafts are collected through the bank clearing house.

[17] See Appendix, Chapter IX (b).

The Accompanying Exchange and Balance Tickets

With its clearance sheet Jenkins and Company also sends the eleven red-and-white selling or deliver tickets of the eleven houses which have sold stock to Jenkins and Company that day. These tickets have come to Jenkins and Company, as we have seen, through the distributing department of the Night Clearing Branch, and serve to establish the accuracy of

STOCK CLEARING CORPORATION (NIGHT CLEARING BRANCH)

THE UNDERSIGNED WILL **DELIVER** THE FOLLOWING **BALANCE** OF STOCK AT THE DELIVERY PRICE.

SHARES	STOCK	DELIVER TO	
300	U.S. Steel Com	Arnold, Mitchell & Co.	300
	95		

DATE 8/2/20 NAME Jenkins & Co. NO. 400

Figure 26. Deliver Balance Ticket. (Size 5⅝ x 3⅝.)
As at completion of clearance, with assigned "name" of Arnold, Mitchell and Company written on it.

the items on the "receive" side of Jenkins and Company's clearance sheet, since they have all originated with the firms which have sold or loaned stock to Jenkins and Company. Likewise, the latter firm sends with its clearance sheet all the black-and-yellow buying or receive tickets of the eight firms to which Jenkins and Company have sold or loaned stock that day. These tickets have also come to Jenkins and Company through the distributing department, and, since they have originated with these various buying or borrowing firms, serve to establish the accuracy of the items on the "deliver" side of Jenkins and Company's clearance sheet. Meanwhile, of course, Jenkins and Company's red-and-white deliver tickets are being similarly sent in with the clearance sheets of Wilkins and Company and the other firms which have bought or borrowed stock that day of Jenkins and Company; and the latter's black-and-

STOCK CLEARING CORPORATION (NIGHT CLEARING BRANCH)

THE UNDERSIGNED WILL **RECEIVE** THE FOLLOWING **BALANCE** OF STOCK AT THE DELIVERY PRICE.

SHARES	STOCK	RECEIVE FROM	
200	Reading 94	T. Long & Co.	200

DATE 8/2/20 NAME Jenkins & Co. No. 400

Figure 27. Receive Balance Ticket. (Size 5⅝ x 3⅝.)

As at completion of clearance, with the assigned "name" of T. Long and Company written on it.

yellow receive tickets with the clearance sheets of Jefferson and Company and the other firms which have sold or loaned stock to Jenkins and Company the same day.

In addition, Jenkins and Company make out and send to the Stock Clearing Corporation its balance tickets. These consist of two special forms, one of which (Figure 26) records the balances of stock the firm has to deliver, and the other (Figure 27) of which records the balances of stock the firm has to receive. In both cases separate balance tickets are made out for each separate stock balance. In this case, Jenkins and Company makes out one deliver balance ticket for 300 Steel, and one receive balance ticket for 200 Reading.

Final Delivery of Clearing Member's Sheet and Tickets

It is a rule of the Stock Clearing Corporation that all these clearance sheets, deliver and receive tickets, and statements of balances of stocks to receive or to deliver, as well as each firm's check or its draft on the corporation, must be turned in by the clearing member at the Night Clearing Branch by 7 P.M. This rule is sometimes relaxed by the corporation during large markets, when the preparation of clearance sheets takes more time than usual. But if there has been a delay which in the judgment of the corporation is unreasonable, the offending firm is subject to fine. Fines are also imposed by the corporation for clerical errors or omissions in either tickets or clearance sheets. The neglect or failure of a member or firm to exchange tickets, in the manner described above, constitutes a default in delivery.

Headquarters of the Night Clearing Branch

Thus far the chief stage setting of our typical daily clearance has been the brokerage office of Jenkins and Company at 500 Wall Street. But after the clearance sheet, with the appropriate check or draft, tickets, and statements, has been prepared and sent to the Stock Clearing Corporation, the part played by the brokerage office in the clearance is over for the day, and the scene shifts to the Night Clearing Branch of the Stock Clearing Corporation at 55 New Street.

The main room of this Night Clearing Branch is not especially impressive in appearance. Its back wall is penetrated by four small windows, not unlike those of a ticket office, through which brokers' clerks deliver the clearance sheets, etc., already described. In the afternoon this room, which is artificially lighted and ventilated, remains practically deserted, although some official is constantly in attendance there, day and night, to answer questions, settle disputes, etc. But by 7 P.M. an ample force of clerks arrives and their nocturnal labors begin.

The room is filled with wide tables where the clerical work connected with the clearance is done, and at 7 P.M. the clerks are usually in their places working on the clearance sheets which have already arrived. None leaves until the whole work of clearance is completed, and thus the volume of sales that day, as well as the errors which may have crept into the auditing of them, determines the hour, whether 10 P.M or far later into the night, at which the clerks can go home. A corps of specialists is also kept in reserve, to run down and eliminate any errors which may be made in the clearance. Of course, the fact that a final balance is obtained is practically proof that the clearance has been made without error.

Separation and Distribution of the Tickets

The clearance sheet of each clearing member, which by 7 P.M. is delivered by his messenger through one of the windows in the back of the Night Clearing Branch office, is, as we have seen, accompanied by a receive or a deliver ticket of another firm for each item on the sheet, the statements of stock balances to receive and deliver, and a check or draft, as the case may require. Clerks at these windows first separate the clearance sheets from the accompanying tickets and credit instruments. The exchange receive and deliver tickets are distributed in the respective boxes of the firms whence they have originated. For example, Wilkins' receive ticket for 100 Steel, which comes in attached to Jenkins' sheet, is detached and placed in Wilkins' box; and Jenkins' deliver ticket for the same stock, attached to Wilkins' sheet, is detached and placed in Jenkins' box.

Next, the statements of stock balances to receive and to deliver which accompany each sheet are checked by a teller against the balance items as they appear on the sheet, and are then turned over to another set of clerks who place each one with the particular allotment sheet (whose function will be considered presently) for the stock in which it is made out. For example, Jenkins and Company's statements that it has a balance of 300 Steel to deliver and a balance of 200 Reading to receive, are separated from its clearance sheet and placed with the two allotment sheets for Steel and for Reading respectively. Finally, the checks or drafts which are delivered at the windows with the clearance sheets are sent to a separate department.

Examination and Checking of the Clearance Sheet

After being divested of the accompanying exchange and balance tickets, checks, and drafts, the clearance sheets are taken in charge by the examiner, who inspects their delivery prices, the cash extensions, and the totals of the stock items. If a sheet is incorrect in any respect, the error is run down and eliminated without delay; if correct, the clearance sheet receives the mark of the examiner after the "EXD" at its top and then passes onward to the checker.

Meanwhile, all the exchange tickets which came in the four windows with the sheets of other firms have been resorted and placed in the boxes of the firms whence they have originated. Hence, when Jenkins and Company's clearance sheet passes from the examiner to the checker, the latter can obtain all the receive and deliver exchange tickets sent out that day by Jenkins and Company. These tickets the checker uses to check against the items on the clearance sheet. For example, he obtains Jenkins' deliver ticket for 100 Steel from Jenkins' box, where it has been placed after being detached from Wilkins' sheet. So it is, too, with all the other receive and deliver

U.S. STEEL COMMON — BALANCES — August 3, 1920

NO.	SHARES		WILL RECEIVE	NO.	SHARES		WILL DELIVER		
1 ✓		400	L. A. Smith & Co.	1		300	Jenkins & Co.	6	
2 ✓		200	Whiting, Todd & Co.	2		200	Le Mar, Burk & Co.	2	
3 ✓		100	E. A. Wilson & Co.	3		100	D. S. Cook & Co.	3	
4 ✓		200	Lee, Tuttle & Co.	4		300	B. P. Robinson & Co.	4	5
5 ✓		100	Johnson, Williams & Co.	5		300	Fisher, Carrington & Co.	1	
6 ✓		300	Arnold, Mitchell & Co.	6		100	C. W. Green & Co.	1	
7				7					
8				8					
9	1	300		9	1	300			
10				10					
11				11					
47				47					
48				48					
49				49					
50				50					

Called by 3 ✓

Checked by 5 ✓

Figure 28. The Allotment Sheet. (Size 12 x 18½.)

The Steel sheet, showing Jenkins and Company's balance of 300 shares to deliver, and number (6) of the firm "name" assigned to it.

tickets which have originated with Jenkins and Company. In this way each stock item on every clearance sheet is checked against the appropriate deliver or receive exchange ticket, and another opportunity to detect any errors or omissions in the sheet is thus obtained. When the checker finishes with each clearance sheet he indicates the fact by leaving his mark after the "CKD" at its top. The termination of checking the sheet marks the point at which the settlement of the intermediate contracts which it records is effected. In Jenkins and Company's sheet, for example, the intermediate contracts for 600 Rubber, 800 Reading, and 500 Steel are thus settled and cleared.

Handling of Checks and Drafts

Meanwhile, in another department the checks turned in with the clearance sheets are added up in a summarized statement. The same is done with the drafts on the Stock Clearing Corporation. The total amount of checks should, of course, always exactly equal the total amount of the drafts. If these totals do not prove by thus balancing each other, it is apparent that an error has been made somewhere, and the clerical force is at once set to work to hunt it down and eliminate it. Fines are levied by the Stock Clearing Corporation in small but by no means negligible amounts upon such clearing members as are guilty of errors or omissions in the preparation of their sheets, tickets, statements, drafts, or checks.

The Allotment Sheet

We must now see how it is that the Night Clearing Branch supervises the delivery of stock balances. It will be recalled that when each clearing member's clearance sheet comes in at the windows, the statements of stock balances to receive and to deliver are detached from it and distributed among the allotment sheets. Every stock which is cleared has its particular allotment sheet; active stocks have each a whole sheet, while several only fairly active stocks may be recorded on one sheet.

The clearance of Liberty bonds is conducted exactly as the clearance of stocks, although in a separate part of the Night Clearing Branch office, and, of course, with separate clearance sheets for the several Liberty issues.

In order to pursue further the sale made by Jenkins to Wilkins, the accompanying illustration of an allotment sheet (Figure 28) has been made out for Steel—the stock in which their bargain has occurred. Since there must always be two parties to every sale—a purchaser and a seller—it necessarily follows that for every 100 shares of stock to be delivered there must be an equal amount of the same stock to be received. Consequently, the total of the stock balances of Steel to be received (recorded on the left side of the allotment sheet) must always exactly equal the total of the stock balances of Steel to be delivered (recorded on its right side). It is, therefore, simplicity itself to find a buying firm or firms to which the stock balances of each selling firm can be delivered. Thus the allotment clerk directs our friends, Jenkins and Company, with a balance of 300 shares, to deliver them to Arnold, Mitchell and Company, who have to receive just that amount. Similarly, he directs Le Mar, Burke and Company to deliver 200 shares to Whiting, Todd and Company; D. S. Cooke and Company to deliver 100 shares to E. A. Wilson and Company; B. P. Robinson and Company to deliver 200 shares to Lee, Tuttle and Company and 100 shares to Johnson, Williams and Company; and Fisher, Carrington and Company to deliver its 300 shares, and C. W. Green and Company its 100 shares, to L. A. Smith and Company.

"Giving a Name"

At the completion of this simple process of allotting deliverable stocks to firms who have stocks to receive, it only remains for the night branch clerks to fill in the blanks on the statements of stock balances to receive and to deliver. We have seen that Jenkins and Company turned in with its clearance sheet one statement that it had 200 shares of Reading to receive, and another that it had 300 shares of Steel to deliver. Since Jenkins and Company could not tell to what firm the allotment clerk would direct it to deliver the stock balance in Steel, or from what firm to receive the stock balance in Reading, it put only its own name on the two statements. We have seen how all the stock balances in Steel for that day have been allotted. A similar process of allotment has meanwhile been completed in Reading. The clerk has only to place on Jenkins and Company's statement of stock to deliver the name of Arnold, Mitchell and Company under the "Deliver to" column, and on its statement of stock to receive, the name of some firm determined by the clerk of the Reading allotment sheet—say, T. Long and Company—under the "Receive from" column. In addition, if Jenkins and Company should have a balance of $10,000 Third 4¼ Liberty bonds to receive, through the same process of allotment it would be "given a name"—say that of Royce and Company—from whom it could expect to obtain them on the next day.

Conclusion of the Night Clearance

When all stock balances have been allotted and all the statements of stock balances to receive and deliver have been "given a name" in the manner described above, that evening's clearance is completed and the clerks can start homeward through the dark and deserted canyons of the Wall Street district.

The next morning at 9 A.M. the messenger of each clearing member calls at the Night Clearing Branch and is given back through the windows his firm's statements of stock balances to receive and to deliver, with the names of the firms from whom it has to receive and to whom it has to deliver the stock balances, before 2:15 P.M. that day. But the exact way in which these physical deliveries of securities are made, as we shall see in the next chapter,[18] is largely conditioned by the operations of the Day Clearing Branch.

Depositing Checks and Approving Drafts

Meanwhile the department of the Night Clearing Branch that supervises the checks and drafts sent to it makes out a summarized deposit slip for all checks received the previous evening. Certification is obtained on all checks over $500 and the entire number of checks is then deposited in the Bank of the Manhattan Company. The accuracy of all drafts against the Night Clearing Branch of the Stock Clearing Corporation, which have been also turned in the previous evening by clearing members, is proved. As stated, the total amount of the drafts must exactly equal the total amount of the checks.

It only remains for the manager of the Night Clearing Branch to approve the drafts by signing them in the space on the left-hand side provided for that purpose, and at 12 M. each noon they are given out to messengers of the clearing firms, who call for them. The firms deposit the drafts to their own accounts in their banks, who collect the proceeds from the Bank of the Manhattan Company through the bank clearing house. Thus all the funds deposited in this bank on a given day's clearance by the Night Clearing Branch are withdrawn by these drafts for the same day. After this the Night Clearing Branch is largely deserted until late in the afternoon, when the current day's clearance begins to demand another repetition of the branch's swift and efficient routine.

Although the operations of the Night Clearing Branch constitute today only a part of the work of clearance performed by the Stock Clearing Corporation, nevertheless before continuing into its subsequent efforts it would be well to gain a

[18] See Chapter X.

clear idea of the achievements of its original and fundamental branch. These have already been explained in the beginning of the present chapter, where the aims and purposes leading to the creation of the old clearing house were outlined. Nevertheless the latter's economic services are sufficiently important to merit a fuller exposition.

Savings in Banking Accommodation

First and most important, of course, has been the large saving effected in the banking accommodation employed. Statistics compiled over a period of years[19] go to show that about 90 per cent of the total sales made on the Stock Exchange have been cleared; and that of this 90 per cent, about 60 per cent represented intermediate contracts which have been settled by the old clearing house (or the present Night Clearing Branch) without the need of any banking accommodation, equivalent to their cash amounts. In other words, a saving in banking accommodation amounting to about 60 per cent has been effected by the operation of the clearing house.

Not only has this huge saving of bank credit been beneficial both to banks as lenders and to Stock Exchange houses as borrowers, but it has also prevented the stock market from being warped out of its proper position by current conditions in the money market. Thus the whole machinery of the Stock Exchange has been rendered more flexible and independent of the money market, and better able to render all its listed securities instantly negotiable at the fairest possible prices, by the broad and continuous market which by this and other means it has been able to maintain.

Economies in Time and Labor.

Secondly, the clearance system has produced a vast saving of time not only through its settlement of intermediate con-

[19] See Appendix, Chapter IX (c).

tracts but also in its supervision of the deliveries of stocks on balance and the payment for them. As this and subsequent chapters show, the work of the Stock Exchange system is arranged according to a time schedule, which is severely limited by the daily settlement system employed. In the large markets which the growth of the United States has produced since 1900 it would have been a physical impossibility, without the clearance system, to complete deliveries by 2:15 the following day. During the past two decades in which American business has experienced its astonishing growth, the clearance of stocks has prevented a breakdown in the stock market, just as the clearance of checks by the bank clearing house has prevented a breakdown in the money market.

A third service rendered by the clearance of stocks is the equally important saving of *labor*—not merely on the part of clerks and messengers but also on the part of firm members themselves. After the fairly detailed descriptions already given of the different ways in which clearing house and ex-clearing house stock contracts are settled, this service should be sufficiently evident to need no further comment. But in addition the old clearing house (and present Night Clearing Branch) has served to lessen the work in commission houses by the central audit it performs in each day's cleared transactions. Lacking this central audit, the bookkeeping and clerical work in brokerage offices would be much greater.

An Added Safeguard to Exchange Contracts

Finally, the Night Clearing Branch imparts a greater degree of security to the whole stock market. Every contract in a cleared stock is carefully examined and its swift and accurate settlement is enforced. Thus, not only are the chances for clerical errors or omissions practically eliminated but the inviolacy of all contracts made in cleared securities on the floor of the Exchange can be more readily maintained.

Elasticity of the Clearance Process

So flexible is this system of settling intermediate contracts that the volume of sales on the Exchange seems to place no practical limit upon it. The heaviest day's trading that ever occurred on the Exchange was on the panic day of May 9, 1901, which aggregated 3,336,695 shares. Yet on the following day clearance occurred in the regular way as follows:

Shares cleared both sides, including balances..........	12,131,600
Total value both sides, contracts and balances..........	$961,300,000
Share balances one side..............................	1,714,800
Value share balances one side..........................	$129,800,000
Cash balances one side................................	$ 5,461,700
Number of parties clearing...........................	452
Bank certification obviated...........................	$221,050,000

The heaviest clearance ever effected in a single day occurred on Monday, May 6, 1901, when the transactions of Friday the 3rd and Saturday the 4th were cleared together. In this record clearance, the shares cleared both sides totaled 13,313,-800, and possessed a cash value of $1,132,200,000. Bank accommodation and certification amounting to $286,100,000 was obviated. The largest elimination of certification for transactions occurring on a single day was made on December 18, 1916, and amounted to $227,000,000.

For steady pressure the record year was 1919, when the unprecedented total of 307,889,450 shares were reported sold on the New York Stock Exchange. Yet never once did its clearance machinery even falter. The old clearing house has handled as many as 100,000 separate items in a single day, while the largest single broker's sheet ever cleared by it contained 1,868 separate items.

Facts Regarding Clearance and Settlement of Security Contracts

This process of settling intermediate contracts which the Night Clearing Branch performs as an agent for its members has sometimes bewildered writers and commentators upon finance, since it cannot be visualized as readily as direct deliveries and payments. Occasionally, indeed, the perennial critics of everything financial have declared that such cleared contracts were illegal because they did not result in direct deliveries of securities and payments of money. Even in the narrower and legal aspect of the matter, however, the courts have held that contracts which show an intent to deliver are legal. That cleared contracts in Stock Exchange securities show such an intent to deliver is at once obvious to anyone who will read a typical clearance sheet with its exchange deliver and receive tickets. An authority in economic matters has said: [20]

> There is no such thing known on any of the reputable exchanges as a contract under which delivery is waived: one obstacle to an understanding of this lies in the way in which transactions are cleared through the Clearing House; but an attempt to prove the legitimacy of the method of clearing would be useless to one who does not understand the way in which bank transactions, for instance, are cleared. It is as ridiculous to say that the clearing of many contracts for delivery on the Stock Exchange, and the settlement of these transactions by a payment of balances, both of stocks and cash, indicates that such transactions are not of a perfectly genuine nature as it is to assert that because the Clearing House for the New York banks arranges for an offset of checks and the payment of only a small balance of cash, therefore, the banking business in New York is not concerned with legitimate business. Speculation could continue without a Clearing House, and in fact, the New York Stock Exchange was very late in adopting this device. Nothing as to the legitimacy or illegitimacy of transactions can be determined from the mere adoption of an up-to-date business method.

The clearance of contracts must, therefore, be looked upon as one of the great inventions of the past century, effecting as

---

[20] H. C. Emery, "Should Speculation be Regulated by Law?" in *Journal of Accountancy*, Apr. 1908.

it does an economy of time, labor, and capital in the major market places of the modern world. For all its technical terminology and its clerical detail, it is based on the simplest common sense principles. Without the employment of these principles by the banks and the security and wholesale commodity markets, the conduct of modern production and distribution with the present ease, safety, and efficiency would be an utter impossibility.

CHAPTER X

THE DAY CLEARING BRANCH

Creation of the Stock Clearing Corporation

From 1892 until 1920 the only clearance employed in Stock Exchange transactions was confined to the clearing of stocks by the old clearing house, whose present operations were described in the preceding chapter. The tremendous strain upon American credit facilities experienced during and after the Great War, however, provided the occasion for a further expansion of the Stock Exchange's clearance system so as to include the clearance of the cash values of security balances and of shifted security loans as well.

This step compelled far-reaching changes in the entire clearance system, which was accordingly organized as a corporation under the name of the "Stock Clearing Corporation," with a capital of $500,000. This corporation is in no sense a bank but simply a credit agency designed to effect the clearance of sales and loans on securities, for such members as choose to belong to it, with the maximum safety, speed, and economy. There are at present about 380 of these clearing members. The funds of the Clearing Corporation, which are deposited as an ever-liquid fund, payable on demand, in such banking establishments as ordinarily handle brokers' accounts, are provided from the clearing fund, to which clearing members of the Stock Exchange contribute in proportion to the extent to which they employ the corporation's services. The clearing fund at present amounts to over ten millions and carries with it an assessable liability of 100 per cent on the part of every clearing member. A clearance charge is made on the money value of such securities as are cleared, and this revenue pays all the expenses of the corporation, all of whose stock is owned by the Stock Exchange.

The work of this Stock Clearing Corporation is performed by two almost separate branches. One, the Night Clearing Branch, is, as we have seen, the former and original clearing house, which has been rechristened and modified in unimportant details to fit into the present and more inclusive clearance system. The other, known as the "Day Clearing Branch," is an almost new but highly successful mechanism, which has been designed after an extensive technical study of the leading European clearance systems and which represents a combination, well adapted to American conditions, of the best features of the foreign clearing houses. It derives its name from the fact that, unlike the Night Clearing Branch, all its work is performed in the daytime between 9 A.M and 5 P.M. Its operations date from April 26, 1920.

Quarters of the Day Clearing Branch

The Day Clearing Branch is housed in the basement of the Stock Exchange building, under the floor on which trading takes place. Its quarters consist of a single large room, fringed on three sides by rows of cages, each of which is occupied by a representative of one of the large New York banking institutions which loan money on call. The operations which take place in these bankers' cages will be described in the next chapter. The center of the room is occupied by a hollow square formed by the ten large cages in which the accounts of Exchange members who employ the Stock Clearing Corporation are kept. Inside this square are the managerial offices of the Day Clearing Branch. In one corner of the room is a separate cage for the distributing department, with a special entrance on Broad Street for the messengers of clearing members who come to deliver or receive the tickets employed in the work of clearance. The two main entrances to the Day

Clearing Branch on Broad and on New Streets are closely guarded, and the whole office is equipped with the most modern and complete protective devices.

Functions of Night and Day Clearing Branches Compared

In comparison with the Night Clearing Branch, which, as we have seen in the preceding chapter, clears only intermediary transactions in stocks on the basis of delivery prices, the Day Clearing Branch is complex and difficult for beginners to comprehend. Not only are its operations in themselves more delicate and more complicated, but their scope is wider, since the Day Clearing Branch clears not only the cash equivalents of these stock balances to receive or to deliver which result from the work of the Night Clearing Branch, but also loans based upon security collateral. Because of the intricate and technical nature of each of these operations, a separate chapter must be devoted to each of these two different functions of the Day Clearing Branch. Accordingly, the clearance of cash balances will be described here, and the clearance of loans will be left for the next chapter.

The Clearance of Cash Extensions of Security Balances

In respect to this clearance of cash balances we must for the moment linger on a practical example. Returning again to the inevitable Jenkins and Company, it will be recalled that at the end of a typical day's clearance of the firm's transactions by the Night Clearing Branch [1] this firm found itself with a stock balance of 300 Steel to deliver and a stock balance of 200 Reading to receive. Since delivery prices that day were 95 for Steel and 94 for Reading, it is obvious that Jenkins and Company must obtain $28,500 for the 300 Steel it must deliver, and pay out $18,800 for the 200 Reading it must receive. Now it is impossible to effect any further economies in the process

[1] See Chapter IX, page 220.

of delivery by balancing different stocks, for the same reason (to use a familiar school arithmetic example) that one cannot add pears and apples. But with the cash extensions of these different stock balances it is a different matter. By their clearance, instead of receiving $28,500 and paying out $18,800 (thus employing $47,300 of bank credit), the whole settlement might be affected by offsetting the two cash extensions and enabling Jenkins and Company to obtain the balance of $9,700.

To anyone who has read the preceding chapter it will be obvious that such a balancing of cash extensions should result in a further saving of banking accommodation, as well as in time and labor, and, as will presently be seen, such is actually the case with operations as they are at present conducted by the Day Clearing Branch. The illustrations of the various documents of the latter organization in this chapter have, as in the previous instance of the Night Clearing Branch, been made out for the typical case of Jenkins and Company, already cited.[2]

Routine of the Day Clearing Branch

Before proceeding into the wonderfully elaborate and flexible system which the Day Clearing Branch provides for the clearance of these cash balances, however, the author must apologize to the lay reader for again plunging him headforemost into a new and still more formidable array of tickets, ledgers, and specialized bookkeeping. Yet the principles involved in this additional clearing process are simple enough, particularly if the background of the Night Clearing Branch is kept clearly in mind.

The daily operations of the Day Clearing Branch with respect to the clearance of cash balances will therefore be described from their beginning at about 9 A.M. to their con-

[2] See Chapter IX.

clusion about 5 P.M. Each successive step necessitated by the work will be numbered, both for the sake of clarity and to make cross-referencing easier.

1. At 9 each morning the clearing member sends his messenger to the Night Clearing Branch and obtains there the statements, prepared by that branch the previous evening, of

STOCK CLEARING CORPORATION
(DAY CLEARING BRANCH)

No. 400
(Clearing Member)
CONTINGENT CREDIT TICKET for value of Security Balance orders to Deliver as per Night Clearing Sheets dated Aug. 3, '20
NAME OF FIRM Jenkins & Co.

	DELIVER TO	Shares or Bonds		Securities	Del'y Price	VALUE STOCKS		√	VALUE BONDS		√
1	Arnold, Mitchell	3	00	U.S. Steel Com	95	28	500	✓			
2											
21											
22											
	TOTALS ~~Bonds~~ Shares					28	500				

Figure 29. Itemzied Credit Ticket of the Day Clearing Branch.
(Size 8 x 9½.)

Recording the $28,500 to be credited to Jenkins and Company, when it delivers 300 Steel to Arnold, Mitchell and Company.

the security balances which he has to deliver and receive that day as a result of his transactions on the Exchange on the previous day.

From these Night Branch statements of security balances the clearing member then fills out two forms, viz:

2. An itemized list, on a white form ruled in red (Figure 29), of the security balances in the various securities which he has to deliver. This form authorizes the Day Clearing Branch to credit his account at the Stock Clearing Corporation with the total value (at delivery prices) of all the balances of stocks or of bonds which he has to deliver, contingent upon their delivery. Balances in bonds are less common than in stocks.

3. An itemized list, on a white form ruled in black (Figure 30), of the various security balances which he has to receive. This form authorizes the Day Clearing Branch to charge his

STOCK CLEARING CORPORATION
(DAY CLEARING BRANCH)

No. 400
(Clearing Member)
CONTINGENT DEBIT TICKET for value of Security Balance orders to Deliver as per Night Clearing Sheets dated August 3, 1920
NAME OF FIRM Jenkins & Co.

	RECEIVE FROM	Shares or Bonds		Securities	Del'y Price	VALUE STOCKS		√	VALUE BONDS			√
1	T. Long & Co.	2	00	Reading Com	94	18	800	√				
2												
21												
22												
	TOTALS ~~Bonds~~ Shares					18	800					

Figure 30. Itemized Charge Ticket of the Day Clearing Branch. (Size 8 x 9½.)

Recording the $18,800 to be charged to Jenkins and Company on its receipt of 200 Reading from T. Long and Company.

account at the Stock Clearing Corporation with the total value (at delivery prices) of all security balances which he has to receive, upon their actual receipt.

Description of the Itemized Lists

These itemized lists (2 and 3) bridge over the gap between the Night and Day Clearing Branches, since they enable the latter to begin its work of handling those stock balances which resulted from the operations of the Night Branch.[3] One side of the itemized list forms reproduces the items on the clearing member's blotter, in respect to his clearing house stock balances to deliver or to receive. Each separate stock balance placed upon the itemized list is assigned the same numbered line as it occupies on the member's blotter. In this way reference can

[3] See Chapter IX, page 227.

conveniently be made to any stock balance by simply giving this "blotter line number," as it is usually called. Not only the name and number of the shares in every stock balance must be recorded on the itemized list, but also their value in each case, and to whom or from whom they are to be delivered or received. The itemized lists are consequently an exact recapitulation of the stock balances entered on the member's blotter from the statements of stock balances to receive and to deliver which he has previously received from the Night Clearing Branch.

On the other side of both itemized list forms, the clearing member must pledge to the Stock Clearing Corporation the stocks mentioned on the reverse side of the ticket to secure payment to the corporation of such amounts as may be due to it from the clearing member during the process of clearing his account that day. Bonds are handled in the same way as stocks but the transactions are entered upon separate itemized list forms.

Division of the Work Among the Cages

4. These two tickets (which because they originate outside the Stock Clearing Corporation are commonly known as "outside forms") are then dispatched by an identified party to the office of the Day Clearing Branch, and delivered there at the particular cage where the account of the clearing member in question is kept. As already stated, there are ten of these cages, with a capacity of 60 accounts apiece, or a total of 600 clearing members. At present, however, there are about 380 clearing members. This work is divided among the cages so that each cage will have about the same amount of work, but not necessarily one-tenth of the total number of accounts. If the given member's clearing number is 45, his tickets will be delivered to the cage handling accounts 1–60; if it is 250, to that handling accounts 240–300, etc. All these tickets should

be delivered to the Stock Clearing Corporation in this wav not later than 10 A.M.

The Control or Record Sheet

5. The record clerk, or "third teller," in the cage then copies the total cash values of the stock balances which each firm expects to receive and deliver that day, from the firm's itemized lists (2 and 3) to its control or "record" sheet (Figure 31). The control sheet of every member's account is ruled into five vertical columns, the first two columns being for its

STOCK CLEARING CORPORATION (DAY CLEARING BRANCH)

No. 400 Jenkins & Co. Name of Clearing Member

Contingent Dr.		Contingent Cr.		Actual Dr.		Actual Cr.		Value of Securities obtained from S.C.C. for Del. of Security Balance		Recd.	Time Deld. to S.C.C.
18 800	00	28500	00	18 800	00						
						28500	00				
18 800	00	28500	00	18 800	00	28 500	00				
9700				9700							
28500		28500		28500		28500					

Figure 31. Record Sheet. (Size 9 x 9.)

Account of Jenkins and Company after it has delivered 300 Steel and received 200 Reading.

contingent debits and credits, and the second two for its actual debits and credits. The fifth column may for the present be disregarded.[4] The value of the balances of stock which the member must deliver that day is entered on his control sheet as a contingent credit, while that of those which he must receive is entered as a contingent debit. Since no actual stock deliveries have as yet been made, only these contingent columns can be filled at this time.

[4] See Chapter XI, page 278.

Entry of Contingent Debits and Credits

6. The record clerk enters the total of the values carried on the itemized lists (see 2 and 3) in the contingent columns of the control sheet (see 5), and then turns them over to another clerk who compares the entries on the itemized lists with that member's Night Clearing Branch balances shown on his clearance sheet. These latter sheets (described in the preceding chapter) are delivered by the Night Clearing Branch to the Day Clearing Branch about 9 A.M. each clearing day. This comparison, and the adjustment of any differences which may be found, together with the operations of the proof department presently to be described in section 9, furnishes evidence to the Day Clearing Branch that the receipt and delivery of the securities which appear on the itemized lists will complete the contracts made in the Exchange on the previous day.

7. The two outside forms of each clearing member are then filed in the rack of post-office boxes in each cage, in the pigeonhole which bears the given member's clearing number.

8. From the figures contained on the itemized lists which it has received, each cage next prepares a special sheet containing a record of all stock balances contingently deliverable and receivable, as well as the cash extensions which these stock balances represent, on the accounts of *all* the firms handled in that cage. This sheet is then sent to the proof department.

Work of the Proof Department

9. The proof department, on the receipt of these ten sheets from all ten cages, adds up the total stock balances and their cash equivalents. In this way is obtained the total number of shares in the stock balances to be delivered and received, as well as the total amounts to be paid out and taken in upon them by *all* the clearing members. Total stock balances to be delivered should equal total stock balances to be received,[5] and

[5] See Chapter IX, page 234.

the total cash value of the one should equal the total cash value of the other. In case both these two total stock items and these two total cash items balance, they "prove" at once the accuracy of the outside forms (2 and 3) sent to the Day Clearing Branch by the clearing members. On the other hand, in case such a balance is not struck, an opportunity is afforded the Day Clearing Branch to inform the clearing members responsible for such clerical or other errors which may have caused the trouble and obtain corrected forms from them. Of course, the Stock Clearing Corporation cannot undertake to make corrections of any kind on its own responsibility. But through its proof department the corporation is able to obtain correct tickets from its members before the actual work of clearance begins.

Summarized Principles of Succeeding Operations

10. The Day Clearing Branch is now ready to proceed with clearing the payments which must be made on stock balances, with a fair idea of the accommodation which this operation will require. The actual delivery of the stock balances is made between members directly, between 10 A.M. and 2:15 P.M. The firm which makes a delivery of a stock balance, instead of demanding a check for it from the receiving member, obtains a receipt for the delivery, which when presented at the Stock Clearing Corporation gives him an immediate credit on the books of the Stock Clearing Corporation for the value of the stock balance delivered. On the other hand, the firm which has a stock balance delivered to it, is by the same means debited for its value at the Stock Clearing Corporation, instead of having to pay out a check to the delivering member on receipt of the stock. At the end of the day the Stock Clearing Corporation balances each clearing member's debits and credits, and pays the members who have a credit balance on its books with the funds it obtains from members who have a debit balance on its

Blotter Line No. 27
(Receiving Member)

Blotter Line No. 1
(Delivering Member)

Stock Clearing Corporation
(DAY CLEARING BRANCH)
DELIVERY TICKET

Clearing No. 400
(Of Delivering Member)

Jenkins & Co.
(Name of Delivering Member)

Time Received by S.C.C.

RECEIVED
STOCK CLEARING CORP.
AUG. 3 1920 12 25 P.M.

Do not use CARBON ON THIS STUB as name and number will conflict.

Blotter Line No. 1 (Delivering Member) CREDIT TICKET Blotter Line No. 27 (Receiving Member)

STOCK CLEARING CORPORATION
(DAY CLEARING BRANCH)

Clearing No. 400 (Of Delivering Member) NEW YORK, August 3, 1920

Delivered to Arnold, Mitchell & Co.

Credit the value of the following Securities to the account of Jenkins & Co.

300 Shares ~~Bonds~~ U. S. Steel Com. @ 95 $ 28,500.00

On Stock Clearing Corporation Security Balance order.

Delivered by them and Received by the undersigned subject to the rules of the Stock Clearing Corporation.

Arnold, Mitchell & Co. 420
(Signature and Clearing Number of the Receiving Member)

Total Delivery
Delivered
Bal. to Deliver

Numbers of Certificates ~~or Bonds~~	TIME RECEIVED
27014 31672 51726	RECEIVED ARNOLD, MITCHELL & CO. AUG. 3 1920 12 20 P.M.

Figure 32. (a) Deliver Credit Ticket of the Day Clearing Branch. (Size 9 x 6.)

As it appears after Jenkins and Company has delivered 300 Steel to Arnold, Mitchell and Company, and has turned in the ticket to the Stock Clearing Corporation.

books. These operations, beginning, of course, with the deliveries of stock balances between members, are conducted as follows:

The Credit and Charge Tickets

11. First of all clearing members with a stock balance to deliver make out a form consisting of: (a) a credit and (b) a charge ticket (Figures 32a and b), each of which has a detachable stub. A carbon sheet is placed under (a) so that (b) is made out simultaneously, thus avoiding the chance of any discrepancy between the credit and charge tickets, and incidentally saving time for the receiving member. On the detachable stubs to both tickets, the delivering member fills out in the indicated place the line number of his blotter (and, of course, on his itemized lists) which the stock balance mentioned in the credit and charge tickets—(a) and (b)—represents, as well as his name and his clearing number.

12. The credit ticket, (a), constitutes both a receipt by the receiving member for the delivering member's stock, and an order by the receiving member to the Stock Clearing Corporation, to credit the delivering member's account with the value of the stock balance delivered. The delivering member also writes in his clearing number and his blotter line number for the stock balance in question.

13. The charge ticket, (b), will also become the acknowledgment of the receiving member for the stock balance which he has to receive, and in addition an order by the receiving member on the Stock Clearing Corporation to charge or debit his account with the value of the stock balance which he receives but does not immediately pay for himself.

14. After filling out both (a) and (b) and their stubs so far as possible, the delivering member sends them to the office of the receiving member, together with the actual stock certificates involved by the delivery.

Blotter Line No. 27
(Receiving Member)

Blotter Line No. 1
(Delivering Member)

Stock Clearing Corporation
(DAY CLEARING BRANCH)
RECEIVE TICKET

Clearing No. 420
(Of Receiving Member)

Arnold, Mitchell & Co.
(Name of Receiving Member)

Time Received by S.C.C.

RECEIVED
STOCK CLEARING CORP.
AUG. 3 1920 12 25 P.M.

Do not use CARBON ON THIS STUB as name and number will conflict.

Blotter Line No. 1 (Delivering Member) **CHARGE TICKET** Blotter Line No. 27 (Receiving Member)

STOCK CLEARING CORPORATION
(DAY CLEARING BRANCH)

Clearing No. 400 (Of Delivering Member) NEW YORK, August 3, 1920

Received by Arnold, Mitchell & Co.

The undersigned hereby acknowledges Receipt of the following Securities subject to the rules of the Stock Clearing Corporation FROM Jenkins & Co.

300 Shares ~~Bonds~~ U.S. Steel Com. @ 95 $ 28,500.00

On Stock Clearing Corporation Security Balance order.
VALUE OF WHICH CHARGE TO OUR ACCOUNT.

Arnold, Mitchell & Co. 420
(Signature and Clearing Number of the Receiving Member)

Total Delivery
Delivered
Bal. to Deliver

Numbers of Certificates ~~or Bonds~~	TIME RECEIVED
27014 31672 51726	RECEIVED ARNOLD, MITCHELL & CO. AUG. 3 1920 12 20 P.M.

Figure 32. (b) Deliver Charge Ticket of the Day Clearing Branch. (Size 9 x 6.)
Carbon copy of Figure 32a except for stub.

Delivery of the Security Balances

15. The receiving member examines the stock certificates to be sure that they are as represented on the tickets and constitute a good delivery. He next writes on the credit and charge tickets—(a) and (b)—the numbers of the certificates, and his debit to the Stock Clearing Corporation created by his receipt of the certificates. He then signs credit and charge tickets—(a) and (b)—as a receipt for the stock certificates which he has just received, and as an order on the Stock Clearing Corporation to credit the account of the delivering member with the value of the securities delivered, and to charge his own account with the value of the securities he has received. He enters on the tickets and stubs the line number where the given stock balances appear as items on his blotter, as well as his own clearing number, and stamps both forms with a time clock, since the amount of money represented by the delivery of stock is from that time on an accommodation given him by the Stock Clearing Corporation. For this reason he does not make payment with his check for the stock he receives.

16. The credit and charge tickets—(a) and (b)—are then returned by the receiving member to the delivering member's messenger, who next takes them to the window of the receiving department of the Day Clearing Branch at 14 Broad Street. Here the tickets are separated from their stubs along the perforated line of the form.

17. The stub of the credit ticket, (a), after the time of its arrival at the Stock Clearing Corporation has been stamped upon it, is then returned to the messenger, who carries it back to the delivering member's office, as a memorandum proving that the stock balance which he had to deliver has been received by the receiving member, and that its value has been credited to his (the deliverer's) account at the Stock Clearing Corporation.

18. The stamped stub of the charge ticket, (b), bearing

record of the same stock delivery and the resulting debit of the receiving member at the Stock Clearing Corporation, is held by the latter for delivery to the receiving member, if he cares to call for it. In practice, few receiving members take the trouble to collect these charge ticket stubs from the Stock Clearing Corporation, since they already have in their possession the actual stock involved.

Separation and Distribution of Credit and Charge Tickets

19. Credit and charge tickets—(a) and (b)—still unseparated, are next delivered by the distributing department of the Day Clearing Branch, to the particular cage where the account of the delivering member is kept. The clerk in this cage in charge of this account examines the credit and charge tickets —(a) and (b)—to see that they correspond in all respects, and then separates the two tickets by tearing the form along its perforated line. The red-and-white credit ticket, (a), is retained in the cage of the delivering member, while the black-and-white charge ticket, (b), is sent to the cage where the receiving member's account is kept.

Function of the Zone Sheets

20. The next step is to enter the value of the stock balances which have been actually delivered and received in the way shown above (see 11 to 19) upon the zone sheets of the delivering and receiving members. These zone sheets are ruled according to the daily hours of 10 to 11:30, 11:30 to 12:30, 12:30 to 1:30, and 1:30 to 2:30. There are two of these zone sheets for each clearing member; on one of them, printed in red on white (Figure 33), the value of the stock balances which the member has delivered and with which his account is accordingly credited, is entered as soon as the red-and-white credit ticket, (a), is delivered at the cage where his account is kept, in the appropriate hourly column; on the other hand, the value of a

stock balance which the member has received is similarly entered on the other zone sheet, printed in black on white (Figure 34). These zone sheets enable the corporation to tell at any moment during the day exactly what proportion of a

STOCK CLEARING CORPORATION
(DAY CLEARING BRANCH)

Jenkins & Co. DELIVER TICKET

August 3 1920

11 30		12 30		1 30		2 30	
		28500	00				
		28600	00				

Figure 33. Zone Credit Slip. (Size 6 x 9.)

Showing that Jenkins and Company has delivered a security balance and received a credit of $28,500 between 11:30 A.M. and 12:30 P.M.

STOCK CLEARING CORPORATION
(DAY CLEARING BRANCH)

Jenkins & Co. RECEIVE TICKET

August 3 1920

11 30		12 30		1 30		2 30	
18800	00						
18800	00						

Figure 34. Zone Charge Slip. (Size 6 x 9.)

Showing that Jenkins and Company has received a security balance and has been debited for $18,800 between 10 A.M. and 11:30 A.M.

member's contingent deliveries of stock have up to that time been actually delivered, and hence, the amount of credit established by each member through the stock deliveries he has made, as well as the amount of his debits through stock balances he has received.

Establishment of Actual Debits and Credits

21. We must now refer back to the clearing member's control sheet mentioned in 5. We have seen that the stock balances which the member is due to receive and deliver are at the beginning of the day entered on his control sheet as contingent credits and debits, respectively. We have also seen (see 20) that an immediate record of stock balances which he actually receives and delivers are kept in hourly columns on his two zone sheets. At 11:30, 12:30, 1:30, and 2:30—the end of these hourly periods—the record clerk enters the total value of stock balances received or delivered by the given clearing member during the preceding hour, from the zone sheets upon the member's control sheet. Stock balances delivered are entered as actual credits, and stock balances received are entered as actual debits.

Thus the Stock Clearing Corporation, when it obtains evidence from the receipt of the credit and charge tickets—(a) and (b)—that a given stock balance has been delivered by one member and received by another, at once debits the receiver's account and credits the deliverer's account, for its value. Meanwhile the receiver has not had to give his check to the deliverer for the stock balance, but instead of giving and receiving such a check the two respective parties accept a debit and a credit entry on their accounts at the Stock Clearing Corporation.

Accommodation Allowed to Clearing Members

22. The amount of daily accommodation allowed to each clearing member by the corporation during the process of

clearing his account is recorded at the top of his control sheet at the beginning of the day. The amount of accommodation permitted in each case depends upon the sum contributed by the given member to the clearing fund. The sum is determined by the member's requirements. The minimum contribution to the clearing fund is $10,000.

If, as a result of his receiving his stock balances early in the day but being slow to deliver them, a member begins to employ a large amount of accommodation at the Stock Clearing Corporation, the latter is, by the record on his zone sheets, able to tell how long he is using such accommodation, and to demand of the member in question that he either hasten his own deliveries of stock, in order to create credits on his account and thus reduce the amount of his indebtedness, or else send to the Stock Clearing Corporation his check for the amount by which the accommodation he is employing exceeds the amount of accommodation allowed him by the corporation. Thus the Stock Clearing Corporation effects a saving not only in the amount of credit accommodation employed by its members but also in the length of time during which it is employed.

Routine with a Failed-to-Deliver Ticket

23. Of course there is always a possibility that for some reason or other a delivering member may find it impossible to deliver his stock balance, either as a whole or in part. In such an event, if it is mutually desirable, the delivering member must give official notice of this failure to deliver, by seeing that a failed-to-deliver ticket (Figure 35a) is properly filled out and presented to the Stock Clearing Corporation by 2:30 P.M.

To this red failed-to-deliver ticket is attached, below a perforated line, a similar black failed-to-receive ticket (Figure 35b). The former states that "we failed to deliver this day to (receiving member) (so many) shares (of such and such a stock) at (its price) $—(value of the stock)." This failed-to-

STOCK CLEARING CORPORATION
(DAY CLEARING BRANCH)

FAILED TO DELIVER TICKET

It will be the duty of the DELIVERER to fill out and sign both charge and credit tickets and deliver same to Stock Clearing Corporation no later than 2:30 P.M.

CHARGE TICKET

Jefferson & Co.
(Name of Member who Failed to Deliver)

Clearing No. 430 (Delivering Member) NEW YORK, August 4 1920

On Stock Clearing Corporation Security Balance Order,

WE FAILED TO DELIVER THIS DAY to Barker & Co.

100 ~~M~~ Shares Union Pacific @ 120 $ 12,000.00

the value of which as stated above charge to our account.

Jefferson & Co.
(Firm Signature of Delivering Member)

STOCK CLEARING CORPORATION
(DAY CLEARING BRANCH)

FAILED TO RECEIVE TICKET

CREDIT TICKET

Barker & Co.
(Name of Member who Failed to Receive)

Clearing No. 440 (Receiving Member) NEW YORK, August 4 1920

On Stock Clearing Corporation Security Balance Order,

WE FAILED TO DELIVER THIS DAY to Barker & Co.

100 ~~M~~ Shares Union Pacific @ 120 $ 12,000.00

and therefore instruct you to credit their account with the value as stated above.

Jefferson & Co.
(Firm Signature of Delivering Member)

Figure 35. (a) Failed-to-Deliver Ticket (upper half). (Size 7 x 4½.)

Showing failure of Jefferson and Company to deliver 100 Union Pacific to Barker and Company, and charging the former's account for its value.

Figure 35. (b) Failed-to-Receive Ticket (lower half). (Size 7 x 4½.)

Crediting the account of the firm failing to receive, for the value of the security balance.

deliver ticket constitutes an order by the delivering member upon the corporation to charge on his account against the contingent credits established by him before 10 A.M. that day (see 2 to 5), the value of the stock which he has failed to deliver. After the delivering member has signed both forms of this double ticket, it is sent to the Stock Clearing Corporation, so that the receiving member may receive the corresponding credit from the failed-to-receive ticket, which states that "we failed to deliver this day to (receiving member) (so many) shares (of such and such a stock) at (its price) $—(value of the stock), and therefore instruct you to credit their account with the value as stated above." The reader will recall that (owing to steps 1 to 9) the corporation knows the value of the stock balances which every member has to receive and to deliver before any actual deliveries have been made.

Consequently, when a properly filled failed-to-deliver and failed-to-receive ticket are presented to the corporation, the two tickets are compared in the cage handling the delivering member's account; if both forms agree, they are then separated. The failed-to-deliver ticket is retained and filed in the delivering member's box, while the failed-to-receive ticket is sent to the particular cage where the receiving member's account is kept. The failed-to-receive ticket constitutes an order by the member failing to deliver upon the Stock Clearing Corporation to credit the account of the member failing to receive with the value of the undelivered securities, and this credit offsets the corresponding contingent charge made on his account for these securities before 10 that morning.

Adjustment of the Record Sheet Account

In the one case, the failed-to-deliver ticket is treated as a charge ticket, and the value of the undelivered stock is added to the contingent debit which has been entered on the delivering member's control sheet described in 5. In the other case, the failed-to-receive ticket is treated as a credit ticket and the value of the "unreceived" stock is added to the contingent credit entered in the similar control sheet of the receiving member. By this double operation the value of the undelivered stock, for which the delivering member received a contingent credit at 10 that morning, now becomes a contingent debit; while the receiving member, who at 10 A.M. received a contingent debit for the amount of the undelivered stock, now receives a contingent credit for its value. The failure to deliver the stock is then treated as an "ex-clearing house contract"—that is, a contract in whose settlement the Stock Clearing Corporation (or, as it used to be called, the "clearing house") will play no further part. As such, the contract may subsequently be settled through the physical delivery of the security or securities involved by the delivering to the receiving member, as in the case of a contract made in non-cleared stocks. Failures to deliver, however, can be and often are put through the Day Clearing Branch the next day if so desired, instead of being handled "ex" in the manner above described.

Delivery by Transfer

24. Another exception to the normal operation of the Day Clearing Branch of the Stock Clearing Corporation arises when stocks are delivered by transfer. Frequently the delivering member will have stock in his possession which he should deliver to the receiving member, but which must pass through the transfer office before it will constitute a good delivery.[6] This condition may arise when the delivering member has two certificates of 50 and 55 shares each, while he has an even 100 shares to deliver, or when other features may make a certificate unsuitable for delivery to the receiving members.

In such a case both the delivering and receiving members

6 See Chapter XVI.

sign a special form "to be delivered by transfer" (Figure 36), which states the number, name, price, and value of the shares to be delivered. Both deliverer and receiver agree that the

Blotter Line No. 12

STOCK CLEARING CORPORATION
(DAY CLEARING BRANCH)
TO BE DELIVERED BY TRANSFER

Clearing No. 450 (Of Delivering Member) New York, August 4 1920

STOCK CLEARING CORPORATION (DAY CLEARING BRANCH),
ON STOCK BALANCE ORDER TO DELIVER.

To C. E. Bowman & Co.

100 shares U. S. Rubber com. @ 84 $ 8400.00

The undersigned have agreed that delivery of above be made by transfer, subject to the rules of the Stock Clearing Corporation and upon its approval Tompkins & Co. (Receiving Member) will hand you immediately after such delivery a certified check to your order for $ 8400.00 the value as stated above, of the stock placed in transfer. Debit and Credit tickets for the value of the delivery must accompany this order so that approval may be stamped thereon by Stock Clearing Corporation.

Deliverer Signs C. E. Bowman & Co.

Receiver Signs Tompkins & Co.

(These notices will not be approved after 1.15 P.M.)

Figure 36. Delivery-by-Transfer Ticket. (Size 8 x 5¾.)

delivery of this stock shall be made by transfer subject to the approval of the Stock Clearing Corporation, and that upon its approval, the receiving member will hand it immediately a certified check to the order of the corporation for the value of the stock placed in transfer.

Final Balancing of the Accounts

25. By 2:30 each day all clearing members' accounts (including failures to deliver and deliveries through transfer) can be closed and settled. First, every member's control sheet

(see 5 and 23) is balanced to discover whether he is a creditor of or a debter to, the Stock Clearing Corporation for the stock balances which he has respectively delivered and received. Thus, if a given clearing member has delivered security balances that day valued at $50,000, and has received security balances valued at $40,000, he is obviously a creditor of the corporation for $10,000, and has a credit on his control sheet for that amount. But if he has received security balances valued at $75,000 and delivered security balances valued at $50,000, he is then a debtor to the corporation for $25,000. In the first case the corporation would expect to meet the member's draft or credit memorandum on it for $10,000; in the second case it would expect to receive the member's check for $25,000. All checks sent to the corporation for $5,000 or over must be certified; for checks under $5,000 certification is not required.

26. Meanwhile all deliveries of stock balances having been made, the individual clearing member, between 2:45 and 3 P.M. prepares a final receipt form. His blotter (see 3) contains a record of all the stock balances which he has had to deliver and to receive that day, a record which is further confirmed by the stubs to his credit and charge tickets—(a) and (b)—which his messenger has brought back to his office from the Stock Clearing Corporation (see 17 and 18). He consequently knows just how much his account with the corporation has been debited and credited during the day.

Use of the Final Receipt

27. If the member owes the corporation a cash balance on his day's stock balances received and delivered, he strikes out the words "credit memorandum" at the top of the final receipt (Figure 37), makes out his check for the sum due the corporation, and sends the check and receipt to it. If, on the other hand, the corporation owes him a cash balance, he strikes out

the word "check" and draws a draft (or credit memorandum) against the corporation, and dispatches the receipt and draft to

STOCK CLEARING CORPORATION
(DAY CLEARING BRANCH)

Clearing No. 400 New York, August 3 1920
Firm Name Jenkins & Co.
We herewith send ~~Check~~ Credit Memorandum for $9700.00 which ~~Credit~~ Charge to our account
Deliver the following for which we hereby acknowledge receipt.

Jenkins & Co.
(Firm Signature)

Figure 37. The Final Receipt. (Size 8½ x 5½.)
Showing final settlement of account of Jenkins and Company. Ruled lines at bottom of form are for securities to be withdrawn and are not involved in the present instance.

it. The receipt form is made out in duplicate. One is retained by the corporation, while the other is returned to the clearing member.

28. The corporation deposits the checks which come into it during the day, in the several banks with which it has accounts.

29. The corporation, on receipt of the various drafts or credit memoranda drawn against it in the course of the day's

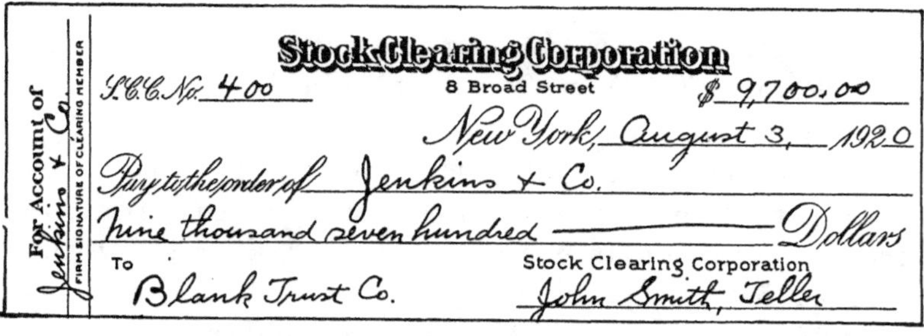

For Account of Jenkins & Co.
FIRM SIGNATURE OF CLEARING MEMBER

Stock Clearing Corporation
S.C.C. No. 400 8 Broad Street $9,700.00
New York, August 3, 1920
Pay to the order of Jenkins & Co.
Nine thousand seven hundred Dollars
To Blank Trust Co.
Stock Clearing Corporation
John Smith, Teller

Figure 38. A Stock Clearing Corporation Check. (Size 8½ x 2⅞.)
Made out to pay Jenkins and Company's credit of $9,700.

business, checks the amount of each against the given firm's account to be sure of its accuracy. Also, this credit memorandum must bear the signature of the clearing member or his authorized signatory. The corporation then determines against which of its bank accounts it wishes to have the draft presented for payment, and writes in the name of this bank on the face of the credit memorandum under "To." The teller of the Stock Clearing Corporation then signs it and returns it to the waiting member or his representative (Figure 38). The member can then deposit the check in his own bank, and through the bank clearing house collect the proceeds from the given depository bank of the Stock Clearing Corporation.

What the Day Branch Accomplishes

30. The checks of members paid to the Stock Clearing Corporation will always provide just enough money to pay the drafts drawn against it. For, since every stock balance to deliver is offset by a stock balance to receive, and since the money to be received on stock balances to be delivered must also equal the money to be paid on stock balances to be received, it is a matter of simple arithmetic to show that in the balancing of the various members' credits and debits in the Stock Clearing Corporation, the total credit balances must always exactly equal the total debit balances. In other words, the total amount of money which the corporation has on deposit at its several depository banks on any given evening, after the day's clearance has been effected, will exactly equal the total sum with which it started in the morning of that day, before any accounts had been cleared. Consequently, the Stock Clearing Corporation in no sense finances the daily purchases or sales of securities made in the stock market on credit each day, but, acting as the agent of its members, simply settles their daily cash debits and credits which arise from the delivering or receiving of stock balances in the most scientific and economical

manner and with the least possible employment of unsecured loans by the banks to the clearing members.

The above account of the credit and debit items entering into the day's reckoning of the given firm has been entirely confined to the clearance of cash extensions from stock balances to receive and deliver. As the next chapter will show,[7] there is another very important factor omitted in this account, namely, the credit and debit items arising from the clearance of loans, also performed by the Stock Clearing Corporation for its clearing members.

Further Saving of Banking Accommodation

The economic functions of the Day Clearing Branch are similar to those of the Night Clearing Branch. As in the latter, the Day Clearing Branch produces a further considerable saving in the amount of banking accommodation needed to settle transactions on the Stock Exchange. It will be recalled[8] that over 90 per cent of total stock contracts on the Exchange are cleared by the Night Clearing Branch, and that by the settlement there of intermediate contracts, a saving in banking accommodation of about 60 per cent of their value is effected. Now the Day Clearing Branch in its clearance of the cash extensions of balance contracts brings about a further saving of banking accommodation, amounting also to about 60 per cent of the value of the balance contracts remaining from the work of the Night Clearing Branch. Thus, through the combined efforts of the two branches only about 20 per cent of the accommodation that would otherwise be needed is actually employed, a saving of about 80 per cent being effected. As the next chapter will show, the clearance of loans by the Stock Clearing Corporation also produces, though in a slightly different direction, an additional saving of accommodation. Owing to the major position among American exchanges

[7] See Chapter XI. [8] See Chapter IX, page 237, and Appendix, Chapter IX (c).

enjoyed by the New York Stock Exchange, the economies in banking accommodation brought about by the Stock Clearing Corporation consequently runs into billions of dollars annually.[9]

Time and Labor Saved

Apart from its major usefulness as an economizer of bank accommodation, the Day Clearing Branch also produces important savings of both time and labor as well. As the president of the Stock Clearing Corporation has expressed it: [10]

> It is figured that a delivery of stock now, where only a receipt is asked for, can be made in seven minutes. In active times, when delivery was made, and a check had to be obtained, the check taken to the bank to be certified, brought back to the office, entered and deposited, it averaged thirty-five minutes. In 1919 it was seldom a boy could make more than two, possibly three deliveries, in an hour. A concrete illustration of the present method was that a certain firm in the Street at two o'clock had forty-four deliveries to make on an active day. It made the forty-four deliveries and settled their difference with the Stock Clearing Corporation by two-twenty, so that the business of the Street has been facilitated and the demands on the New York banks reduced.

Thus the whole business of delivering securities has been wonderfully speeded up, and not only has the amount of accommodation needed to pay for them been greatly reduced, but also the time over which this reduced amount of accommodation is actually extended.

Increased Flexibility and Safety

A more important consequence of the Day Clearing Branch, however, is the increased flexibility it imparts to the stock

---

[9] See Appendix, Chapter X (a).

[10] Samuel F. Streit, President, "Function of the Stock Clearing Corporation," *Acceptance Bulletin* for May 1921, p. 10.

market by freeing it still further from technical conditions in the money market. An even more significant result obtained is the enhanced safety of all firms and their customers dealing in the Stock Exchange, which follows from the careful supervision exercised by the Day Clearing Branch over the actual deliveries of stock balances. For through its control and zone sheets in particular (see 5, 20, 21, and 22 above in this chapter), this new branch of the Stock Clearing Corporation can efficiently direct, and, if need be, hasten the delivery of stock balances, in such a way as to minimize the danger of failures.

The new branch also largely relieves bankers from the difficult task of estimating the daily condition of the various brokerage houses, and consequently protects them from the danger of loss during periods of financial stress, for the reduced amount of accommodation granted by bankers to clearing members to receive cleared stocks is protected during the process of settlement by the whole clearing fund, instead of merely by their deposits in the banks giving this accommodation. This clearing fund at present aggregates $10,000,000, and in addition bears a 100 per cent liability. This, together with the fact that all the debts of the Stock Clearing Corporation are daily offset by its credits, is the reason why the banks are willing to accept the checks of the Stock Clearing Corporation without certification.

Present Physical Limitations Upon Stock Clearance

But while the Stock Clearing Corporation should easily be able to handle larger markets than the Exchange may see for many years (if indeed the volume of transactions ever really can succeed in burdening its clearance system at all), nevertheless practical considerations at present to a certain extent prevent the expansion of the corporation's activities into new fields, where it may some day perform equally notable tasks. Until the new twenty-story addition to the Stock Exchange building is completed, the Stock Clearing Corporation, perhaps to a greater degree than any other part of the Exchange machinery, will be more or less hampered by the insufficient floor space and housing facilities in rendering its maximum possible service. Yet the time is not far distant when the corporation can, and doubtless will, expand its operations and increase its service very considerably. For one thing, more ex-clearing house transactions in securities not regularly cleared can be cleared on special occasions at the request of the clearing members. Moreover, the number of stocks and bonds which are regularly cleared can be considerably increased, whenever their activity enables a saving of credit to be brought about by so doing. Lastly, the clearance of odd-lot transactions in clearing house stocks may some day be undertaken.

In spite of its bewildering intricacy of detail, therefore, the Stock Clearing Corporation is really one of the most interesting and delicate parts of the Stock Exchange machinery, and one whose future evolution seems destined to be as swift and brilliant as its recent development has been. By replacing the old chaotic and clumsy custom of the direct delivery of stock and payment of money between brokers for stocks sold on the Exchange with the present highly scientific and economical system, it has made possible vast annual economies of labor and credit, and tended to stabilize the whole vast market it serves. Like so many other departments of the New York Stock Exchange, the economic value of the Stock Clearing Corporation is not confined simply to the securities market. The beneficial effects of its operation are felt, indirectly perhaps, but none the less certainly, throughout the whole credit structure of the nation.

CHAPTER XI

THE CLEARANCE OF LOANS

Financing the Loan Turnover

In Chapter VIII the system was described whereby the commission house finances its transactions in securities requiring credit accommodation, by means of collateral time and demand or call loans. The latter class of loans, since it comprises obligations payable upon demand, is naturally shifting constantly, and one of the major tasks of the Stock Exchange system consists in enabling call loans to be paid off and new call loans to be made. Furthermore, this constant obtaining and repaying of call loans, until quite recently, placed a considerable burden upon the New York banks, which arose in the following way.

In case Jenkins and Company had its loan for $100,000 called by the lending bank A, the commission house would make an agreement with bank B to borrow a similar sum there upon the security collateral then reposing in a loan envelope in bank A's vaults. But Jenkins and Company could not obtain its collateral from bank A until it had bank B's check for $100,000 with which to pay off its loan from bank A; and Jenkins and Company could not obtain such a check from bank B until it delivered the aforesaid collateral at bank B's loan window. Thus, Jenkins and Company found itself in the apparent dilemma of not being able to get a money loan until it got its securities, and not being able to get its securities until it had obtained a money loan.

This situation was somewhat similar to the one previously described[1] in connection with the receipt and delivery of

[1] See Chapter IX.

securities which the firm had purchased and sold, and it was solved in practically the same way. Just as the banks made day loans to brokers which enabled the latter to pay for the securities which the latter had purchased and were to receive, so too they furnished temporary accommodation wherewith the broker could shift his loans. Accordingly, Jenkins and Company would draw a check for $100,000 upon bank C, where it kept a standing deposit, and request bank C to certify it. It would then turn over this certified check to bank A, obtain its security collateral, deliver the latter to bank B, obtain bank B's check for $100,000 as a loan upon it, and deposit this check with bank C, thus retiring the firm's temporary obligation at the latter institution.

The Work of Loan Clearance

We have already seen how the Night and Day Clearing Branches of the Stock Clearing Corporation, acting in respect to deliverable and receivable securities as a central and supervisory agent for its members, have been able greatly to reduce the amount of banking accommodation required to pay for the stocks bought each day on the Stock Exchange. In order to effect a further economy in the use of accommodation, the Stock Clearing Corporation accordingly clears call and time loans, upon somewhat the same general principles as in the instance of contracts calling for the delivery of and payment for stock balances. By intervening as an intermediary in the shifting of loans, it has rendered the certification of a check by a third bank (C in the above example) unnecessary. This task of clearing loans is a recent undertaking on the part of the Stock Clearing Corporation, having been inaugurated on March 22, 1921.

The clearance of loans is performed in the offices of the Day Clearing Branch in the basement of the Stock Exchange building. These offices have already been described, in connection with the work of clearing cash extensions performed there.[2] The clearance of loans, as will shortly be apparent, has imposed new duties upon the ten cages in the middle of the office, where the clearing members' accounts are kept. An additional feature of the office made necessary by the clearance of loans is the lenders' booths which are situated side by side along the walls of the office. The present lack of space has allowed room for only 29 of these booths, and hence has limited the number of lending institutions which can participate in the clearance of loans. But when the new addition to the Stock Exchange building is opened it is expected that the ampler physical accommodations then available to the Stock Clearing Corporation will permit the erection of many more booths, and the inclusion of many more lending institutions in the system of loan clearance.

The Lending Members

The Stock Clearing Corporation, of course, undertakes the work of clearing loans only for its regular clearing members.[3] But in addition to these, who in the main appear only as borrowers, the representatives of the banking institutions which lend money on call constitute a class of "lending members." The lending institutions have signed an agreement with the Stock Clearing Corporation which permits the routine of loan clearance to be carried on smoothly and efficiently. These lending members pay no charges to the Stock Clearing Corporation and own none of its stock. Sometimes the clearing members appear as lenders of money. As we shall see, special provisions have been worked out to meet this contingency.

The Return Loan Agreement

In discussing the various phases of the clearance of loans, the clearest and simplest way is to start with the operations by

[2] See Chapter X, page 243. [3] See Chapter IX.

which an existing loan is paid off; next to consider how the Stock Clearing Corporation holds the collateral and enables it

FIRST ORIGINAL

STOCK CLEARING CORPORATION

(Day Clearing Branch)

Clearing No. 400 Called Returned

RETURN LOAN AGREEMENT

New York August 10, 1920

Jenkins & Co. has agreed with Fiftieth National Bank to pay off this day a Loan dated Aug. 9, 1920 $ 100,000.00 and interest $ 16.67

Total Charges $ 100,016.67 in accordance with and subject to the By-Laws and Rules of the Stock Clearing Corporation.

	Securities	Price	Value	
400	Southern Pacific	97	38	800
200	Canadian Pacific	121	24	200
200	U. S. Steel Com.	86	17	200
200	U. S. Rubber Com	73	14	600
300	American Sugar	103	30	900
			125	700

The securities held by the lender as collateral for the above loan are to be delivered to the Stock Clearing Corporation. The borrower directs the Stock Clearing Corporation to pay the amount of said loan with accrued interest and to hold said securities for his account subject to the By-Laws and Rules of the Stock Clearing Corporation.

Fiftieth National Bank — Lender Signs

Jenkins & Co. — Borrower Signs

The delivery to the Stock Clearing Corporation of the securities named above is hereby acknowledged.

Fiftieth National Bank — Lender Signs

Jenkins & Co. — Borrower Signs

Figure 39. The Return Loan Agreement. (Size 6 x 9½.)
Employed in payment of loan by Jenkins and Company to Fiftieth National Bank.

to be shifted and withdrawn in whole or in part; and finally, to describe the methods employed in making a new loan.

The repayment of loans starts at 10 A.M. each full business day. Of course, a loan may have to be paid off because either the lender has called it, or because the borrower desires to pay it off. Notice to this effect is given direct between borrower and lender, usually over the telephone. When a loan is paid off by a non-member of the Stock Clearing Corporation the borrower obtains his security collateral from the lender by delivering at the latter's office a certified check for the principal and interest of the loan, in the manner previously described in the present and an earlier chapter.[4]

When a clearing member pays off a loan through the Stock Clearing Corporation the borrower first fills out a quadruplicate return loan agreement in his office. This form (Figure 39) contains the borrower's clearing number, the names of the borrower and lender, the amount of the principal and interest

For Account of
Jenkins & Co.
FIRM SIGNATURE OF CLEARING MEMBER.

Stock Clearing Corporation
S.C.C. No. 400 — 8 Broad Street — $100,016 67/
New York, August 10 1920
Pay to the order of The Fiftieth National Bank
One hundred thousand sixteen and 67/x Dollars
To — Stock Clearing Corporation
Fiftieth National Bank — John Smith, Teller

Figure 40. Stock Clearing Corporation Check. (Size 8½ x 2⅞.)
Made out to pay to Fiftieth National Bank, principal and interest of loan to Jenkins and Company. Note that check does not require certification.

of the loan, as well as an itemized list of the securities pledged as collateral for the loan and held in the envelope by the lender, together with the number of shares, the price, and the value of each. The borrower signs the three forms of this agreement with a signature recognized by the Stock Clearing Corporation, for although the form is in quadruplicate, only three forms are

[4] See Chapter VIII.

used in paying off loans. At the same time the borrower fills out a credit memorandum (Figure 40) form which he signs on the left edge, making payable to the lender the amount of the principal and interest of the loan in question. The form, of course, possesses no value as a check until it is signed by an official of the Stock Clearing Corporation, and until the latter designates one of its depository banks to which the lender should present it for payment. At first, therefore, the borrower fills out all but the bottom line of the form, where space is left for these two important items to be filled in later.

Notification of the Lender and the Clearing Corporation

The borrower's representative then takes the return loan agreement to the lender's office. The receipt of the return loan agreement by the lender constitutes a notification to him from the borrower that the loan will be paid off. The lender detaches one of the three forms of the return loan agreement, signs the other two forms, and returns them to the borrower's representative. The latter then takes these two forms, together with the credit memorandum above described, to the Day Clearing Branch of the Stock Clearing Corporation, and delivers both agreements and memorandum to the particular cage in which the account of his firm is kept. Thus the Stock Clearing Corporation is notified concerning the clearance to be made, and has on the face of the agreement the list of securities which it must receive from the lender in behalf of the borrower. The corporation, of course, reserves the right to refuse to act, in which case the loan must be paid off "ex," in the manner described in Chapter VIII.

Making Payment to the Lender

The next step in the clearance is made by the lender's representative, who comes to his booth in the Stock Clearing Corporation with his copy of the return loan agreement and the envelope of security collateral itemized on its face. He goes to the cage where the borrower's account is kept and delivers the loan envelope and its contents. The clerk in the cage compares the securities in the envelope with the itemized list on the face of the return loan agreements previously received from the borrower. If the securities in the envelope agree with this list in all respects, the clerk retains the security collateral for the account of the borrower. The head teller of the cage, as an authorized representative of the Stock Clearing Corporation, then signs the credit memorandum (Figure 40) previously left there by the borrower, and under the word "To" fills in the name of a bank where part of the clearing fund is deposited. Thus the credit memorandum becomes the check of the Stock Clearing Corporation, drawn on the depository bank in favor of the lender. This check is then handed to the lender. So financially sound is the corporation, with its large clearing fund always on deposit as a liquid and revolving fund, that its checks are not certified. The lender collects the proceeds of the check he receives, through the bank clearing house.

If the lender desires a receipt for the securities he has delivered to the Stock Clearing Corporation, the latter will sign to that effect on the return loan agreement form brought to the Stock Clearing Corporation by the lender.

"Secured" and "Unsecured" Accommodation

Meanwhile, in the borrower's cage at the Stock Clearing Corporation, the securities constituting the collateral to the loan paid off are held for the borrower's account, and he is debited with the amount of the principal and interest of the loan which the Stock Clearing Corporation has just paid to the lender on the borrower's behalf. But it must be noticed that this debit item is not "unsecured accommodation," as is the case with debits incurred by clearing members through receiving stock balances, as described in the previous chapter.[5] For, to balance the debit of the borrower on the Stock Clearing Corporation's books which was created when the latter paid off the loan to the lender, the corporation holds the security collateral. Consequently, this debit item is "secured

STOCK CLEARING CORPORATION (DAY CLEARING BRANCH).

No. 400 Jenkins & Co Name of Clearing Member

Contingent Dr.		Contingent Cr.		Actual Dr.		Actual Cr.		Value of Securities obtained from S.C.C. for Del. of Security Balance		Recd.	Time Deld. to S.C.C.
				100 016	67						
						100 000	00				
				100 016	67	100 000	00				
						16	67				
				100 016	67	100 016	67				

Figure 41. Record Sheet. (Size 9 x 9.)

Entries record payment by the Stock Clearing Corporation of principal and interest of loan for the account of Jenkins and Company, and the receipt of principal of a new loan. Note debit balance of $16.67, to be settled on Jenkins and Company's final receipt (Figure 46).

accommodation" and is dealt with as such on the books of the corporation. A separate sheet (Figure 41) in each cage contains the summarized account of both the secured and unsecured accommodation employed by each member, as well as their offsetting credit items. Thus the Stock Clearing Corporation at all times can tell to a penny the exact financial position with it of the clearing member in question. The collateral received by the Stock Clearing Corporation is almost automatically acceptable to it, since the lender was willing to hold it overnight.

The above operations take place during the morning in

[5] See Chapter X, page 249.

two shifts. If the borrower takes the return loan agreement to the lender's office by 10:15 A.M., the lender delivers the security collateral to the Stock Clearing Corporation by 10:30 A.M. But if the agreement does not reach the lender until after 10:15 A.M. the matter goes over until 12:30 P.M., by which time all agreements for the paying of loans to be effected through the Stock Clearing Corporation that day must reach the lender. The lender then leaves his office immediately after the last loan agreement has been received, and comes to the Stock Clearing Corporation, bringing with him the collateral to the loans which are to be paid off to him. It is an unwritten law in Wall Street that "no loans are called after 12:15."

Against such checks as the Stock Clearing Corporation pays to lenders in behalf of borrowers who are paying off loans, it deposits in the banks upon which these checks are drawn funds arising from certified checks, or bank checks received by it during the day representing payments to it by its clearing members either for security balances received, or for new loans made, or for the final daily settlement of its account by the clearing member with the Stock Clearing Corporation.

Withdrawal of Collateral Securities "Free"

We must now consider some of the problems which arise after the Stock Clearing Corporation has paid off a loan for a borrower and while it holds the borrower's collateral securities. Usually the borrower will need some or all of the securities held in this way by the Stock Clearing Corporation for the routine business of the day. Perhaps the envelope at the corporation contains a certificate for 100 shares of United States Steel which he must deliver on balance to another clearing member whose name the Night Clearing Branch has given him; or perhaps the borrower may wish to get this 100 shares of Steel in order to substitute it for 100 shares of Reading which he has to deliver but which is at present in another loan envelope at a bank as collateral for another loan. Under certain conditions the Stock Clearing Corporation will permit the clearing member to withdraw such certificates from his collateral "free" —that is, without at the same time having to give in return to

STOCK CLEARING CORPORATION
(DAY CLEARING BRANCH)

Clearing No. 400 New York, August 20, 1920
Firm Name Jenkins & Co.

No. of Shares	SECURITIES	Price	VALUE		1 Said Securities are to be delivered immediately under existing contracts for cash	2 Said Securities are to be substituted or exchanged for Securities as stated below, which are to be delivered under existing contracts for cash	3 Said Securities are to be exchanged for Securities as stated below, which are to be delivered to receiving party pursuant to security balance order of the Stock Clearing Corporation
100	Atchison	85	8	500			
100	Bethlehem Steel	55	5	500			

Received the above mentioned securities,
Jenkins & Co.

Figure 42. Withdrawal of Securities Ticket. (Size 9½ x 6.)

In this instance Jenkins and Company is withdrawing 100 Atchison and 100 Bethlehem Steel "free" from security collateral left at the Stock Clearing Corporation after a loan has been paid off.

the corporation his certified check for the value of the securities withdrawn. The form used in connection with such withdrawal is shown in Figure 42.

The restrictions upon this practice are several. In the first place, a member is only allowed to withdraw free securities to a value equal to the amount of the credit balance in his account with the Stock Clearing Corporation, which has been created by his delivery of securities, or the receipt by the corporation of a check or checks for his account previous to the time when the report is made to withdraw the securities. Securities may be withdrawn free for the purpose of delivery against cash contracts either by delivering them and thus obtaining a credit for their value on the corporation's books, or by substituting them for other securities which are to be delivered and credits with the corporation similarly established, or by obtaining funds in exchange for them, or as a loan upon them as collateral, which will enable the clearing member to present the corporation with a check for their value. The clearing member is not allowed to place in transfer securities delivered to him free out of his collateral with the corporation, since in this case they would pass out of the control of the corporation, which would thereby release the pledge it holds on the securities. For securities withdrawn to be placed in transfer, therefore, the clearing member must deliver to the corporation a certified check for their value.

Secondly, securities delivered free are released for two hours only, at the end of which time the clearing member is expected to have financed himself and be prepared to establish credits or present a check at the Stock Clearing Corporation equivalent to their value.

In the third place, the value of securities delivered free in this way is treated as unsecured accommodation extended to the member by the corporation, and hence is debited to his account, along with the value of the security balances he has received, in the fifth column of the control sheet for his account, described in the previous chapter.[6] Of course, the clearing member, whether for security balances received or for securities withdrawn free, cannot obtain a greater total of unsecured accommodation from the corporation than the amount regularly allowed him. For any accommodation above his allotted amount he must give his certified check or other securities of equal value to the Stock Clearing Corporation. Consequently, if the member were to withdraw securities from his collateral unnecessarily, he would to the extent of their value needlessly increase the amount of his debit for unsecured accommodation extended to him by the corporation. In an active day particularly, it is necessary for the clearing member

[6] See Chapter X, page 249.

to keep this accommodation as liquid as possible. If he withdrew too many securities he might overextend his position on the corporation's books and be forced to send it a check or other securities. Thus, the member's account almost automatically prevents him from abusing the privilege of withdrawing securities free from his collateral with the corporation.

Procedure with Withdrawal of Securities

The routine for withdrawing securities free from collateral at the Stock Clearing Corporation is very simple. The clearing member fills out a duplicate form, which is a receipt by the clearing member for the securities to be withdrawn and which states the number of shares, name, price, and value of these securities. On the reverse side the member pledges the securities to be withdrawn, or the proceeds obtained from them, to the Stock Clearing Corporation. If the securities to be withdrawn are to be substituted in another loan envelope for some other securities there, then these latter securities or the proceeds from them are pledged to the corporation. This form, when properly filled out, is presented by the clearing member's representative at the cage in the Stock Clearing Corporation in which his account is kept. If the operation does not involve a breach of the restrictions upon the process above outlined, the clerk in the cage retains one of the duplicate forms, delivers to the clearing member's representative free the securities he desires to withdraw, and debits his unsecured accommodation account with their value.

Subsequent Employment of Remaining Securities

The securities left with the Stock Clearing Corporation as collateral for a paid off loan, subject of course to this process of withdrawals, may remain with the corporation until the end of the day, when, if the clearing member's account is in debit, he may settle with the corporation for their value with his final check, and take them away. Often, however, they are employed as collateral for a new loan to be made, the proceeds of which the clearing member will usually need either for settling his indebtedness with the corporation at the close of the day's business, or in connection with his ex-Stock Clearing Corporation operations. We must, therefore, next consider exactly how new loans are made through the agency of the Stock Clearing Corporation.

The borrower's purpose in contracting a new loan may, of course, be to enable him to finance his customer's margin transactions, or for financing on account of a loan which has been paid off earlier in the day, or for various other purposes as the day's business may require.

We have seen [7] that call money can be borrowed either direct between borrower and lender, or through a money broker, or at the money desk on the floor of the Stock Exchange. But whichever way the loan is made, so long as it is between members of the Stock Clearing Corporation, or between a member and a lender who has signed an agreement with the Stock Clearing Corporation, the new loan must be handled by the Stock Clearing Corporation, as a third party and the agent of the borrower.

The New Loan Agreement

The borrower first makes out in his office a new loan agreement, which in several respects resembles the return loan agreement already described. The new loan agreement form (Figure 43) is in quadruplicate and contains the borrower's clearing number at its head, as well as a formal agreement stating that the lender has agreed to loan to the borrower in accordance with and subject to the By-laws and Rules of the Stock Clearing Corporation a stated sum of money at a stated interest rate, upon the collateral of an appended itemized list

[7] See Chapter VIII, page 176.

FIRST ORIGINAL

STOCK CLEARING CORPORATION
(Day Clearing Branch)

Clearing No. 400

NEW LOAN AGREEMENT

New York August 10, 1920

The Blank Trust Co. has agreed to loan this day to Jenkins & Co. in accordance with and subject to the By-Laws and Rules of the Stock Clearing Corporation $ 100,000 00 on the following securities at 5 %

	Securities	Price	Value	
400	Southern Pacific	97	38	800
200	Canadian Pacific	121	24	200
200	U.S. Steel Com.	86	17	200
200	U.S. Rubber	73	14	600
300	American Sugar	103	30	900
			125	700

Lender's check for the amount of the above loan is to be payable to the Stock Clearing Corporation and to be delivered to it.

Lender Signs: The Blank Trust Co, Thomas Brown, Cashier

Borrower Signs: Jenkins & Co.

Figure 43. New Loan Agreement. (Size 6 x 9½.)

Jenkins and Company obtains a new loan of $100,000. Note credit entry for this loan on its record sheet, Figure 41.

of securities. This itemized list states the name, number of shares, price, and value of the securities to be pledged for the loan. After filling out the four forms of this new loan agreement, the borrower signs them at the bottom, and his representative takes the agreement to the office of the lender.

Here, the lender passes on the desirability of the security collateral itemized on the face of the agreement. If the collateral is acceptable to him, he detaches two of the four forms of the agreement for his own use, and, after signing the other two forms in the space provided for that purpose at the bottom, returns these to the borrower's representative. But in case the collateral for the proposed loan is not acceptable to the lender, the latter rejects the agreement and requests the borrower to pledge other securities than those on the list as collateral. In such cases the borrower proceeds to make up a new list of securities and a new agreement which will be acceptable to the lender, and sends it back to the latter for his approval and signature in the manner above described. These new loan agreements for new loans to be "put through" the Stock Clearing Corporation are accepted by lenders up to 2:45 P.M. In case a borrower sends his agreement to the lender after that time, the lender can insist that the loan be made "ex," in which case, of course, the Stock Clearing Corporation does not figure further in the matter.

Notifying the Stock Clearing Corporation

The borrower's representative next takes the two forms of the new loan agreement, which have by this time been signed by both borrower and lender, to the Stock Clearing Corporation. He delivers them at the particular cage there where the account of the borrower as a clearing member is kept, and the clerk in the cage files them for future reference. Thus, the Stock Clearing Corporation is officially notified that it must be prepared to act as agent for borrower and lender in handling the loan about to be made. Under certain circumstances, however, the Stock Clearing Corporation reserves the right to refuse to act, in which case the loan must be made "ex."

The representative of the lender arrives at his booth in the Stock Clearing Corporation at about 1:30 P.M., and remains there until his business with the corporation for that day has been concluded. He brings to the corporation's office the two forms of the new loan agreement previously detached and retained at the lender's office, as well as the check of the lending institution made out payable to the Stock Clearing Corporation for the account of the borrower, for the principal of the new loan to be made. It may be that all the securities to be used as collateral for the new loan have already been deposited with the Stock Clearing Corporation as the result of a previous loan which the corporation already has paid off in behalf of the borrower.

Making the New Loan

In consequences of the lender's having shown that he has approved the collateral pledged for the loan by signing the new loan agreement, the lender's representative has only to see that the securities he obtains are identical with those stated upon the new loan agreement form which he has, and that the certificates are in such negotiable shape as to conform with his requirements. The lender's representative, therefore, obtains the security collateral for the new loan from the cage where the borrowing clearing member's account is kept, and at the same time delivers to the clerk in that cage the check of the lending institution for the amount of the loan, made payable to the Stock Clearing Corporation for the borrower's account. Thus the lender has his collateral, has paid over the principal of the loan, and is now finished with his part of the loan.

Further details of the operation, however, remain to be concluded between the borrower and the Stock Clearing Corporation. The latter, on receipt of the lender's check, credits it to the account of the borrower. If this leaves the borrower with a large credit balance at the corporation, he can under certain restrictions draw this down, as we have seen in the preceding chapter.[8] On the other hand, if before the receipt of the lender's check by the Stock Clearing Corporation the borrower's account with the corporation contained a heavy debit balance, the deduction from this debit balance of the check for the new loan turned over to the corporation will materially assist in restoring the borrower's credit or debit balances with the Stock Clearing Corporation nearer to a proper proportion.

The Case of Lending Clearing Members

In the routine for the paying of old loans and the making of new ones above described one important variation should be noticed. In case the lender is also a clearing member his account is, of course, kept at the Stock Clearing Corporation along with that of the borrower. This fact enables a still more economical method to be employed in clearing loans made between the two, which is in several ways analogous to the method employed by the Stock Clearing Corporation in crediting or debiting its members' accounts for stock balances which have been delivered or received.[9] The same forms are employed in a clearance of loans between two clearing members as in the clearance of loans between a clearing and a lending member already described, with the exception of the payment of the principal of a new loan, or the repayment of the principal and interest on an old loan. The clearing member who acts as a lender is assigned a booth in the Stock Clearing Corporation where he must have his representatives to handle the security collateral and other matters involved in the same way as other lenders of money. But instead of a credit memo-

[8] See Chapter X.

[9] See Chapter XII

Date Aug 16 '20
Clearing No. 470
Lender
Clearing No. 400
Borrower
Principal & Int. of loan $100,016 67

Entered:

STOCK CLEARING CORPORATION
8 BROAD STREET

S.C.C. No. 470
Lender

$100,016 67

New York, August 16, 1920

CREDIT the account of Harrison & Co.

One hundred thousand sixteen and 67/x Dollars

PRINCIPAL AND INTEREST OF A LOAN TO BE PAID TO-DAY as advised on quadruplicate agreement previously filed with Stock Clearing Corporation against which we have received as stated the securities held by them as collateral.

Approved.
STOCK CLEARING CORPORATION
John Smith
Teller

Jenkins & Co.
Borrower

Figure 44. (a) Pay-off Loan Credit Ticket. (Size 9½ x 4.)

Used when one clearing member pays off principal and interest of a loan made to it by another clearing member. This ticket is used to credit the proceeds to the account of the lender.

Date Aug. 16 '20
Clearing No. 470
Lender
Clearing No. 400
Borrower
Principal & Int. of loan $100,016 67

Entered:

STOCK CLEARING CORPORATION
8 BROAD STREET

S.C.C. No. 400
Borrower

$100,016 67

New York, August 16, 1920

Credit the account of Harrison & Co.

One hundred thousand sixteen and 67/x Dollars

Charge ~~my~~ our account for the payment as advised on quadruplicate agreement previously filed with Stock Clearing Corporation of principal and interest of a loan against which we have received the securities held by them as collateral.

Approved.
STOCK CLEARING CORPORATION
John Smith
Teller

Jenkins & Co.
Borrower

Figure 44. (b) Pay-off Loan Charge Ticket. (Size 9½ x 4.)

This ticket is used to charge to the account of the borrower the principal and interest of the loan paid off.

randum which becomes a check of the corporation, or of a bank check, credit and charge tickets are employed in the manner about to be described.

Paying Off Loans to Lending Clearing Members

When a loan is to be paid off, the lending clearing member delivers its collateral securities to the Stock Clearing Corporation at the borrower's cage. The borrower, in the meantime, has brought in a special gray form, which is in duplicate, consisting of a credit ticket, printed in red (Figure 44a), and a charge ticket, printed in black (Figure 44b). Attached to each is a stub which serves as a receipt for the lender and the borrower respectively. The credit ticket consists of an order signed by the borrower upon the Stock Clearing Corporation to credit the lender's account for the principal and interest of the loan to be paid. This ticket must also be approved by the corporation, and signed by one of its tellers. The charge ticket, on the other hand, which is the other half of the form, is a signed order by the borrower upon the Stock Clearing Corporation to charge his account with the amount of the principal and interest of the loan.

The clerk of the borrower's cage then detaches the charge ticket, in order to debit the account of the borrower for the principal and interest of the loan paid off, and gives the credit ticket to the lender. The latter then files this ticket at the cage where his own account is kept, and thereby receives credit on the books of the Stock Clearing Corporation for the principal and interest of the loan paid off. The clerk at his own cage detaches the stub to the credit ticket and returns it to the lender as a receipt for the credit he has obtained on the books of the Stock Clearing Corporation for the principal and interest of the loan paid off. Thus it is not necessary for the Stock Clearing Corporation to pay the lender with one of its own checks; the whole transaction is finally settled when

Date Aug. 15 '20
Clearing No. 470 Lender
Clearing No. 400 Borrower
Principal of loan $ 100,000 00
Entered:

STOCK CLEARING CORPORATION
8 BROAD STREET

$ 100,000 00

S.C.C. No. 470 Lender New York, August 17 1920

CREDIT the account of Jenkins & Co
One hundred thousand Dollars

PRINCIPAL OF A LOAN MADE TO THEM as advised on quadruplicate agreement previously filed with Stock Clearing Corporation and from whom we have received as collateral the securities mentioned thereon.

Approved:
STOCK CLEARING CORPORATION,
John Smith
Teller

Harrison & Co.
Lender

Figure 45. (a) New Loan Credit Ticket. (Size 9½ x 4)

Used when one clearing member makes a loan to another clearing member. This ticket credits the account of the borrower with the principal of the new loan.

Date Aug 15 '20
Clearing No. 470 Lender
Clearing No. 400 Borrower
Principal of loan $ 100,000 00
Entered:

STOCK CLEARING CORPORATION
8 BROAD STREET

$ 100,000 00

S.C.C. No. 400 Borrower New York, August 15 1920

On account of loan to Jenkins & Co. for
One hundred thousand Dollars

CHARGE ~~my~~ our account with the above stated amount as advised on quadruplicate agreement previously filed with Stock Clearing Corporation representing the principal of a loan against which we have received as collateral the securities mentioned thereon.

Approved:
STOCK CLEARING CORPORATION,
John Smith
Teller

Harrison & Co.
Lender

Figure 45. (b) New Loan Charge Ticket. (Size 9½ x 4.)

This ticket charges the account of the lending clearing member with the principal of the loan made to the borrowing clearing member.

the lending and borrowing clearing members make their final settlement with the Stock Clearing Corporation for the day.

New Loans Made by Lending Clearing Members

An analogous procedure is followed in the making of new loans where the lender is a clearing member. The lender first makes out a duplicate white form consisting of a credit ticket, printed in red (Figure 45a), and a charge ticket, printed in black (Figure 45b). Attached to each is a stub later used as a receipt. The credit ticket is a signed order by the lender upon the Stock Clearing Corporation to credit the account of the borrower with the principal of the new loan. The charge ticket, on the other hand, is an order signed by the lender upon the Stock Clearing Corporation to charge the lender's account with the principal of the loan, and states that the lender has received as collateral the securities pledged to obtain it. Both credit and charge tickets must be approved by the Stock Clearing Corporation and to that effect bear the signature of one of its tellers.

The lender delivers this form to the cage in the Stock Clearing Corporation where his own account is kept. The form is then torn apart along the perforated line, and the charge ticket is retained in the cage to debit the lender's account for the amount of the loan. The lender is given its stub as evidence of this charge. The credit ticket is then given to the borrower, after he has delivered the collateral either to the lender or at the lender's cage, and the borrower's account is credited with the proceeds of the new loan.

Loan Items on the "Final Receipt"

When the various transactions of the day between the Stock Clearing Corporation and its lending and clearing members have been concluded (including the delivery and receipt of stock balances to receive and to deliver, and the clearance of loans as above described), the clearing member, as has been explained in the preceding chapter,[10] makes out a final receipt form (Figure 46) in settling his balance with the corporation for that day. This final settlement form is accompanied by the member's check payable to the corporation, or his draft

STOCK CLEARING CORPORATION
(DAY CLEARING BRANCH)

Clearing No. 400 New York, August 10 1920
Firm Name Jenkins & Co.
We herewith send Check ~~Credit~~ Memorandum for $16.67 which Credit ~~Charge~~ to our account
Deliver the following for which we hereby acknowledge receipt.

Jenkins & Co.
(Firm Signature)

Figure 46. Final Receipt. (Size 8½ x 5½.)

Showing settlement of balance of Jenkins and Company from transactions recorded in Figures 39, 40, 41, and 43.

drawn against the corporation, according to whether his final balance with the corporation is a debit or a credit balance. Both secured and unsecured accommodation are settled by one check or draft. The clearance of loans by the Stock Clearing Corporation, therefore, complicates the daily settlement between it and its members, as described in the preceding chapter, in only a few details.

Often there remains at the Stock Clearing Corporation, in the account of a clearing member, a residue of security collateral. This residue results from the fact that not all the securities placed with the corporation are withdrawn "free" during the remainder of the day, for reasons already given. At the end of the day the clearing member takes up the securities remaining in his account at the corporation, after his final balance with it has been settled.

[10] See Chapter X, page 265.

Obviation of Certification

The exact economic services rendered to the financial and the general community by the clearance of loans are largely analogous, if not entirely identical, with the services rendered by the Stock Clearing Corporation in clearing intermediate contracts in stocks and cash extensions of contracts on balance. First of all, there is the further reduction of the day loans and certification of checks obtained at the banks by stock brokerage firms. It is important to realize exactly how this reduction is brought about.

It will be recalled that in a loan shifted "ex-clearing house" from one lender to another, the borrower must obtain a day loan at a third bank in order to obtain the funds needed to pay off the first lender and obtain his security collateral. But with the assistance of the Stock Clearing Corporation this certified check from a third banking institution is no longer needed, for, as we have seen, the Stock Clearing Corporation pays the first lender with its own check (which is not certified) on receipt of the security collateral to the loan, debits the borrower with secured accommodation to the extent of the principal and interest of the loan thus paid off, and later turns over the security collateral to the second lender in exchange for the check of the latter. Thus the clearance of the loan is effected with the uncertified check of the Stock Clearing Corporation, instead of the certified check of a third bank. Consequently, the clearance of loans does not directly reduce the amount of accommodation needed to shift loans, but it does largely obviate the need of certifying checks for this purpose. The saving in certified checks obtained through the clearance of loans is estimated at about 60 per cent. In the comparatively dull month of April, 1921, the saving in certification effected by loan clearance amounted to $128,749,000. In heavier markets, and with a higher general level of stock prices, this total would of course be considerably exceeded.

Saving in Amount of Accommodation Employed

But it is not wholly correct to say that loan clearance does not reduce the total sums needed to shift loans. Actually, an indirect but considerable saving in the amount of banking accommodation which would otherwise be employed, is effected.

Let us suppose that a given clearing member at the beginning of the business day had a stock balance of 1,000 shares of Steel to deliver at par, and a stock balance of 200 shares of United States Rubber to receive at 80. In addition, the same firm has a loan of $100,000 called by the bank. Through the operations of the Day Clearing Branch, when the firm has delivered its 1,000 Steel it will have a credit of $100,000 and when it has received its 200 Rubber it will have a debit of $16,000. Consequently, the firm will have a credit balance on the books of the Stock Clearing Corporation for $84,000, which is applied against the principal and interest of the call loan, amounting to $100,016.67. Before loans were cleared, the member would have had to obtain $100,016.67 to pay off his old loan elsewhere. But now he can settle the whole matter through the Stock Clearing Corporation with a check to the latter institution for $16,016.67 at the end of the day. In other words, by balancing the firm's loan account with its stock account, a net debit or credit balance at the Stock Clearing Corporation can be obtained which represents a considerable saving in the employment of bank credit which would otherwise prove necessary. Owing alike to the clearance of loans and to the clearance of cash extensions of balance contracts performed by the Day Clearing Branch, a very large saving in the number of checks which must be drawn to settle each day's business is effected. This is mainly due to the fact, already cited, that the clearing member draws one final check to settle both his loan and his contract account with the Stock Clearing Corporation. Statistics show that this saving in the number of checks drawn amounts to about 92 per cent.

The stability of the entire mechanism of American finance is enhanced by the operations of the Stock Clearing Corporation. So sound and firmly founded is the latter institution, with its $10,000,000 of liquid funds on deposit in New York banks, and with the 100 per cent assessable liability accompanying contributions to this clearing fund, that, as we have seen, Stock Clearing Corporation checks to any amount go without certification. Furthermore, the corporation in its granting of unsecured accommodation to its members is able to know for just what purposes this accommodation is being employed, and even to check hour by hour the progress its members are making in meeting the problems of financing they encounter during the day. Other functions, as has already been suggested [11] will doubtless be undertaken by the corporation when the practical limitations imposed upon its further growth by lack of space and other factors will permit. But today, although admittedly in an intermediate stage in its evolution, it is able to perform a vast and genuine service to the entire financial community, and, therefore, to the entire world of commerce and industry.

[11] See Chapter X.

CHAPTER XII

THE COMMISSION HOUSE

Importance of the Commission House

In our second and third chapters it was pointed out that the human machinery of the stock market consists of two separate types of Exchange members, the brokers and the traders or dealers. The offices of the latter are for the most part confined to the Wall Street district. But owing to the establishment of a huge network of private wires reaching out from the commission houses of Wall Street to their branch offices and correspondents in all parts of America,[1] the commission brokers, who years ago were also located mainly in lower Manhattan, are now to be found all over the nation. The Stock Exchange of today is, therefore, a national market, meeting national needs and available for instant service to Americans over our whole vast national area.

Since it is through the commission houses, whether their head offices in Wall Street or their branch or correspondents' offices scattered from upper Manhattan to California, that orders from the American investing and speculating public are relayed to the Stock Exchange floor, the commission broker's office is an integral and extremely important part of the whole Exchange system. Indeed, much of the most difficult and necessary work of marketing Exchange securities is done, not in its headquarters, but in the hundreds upon hundreds of commission houses all over America, and even abroad. We must therefore give some time and attention to the problems, the methods, and the typical activities of the commission house,

[1] See Chapter XIV, Figure 55.

if we are to gain an adequate conception of the work and true significance of the Stock Exchange.

Almost everyone has seen the outside of a commission brokerage office, whether in the lofty cliff dwellings of the Wall Street district, or elsewhere in the United States. In the banking section of even small American cities one can almost invariably discover a brokerage office, built sometimes of cut stone like a small bank, or, if less ostentatious, with its green silk window curtains, and its stereotyped legend in gold letters,

JENKINS & CO.
Members of the New York Stock Exchange

Not so many people, however, have inspected the inside of such offices, and still fewer are sufficiently acquainted with their machinery to understand thoroughly the business which is transacted there.

All commission houses are partnerships, one of whose partners is a member of the New York Stock Exchange. Corporations are not permitted to own a seat there. But a considerable difference, of course, exists between the various commission houses in the scope and variety of the service they render the public. There are also fundamental differences between the main office and its branch or correspondents' offices beyond the Wall Street area. But in order that we may see as much as possible of the brokerage house machinery, we will elect to visit the main office of a fairly large commission house located at 500 Wall Street.

Appearance of a Typical Commission Office

As we enter the outer door we come into a hallway, the inner wall of which is pierced by several windows marked "Cashier," "Telegrams," and "Deliveries," and by a door inscribed "Customers." Since we are neither creditors or debtors of the firm, nor messenger boys or stock runners, we open the latter door and enter the customers' room—the largest and most important in the office.

The first item of furniture which strikes our eye is the large quotation board on the wall. Many present-day brokerage offices still prefer the older type of quotation board, which consists simply of a large blackboard upon which current prices are chalked up. Other commission houses favor the oak or mahogany board with cardboard tickets. This latter type of board is equipped with horizontal ledges in which green cardboard price tickets printed with black figures are inserted. The record of the active stocks which the board contains, runs vertically, giving the highest, lowest, and last current quotations for the day. Above each individual stock record is usually a red plate, containing the ticker symbol of the given stock in white letters, as well as its latest dividend rate. On one side of the board (if the house executes orders in other stock or produce markets) is a space for stocks listed only on out-of-town exchanges, and for such speculative and staple commodities as cotton, wheat, corn, pork, sugar, etc., etc.

The "board boy" ceaselessly paces up and down in front of the board, changing the latest quotation by inserting new cards, as new prices are called out to him by another employee of the house standing beside the stock ticker, to one side of the board. This latter instrument, together with the somewhat similar news tickers containing a record of the latest announcements and events occurring all over the world, fill the room with a low metallic stuttering. Thus the spectator can see easily and quickly just what the various markets are "doing."

Difficulties of Financial Abbreviation

But to read stock quotations, considerable knowledge on his part is necessary. The various stocks are each indicated, not by their full titles, but by a system of abbreviations or symbols which the exigencies of time and space—both precious in Wall Street—make necessary. Some symbols are obvious enough—even the amateur might suspect that "CAN" referred to the American Can Company, or that "PA" indicated the Pennsylvania Railroad. But most stock symbols are more difficult to identify than these, and before they all become at once recognizable constant reference must be had to the explanatory list of symbols hung near the stock ticker. The amateur's difficulty is only increased by the hasty and unintelligible explanations given him by experts. If he asks to what stock "MN" may refer, he will probably be told "Mexican Pete," which is not the sobriquet of some southwestern desperado but an abbreviated way of saying "Mexican Petroleum." But in time he too will learn to refer to the Southern Pacific Railroad (SP) inelegantly but concisely as "Soup," or the Missouri, Kansas and Texas Railroad (MKT) as "Katy." This queer and sometimes fantastic slang used in brokerage circles undoubtedly saves valuable time, and is convenient, practical, and simple enough—once it is understood.

Departments of the Commission House

Facing the stock board are several rows of armchairs where the customers or prospective customers of the firm can sit and watch the fluctuations in prices shown on the board. Close at hand to the customers' chairs is the cage of the order department, which handles the execution of such orders as the customers in the office may tender it, and such telephoned, telegraphed, or written orders as come in to the firm. Nearby is the cashier's cage, in many ways the real executive center of the office. In adjoining rooms are the private offices of the firm partners, the accounting department where the company's bookkeepers work, and perhaps an unlisted department, which handles orders for securities not listed upon the Stock Exchange, and which usually consists of a desk, a telephone, a few financial manuals, and one of the quickest and most incisive brains in the office.

In addition, there is the statistical department, which often carries on general financial educational and publicity work, prepares special reports for the firm or its customers on various financial topics, issues circulars and market letters, and performs a variety of other practical and necessary routine work for the firm. The educational work done by Stock Exchange brokerage offices all over the country is valuable from a national standpoint, since it acquaints the public with current economic problems, and makes available everywhere information regarding investments—a significant service when the ignorance of many investors and the persistence of clever and daring stock swindlers are remembered.

The Romance of Gauging the Future

There are few more fascinating aspects of the modern business world than that revealed to the thoughtful spectator of the stock board. As one sits in the customer's chair, he is, through the news ticker, placed automatically in touch with the latest news of the world—news which the linotype batteries of the great metropolitan papers have not yet even started to cast into columns and pages. But the stock board itself goes even this instantaneous news service one better, for the ever-restless and ever-changing security prices which it records are the estimates in dollars and cents of *future* rather than present conditions in the whole country's industry and trade.[2] The hopes, the fears, the aspirations and dreams and dreads of the whole nation thus find an expression here in the ceaseless fluctuations of stock prices.

The sheer romance of this constant attempt to discount the future which causes much of the price fluctuation in speculative stocks makes a particularly strong appeal to the imaginative

[2] See Chapter XIV.

mind, for the thoughtful student of modern society and civilization can see in it the true significance of the stock market as a barometer of the future. Moreover, many hard-headed American business men, who never engage in marginal transactions in securities, nevertheless follow the course of stock market prices very closely in order to foresee the probable future tendencies of their own particular business.

But the commission broker, being of necessity an eminently practical man, can scarcely be expected to maintain expensive offices, engage numerous highly trained technical employees, buy a Stock Exchange seat at around $100,000, obtain extensive credit facilities at the banks, and undergo great and constant business risks, merely for the philosophic pleasure of furnishing amusement to day-dreaming students of industry and trade. Although some brokers occasionally speculate in securities themselves, their business consists mainly of earning commissions on their customers' orders. Let us see exactly how this is done.

Perhaps the simplest and most graphic way in which to describe the operations occurring in a typical broker's office, is to follow a transaction of a single customer from beginning to end. In an earlier chapter [3] this method was in part employed. But at that time many details of the typical transaction cited were omitted, since they involved technical procedure still unexplained. But now that the manifold and complex activities of the Stock Clearing Corporation, as well as the call and time loan markets have been outlined, we can retrace the various stages of a similar transaction in more complete detail.

Opening a Brokerage Account

Accordingly, we will suppose that Mr. Blank has for the first time found his way into the customers' room of Jenkins

3 See Chapter III.

and Company's main office at 500 Wall Street. Before he can buy or sell any securities there, however, he must open an account with the firm, a proceeding which closely resembles opening a bank account. Usually the customer will be personally introduced to the broker by a mutual acquaintance, and will then be given a card upon which to fill out his name, address, and present occupation. In some brokerage houses the prospective customer is also requested to sign an agreement that he will maintain with his broker sufficient margin on his account, and that in the event of his failure to respond promptly to a call for additional margin the brokerage house is authorized to take such action as it may deem necessary to protect its interests. Under the rules of the Stock Exchange [4] no employee of a bank, Stock Exchange house, trust or insurance company is permitted to open a speculative account. Apart from this restriction, and, of course, the inevitable deterrent of insufficient capital, the Exchange is open to all Americans on an absolutely equal footing.

As a necessary consequence to opening his account, Mr. Blank deposits with Jenkins and Company, say, a $1,000 Baltimore and Ohio Railroad 6 per cent bond, ten shares of United States Steel preferred, and his check for $2,000—or about $4,000 altogether—to provide margin for such transactions as he may later desire to enter into. The value of the securities thus deposited as margin does not, however, serve to reduce the customer's debit balance with the firm. Some commission houses frown on accepting security collateral for marginal purposes, although the practice is sufficiently extensive to justify the above example.

Blank may next ask the broker point blank to tell him which securities he should buy. Such questions place the broker in a delicate position. He will probably reply that he will take no "discretionary orders," meaning that he does not care to

[4] See Appendix, Chapter XII (a).

assume the responsibility of having the customer's orders left to his discretion. The broker's unwillingness to "handle his customer's account" is natural enough, for the broker is after all merely the customer's agent, and it is consequently the broker's business to take orders, not to give them. Furthermore, he cannot guarantee to have a more accurate idea of security values than the customer himself. But, as a compromise, he will usually express his opinion upon the various securities which the customer may name, or himself indicate securities which in his opinion deserve special consideration.

Giving a Buying Order

During the ensuing week Blank decides to purchase 200 shares of the Southern Pacific Railroad Company. He might, of course, simply write or telegraph or telephone his order to the brokerage office. But in order to visualize the course of his order more concretely, let us suppose that he goes to the office of Jenkins and Company a few days after opening his account with the firm and, having watched the board for a while, fills out an order blank (Figure 47) for the 200 shares of Southern Pacific.[5] This order blank instructs Jenkins and Company to purchase the stock, as the customary phrase goes, for his "account and risk." Blank may, of course, put a time limit upon this order, or mark it "G.T.C." (good till countermanded); he may likewise make a limited order of it by placing a price upon the slip at or under which he is willing to purchase the stock, or he may leave it a market order to be executed at the prices prevailing in the market at that time. Market orders, of course, never have a time limit placed upon them. These various limitations placed by customers upon their orders have already been sufficiently outlined in an earlier chapter.[6] In this particular case, let us suppose that Blank marks his order "G.T.C." and puts a limit upon it at 90.

[5] See Chapter III, page 54.

[6] See Chapter III, page 53.

Since, as we have seen, Blank deposited in all about $4,000 with Jenkins and Company, and since the 200 Southern Pacific he has just ordered at 90 will be worth $18,000, he is purchasing on a margin of about 20 per cent.

The Necessity for Maintenance of Margins

Since the broker is merely the agent of his customers and cannot share in any profits which they may make in their purchases and sales of securities, naturally he cannot be expected to share with them any losses which they may experience. But, as we have seen,[7] the commission house contracts for the purchases and sales of securities which its customers may direct, in its own name, and other similar purchasing and selling houses, aided by the Stock Clearing Corporation, will hold it very strictly to account for the payment of money or the delivery of stock called for by these contracts. When the market moves adversely to his customers' interests, and when in consequence his customers' margins tend to diminish and expose him to risk, the broker will, therefore, by the terms of the agreement between him and his customers, demand additional margin from them in order to protect himself against incurring losses on their accounts. If a customer does not respond to such a call for more margin within a reasonable time, then by the terms of the same agreement the broker is authorized to close out the account of his customer, by selling the latter's long stock or buying in the stock of which he is short.

The soundest and most conservative brokerage practice favors strict insistence upon "margin calls," and disagreeable though such a call may sometimes be to a customer, he should respect his broker all the more for his promptness in demanding more margin. On the other hand, the best interest not only of brokerage houses and banks, but also of the given customer

[7] See Chapter IX, page 220.

himself and other similar customers, requires a prompt response by him to calls for more margin.

The Pledging of Customers' Securities

The marginal customer must also agree that all securities purchased and carried on margin for him by his broker, or those deposited as margin on his account, may be loaned by the

BUY

200 Southern Pacific

90

G.T.C.

John Blank

Figure 47. Office Buy Slip. (Size 4⅛ x 3½.)

Containing Mr. Blank's order to buy 200 Southern Pacific at 90, good till countermanded.

BOUGHT

200 Southern Pacific

90

Figure 48. Office Report Slip. (Size 3¼ x 4⅛.)

Containing report of purchase of stock for Mr. Blank.

broker, or may be pledged by him, either separately or together with other securities, without further notice from the broker.[8] Except for the constant hypothecation at the banks of securities purchased on margin by customers, the broker would be unable to extend credit to his customers and enable them to purchase on margin.[9] But securities which the customer has purchased outright and has left in his broker's hands, cannot be pledged for loans in this way without the customer's consent,

[8] See Appendix, Chapter IV (c).

[9] See Chapter VIII, page 172.

since they are entirely the customer's property, unless, of course, they have been used to furnish margin on the customer's account.

Blank's order for 200 Southern Pacific, let us suppose, is limited to the price of 90, and is marked "G.T.C." He hands it through the window to the order clerk, who first passes it to the margin clerk, to learn if Blank's account has sufficient margin. If his margin with the firm is insufficient to justify taking on additional stock on margin, the order clerk will not execute the order until Blank produces sufficient additional margin, either in the form of a check or in readily marketable securities. But since in this case Blank's margin is ample, the order clerk at once telephones the order to the Stock Exchange over the firm's private wire direct to the floor. The order is received there at the firm's telephone booth, and given by the telephone clerk to the firm's floor broker, who at once goes to the Southern Pacific post, executes the order,[10] and so informs the telephone clerk, who in turn reports the purchase back to the order clerk in the office(Figure 48). Simultaneously, the reporters on the floor have "caught the sale" and turned it in to the Quotation Company; perhaps before the order clerk has been notified that the sale has been effected, Blank may see the brief but confirmatory message "SP. 2.90" appear on the stock ticker in Jenkins and Company's office. But Blank must not jump to the conclusion that such a price on the tape will necessarily represent the purchase of his own stock, for reasons previously stated.[11]

The Commission House Machinery in Motion

When he first receives the order, the order clerk stamps the time of its receipt upon it, in order to be able to run down any possible future questions about its execution, and files it alphabetically. When the report of its execution is received

[10] See Chapter III, page 58. [11] See Chapter VI, page 143.

from the Exchange, the order clerk pulls out the order blank again, marks upon it the price at which the purchase was made, and again stamps it to check the time at which it was executed.

JENKINS & CO.,
500 WALL ST.

New York, August 4th 1920

Mr Blank

We have this day **BOUGHT** for your account and risk, in accordance with the rules of the New York Stock Exchange.

No. SHARES	DESCRIPTION	PRICE	TIME	FIRM NAME
200	Southern Pacific	90	2.03	Jefferson + Co.

It is agreed between broker and customer:
1. That all transactions are subject to the rules and customs of the New York Stock Exchange and its Clearing House.
2. That all securities carried from time to time in the customer's marginal account, or deposited to protect the same, may be loaned by the broker, or may be pledged by him, either separately or together with other securities, either for the sum due thereon or for a greater sum, all without further notice to the customer.

Respectfully yours,
JENKINS & CO.
By William Jones

Figure 49. Broker's Confirmation. (Size 5⅜ x 8⅜.)
Showing purchase by Jenkins and Company of 200 Southern Pacific at 90 from Jefferson and Company, at 2:03 P.M.

In most offices the order is then listed on triplicate forms in order to provide the accounting, clearing house, and report departments of the brokerage house with a record of the purchase. The report department at once makes up a memorandum of the purchase (Figure 49), which states from what Exchange member the 200 Southern Pacific was purchased, as well as the price, the date of the purchase, and other data. This memorandum,[12] is commonly known as a "confirmation," and is at once dispatched by mail to the customer's address. The accounting department, on receipt of its copy of the order form, enters the item on Mr. Blank's account with the firm, and the margin clerk carefully revises the figure of Blank's present margin.

Lastly, the clearing house department enters the item of the 200 Southern Pacific purchased on the firm's clearing house blotter (since transactions in Southern Pacific stock are regularly cleared).[13] That evening, when Jenkins and Company makes up its balance or clearance sheet to send to the Night Clearing Branch, the item of 200 Southern Pacific appears as stock to be received. If Blank's transaction was the only one handled that day by the firm in this particular stock, it will on the morrow obtain from the Night Clearing Branch in its statement of "stock balances to receive" instructions to receive 200 Southern Pacific from some designated Exchange member. The stock is paid for by Jenkins and Company under the supervision of the Day Clearing Branch described in a previous chapter.[14] The 100-share certificates, when received, may be put in a loan envelope by the cashier and sent to the Forty-first National Bank of New York as collateral for a loan;[15] or they may be loaned to some other broker who has sold this amount short and wishes to make a delivery to his purchaser.[16]

Sequel to a Margin Purchase

But sooner or later Blank will either sell out this stock at a profit or loss (see Figures 50 and 51), or else pay up what he owes upon it and "take it up," to hold outright as an invest-

[12] See Appendix, Chapter XII (b).
[13] See Chapter IX, page 220.
[14] See Chapter X.
[15] See Chapter VIII, page 184.
[16] See Chapter IV, page 82.

ment. If Jenkins and Company have loaned the certificate to some other broker, they will request its return, upon which they will return to the borrower its money equivalent which he loaned them in exchange for it, and deliver the stock to Blank, or to some other firm to whom they have sold it upon his subsequent instructions. While if Blank's stock is reposing in a loan envelope at the bank, Jenkins and Company may substitute some other equally valuable security or securities in place of it, obtain the certificate, and deliver it to Blank,[17] on receipt of his check for the sum which he still owes upon it.

SELL

200 Southern Pacific
Mkt.
John Blank

Figure 50. Office Sell Slip. (Size $4\frac{1}{8}$ x $3\frac{1}{2}$.)

Containing Mr. Blank's order to sell 200 Southern Pacific "at the market."

SOLD

200 Southern Pacific
92

Figure 51. Office Report Slip. (Size $3\frac{1}{4}$ x $4\frac{1}{8}$.)

Containing report of sale of stock for Mr. Blank.

The Practice Regarding Transfers

One frequently troublesome detail, however, has been disregarded in the above operations—the matter of transfer.[18] So

[17] See Chapter VIII, page 190.

[18] See Chapter X, page 263.

long as a share certificate is irrevocably assigned by a Stock Exchange house, it constitutes a good delivery. Hence, stock held by a firm on marginal account for its members, if so assigned, may be made out in the name of any firm, and still be readily salable or constitute satisfactory collateral for a loan. If the stock is non-dividend paying, there is little purpose in having it retransferred every time it changes hands. But if it pays dividends, they will, of course, be paid to the firm or individual in whose name the stock stands. In consequence, it is customary for firms holding stock on margin account to have it transferred into their own name before the corporation books close for dividends, in order to receive the dividends accruing on the stock.

In the previous chapter upon the bond market,[19] an explanation was given of the custom of selling bonds with accrued interest added to the selling price. Somewhat the same thing occurs in the case of dividend-paying stocks, although in a less mathematically exact manner. As the day approaches when the books of a corporation are closed for the payment of a dividend, the stock tends to sell at a higher price which roughly equals its regular price at that period, plus the dividend about to be paid. Once the books are closed, however, the new purchaser of the stock will not receive the dividend, which will go to the holder of the stock at the time when the books were closed. Hence, the amount of the dividend to be paid is promptly subtracted from the price of the stock, which under such circumstances is said to sell "ex-dividend." Sometimes, however, in strong bull markets, when stock prices are rising swiftly, the price of the given stock may rise sufficiently to offset the amount of the dividend. In such a case the subtraction of the dividend would not be revealed in the current price of the stock.

---

[19] See Chapter VII.

Functions of the Cashier

The work of overseeing the prompt and proper transfer of stocks, like so many other of the technical details of the brokerage office, falls to the cashier of the firm. The cashier is in many respects the practical executive of the office and supervises its entire routine. It is he who borrows money on the firm's stock, either at the banks or on the Exchange, who deposits money at the banks and checks it out again, who oversees the receipt and delivery of the firm's daily stock balances, and who pits his judgment against the loan officers of the banks and trust companies in obtaining loans for his firm. It is little wonder that so many cashiers ultimately become partners in their firms, or, on the other hand, that so many governors of the Stock Exchange have in their younger days served their apprenticeship in the cashier's cage.

The Bookkeeping Side of Stock Brokerage

But we are getting far afield from the office of Jenkins and Company at 500 Wall Street. While Blank and other customers of the firm have been ordering the purchase and sale of securities, the bookkeeping or accounting department of the firm has not been idle. We have already seen that a copy of every order received by the order clerk is dispatched at once to this department, where an up-to-the-minute record of every customer's account is kept. Thus Blank can obtain an accurate and detailed statement of his account with the firm any time he asks for it. Few visitors to Wall Street have any conception of the importance or the amount of bookkeeping which the Stock Exchange necessitates. But for the army of bookkeepers which invades the financial district early each morning, and does not leave until the accounts of the various houses are completed for the day, the whole system would at once break down. Even a moderate-sized brokerage house must employ a large bookkeeping force to handle accurately and promptly the almost infinite detail of the day's business. During the tremendous markets of the spring and summer of 1919, it was mainly the bookkeepers who kept the office lights blazing in

DR JOHN BLANK,
13 FOREST STREET,
N. Y. C.

IN ACCOUNT WITH JENKINS & CO., 500 WALL STREET, NEW YORK

1920	Bought or Received	✓	Sold or Delivered	Description	Price	Debit	Credit
AUG 4	1M			BALT OHIO 6S 1929 J&J	RECVD		
	10			U S STEEL PFD	RECVD		
				CHECK			2000 00
3	200			SOU PAC	90	18030 00	
6			200	SOU PAC	92		18362 00
9			100	READING	75		7483 00
10	100			COL GAS & ELECT	60	6015 00	
12				DIVD 100 READING		100 00	
16				DIVD 100 COL GAS ELECT			150 00
18	100			READING	75 1/2	7565 00	
20			100	U S STEEL	88 1/2		8831 00
	100			CHES OHIO	40	4015 00	
25	100			MEX PETE	150	15020 00	
			100	CRUCIBLE	110		10981 00
28	100			CRUCIBLE	100	10015 00	
				PREM 100 CRU 30DAYS ¼		75 00	
31				INT 6 C C 1 1/2		47 01	
				INT 3%			95
AUG 31				BALANCE		13074 06	
	1M			BALT OHIO 6S 1929 J&J			
	10			U S STEEL PFD			
	100			COL GAS ELECT			
	100			CHES OHIO			
	100			MEX PETE			
			100	U S STEEL			

Balance	Date	[illegible]	Interest Days	Interest Debit	✓	Interest Credit
CR 2000 00	4	2 000 CR	L			33
16030 00	5	16 030	L	2 67		
CR 2332 00	6	2 332 CR	3			1.17
CR 9815 00	9	2 332 CR	1			39
CR 3800 00	10	3 603	2	1 23		
CR 3700 00	12	3 783	4	2 52		
CR 3850 00	16	3 633	2	1 21		
3715 00	18	3 715	2	1 24		
CR 1101 00	20	7 730	3	6 44		
2938 00	25	22 750.	3	11 37		
13028 00	28	21 859	3	10 93		
13074 06	31			37 61 9 40 47 01		1 89 94 95

E. & O. E.

Figure 52. Customer's Statement. (Size 12 x 9.)

the dark canyons of the financial district after even the Night Clearing Branch men had gone home, and who slept on hastily installed cots in the brokerage offices, in a strenuous but successful effort to keep up with the extraordinary succession of 2,000,000-share days on the Exchange.

Since, therefore, the broker's bookkeeper is so fundamental in the machinery of the Stock Exchange system, it were well to inspect a typical piece of his handiwork—the more so, too, since customers of brokerage houses rarely seem to understand the statements rendered to them by their brokers. Brokerage houses at stated intervals render statements to their customers of their accounts, as well as at any time when the latter demand them. These statements of the customer's account must not, of course, be confused with the confirmation of each particular transaction which, as has been noted, is sent to the customer as soon as possible after the execution of the order which it reports. Commission houses also make it a practice promptly to send notices to their customers of any dividend paid on stocks in their accounts, with a credit if it is long stock and a debit if it is short stock.

A Typical Customer's Statement

Figure 52 represents a typical modern monthly statement of the account of Mr. Blank, rendered to him by his brokers, Jenkins and Company. It contains columns for the dates of the customer's various transactions and for the amounts of the securities bought or sold. In addition, other columns contain a description of the item, the price at which it was bought or sold, the debit or credit thus incurred by the customer, and his debit or credit balance. At the extreme right of the statement the interest items are calculated upon a detachable slip in the manner shortly to be described. Such statements are made out with two carbon copies, and the originals usually record credit cash items in red. The original is kept as an office record, while one of the duplicates goes to the customer and the other is available for transmission to the branch office or correspondent in case the customer's order came in to the commission house from either of these sources. The statement is, of course, expressed in terms of cash rather than of securities. The customer is credited with long stocks and with the cash extension of stock sold, and debited with short stocks and the cash extension of stocks purchased.

Summary of Mr. Blank's Transactions

In the typical account of Mr. Blank under consideration, the customer in the beginning deposited as margin a $1,000 Baltimore and Ohio Railroad 6 per cent bond, 10 shares of United States Steel preferred, and his check for $2,000. He then bought 200 Southern Pacific at 90 and one day later sold it at 92. He next proceeded to sell 100 Reading short at 75, but some time afterwards covered the sale of 75½—an unprofitable transaction. He also purchased 100 Columbia Gas and Electric at 60, 100 Chesapeake and Ohio at 40, and 100 Mexican Petroleum at 150, and sold short 100 United States Steel common at 88½, and 100 Crucible at 110. The latter short sale he later covered at 100. Let us see how the bookkeeper of Jenkins and Company has posted these items, and others arising from them, upon Blank's monthly statement.

At the outset Blank's securities deposited as margin are entered as "Received," and he is credited with his check for $2,000. His first transaction was his purchase of 200 Southern Pacific at 90, which occurred on August 4. It is to be noticed that the date of this item on the statement, however, is August 5, for items are dated, not according to the dates when contracts for the purchase and sale of securities were made on the floor of the Exchange but when such contracts were settled by delivering the securities. If Blank's order was executed on a Monday, the contract would ordinarily be settled Tuesday, etc., according to the daily settlement system employed on the Stock Exchange.[20] So it is, too, with all the other purchases and sales entered on the statement—they are posted on the day when the contract is settled.

[20] See Chapter IX, page 203.

How the Brokerage Commission Is Entered

In connection with this purchase of 200 Southern Pacific at 90, the reader will also observe that Blank is debited for $18,030. The extra $30 represents the commission [21] charged by Jenkins and Company for making the purchase for him, and is added into the extension instead of being posted as a separate item. Since the customer's purchase of stock creates a debit cash extension, commissions are in this way added to it. On the other hand, since the customer's sale of stock creates a credit cash item, the commissions on sales are subtracted from the cash extension. Thus, when Blank sells his 200 Southern Pacific at 92, he is credited with $18,400 less commissions of $30 and taxes of $8, or with $18,362.

The Item of Taxes on Sales

This matter of taxing sales of securities, already alluded to in its economic aspects,[22] also should be watched as it affects the customer's statement. On the sales of stock of no-par value or of $100 par, there is a federal and a state tax of $2 each per 100 shares, or $4 for both. When Blank sold his 200 Southern Pacific, taxes amounting to $8 were therefore deducted from his credit extension, along with commissions. Since this tax applies only to the sale and not to the purchase of stocks, he was not taxed when he bought the stock. Southern Pacific stock has a par value of $100, while Reading has a $50 par. Accordingly, when Blank on August 9 sold 100 Reading his tax amounted to $2 instead of the $4 he had to pay for selling 100 United States Steel (another $100 stock) on August 20.

Dividends and Premiums

In a previous chapter it was stated that dividends upon the customer's long stock were paid to the customer, while divi-

[21] See Appendix, Chapter XII (c).

[22] See Chapter V, page 104.

dends upon his short stock he was himself forced to pay.[23] The accompanying statement gives illustrations of both cases. When the dividend on Reading is paid, Blank is already short 100 shares of this stock, and accordingly he is debited $100 for the quarterly $1 per share. But when the $1.50 per share quarterly dividend on Columbia Gas and Electric is declared, Blank is long of 100 shares, and consequently he is credited with $150.

Still another item remains to be explained—the charge for a premium for three days of 1/4 on the 100 shares of Crucible Steel of which the customer is short. We have seen [24] that when the floating supply of a given stock becomes scanty and and it is difficult to borrow it, the borrower must sometimes pay a premium to get the desired stock. Evidently this was Blank's experience with Crucible. On August 25 he sold 100 shares short at 110 and did not cover the sale until the 28th, when he purchased the same number of shares. In the interim, of course, Jenkins and Company had to borrow the 100 Crucible for him and, owing to its temporary scarcity, had to pay a daily premium of 1/4 per cent, or $25, for it, for three days. Accordingly, Blank is debited for $75.

Computation of Interest

Lastly, there remains to be considered the important factor of interest charges. These are calculated upon the detachable slip on the right of the statement. The column headed "Interest Adjustment" contains the cash amounts upon which the customer is due to receive or pay interest. To save time, all interest charges or credits are first calculated at 6 per cent, and the total credits and debits are then adjusted to the correct and actual rate, which, of course, may be either more or less than the flat 6 per cent rate first employed.

Referring again to the accompanying statement, it will be

[23] See Chapter IV, page 83.

[24] *Ibid.*

noticed that Blank's account has a credit balance of $2,000 (the amount of his check) for one day. Accordingly, he is credited with 33 cents interest upon it. But by his purchase of 200 Southern Pacific at a total cost of $18,030, he creates a debit balance of $16,030 which remains one day until he sells this stock. He is therefore charged interest upon $16,030 for the one day, and thus receives a debit of $2.67. This interest charge serves to repay his brokers the interest and commissions they may have had to pay on their loans.

At the end of the month a total debit and credit interest item is obtained. As shown in the illustrating statement, Blank is thus debited with $37.61 and credited with $1.89. These figures, as has been stated, were arrived at on the basis of a 6 per cent rate. But the brokerage house will rarely if ever pay as much as that on customers' temporary credit balances. In this case, indeed, Jenkins and Company pay 3 per cent, and, comparatively speaking, this rate is high. If the customer's credit interest item at 6 per cent was $1.89, at this actual 3 per cent rate it would amount to 95 cents. Accordingly, Blank is credited with this sum at the bottom of his credit column.

The Rate of Interest Charged

On the other hand, since our example is taken during a period of tight credit, the money which the firm had to borrow for Blank probably cost much more than 6 per cent. The exact rate of interest at which he is charged is derived by averaging the rate paid by the house on all of its various loans during that month. Let us suppose that this average rate of interest amounts in this case to 7 per cent. The firm add ½—let us say—to compensate it for its trouble, expense, and risk in making these loans for its customers and accordingly charges the latter 7½ per cent. This means that in addition to the 6 per cent, a carrying charge of 1½ per cent must be made. Therefore the $37.61 (or interest at 6 per cent) is increased by 25 per cent, giving $47.01 as the interest at 7½ per cent. This sum is then entered as a debit on the customer's statement. A special rule in the Constitution of the Exchange[25] forbids its member firms from competing unfairly with each other for business by charging "special and unusual rates of interest." Such a practice is looked upon by the Exchange as tantamount to a breach of its commission law.[26]

After these interest items are figured in, Blank is shown to have a total debit balance at the end of the month of $13,074.06. In addition, his account shows that he is long of the securities which he originally left with Jenkins and Company as margin—namely, his $1,000 Baltimore and Ohio 6 per cent bond and his 10 shares of United States Steel preferred, as well as the 100 Columbia Gas and Electric, the 100 Chesapeake and Ohio, and the 100 Mexican Petroleum which he bought on margin during the month. At the same time he is still short of 100 United States Steel common.

Determining the Customer's Margin

But what Mr. Blank is principally interested in is what his equity in the account, or the sum of money belonging to him in it, amounts to. This can be determined only by first imagining that his account has been completely closed—that is, that all his long stocks have been sold and all his short stocks bought in. Let us suppose that this is done on August 31, when Baltimore and Ohio 6's are selling at 91, United States Steel preferred at 107, Columbia Gas and Electric at 62, Chesapeake and Ohio at 44, Mexican Petroleum at 148, and United States Steel common at 85. At these prices we find that Blank's 320 shares of long stock possess a market value of $27,380, and his 100 shares of short stock a market value of $8,500. In addition,

[25] See Appendix, Chapter XII (d). [26] See Chapter XIII, page 345.

we learn from his statement that his debit balance owed to his broker amounts to $13,074.06.

Had Blank's account contained only long stock, his equity in it could be determined simply by subtracting his debit balance (which he owes his broker) from the total market value of his long stock (which is credited to the customer). On the other hand, had the account consisted entirely of short stock, Blank's equity would be determined by subtracting from his credit balance (for in such a case he would necessarily have a credit rather than a debit balance), the total market value of his short stock.

But in the somewhat more complicated instance above cited the customer's account contains both long and short stock. Perhaps the simplest way to reckon the customer's equity in such an account is to consider the account long or short according to the preponderance of its commitments, and figure in the lesser of the two afterwards. In this case Blank is long 320 shares and short 100 shares. His account is thus mainly a long account. In reckoning Blank's equity, therefore, we would naturally subtract his debit balance of $13,074.06 from the total market value of his long stocks, or $27,380, which would give us $14,305.94. But this last figure does not represent Blank's equity in his account, for there is another subtraction still to be made—namely the $8,500 which he must pay to cover his short stock at its market price. When this is subtracted, then Blank's true equity of $5,805.94 is obtained.

This figure represents the value of his Baltimore and Ohio 6 per cent bond ($910) and his 10 shares of United States Steel preferred ($1,070), or $1,980 altogether, which he originally put up as margin. It also contains the $2,000 originally deposited with the broker for the same purpose. When these two items are subtracted from Blank's total equity in the account, we find that his profit from his transactions amounts to $1,825.94.

The Margin Card

A current record of Blank's equity in his account—or his "margin," as it is more often called—is constantly kept by the margin clerk of the brokerage house. The broader economic significance of margins has already been discussed in a previous chapter.[27] The margin clerk keeps a separate card for the margin of every customer of his house, and constantly adjusts the customer's margins as the trend of security prices dictates. In this way the commission house is always in touch with the amount of margin maintained by each of its customers, and in a position to call the given customer for more margin, or to know whether he can safely make new transactions on the basis of his existing margin. The margin cards used by different Stock Exchange commission houses differ more or less in their details. Figure 53 represents one of the simpler forms of margin card. The items which it contains show the condition of Mr. Blank's margin at the time when his monthly statement above included was issued. It will be noted that the securities which the customer originally owned outright, but which he deposited as margin, are entered exactly like the securities which he subsequently bought on margin.

At the top of the margin card the customer's debit or credit balance, and the market value of his long and short stock are entered. These figures, as well as the margin derived from them by methods already outlined, are erased and changed as the fluctuations in market prices or other factors necessitate. Exchange houses differ somewhat in the exact way that they figure margin, particularly on an account containing both long and short stock. In the example given, margin on the short stock is not separately reckoned, inasmuch as in the event of a sudden and general decline in the security prices Blank would tend to benefit by the decreasing value of his short stock at the same time that he suffered by the lessened value of his long

[27] See Chapter IV, page 78.

stock. Thus his short stock tends to buttress his margin on his long stock, and hence his margin can be figured simply on his 320 shares of long stock.

JENKINS & CO.

NAME *John Blank*	TELEPHONE *1234*
ADDRESS *13 Forest St., N.Y.C.*	
OCCUPATION *Manufacturer*	

BALANCE	VALUE OF SECURITIES	MARGIN	%	POINTS
DR.	LONG			
$ 13074.06	$ 27380.00	$ 5805.94	21	18
CR.	SHORT			
$	$ 8500	$		

LONG	SHORT	SECURITIES	@	AMOUNT	
1 M		B. & O. 6s	91		910
10		U.S. Steel pfd.	107	1	070
100		Col. Gas & Elect.	62	6	200
100		C. & O	44	4	400
100		Mex. Petrol.	148	14	800
	100	U.S. Steel	85	8	500

Figure 53. Customer's Margin Card. (Size 5 x 8.)
Showing Mr. Blank's margin, debit balance, securities, etc., as of August 31.

Margin in Points and in Percentage

Margin is usually figured in points—that is, in the number of dollars per share which stock prices would have to decline before the margin became exhausted. Since Blank's margin on his 320 long shares amounts to $5,805.94, it amounts in even figures to $18 or 18 points on every single share of the long stock. In other words, every one of the 320 long shares would have to decline on the average 18 points (or $18 per share) before Blank's margin would be exhausted.

Margins may also be figured in percentages. Thus in Figure 53 Blank's margin is stated to be 21 per cent, because his equity of $5,805.94 bears that proportion to the total value of his long stock, $27,380. In very high- or very low-priced stocks, the percentage of the customer's margin is especially important. If, for example, a customer happened to hold shares whose price stood at about $600 or $700 apiece, a 20-point margin would be insufficient and a 10-point margin would be perilous. On the other hand, if the customers' shares were low-priced stocks, selling, let us say, at $5 apiece, a 20- or a 10-point margin would be impossible, and a 2-point margin probably conservative. In such cases the percentage relation of the amount of the margin to the value of the shares would have to be reckoned. A customer might have a 50-point margin on a $500 stock, and have only a 10 per cent margin, and yet his margin on $5 stock would be 20 per cent if it were 1 point. Thus it can be seen that the number of points of margin demanded by the broker varies with each individual case, and cannot be set at any one limited figure, either by law or by regulations of the Stock Exchange itself. It would be equally impractical to attempt to establish a fixed percentage between the margin and the value of the securities of which the customer is long or short. It is significant, however, that the Constitution of the Exchange contains the following provision:[28]

> That the acceptance and carrying of an account for a customer, either a member or a non-member, without proper

[28] See Constitution, p. 100, also see Art. XVI, Sec. 5.

and adequate margin may constitute an act detrimental to the interest and welfare of the Exchange, and the offending member may be proceeded against under Section 8 of Article XVII of the Constitution.

Safeguarding the Broker's "Box"

From the foregoing description of a single customer's experience with his brokerage house, as well as from what has already been said concerning the general machinery of the Stock Exchange in earlier chapters, a fair idea can be obtained of the daily routine of a typical Wall Street commission house. One picturesque feature of this routine, however, remains to be mentioned. Many Exchange houses, because of their unwillingness to leave security certificates of considerable value "in the box" in their offices overnight, rent safe deposit vaults of the New York Stock Exchange Safe Deposit Company in the basement of the Stock Exchange building.[29] Before the opening of the market each morning employees of the various Exchange houses may be seen, followed by their guards, removing from the Broad Street entrance to the Safe Deposit Company's vaults the heavy steel boxes of their firms containing the securities belonging to them, their partners, and their customers. And later on, after the Exchange has closed and business for the day is over, they return with their closely guarded burdens, and redeposit them in the Safe Deposit Company's vaults for the night.

The Stock Exchange was originally created to provide a free and open organized securities market where the American public could purchase and sell the leading American stocks and bonds. For over a century it has rendered indispensable economic services to the whole nation. On the other hand, without the public buying and selling, and without the commissions earned by the Exchange houses for executing the

[29] See Chapter II, page 40.

orders of the public, the present broad and continuous securities market on its floor would, of course, be impossible to maintain. These orders from the public at large can enter the securities market on the Stock Exchange only through the commission house. For this reason the commission broker is the principal if not the only representative of the Stock Exchange with whom the average man comes into personal contact. Usually, too, he is a partner or employee of a member of the Exchange, rather than a member himself.

Present and Former Scope of the Stock Market

In the earlier years of its history it was inevitable that the facilities of the Stock Exchange should have been employed locally rather than nationally. Even apart from the fact that the telegraph was invented as late as 1844, and not practically perfected until after that date, the economic growth of the United States did not until the past few decades really demand its services in extending the scope and availability of the organized markets. For while our Great West was still hewing down the primeval forest, laying road beds, and establishing those villages which were destined in after years to experience so remarkable a growth, its inhabitants, still pioneers, were naturally possessed of no surplus to invest in stocks and bonds.

But with the steady westward thrust of population and wealth into our southern and western states, the demand for stock market facilities has led to a similar extension of the Stock Exchange system into all parts of the nation, through the rise of the "wire house" type of Stock Exchange commission firm. The first sign of this coming development was shown in 1873, when a prominent Wall Street firm established a private telegraph line to its up-town office at 23rd Street—a great convenience at a time before the elevated railroad or telephone system, when it took over an hour to communicate between the two offices. The obvious advantages of such speedy means of communication soon bore more extensive results. In 1879 private wires were obtained by various Wall Street firms to their offices in the neighboring centers of Boston and Philadelphia. A similar connection with Chicago was inaugurated in 1881, and with San Francisco in 1901. Since that date the wire systems of several large Stock Exchange commission houses have crossed the border to various Canadian cities. Recently, one Wall Street firm has even installed a private wire by cable to Havana, Cuba. And when the steady growth of the Stock Exchange as an international market and credit center is realized, it seems patent that the future may witness the extra-national extension of the wire systems of many Stock Exchange houses.

At first considerable prejudice was shown against the new "wire house." It was thought that no firm could properly control its business over such distances. There was even a tendency to discriminate against the loans made by such houses, because of the supposed unreliability of the business. If anything, just the opposite attitude is taken today, for, other factors apart, the wire house represents a diversification of business risk over many parts of the country.

The Wire Systems of Today

Speaking of the extensive use of private wire systems today by financial and commercial firms, a recent writer[30] has the following to say:

> Now there are about a thousand private wires in operation, tapping every city or locality of any importance in the United States and Canada. It is estimated that they are more than 500,000 miles in length, and represent a yearly expenditure of more than $15,000,000, to which must of course be added the wages of the operators who man them and the other expenses for which their lessees are liable. It is therefore probable that

[30] "The Nerves of Wall Street" in *Commerce and Finance*, June 22, 1921, p. 879.

the private wire system of America costs more than twenty million dollars a year, and perhaps the total is a great deal higher . . .

Between New York and Chicago it is estimated that there are 100 leased wires; eight between Chicago and the Pacific coast; 100 between New York and Boston; 75 between New York and Philadelphia, Baltimore and Washington; 10 between New York and points south of Washington; 15 between New York and Montreal; 25 between New York, Pittsburg and Buffalo; and about 25 from New York to other nearby cities . . .

The private wires now in operation are mainly employed by those who are engaged in business on the great speculative exchanges of the country, the New York Stock Exchange, the Chicago Board of Trade, the New York Cotton Exchange, and the smaller stock and commodity exchanges of the country, of which there are about fifty . . .

Then there are many large industrial and financial concerns that operate private wires in handling their business. The Federal Reserve Banks have a private wire system connecting them and their branches with each other and the Federal Reserve Board in Washington. The United States Steel Corporation and most of the big packers have their own private wire systems. Many of the large banks and banking firms lease private telephone circuits between New York and their home offices.

Incidentally, not merely the figures relating to the extensiveness of these wire systems should be noted, but also those respecting their large annual cost. When those who may consider that the Stock Exchange brokerage firm's commissions are easily earned, or that the business is a royal road to fortune, realize that the house engaged in it must, in addition to earning interest upon an Exchange seat worth about $100,000 and upon business capital probably several times that sum, bear this heavy overhead cost of its leased wires, a more just and accurate idea of what the average commission house does for its customers can be obtained.

The Modern Wire Room

In the investment transaction traced in an earlier chapter,[31] Jenkins and Company was a typical wire house, with a branch office in Baltimore and its main office at 500 Wall Street and a private wire connecting the two. In addition, the firm probably had other private wires, reaching out from the New York headquarters to branch offices and correspondent houses at other points. In the Wall Street office of the firm, if these private wire connections were numerous, the order department might well occupy a whole room by itself, with expert telegraphers in charge of the far-flung wires. This work calls for vastly more accuracy and speed than ordinary telegraphy, and such operators must be unusually skilled in it to meet satisfactorily the tense pressure and unusual demands put upon them. Practically all such wire rooms have a device known as a "tell-tale," which records all messages passing through it. Its records are filed, and thus the responsibility for the rare errors which occur can quickly be determined.

The speed with which such a wire system (including operations on the Stock Exchange floor) works, is truly surprising, when its complexity and the distances it covers are remembered. The same authority [32] quoted above relates the following instance:

> A large New York and Chicago firm has an interesting speed record that has not yet been duplicated. Their correspondents in San Francisco sent in an order to buy a security on the New York Stock Exchange. The order was executed and advice of its execution received in San Francisco 56 seconds after it was given.

According to the same writer, one of the large Exchange commission houses has in the "regular order of business" received orders over their Havana cable, executed them, and

[31] See Chapter III.

[32] "The Nerves of Wall Street," in *Commerce and Finance*, June 22, 1921, p. 880.

had the report of the execution back in Havana in less than a minute.

Arrangement of a Wire System

The wire house arranges its wires much as the railroad its lines of track, so as to pick up along their length sufficient traffic to justify their expense. Hence the house places correspondents along its wire routes. No contract is entered into regarding the length of time the connection will be maintained. The house can discontinue it on a single day's notice if the business done by it fails to justify its expense. But the wire house notifies its correspondents in the beginning of its requirements with regard to such other matters of business between them as margin requirements, etc. It is, of course, usually much easier for the wire house in Wall Street to call its correspondents for more margin than its customers in or out of New York City.

Taken as a whole, the Stock Exchange system, with its various units of the board room, the Wall Street commission houses, their branch offices and correspondents, and the thousands of miles of private leased wires which connect them, has practically annihilated the considerations of space and time in the operation of America's principal securities market. A San Francisco customer has access to the board room market practically as ready and immediate as a customer in William, Nassau, or Broad Street offices—a stone's throw from the Stock Exchange building. By the magic of applied science and the phenomenal skill of the operators, Los Angeles is rendered as close to the Exchange floor as Boston, or New Orleans as Philadelphia. Of course the private brokerage wires are used to transmit news as well as orders to buy or sell, and in consequence the system makes for uniform intelligence and knowledge all over the land regarding security values, as well as an equalized instancy of dealing in the market.

National Character of the Stock Market Today

One practical result of this accessibility of the Stock Exchange to all parts of the United States and to nearby countries has been that its securities market is vastly less subject than formerly to local influence. Before the era of the fully developed wire house, the Stock Exchange was to a considerable extent a New York institution. There were bull leaders and bear leaders in Wall Street, and the stock market was to some extent subject to their personal attitude and operations. But, although the memory of these earlier generations of Wall Street men has given rise to a swarm of modern legends and modern superstitions regarding the Exchange, the stock market is today a national, not a local market, and has long since grown too big for the operations of yesteryear. An investigation of the Exchange market with respect to the origin of the orders coming into it,[33] undertaken in 1909 by the Hughes Commission, showed that on a selected day "52 per cent of the total transactions on the Exchange apparently originated in New York City, and 48 per cent in other localities." Since that date, and particularly in 1919, the out-of-town business transacted upon the Exchange has experienced a huge proportional increase, estimated by some authorities at 80 per cent orders from outside of New York City to 20 per cent New York City orders.

While no statistics comparable in exactness to those of the Hughes Commission exist for recent years, nevertheless a great increase in the proportionate amount of out-of-town orders on the Exchange, apart from being a matter of common knowledge in Wall Street, is shown by the increase in the number of correspondents from about 1,500 in 1909 to about 2,500 in 1919, as well as by the greater number of shareholders in the large corporations the stocks of which are listed on the Exchange.

[33] See Appendix, Chapter XII (a).

Benefits of the Extension of Brokers' Wires

Certain valuable economic results have flowed from this evolution in the market. A broader market has been created by it, representing more buyers and sellers than formerly, and hence with more power to render its listed securities negotiable and to distribute them among investors. And this has been accomplished despite the onerous tax on stock sales, and the burden of the surtaxes on the investable income of former large investors.

Moreover, the swift extension of branch offices and correspondents has made it possible for American business men to travel extensively, either in the United States or abroad, and at the same time keep in perfect touch with the market. The necessity for such accommodation has created what is known as "give up business." If, for example, a customer of a commission house with offices only in New York should be called away to some other city and while there should wish to have an order executed on the Stock Exchange for his account, he can go into any branch office or correspondent of any Stock Exchange commission firm there and place his order, "giving up" the name of the firm with whom he has his account. The branch office or correspondent, after verifying the facts over its wire system, will at once permit his order to be executed. Thus, any customer of any Stock Exchange firm is always as near the stock market as the nearest branch office or correspondent of any Stock Exchange house. In consequence, the New York securities market is readily accessible to practically all American business men at all times.

Overcoming Time and Space

Until the last century it had been one of the perennial problems of government to control large areas of land. Lack of facilities for communication and transportation had in the end frustrated even the ambitions of the Cæsars and Napoleons of history. That this difficulty was realized by the founders of this nation is attested by a recent writer [34] upon the present-day wire house:

> George Washington advised against including the Mississippi River in the Union. Webster opposed taking in Texas and Oregon. Monroe once warned Congress that a country which reached from the Atlantic to the Middle West was "too extensive to be governed except by a despotic monarchy." But they spoke in the days when mountains still retained mastery over man, when distances were measured in miles rather than in minutes.

By the achievements of scientific inventors and business organizers (and, incidentally, by the investors and speculators in the stock market who financed them, too) this former supposed limitation upon the physical size attainable by free governments has been dissipated. An almost equally notable triumph has occurred in the economic realm of business through the growth of free markets, and by the same means. The telegraph has made possible the rise of world markets, accompanied by an international stability in industry and trade. Without facilities for instant communication the present international market places would crumble and again resolve themselves into local markets, with scanty and precarious trading, and a parochial outlook.[35] In the instance of the Stock Exchange, therefore, its national and even international free market for securities, while fundamentally due to increased national wealth and natural economic forces, has been in a practical and immediate way due to the extension of the commission brokerage house through its wire system to thousands of branch offices and correspondents all over the nation, and even beyond its borders.

---

[34] T. S. Brickhouse, "The Back-Stage Side of the Wire Business," *Commerce and Finance*, June 22, 1921, p. 884.

[35] See Chapter XIV.

CHAPTER XIII

THE GOVERNMENT OF THE STOCK EXCHANGE

"What Is the Stock Exchange?"

Something has been said in Chapters I and II as to why and how the New York Stock Exchange was created and grew to its present magnitude as a securities market, while in Chapters III to XII a brief description of its present-day machinery and operating methods has been given. We must now consider another aspect of the Stock Exchange—its methods of government and administration.

It is first necessary, however, to answer a common question, concerning which considerable confusion exists in the popular mind—"Exactly what is the Stock Exchange?" The term "Stock Exchange" is commonly and correctly employed to denote: (1) the building at Wall and Broad Streets where trading in securities takes place; (2) the association of brokers and dealers who own this building and conduct trading operations inside it. But in addition, the words "Stock Exchange" are also often used in a loose and utterly inaccurate way with reference to everything and everybody in the Wall Street financial district, including not merely all types of banking establishments and corporation offices, and indeed the whole machinery of the money market located there, but also every fly-by-night promoter of worthless securities who may hire an office for a few weeks between City Hall and the Battery. Frequently these gentry are suddenly impelled to seek a healthier climate over the Canadian or Mexican border, while the permanent and legitimate financial houses and institutions in the Street remain to inherit the odium of their swindles and misdeeds. At most, the Stock Exchange is only a part of what is known as "Wall

Street." It must not be confused with the large number of enterprises, companies, and individuals, both legitimate and naturally beneficial, and illegitimate and naturally harmful, which are located in its immediate neighborhood.

The exact purpose of the Stock Exchange (using the term in its second meaning of an organization) can best be stated by quoting Article I of its Constitution:

> The title of this Association shall be the "NEW YORK STOCK EXCHANGE."
>
> Its object shall be to furnish exchange rooms and other facilities for the convenient transaction of their business by its members, as brokers; to maintain high standards of commercial honor and integrity among its members; and to promote and inculcate just and equitable principles of trade and business.

This simple and straightforward statement of fact will repay both thought and study, for it defines with exactness the limits within which the Stock Exchange operates.

Stock Exchange Membership

There are 1,100 members of this voluntary association, of whom some 200 or more live and do their principal business outside of New York City. A full membership is always maintained. Some members of the Exchange are in business entirely for and by themselves, while others are partners and representatives of various types of financial houses.[1] The total membership has long been limited to 1,100.[2] A nonmember secures a seat (as it is still called) either by purchasing that of some recently deceased or retiring Exchange member, or by bidding high enough for one to induce some member to sell. The price of a seat of course varies with supply and demand—prices in 1920 averaged around $100,000.[3] But membership in the Exchange is not simply a matter of money

[1] See Chapter II, page 45.

[2] See Chapter II, page 34.

[3] See Appendix, Chapter XIII (a).

To quote the first assistant secretary's comprehensive and succinct summary of the requirements for elegibility:[4]

> . . . the applicant must be a citizen of the United States, be of high character; have secured the agreement of a member to retire in his favor; be sponsored by two members who have known him at least two years; be in good health; free from debt; solvent; free from judgments; if engaged in lawsuits, must explain their nature; must present a written statement, as to date of birth, place of birth, and business career; and letters from at least three persons of standing, testifying as to his integrity; if unable to pay for the membership with his own means, the funds for the purpose must be a free gift to the applicant and released, otherwise he would not be free from debt, and he must agree not to allow the gift to become a debt; he should have some capital; and must receive at least ten favorable votes of the Committee on Admissions.

Thus the efforts of the Stock Exchange to safeguard both its own members and the investing public in all security transactions conducted under its auspices commence at the very outset of each member's career.

Constitution of the Stock Exchange

The new member is also required to sign the Constitution of the Exchange, thereby promising to abide by its requirements and making himself subject to the rigorous discipline for which it provides. The rules which the Exchange enforces are so just and necessary that for their own sake Exchange members heartily advocate their strict and instant enforcement, even on occasion against themselves.

This Constitution of the Stock Exchange has evolved from the original brokers' agreement made under the buttonwood tree in 1792,[5] and represents the results of more than a century's experience on the part of several generations of stockbrokers, through all the trying and difficult periods of our past

[4] Martin, p. 236.

[5] See Chapter II, page 29.

national economic life. It makes no pretense at specifically settling by a priori dogma or rule-of-thumb, all the possible eventualities in a highly complex and ever-changing business. Rather, it makes provision for determining future perplexing problems justly, swiftly, and with open minds. It has made precedents as circumstances have arisen, and for this reason is of interest and value to the historian of America's past economic life. It lacks the ponderous inclusiveness and meticulous detail of some of our present-day statute books. But it is superbly clear and practical, and leaves the way open for the enforcement of its provisions according to the substance and spirit as well as the mere letter of the law.

The Governing Committee

Subject to the Constitution the legislative and judicial powers of the Stock Exchange are placed without qualification in the hands of its Governing Committee.[6] This body consists of forty members of the Exchange, together with its president and treasurer. Ten governors are elected each year by vote of the entire membership.[7] This method of election makes for conservatism in the policy of the Exchange, as well as for the retention as governors of those members which the entire body deems best fitted by character and ability to serve the association in this capacity. Moreover, for the same reason, the same governors are often re-elected term after term.

The officers of the Exchange consist of the president, vice-president, treasurer, and other members of the Governing Committee, as well as the secretary, the first assistant secretary, and the accountant. The executive power of the Exchange is vested in its president, who directs the enforcement of its rules and regulations and presides over the Exchange and its Governing Committee. In the absence of the president, his duties are discharged by the vice-president. The treasurer

[6] See Constitution, Art. II.

[7] *Ibid.*, Art. IX.

receives, has charge of, and disburses the funds of the Exchange under instructions from the Finance Committee. The secretary, usually a former member and governor of the Exchange who has given up his seat and retired from active business, is appointed by the Governing Committee, and performs a wide variety of important duties, some of which are specified in the Constitution.[8]

The governors of the Stock Exchange are heirs to a long and honorable tradition, and to be elected a governor is considered one of the highest honors which American finance can bestow. The ability and conscientiousness which they lend to their responsible tasks is proverbial in Wall Street and out of it. Sheerly out of a sense of duty and loyalty to the Exchange and the public whom the Exchange serves, these forty carefully selected and experienced members, whose time and ability possess a constant cash value and are constantly demanded by their own interests and by other business enterprises, willingly give no small amount of service gratis to the Stock Exchange each year.

Powers of the Governors

In the hands of its Governing Committee is invested the real power of the Stock Exchange organization.[9] Its power to discipline members of the Exchange is practically absolute, owing to two fundamental provisions of the Constitution. The first of these[10] (italics are the author's) reads as follows:

> A member who shall have been adjudged by a majority vote of all the existing members of the Governing Committee, guilty of wilful violation of the Constitution of the Exchange or of any resolution of the Governing Committee regulating the conduct or business of members, *or of any conduct or proceeding inconsistent with just and equitable principles of trade,* may be suspended or expelled as the said Committee may

[8] See Constitution, Art. VII. [9] *Ibid.*, Art. II. [10] *Ibid.*, Art. XVII, Sec. 6.

determine, unless some other penalty is expressly provided for such offense.

The latitude and degree of the governors' authority is further extended by another section of the same article[11] reading:

> The Governing Committee may, by a vote of a majority of all its existing members, suspend from the Exchange for a period not exceeding one year, any member who may be adjudged guilty of any act which may be determined by said Committee to be *detrimental to the interest or welfare of the Exchange.*

Thus the power exercised by the governors is conferred in the most comprehensive terms. As the above and still other sections of the Constitution indicate,[12] they sit in absolute authority over every member and his partners. Penalties are often inflicted for acts that violate no formal law and that would not give a plaintiff any technical standing in a court of law. In their nature, therefore, Stock Exchange rules are searching and ethical rather than merely legal rules. The high standard of conduct enforced by such thoroughgoing regulations as these is necessary for the absolute mutual confidence enjoyed by members in each other, in the exercise of their trading privileges.

Disciplinary Methods

The methods employed in disciplining members are swift and equitable. Having been presented with the charges made against him in writing, the accused member appears before the Governing Committee, sitting as the jury in his case—a jury which is expert in the complexities of Exchange transac-

[11] *Ibid.*, Sec. 8.

[12] The closer student of Stock Exchange administrative methods is referred to the following additional references in the Constitution for further powers of the Governing Committee: Arts. III, 2, 3; XII, 1; XVI, 5; XVII; and pp. 96–97 and 100.

tions and which gets at the true facts of the case directly and keenly. They decide whether the accused member's conduct has or has not violated the rules and principles of the Exchange. From their decision the member on trial can, of course, appeal to the courts.[13] One such case—it might be noted in passing—caused six years of litigation in the courts. The remarkable and significant fact that in every one of the many instances where this has occurred the courts have sustained the action of the board of governors, speaks well for the justice and ability with which the latter conduct the affairs of the Exchange.[14] The decisions of the governors are quickly effected and are governed by the merits of each individual case. Because of their complete authority in disciplinary matters, the morale and spirit of the Stock Exchange are in the keeping of its Governing Committee.

Other Stock Exchange Committees

The work of the Stock Exchange, however, is too extensive and too intricate to be conducted by a single committee of forty-two members. Accordingly, several standing and special committees composed of members of the Governing Committee and appointed by it [15] are delegated to supervise and conduct special departments of the work. Appeals from the decisions of any of these committees can, of course, be taken to the Governing Committee, as the final governing authority of the Exchange.[16]

A brief survey of these subcommittees of the Governing Committee is therefore needed for an adequate understanding of the administrative side of the Stock Exchange.

The Committee of Arrangements (7 members) maintains the Stock Exchange building and controls the telegraph and telephone lines running into it. It supervises the conduct of

[13] See Appendix, Chapter XIII (b).
[14] *Ibid.*, (c).
[15] See Constitution, Art. XI.
[16] *Ibid.*, Art. XII.

business on the floor, considers complaints of violation of rules, purchases supplies, and engages, pays, and discharges employees.

The Committee on Admissions (15 members) passes on applications for membership in the Exchange, along the lines already outlined as well as the claims of suspended members for reinstatement.

The Committee on Arbitration (9 members) investigates and decides claims or matters of difference involving contracts subject to the rules of the Exchange between members, or at the instance of a non-member, between a member and non-member. Members possess the right of appealing from its decisions to the Governing Committee.

The Committee on Business Conduct (5 members) considers the business conduct of members with respect to their customers' accounts. It also has the duty of keeping in touch with the course of prices of Stock Exchange securities, in order to prevent improper transactions. It can at any time examine into the dealings of any member and report its findings to the Governing Committee.

The Committee on Commissions and Quotations (9 members) is a recent amalgamation of two former separate committees. As was the case with the old Committee on Commissions, it enforces the rules of the Exchange relating to commissions, partnerships, and branch offices by reporting violations of them to the Governing Committee. It also has charge of all matters relating to quotations, and can approve or disapprove any applications for the ticker service which reports them.

The Stock Exchange has always waged unrelenting war on the "bucket-shops," and in 1914 organized the original Committee on Quotations to exert more efficiently all its possible powers in their extermination. As these bucket-shop operators pretended to deal in securities listed on the Stock Exchange, they were dependent upon the use of the stock tickers which report the latest prices there for these securities. By placing restrictions as to whom the use of the tickers is granted, as well as upon the uses to which tickers shall be put, the Stock Exchange has been mainly responsible for the gradual but steady elimination of the nefarious bucket-shop operators throughout the nation.

To the Committee on Constitution (5 members) are referred all proposed additions, alterations, or amendments to the Constitution of the Stock Exchange.

The Finance Committee (7 members) examines and audits the accounts of the Stock Exchange, pays its bills, and reports to the Governing Committee.

The Committee on Insolvencies (3 members) is selected from the Committee on Admissions and investigates the cause for any failures of members.

The Law Committee (5 members) considers all questions of law affecting the interests of the Exchange, advises the president at his request, represents the Exchange in conference with other interests, and in the interest of the Exchange can examine the dealings of any member of the Exchange.

The Committee on Securities (5 members) makes rules defining the requirements for regularity in delivery of securities dealt in on the Exchange, and decides all questions relating to the settlement of contracts subject to the rules of the Exchange, with respect to due bills, irregularities thereof, and all questions of reclamations therefor.

The Committee on Stock List (5 members) receives and considers all applications for placing securities upon the list of the Exchange, and hence making it possible to trade in them on its floor. Its exact functions in this and other respects are discussed with some detail in a later chapter.[17]

In addition to these standing committees, the Governing

[17] See Chapter XVI.

Committee also appoints certain of its members to serve on special committees. Of these perhaps the most important is the Committee on Library (5 members) which maintains statistical records and a library upon financial and economic subjects. It co-operates with schools, colleges, and economists generally to give information regarding the Exchange, and serves as a committee on public information with respect to the Stock Exchange's functions and activities.

Employees of the Stock Exchange

This general account of the human mechanism of the Stock Exchange administration must include mention of its many and various employees. These range from experts of long experience who, under the supervision and control of the Governing Committee and its subcommittees, are in immediate charge of responsible and highly technical operations, down to the army of cleaners and scrub-women who invade the building after the close of each day's market, to put the Exchange in condition for the next day's business. A brief description of the many adjuncts to the securities market which are housed under the Stock Exchange roof was given in Chapter II,[18] and a running account of the Exchange employees on its floor in Chapter III.[19] In number, the employees of the Exchange aggregate several hundred persons, and include tube attendants, pages, bond clerks, phone attendants, price-reporters, and telegraph-operators. In the Night and Day Branches of the Stock Clearing Corporation a large group of highly trained and efficient clerks and executives carry on the vital work of clearance. Over all a corps of watchmen stand guard day and night.

Association of Stock Exchange Firms

To correct prevalent misunderstanding and confusion, a word should also be added here concerning the Association of

[18] See Chapter II, page 40. [19] See Chapter III.

Stock Exchange Firms, which is composed of the partners of Stock Exchange members. While this association has no official connection with the Stock Exchange, nevertheless it co-operates with the Exchange in many ways to improve conditions and correct defects in the New York securities market. The purpose of this association is "to promote more friendly relations among its members, and urge the maintenance of high standards and just principles of business." The cashier's section of this association is composed of the cashiers of the various Exchange houses. In a previous chapter [20] we have noted the responsible part played in the commission houses by the cashier. This cashier's section is therefore an organization of experts and besides carrying on its monthly publication, *The Cashier,* it does a splendid work as a clearing house for the discussion and investigation of the many technical practical problems constantly arising in the stock brokerage business.

Disputes Regarding Contracts

With this brief but fairly comprehensive sketch of the organization and methods by which the Stock Exchange is governed, we can pass on to a few of the common and typical problems which call for solution and settlement by its authorities. And first, something should be said regarding such disputes as arise from bargains made on the floor of the Exchange. In previous chapters [21] the conditions under which contracts are entered into on the Stock Exchange have been briefly described. Often, indeed, a single word or even a mere nod of the head constitutes an agreement to buy or sell securities worth many thousands of dollars. Occasionally, however, in the speed and rush of the trading, misunderstandings will arise. Some of these are settled on the spot by the parties concerned.[22] The rule of the Exchange is that, once entered into, a bargain must stand, unless *both* parties to it agree to

[20] See Chapter XII. [21] See Chapters II and III. [22] See Chapter III, page 58.

alter its terms. Exchange contracts are looked upon as sacred and neither buyer nor seller may cancel them. Accordingly, any serious disputes are taken before the Arbitration Committee and judged entirely on their merits, justice being done quickly and effectively.

"Wash Sales"

So much is said concerning "wash sales" that a word concerning them is necessary here. A "wash sale" occurs when two parties engage in fictitious transactions in order to establish artificial prices, with no real intention of exchanging money or goods. This indefensible practice is non-existent on the floor of the New York Stock Exchange. We have seen [23] that the original Constitution of the Exchange provides expulsion for any member of the Board "making a fictitious sale or contract." The present Constitution [24] states:

> Fictitious transactions are forbidden. A member of the Exchange or a member of a firm represented thereon who shall give or with knowledge execute an order for the purchase or sale of securities which would involve no change of ownership, shall be deemed guilty of conduct or proceeding inconsistent with just and equitable principles of trade, and punished as prescribed in Section 6 of Article XVII of the Constitution.

The above section provides either suspension or expulsion as the Governing Committee may determine. Moreover, as has previously been stated,[25] the broker is compelled both by the custom of the Stock Exchange and the laws of New York State to render his customers on their request a confirmation of every order executed for them, which states the name of the firm from whom the customer's securities were purchased, or to whom they were sold. This important safeguard obviously prevents the broker from only pretending to execute

---

[23] See Chapter II, page 30.

[24] Constitution, Art. XXIII, Sec. 7.

[25] See Chapter XII, page 307.

the customer's orders, since it enables the customer to verify their execution readily and quickly.

Matching Orders

A similar but subtler evil consists of "matching orders." An outside party might conceivably hire two brokers, and by giving orders to one to buy and to the other to sell, at identical prices, manipulate the price of a security listed on the Exchange. Both brokers could be quite innocent of any intention of misdoing, and still be the unconscious agents of collusion. Yet such a practice is contrary to the rules of the Stock Exchange, as can be seen in Article XXIII, Section 7, quoted above, which forbids the execution of "an order for the purchase or sale of securities which would *involve no change of ownership.*" In practice, however, two Exchange brokers, even if so inclined, could scarcely match sales often enough to cause any considerable manipulation of price in the open market, without attracting the attention of other members. The Business Conduct Committee is constantly watching any peculiar price movements occurring on the Exchange, with full authority to investigate and report them to the Governing Committee.

A few other instances where there is danger of matched orders also deserve brief explanation. It may happen that a broker may receive two separate orders from two distinct sources over the telephone from his firm, one to buy and the other to sell the same security at the same price. To avoid any doubtful practices arising from such cases, the Constitution (Article XXIII, Section 9) provides that:

> Where parties have orders to buy and orders to sell the same securities, said parties must offer said securities, if they be bonds at ⅛ of 1%, and if stocks at ⅛ of one dollar, higher than their bid before making transactions with themselves.

Another regulation [26] forbids any member of the Exchange, whether a specialist or not, from acting as both a broker and a dealer in the same transaction.

Significance of the Commission Law

Great emphasis is also laid upon the enforcement of the commission law,[27] which establishes the minimum rate of commission that Exchange members may charge as brokers for the execution of orders in the various classes of listed securities. This commission averages about 1/6 per cent [28]—a very low figure when the elaborate and expensive machinery made necessary by the securities market and described in the foregoing chapters is taken into consideration. Certainly in the modern world of business a smaller rate of commission is nowhere paid for the purchase or sale of any commodity, while a wealth of instances might be cited where commissions in certain classes of goods amount to 25 and even 50 per cent. Early in the history of the New York securities market, however, it was deemed advisable to establish a minimum rate of commission; the historic brokers' agreement of 1792, indeed, owed its existence principally to the minimum rate of 1/4 per cent which the original twenty-four eighteenth century brokers agreed to charge in it. The minimum rate of commission has always been severely insisted upon, and infractions of the rules relating to it have always been sharply punished, because cutting the commission below the established minimum would not only be unfair to houses which adhered to it, but would also deprive the public of a uniform and constant minimum cost for the services rendered it by Stock Exchange members. A century and a quarter of experience has completely confirmed the opinion of the original brokers under the buttonwood tree that business in securities could not otherwise be

[26] See Constitution, p. 85.
[27] *Ibid.*, Art. XXXIV.
[28] See Appendix, Chapter XII (c).

conducted permanently, conservatively, and safely. For without a commission law the business of executing orders in the stock market would tend to flow into new and rash Exchange houses which, to "get business," would be willing to assume risks likely at any time to overwhelm them and the other firms which did business and made contracts with them.

Another rule of the Exchange [29] relates to the advertising which its members are permitted to do, which is restricted to "a strictly legitimate business character." A glance at the financial section of any leading metropolitan newspaper will reveal how thoroughly this regulation is enforced. In England, indeed, members of the London Stock Exchange are not allowed to advertise at all, but in the United States such a flat prohibition would not prove salutary, both because of the more extensive employment of advertising with us, and because of other even more fundamental differences between British and American business.

The Circulation of Rumors

Still another cause for constant vigilance by the Exchange authorities lies in its provision regarding rumors: [30]

> That the circulation in any manner of rumors of a sensational character by members of the Exchange, or their firms, will be deemed an act detrimental to the interest and welfare of the Exchange.

In spite of occasional assertions to the contrary, this rule is enforced unsparingly and without favor by the Exchange. Yet its enforcement is from the nature of things difficult to effect, and of course can be carried out only with respect to members of the Stock Exchange. More than this the governors can hardly do, for they have no authority to regulate the conversation of everyone even on Manhattan Island, let alone

[29] Constitution, p. 79.

[30] *Ibid.*, p. 102.

other apprehensive and talkative sections of the inhabited world.

Rumors, as a matter of fact, never start on the floor of the Exchange but outside it; yet, since their effects are principally felt in the stock market, the opposite is commonly supposed. The tense and imaginative atmosphere of Wall Street is peculiarly liable to magnify trifles into bonanzas or catastrophes —but we must remember that the Stock Exchange and Wall Street are not synonymous. A rumor widely circulated by word of mouth (and in the press also, for that matter) in recent months concerning the supposed shaky financial condition of an old, conservative, and deeply rooted business house in New York, was, after a painstaking study, finally traced to a well-meaning but inaccurate trade publication in another continent.

The circulation of false news and rumors by unprincipled speculators to affect security prices is mentioned by Macaulay as common to the British securities market of the early eighteenth century. Certainly the amazingly swift and accurate news service of the New York financial district, its impartial news tickers and keenly analytical financial press, has vastly reduced the ability of artifically circulated rumors to affect security and wholesale commodity prices, either upwards or downwards—and both price movements proceeding from such a cause are equally bad. If those unsparing critics of the Stock Exchange would only inform its governors as to some new and practicable method of preventing the circulation of sensational rumors, they would deserve and obtain the thanks of that able and conscientious but not omniscient and omnipotent body.

Closing Contracts "Under the Rule"

A further set of regulations [31] relates to the methods employed in closing contracts "under the rule." Such contracts

[31] Constitution, Art. XXVIII, also Chapter IX.

are occasioned when a house either announces its insolvency, or fails to make deliveries of stock or payment for stock by the proper time. The member to whom money or securities are due but have not been delivered, is permitted to make a new contract involving the same transaction in the same security, and substitute it for the old contract which has not been fulfilled. Any profit or loss occasioned to the member who is forced to make such a second contract is credited or charged to the member who has failed to keep his contract. Owing to this method of closing contracts under the rule, all unnecessary delay and risk by the party closing the contracts is eliminated.

Suspension of Trading

It sometimes becomes necessary to halt the trading in securities upon the Exchange, either in a single security or in all securities. In the former case of a given security, trading in it may be temporarily suspended, or it may be permanently stricken from the list, in the manner and for the reasons outlined more fully in a subsequent chapter.[32] But upon two wholly exceptional and extraordinary occasions the entire Stock Exchange has failed to open its doors and all its operations have ceased.[33] This has happened only twice since 1792—in the panic of 1873 and at the outbreak of the Great War in 1914. So drastic a step has been resorted to only in an economic convulsion, when the maintenance of a security market beneficial to the public has been rendered an impossibility. Needless to say, to close the Stock Exchange requires the affirmative vote of the Governing Committee. So harmful to the well-being of the entire nation has the closing of the Exchange proved (even though this harm was more than counterbalanced on both occasions by stern necessity) that it is never resorted to except under the most unusual circumstances.

---

[32] See Chapter XVI.

[33] See Chapter II, page 37.

Past Criticism of the Stock Exchange—Question of Incorporation

The Stock Exchange has by no means escaped criticism and even governmental investigation in the past, both with respect to the nature of the services which it daily renders to American business and to the manner in which its business is conducted and administered. On the whole, the Exchange is today undoubtedly the gainer by this searching criticism; it has adopted in toto many practical and constructive suggestions made to it, and successfully adapted others to improve its methods in a practical way. But unfortunately, during the course of the Hughes Committee investigation of 1909, the so-called Congressional "Money Trust" investigation of 1913, and the hearings on the proposed Bill S. 3895 before the Banking and Currency Committee of the United States Senate in 1914, many inaccurate criticisms of the Exchange were uttered and given widespread publicity. Fanciful remedies for fancied grievances also were not merely proposed, but urged with insistence. Some of these have already been dealt with in the preceding pages. It remains necessary here to examine the proposal to force the Stock Exchange to incorporate.

The mystical benefits of incorporation are vehemently urged with a rhythmical recurrence which is analogous to the tidal swings of the stock market, and perhaps occasioned by them. For every bear market results in financial losses and indignation on the part of speculators, who, being unable to understand the intangible laws of economics, vent their feelings upon the tangible Stock Exchange. Someone, as by a stroke of inspiration, cries "Incorporate the Stock Exchange," and again it is necessary to point out the fallacy of this proposed remedy.

The Stock Exchange is regulated by law to the extent of the law's constitutional limitations.[34] As an association, sub-

[34] See Regulation of the Stock Exchange, pp. 556–557.

ject to the laws of the state, it possesses enough property to satisfy any ordinary claims against it. As a market place it is subject to the law of the state of New York, many of whose statutes relate to the stock brokerage business. Recourse from the decisions of its Governing Committee can always be had to the courts of the land. The Stock Exchange is consequently just as subject to the law as an association as it would be if incorporated, and no benefits in this respect would therefore be derived from incorporation.

Instant Action Necessary

The Stock Exchange has consistently opposed forcible incorporation not because of any hostility to proper governmental regulation but for entirely different reasons, which inevitably arise from the nature of the business conducted beneath its roof. To begin with, there is the very important necessity for swift and expert decisions. The Stock Exchange more than any business organization on earth demands instant action. The government of the stock market cannot be halted, not merely for six months but for even a second, without grave dangers. It is the balance wheel of irresistible tides of emotional public feeling. Cripple its power to steer and brake itself, and it might well become a public menace instead of a public benefit.

As it is, instant action can be taken in the conduct of its affairs by experts in a highly technical and complex business, who are responsible and can be subjected to the processes of the law later on, if need be. The present safe and efficient methods are in striking contrast to what might happen were the Exchange incorporated, and subject in a crisis to an injunction by an irresponsible party or a national enemy. It is generally appreciated that in the unprecedented summer of 1914, the governors of the Stock Exchange literally averted what would have been the most appalling panic in our history, by closing the Stock Exchange at the psychological and economic moment. The delay of a day—yes, of even an hour—in closing might have spelled ruin and disaster to America. It might have proved no little advantage to Imperial Germany, for example, had the Stock Exchange on July 31, 1914, been incorporated, and at the mercy of her swarm of spies and propagandists then in our midst, unknown and unsuspected, who by court proceedings could have brought an injunction to prevent the prompt closing of the Exchange.

Neither are such occasions when instant and expert action is needed only to be found at the outbreak of wars. In the every-day conduct of the Exchange there must always exist authority, complete and unhampered, to act without a second's delay. There was no war in the fall of 1920, nor epoch-making international crisis. Yet at noon on September 16, 1920, a tremendous explosion occurred only a few score yards from the Stock Exchange building, which shattered the windows throughout the heart of the financial district and killed some forty men, women, and children. Only the lowered curtains in the lofty Stock Exchange windows prevented possible casualties upon its floor. At once the news of the explosion was flashed over the tickers to all parts of the country. In the light of the subsequent severe but gradual decline in security prices, it is not unreasonable to imagine that, had this bomb accomplished its purpose and had the Exchange attempted to remain open that day, an avalanche of selling orders might have swept into it from all parts of the nation, and a narrowly averted panic might well have occurred then and there.

Fortunately, the president of the Exchange almost instantly rang the gong and suspended trading, and shortly afterward the governors voted to close the Exchange until the morrow. Had the authorities of the Exchange, who handled that dangerous and wholly unexpected crisis so efficiently that today it has been almost forgotten, been restrained by the restrictions to which, by the terms of their franchises, many incorporated bodies are subject, there might have been a very different story to tell. The Stock Exchange members heartily share with the public a distaste for panics. It is small wonder that they do not agree with the recurrent proposal to incorporate the Exchange.

Enforcement of Discipline

A less fortuitous but perhaps even graver danger which would result from incorporating the Stock Exchange would be that its present morale and strict discipline over the conduct of its members would be profoundly shaken and impaired. We have seen that the regulations of the Stock Exchange relating to the business conduct of its members go even beyond the common law in the earnest attempt to maintain "just and equitable principles of trade," and that these regulations are immediately and thoroughly enforced. From the inherent nature of the transactions which take place in an organized securities market, such a high and ethical spirit of legislation is necessary. The general recognition of this necessity by Exchange members, in fact, is responsible for the severe and instant punishment to which they have voted to make themselves liable. "Under a legislative charter the terms of membership and the relations of the members to the governing body of the Exchange would be subject to legislative control, whereas they are now a matter of contract. The present disciplinary power of the governing body is based on this contractual relationship. Under the contract fixing the terms of membership every member agrees to observe the rules of the Exchange and submits himself to the jurisdiction of the Board of Governors to punish any violation of the rules by fine, suspension, or expulsion, as the case may be. The most effective of these rules are couched in the broadest language to bring within their sweep not only acts that are wrongful from a legal point of view, but also acts that are inconsistent with fair dealing and in any way detrimental to the Exchange as a great market for securities."[35] As Mr. Horace White, chairman of the Hughes Commission, expressed it, "Forcing upon the Exchange an act of incorporation would impair this disciplinary power and involve the Exchange in extensive litigation at heavy costs without any advantage to the public."[36] The morale which exists on the floor of the Exchange is not a condition isolated from and unrelated to the prosperity of the nation. It is a national asset. As a subsequent chapter[37] will demonstrate in some detail, it performs economic services of profound benefit and significance to all classes of our population. Any disruptive and weakening force exerted upon the organization or standards of the Exchange would consequently constitute a drag upon the economic progress of the United States.

But the danger to the public from an incorporated Stock Exchange would not be merely general and abstract. Apart from the profound public harm, as outlined above, a constant liability of personal and individual injuries would likewise ensue. Why should the investing public, it might be asked, be compelled during years of litigation to make contracts for large sums through their brokers with a possibly unscrupulous member, whose very solvency might easily be impaired while his case unavoidably hung fire in the courts? Yet this would become a disquieting possibility were the present summary powers of the governors crippled by incorporation of the Exchange. In this, as indeed in other respects, the interest of the public is consequently much more adequately protected in its dealings in the Exchange under its present régime, than could possibly be the case under an incorporated Exchange. It

[35] See Regulation of the Stock Exchange, p. 557.
[36] *Ibid.*, pp. 294 and 557–558.
[37] See Chapter XVII.

has nothing to gain and almost everything to lose by incorporation.

Not a Profit-Making Organization

Another aspect of the matter not without bearing upon the question is furnished by the fact that the Stock Exchange is quite unlike the typical business partnership or corporation. It has never sought or obtained any special franchise from the state. It is not run for a profit, but simply as a necessity to its members and their customers. Financially speaking, it only aims to pay its expenses. Its members' income is derived from their personal business, and not unnaturally they are best satisfied when their dues to the Exchange are lightest. Corporation laws, which are primarily aimed at institutions run for the maximum obtainable profits, are therefore in many ways inapplicable when applied to an organization which generically is and always has been a voluntary association. It must likewise be borne in mind that an organization such as the Stock Exchange, with 1,100 members located all over the nation, has the same interest as the public at large in the conduct of its affairs, rather than a narrow and specialized interest opposed to the public interest.

In concluding this scanty and yet already overlong discussion of the dangers of incorporating the Exchange, the fact should be noted that the Hughes Investigation of 1909 refused to recommend incorporation,[38] and that after a careful investigation by the British Royal Commission of 1877, the London Stock Exchange was likewise not required to incorporate, but was permitted to continue its internationally beneficial work as a voluntary association.[39] In both the largest stock exchanges of the world, then, as indeed in smaller ones, of lesser general significance, the argument for incorporation has been thoroughly exploded.

[38] See Appendix, Chapter XIII (d).

[39] See Van Antwerp, pp. 231-234.

Jurisdiction of Stock Exchange

To approach the question of the extent of the Exchange's jurisdiction, we have seen that it is essentially a market place with provisions for the maintenance of "just and equitable principles of trade" therein. Over its membership it has full and necessary power, but there its authority naturally and rightfully ends. John R. Dos Passos, an acknowledged authority on the laws of the Wall Street securities markets, states that the jurisdiction of the Stock Exchange should be confined and limited "to those matters which arise between its members in the course of their business with each other as brokers; otherwise its judicial powers might be extended to embrace every affair of human life, which was never intended and which the law would not permit." And this general position in regard to its proper jurisdiction, the Exchange itself takes also.

The possible extension of the Exchange's powers, curiously enough, has been urged more strongly by amateur critics than by the Exchange itself. Frequently in the past they have attempted to make a club of the possible but undesirable extension of the Exchange's powers to regulate evils, real or fancied, in our larger corporations. Of course, no Exchange in the world has ever been made use of in this way, or ever should. The Exchange is clearly conscious of the fact that no one has appointed it to supervise the affairs of all listed corporations, to discriminate among the customers of its members with a superhuman and infallible eye for hidden motives, oversee all the banks and financial institutions of all kinds in Wall Street and elsewhere, and to try to change the fundamental and eternal laws of economics to suit the erstwhile complainant's every passing whim. Indeed, should the Exchange be foolish enough to rush in whenever someone indignantly demands, "Why doesn't the Stock Exchange stop this?" the other camp of critics might for once have some justice behind its ancient and threadbare but ever-recurring outcry against the "tyranny of Wall Street, etc., etc."

Responsibility to Public Keenly Felt

The Exchange sticks to its last. It maintains a market place, and enforces just and equitable principles of trade within it. Yet the Exchange has always been ready and willing, so far as its inherent limitations permit, to co-operate in any movement looking to the benefit of the investing public. Something has been said regarding the unremitting and successful fight it has waged against the bucket-shop. While a very conservative force, it none the less has always been emphatically patriotic and public spirited. The Exchange realizes its essential community of interest with the public and its responsibility to the public. The governors of the Exchange take vastly more concern over this responsibility than the public has any idea of.

The reader of these pages must have gleaned from them some idea of the complexities of the business conducted in the Stock Exchange. A more lengthy and searching study of the source books here quoted, or of actual conditions in Wall Street today, would only increase his realization of its infinite detail and subtle technicalities. It must therefore appear as a unique tribute to the manner in which the Exchange is administered that no business community in this or any other country can be cited where higher standards of good faith and fair dealing prevail than on the floor of the New York Stock Exchange; that inviolable contracts can be made there by a word or a nod, even in periods when the commercial world is swept with the cancellation, repudiation, and "welching" on contracts.

The present organization of the Stock Exchange has, as we have seen, resulted from an intensely practical and varied experience since 1792. The vast spread of corporate enterprise in America since 1830 is in itself a pragmatical tribute to the management as well as the work of the Exchange. Another impressive tribute is likewise furnished by the steady growth and extension of the Exchange system to all parts of the country. Ill-managed and economically dangerous institutions do not continue to grow in this way from century to century.

CHAPTER XIV

ORGANIZED MARKETS AND THEIR ECONOMIC FUNCTIONS

Antiquity of Markets

In the preceding chapters a description has been given of the daily operations of the New York Stock Exchange. It now remains to say something about the economic significance of these operations. And lest, in examining it so closely, the Stock Exchange should seem to stand out as an isolated exception among our modern market places, it will first be necessary to say something about the broader significance of market places in general.

To establish markets is one of the most ancient and fundamental instincts of civilization. From the earliest times the development of industry has necessarily been accompanied, step for step, by the constant creation and expansion of markets which could *distribute* the products of industry. Travelers tell us that even in darkest Africa natives, still in a state of savagery, are perfectly accustomed to market places, where the buyers and sellers among them can meet to barter with each other their simple products of the chase and the fields. The oldest civilizations of the world had established market places prior to the earliest times of which any records have come down to us. The battered temple pylons of ancient Egypt, for instance, show us the fisherman, the weaver, the potter, the poulterer, the farmer, and the metal-worker bartering their several products in market places centuries before currency was invented.

The markets of the classical world, developing from equally crude and primitive trading, attained a broader scope and a higher degree of organization and played a more significant part in the processes of civilization than most historians seem to appreciate. The famous Agora, long the center of Athenian political life, where the just Aristides and the shrewd Themistocles were ostracized from the state, was originally a market place which had sprung up at the foot of the Acropolis where the seven roads of Attica converged. Long before Solon instituted the Athenian coinage system, the fisherman from the Piræus bartered his fish here for the barley of the Attican farmers.

The Roman Forum

Such, too, was the origin of the great Forum of Rome, the most famous spot in classical antiquity. For half a thousand years all European civilization was ruled from this spot. But long before there was any Roman state and while the Romans were still a small and struggling provincial people, this forum had been a market place for cattle. Before the dawn of history the Campagnian peasant drove his herds into what was later destined to be the political center of the world, to barter them for the goods of other traders who also congregated there. There being no currency, goods were at first valued according to the number of cattle they sold for—a custom which was responsible for the derivation of the Latin word *pecunia* (money) from *pecus* (a herd).

But the most remarkable thing about the great Roman Forum is that it is again performing its original function. Centuries have passed since the fall of the Roman Empire. The temples, the triumphal arches, the rostra with its war beaks of the captured fleets of Carthage where Cicero and Antony spoke—all these former symbols of the might of Rome have long since disappeared. The Forum today is a forlorn and desolate spot, marked only by shattered masonry and broken columns. The Roman people itself as a racial entity has long since ceased to exist. But today the Forum has again become a cattle market —the *campo vacchino,* as the Italians call it—into which the Campagnian peasants again drive their cattle to sell. Thus this spot between the seven hills of Rome, which started as a cattle market, then became the political center of the world, and has finally reverted to a cattle market, affords a striking illustration of how deeply rooted and fundamental market places often are to mankind.

Marketing in Imperial Rome

The purchase and sale of debts and money were conducted in imperial Rome, and perhaps even earlier in republican Athens. It is interesting to note that even in ancient Rome the financial and commercial markets were already clearly differentiated. Of the nineteen *fora* of Rome, those devoted to the purchase and sale of commodities were known as the *fora vendalia,* while the bankers and usurers (or *argentarii*) used to take their stand in the *fora civilia* or *judicialia,* where political activity centered and where popular assemblies and courts of justice were held. Of the exact extent of financial operations in those days little is really known. But some of the comments upon the daily life in Rome made by the later satirists are of interest to the Wall Street banker and broker of today. "Why," asks Juvenal [1]—no feeble "muckraker," even by modern standards—"do you look as woebegone as Creperius Pollio when he goes around offering a triple rate of interest and can find no fool to trust him?" The perennial outcry that the interest rates are "juggled by insiders" for their benefit is at least as old as Persius, who qualifies a sentence with the significant clause, "if by some crafty trick you flog the money market with a whipcord." Verily, there is little new under the sun!

[1] "Non erit hac facie miserabilior Creperius Pollio qui triplicem usuram praestare paratus circumit et fatuos non invenit?" (Juvenal, Satire IX, 11, 6–8.)
" . . . . si puteal multa cautus amarum vibice flagellas." (Persius, Satire IV, 1, 49.)

The limits of space preclude further mention of the extensive market places of the ancient world. Neither can we linger in the largely cityless era of the Middle Ages to follow the wandering fairs, which sprang up in response to the eternal laws of supply and demand even in the face of an unstable political life and a hostile theology. In these medieval fairs future trading seems to have been practiced to some extent, and their pie powder [2] (or "dusty foot") courts, which administered a rough and ready justice to contentious and quarreling buyers and sellers, were the historical forerunners of the governing committees of our modern exchange. Nevertheless before proceeding to the discussion of the latter organizations, the significance of market places as fundamental economic factors in the progress of civilization deserves at least a few general remarks.

Civilization's Debt to Market Places

The social life and culture of even the most ancient cities cannot be adequately understood without considering them as market places dependent on the ever-shifting routes of trade. Most of the cities of the ancient and modern world—whether prehistoric Cnossus or the London of today—have owed their location and much of their political power and cultural eminence to their usefulness as market places for goods. This fundamental relationship of the market places to the wider cultural and political aspects of the cities which have in time grown up about them is most obvious and apparent in the earlier stage of city development. Within their market places the growing cities of history have often come to set up the statues of their gods, organize armies, talk politics, hold assemblies, and sometimes rule whole empires.

Although often hidden by the rhetorical flights of orators and patriots, the celebration of military triumphs, and even

[2] An Angelicized corruption of the French, *pied poudré*.

the more enduring artistic and social achievements of the superstructural city life built about it, the parent market place of the city steadily performed its less striking but more basic economic functions. The steady exchange of goods among unremembered merchants, the influx of imports, and the outflow of exports, went quietly on. While on the Acropolis Pericles was planning a greater Athenian empire, while Phidias was carving the white loveliness of the reliefs on the Parthenon, or while Plato was discoursing of immortality in the Academy, the purchase and sale of goods proceeded steadily in the Piræus—in the main unremarked by the historians and unsung by the poets, and yet fundamentally vital to the glory and power of the Athenian state.

On the other hand, once its market place had decayed, the city which so often scorned it, so often viewed it as an objectionable congregation of noisy sharpers and rascals, was smitten as if with a palsy. Indeed, the ever-shifting routes of trade and the stern competition between market places has left a wake across the world of ruined cities, of abandoned or decayed communities, of rotting harbors, whence in better days intrepid tradesmen went down to the sea in ships to satisfy the clamor of the market place for the goods of distant lands and strange peoples.

The mere passage of time has not altered this inexorable economic law. The great cities of the present day exist at the sufferance of supply and demand. As market places they arose, and as market places they will continue to prosper, or else go the way of Venice and Carthage. America is still too young a nation to realize the full significance of her market places. There seems no particular limit set against the continual growth of her cities. Yet we too must cherish our market places, lest in the end we learn the bitter lesson which was forced upon the Phœnicians of Tyre or the Greeks of Corinth.

Evolution of the Market Place

Thus far, the term "market place" has for the most part been employed in its widest sense, as a general meeting place for all sorts of merchants interested in the exchange of all sorts of goods. We must now examine more closely some of the practical and immediate aspects of markets, in order to differentiate between their widely varying types.

The earliest and simplest markets were formed by the congregation in one place of buyers and sellers, driven together by the economic necessities of trade. These original markets did not in the beginning specialize, but dealt in all kinds of goods and were located for the most part in the streets or open places of the town. Farmers drove in from the country with foodstuffs to sell, weavers displayed their textiles, and smiths their manufactured articles. Markets of this primitive type, at least in foodstuffs, still exist in some American and European cities, and are common in the bazaars of the immemorial East.

But as communication became easier, population (and hence the consumption of goods) greater, and political and social conditions more stable and tranquil, a process of specialization began. At first, of course, this tendency appeared within the single original market place itself. Traders in textiles took their stand in one part of it, traders in foodstuffs in another—just as, in the Stock Exchange today, the Steel crowd always gathers about the Steel post, the bond crowd in the bond market, etc. But with the increase in trading, certain commodities which experienced the heaviest trading would break away from the single original market and form separate markets exclusively for themselves.

At first these special markets were often conducted in the open streets. But with a further increase in their transactions they have tended to assume the more dignified title of "Exchanges," and finally to go under a roof with a restricted membership. As a part of the same evolutionary process, contracts for the receipt and delivery of the given commodity or article replaced on the trading floors of the exchanges the actual commodities or articles themselves. Systems of clearing and settling these contracts were then instituted.

This entire evolution is well illustrated by the London Stock Exchange. Securities were at first dealt in at the Royal Exchange, along with goods and commodities of all kinds; at length outgrowing this general market, they overflowed into a street market in Exchange Alley; this outside market, in turn, after lodging precariously in various coffee houses, finally erected its own building and became the London Stock Exchange. The shorter but similar evolution of the New York Stock Exchange has already been described.[3]

Prerequisites for the Creation of Exchanges

In the case of every exchange, however, such a complete evolution has depended both on the volume of trading in the particular commodity and on the nature of the commodity itself. Unless it was a staple article, widely demanded by consumers and hence produced in considerable quantities, there would not be sufficient trading in it to justify the creation of an exchange. Moreover, unless it could be easily graded and standardized, trading in it would usually involve small retail transactions in various grades of the commodity rather than wholesale transactions in large and uniform units of a standardized quality. Furthermore, many widely produced and widely consumed articles have proved too perishable to permit their handling through the most highly organized type of wholesale market. Other factors, too, such as the proportion of production obtained from a single source or institution, etc., also have a vital bearing on whether or not an exchange might evolve for the given commodity.

---

[3] See Chapter II.

In the gradual and confused process which has attended the higher development of markets, therefore, a considerable number of articles—and in particular, perishable foodstuffs and articles of widely varying quality and relatively small demand—have lagged behind, and have either remained in the old markets made in the street or else have moved back across the sidewalks into the retail stores. Trading in such commodities is usually sluggish and speculation in them occurs on too narrow and limited a scale to afford the fullest economic benefit to the public. In consequence, the risks involved by carrying them are considerable and the profit on their occasional sales for that reason has to be very large.

But with the heavily demanded and more easily standardized commodities, as we have seen, a further evolutionary stage has been attained. As the Hughes Commission report clearly and directly states, "markets have sprung into being wherever buying and selling have been conducted on a large scale. Taken in charge by regular organizations and controlled by rules, such markets become exchanges."[4] These exchanges—or wholesale markets in staple and carefully graded articles—are commonly called "organized markets" because of the elaborate organization, comprehensive rules, and sometimes extensive mechanical equipment which they develop in the furtherance of their business.

We have already followed in some detail how such an organized market in securities developed during the last century in New York City. A similar evolutionary process has left us with organized markets for cotton, wheat, and other cereals, and other staple commodities. All these organized markets are usually called "exchanges"—as, for example, the Stock Exchange, the Cotton Exchange, or the Metal Exchange—although they sometimes take other titles, as for example, the Chicago Board of Trade, the world's greatest cereal exchange.

[4] Hughes Report in Van Antwerp, p. 415.

The Exchanges and Speculation

One fundamental characteristic of these highly organized markets is that they permit the free play of speculation in them. Something has already been said concerning the methods in the Stock Exchange by which speculative commitments are often made, such as margin purchasing and short selling,[5] as well as concerning the dealers by whom much of this speculation is carried on.[6] Subsequent chapters will show the beneficial economic effects of speculation in the Stock Exchange as a free and open market. Here it is enough to note that while one-sided or restricted speculation, like a little learning, may be a dangerous thing, the free play of speculation in our organized markets is an economically beneficial force and arises naturally in the development of the exchange as a means of absorbing and minimizing the risks of sudden change in prices and values.

International Competition Between Exchanges

The last and final step in the evolution of organized markets has been the competition between different exchanges dealing in the same general commodity—that is, in securities, or wheat, or cotton, etc.—which has resulted in the rise of certain exchanges to a dominant national and even international position, while others dealing in the same article tend to function only locally or in a supplementary capacity. From the economic standpoint this competition between the exchanges is an inevitable development, for the purchases and sales of a particular commodity tend to gravitate into a single market, since the greater the number of buyers and sellers that appear in a market, the broader the market becomes and the fairer are the prices established there. It is necessary to observe, however, that competition between the exchanges could not become intense, nor could any few organized markets emerge as

[5] See Chapter IV.

[6] See Chapters V and VI.

dominant world exchanges in their respective fields, until the means for effecting swift and dependable transportation and communication were developed. This final step in the rise of the international dominant exchanges, therefore, occurred during the past century after the development of steam railways, telephones, telegraphs, tickers, and cables.

The markets for securities are a comparatively recent addition to the list of the world's market places. Credit was not extensively employed until the eighteenth century, and corporate securities in their present form are an invention of the past hundred years. Yet it was inevitable that corporations with securities to sell, as well as investors who wished to buy or sell them, should, after a little blind groping about, create organized markets for this new but rapidly multiplying species of property, precisely as the older wholesale producers and consumers of staple commodities had previously learned to direct their sales and purchases into centrally located and wholesale markets. The lately created securities exchanges, however, have as a rule outstripped the commodity exchanges in size and economic significance, owing to the vast shift in all modern countries toward large-scale corporate enterprise, following the successful application of steam power to transportation and industrial production.

The World's Chief Organized Markets Today

When we survey the vast panorama of the world's present-day international marketing machinery, it seems indeed a far cry to the few scanty and localized markets of the eighteenth century. In securities, the principal exchanges of the world are: the London Stock Exchange (an international market of huge scope); the New York Stock Exchange, the leading American exchange, with a smaller but rapidly growing list of foreign securities; and the Paris Bourse, the headquarters of French financing and a large market for foreign government bonds of all descriptions. In addition, there are smaller but internationally significant security exchanges at Amsterdam, Berlin, Vienna, Rome, Madrid, Petrograd, Tokio, and other foreign financial centers. But these are only the leading stock exchanges—almost every country possesses in addition many smaller exchanges. There are over twenty such stock exchanges in the United States, some of which—as for example, the stock exchanges of Boston, Philadelphia, Chicago, or Pittsburgh—are important centers for local financing. The tendency to found stock exchanges is consequently present wherever investors and corporate enterprises exist.

As it is with security exchanges, so it is, too, with the exchanges or even the less organized markets in other commodities. The main commodity producing and consuming centers of the world, as well as its vitally helpful money centers, have inevitably fostered the development of an elaborate chain or system of market places all over the civilized world today. The leading gold market has in the past been London, although New York, Paris, and other financial centers have been and are also important factors. The main market for silver is divided between New York as the headquarters of the great American silver-producing areas, and London as the center for its distribution, particularly to the Far East, where the silver-using countries, such as China and India, have important local markets for the white metal.

The leading cotton markets are on the New York, Liverpool, and New Orleans cotton exchanges, with important subsidiary markets in Alexandria, Bombay, and the continental ports. The staple cereal crops find their dominant market on the Chicago Board of Trade, but the exchanges of Liverpool, Buenos Aires, Minneapolis, Kansas City, and other producing and consuming centers are also noteworthy factors. Sugar is largely disposed of on the New York Sugar and Coffee Exchange, with the help of local markets in Cuba, Java, Hawaii, and the consuming centers of Europe. The same New York exchange is perhaps the dominant market for coffee, although in its production and consumption Rio de Janeiro, Santos, and London play a significant part. The dominant market for wool before the war was the London wool auction, but Boston and other consuming centers have recently risen to great influence in the disposal of the world's annual clip. The most important steel and iron market is at Pittsburgh, but London and continental points are also prominent factors. London and New York are the chief markets for rubber, as well as for copper, tin, lead, zinc, and other non-ferrous metals. Silk and rice are marketed upon specialized exchanges in Japan.

This list of world markets could be amplified and extended almost indefinitely. Its inclusion here, even in its present abbreviated and superficial form, will at least indicate to the general reader on what a vast scale the markets of the world have developed, and how completely their creation has been due to the necessities of industry and commerce. Commodity exchanges in various parts of the world often stand in closer relationship to each other than do stock exchanges, since the former deal in a single commodity of huge volume which is needed all over the world, while the latter deal in hundreds of different security issues of a more localized interest and demand.

Economic Significance of Organized Markets

We now come to the central theme of the present chapter—the economic significance of these highly organized markets, the exchanges. Almost all exchanges possess, if not identical at least analogous economic functions. Hence, although the subsequent analysis is chiefly concerned with stock exchanges, yet the student may in most instances discover in the commodity exchanges, too, similar economic features and functions. In order to avoid an interminable recital of the various economic benefits, great and small, performed by organized markets, it has been found best to group these benefits under ten leading headings.

1. Negotiability

The foremost and perhaps most fundamental economic service performed by the commodity and stock exchanges is that they render instantly negotiable the respective articles in which they deal. The full value of this service to business can be gauged only by what happens when the vital quality of negotiability is lacking. It is a well-known and yet frequently overlooked axiom in practical business life that "a thing is worth what you can get for it." Your automobile, for which you paid $2,500 and which you cheerfully inventory at $1,500, is in reality worth to you only what you can actually sell it for, whether it be $2,000 or $200. It is, of course, equally true of securities, that at any given time they are actually worth what you can sell them for, no more and no less. But there is this important difference. There is no organized market for used cars. If you suddenly find you must sell your automobile, you must call on your friends, and your friends' friends, and skilfully talk automobiles to them. You must consult garages and agencies, and perhaps in addition spend both time and money in advertising your car in the newspapers, in order to find a buyer. In a word, you are forced yourself to create a market in which to sell your automobile.

But when you wish to sell your 100 shares of United States Steel or any other stock listed on an organized exchange, for that matter, you can do so instantly and without effort or exertion on your part, for the stock market on the New York Stock Exchange is already organized and is ready at all times to absorb instantly your buying or selling orders. As it is with stocks listed on a stock exchange, so it is with any commodity, such as cotton, wheat, or corn, which possesses an organized market. These commodities are instantly salable at all times. It is obvious, therefore, that this quality of instant negotiability imparted by organized markets to securities and commodities, has the practical result of considerably enhancing their present and actual worth in dollars and cents to necessitous sellers.

Scope of Marketing Through Exchanges

The full significance of this ability of the exchanges to render their listed articles and commodities instantly purchasable and salable can only be realized when the colossal value of the latter is recalled. The value of the American wheat crop in 1919 was $2,024,008,000. During the same year that of the American corn crop was $3,934,234,000, and that of the American cotton crop was $1,967,143,000.[7] These, and other large crops were marketed and distributed through the agency of the Chicago Board of Trade, the New York Cotton Exchange, and other highly organized markets, both here and abroad.

Even more impressive are the figures relating to the New York Stock Exchange. The present total amount of stocks and bonds listed for trading in that mighty market aggregates roughly some sixty billions of dollars. This gigantic sum is more than the estimated national wealth of many important countries, and is equivalent to about one-fifth of our own total national wealth, assuming that certain economists are correct in estimating the latter at three hundred billion dollars. Through its organization, and the national and even international extension of the branch offices of its members in all parts of this country and abroad, the New York Stock Exchange has been able to attract to itself practically all buyers and sellers of its listed securities. The broker "puts his firm name on the certificates as witness of the stockholder of record, thus facilitating either its transfer or its sale, just as the indorsement of a bank

---

[7] See Statistical Abstract, pp. 149, 161.

would help in establishing the legitimacy of any document or instrument which was to be pledged for a loan or sold." [8] (See Figure 54.) As a result, this large proportion of the total wealth of our nation has been rendered instantly negotiable,

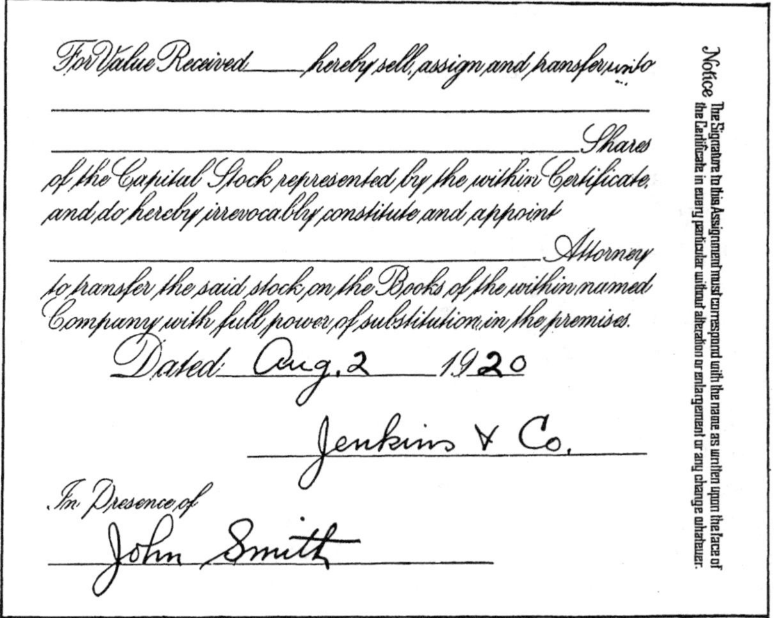

For Value Received ______ hereby sell, assign, and transfer unto
______
______ Shares
of the Capital Stock represented by the within Certificate, and do hereby irrevocably constitute and appoint
______ Attorney
to transfer the said stock on the Books of the within named Company with full power of substitution in the premises.
Dated Aug. 2 1920
Jenkins & Co.
In Presence of
John Smith

Notice. The Signature to this Assignment must correspond with the name as written upon the face of the Certificate in every particular without alteration or enlargement or any change whatever.

Figure 54. Reverse of a Stock Certificate
Showing method of assigning stock "in blank."

suitable for the investment of temporary or permanent funds, and hence in some cases even an acceptable medium of exchange in international trade.[9]

The New York Stock Exchange in 1920

This quality of instant negotiability imparted to so large a proportion of our national wealth, whether securities or crops,

[8] Duncan Macgregor in the *Financial Barometer*.

[9] See Chapter XVIII.

is naturally appreciated most when selling pressure is greatest. During the autumn of 1920 various economic forces had conspired to bring on a drastic decline in all prices, and the eagerness of business men to sell was matched only by their unwillingness to buy. Holders of securities or commodities traded in on exchanges, whatever losses they might have been forced to take, could always sell their goods in the organized markets for cash. But under the tremendous pressure of the wave of liquidation which ensued, many loosely organized markets ceased to function for the time being, with the result that the commodities traded in there were rendered quite unsalable. Such was the fate of many unlisted securities, and commodities with unorganized markets, such as silk, wool, and leather. Under the circumstances the banks naturally hesitated to advance large sums upon collateral which had proved unsalable.

In consequence, business men all over the United States who found themselves in a serious predicament to obtain ready funds, had final recourse to the Stock Exchange. Great numbers of them went to their deposit vaults, withdrew their listed securities, and at once sold them on the Stock Exchange for cash. The ability of the organized securities market to render instantly negotiable the huge amounts of securities suddenly dumped upon it underwent in consequence one of the severest tests in its history, and the Stock Exchange scored a signal triumph by the manner in which it acquitted itself in that emergency. During the most critical period of the decline there was never a moment when listed securities could not be exchanged there at once for cash. The Stock Exchange therefore served as a shock-absorber to the less organized and less liquid markets, and hence, to the whole price and credit structure of the country. Due to the Exchange no less than to the federal reserve system, a real business crisis was averted. Yet countless critics, embittered perhaps by their losses in the declining market, did not hesitate to condemn the Stock Exchange at the very time when it was saving them from disaster.

2. Collateral Value

A second service performed by the exchanges, growing out of the one discussed above, is that of rendering their listed securities or commodities desirable collateral for loans at the banks. The unfitness of unsalable commodity collateral during the 1920 decline in prices has already been remarked. It is also generally recognized that unlisted securities are often sharply discriminated against by bankers in making loans on security collateral,[10] not from any inherent defects in the securities themselves nor in the companies behind them, but solely because, not being listed, they cannot be sold instantly, and there is consequently involved a distinct chance of the lender suffering a loss.

3. Establishment of Fairest Prices

The exchanges also permit the fairest possible prices to be made for the securities or commodities listed for trading upon them. Concerning this aspect of organized markets Judge Grosscup, of the United States Circuit Court, once said:

> The exchanges balance like the governor of an engine the otherwise erratic course of prices. They focus intelligence from all lands and the prospects for the whole year by bringing together minds trained to weigh such intelligence and to forecast the prospects.

The truth of this remark becomes apparent when the contrast between selling an automobile and a listed security is recalled. The car may possess an intrinsic value of $1,500, and there may be hundreds of people in the United States who would welcome the opportunity of purchasing it at that figure.

---

[10] See Chapter VIII, page 187.

But this does the owner no good. He cannot locate them and arrange a sale, because there is no organized market through which he can readily be put in touch with them. He must therefore accept whatever price the few buyers whom he is able to interest may be willing to bid for his car, and the highest bid he can obtain may not reflect its actual value.

Very different is the situation in a nationally organized market like the Stock Exchange, the leased wires of whose members reach to all important centers in the nation (Figure 55). Practically all the possible buying orders regularly compete to raise prices, and simultaneously all the possible selling orders compete to lower them. As a result of the balance struck between these mutually opposing forces, the fairest price to both buyers and sellers results. Moreover, the system is self-corrective, owing to the constant speculation in the stock market. Whenever a price of a stock deviates temporarily from its intrinsic value, an opportunity for a profit is at once afforded to thousands of keen and experienced speculators, who are not slow to seize it. If the price is below the value, they buy "for the rise"; while if the price is above the value, they sell "for the decline." As a result of this speculative buying or selling, the inaccurate price is speedily driven back to conform with the inherent value of the security. The effect of inaccurate judgment on the part of the speculator is quickly dissipated by the surest method that could possibly be devised—he loses money. It is to be noticed that only in a highly organized market can short sales be readily and safely effected. In consequence, only in such a market do current prices have the full benefit of the free and unhampered interplay of speculative forces.

Concentration of News

In this connection, the concentration of the very latest information bearing on values which results from an organized

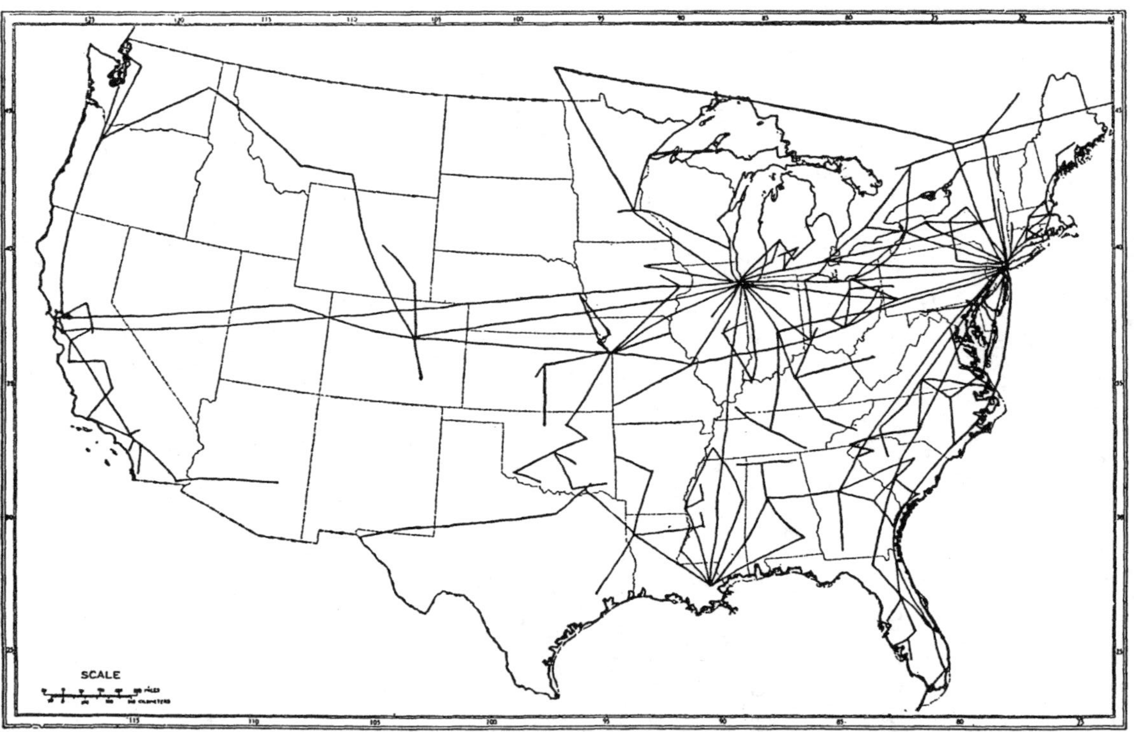

Figure 55. Map of Wire System of New York Stock Exchange Firms

Including branch office and correspondents in cities of over 20,000 population. Duplicate wires are omitted. The concentration of wires at Chicago and New Orleans is due in large measure to the Chicago Board of Trade and the New Orleans Cotton Exchange.

market should also be remembered. All the news from all over the world which has any bearing on current prices is instantly distributed over the country by the press and the even speedier news tickers. As a result, the best trained collective intelligence of the nation is kept constantly informed of the latest developments, and can quickly exert itself through the Stock Exchange system to keep security prices close to their real values—so far as those values can humanly be determined. This same process is greatly assisted by the complete and instant publicity given to transactions on the Stock Exchange by the stock and bond tickers.

Thus prices in an organized market adjust themselves through the forces of supply and demand almost automatically, and usually in advance, to changes in the basic values. If values improve, demand tends to outrun supply, and prices accordingly rise; while if values diminish, supply tends to overbalance demand and prices decline. In either case, the price at once adjusts itself to conform with the new value. But as a rule, owing to speculative factors, prices will rise before the rise in values occurs, or will decline before values actually diminish. This prophetic quality of Stock Exchange prices is imparted to them by the invariably accurate group judgment of thousands of buyers and sellers throughout the nation, regarding future or prospective values. The reader of course realizes that the Stock Exchange does not itself "make prices," although accurate prices could scarcely be made without its help. Prices are "made" by the buying and selling orders of the nation, as they find expression in the market place for securities organized and maintained by the Stock Exchange.

4. Prevention of Artificial Control

The more highly a market is organized, the more easily are monopoly and artificial control prevented. The late Chief Justice White once remarked concerning this aspect of the exchanges, or "boards of trade," as they are sometimes called:[11]

> What are these boards of trade? They are merely the aggregation of merchants who meet in a room to collect the information necessary to enable every man to trade on an equal footing.

Experience of over a century in maintaining America's largest and most important organized market has taught the members and governors of the New York Stock Exchange the vital necessity of keeping their great market free and open. In fact, this very phrase—"a free and open market"—is constantly on the lips of Stock Exchange men as an ideal for which they must invariably strive.

Meaning of "Free and Open Market"

By a "free" market the Stock Exchange members and officials mean one which is not dominated by any single man, or any single group or class of men, in defiance of the law of supply and demand. Students of the exchanges all recognize that a national and highly organized market, where the full force of the buying and selling orders of a nation is constantly reflected, cannot be manipulated nearly so easily as a non-speculative, unorganized market. A combination of wholesale dealers in fountain pens or shaving soap, for example, could easily adjust the price of the article to suit themselves. These articles have only a sluggish, unorganized, and intermittent market, which does not permit of adequate short selling. To counteract an artificial advance in prices there is only the very slow resistance of public opinion. But the would-be manipulator of Stock Exchange securities encounters a very different situation. He is forced by the rules of the Exchange to buy and sell in the open; every price affected by his purchases

[11] See Martin, p. 249.

or sales is instantly reported all over the nation, and if such price becomes at variance with the inherent value of the security, a chance for profit is at once afforded to speculators from coast to coast. The tremendous counterpressure which this national and readjusting speculation exerts, no manipulator or group of manipulators can withstand.

By an "open" market is meant one which is maintained, not for any limited or chosen few, but for every honest investor and speculator in the country—a market, too, where all trades are made in the open and out loud, and not by secret negotiations and whispered agreements. An exchange is the most democratic type of market. Nothing could be more fundamentally democratic than the way in which purchases and sales are made in the Stock Exchange. All buyers and sellers in that market are put on an absolutely equal footing. Through the ticker system everyone gets the latest news of Exchange transactions as nearly at the same time as the vast area of the United States will permit. As a rule, no broker on the floor knows at the time whose orders he is executing—whether those of some great capitalist or of some very ordinary citizen; to each he gives his best efforts, and only at the close of the day does he perhaps learn whose orders they were. No member of the Exchange can refuse to deal with any other member on the floor. There are no rebates made to wealthy or powerful men, nor any discrimination against the man in moderate circumstances. As we have seen,[12] the Stock Exchange rules establish a minimum rate of commission which all its members' customers—great or small, rich or poor—alike shall pay for the execution of their orders. Even when a member executes an order for a fellow-member, the commission rate is similarly fixed.

The reader does not need any vast experience in the business world to realize that very few indeed of the articles which

[12] See Chapter XIII, page 345.

he buys possess any such free and open market as this. Indeed, this democratic quality can be possessed only by a highly organized market.

5. Prevention of Fraud

One of the principal reasons for the formation of organized markets is their ability to prevent fraud. The proper functioning of an exchange makes impossible both of the two leading kinds of fraud—the placing on sale of misrepresented and worthless goods, and inequitable methods of effecting purchases and sales. All exchanges have regulations by which the goods in which they deal are first standardized and graded. The reputable boards of trade, for example, enforce strict rules regarding the various classes and grades of the cereals dealt in there; similarly, the Committee on Stock List carefully investigates every new security before it is listed on the Stock Exchange.[13] Also, by their restricted membership and rigid regulations the exchanges succeed in regularly maintaining more honorable conditions and methods of trade than the average unorganized market can possibly attain.

The Problem of Fraudulent Securities

Particularly is this true of the New York Stock Exchange. It is sometimes held responsible by loose thinkers for the huge amount of stock swindling which annually takes place in the country, in spite of the fact that the whole character and effort of the Exchange has long made it one of the most consistent and inveterate enemies of the promoter or vendor of worthless securities in this country. Indeed, it is only common justice to say that much of the prejudice against stock exchanges results from the deliberate attempt of swindlers themselves to create suspicion against the Exchange, whose efforts to put them out of business they realize only too well. "Fake" securi-

[13] See Chapter XVI, page 446.

ties are not listed on the Exchange—even if by some miracle the Committee on Stock List should approve their listing, speculators from all over the nation would at once pulverize their prices to nothing on the Floor. The Stock Exchange cannot guarantee purchasers or sellers of its listed securities against loss, as the familiar example of Liberty bonds will demonstrate. It can and does, however, protect them absolutely against fraudulent securities.

Moreover, the Exchange by its sternly administered regulations throws about investors and speculators a great variety of safeguards against fraud through the methods whereby securities are bought and sold there. Many of these safeguarding regulations have already been explained in detail,[14] and only a few of them will therefore be summarized here. The investor has the benefit of a free and open market, and the fairest possible prices. The ticker system assures him of complete publicity. The inviolacy of contracts is more strictly insisted upon than in any other existing market. Forged certificates, as we shall see,[15] are rendered practically impossible. All these and other innumerable factors which constantly operate to prevent fraudulent transactions of any kind on the Stock Exchange, owe their existence to the fundamental fact that the Exchange is an organized market. Analogous factors can be found in the other organized markets of this and other countries, while their absence in almost all unorganized markets becomes every now and then glaringly apparent. Certainly, the cynical old adage of *caveat emptor* (let the buyer beware) is less applicable in the organized than in the unorganized type of market place.

6. Stock Exchange's Services to Investors

The exchanges perform a further economic service by *stabilizing the processes of consumption or investment.* In this

[14] See Chapter XIII. [15] See Chapter XVI, page 449.

respect the exact functions of security and commodity exchanges differ widely, for while commodities such as cotton or wheat are destroyed through consumption, securities can be said to be consumed only in the sense that they are purchased by investors and held "off the market" for long periods of time. Nevertheless, the consumer and the investor alike derive great benefit from organized markets through the prevention of fraudulent goods or fraudulent dealings, the continual negotiability and collateral value of the goods, and the fair prices made for them there. Buyers can also better employ their judgment as to the proper time and the proper amounts to purchase in an organized market which insures full publicity to all its transactions. Furthermore, the buyer has greater choice as to the methods of purchase he should adopt: if a purchaser in the Cotton Exchange, for example, he can hedge against his holdings to insure himself against loss, or he can buy any one of the several different futures which he may consider most advantageous.

The Stock Exchange opens to the investor a huge panorama of securities of all kinds, representing the debts or shares of a hundred different industries. He can instantly purchase any type of security to which his particular needs and preferences incline him, whether the most gilt-edged and conservative bond in the Bond Department, or the riskier but sometimes more profitable common industrial stock. In addition, the investor in listed securities can benefit by the seasoning process which they undergo on the Exchange. Furthermore, thanks to the Exchange, he is able to obtain information concerning the company whose securities he is thinking of purchasing, which would otherwise probably be unobtainable.[16] That the Stock Exchange serves to stabilize investment, no one acquainted with the "over-the-counter" market in unlisted securities would for a moment attempt to deny.

[16] See Chapter XVI, page 453.

7. The Stock Exchange as a Source of Capital

Another signal service rendered by the Exchanges consists in *stimulating the flow of large amounts of capital into industry.*[17] Owing to the ready market provided by the commodity exchanges the production of commodities has been vastly increased and is often financed directly by dealers and speculators in the commodity markets.[18] The buyers' money thus becomes available to farmers and other producers. The same tendency is present to an even greater extent on the security exchanges. Walter Bagehot, in a celebrated passage,[19] declared that:

> A million in the hands of a single banker is a great power; he can at once loan it where he will, and borrowers can come to him, because they know or believe that he has it. But the same sum scattered in 10s and 50s through a whole nation has no power at all; no one knows where to find it or whom to ask for it.

What is true of the bank is also true in a slightly different way of the Stock Exchange, which as our leading organized security market collects the funds of individual investors and speculators from all over the nation, and even at times from other countries, and directs their flow into the productive industry of America. Of course, the money does not pass directly from the purchaser of listed securities to the manufacturer, but instead, as a subsequent chapter[20] will demonstrate, through a number of speculative hands, including underwriting houses.

Nevertheless, by making this process possible the Stock Exchange renders every day an indispensable service to the industrial corporations of the nation. Silently, day after day,

[17] On the function of the stock market as a market for new industrial capital, consult the statement and testimony of Governor Benjamin Strong of the New York Federal Reserve Bank before the "Agricultural Inquiry" Commission (Washington, August, 1921), pp. 685–687.

[18] See Chapter IV page 72.

[19] Bagehot, Lombard Street.

[20] See Chapter XVI, page 468.

week after week, year after year, this great flow of capital through the Stock Exchange into industry, and the ebb of dividends, interest, and profits (or losses) back from industry to the public, goes on. In the past it has spanned our continent with a steel network of railroad tracks—the arteries of our inland transportation system; it has built the vast factories and mills, and sunk the countless oil wells and mine shafts which have made this country the industrial marvel of the century. It has ceaselessly operated to bring forth from the inventor's shed and make available for daily use by the people those inventions which have so powerfully contributed toward making life today more worth living than at any other period in history.

8. The Carrying of Surplus Production

Another extremely important and often forgotten task of the exchanges is to facilitate the *carrying of surplus production over into consumption.* Any practical business man knows that the exact amount of goods of any type which is demanded for consumption at any time cannot be predicted beforehand. He also knows that the inevitable risks of production render the amount of goods which can be produced by a given time equally uncertain. Under ideal conditions production should just meet consumption, but any farmer who has struggled against insects and the weather, or any manufacturer who has had to contend with insufficient capital, labor difficulties, material shortages, or poor transportation, can testify that such a Utopian state of affairs is not yet on the horizon.

A Thought for Socialists

In the Middle Ages—whose economic system evokes a curious partisanship among the socialists of today (perhaps because, for all their vaunted interest in the future, they are in reality several centuries behind the present era in many of their ideas)—there were no exchanges or markets except of the most local and primitive kind. Hence, only just enough goods were produced to satisfy the immediate local demand. If, for example, more wheat was grown than was immediately needed, it was for the most part thrown away as unsalable and worthless; while if not enough wheat was grown to satisfy the demand, the account was balanced by starving the necessary number of consumers. Both the modern capitalistic system and the proposed neo-medieval socialistic system are thus necessarily speculative. They differ in that capitalism speculates in commodities, while socialism would speculate in human lives.

Owing largely to the organized markets, producers today can boldly produce their maximum, confident that even should a surplus over the immediate demands of consumption result, the surplus will be carried by speculators on the various exchanges until it is distributed. The capitalistic order of society constantly tends to overproduce, and thus gradually render more and more goods available per human being. To state the same truth the other way round, this steady overproduction has not only made it possible for more and more people to live on earth, but has also tended gradually but surely to raise their standards of living as well. Many other economic factors have contributed to achieve this result, of course, but the work of our speculative exchanges is not the least important of them.[21]

Significance of the Floating Supply

What is true of the commodity exchanges in this respect is likewise true of the security exchanges, although in perhaps a more indirect and less concrete way. The New York Stock Exchange, we have said, has made it possible for large-scale corporations to obtain *at once* the large amounts of capital they

[21] See Chapter XVII.

have needed to set up gigantic enterprises producing goods and services wholesale. But if the large corporation could only obtain as much money as investors at any one time would put up, large-scale enterprise would have been seriously hampered, if not made entirely impossible. As it is, the "floating supply" of a security—that is, the surplus amount of it remaining in excess of investment demand—can be carried by speculators in the Stock Exchange until it is gradually distributed among permanent investors. The details of this process will be explained more fully in a later chapter; it is sufficient here to point out the economic significance of carrying this floating supply, which can be done with ease in an organized market, but only with great difficulty, if indeed at all, in an unorganized market. Anyone who will examine the list of companies whose securities are now traded in upon the Stock Exchange will realize that they, too, have done a vast work in raising the standards of living of the average man and woman of today.

9. The Stock Exchange as a Business Barometer

All organized markets to some extent, and the Stock Exchange very especially, serve as a *barometer of future business conditions.* In section (3) above, relating to the making of prices, it was stated that prices on the Exchange, owing largely to speculative forces in the market, tend to discount future changes in security values, which of course quite accurately reflect the current business situation. So eminent an authority as Professor S. S. Huebner has stated, "Without an exception every business depression in this country has been discounted in our security markets from six months to two years before the depression became a reality." [22] Well known as this prophetic character of Stock Exchange prices is, nevertheless they

[22] *Annals of the American Academy of Political and Social Science*, Vol. XXXV, No. 3, May 1910, p. 13.

are very largely disregarded by business men before every business crisis. In the winter of 1906-1907 the Stock Exchange clearly predicted trouble ahead, yet the warning went mainly unheeded in the commercial world—and the result was the panic of 1907. So, too, in the late fall of 1919 and the winter of 1919-1920, price declines on the Stock Exchange gave notice to the business world of "breakers ahead"; but to as little purpose, so far as the "hard-headed" business man was concerned.

It is a curious commentary upon the inherent thoughtlessness and credulity of many American business men that they will pay considerable sums of money to glib and superficial "business experts" and their ilk for advice on future policy, and yet disregard the best and most unerring advice in existence, although it can be obtained for nothing from the newspaper or the stock ticker. Indeed, the Stock Exchange seems fated to endure the unhappy lot of the prophetess Cassandra, whose predictions brought upon her the charge of being both demented and ill-natured, until the foreseen calamity fell, when with equal inconsistency she was blamed as the cause of it all. There is, however, a rapidly growing class of business men in America who, although they rarely if ever speculate in securities, nevertheless follow the trend of stock prices closely as an index to future conditions in trade and industry. When a period of stress comes, these men are rarely caught with large, high-priced, and almost unsalable inventories. By that time they have sold out and with cash in the bank await the inevitable depression almost with serenity.

Comparative Barometrics of Different Industries

Not only does the trend of general price levels of Stock Exchange securities forecast with uncanny accuracy the general business conditions of the future, but the price tendencies of securities of each separate industry also forecast comparative future conditions among the various industries. If over a period of time steel stocks are "strong" while copper stocks are "weak," business men as well as investors are automatically given notice that more production and more capital is needed in the steel industry, while a surfeit of both exists in the copper industry. Thus the Stock Exchange provides a universally accessible and unfailing index as to the proper channels into which new investment funds can most usefully and profitably flow, as well as to the channels into which further investment for the time being will probably prove less useful and less profitable.

In the long run the comparative levels of security prices reflecting this situation cannot go unheeded. Sooner or later funds shun the copper industry and seek the steel industry until a better balance between supply and demand is struck. Hence it may be said that the Stock Exchange in the interest of everyone, plays a vital part in guiding or checking the flow of funds into the various industries. In this way the Exchange serves as a balance wheel to our whole business machine.

The commodity exchanges fill a similar function. When there is a surplus of corn, prices fall and farmers in discouragement limit their corn crop. Gradually the surplus is consumed and a shortage threatens; prices soar upwards, and the farmer is thus given notice that a larger corn crop is needed. In this way, the exchanges, by accurately forecasting the changes in values, stabilize and equalize conditions of supply and demand. Not only do they tend to assure funds for needed industries and needed crops, but they save incalculable billions of dollars to the American people by tending to check needless production and wasteful investment.

10. Sustaining the Risks of Industry and Trade

Finally, the organized markets perform an intensely useful and practical purpose in *segregating the risks of industry and trade.* Since this function of the Stock Exchange is performed through and because of the active speculation centering in the Exchange, it will be described at greater length in the next chapter.[23] It is sufficient here to note that owing to the constant readiness of various kinds of speculators to purchase and sell securities listed on the Stock Exchange, the conservative investor or manufacturer can at all times rid himself of the risk arising from ownership of any given stock or bond by selling it at once to a speculator through the Stock Exchange. The same is true of the grain farmer and miller with respect to the grain exchanges, and to the cotton-planter and spinner with respect to the cotton exchanges. Or by selling short to the extent of their holdings the owners of securities or commodities can "hedge" and thus insure themselves against loss—a practice which cannot be carried on except in highly organized markets. Furthermore, the holder of Stock Exchange securities can as a rule automatically limit his losses by the use of stop orders, previously described.[24] Thus, granted their intelligent employment, the organized markets provide a means whereby the individual can always avoid or limit his losses, and pass along risks which are greater than he feels justified in assuming, to the speculators, whose business it is to assume them.

Social Dangers Attending Organized Markets

Of course, this tendency of the organized market to segregate risks is not without a certain element of social danger. While the factor of speculation is equally as fundamental in the unorganized market as in the exchange, nevertheless it is not as accessible to the individual in the former as in the latter. There are speculators in overcoats, or tomatoes, or furniture, just as there are in stocks, but owing to the lack of organization in these markets the average person cannot speculate in

[23] See Chapter XV.

[24] See Chapter III, page 52.

them as readily as in securities. Consequently, it is easier for reckless and uninformed people to injure themselves in an exchange than in an unorganized market, just as it is easier today to be killed by being run over by a railroad train than it was formerly by stagecoach. Yet, just as the latter fact does not constitute a valid reason for urging the demolition of steam railroads and a return to stagecoaches as a means of transport, so there can be no justification for condemning the exchanges because those who elect to misuse them occasionally come to grief. The truth is that people must somehow be taught not to speculate foolishly, just as they have been taught to avoid getting in front of locomotives.

Future Marketing Probabilities

That the organization of exchanges has been accomplished in comparatively recent times was pointed out early in the present chapter. So important a factor in the economic and social progress of world civilization have they already proved, that not only their permanence in the present economic machinery of the world, but also their continued evolution in the future along significant lines is assured. Great as are their functions and beneficial services to mankind today, nevertheless it is obvious to the economic historian that their present development is only a stage in their larger and continuous evolution. In so sober and matter-of-fact a study as the present volume, fanciful predictions should, of course, have no place; nevertheless it is an irresistible temptation to conjecture along what lines this future evolution of the organized markets is likely to be. Nor need such conjecture be founded wholly on imagination. If we analyze the past economic evolution of the exchanges and note the direction of its trend, we can with some confidence follow this main tendency into the future.

In the first place, it seems inevitable that the production and consumption of many commodities will considerably increase during the coming century, and that they will consequently come to be considered as staples. It will become more and more dangerous, expensive, and impossible to buy and sell such commodities in their present loose-jointed, unorganized, and precarious markets, and accordingly exchanges will gradually be established for their more economical sale and distribution. Many preliminary steps in this direction can already be seen. Every year the marketing of all manner of goods and services is being investigated in a more thorough and scientific spirit. On the Pacific Coast growers are apparently developing what one day may become an organized market in fruit. Farmers, too, are everywhere experimenting to effect improved markets for produce of various sorts. Some commodities, either because they are perishable or difficult to standardize, may never develop markets of the most completely organized type. Yet for such commodities as wool, crude rubber, coal, or tobacco, it is not unlikely that organized exchanges will spring up during the next hundred years. Our present exchanges, whether in commodities or securities, seem likewise destined to experience a steady growth in the volume of their annual turnover, and a more delicate adjustment of their internal mechanism.

The United States and the World's Markets

Secondly, it also seems inevitable that as time goes by competition between exchanges of like character in various parts of the world will continue, and if anything increase, with the result that single exchanges more internationally dominant than at present will emerge. The location of such leading world exchanges will depend chiefly upon three different factors—nearness to the main center of production, nearness to the main center of consumption, and nearness to the money markets which enable surplus production to be carried into consumption. Americans can face this probable future evolution with equanimity. When the unequaled natural resources of this country, the vast consumptive demands of its mighty and constantly mounting population, and the rapid development of its money centers—particularly, of course, in the Wall Street district of New York—are remembered, it seems altogether likely that many of the internationally dominant exchanges of the year 2000 A.D. will be found within the United States.

If, then, the volume of transactions in organized markets will experience a large increase in the future, whether through the creation of new or the expansion of old exchanges, it follows that the volume of speculation in securities and commodities will increase in proportion. The business man of 2000 A.D. will probably be able with the greatest ease to make short sales in crude rubber or tobacco, or purchase futures in coal and crude oil, whether in the course of his business, or for the sake of speculative profits. To the blind and unreasoning opponent of speculation this may seem a dire fate, indeed, to be visited upon business and society at large. Yet a few of the corollary facts regarding speculation as it occurs in our organized markets must also be borne in mind. The violent changes in prices, and the considerable disparities between prices and values, which occasionally are seen in the unorganized markets, are not due to too much speculation but to too little and therefore too one-sided speculation. In a free and open organized market, however, the fuller and more equalized play of speculative forces operates, as we have seen, to stabilize prices and business conditions generally. In an exchange undue speculation for the rise quickly leads to corrective and counterbalancing speculation for the decline, and vice versa. The practical effect of speculation, when it is not hampered or restricted but given full play, is to produce more tiny fluctuations in price within vastly narrowed limits or extremes.

The past century has seen a gradual stabilization in business, largely through the operations of our organized markets. The next century will see the further stabilizing of prices and minimizing of risk. The accomplishment of these desirable ends will depend principally upon the creation and growth of organized markets.

CHAPTER XV

THE DANGERS AND BENEFITS OF STOCK SPECULATION

Attitude of Uninformed

The topic of speculation is an old and favorite theme with moralists as well as economists. Probably no factor in modern economic life is more frequently discussed, more generally condemned, and more rarely studied. Nor is this any new condition of affairs. Even the Middle Ages resounded with complaints against the "forestaller," as the "bull operator" of that far day was commonly known. Something magic there is about the ten-lettered word "speculator" today, which in a moment can make the average man exceedingly indignant, although in most cases he could not to save himself explain clearly and from an economic standpoint just what speculation is or why it is so reprehensible. In his mind, too, the subject of speculation is almost always exclusively related to the Stock Exchange, in spite of the fact that speculation is a universal economic force and pervades practically every class of business. But in all probability this same theoretical average man has heard of great fortunes gained or lost "on the Stock Exchange," and, without endeavoring to ascertain the accuracy of his information in any way, he is left with the feeling that there must be something fundamentally wrong about any place or institution where such things can occur. The prejudice against speculation and speculators, although almost never based upon actual facts or upon any real knowledge of the science of economics, is nevertheless widespread and deeply rooted.

Certain Undoubted Evils of Speculation

There is, of course, a genuine basis in both theory and practice for this perennial protest against speculation. Not even the stoutest defender of speculation, whether in securities or in anything else, can declare it to be an unmixed blessing. But neither can the sincere but insufficiently informed critic afford to proclaim it to be a pure and unadulterated evil. And there is this difficulty about arriving at a fair conclusion regarding its comparative benefits and dangers, that the undoubted harm which it inflicts upon many speculators is very human, graphic, and easily described, while its economic benefits are abstract, indirect, and almost impossible to explain without the use of technical and unfamiliar words and expressions. It is natural, therefore, that our economists have rarely attempted any popular presentation of the subject, but instead have abandoned that field almost entirely to the editor who must get his paper to press without delay, and to the politically minded minor statesman. So long as the human race prefers watching motion pictures or reading fiction to struggling with the "dismal science" of economics, the harm of speculation will in the popular mind probably possess an emotional quality which even a thorough realization of its invaluable services to society never can have.

Speculation No Topic for "Snap Judgments"

And yet the average citizen invariably wants to be fair in his judgments. He has a passion for "fair play" and the "square deal." He is perfectly aware that an element of entertainment as well as a scientific attempt to furnish the exact truth enters into the composition of moving pictures, newspapers, and political discourses. He will quite frankly admit that he has never studied speculation, either in the Stock Exchange or elsewhere, thoroughly or at first hand. If only the truth about this baffling and many-sided subject could be clearly and honestly presented to him, he would not be slow in seeing that a force which is so universal and fundamental to almost every phase of modern life cannot be wholly bad—that in fact speculation must fulfil some economic functions which are indispensable and vital to business and society. What speculation needs, therefore, is not so much an attempt at justification, as simply a clear, thorough, and unprejudiced explanation.

Preliminary Definitions

Probably nine-tenths of the erroneous notions that are current concerning speculation are founded on a vague or incorrect definition of the terms employed. It is therefore particularly necessary, before proceeding further, to distinguish as clearly as possible between "investment," "speculation," and "gambling" in the economic sense, for ordinarily these three terms are employed confusedly and without any pretense of clarity or accuracy.[1] Reference to the New English Dictionary —that final and most scholarly authority upon the origin, use, and definition of English words—shows that despite much current loose thinking on the usage of these three words, they are nevertheless in their ultimate economic denotation fairly distinct and separate terms. "Investment" (Latin, *investire*) is defined there as "The conversion of money or circulating capital into some species of property from which an income or profit is expected to be derived in the ordinary course of trade or business." On the other hand, "to speculate" (Latin, *speculari*) is defined as "To engage in the buying and selling of commodities or effects in order to profit by a rise or fall in the market value."[2] Lastly "to gamble" (ME *gamenen*) is defined by the same authority as "To stake money on some fortuitous event."

[1] See Appendix, Chapter XV (a).
[2] *Ibid.*, (b).

In order to realize more clearly the correct application of these definitions to transactions which relate to securities, the following examples are pertinent: If a man purchases 100 shares of United States Steel common stock mainly to secure the dividends to be declared upon it, he would be an investor. If he purchased the same stock mainly to make a profit by selling it later at a higher price, he would be a speculator. If he did not buy or sell the stock at all, but simply said to some-one else, "I'll bet you $10 that this stock will sell at par within the next month," or made some similar betting wager, he would be a gambler.

Distinctions Between Investment and Speculation

By definition, therefore, the theoretical distinction between investment and speculation seems fairly clear—the one is mainly founded on a desire for income, and the latter on a desire for a profitable difference between the buying and selling prices. Yet in actual daily life this distinction usually becomes almost impossible to establish, owing to the usually inextricable connection between income and profits in securities. Of course, some cases of almost pure investing and of almost pure speculating exist. A savings bank account is an almost completely non-speculative investment, for there is no chance for appreciation of principal, but simply an income derived from it. Yet even here the failure of the bank and a consequent depreciation of the principal might conceivably enter into the case.[3] So, too, the purchase of a non-dividend paying stock in order to profit from a possible rise in its price is almost a pure speculation; nevertheless, the rise in price will probably be due to an actual dividend or the hope of a declaration of a dividend upon it.

As a matter of fact, the purest cases of speculation occur, not in securities but in commodities, which do not of course

[3] See Appendix, Chapter XV (c).

pay interest or dividends, and hence do not involve this element of income which so extensively pervades the consideration of securities. In the field of articles and commodities the prototype of the investor is the consumer or user, and the distinction between speculation and investment consumption there depends upon whether the individual purchases goods to use or consume himself, or to sell to some other consumer with an attempt to get a profit. In the latter case he is just as truly a speculator as the margin purchaser of stocks or the short seller of cotton futures.

Returning to the instance of securities, however, the average man who buys 100 shares of stock wants both an income and a profit to be derived by selling it at a higher price later on, and is therefore part speculator and part investor. Conversely, the practical speculator bases his purchases and sales of securities upon prices which are fundamentally determined by the income or the expectation of income to be derived from them. The margin purchaser, who is in the main a speculator, often selects dividend-paying stocks in order to offset his interest charges,[4] while the short seller gives careful attention to the dividends paid on his short stock, since he must pay them to the loaner of the stock. Moreover, many an investor who purchases for income will, after a swift rise in price, sell out for a profit and consequently become a speculator. Thus, in actual practice, the difference between investors and speculators in securities is one of degree rather than of kind, and it is especially difficult to state in any given case just where the one ceases and the other begins. It should be noticed that investment and speculation are alike in that they both involve a genuine exchange of ownership of actual property. As has been pointed out earlier in the present volume,[5] all orders, whether for investment or speculation, are executed and cleared in exactly the same way in the Stock Exchange.

---

[4] See Chapter IV, page 76.

[5] See Chapters III and IV.

Meaning of the Term "Investment Transaction"

It should be noticed that the common Wall Street expression of "investment transaction" refers to an outright purchase and sale of securities, and that of "speculative transaction" to a margin purchase or short sale. So current are these expressions that Chapter III was entitled "A Typical Investment Transaction" because it described an outright purchase and outright sale of 100 common shares of the United States Steel Corporation. Usually, of course, margin purchasers and short sellers are actuated principally by a desire for profits rather than for income, and the presumption usually is when a security is bought or sold without the use of credit that the primary motive is income. Yet investors sometimes purchase securities on margin by the "part payment plan"; sometimes short sales are caused by the liquidation of investments from out of town or from abroad; and many people purchase securities outright in order to sell them later at a higher price. As working definitions, then, these expressions, while of considerable practical value in the daily work of the Street, are nevertheless too superficial and mechanical to penetrate to the bottom of the matter.

Distinction Between Speculation and Gambling

Coming now to the equally important distinction between speculation and gambling, this is not only clear in theory but, despite a few technical details, also quite clear in practice. There are at least four principal differences between speculation and gambling, which deserve careful consideration by the student:

1. Speculation involves the purchase or sale of some form of property, while gambling does not.

2. The risks entailed by the speculator arise fundamentally from risks inherent in the property which he buys or sells, while the risks of gambling are created by the gambler and are

based upon future events without any necessary relation to ownership of property.

3. The speculator's buying or selling operations affect the forces of supply and demand, and tend to bring about the very change in price for which he hopes, while the bets placed by the gambler have no effect whatsoever in determining the actual outcome of the fortuitous events upon which he stakes his money. In other words, a speculator who purchases 100 shares of Northern Pacific because he anticipates a rise in its price, assists by this very purchase in bringing about the rising market for which he hopes, while a gambler who bets $10 that it will rain next Thursday, or that Yale will win the Harvard football game, exerts absolutely no effect upon atmospheric conditions, and in no way strengthens the sinews of the team of his preference.

4. In gambling transactions the winner makes what the loser loses. But in speculation, in the alternate rise and fall of prices, there are occasions where practically everyone profits, and where practically everyone incurs losses. Gambling has no economic justification, and of course performs no little social harm, while, as we shall presently see, speculation is a profoundly necessary economic force. Some critics of stock exchanges, in lieu of refuting these primary and fundamental distinctions, advance the claim that they are only formal distinctions and legal subterfuges. But they do not meet them nor answer them, because they cannot.

Superficial Resemblances

Speculation and gambling, of course, sometimes possess superficial resemblances. The motive for both may alike consist in a rash and unintelligent willingness to take large risks for large possible profits. A man can, of course, lose just as much money in unwise speculation as he can by "playing the races," yet it does not follow that a stock market is a race-course, or that a race-course is a stock market. It is also true that some speculators use no more intelligence in purchasing or selling securities than as if they were blindly gambling upon an undeterminable future event. One worthy citizen is said to have taken a "long position" on certain speculative securities in a "bear market" because of the advice of a medium, who evoked the spirits of great American financiers at a profitable rate per spirit. He was, extraordinarily enough, not inclined to blame the Stock Exchange for his losses, although perhaps some of the readers of his plight unconsciously did so.

Yet just such episodes as this raise the query why the Exchange should be visited with righteous wrath because speculators lose money through unwise ventures, when the similar lack of intelligence in other speculative lines of business evokes no such bitterness. A large proportion of all business enterprises undertaken in this country ultimately result in failure, and undoubtedly the cause is mainly ignorance and folly on the part of the management. America, too, has its share of poorly trained, inefficient business men who speculate with their savings and inheritances in poor real estate, impossible retail shops, and all manner of harebrained and unlikely enterprises every year, which soon exhaust their funds and leave them bankrupt. But they have no target later to direct their resentment against, while the losing speculator in securities can always blame the Stock Exchange for his own folly and usually obtain a sympathetic hearing.

Gambling Forbidden on the Stock Exchange

It is one of the principal services of the Stock Exchange to maintain a speculative market for speculative securities. But any form of gambling on the Exchange floor has long been prohibited absolutely by Article XXXVI, Section 4 of the Constitution, which reads, "Betting or offering to bet, upon the Floor of the Exchange is forbidden." From the foregoing it is therefore only common justice to declare that such current phrases as "stock gambler" or "gambling in stocks" are, so far as the Stock Exchange is concerned, a contradiction in terms, which reflect rather upon the economic knowledge of the speaker than upon the ethical character of the Exchange or its members.

Economic Function of Speculation

Broadly speaking, the economic service of market speculation may be defined as the assumption of those necessary risks which always exist during the process of distributing any kind of property. So fundamental an economic factor as speculation inevitably pervades every type of market and not simply the organized markets, although in the latter, owing to their tendency to segregate risks,[6] it is no doubt exhibited in a more naked form. To take a simple example: the corner grocer who buys 100 pounds of sugar at 8 cents to distribute among his customers at 10 cents is essentially a speculative dealer. He has no intention of consuming himself all this sugar, but buys it with the hope of profiting by selling it at a price above its purchase price. This profit is earned because of the services which he renders in distributing the sugar, and is justified because of the risk which he assumes in holding it himself ready for sale. For, as many American retailers in 1920 would agree, if the price of sugar declines below the purchasing price before the grocer has sold out his stock, he may incur a loss on his inherently speculative dealings in it.

The economic functions of the speculative dealer in Stock Exchange securities, including such customers of the commission houses as Mr. Blank of Chapter XII, are in their main features identical with the dealer in sugar, as the next chapter will illustrate in more detail.[7] Like the latter the stock speculator also buys and sells at his own risk with the aim of making

[6] See Chapter XIV, page 388.

[7] See Chapter XVI, page 461.

a profit, and plays a similar part in distributing securities among investors.

Economic Education and Progress

Unfortunately, however, the economic education of the public has been very slow, while the evolution of our organized markets, particularly during the past half-century, has been extraordinarily swift. The paradoxical result is that the general public, although living by means of the economic institutions of 1920, are for the most part still thinking in terms of the economic America of 1850. This is particularly true in respect to the whole general subject of distribution.

In consequence, the public is only too apt to mistake superficial and incidental differences between the modern organized exchange and the older and more familiar unorganized type of market for fundamental and basic differences, and to criticize and suspect the former because it does not conform in the details of its operation to the methods customary in the latter. Thus through ignorance or misunderstanding of the system for clearing contracts in vogue in all the modern exchanges, many lawyers, economists, and men of affairs are inclined to think speculation for small profits which is accompanied by a frequent clearance of intermediate contracts,[8] amounts to gambling, because, forsooth, there is no precedent for such a practice in the older unorganized markets! A similar method of thinking led Ruskin and other mid-Victorian writers to decry mass production in the steam factory, because it was conducted by methods differing considerably from those in vogue during the era of hand production which preceded the Industrial Revolution.

Speculation in securities on the Stock Exchange of today, therefore, must be judged by its conformity in fundamental economic principle rather than in technical mode of operation,

---

[8] See Chapter V, page 101.

with speculation in other and less highly organized markets. Moreover, the *modus operandi* of the present Stock Exchange must be carefully studied before any intelligent conclusion can be drawn regarding either the benefits or the dangers of speculation there. It is for this reason that the whole matter of stock speculation has in the present volume been deferred until the machinery of the Stock Exchange was described in some detail.

Stock Speculation and Panics

Coming, then, to this question of the harmful results of stock speculation, we must first disabuse our minds of a few hoary fallacies, for speculation in securities has serious enough faults without attributing to it many others for which in fact it is in no way responsible.

The first of these fallacies is that "stock speculation causes panics." Whenever a violent catastrophe overtakes business, the man in the street at once and quite naturally begins to look around for its cause. He does not understand the inflated condition of bank credit, nor the veering relationship of production to consumption, nor many other fundamental economic factors responsible for the crisis. He simply notices that a few months before, when the sky was apparently unclouded and serene, the stock market had experienced a decline in prices. At once a hundred myths and legends he has heard about "Wall Street" spring up in his mind. And since the disturbance first made itself manifest on the Stock Exchange, he leaps to the conclusion that somehow or other speculation in stocks must have started it all.

Sensitiveness of Security Contracts to Future Conditions

We have seen [9] that it is one of the economic functions of the organized and speculative markets to reflect in advance, like

[9] See Chapter XIV, page 386.

a barometer, future developments in the field of business. Particularly in the highly organized and sensitive Stock Exchange, "coming events cast their shadows before," and accordingly stock prices begin their adjustment to the future diminished net earnings and dividend rates which oftentimes general business is not equally quick in foreseeing. If contracts made in general merchandise were as sensitive to probable future conditions as contracts in securities made on the floor of the Stock Exchange, our business crises would be both much more infrequent and much less severe. At any rate, it is obvious that the decline in the stock market is simply the first indication of a general declining movement in practically all markets. It is therefore an effect, not a cause. What then is the fundamental and ultimate cause of panics and depressions?

Upon this subject so much controversy has arisen among students of economics that the writer may be pardoned for avoiding any further discussion of the matter than merely to remark that an important causal factor is a suddenly discovered surplus of goods over the amount demanded for immediate consumption. Organized markets perform a valuable economic service, as we have seen,[10] in that they tend to equalize the supply and demand conditions governing the rate of production of goods and services, and also make possible the carrying of a considerable surplus over consumptive demand. The Stock Exchange is, therefore, if anything, an automatic check against a condition of undue inflation and overproduction, rather than a stimulus to such a condition.

Organized and Unorganized Markets in a Crisis

As a matter of fact, the acute crises which have befallen American business in the past have usually followed a period of prosperity and mounting prices. The unorganized markets, in which short selling and hence quick and ready price adjust-

[10] See Chapter XIV, page 381.

ment is impossible, are the scene of steadily ascending prices for real estate, merchandise, etc. Here an unbalanced, one-sided, and dangerous speculation sets in, and it is here that the most acute economic convulsions occur. Usually at a time when prices on the organized exchanges are already declining in the anticipation of future trouble, this ballooning and unhealthy speculation in the imperfectly organized markets is at its height (Figure 56). At length, the huge disparity between prices and values of semiliquid commodities becomes too great

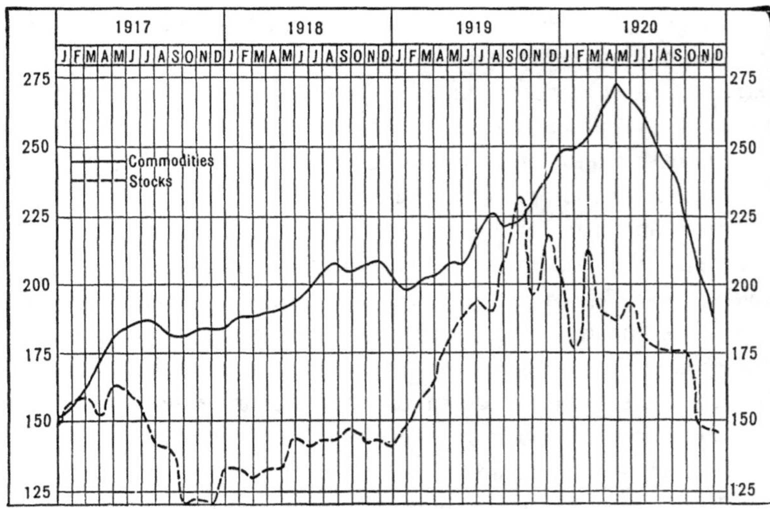

Figure 56. Price Movements of Industrial Stocks and Wholesale Commodities, 1917–1920

Note how break in stock prices in the fall of 1919 discounts similar break at higher levels of commodity prices in spring of 1920. For stock prices, the *Annalist* index numbers were taken; for wholesale commodities, index numbers of the United States Department of Labor. In both cases, these index numbers were rescaled on the basis of 1913 average =100.

and the catastrophe follows. There is therefore a very great difference between the sensitive, alert, and two-sided speculation in the stock market, and the crude, insensitive, and one-sided speculation in the unorganized markets. And when the crisis commences, the Stock Exchange, by functioning as a shock-absorber to the national credit structure,[11] performs still another service in counteracting the ill effects of the crisis. It is therefore illogical and contrary to all the facts of economics and financial history to attribute business panics to the Stock Exchange or its securities market.

The explosion of this fallacy, however, only serves to bring up still another common and in some ways closely allied misstatement concerning speculation on the Stock Exchange, namely, that it absorbs undue amounts of credit and thus imposes a dangerous strain on the money market. There is the added implication, sometimes expressed and sometimes not, that money needed for the production of goods is, on account of speculative activities on the Exchange, diverted into collateral loans made for speculative purposes, which serve no useful economic purpose. Let us see exactly what this oft-repeated charge against speculation on the Stock Exchange amounts to.

The Flexibility of Speculative Funds

It is of course true that in an active period on the Exchange, when speculation is comparatively heavy and prices are high, more money is borrowed on collateral loans than in a dull period when speculation is comparatively light and prices are low. But exactly the same thing may be said of practically all other commodities. In the economic cycle which results in a money stringency, heavy speculation on the Stock Exchange is only the first wave of a vast tide of speculation which sweeps through all markets, and which soon produces rising prices and extensive one-sided speculation in the unorganized markets. Such great speculative impulses are imparted to business by profound economic world forces which the Stock Exchange could not possibly either evoke or terminate. But at the first suggestion of an impending shortage of money the securities

[11] See Chapter XIV, page 372.

market at once begins almost automatically to put its house in order to meet it.[12] Prices on the Stock Exchange decline and the volume of speculative trading begins gradually to fall off. In consequence, the demands made on the credit market for collateral loans invariably experience a marked decrease, long before the crisis arrives.[13] Meanwhile, however, the speculative "boom" in the unorganized markets continues. Short selling is impossible there and hence there is no adequate check to the uneconomic "ballooning" of prices. As a result, greater and greater sums of bank credit are tied up in loans on farm land, real estate, illiquid raw materials, and general merchandise. At a time when Stock Exchange loans are dwindling in number and total amounts, loans for the speculative carrying of commodities for which no organized markets exist, increase rapidly—and then the crash comes.

During the severe decline in prices which occurred in 1920, we heard no complaint that collateral loans were illiquid, while the vast amount of bank credit tied up in frozen loans on illiquid real estate, raw materials, and general merchandise became one of the most serious economic problems of the country. Moreover, as has been pointed out,[14] wholesome speculation in the Stock Exchange enabled that institution to act, not as a burden, but as a shock-absorber to our entire credit structure during the same critical period.[15]

Credit Shortages and Call Loans

There is another reason why collateral loans do not materially strain our money market. We have seen [16] that the money which flows into call loans arises from surplus banking funds. This tends of course to restrict the amount of such loans, as the high call rates for money frequently indicate.

[12] See Appendix, Chapter XV (d).
[13] See Appendix, Chapter XV (e).
[14] See Chapter XIV, page 372.
[15] See Appendix, Chapter XV (f).
[16] See Chapter VIII, page 177.

Moreover, collateral loans are in a practical way often undesirable to lenders, since they cannot be rediscounted at federal reserve banks.[17] Furthermore, it is always easier for the reserve authorities to discourage collateral loans, which are so largely centralized about the Stock Exchange, than it is to discourage borrowing for speculative purposes on other collateral, such as real estate or merchandise, which occurs in no one place, but throughout the length and breadth of the United States. When, therefore, we get a proper and full perspective of security collateral loans in their relation to other loans, we cannot help realizing that they cannot be held responsible for credit shortages. Neither are collateral loans an economic waste, but, as has already been demonstrated,[18] a very necessary financial operation in behalf of the indispensable and necessary work which the stock speculator performs for business and society.

Effect of Speculation Upon Prices

This brings us to another charge frequently made against speculation in securities—that it "unsettles prices." This is true in much the same sense that it is the sails which make the ship go. The fundamental cause for changing prices is, of course, changing values. In a market where values never changed there would never be any speculation. The more speculative character of the stock than the bond market is due to the fundamental fact that as a rule the value of bonds are less subject to change than the value of stocks. Speculation merely intervenes to adjust present prices to more or less future but seemingly probable values. In this remarkable process of discounting future conditions which results from speculation in stocks we have seen how accurately Stock Exchange price changes in the past have anticipated future changes in values. Naturally, such prophetic price changes are only as accurate

[17] See Chapter VIII, page 172. [18] See Chapters VIII and XVI.

as the consensus of the most experienced and expert human opinion can make them. Everyone, of course, knows that at the climax of a "bull market" prices for a time arise above what eventually turn out to be future values, and similarly at the end of a decline in the market, prices get below future values. Yet such conditions are only temporary, and it is speculation which subsequently readjusts the prices to inherent values.

Moreover, hindsight is always better than foresight. It is easy to detect afterwards occasions when market prices, which so largely represent human opinion, temporarily misjudged the trend in values, but it is a very different matter to stare into an inscrutable future and invariably fit prices to future values. Furthermore, the distance into the future which present prices may be discounting is also a variable factor. But with all due allowance for such exceptions, no man who has ever studied the relationship between prices and subsequent values on an organized market over a period of years can fail to recognize that the general effect of speculation, if allowed freedom and permitted to proceed with equal ease whether for the rise or for the decline, is to stabilize prices,[19] by adjusting them even in advance of changes in intrinsic values.

Relation of Organized Speculation to Manipulation

Another public misconception of speculation seems to arise from a tendency to associate it with manipulation of prices. An important section of a previous chapter [20] has been written in vain if the reader does not recognize that in reality free speculation is the only known foe and corrective to the manipulation of prices. Professor H. C. Emery, speaking of the utter failure of the German attempt to regulate her speculative markets,[21] has stated this whole matter with his usual clearness and acumen:

---

[19] See Chapter XIV, page 374. [20] *Ibid*, page 377.

[21] See testimony of Prof. H. C. Emery in Regulation of the Stock Exchange, p. 330.

> The result of this experience was to prove practically what I have maintained for years from my theoretical study of this subject, that the most easily manipulated market is the limited market. The market you cannot manipulate is the big, open, easy, facile market, where everybody can trade with the least restriction. . . . There is no man so big he can manipulate a market into which the whole public comes. The idea that a big man can manipulate a market is greatly exaggerated anyway, but the bigger the market the harder it is for the big man to manipulate it. If the market is bigger than the man he cannot manipulate it. If you have a little market a big man can manipulate it. . . . The big man cannot manipulate a market into which the public comes freely. The public determines the price of the stock in the long run, and the more easily you let the public come in the harder it is for the big man to manipulate.

Losses from Speculative Ventures

After this extended account of the ills for which speculation is not responsible, the reader may think that the present study is an attempt to "whitewash" the speculator and his speculation. This is far from the purpose of this book. For having disposed of these incorrect notions concerning speculation, there still remains a residuum of possible danger and harm to the individual which no one would attempt to deny—least of all members of the Stock Exchange, who, if only from their own experience, appreciate just how dangerous speculation can be.

This story of the real injury done by injudicious speculation is older than the South Sea Bubble and as universal as trade itself. For generations men have rashly undertaken speculative commitments in the stock market and out of it, have recklessly traded beyond their means, have been influenced in their commitments by "tips" and jumbled, absurd reasoning—and have lost their money. Usually, despite the fiction-writers, speculative losses in securities simply deprive the individual of a part of his surplus funds, just as financial losses arising from business or investments do. Yet such losses only too often cause hardships, not merely to the speculators themselves, but to their families and dependents, for whose sake, perhaps, they mistakenly engaged in the risks of speculation with no knowledge of securities, of business, or of those vast economic factors which shape prices in all the markets of the world. Such losses by people who can ill afford them are the real source of the considerable public prejudice against speculation and stock exchanges, and indeed are profoundly human and moving to any man who has been long in Wall Street.

Furthermore, speculation is only too apt to distract the ordinary business man from his regular work. He becomes possessed of "an impatience to be rich, a contempt for those slow but sure gains which are the proper reward of industry, patience, and thrift."[22] If he has a weak and vacillating character, he is always fidgeting to finger a ticker tape. Often he is utterly ignorant of the economic currents and cross-currents to which he is so blithely entrusting his funds. In fact, he is apt to be the first to deny the significance of economic laws and principles as they affect security prices, and declare cynically that "It's all a gamble, anyway." Or else he will assume an owlish wisdom and discourse, with the jargon of the "Street," on a nondescript lot of economic fallacies and platitudes. It was of this type of individual, who almost always loses his money in the end, that Carnegie once said, "The man who grasps the morning paper to see first how his speculative ventures on the Exchanges are likely to result, unfits himself for the calm consideration and proper solution of business problems."

Speculation Impossible to "Abolish"

Because of the all too frequent losses which men suffer by overtrading and which they cannot afford, and also because of

[22] Macaulay, History of England, Chap. XIX.

the deteriorating effect of speculation on weak and shallow natures, many honest and sincere, but short-sighted and hasty, people rush to the conclusion that speculation and speculative markets should be abolished. Just as the king in the old play cried, "Off with his head! So much for Buckingham!" so, too, these people seize upon the seemingly simple expedient of curing headaches with the guillotine. But in spite of laws, in spite of threats, penalties, and restrictions, made in many lands by many peoples over the course of many centuries, speculation and speculative markets have stubbornly endured. The attempt at their abolition has invariably failed. As recently as 1896 the German government attempted to do away with speculation in securities and commodities.[23] Yet in spite of the characteristic Teutonic thoroughness, in spite of the despotic powers of the Prussian state, this attempt not only failed of adequate enforcement to such an extent that its regulations came to border on farce and absurdity, but it directly resulted in crippling the Berlin financial markets so thoroughly that when the law was repealed in 1909, their power had permanently passed to London and Paris. What this blunder meant to the economic staying power of Germany during the war, future economists will doubtless relate.

But still more recently an even more thoroughgoing attempt to abolish speculation has been made in Bolshevist Russia and has failed even more completely. The ingenuous but fanatical theorist, Lenin, at first ordered the traders and dealers lined against the wall and shot. Yet speculative trading went on, at extortionate prices and with unwholesome economic consequences. And instead of the glittering Utopia which this theorist and his confederates expected to establish, what actually followed? Russian industry collapsed, unemployment spread. In the cities starvation and the plague wrought a havoc unparalleled since the Thirty Years' War, until city life itself became

---

[23] See Emery, p. 822.

impossible there and the citizen either rotted in his decaying home, or went back to the country to grub in the soil for his existence. It is typical of all such attempts to abolish speculation that at this writing Lenin is apparently admitting that "trading must be resumed" and is confessing the complete futility of his witless and deadly experiment.

Other more intelligent critics, who realize the inevitable existence of speculation, have frequently taken the Stock Exchange to task for the way speculation is conducted by brokers' customers. Especially the amount of margin required by Stock Exchange houses [24] has been attacked, since so many cases of loss to customers can be traced to buying stocks on small margins. Often, it is demanded [25] that the Stock Exchange compel everyone to trade on a given margin—say, 20 per cent.

Stock Exchange Attitude Toward Margins

The members of the Stock Exchange must not for a moment be thought of as desiring to see their margin customers lose money. It must be remembered that the commission broker, through whom the public comes in contact with the Exchange, is not a dealer but a broker and the agent of his customer. Far from making what his customers lose (like a croupier or other kind of gambler) the broker can derive no possible benefit from his customers' losses. On the other hand, these can frequently do him no little harm. For one perfectly selfish reason, he loses the account of that customer and the future commissions it might otherwise bring him. Between the hundreds of Exchange commission houses there is a keen competition for accounts.

Moreover, the broker may himself become involved in his

---

[24] See Chapters IV, page 78, and XII, page 321.

[25] "We urge upon all brokers to discourage speculation upon small margins, and upon the Exchange to use its influence, and if necessary its power, to prevent members from soliciting and generally accepting business on a less margin than 20 per cent." (Hughes Report, 1909, in Van Antwerp, p. 420.)

customer's catastrophe, by attempting to "carry him" after his margin is exhausted. Most failures of brokerage houses are due to such overextension of credit to customers, who may be unable or simply unwilling to respond to margin calls. And the failure of a Stock Exchange firm may entail losses, not only to its customers but also to the other houses with whom it has done business and concluded contracts on the Exchange. Even if the customer escapes with a slight loss, he is apt to blame his misfortune on his broker, whose good-will suffers thereby. Stock Exchange brokers, therefore, are not anxious to accept any more of such risky business than they can help, if only for their own sake.

The Stock Exchange takes all the precautions it can to protect margin customers against loss. It enables the margin purchaser to place a stop-loss order in the market to limit a possible loss. It provides unequaled ticker publicity for its transactions, besides exercising great care in the securities which are listed in its market. Furthermore, it expressly provides in its Constitution:[26]

> That the acceptance and carrying of an account for a customer, either a member or a non-member, without proper and adequate margin may constitute an act detrimental to the interest and welfare of the Exchange, and the offending member may be proceeded against under Section 8 of Article XVII of the Constitution.

If, then, the Stock Exchange has not hitherto adopted a flat minimum amount of margin, it is not because its members do not wish to see reckless dealing prevented, but because such an inflexible margin rule would prove impractical and impossible. For one thing, as the chairman of the Hughes Commission pointed out,[27] "the right of one private person to extend

---

[26] See Constitution, p. 100.

[27] See Horace White, "The Hughes Investigation," *Journal of Political Economy*, Oct. 1909, p. 537.

credit to another is simply the right to make a contract, which, under the Federal Constitution, cannot be impaired by any State Legislature." Moreover, such a uniform and absolute requirement regarding margin would make no allowance either for the personal nature of all credit, or the vast difference between the price movements of different securities. Most Exchange houses would willingly execute orders from many prominent and well-known American business men without margin, while they would demand large margins of a stranger. Similarly, there are many bonds and some preferred stocks which could be purchased with relative safety on a 5-point margin, while other securities, particularly speculative common stocks, would be a riskier purchase on a 30-point margin.

It is a fact, however, that the tremendous credit shortage prevalent since the armistice has not only raised the interest charged on credit advanced to purchase securities, but has also compelled brokers to demand heavier margins to conserve their own capital. As a result, the margin requirements are larger today than ever before. Of course easier money may abate this condition and to some extent tend to lower margin requirements in the course of time; but in all probability a higher general level of the margins required of customers by brokers will permanently result.

Inevitable Risks of Business Enterprise

Speculation is fundamental to our present economic order of society and business, because it arises from the inevitable and basic risks and the inherent vicissitudes of all industry and trade. Of course that extremely knowing class of people who write letters to the editors and orate from the soapbox on every possible occasion will deny that there are any particular risks in industry. They delight to picture our larger industrial companies as fat jovial men labeled "Sugar Trust," "Oil

Trust," "Beef Trust," etc., who have not a care in the world except their riotous pastime of squeezing and robbing a small, frightened, bristly haired, unprotected figure labeled "The People."

But the business man who has a responsible part in some enterprise with the avowed and shameless purpose of "making money"—and it matters little whether the enterprise is a village grocery store or a metropolitan bank—will tell you a very different story concerning the risks of business. He is under no fond delusion that business enterprises "run themselves." He will tell you of the shifting prices and supplies of raw materials, and the danger of carrying either too large or too small inventories. He will discuss labor shortages and unemployment, wage scale agreements, efficiency, strikes, boycotts, walkouts, lockouts, picketing, arbitrations, injunctions, and accident compensation. After briefly touching upon insurance, advertising, and the problem of obtaining loyal and efficient management, he will have something to say also concerning sales managers and salesmen, expense accounts, sales policies, the protection of trade-marks, and the ever-changing markets for his products, with a few concluding remarks upon competition here and abroad, tariffs, bank accommodation, foreign exchange rates and (possibly with a rising inflection) canceled contracts and excess profits and income taxes.

Anyone who has followed him, except the purblind doctrinaire, will gather from his remarks some idea of why corporation net earnings and dividend rates vary so greatly, not merely from year to year, but even from month to month, and will begin to appreciate the truth of Dr. Arthur T. Hadley's statement that "The success or failure of a man engaged in manufacturing, transportation or in agriculture depends more upon his skill as a prophet than upon his industry as a producer." [28]

---

[28] See President A. T. Hadley of Yale, Economics (1896).

Assumption of Risk in the Modern World

These risks of business pervade the entire field of human enterprise. They are fundamental to and must be borne by the manufacturer, the wholesaler, the jobber, and the retailer in every line of trade. In a large measure the contractor, the builder, the banker, the real estate dealer or owner, or anyone who creates or constructs anything in the present to sell in the future—all are speculators. The farmer, who continually stakes his capital and his judgment against even the blind forces of nature, is probably the most persistent, heroic, and useful speculator in the country. Professional men also are frequent if not universal speculators. The lawyer and the doctor who spend money (sometimes borrowed) now in order to obtain their technical training, with the hope of later recovering it from future earnings, are speculators of the purest dye. Even the grim old New England adage, "There's nothing sure but death and taxes," is belied by the insurance companies and the tax experts, two highly speculative pursuits.

Everywhere in the world that inevitable business risks have arisen, some speculator has been forced to assume them, either of necessity, or voluntarily and in the hope of a large possible profit. These risks can no more be abolished by legislative fiat than the tides can be halted or water be prevented from flowing downhill. They are inherent in the nature of things. And thus modern corporations pass on their risks to their share certificates and to those individuals who own them. With the augmentation of the volume of business and the processes of specialization rising to sustain it, a special class of speculators has been created who make it their business to assume the risks of enterprise for a possible profit, by buying and selling corporate shares. For the same reason organized markets have sprung up for securities, where this necessary and inevitable traffic in the risks of business by speculators can be conducted in the fairest, most efficient, and least hazardous manner.

Antiquity of Speculation

Speculation is an immemorial handmaiden and companion of trade. Every schoolboy has read how, in the dawn of history, Joseph anticipated the "cycle theory" of prices by his dream of seven fat and seven lean years, and by accumulating and "cornering" wheat, prospered exceedingly in the land of Mizraim, in the shadow of the recently erected Pyramids. The more curious student of history may likewise have run upon the story of the ancient Greek philosopher, Thales,[29] who, upon being jeered at by the king for having fallen down a well while gazing at and theorizing upon the stars, proceeded to give a startling proof of his practical ability by cornering the supply of olive presses and making the king and his subjects pay through the nose for them. Even the much regretted short sale is at least as old as Esau, who sold his inheritance ("which he didn't own") to his brother for a mess of pottage.[30]

Speculation and the Growth of America

Of all the peoples of history the American people can least afford to condemn speculation in those broad sweeping strokes so beloved of the professional reformer. The discovery of America was made possible by a loan based on the collateral of Queen Isabella's crown jewels, and at interest, beside which even the call rates of 1919-1920 look coy and bashful. Financing an unknown foreigner to sail the unknown deep in three cockleshell boats in the hope of discovering a mythical Zipangu cannot by the wildest exercise of language be called a "conservative investment." Later, the two dominant colonies on our Atlantic seaboard, Massachusetts and Virginia, were established as the direct result of stock speculation in London in

---

[29] "Thales, being a man of moderate means, worked his corner by securing options on the use of the presses at the next harvest season." (H. C. Emery, Speculation on the Stock and Produce Exchanges of the United States, p. 33).
The original citation of Thales' corner can be found in Aristotle's Politics (Jowett's translation) I, II, 58.

[30] See Genesis, XXV, 29.

the shares of the Plymouth and London companies.[31] Neither was the 6 per cent loan of the newly established United States of America, by which this country was originally financed, in the modern sense of the word "a conservative investment," as the old brokers under the buttonwood tree could testify. Moreover, our government has time after time speculated in real estate to an advantage to the public which is simply incalculable.

When enterprise assumed corporate form in the last century, our vast present-day railroad system was built primarily by speculators. Railroad pioneers, like the late James J. Hill, boldly projected their lines through the pathless forests, across rivers and lakes, through mountains and over mountain ranges with unbuilt cities and non-existent traffic in their vision. In the industrial field, similar leaders successfully capitalized the future conditions of demand by creating vast industrial units like the United States Steel Corporation. From its foundation to the present day, America has been pre-eminently the nation of the pioneer and the trail-blazer. Its present wealth has been mainly due to bold and yet wisely conceived and skilfully executed speculation, rather than such universal thrift and saving as characterizes France and other continental nations. France has long been known as a "nation of investors," while thus far America has been rather "a nation of speculators." It is after this unparalleled historic record of national energy, foresight, and speculation in almost every manner of business that the American public, with that mental capriciousness which is at once the admiration and despair of those who seek to serve it, solemnly shudders and condemns "speculation" as an innate and quite unnecessary piece of wickedness! For once we would do better to consider the words of the great German economist Cohn, who said that speculation is in reality "the struggle of intelligence, armed with a knowledge of the ascertainable conditions, against the blind workings of fate."

---

[31] See Chapter I, page 11.

A Socialist's Testimony Regarding Speculation

Unexpectedly enough, the necessity of speculation is confirmed even by the ablest socialistic thinkers, such as P. J. Proudhon, the "Father of Anarchism," who declared:[32]

> Speculation is nothing else than the intellectual conception of the different ways in which labor, credit, transportation and exchange can unite in production. It is speculation which discovers riches, which invests the most economical means of securing them, and which multiplies them by new forms or combinations of credit, transportation, circulation, and exchange by creating new wants or by the incessant redistribution of fortunes.

The ablest socialists object to private property, either absolutely or relatively, but they realize quite clearly that so long as we have private property, speculation in it will occur. This is not the place to ask our socialist friends exactly how in their nebulous superstate of the future the risks of industry will be borne, if not by the private speculator, nor to inquire what is the moral of Lenin's recent experiment in Russia in "abolishing" both speculation and private property. Yet it surely argues little for the wisdom or consistency of those who condemn socialism as roundly as the writer could wish, that they should be equally ready to attack speculation, which even socialists recognize as one of the cornerstones of private property and private ownership.

But we must not hold the ideà that speculation, with all the harm it occasionally works to the individual, is simply a necessary evil in our modern economic scheme of things—an ancient and unshakable evil which fate has condemned us to endure with what grace we can muster. Speculation in several distinct ways is a positive and constructively beneficial factor in modern civilization, as a moment's reflection will show.

---

[32] See *Manuel du Speculateur à la Bourse* (Paris 1854).

Speculation a Phase of All Pioneering

In the first place, we must recognize that financial speculation plays an integral part in all pioneering and in all the preliminary and experimental stages of new enterprise. In almost every instance, financial speculation has been the mainspring and economic basis of those bold and hazardous explorations which have discovered and opened up new continents, and of those inventions which have subjected even the blind forces of nature to man's will. Behind almost every pioneer whom history has declared a hero stood the financial speculator, unhonored, unsung, and usually forgotten, who nevertheless must have possessed some of the hardihood and imagination of the actual adventurers whom he financed. Even good Queen Bess, so the story goes, did her share in financing the bold Francis Drake in his amazing forays upon the plate-ships of the Spanish Main, which cleared the way for the British colonization of North America. And so it has been since her day with adventurers and pioneers, successful and unsuccessful.

No business in the world is so entirely judged by results as speculation; if the adventure suceeds, the speculator is proclaimed a genius, while if it fails, he is ridiculed as a credulous fool. This admittedly is a harsh and severe criterion by which to be judged. And yet, however valuable or practical the inventor's model or the scientist's discovery may seem, the financial speculator must actively intervene before they can be placed at the daily service of mankind. As Hirst so well says: [33]

> The rapid development of material resources, mining, agriculture, manufactures, transportation, is of necessity associated with speculation. For speculation in the best sense is the investment of capital and the use of credit to finance enterprises which promise to yield handsome profits. But for a verdant

[33] Hirst, The Stock Exchange, p. 244.

and evergreen faith, salted with the love of risk and adventure for their own sakes, how could mountains be bored and waters bridged? If there were not superstition, there could be no religion; if there were no bad speculations there could be no good investments; if there were no wild ventures there would be no brilliantly successful enterprises; the same sort of sentiment which gave Dr. Cook a temporary notoriety invested Hansen with permanent fame. New York, then, must be valued fairly, not as a sort of gambling hell, but as a nerve center of North American enterprise.

The Economic Value of Unsuccessful Speculation

In this age, when the inductive method of reasoning prevails and the only test of a proposal is to "try it and see," almost all intelligently conducted experiments serve a useful purpose in the long run. The real invention, like the telegraph or the combustion engine, which is at first usually deemed only a "cracked inventor's dream," provides a direct illustration of the value to society at large of the speculators who finance it. But even failures may not be without an ultimate economic benefit. Just as in science there have been no striking discoveries without many futile experiments, so too in finance there have rarely if ever been great successes which have conferred services upon millions, without preliminary unsuccessful speculations. If the Anglo-Saxon race had always waited for a "sure thing," it would still be tending goats on the foothills of the Himalayas, instead of directing the destinies of most of the civilized world today. It was not until railroading on wooden rails, with sails, mules, and hand-cars as motive power, had been eliminated from the field of practical possibility by actual and costly trial that steam railroading on steel rails finally became a success. If the successful speculator is the hero of progress, the unsuccessful speculator is often the martyr to progress.

Moreover, in the course of unsuccessful experimentation financed by the speculator many invaluable by-products have been accidentally discovered. The medieval alchemists failed to discover the philosopher's stone which would turn base metals into gold, but they laid the foundation of modern chemistry. The original American oil men sought only the raw material for a patent medicine, but they laid bare the Pennsylvania petroleum fields. Raleigh mistook iron pyrites for gold, but he started the colonization of North America. It is probably no exaggeration to say that most of the scientific discoveries upon which modern civilization is so largely based, have resulted from the accidental discoveries of a disappointed and unsuccessful speculator.

Thus, in the onward march of civilization the speculator is the advance scout and pioneer of economic civilization. It is he who reconnoiters the posts of danger, who first attracts the enemy's fire and bears the first brunt of his resistance. From Friar Bacon to Edison, inventors and the speculators who financed them have been the eyes of business, without whom industry and trade would lose its sense of direction. Very often the speculator is quite unconscious of the larger economic significance of his work. He simply wants a profit. Yet just this willingness to take risks for possible profits has made the United States what it is today. It has been by such blind groping and stumbling toward the light that modern civilization has been achieved.

Exploration Replaced by Exploitation

The age of Balboa and Magellan is past. In the field of pioneering the risks of exploitation have replaced the risks of exploration. Speculation today is concerned, not with "lands beyond the sunset" or "perilous seas forlorn," but with new oil concessions, new railroads, and new industrial projects organized as corporations, with shares to sell. In consequence, Wall Street has become the last frontier and the true haunt of the modern pioneer. It is here, through the great banking institutions, the investment houses, and the Stock Exchange, that the pioneering capital of the nation sustains the present-day adventures of discoverers and inventors. This adventurous spirit of the modern capitalist, expressed in the acquisition of speculative shares, is a most essential forerunner to progress. It is closely akin, as Mr. Van Antwerp has pointed out,[34] to that spirit of "divine unrest" which every active and enterprising man possesses. Remove speculation from society and you would emasculate the creative instinct and the forward-looking energies of the human race.

Modern Civilization Built Upon Risks

But, even if suddenly speculation could be abolished, not merely new inventions and further progress would be halted; it is not until speculation is crippled or temporarily withdrawn that we see it in its true perspective as a necessary, energizing, and creative economic force. Even established enterprises and existing organizations could no longer be carried on without it, especially of course in times of economic stress and uncertainty. It is not until such periods come on, that men realize upon what frail and tenuous foundations our boasted modern civilization rests. Governments, as well as private corporations, have their financial risks, which are borne largely by investors and speculators who purchase their bond issues through the stock exchanges. The modern world has thus permitted the manufacture of credit instruments by its government and its banks. It has permitted its governments to capitalize their future taxing power, and its business corporations to capitalize their future earning power. It has built up a vast city life upon the sensitive and delicate mechanism of paper and metallic currency. It has become so accustomed to presuppose the speculator in all these things and countless others as well that it no longer appreciates the risk and burden of the world's business which he bears. And when the ignorant and violent political

[34] See Van Antwerp, p. 35.

theorist lays violent hands upon the speculative mechanism of modern life, as has so recently happened in Russia, the economist can afford to predict with Prospero: [35]

> The cloud-capped towers, the gorgeous palaces,
> The solemn temples, the great globe itself,
> Yea, all which it inherit, shall dissolve
> And, like this unsubstantial pageant faded,
> Leave not a rack behind.

Speculation in Times of Calamity

In times of adversity, when business is faced with an apparently cheerless future, at what might be called the "zero hours of industry," the speculator, who is so often falsely considered the villain of our whole economic drama, clearly and unmistakably becomes its hero. A striking example of what speculation can do in a national crisis occurred in France in 1871, after her overwhelming defeat by the Prussians. In that dark hour of France's destiny a revolutionary commune composed of the dregs of Paris ruled her capital; her armies were crushed and all but her unconquerable soul prostrate; two of her most valuable industrial provinces were lost; the Prussian armies stood victorious on her soil, and she faced the huge indemnity of five billion gold francs. If ever the outlook for French business—yes, and for the solvency of the government itself—seemed hopeless, it was then. And yet, as is well known, France's recovery from her prostration was so swift that it astonished the world. How was this remarkable recovery brought about? Let one of the foremost historians, economists, and publicists of France, M. Anatole Leroy-Beaulieu, answer this question for us: [36]

> Let us recall the already remote years of our convalescence, after the invasion, years at once sorrowful and comforting,

[35] See The Tempest, IV, 11, 152–156.

[36] See "*La Regence de l'argent,*" in *Revue des Deux Mondes*, Feb. 25, 1897, pp. 894–895, or Van Antwerp, pp. 383–387.

when with the gloom of defeat and the suffering of dismemberment, mingled the joy of feeling the revival of France. Whence came our first consolation, our first vindication before the world? Whether glorious or not, it originated on the Bourse. . . . When more than one political skeptic and discouraged thinker allowed themselves to write down upon the crumbling walls of our burned-down palaces "Finis Galliae," the Bourse kept its faith in France and her fortune, and that faith in France was spread by it all around, at home and abroad.

Speculation was patriotic in its way; it exhibited a confidence in our resources which the discretion of many a wise man rated as foolhardy. Have we already forgotten our great loans for liberation? Without the Bourse, these colossal loans, the amounts of which exceeded the dreams of financiers, would never have been subscribed for, or, if ever, it would have been only at rates much more onerous for the country. . . .

If France regained her rank among the nations of the world so quickly, the credit for it should be given mainly to the Bourse. And to its services in war, we should, if we wanted to be just, also add its services in time of peace. Without the extensiveness of the Paris market, and the stimulus given to our capitalists through speculation, how many things would have remained unaccomplished in the recklessly overdriven condition of our finances? We should have been unable to complete our railroad system, or renew our national stock of tools, or create beyond the seas a colonial empire which shall cause France to be again one of the great world powers. When the Bourse is on trial, such credentials should not be overlooked. Before condemning it in the name of morality and private interests, a patriot should give due consideration to its services rendered for the national weal; if all its defects and misdeeds be heaped up on one scale tray, then services of like importance will easily counterbalance them.

This is the testimony, bear in mind, of a member of the Academy of Moral and Political Sciences, and a citizen of France, that thriftiest and most cautious race of investors in the world.

A More Recent American Example

Nor do we need go so far afield as France, nor so far back as a half-century, to cite equally significant instances of the intervention of the speculator to maintain civilization during a time of stress and doubt. In the gloomy and anxious winter which succeeded the outbreak of the Great War in 1914, American finance, commerce, and industry were for the time being demoralized. So risky were even our soundest corporate shares considered that their prices had declined to astonishingly low levels. For the first time in its history the New York Stock Exchange had closed for several months, and was gradually and very cautiously restoring trading in securities on its floor. Everyone realized that the crisis which had thus suddenly overtaken the world was unprecedented. We were told that civilization was committing suicide, that our credit machinery was irreparably shattered, that international trade would never recover, that the gold standard had been destroyed, that American industry and trade had received their deathblow. Only a ruinous period of economic and business stagnation seemed to lie ahead of us.

It was in the face of such depressing opinions and the hazardous conditions which gave rise to them that the speculator alone among our business men dared to sustain public and private credit by purchasing stocks and bonds, and to assume himself the threatening risks of industry and enterprise. While that much lauded individual, the "shrewd investor," stood irresolute or else dumped his securities overboard on the Stock Exchange in terror, the much despised speculator backed his belief in the future of the country and its industries, not with mere talk, but with his money. His speculative purchases in the stock market had the result of at first stabilizing and then advancing prices. Public confidence followed the ticker tape's ascending prices upward. That virile spark of faith in America, first imparted to the American people by American speculators on the Exchange, fired the train of public confidence. And soon our factory chimneys smoked again, our harbors swarmed with the bustle and clamor of commerce, and our mills shook with the roar of renewed production.

Function of the Stock Speculator

The stock speculator, then, is needed at all times by American industry to absorb and largely segregate its risks, and thus make conservative investing possible for less daring men. New enterprises, and weak uncertain enterprises particularly, call for his constant courage and audacity. In more normal times we may perhaps complain of his occasional fits of overenthusiasm or overdespondency, albeit he has in general an uncanny way of correctly forecasting values. But we have and will invariably rely upon his courage and daring when the industrial clouds gather and business men fear for the darkening future

So long, therefore, as the pioneer spirit is strong in our people, so long as new business enterprises are attempted or old enterprises entail risk, we will have the speculator with us. And, if we are to maintain our amazing rate of industrial progress, we will need the speculator to bring forth the inventor's dream and the scientist's discovery out of the workshed and the laboratory and place them at the practical service of mankind.

Speculation Necessary to Improved Marketing Methods

Finally, there is another economic service performed for society as a whole in which speculation plays a prominent and essential part—that of assisting in the creation and maintenance of the exchanges. The several signal economic benefits rendered by these organized markets have been noted with some detail in an earlier chapter.[37] All but a few of these services rendered by organized markets depend directly and funda-

[37] See Chapter XIV.

mentally upon speculation. It has been pointed out that listed securities, both stocks and bonds, are in a practical way rendered negotiable by the Exchange, because of the willingness of speculators there to sell on a slight advance and purchase on a slight concession.[38] Without this continuous stream of speculative bids and offers coming into the stock market the investor would not invariably and quickly be able to buy or sell, because he would not be able to find a seller or buyer with whom to strike his bargain. The superior collateral value of listed securities is also basically due to speculation, because it is based upon their instant negotiability. It is likewise true that the capital made available for industry through the Stock Exchange, as well as the direction given to this capital into one rather than another industry, comes in the first instance from speculators.[39]

Reciprocally, the Exchange is of vast significance to thrift and investment, not only in rendering the investor's securities always negotiable, but also because a speculative "floating supply" is maintained through its efforts, in which securities can rest until they are sufficiently seasoned to warrant their purchase by investors.[40] This same floating supply represents the surplus production which is speculatively carried into consumption. Furthermore, the distinctive ability of an organized market to frustrate attempts at manipulation or monopoly is due to the free play of national speculative forces in it. The fact that an exchange can establish the fairest prices is likewise due to the fact that any disparity between price and value makes speculative profits possible. And, of course, the usefulness of Exchange prices as a barometer is due to the constant attempts of speculators to anticipate future changes and conditions in the value of securities. It is therefore apparent that a stock exchange in which speculation was either forbidden or else

---

[38] See Chapter V, page 98.

[39] See Chapter XVI, page 443.

[40] *Ibid.*, page 457.

restricted in any artificial and unnatural way by taxation or legislation, could not perform those vital economic functions without which corporate enterprise of any magnitude in this country would soon be dangerously impaired, if not rendered altogether impossible.

Relation of Speculation to Organized Markets

That they serve as speculative markets for securities is perhaps the principal virtue and chief economic justification of the stock exchanges. It should be noted, however, that the latter are comparatively recent additions to the mechanism of credit and business, while speculation is an ancient force in the world's business and inseparably bound up with the processes of trade. Speculation existed centuries before the organized markets in which much of it is today conducted.[41] It is therefore obvious that speculation created the exchanges, not the exchanges speculation. The Stock Exchange, as in the case of other organized and speculative markets, resulted from a natural economic evolution, and serves to segregate speculation, to minimize its dangers, and to intensify its practical and abstract benefits. It is as illogical to blame the sometimes costly shifts of speculative forces upon the Exchange as it would be to accuse the life insurance company of murdering a policy-holder.

Adjusting Prices to Values

We have seen that the occasion for a successful speculation comes only when a disparity exists between the price and the value of some commodity or enterprise. The principle is exactly the same, although, of course, on a smaller scale, with a speculation in the stock market, or with the founding of a new industry, wherein a large potential value seems creatable for a small price. It is this fundamental fact with regard to

[41] See Chapter XV, page 419.

speculation which led Justice Holmes of the United States Supreme Court to remark, "Speculation is the self-adjustment of society to the probable." The speculator, therefore, as M. Bloch, the French economist, has declared, renders an economic service every time his speculation succeeds. For this service, when he succeeds in rendering it, the speculator of course obtains a profit, and this profit, considering the profound economic benefits of speculation, is as well deserved as any other.

Many times the profits of the stock speculator result from rendering a much more genuine and valuable service to society than profits arising from production. Surely few will care to deny that profits obtained by bulls in the stock market of 1914-1915, when the credit of industrial America was at stake, did vastly more benefit to business generally than the profits of manufacturers of silk shirts in the extravagant year of 1919. For distribution is fully as important, if not more important, than production, and since speculation is a necessary factor in distribution, speculative profits represent the profits of distribution and are equally justifiable from the economic standpoint as profits arising from production.

One logical deduction from the premises stated above is that unsuccessful speculation is economically harmful, and this is in many practical ways true. But such speculation is always kept from becoming an excessive economic harm for the simple reason that the speculators suffer losses and are penalized for running counter to the trend of true values.

Economic Moral of Norris' "The Pit"

The whole theory of the service rendered by the speculator, as well as the economic significance of his profits and his losses, was graphically and correctly epitomized by Frank Norris some years ago in his celebrated novel, "The Pit," dealing with speculation in wheat in the Chicago Board of

Trade. Jadwin, a speculating member of that institution, correctly foresees a world shortage of wheat. The prospective value of wheat would under such circumstances be almost double its present price. He accordingly becomes a bull, and by enormous purchases of contracts forces the price up to higher levels. Subsequent events justify his predictions, and the value of wheat rises to its market price so established. At once farmers, seeing profits in the production of wheat (and basically speculative profits, bye the bye), immediately set about raising as much wheat as they can, with the result that the supply of it is again made to balance the demand and its value is accordingly lessened by the inevitable operation of economic laws.

But meanwhile Jadwin, who until this time has profited by correctly anticipating the rise in values, now incorrectly interprets these values and attempts to maintain by manipulation the high price which, as agent for the larger forces of supply and demand, he was responsible for creating. His speculating now serves no useful purpose; but he persists in it and as a result he is overwhelmed and ruined under an avalanche of liquidation and short selling, the latter now serving the useful purpose of reducing the high prices to the new and lower actual values.

While to the Wall Street man Jadwin seems a somewhat sententious and conceited character, yet the exposition of the economic significance of his alternate success and failure reveals not only a splendid imaginative power on the part of the author, but a clear and accurate understanding of economic principles. For one thing which the innumerable romance-writers of financial life—and how few of them ever glimpse the real romance of it!—seldom recognize, is that any economic misalignment of stock prices is self-correcting, just as the disease which brings with it a swift and powerful toxin for its own cure.

American Fondness for New Legislation

Something has already been said concerning the hopelessness of attempting to legislate speculation either out of existence or into absolute harmlessness to the individual speculator.[42] We Americans, probably more than any people on earth, have contracted the habit of rushing headlong into statute-making whenever we suffer the slightest grievance. That so many of these ill-considered and superficial attempts to inaugurate the millennium with a new law are actually enacted, is emphatically more our own fault than that of our elected representatives, whom, nevertheless, we invariably blame for the whole affair later when the law is found impossible or else dangerous in its enforcement. However we may rail at Washington or the state capitols, most of the uneconomic and useless statutes which are enacted each year are primarily due to our own unwillingness to perform the duties of intelligent citizens. If we get bad laws, we have ourselves to blame for it.

One of the seemingly perennial sources of economic legislation that is unenforceable and harmful is speculation and the various forms it takes in the business world of today. Justice Holmes of the United States Supreme Court has tersely and shrewdly stated the situation regarding such legislation:[43]

> It's true that the success of the strong induces imitation by the weak, and that incompetent persons bring themselves to ruin by attempting to speculate in their turn. But legislatures and courts generally have recognized that the natural evolutions of a complex society are to be touched only with a very cautious hand, and that such coarse attempts at a remedy for the waste incident to every social function as a simple prohibition and laws to stop its being, are harmful and vain.

The same general point—the impossibility of adequately and successfully halting speculation by statute—is testified to by

---

[42] See Appendix, Chapter XV (g).
[43] Chicago Board of Trade Case, May 8, 1905.

Professor H. C. Emery, probably the highest economic authority on speculation in America:[44]

> You cannot stop speculation in industrial securities, and you cannot stop speculation in anything by any process of law. Just as long as the value of property fluctuates, men will buy and sell with a hope of profit. There will be speculation of some kind. If you throw it out of an organized exchange, you throw it out into the street. If you throw it out of Berlin you can throw it into London. But somehow and some way, just as long as wheat fluctuates in value, people are going to buy and sell wheat; just as long as land fluctuates in value people are going to buy and sell land. Just as long as stocks fluctuate in value, people are going to buy and sell stocks.

Legislation and Economic Principles

That this view of the matter is correct is borne out by the experience of all nations at all times. Particularly in the typical instance of the much abused short sale, the cases previously cited[45] of most meticulously drafted laws passed in England, Germany, France, and this country to regulate it, tell only of failure and final repeal. The fact of the matter is that in attempts to legislate concerning so universal and fundamental a matter as speculation, the statute-makers set themselves against more powerful laws than any statute which ever adorned the printed page—the immutable, eternal, and irresistible economic laws, by whose processes nations have risen and fallen, and owing to whose unimpeded operation not merely progress, not merely the maintenance of the present business and social order, but the ability of the human being to find the food, shelter, and clothing necessary to mere existence and life itself, are basically and necessarily due. These principles defy the passing fiat of unwise legislators and hasty public opinion almost as completely as the law of gravitation. The

---

[44] Regulation of the Stock Exchange, p. 325.

[45] See Chapter IV, page 96.

law-makers who attempt to hamper with unscientific legislation the life-giving economic energies released by speculation are embarking on perilous waters; any temporary success of their efforts only intensifies the ultimate recoil of pent up economic forces to the destruction of civilization and human life.

Education the Only Genuine Remedy

This is as true of speculation in the stock exchanges, although the bearing here is less direct and obvious, as it is of speculation in the wider fields of agriculture and commerce. The account already given of the complex and tested machinery by which the New York Stock Exchange practically and successfully administers the principal American market place for securities, with constant regard for the fundamental economic forces exerting themselves within it, affords a steady contrast in the swiftness and flexibility of its operation to the dogmatic and futile statutes concerning speculation with which the history of legislation from the Middle Ages to the present day is replete. Evils in the speculative factors inherent in production and distribution there undoubtedly are, but there exist no possible legislative short cuts or panaceas for their abolition. Only the slow and tedious but old and sure method of educating the people into an understanding of economic law, and particularly as it exerts itself in the organized and unorganized markets, can be of practical value in reducing the harm which so universal, inevitable, and powerful an economic force as speculation occasionally works upon the individual.

In conclusion, one can at least take consolation in the fact already stressed, that so far as prices are concerned speculation swiftly readjusts and eliminates the results of its occasional excesses. Leroy-Beaulieu not inaptly sums up the matter by stating that "the evils which speculation prevents are much greater than those it causes." But the best summary of a difficult question has probably been made by the brilliant British logician, philosopher, and economist, John Stuart Mill:

> The operations of speculative dealers are useful to the public whenever profitable to themselves. The interests of the speculators as a body coincide with the interests of the public, and as they can only fail to serve the public interest in proportion as they miss their own, the best way to promote the one is to leave them to pursue the other in perfect freedom. Neither law or opinion shall prevent an operation, beneficial to the public, from being attended with as much private advantage as is compatible with full and free competition.

CHAPTER XVI

THE DISTRIBUTION OF SECURITIES

Listed Securities Considered

In a preceding chapter [1] the broad, fundamental economic benefits and services performed by all organized markets have been discussed. But in order to give fuller and more definite illustration of the practical workings of several of these principles as they manifest themselves each day in the Stock Exchange, we must consider in some detail the chief successive stages by which securities are distributed—from their first issuance by corporations until they at last find a permanent resting place in the investor's deposit box. With listed securities, traded in on the Stock Exchange, a very important part of the process of distribution is effected through the Exchange; on the other hand, there is a huge amount of unlisted securities which are not traded in upon the Stock Exchange and in whose distribution the Stock Exchange plays no part whatsoever. These latter securities vary all the way from many gilt-edged and extremely conservative bonds issued by the oldest and most reputable underwriting houses in America, down to the rank fraudulent stocks of spurious oil companies, glass casket concerns, crooked motor and moving picture enterprises, and the like, which swindlers peddle out to the American public in such huge quantities each year. The present chapter is limited to the distribution of the strictly legitimate although frequently speculative securities which are listed on the Exchange, and therefore does not describe the methods employed to distribute either good unlisted securities, or the fraudulent issues of the stock swindler.

[1] See Chapter XIV.

Basis of Corporate Security Financing

Our first chapter, by citing the example of an imaginary railroad company which obtained its capital through the issuance of stocks and bonds, touched the roots of our present-day securities market. Such corporations are constantly in need of fresh capital to carry on their business. Their frequent need for small sums for short periods can of course be supplied by the banks on their notes and commercial paper. But reorganizations, extensions, or large permanent improvements and the like, usually call for larger sums and over longer periods. Generally speaking such demands can be supplied only through the sale of the corporation's stocks or bonds.

Small corporations under exceptionally favorable circumstances are sometimes able themselves to dispose of small issues of their stocks or bonds direct to their stockholders or to purchasers of their products. Such a procedure, however, is impossible with a large security issue, and is usually impracticable even with small ones. The large sums needed by corporations must usually be had all at one time rather than in small successive payments over a period of time. Hence, if the average large-scale corporation had to depend on the gradual sale of its securities direct to chance investors, it could not be successfully financed. Moreover, the average railroad or industrial corporation lacks the long experience and necessary facilities to engage in the security business on its own account. In most cases, therefore, it becomes necessary for the corporation needing extensive and long-term financing to sell its stocks or bonds to some investment house which will underwrite and market them.

The Security Underwriting Business

This business of underwriting and marketing new security issues is of course carried on in every considerable city in the country. But the national headquarters of the business—

so to speak—is centered in the financial district of New York City, where the largest underwriting houses and the Stock Exchange are located. Most of the larger issues of securities, representing industries of national scope and significance, are in consequence "brought out" in that city, while the smaller and more localized banking and brokerage groups in Boston, Chicago, Philadelphia, and lesser centers, for the most part underwrite smaller and more localized enterprises. In addition, as we shall presently observe, these "out-of-town" centers give invaluable local assistance to the larger New York underwriters in selling and distributing large security issues.

The vast volume and wide variety of securities underwritten in New York have naturally led to the establishment there of many different sorts of security dealers. Some underwriting houses are members of the Stock Exchange and some are not. The inevitable process of specialization has induced some investment houses to limit their business mainly or even exclusively to securities of a single class, such as railroad or public utility or foreign securities.

Function of the Security Underwriter

The underwriting security house is an invaluable part of the financial mechanism, since it enables the manufacturer to sell his entire block of securities and obtain his money at once. As a rule, as soon as the manufacturer turns over his securities to the underwriter and gets his money for them, he can go about his business with only a sentimental interest in the underwriter's further proceedings. The underwriting house thus assumes the risk, expense, and trouble of reselling to investors and speculators the securities it purchases, for the consideration of a profit between the purchase and selling price. The purpose of the underwriting firm is not, of course, to invest its funds in securities which it intends to hold as investments for the sake of their dividends or interest coupons, but rather to resell them at a profit. Its business is in consequence essentially speculative. Indeed, if the underwriting house cannot sell out its issues readily, and thus turn over its capital rapidly, it cannot profitably engage in the underwriting business at all.

Any investment banker will testify to the fact that real and ready investors in a new security are difficult to find in a hurry, even by a firm of long experience and conspicious energy and ability in that very business. For this reason the task which the underwriting house faces in marketing the securities it purchases usually involves hard work over a considerable period of time. If the issue underwritten is small, the underwriting firm may handle it alone without the assistance of other investment houses. But with a larger issue the underwriter will usually organize a syndicate, composed of several firms which agree to share the risks, profits, and expenses of marketing it with him.[2] The number of firms in such a syndicate depends upon the size of the issue to be sold, as well as the current economic condition of the market. The average syndicate consists of from three to five firms, all of which may or may not be located in New York. On the other hand, the gigantic $500,000,000 Anglo-French 5 per cent loan floated under the leadership of J. P. Morgan and Company in 1915, was handled by a huge syndicate comprising almost all the wholesale security houses in the country.

Allotment of Syndicate "Participations"

After the syndicate has been organized, the original underwriting house, as its organizer and manager, proceeds to arrange the "syndicate allotments" or "participations"—that is, the exact portion of the total security issue which each member of the syndicate agrees to purchase and attempt to resell. It is a significant fact that prior to 1914, while the United States

[2] See Money Trust Investigation, Vol. III, p. 1661.

was still on the whole a debtor nation, foreign financial houses participated largely in American syndicates. Since the war, however, after we became a creditor nation, this former practice was reversed and at present the tendency is for this country to finance itself entirely and, in addition, to underwrite and distribute here the securities of foreign countries.

With the larger security issues, members of the syndicate often organize subsyndicates composed of the smaller investment houses, which do a retail rather than a wholesale business in securities. The syndicate member is thus enabled to dispose of his allotment to the subsyndicate, in part or in whole, at a slight profit to himself. As might be inferred from the foregoing, the business of underwriting and selling securities, like most other large-scale lines of business today, is highly organized and includes wholesalers, jobbers, and retailers.

The Public Offering

The next step, after these preliminaries have been arranged, consists of the "public offering." Under direction of the syndicate manager the new security issue is advertised for sale in the newspapers and magazines on a set date, and simultaneously syndicate and subsyndicate members release to their prospective customers circulars in which the characteristic and essential facts relating to the new security are set forth. The price at which it is offered for public subscription is, of course, above the purchase price paid by the subsyndicates and still further above that paid by the syndicate to the issuing corporation. If, for example, the "subscription price" of a bond issue was 100, the price to the subsyndicate might be—say—97, and the price paid to the corporation 96. Such arrangements vary, of course, according to the size and attractiveness of the issue, the condition of the investment market at that time, and other factors.

It may be noted in passing that the public advertisements

sometimes contain a statement that "Application will be made to list the above issue on the New York Stock Exchange." This is especially true of the larger issues, which will presumably need a broad market later. Since the underwriting syndicate houses, if they are firms of standing, are thoroughly acquainted with the listing requirements of the Exchange, the supposition is that such an issue will probably fulfil these requirements and ultimately find an active market there. Certainly no investment house would make such an announcement, were there much danger of being discredited in the eyes of the public by having the issue later refused the privilege of listing by the Exchange. Sometimes, too, the advertisement of a new issue contains at the bottom the statement that "All the above issue having been sold, this advertisement appears as a matter of record only." This does not mean that all the subsyndicates have disposed of their securities, but simply that the syndicate, the names of whose members are printed beneath the advertisement, have sold out all their securities.

Distribution Following the Offering

After the announcement to the public that the security is for sale, the syndicate or subsyndicate members, or both, endeavor to dispose of their respective allotments of the new security as rapidly as possible. The buyers "on the offering" might be divided into three chief classes: (1) pure investors, who subscribe to the security in order to hold it for the sake of the income to be derived from it; (2) speculative investors, who are willing to hold it for income but who hope to be able to sell it out at a profit to themselves sooner or later; and (3) speculators, who plan to resell it as quickly as possible for a slight profit.

The proportion of these several classes of buyers in the case of any given security depends primarily upon the nature of the security, as well as the condition of the market at that particular time. In the case of a small but very attractive and gilt-edged bond issue, investors may conceivably purchase a large portion of the issue at once. But under most circumstances and with most securities, particularly if the issue is a large one, probably at first the greater part will be sold to speculators. This is natural enough, for the intelligent investor almost always demands "seasoned securities" and is apprehensive of those which are new and yet untried. Since, therefore, in most cases there is not sufficient investment demand to absorb the entire new offering at once, the speculator must be relied upon to absorb the surplus remaining in excess of this demand, at least for the time being.[3] Frequently in a new issue of stock as much as 90 per cent will rest in speculative hands and only 10 per cent with investors after the public offering has closed.

Further Preliminary Distribution

As a rule, this preliminary distribution of a new security is not sufficiently stable and complete to meet the listing requirements of the Stock Exchange. In consequence, the new issue may undergo a further process of distribution on the New York Curb Market. Some Stock Exchange houses have representatives there, as have also houses not connected with the Exchange; nevertheless the Curb Market is absolutely different and completely separate from the Stock Exchange, and must not be confused with it.

The chief economic function of the Curb is as a preliminary market, and the service it renders as such can be realized when it is recalled that wherever in the world there is a large organized securities market, there also is found some sort of preliminary or curb market. The New York Curb frequently anticipates the termination and even the opening of a public offering of new securities, by allowing contracts for their purchase and sale to be made "when, as and if issued."

[3] See Chapter XIV, page 384.

After a new security has been traded in upon the Curb for a period, its distribution may of course undergo further changes. The principal sellers there are: (1) members of the syndicate or subsyndicate (provided, of course, that their allotments have not already been sold out); (2) speculators who purchased on the public offering; and (3) speculators who wish to resell the securities also purchased there. The principal buyers are as before: (1) pure investors, (2) speculative investors, and (3) speculators "for the turn."

The chances are that a considerable proportion of the new issue will still remain in speculative hands, however, since few investors purchase on the Curb. Nevertheless, the investment holdings usually tend to increase, provided of course that the security is of the sort which warrants purchase by investors. In this way a more stable and satisfactory preliminary distribution is attained. This is sometimes as far as the matter goes, either because the issuing corporation or the Stock Exchange authorities are unwilling to have the particular security listed on the latter market.

Part of the Stock Exchange in Distributing Process

Thus far the operation of the underwriting syndicate or subsyndicates in their mutual transactions, the subscription offering made to the public, and the transactions in the new security on the Curb, have not in any way involved the Stock Exchange. This fact is reiterated because of the vague idea which many people seem to have that "Wall Street" consists simply of the Stock Exchange and that the latter institution supervises all new security issues from their very inception. Nothing as a matter of fact could be further from the truth. The Stock Exchange begins to figure in the distribution of any given security only when the latter is listed for trading on its floor.

Most large corporations, whose security issues aggregate

large sums of money, naturally desire to list upon the Exchange in order to gain the advantage of its broad and reliable marketing facilities. But first a formal application must be made for listing by the corporation itself. The Stock Exchange never solicits new listings lest it appear to indorse them. Such applications for listing are referred to the Committee on Stock List,[4] composed of five governors of the Exchange, whose function it is to receive and consider such applications and to make recommendations concerning them to the Governing Committee.

Requirements for Listing on the Stock Exchange

When application is first made, the applicant is given three separate documents—a list of requirements[5] which must be met by the formal application later submitted, a questionnaire (Figure 57), and a distribution statement (Figure 58). Since the requirements are too elaborate to permit of detailed comment here, only a few of their chief features will be briefly remarked; they are reprinted complete as an appendix to the present chapter. These requirements have resulted from many years' experience by the governors, and are modified from time to time as new conditions warrant. In formulating them the Committee on Stock List has had the benefit not only of its own knowledge of securities and securities markets, but also of the most expert industrial advice obtainable. Before composing its requirements concerning mining securities the Committee consulted the Metallurgical Society, whose suggestions are embodied in the present form. Similarly, before listing oil securities recourse was had to the American Institute of Mining Engineers.

All applicants for listing must comply with these requirements, which tend to become more rigid and exacting year after

[4] See Chapter XIII and Appendix, Chapter XVI (a).

[5] See Appendix, Chapter XVI (b).

Questionnaire 1921

Are you an officer of the Company? . . . .

Do you appear as representative of the applicant company for the listing of. . . . .? . . . .

Is the application made by action of the Stockholders, Board of Directors, or Executive Committee?

. . . .

Is there any syndicate or concentrated holdings of this security?

. . . .

Is there any restraint on any portion of the security? . . . .

Is the control of the property vested in any minority holding?

. . . .

Have any dividends been declared and not paid subsequent to date of the present application? . . . .

How frequently do you make reports to shareholders?

. . . .

The Committee desires publications of quarterly statements of earnings. Will you agree to do so? . . . . . .

The Committee prefers that the transfer books of the Company do not close, but a record be taken. What is your practice?

. . . .

The Committee desires it understood that all future financial statements of the Company published for the benefit of stockholders are to be in the form contained in the listing application.

. . . .

Is there any litigation pending or threatened that would affect the Company's source of income from, title to, or possession of any of its property?

. . . .

Has there been any change in your Charter or By-Laws since previously filing with the Committee?

. . . .

Do you desire additional copies of this application, at your expense, for distribution to your stockholders, if the Committee acts favorably upon application? If so, how many? . . . . .

In the event any additional papers should be filed, will the same be furnished on request?

. . . . .

. . . .

By . . . .

Figure 57. The Questionnaire Form. (Size 8 x 13.)

COMPANY.

DISTRIBUTION OF STOCK

ON

No.				Shares.
	Holders of	1 - 100	share lots	________
	" "	101 - 200	" "	________
	" "	201 - 300	" "	________
	" "	301 - 400	" "	________
	" "	401 - 500	" "	________
	" "	501 -1000	" "	________
____	" "	*1001 - up	" "	________
	Stockholders			________

* The ten highest holders on the above date were as follows:

1-________	Shares	6-________	Shares
2-________	"	7-________	"
3-________	"	8-________	"
4-________	"	9-________	"
5-________	"	10-________	"

All stock is free for sale and is held under no syndicate, agreement or control.

Certified Correct,

(To be made out for each class of stock applied for)

Figure 58. The Distribution Statement. (Size 8 x 13.)

Showing distribution of a security issue for which listing on the New York Stock Exchange is sought.

year. It must be remembered, however, that extensive corporate enterprise in many different industrial fields is still relatively new, and hence, what should constitute proper listing requirements for such securities has been a question to be decided on little practical evidence. Until as late as 1910 the Exchange maintained an Unlisted Department for its industrials, but in the past decade strict and yet equitable requirements for this increasingly large group of stocks have been developed.

Regulations Regarding Security Certificates

Certain requirements in respect to the form of the security certificates to be listed are prescribed. They must be fully engraved and printed from at least two steel plates in a manner satisfactory to the committee, and specified features of the issue must be clearly set forth on their face. The Exchange also requires that the work be done by an engraving company upon whose work the committee is authorized by the Governing Committee to pass. When the capital sums into which such security issues frequently run is remembered, the need for the strictest measures to prevent forgeries or overissues of certificates is apparent. The same general problem with respect to American paper currency forced the United States government to organize its Bureau of Engraving and Printing.

As a result of this strict supervision over the preparation of certificates to be listed on the Exchange, the purchaser of its listed securities is protected from unknowingly receiving a forged and worthless certificate. "The part that the New York Stock Exchange plays in this regard," declares a financial expert of long experience in Wall Street,[6] "may be compared to the creation of the national banks and their notes of issue, after the era of wild cat private bank note currency." This prevention of forgery is, of course, basic to the ready negoti-

[6] Article by Duncan MacGregor in the *Financial Barometer*.

ability which is so important and advantageous a characteristic of securities listed on the Exchange.

Purpose of Transfer and Registry Offices

The requirements also seek information regarding the organization of the given corporation, the nature of its business, its indebtedness, a description of its properties, etc., etc. Moreover, corporations seeking to list their securities on the Exchange must also maintain two separate offices or agencies in the Borough of Manhattan, City of New York, one for the transfer and one for the registry of their securities. The large trust companies frequently act as transfer agent or registrar for many corporations which are unwilling to maintain such offices of their own. Certificates listed on the Exchange are not valid until countersigned by the transfer agent and registered by the registrar, thus providing an additional safeguard against fraud or forgery. As the secretary of the Committee on Stock List [7] explains the matter:

> The transfer agent in such cases represents the corporation and is a check on the part of the corporation against over-issuance. The registrar, however, is not the agent of the corporation, although its services are paid for by the corporation. The registrar represents the Stock Exchange and will not register any stock until authority is given by the Committee so to do, and that restriction is one of the greatest safeguards against over-issuance.

Responsibility of the Stock Exchange

The purpose of these requirements is to obtain essential information concerning the company seeking a listing, which shall be adequate for the investor to form his own opinion as to the value of its securities. Naturally the Stock Exchange cannot be responsible for the final outcome of the corporate

---

[7] W. D. Williams, pamphlet, "The Committee on Stock List," pp. 4–5.

enterprise in question, for, after all, the Exchange is not running the business, but simply furnishing a market place for its bonds and shares. The fact that a given security is listed on the Stock Exchange is not and cannot be any guaranty of its value, nor does it even imply that the Exchange recommends it for the favorable consideration of speculators or investors.

An exception to the rule was, of course, made during the war in respect to Liberty bonds. For once in its existence the Exchange heartily indorsed them and did its utmost to persuade investors of their undoubted merits. Yet, unfortunately enough, even what was generally and correctly termed "the soundest security in the world," ultimately caused huge losses to investors, including among others practically the entire membership of the Stock Exchange itself. After this instance it is easier to realize why the Exchange cannot indorse its listed securities. It does everything in its power, however, to safeguard the investor by requiring the issuing corporations to give wide publicity to the salient features of their business.

The Test of Distribution

As to the questionnaire mentioned above, an examination of it as it appears in the accompanying illustration suffices to reveal its purpose. A further word is, however, necessary concerning the distribution statement (see Figure 58), which is reproduced on an accompanying page. Here the applicant for listing must state the number of shares held in blocks of different sizes, and also the number of shares held by the ten largest stockholders of record. It is imperative for the establishment of a free and open market for the new security that not too much stock shall be held in large blocks, or by too few shareholders. The Stock Exchange cares nothing about who the shareholders are, and in fact will not receive a list of them, but it is keenly interested in the proportionate amount of the total issue which the largest of them holds. A stock is considered to be poorly distributed if a few shareholders own the bulk of it in large blocks, and well distributed if many shareholders own it in small lots. By means of the distribution statement, the Exchange gets an idea of how readily a free and open market can be created for a new security on the floor, and it thus minimizes the danger of corners or of large blocks being dumped suddenly on the market.

The Routine with Applications to List

When the applicant has filed with the Secretary of the Stock Exchange the application meeting the listing requirements, and the other papers called for, including the questionnaire and distribution statements, the papers are gone over carefully; and after any necessary corrections have been made by the applicant they are turned over to the Committee on Stock List and a date is set for a hearing upon them. At the time of its receipt the application is posted on the floor of the Exchange, so that members may familiarize themselves with the facts it sets forth, and communicate to the Committee any knowledge they may have concerning the enterprise.

The Committee on Stock List meets Mondays at 3:15 P.M. and carefully examines and considers any application which has been submitted to it. If it finds that the various requirements have been satisfactorily met by the applicant, it recommends to the Governing Committee that the application be granted. Usually, although by no means always, an application recommended by the Committee on Stock List will be favorably acted upon by the governors.

When the recommendation of the Committee on Stock List in the matter of an application to list securities is adopted by the Governing Committee, authority is granted for such listing of such securities. A notice is then prepared and sent over the tickers throughout the Wall Street district the next morning and trading in the securities on the floor of the Exchange begins, unless in the authority granted by the Governing Committee some condition is stipulated, which must be met before such trading can take place.

Insistence by the Stock Exchange Upon Corporate Publicity

Enough has been said in a preceding chapter concerning the economic services rendered by organized markets to demonstrate the many advantages of listing securities on the New York Stock Exchange. A few concluding observations on the listing process, however, remain to be made. The demand by the Stock Exchange that corporations listing their securities upon it give wide and adequate publicity to their affairs, is made primarily on behalf of the public. All the information received by the Committee on Stock List concerning any security which is listed is available to the public. The Committee in fact refuses to receive any statements from corporations which cannot be printed in the listing application, or be made accessible to its stockholders and investors generally. Corporations with securities listed on the Stock Exchange are also required to make public at suitable intervals their earnings and other essential and current statistics. It is not the general custom for the Stock Exchange to give out this information itself, for, of course, the Exchange is not a news agency but a market place. But for the protection of the public the Exchange requires the companies in question to publish such information in the press and thus make it readily available to people all over the world.

The Stock Exchange has and seeks no power over the corporations of the country. If it set itself up as a self-appointed censor of all American business, the Exchange would invite and deserve public condemnation. If its regulations with regard to listing should become excessive and inequitable, they would soon prove valueless, since the corporations would refuse to list their securities there. The Exchange can and does, however, employ moral suasion with the corporations of the country, and thus is a factor in the constantly rising standard of corporation ethics that is apparent in this country.

The "free and open market" maintained by the Stock Exchange demands, as is made clear in the distribution statement, that "all stock is free for sale and is held under no syndicate, agreement or control." This requirement is, of course, designed to prevent blocks of the new issue being held off the market by a syndicate to maintain an unduly high price for it.

The Creation of an Active Market

An underwriting syndicate invariably feels a keen responsibility for the market action of its newly listed security during its initial career on the Exchange. The syndicate members realize that the financial reputation of their respective firms is largely at stake over the success of the issue. But while there is a considerable element of self-interest in the syndicate's attitude toward the initial career of its new issues on the Exchange, there is also a large ethical element involved. An integral part of the work of an underwriting syndicate is to see not only that its issues are initially distributed among investors and that other investors can at all times readily buy them, but also that such investors shall be protected by being able, if need be, to sell them with equal readiness. Now there is no inherent magic in listing on the Stock Exchange which would produce automatically an active and stable market in a new security as soon as trading in it is permitted. Active markets in any security result from many buyers and many sellers, and their stability depends in large measure upon the orders to sell above and buy below the current price, which stand on the brokers' and dealers' books.[8] But it takes time for the investing and speculating public to become enough interested in a security to buy and sell it in equal enough and

[8] See Chapter V, page 115.

constant enough volumes to create an active market for it. Moreover, when it is first listed there has been no opportunity as yet for the stabilizing orders "away from the market" to accumulate in dealers' and specialists' books. During this uncertain initial period of trading in a new issue most underwriting houses consequently feel under the necessity of stimulating its activity and stabilizing its price.[9]

This they do by putting orders in the market to buy the new security "on a scale down," or sell it "on a scale up." A given syndicate manager, for example, might give orders to buy 1,000 shares of a given newly listed stock at 99, 1,000 shares at 98, at 97, and 96 respectively; together with orders to sell 1,000 shares at 101, 1,000 at 102, at 103, and 104 respectively. The giving of such orders in no way constitutes "matching orders," for the syndicate manager's buying and selling orders are fixed at such prices that they cannot meet but simply make it possible to execute any buying and selling orders which may come into the market, at approximately par.

By such operations any investor who wishes either to buy or sell the new security can be certain of being able to do so. In due course orders away from the market are sent in by investors and speculators, just as in the case of long-listed securities, and accumulate in the dealers' and specialists' books. Gradually, but as rapidly as they can, the syndicate members reduce the amounts of their "scale orders" until at length, the dangerous initial stage having been past, the new security is left to follow its own devices. It should be noted that this effort of the syndicate to provide an active market is not undertaken for the purpose of speculative profit; it tries to avoid heavy losses, of course, but usually incurs small ones by the operation. From the standpoint of the syndicate, it is an irksome, dangerous, and not inexpensive moral duty which it owes to its investors and to its own good name.

[9] See Appendix, Chapter XVI (c).

The Question of "Scale Orders"

The grounds for objection to this practice of employing scale orders are not that it stimulates the activity of trading in the new security so much as that it may amount to a manipulation of prices at which sales are made. Scale orders cannot be used without fixing upon some one figure above which the syndicate will sell and below which it will purchase. This of course tends to confine the price approximately to this figure, since, if heavy selling orders come into the market, they will meet the syndicate's scale buying orders and thus prevent the price from declining severely, while heavy buying orders will similarly meet the syndicate's scale selling orders and prevent a sharp rise in price. If the figure around which the syndicate tends temporarily to confine the movement of prices is a fair one and in accord with the real value of the security, no economic harm is done. On the other hand, should the price set by the syndicate be higher than the inherent value of the security warrants, the possibility of causing losses to investors arises.

Practical Power of Syndicates in the Market

But it must not be forgotten that the syndicate manager is, after all, dealing in a national market. He has given publicity to the essential details of the equity and earning power behind the new security. Every sale of it made on the Exchange is instantly reported all over the country. Any disparity between price and value immediately makes speculative profits possible. If, therefore, he attempts to stabilize its price at a figure in excess of its inherent value, the new issue will at once become a target for speculators from every corner of the nation. Against the combined pressure which they can quickly exert, no syndicate could hope to hold its ground.

In consequence of this irresistible and immediate corrective force which national speculation exerts, the power of syndicates to do harm by attempting to stabilize prices is reduced to a minimum, although it is not wholly eliminated. On the other hand, the stimulation of activity and stabilization of price is a temporary but inevitable practical necessity in the case of newly listed securities. In this connection, it is interesting to note that in 1917 the United States Treasury Department, in co-operation with the federal reserve authorities and many patriotic security dealers in Wall Street, formed a syndicate to oversee the initial marketing of Liberty bonds on the Exchange. Whatever the theorist may allege—and there are theoretical objections to such operations unless they are skilfully and judiciously conducted—the Liberty bond syndicate was absolutely necessary to the successful distribution of the first and the later issues.

The "Seasoning" of a New Security

The length of time during which underwriting syndicates maintain scale orders in the market to buy and sell a newly listed security varies considerably. It depends in the main upon the attractiveness of the issue and the condition of the general securities market at the time. But as soon as an active market has been created for it and there is promise that its prices will not be violently deflected by technical conditions in the market incident to its recent appearance there, the syndicate will gladly withdraw its buying and selling orders, and leave the new security to go its own gait unsupported and unassisted. In this way, the process of "seasoning" the new issue begins.

Pitiless publicity has already been turned upon the security. Investors and speculators from coast to coast study its merits and defects. Analytical articles are written upon it in the financial and the general press. Its sales on the Exchange are instantly flashed to the four corners of the United States. In consequence the new security at once encounters what has well been called "the bloodless justice of the market place." Its prices will depend upon what the vast investing and speculating public of the whole nation thinks about it, and will fluctuate accordingly as these hundreds of thousands of people think better or think less of it.

Sometimes the result is gratifying to the underwriters and the original investors alike, and its price either holds firm or else advances. Sometimes, too, affairs do not turn out so pleasantly. If any inherent weakness develops in the security itself, or the government or corporation behind it, no sentimental regard is shown it on the Exchange. On the other hand, its genuine merits will usually be recognized there quickly and accurately.

This seasoning process is naturally of vast benefit to conservative investors. The latter can wait until a security is well seasoned and avoid losses due to any weakness in it which has been revealed, and benefit by the constant readjustment of the price accurately to fit the risk entailed by its ownership. Since this seasoning is performed in the main by the speculator, he thus renders at his own risk a real service to the conservative investor, without cost to the latter.

Speculative Maintenance of the Floating Supply

Meanwhile, of course, the same speculators do not as a rule hold the same stocks for long periods of time. Instead, there is a constant "churning" of the speculative floating supply of listed stocks in the market. Frequently, a given portion of a fairly speculative stock may be held in rapid succession by hundreds of different speculators before it becomes sufficiently seasoned to justify the investor's purchasing it and locking it up permanently in his deposit box. But for all the swift changes of speculative ownership experienced by any one share of stock, the whole floating supply of the stock issue in question continues to be sustained at all times by all the speculators in the market, including the floor trader, the specialist, the odd-lot dealers, and the speculating customers of commission houses. Anyone can sell at any time at a concession in price, and no speculator or investor need be "stuck" with an unsalable certificate, as is so frequently the case with unlisted stocks.

Striking Securities from the List

Sometimes, however, this process of seasoning and distributing a security upon the Stock Exchange will suffer a rude interruption, owing to the security being either suspended or stricken from the list by the Committee on Stock List. The conditions which commonly necessitate this drastic action, have been clearly stated [10] by an eminent ex-president of the Stock Exchange:

> Our experience of many years as Governors of the Exchange, and the experience of previous Governing Committees, is that a small amount of stock in the list leads to a condition that is dangerous to ourselves and to our customers, the public; and therefore, in order to obviate the danger, when in our opinion that condition has been reached, we remove the stock from the list or suspend it from dealings. . . . The danger may arise from two causes. A small quantity of stock is more easily subject to manipulation than a large quantity, and by means of manipulation people may be induced to buy stock at very much greater prices than it is worth. The other danger, which of course is the greatest one we fear, is the subject of a corner in the stock, which not only hurts the broker and his customer, but demoralizes the whole country, the Northern Pacific corner being a case in point.

The Stock Exchange therefore is usually unwilling to list a very small security issue in the beginning. Moreover, it watches with particular attention, listed issues whose outstanding amounts have for any reason been considerably decreased. This sometimes happens when an issue of serial bonds has

[10] See testimony of H. K. Pomroy in Money Trust Investigation, Vol. I. p. 494.

almost all been retired, or when in a reorganization some old stock issue has almost all been converted into a new security issue. Like many other functions of the Governing Committee, the power to suspend dealings in any listed security, or to strike it from the list entirely, is and must from the nature of things be instantly exercised. Such action is usually taken at the direction of the Committee on Stock List.[11]

The Problem of "Corners"

It is particularly necessary when the free and open market for a security has been destroyed by the establishment of a "corner" in it that, for the protection of the public, trading in it should quickly be halted on the Exchange. Corners are more difficult of exact definition than might at first appear. A partial corner in a security may occur when a single individual or group of individuals gain possession of either a large majority or all of its floating supply. A complete corner arises from such an ownership of all or almost all of the outstanding amount of a given issue. When such a situation develops, anyone short of the security (and therefore under the necessity of purchasing it) is at the mercy of those holding the corner, who can either extort a premium from him on the stock he has borrowed to deliver to the original purchaser, or compel him to buy in his short stock at an exorbitant figure. In the ordinary course of trading the possibility of a premium being charged on stock when borrowed, as well as that of its price rising, are in themselves strong safeguards against the creation of an excessive short interest. But when the remedy becomes more dangerous than the disease, it is the Stock Exchange's view of the matter that what was a slight and necessary economic readjustment becomes a deliberate and premeditated attempt at extortion by a few individuals, which is contrary to the just and equitable principles of trade. The Exchange accordingly

[11] See Chapter IV, page 89.

acts to halt the offense by suspending dealings in the cornered security.[12] The sensational interest attending a corner is in itself a proof of their rarity on the Stock Exchange.

The mechanical and statistical side of the normal process of seasoning securities is important and essential to any real understanding of securities markets. We have seen that prior to the listing of a new issue upon the Exchange the larger part of it is usually held by speculators who stand ready to sell out their holdings quickly, while usually the smaller portion of it is held by investors who desire to hold it for a longer period. The latter part of the issue is said to have been absorbed by investors, while the former part, held by speculators, is known as the "floating supply."

Function of the Floating Supply

In the course of time, if the given company is successful and general economic conditions are favorable, investors will tend to buy its stock from the speculative holders of the floating supply at rising prices. Under such circumstances the stock gradually passes from a speculative into an investment stage, and its floating supply decreases. But if the company encounters difficulties, or if economic conditions prove adverse, not only do no new investors purchase the stock, but former investors sell out to speculators at falling prices, being unwilling or unable to assume the risks and dangers then attending it. As a result the floating supply of it increases. Thus, speculators hold the stock during the periods of greatest risk and enable investors to sell or buy it more safely and conservatively at all times.[13] For assuming these greater risks involved by the inherent vicissitudes of industry, speculators sometimes,

---

[12] "Whenever it shall appear to the Committee on Stock List that the outstanding amount of any security listed upon the Stock Exchange has become so reduced as to make inadvisable further dealings therein upon the Exchange, the said Committee may direct that such security shall be taken from the list and further dealings therein prohibited." (Constitution, p. 96.)

[13] See Chapter XIV, page 384.

(but by no means always) obtain those larger profits which the assumption of this greater risk justifies.

In a preceding chapter,[14] the carrying of surplus production into consumption was cited as one of the economic services performed by organized markets. The floating supply of a security is just such a temporary surplus over consumptive (or investment) demand, and by making it possible for it to be carried by speculators, the Stock Exchange, as we have previously noted, performs a most necessary economic service to the country. It is also this floating supply which lends negotiability to the security, since any investor can at any time add to it by sales or subtract from it by purchases.

Time Needed to Complete Distribution

The size as well as the attractiveness of the particular security issue also does much to determine how long its distribution among investors will take. Naturally, other factors being equal, it takes longer to distribute a large issue than a small issue, simply because there is more of it. Distribution, as a rule, is effected most quickly in the case of a small and attractive bond issue. Furthermore, the floating supply of the average bond, because of the superior features which bonds offer to the investor, is usually reduced to smaller proportions than that of the average stock. This is another aspect of the fact noted in the previous chapter [15] that the bond market is as a rule less active than the stock market, and serves to explain why many listed bonds are harder to buy or sell than most listed stocks. The floating supply of bonds, as well as of stocks, however, will increase when some doubt springs up as to their value as investments, and with a larger floating supply their market tends to become more active.

In connection with this general tendency of securities to shift from speculators to investors it must of course be rec-

---

[14] See Chapter XIV, page 384.

[15] See Chapter VII, page 156.

ognized that many years often elapse before the process approaches relative completion and the floating supply is reduced to small proportions.[16] In the meantime the general trend may be halted from time to time by various adverse incidents. Sometimes, indeed, the trend may temporarily turn in just the opposite direction. Nevertheless, over a considerable period and in the instances of successful and well-managed companies, the general drift of shares from speculators to investors, together with a gradual decrease in the floating supply, is the normal tendency. Thus the average 100-share lot, after an adventurous and speculative youth in broker's boxes and call loan envelopes, slowly settles down into a calm and dignified old age in the deposit box of some private or institutional investor.

The Distribution of Steel Common

In order to illustrate this general trend in the large-scale distribution of securities, the case of the common and preferred stocks of the United States Steel Corporation is cited.[17] Both issues, and particularly the common (5,083,025 shares), are large enough to preclude any abnormal conditions in their distribution arising from any unusual speculative purpose or condition. The United States Steel Corporation has endeavored to distribute its stock to investors for the past twenty years—a period in which the company has proved a conspicuous financial success. The quarterly reports published by the corporation give the proportion of both its stock issues which stand respectively in brokers' and in individuals' names. While a little of the former may really represent investment, and a very little of the latter be held for speculative purposes, nevertheless in a general way it is fair to consider stock standing in a broker's name as part of the speculatively held floating

[16] See Appendix, Chapter XVI (d).
[17] *Ibid.*, XVI (e).

supply, and that standing in the name of an individual as investment stock.

On the basis of this assumption, a comparative examination of these quarterly reports of the United States Steel Corporation from 1909 to 1920 shows that on December 31, 1909, 66.41 per cent (or about two-thirds) of the common stock was in the floating supply, and only 33.59 per cent (or about one-third) held by investors. Six years later, on December 31, 1915, 49.80 per cent (or about one-half) of the same issue was speculatively held, and 50.20 per cent (or about one-half) held by investors. On December 31, 1920, 25.17 per cent (or only about one-quarter) remained in the floating supply, and 74.83 per cent (or almost three-quarters) had been absorbed by investors. This is a striking illustration of the tendency of a stock to shift from speculative to investors' hands as it becomes seasoned.

The more complete diminution of the floating supply of an investment security as contrasted with that occurring in a more speculative common stock is furthermore shown by the similar statistics relating to Steel preferred, which has long been considered by many to possess investment features almost comparable to those of the average bond. On December 31, 1909, 17.57 per cent of this preferred issue constituted its floating supply, but by December 31, 1915, this had shrunk to 11.15 per cent, and by December 31, 1920, to only 7.53 per cent.

The Floating Supply of Commodities

The necessity of gaining distribution by the intermediate aid of the speculatively held floating supply is nowise peculiar to securities. With the possible exception of the financial metals, gold and silver, no ordinary commodity or article in the world today can normally be sold by producer to consumer as fast as production takes place. Whether in the wholesale cereal or textile commodities, or in manufactured products like automobiles and shoes, distribution inevitably involves a carrying process between the time when production is completed and the time when the final sale to the consumer is made. Since in this interval demand may slacken and prices fall, this carrying process which attends the sale of practically all classes of goods necessarily involves a speculative risk, and an accompanying chance for speculative profit.

In most cases goods are carried by several different types of speculative dealers, such as wholesalers, jobbers, and retailers, and reach the consumer only through the last class. All such dealers, since they attempt to make a profit by purchasing cheap and selling dear, are essentially speculators. Neither are they parasites in any sense, since they perform an indispensable service in carrying stocks of goods at their own risk in the hope of selling them later at a profit. Without the stocks ready for sale which such dealers constantly carry, most modern consumers could not even obtain food, clothing, and shelter for themselves, let alone any of those articles demanded by the refinements of modern civilization. Thus, the stock speculator who buys 100 Steel on margin in the belief that its price will increase, is performing much the same service to society as the grocer who buys his canned goods on credit and in hopes of disposing of them at a profit. The higher degree of organization which characterizes securities markets, however, permits the stock dealer to enter into his transaction more safely and easily. But in an economic way, that is about the only difference between these two types of speculative transactions.

Slowness of Security Distribution

For several reasons the distributing process occurring in securities on the stock exchanges is necessarily slower than in agricultural or industrial products. To begin with, securities, which from the investor's standpoint are simply the right or the assurance of receiving an income, are to the average man a luxury rather than an absolute necessity. All modern men must pay rent to obtain shelter, buy food in order to eat, and buy clothing to preserve their health. But they can get along without buying stocks or bonds. Hence, from the standpoint of the individual, the purchase of securities is made with surplus funds.

Since the tendencies in the stock market are only the aggregate results of the hundreds of thousands who buy and sell securities in it, the factor of demand in the securities market is perforce more variable at different times and under different economic conditions than in the case of demand for commodities and articles absolutely necessary to the daily existence of mankind. In consequence, securities are on the whole harder to distribute among investors than many articles are among consumers, and from this fact it follows that the process of carrying the surplus of securities over investment demand in the speculatively held floating supply involves a greater proportion of many new stock issues, takes a longer period of time, and thus necessitates a more constant and considerable amount of financial speculation in them, than is the case with the similar carrying, from production to consumption, of temporary surpluses of other articles and commodities by speculative dealers.

Listed Securities Always Salable

Moreover, it must be always remembered that unlike wheat, corn, and beef, which are destroyed through being eaten; or cotton, wool, and silk, which are destroyed by being worn out; or pig iron, bar copper, or lumber, whose immediate and more general usefulness is destroyed by being fabricated into special forms, shapes, and articles, securities are not thus destroyed or rendered unsalable in any way by their purchasers. The investor in stocks and bonds simply holds his purchased certificates in his deposit box, in exactly the same form as when he received them, for the sake of the income accruing to him from them. He is at liberty to sell them again at any time he wishes, and very often he does so. Thus, after being held for a few years by an investor, a given security certificate may be sold by him through the Stock Exchange to some speculator, and thereby added to the floating supply. In consequence, it is one thing to sell listed securities to investors, and another to keep them sold to investors.

Of course, some securities disappear in the course of time, either through the dissolution of the issuing corporation or through being paid off or converted into other securities. Nevertheless, there are bonds listed on the Stock Exchange which will not mature until after 2000 A.D., while stocks represent shares in corporations which in theory at least are deathless and perpetual. In consequence, the floating supply of any given listed security is constantly being augmented by the selling of whilom investors, and this fact provides another reason why it is comparatively difficult to reduce this floating supply and permanently distribute stock issues among investors. And, as we have seen, this difficulty of reducing the speculatively held floating supply furnishes an additional reason why speculation in any average security must be both extensive and of long duration.

For these and other equally fundamental reasons the distribution of securities necessarily demands considerable financing through the collateral loan market, already described.[18] Funds thus employed perform in general the same economic service as funds employed by speculative dealers in effecting the distribution of any commodity or article to the consumer.

Professor H. C. Emery has epitomized this whole seasoning process experienced by listed securities in the following words:

---

[18] See Chapter VIII.

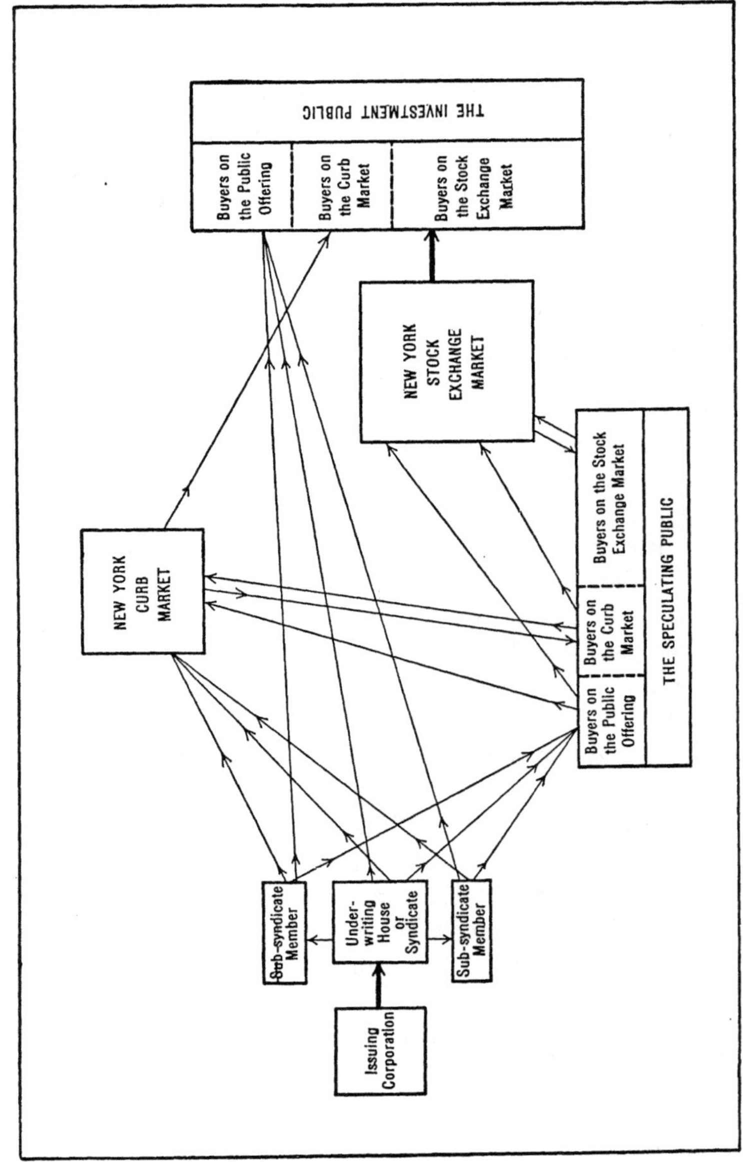

Figure 59. The Distribution of Listed Securities

Showing their course from the issuing corporation to the permanent investor. The flow of capital from investors into industry occurs in exactly the opposite direction in each instance to that here indicated.

Each new enterprise must stand the test of criticism, and unless unusually sound will be the subject of active speculation. Its ups and downs follow the changes of opinions, until gradually a continuous flow of dividends of moderate amount show the stability of real value (or lack of dividends shows the valuelessness) of the security and speculation ceases. The particular investment has been put through the ordeal and come out whole. It then becomes a field for the private investor. Many of the more active stocks of today may run their course and fall into the honorable obscurity of certainty.

The Reciprocal Flow of Money Into Industry

With respect to the whole process of distributing securities above outlined, the reader, of course, realizes that each time anyone disposes of stock he obtains money in exchange for it. The wider significance of this apparent platitude, however, deserves a further word of comment. The chart shown in Figure 59 illustrates the course of security distribution, beginning from the issuing corporation and ending with the permanent investor. But we must not forget the reciprocal flow of funds which this process of security distribution sets in motion, in precisely the opposite direction. The manufacturer gets his funds from the underwriting house, and frequently neither knows, understands, nor cares about the further stages of the process. The underwriters in turn sell the purchased security, perhaps at a profit and perhaps not, and obtain funds from the members of the subsyndicates and from speculative and investing buyers on the public offering, and perhaps on the Curb. The speculators to whom most of the security has been sold in turn shift it about among themselves, either for a profit or a loss, but, as we have seen, gradually sell out the floating supply, which they hold, to investors on the Stock Exchange and thus get their money back.

Disregarding minor exceptions, therefore, it can be said in general that underwriters cover their advances to the issuing corporation by cash receipts from speculators and investors, and that speculators as a whole cover their cash advances to the underwriters by cash receipts from investors in the Stock Exchange. In this process by which funds flow into industry, then, the Stock Exchange is an indirect but vital link. For the syndicate would not advance money to the corporation unless it thought it could get its money back mainly from the speculators, and speculators in turn would not advance their money to the underwriters unless they thought they could sell out to investors in the long run. It is, of course, the Stock Exchange which enables investors over a period of years gradually to purchase securities out of the speculative floating supply, and this is the real foundation of the whole process. Hence, it is quite correct to attribute mainly to the Stock Exchange the present continuous flow of large capital into industry,[19] even if manufacturers and investors are often unconscious of the fact and although a detailed explanation of the process such as the above is maddeningly reminiscent of "the house that Jack built."

The Stock Exchange as a Capital Market

This function performed by the Stock Exchange in distributing capital to industry has been described by Charles A. Conant, the eminent banker and economist,[20] with the following suggestive simile:

> The stock market acts as a reservoir and distributor of capital, with something of the same efficiency with which a series of well-regulated locks and dams operates to equalize the irregular current of a river. The hand of man is being stretched out in the valley of the Nile to build great storage basins and locks, and the waters which flow down the great river may be husbanded until they are needed, when they are

[19] See Chapter XIV, page 383.
[20] The Uses of Speculation, *Forum*, August 1901.

released in small but sufficient quantities to fertilize the country and tide over the periods of drought. Something of the same service is performed for accumulations of capital by the delicate series of reservoirs, sluice gates, and locks provided by the mechanism of the stock market. The rate of interest measures the rise and fall of the supply of capital, as the locks determine the ebb and flow of the life-giving water. The existence of negotiable securities is in the nature of a great reservoir, obviating the disastrous effects of demands which might drain away the supply of actual coin, and prevent the panic and disaster which, without such a safeguard, would frequently occur in the market for capital.

Pre-War Importation of Investment Funds

In the present volume the vital economic usefulness of the investor to business and society has been only occasionally alluded to, while constant stress has been placed on the economic services rendered by the speculator. The reason for this different treatment of two equally vital economic forces in our business structure is that the beneficial functions performed by the investor are quite generally known, while the intermediate but also indispensable functions of the speculator are constantly misunderstood. But in concluding this brief survey of the usual channels through which the distribution of large security issues takes place, a few final remarks upon investment, and the services performed for it by the Stock Exchange are needed.

Before the war it was generally recognized that the growth of security investing in the United States had not kept pace with the tremendously swift and enormous growth of corporate industrial enterprises here. In consequence, although even then we probably possessed more wealth; and certainly were accumulating wealth more swiftly, than any other nation in the world, we nevertheless were unable to supply sufficient investment funds to finance our own trade and industry. We had constantly to import for this purpose capital furnished by British,

French, Dutch, and other foreign investors in our stocks and bonds. But the Great War has changed this condition, probably forever. Not only must large-scale American industry henceforth depend upon the American investor alone, but, in addition, the latter must learn to supply capital to governments and corporations abroad by purchasing foreign securities.

The New American Investing Public

Naturally, so sudden a reversal of investment conditions in the United States at first resulted in considerable confusion of mind, both on the part of investors and security dealers. Certainly a vast amount of educational work must be done before the fruit-grower of Oregon or the farmer of Kansas will be able to diversify his investments here and abroad with skill and success. Nevertheless, during the recent trying years of the war a vast and wholesale education with regard to security investments resulted from the distribution of the enormous Liberty bond flotations among all classes of our people and in all sections of the nation. A former Assistant Secretary of the United States Treasury Department once told the writer that when the first interest date on the earlier Liberty bond issues arrived, the government Treasury in Washington was flooded with remittances from the new American investors, who stated that they had bought bonds and were therefore sending in the interest due upon them! Such an episode as this furnishes as appalling an example of the ignorance of many of our people concerning security investment as it is a touching instance of their whole-hearted patriotism. But literally millions of people since those early days of the Liberty Loans have learned the "feel" of bond certificates, have experienced the by no means ignoble pleasure of "cutting coupons" and cashing them at the bank, and best of all have experienced at first hand the personal benefit of saving money and investing it in sound securities. This tendency has naturally been furthered by the wonderfully prosperous business years experienced by this country since 1915, and the wider diffusion of wealth among all classes in our population. Incidentally, the old demagogic expression, "bloated bondholder," seems to have become obsolete and to have disappeared altogether.

Broadening of American Investment

The stimulus furnished to thrift and investment among the masses by the Liberty Loans has shown itself in many other directions also. The odd-lot business on the Exchange, described in an earlier chapter, has grown rapidly since the armistice, owing to the small investor and small trader in stocks. There has been an increasing tendency on the part of underwriting houses to reduce the denominations of new bond issues to $500 and even to $100 pieces. Moreover, our large and more stabilized corporations, such as the United States Steel Corporation, the American Telephone and Telegraph Company, or the Pennsylvania Railroad Company, can today show more stockholders of record and fewer shares per average holder than at any previous time in their history.[21] These tendencies are simply straws which show in what direction the economic winds are blowing. To these new small investors the Stock Exchange performs a variety of useful services. As a previous chapter has pointed out,[22] a highly organized market like the Exchange places the small buyer and seller more nearly on a level with the larger trader than any other type of market can possibly do.

Were the total annual wastage of funds by the masses rendered available for investment in sound securities through increased thrift and a more widespread knowledge of the principles of investment, there seems to be almost no limit to

[21] See Appendix, Chapter XVI (f).
[22] See Chapter XIV, page 379.

the possible economic benefits which would result. It has often occurred to our business leaders as well as to our economists, that a practical solution of the recurrent quarrels between capital and labor might some day be found by enabling employees to participate in the management of corporate enterprises through becoming stockholders in the companies themselves. Indeed, several large and far-sighted corporations have already been experimenting in a practical way with this idea.

Economic Immaturity

The growth of security investing in this country, however, must encounter certain retarding forces also. For one thing America is still throughout much of its area a new and undeveloped country. In many agricultural states of the Great West it is inevitable that the land mortgage should be almost the only form of investment as yet demanded or supplied by the economic life of the inhabitants. Our eastern states at present represent a stage of greater economic maturity, and consequently securities are on the whole better understood and oftener purchased than in the West. Yet with further urban and industrial development west of the Mississippi, the present condition of investment needs and resources will automatically change. Such a transformation will probably occur gradually; nevertheless the ultimate outcome seems certain.

The Menace of the Stock Swindler

The most serious foe to sound investment is, of course, the stock swindler, whose operations not only injure his unfortunate victims, but also tend to undermine the faith of the people in legitimate securities and reputable security dealers as well. From the bitter experience which Americans, more particularly in our undeveloped states, have had with these jackals of finance, it is little wonder that their victims, who understand little about securities or the security business, should be inclined in their righteous and naturally indiscriminating wrath to lay the blame for their misfortunes upon stock exchanges, reputable investment houses, and in fact upon everything and everybody connected with the security business. The enormous amount of stock swindling in America today serves both as a brake upon all legitimate business in securities and as an indication of the great need for educating the American investor, in the East as well as in the West, in the underlying facts and principles of security investment. In this work of popularizing a knowledge of economics and investment the Stock Exchange has co-operated with the leading bankers, universities, and advertising men, and in this respect stands ready at all times to render any service within its power.

CHAPTER XVII

THE STOCK EXCHANGE AND AMERICAN BUSINESS

Sensitiveness of Security and Money Markets

Practically every significant economic force in America, and the principal economic factors in the life of foreign nations as well, make their influence felt instantly and often in advance, upon the course of the security prices established on the floor of the New York Stock Exchange.

The newcomer in Wall Street is always astonished at this tremendous sensitiveness of the money and securities markets to domestic and foreign happenings, present and future. Stock Exchange prices fluctuate as constantly and as unexpectedly as life itself, and possess some of the inevitable rhythm of progress. Not only crop reports and crop prospects, banking and money conditions, steel production, commodity prices, and the lurking possibilities of war, but also labor conditions, unemployment, strikes present or prospective, idle freight cars, business failures, interest rates, building reports, retail sales, the legislative enactments and judicial decisions of Washington, and a thousand other events—all directly and profoundly affect the course of security prices on the Exchange. In addition, the stock market must reckon with all manner of cabled foreign news, the British bank statement, the progress of French taxation, the production of gold in the Rand, of copper in Spain, of tin and rubber in the Straits, the foreign exchange rates, the foreign exports and imports of this and other leading nations, and the decisions and strategy of the chancellories of Europe.

The writer once found a well-known business man pacing

up and down his Wall Street office in evident anxiety. On inquiring what the trouble was, he was informed that "the Indian monsoon was not blowing well." Failing to see the connection between the climate in India and the speaker's business in securities, an explanation was requested, and he was told, "If the monsoon fails, there will be a drought in India, and the bazaars will be forced to sell silver. If oriental silver comes on the market, it will depreciate the oriental exchanges, which are founded on silver. This will in turn temporarily ruin the market there for cheap British textiles, because it will decrease the buying power of the purchasers' money. If the Lancashire district in England slows down, it will not buy textile machinery, and I am vitally interested in the stock of an American company making textile machinery." Far-fetched as this chain of hypotheses may seem, nevertheless almost exactly this sequence of events actually occurred some months afterward. It is consequently natural that a leading tenet in the philosophy of Wall Street men is the old adage of the Greek philosopher, Heraclitus, to the effect that "all things flow," and that the only changeless feature of life is the principle of change itself.

The Wall Street Point of View

From one standpoint the vision of Wall Street and of the business men all over the country who do extensive business there is as wide as the world, as deep as the deepest mineshaft, and as high as the loftiest soaring cloud or aeroplane. And yet, because its inhabitants and its customers are human beings, its viewpoint is in many ways limited and parochial, too. The intense stress and strain under which most men live there has made them only too apt to credit glib assertions and superficial deductions, and to have a highly specialized but hazy and limited conception of the vast economic forces which converge upon the narrow Stock Exchange floor. Men who year after year are cliff dwellers in the great gray canyons of the New York financial district are through force of circumstances often unable to look further into the future than the prices on the stock ticker. As we have seen, this amounts to seeing into the future some three to six months further than most business men do, yet of course the thoroughgoing student of practical business economics would not wish to confine his attention solely to it. And as it is with the vision of Wall Street men, so it is too with their temperament. When ticker prices climb, they are joyous optimists, but the next day, when the ticker reports declining prices, they become sad and melancholy indeed.

But if the average Wall Street man is in a human way the victim of intense specialization and absorption in his own immediate environment to the exclusion of a wider and deeper understanding of economic forces and tendencies, the same thing may be urged against the average American business man who judges the work of Wall Street only from rumor and hearsay evidence. Manufacturers often wonder at the occasional gyrations of their stocks in the stock market, and their habitual assumption that somehow or other the Stock Exchange itself must be responsible for them is a fallacy as natural as it is erroneous.

No Royal Road to Understanding Price Changes

The real understanding of prices and price changes in our organized markets involves not so much romantic mysteries or astonishing human-interest stories, as a painstaking and unenlivening study of the "dismal science" of economics. The student must become familiar with abstract conceptions and much technical terminology; he must pore over many initially bewildering statistical tables and graphic charts; and in addition he must gain by equally laborious means a knowledge of many markets and marketing methods. In this formidable and superficially dull undertaking there are no short cuts or simple but secret formulas, nor, despite the assurances of those philanthropic individuals who occasionally advertise "How to make money in the stock market in 10 easy lessons," is there any royal road to learning.

The Universal Habit of Personifying

Now the great majority of mankind, whether through preoccupation or laziness, are not and never will be deeply moved by abstract philosophers or recondite economists. We all of us base our opinions on every conceivable subject, not upon the results of hard, slow, and painful thought and study, but upon the whispered rumor, the contagious suspicion, or the vehement, picturesque, and reiterated accusations of the fiction writer. Moreover, being still only some hundred generations removed from barbarism and savagery, we all still have deep in our methods of thought that instinctive habit of personifying everything, which the scientists call "anthropomorphism." For primitive and ancient man always personified as human beings those abstract forces in life and nature which he could not otherwise comprehend, and modern man in hundreds of ways still follows in his footsteps.

The ancient Greek, for example, without our scientific knowledge, was naturally puzzled in trying to determine why the sun rose and set, why there were storms over sea and land, or why the seasons recurred in endless succession. As we know, he finally concluded that in each instance some semihuman, semidivine person was responsible for it all. The sun consequently came to be thought of as a charioteer who drove flaming horses across the sky, and the winds as winged beings who flew through the air. Thus, a whole pantheon of pagan gods finally resulted from the primitive man's inability to think in abstract, scientific terms about the universe.

So, too, the American Indian who could not understand

the destructive and terrifying force of the lightning, finally decided that there must be a personal devil behind it, who, for all his evidently superior powers, was after all only another Indian like himself with a more cruel and disagreeable disposition. This natural theory proved so satisfactory that thereafter he had not the slightest doubt that he really understood practically everything worth while knowing about lightning.

Modern Myths and Myth-Makers

This plunge into ancient myths and myth-making is not such a digression from the ways of current thought, both in Wall Street and out of it, as might at first appear. Every modern man also personifies the abstract forces of life, of nature, and even of international politics. Uncle Sam and John Bull are much more real individually to millions of people than the President of the United States or the Premier of Great Britain. And when it is not as vivid and graphic a matter as international relationship, but instead the dim and dreary realm of economic forces, how natural and inevitable it is that we should all more or less yield to the old instinctive tendency of personifying the abstract forces of the shop and the market place which, without hard and difficult study, would otherwise elude our understanding.

Wall Street, therefore, has its own mythology, and a very colorful and picturesque mythology it is! The chief demigods in this modern financial pantheon consist of the imaginary group of men "Who Put Prices Up and Then Put Them Down Again." For prices certainly rise and fall, and somebody must be consciously responsible for it! It is useless to point out that the Exchange is a national market, and that prices established there result from the transactions of thousands and thousands of people all over the country. These thousands of people cannot be visualized, and so honestly indignant and sincerely superstitious individuals heatedly declaim against these mythical figures, as "a little clique in Wall Street," or "the powers that be." Even the broker's clerk, as he watches the tape, murmurs, "I see *they* are putting prices up again."

It is as useless to talk about supply and demand, or interest rates, liquidation, or prospective earnings to these simple souls as it would be to mention the theory of sidereal revolution to the Greek worshipper of Apollo, or the theory of air currents and electricity to the Indian worshipping his lightning devil. And so the Stock Exchange, at least in many men's minds, is thronged with a ghostly and devilish company of "insiders," "big manipulators," "operators," and "scalpers"—lineal descendants, all of them, of Satan, Mephistopheles, Beelzebub, and every other pleasing personification of the forces of evil that mankind has ever evoked in order to shudder at. Particularly villainous in this demonic financial company is the "bear raider," who in the popular mind combines the daring bloodthirstiness of Captain Kidd with the grisly hideousness of Fi-fo-fum. Such conceptions are an immemorial heritage of the human imagination. After the bear raider has changed his smart metropolitan attire for a tropical costume, the West Indian negro voodoo-worshipper is waiting to sacrifice his white cock to him. And so it goes.

The Human-Interest Factor in News

If all these supposed personal factors in the stock market are to such a degree mythical and imaginary, it might well be asked why the papers continually give this personal touch to what should be a cold, impersonal, and statistical account of the stock market. The younger and less experienced reporters and editors can hardly be blamed if they quite sincerely believe some of the commoner myths of Wall Street, particularly when it is realized that even members of the Exchange themselves occasionally lapse into this almost instinctive and yet fallacious mode of thought. The older financial writers, as a matter of fact, are well aware of the impersonal economic forces which really create Stock Exchange prices. Nevertheless they help more or less to keep alive these superstitious myths which haunt the market place, because after all they have to write in a language which the great mass of people can understand. If an editor states that, "The short interest having been depleted by previous covering, liquidation and short selling found little resistance, and lower prices resulted," he might in a given case quite accurately describe the factors in the market making for a price decline. But lest such technical abstractions prove "caviar to the general," he will usually garnish his report with an inaccurate but vastly more appealing human-interest motif. He will hint at "a prominent bear raider" to whom the decline may be attributed, or suggest that the "Waldorf crowd" or the "Palm Beach crowd" or "the West," or some equally far-off and indefinite set of men, had "decided to smash prices." This suggestion of a deep-laid plot by mysterious conspirators is as old as Hindoo mythology, and rarely fails of popular appeal—witness the motion pictures! The editor's position has recently been stated quite candidly by a well-known financial journalist:[1]

> It is always easier to say that the market is going down because it is being raided by powerful and conscienceless bears than merely to call attention to the undoubted fact that no one wants to buy stocks. It not only sounds better, it reads and writes more easily. The writer knows what he is talking about, for he had to fill a column in a New York newspaper with stock market gossip every day for five or six years.
>
> The public must always personify what is going on. There is no way of personifying the cold fact that people do not want to buy stocks, and a financial editor cannot find new ways of stating this naked, unadorned and comfortless truth every day in the year. But once you introduce the bear, there is something the public imagination can fasten itself upon.

[1] See Albert W. Atwood, "Vanished Millions," *Saturday Evening Post*, Feb. 26, 1921, p. 9.

Effect on the Public Mind

The effect of such picturesque financial columns on the general public is only too evident. Amid the murky fog of vague and unfamiliar economic and financial terms which he doesn't understand, the average citizen finds, in this human side of the story, something that he can really comprehend. Prices went down and some mysterious person did it—that to him is the crux of the matter. Unless he makes so thorough and complete study of the economics of the stock market that he can realize what absurd nonsense this personifying of economic forces really leads to, the more he investigates the mystery, the more strange and mysterious it all becomes. He never learns who the "Palm Beach crowd" is, or exactly how even the Argus-eyed editor knows that it is responsible for the decline. Neither is he ever told who the real "insiders" in the market are. Many knowing nods, wise looks, and vaguely cynical adages he may encounter, but no genuine information. And so the mystery deepens and the greater grows his superstitious fear and hatred of the imaginary demigods and demons of Wall Street. This is human nature—but it is not economic fact.

Services of the Stock Exchange to Investors

In previous chapters the functions and benefits of the Stock Exchange as they touch society generally, have been described with abstract and dull veracity. In the present chapter the attempt will be made in the same unromantic but truthful fashion to particularize and speak more specifically of the contacts which the Stock Exchange has with different types of men and of business. For even at the risk of repeating in other words much which has been said before, it seems essential to summarize the many powerful though often indirect links which exist between stock exchanges on the one hand, and even those sincere but misguided persons who regard them with undisguised horror on the other.

First of all, a word concerning investors and investment is called for. Previous chapters [2] have sufficiently recounted the services to investors rendered by the Stock Exchange to make unnecessary their re-enumeration here. But we should realize that in one way or another a vast majority of Americans are investors. The number of people who directly invest in small lots of stock [3] or in bonds of small denominations [4] has experienced an astonishing growth during the past decade. But in addition, millions of individuals today invest their savings in listed securities by proxy, often without knowing it. Only a relatively small proportion of the hundreds of thousands of people who have savings bank accounts realize that the latter institutions are able to pay interest upon their accounts only through reinvesting their money, and that largely in listed securities. The savings banks are among the largest institutional investors in this country and, through their shrewd and extensive purchases of seasoned railroad and other bonds, are an important factor in the Stock Exchange Bond Department.[5]

So it is, too, with the insurance companies, whose large surplus funds are steadily invested in Stock Exchange securities. The economic importance of insurance to the country today as a stabilizer of the risks of death and disaster to property is generally realized, yet the assistance which the Stock Exchange gives to this beneficial business is often forgotten. The ability of the insurance companies to pay their policyholders promptly largely depends upon the ability of the Stock Exchange to render its listed securities speedily negotiable.

The San Francisco Earthquake

A striking instance of this fact was afforded in the great San Francisco earthquake. At that time the ease and readi-

[2] See Chapters XIV, page 381, and XVI, page 457.

[3] See Chapter VI, page 150.

[4] See Chapter VII, page 165.

[5] See Chapter VII.

ness with which the insurance companies indemnified their policy-holders caused very general and flattering comment. Yet the fact that the companies were able to get cash mainly by liquidating securities in the Stock Exchange and that no small part of the economic burden imposed by the great catastrophe consequently fell on the organized securities market in New York, is not so often remembered. Many men and many companies carry insurance, not only as a protection, but as an investment, and in large measure they unconsciously depend upon the steadiness and liquidity which the Stock Exchange imparts to its listed securities.

Importance of Agriculture to the United States

Coming now to the various classes of American citizens for whom the Stock Exchange renders a daily though often little recognized service, one instinctively thinks first of all of our great farming population. The tremendous economic significance to this country of our vast and fertile fields, and of our great and progressive farming population is sometimes overlooked in the turmoil and clamor of city life. It is only when the city dweller delves into statistics, when he learns of the several "billion-dollar crops" which these men raise each year, and their importance to our entire foreign and domestic commerce, or when he discovers the vast quantities of city products which are purchased annually by American farmers, that he begins to realize that this nation, in spite of its huge and increasing industrial progress in recent years, is still mainly an agricultural country. The national functions of the Stock Exchange, as a matter of fact, are in no way more clearly emphasized than by the services which it renders to farmers all over the United States.

The latter of course benefit from its operation to some extent simply through being investors, although it is of course true that the favorite farmer's investment is, and may always be, the farm mortgage. Still, the idea that all farmers are over-credulous victims of the stock swindler's wiles is far from the truth. Some farmers are as shrewd judges of sound securities as could easily be found among most other classes of American business men. Moreover, farmers invest indirectly to an even greater extent by being patrons of savings banks and insurance companies in great numbers and for large aggregate sums.

The Stock Exchange and the American Farmer

Yet undoubtedly the principal assistance which the Exchange has been able to render the farmer consists of having been so largely instrumental in establishing the machinery of transportation and distribution upon which the agricultural communities must depend to sell their produce. The farmer who sends his wheat to market over the iron pathway provided by our western railroads benefits unconsciously and yet profoundly from the work accomplished by the Stock Exchange during the preceding half-century in marketing and distributing our railroad securities. The American farmer could obviously never have become the progressive and, compared with the agricultural workers of other countries, the extremely prosperous individual that he is, were it as difficult for him to market his produce as it is for farmers in other less developed countries. Without the network of steel rails stretching all over the United States, he would be engulfed and isolated in its vast interior areas, as are the peasants of Russia or China.

But the problem of marketing and distributing the great crops of this country does not simply consist of getting them aboard the freight cars. Many other factors are also involved. There is the country bank, which finances the farmer's undertakings and often sends in its surplus direct or by proxy to Wall Street to loan on security collateral.[6] In addition, even besides the great organized markets for agricultural staples,

[6] See Chapter VIII, page 177.

whose operation, as we shall presently see, is materially assisted in several ways by the existence of a ready securities market of national scope, there are still other vital parts of the crop-marketing machinery beyond the blue horizon of the farmer's world. The elaborate mechanism of foreign exchange and foreign trade, the exporting, shipping, and insurance companies have to perform their separate parts of the work. And to each of these additional factors the Stock Exchange renders one important service or another.[7] Thus, while the Exchange has nothing to do directly with marketing the farmer's wheat, corn, or cotton, nevertheless it renders indirectly a hundred often unnoticed and yet genuine services.

The Modern American Farmer's Needs

Nor does the contact between the stock market and the farmer end here. For the American farmer of today has in many ways become an agricultural engineer, who uses machinery extensively and to an increasing extent in place of the slower and less profitable manual labor employed in our fields fifty years ago, and which is still so employed in most other countries. If the industrial portions of this country have imposed a constant burden upon our farmers by attracting their labor into the cities, they have repaid the debt by furnishing the farmer with iron slaves capable of outworking hand labor both as to speed, efficiency, and cheapness. Nowadays, machinery can be depended upon to shell and grind corn; plant, reap, and shock wheat; cut silage; hoist hay, thresh grain, and perform many other tasks essential to wholesale farming. Neither has the farmer's wife been slow to adopt such mechanical, labor-saving devices for her churning, washing, milking, and separating.

All these invaluable machines are manufactured by corporations, many of the larger of which have in the past depended

[7] See Chapter XVIII.

upon the Stock Exchange for their capital. Still other corporations which have similarly financed themselves furnish the farmer with various petroleum products, fertilizers, tractors, etc. Moreover, apart from the tools of his trade, the farmer is enabled, along with the city dweller, to obtain the innumerable comforts and luxuries of life through corporations with listed securities. These days the farmer drives his pleasure car, uses a telephone, buys merchandise by mail from the great mail order houses, and employs electric lights in his home and in his barns. In the creation of all these things, also, the Stock Exchange plays an indirect but essential part.

For all the perennial misunderstanding which has existed between town and country even before the days of Horace, the farmer is not at all antipathetic to city life or city institutions, nor insensible to the main economic services which they render to him. For the farmer is a hard-headed thinker, with a firm and stubborn grasp upon the realities of life. Far from the many superficial and time-wasting attractions of the city, he has both the time and the inclination to read and to think. He is, too, a conservative and constructive individualist. It is a real tribute to the sound sense of the farmer that Socialism and its glib theories about abolishing property and the like almost invariably make little appeal to him. Even in Russia this has been so, for although Bolshevism swept the cities and towns, it made no progress out in the country. Now the average American farmer has been bombarded too long and too steadily with misleading and distorted statements concerning the Stock Exchange to have a clear idea of just what it is or what use it serves. Offhand, he might perhaps be inclined to suspect and condemn it on this fallacious yet oft-repeated hearsay evidence. Yet the fact remains that the Stock Exchange has played a continuous and highly important part in making American farmers generally the most progressive and prosperous class of agricultural workers in the world.

American Labor's Stake in the Stock Exchange

When we pass from the country to the city the connection between the Stock Exchange and the daily lives of the city dwellers becomes even more direct, graphic, and thoroughgoing. And yet this vital and necessary connection is probably understood even less by the classes of the employed than it is by the farmers. The working man's very employment, in fact, is tied up with general conditions in industry and trade which depend to so large a degree on organized security markets. A former writer [8] upon the Exchange has clearly and trenchantly explained this connection:

> The last census shows that 32½% of the population of the United States is composed of laboring men, not counting agricultural workers. This large army of men is by no means independent; on the contrary it is strictly dependent on the ability of others to give it employment. Shut down the factories, curtail the operations of railways, close the mines and quarries, stop building and new construction, and in greater or less degree suffering and privation among these large masses must ensue.
>
> Now go a step further, and we find that the managers of these railways, mines and factories are in turn dependent—wholly dependent upon capital. They cannot go ahead with the extensions and improvements necessary to efficiency without borrowing money; and credit, in turn, will not come to their support unless a broad market is provided, through the Stock Exchange, for the securities which represent these obligations. Hence we see that just as every farmer in the West and every cotton-grower in the South must have a stable market for his products, so every laborer in our great industrial field is directly concerned with the maintenance of a stable market for the securities of the company that employs him. The interests of one are the interests of all, and speculation, in one form or another, underlies all industrial progress.

From the previously recited fact [9] that the Stock Exchange stabilizes the flow of capital into industry, it follows that it

[8] See Van Antwerp, pp. 42–43.

[9] See Chapter XIV, page 383.

likewise is an indirect but powerful force in stabilizing the conditions of employment, and thus performing a genuine though little recognized service to the laboring man.

The Worker as an Investor

In addition, the employed classes are rapidly becoming investors. They are absorbing odd lots of stock, "baby bonds" of less than $1,000 denomination, and investing in other listed securities by proxy, through opening savings bank accounts and taking out insurance policies. The fact that many far-sighted and progressive corporations are encouraging their employees to become stockholders by purchasing the stock of the employing company, and the possibility of largely composing the difficulties which arise between capital and labor by thus merging the two classes, has already been pointed out.[10]

But there is also a profounder although even more imperceptible service which the organized markets render to the laboring classes. Owing to the ability of these organized markets speculatively to sustain surplus production, as has been already pointed out,[11] the purchase price of goods has been gradually cheapened in terms of wages and salaries, with the result that the standard of living has gradually been raised. We shall say something later in the present chapter concerning this great although indirect and slow-moving service of the organized markets, and particularly of the Stock Exchange, to labor. If the working classes realized the full value to their economic status of the Stock Exchange, they would be the first to spring to its defense when it is unjustly assailed.

The Stock Exchange and Our Middle Class

Passing on to our so-called "middle class"—our tradesmen, salaried executives, doctors, lawyers and the like—the Exchange likewise has its appropriate service to perform for them.

---

[10] See Chapter XVI, page 473.

[11] See Chapter XIV, page 384.

The typical fairly successful man derives in many respects the same general benefits from the Exchange as does the laboring class. But he begins to experience to a greater degree the problems arising from the saving and accumulation of wealth. With the first few thousands he saves, he will probably buy real estate, get his life insured, and start a savings bank account, thus at least becoming a security investor by proxy. But after that point has been passed the problem of how to invest his money safely and yet profitably becomes a vital rather than merely an incidental part of his economic existence. The problem may be intensified by his inheriting money from relatives. If he is overcredulous the stock swindler may do him harm. If he is reckless or unwise, speculation in the Exchange or elsewhere may injure him and his family. But if he pursues this business—and it must be looked upon as a business—of investing his surplus savings carefully and intelligently, the Exchange opens to him the means of securing the best and most negotiable security investments in the country. And this continual investing on his part—together with such successful speculations as he may make—are an economic benefit, not only to himself but to the whole community, since he provides the capital so steadily needed for the development of our industries.

The Purchase of Income

The ease with which modern man can buy incomes is, in fact, one of the most significant testimonials to our economic progress in the past two centuries. In the late seventeenth century the father of Alexander Pope, the poet, who had been a highly successful London merchant, decided to retire from business. From his experience he was fitted to know of the best existing methods of investing his money so as to enjoy his old age comfortably and securely. But that was before the era of anything but highly speculative corporations, before the creation of the government debt and its sale in interest-bearing obligations, and, of course, long before the establishment of an organized securities market. The only established investments were real estate or loans upon it, or the purchase of a partnership in an active business. As a result the best scheme Pope *père* could hit upon was to turn his wealth into gold and take it with him into the country. It is consequently true that the poorest and most inexperienced rancher in New Mexico today finds it easier to invest his money safely and profitably than a conspicuously successful business man familiar with the international center of trade and commerce did only two hundred years ago. Naturally, no small part of this amazing transformation has been directly due to the development of organized securities markets.

The Stock Exchange is naturally of increasing value and significance to the investor in proportion to the sums of money which he has to invest. To the man of wealth the Exchange is as much a part of the daily machinery of business life as the bank or the stock corporation. While he gets no greater concessions made to him on the Exchange than the small investor, still the Exchange is to him a protector and a safeguard, since it enables him to shift his investments to suit his needs or sell them quickly in case of necessity.

Services of the Stock Exchange to the Manufacturer

Turning next to the manufacturer, we have seen that economic forces have favored the creation of large-scale corporations in the industrial world,[12] and that the Stock Exchange provides an indispensable machinery for the gradual distribution of their securities among investors.[13] Without a Stock Exchange which makes it possible for speculators to carry the "floating supply" of a particular stock and thus largely segregate and stabilize the risks of industry as they exert themselves

[12] See Chapter I, page 16. [13] See Chapter XVI.

upon it, the manufacturer himself would have to sustain the risk of his company entirely alone, and probably have to go into the security business himself. In the swift and continual expansion of American productive facilities to supply a steadily growing domestic market, and new and increasingly profitable foreign markets, there is a constant tendency for manufacturing and commercial firms to expand their small and closely owned companies into large stock corporations with a greatly augmented industrial equipment and output. This healthy and desirable development of American manufacturing and commercial firms makes necessary in its initial stages additional capital, which is mainly obtained by the distribution of the expanding company's stocks and bonds to the speculating and investing public through the free and open market provided by the stock exchanges.

In recent years the experience of our manufacturers in this respect is only a vivid and contemporary instance of the long-established fact that the creation and operation of large units of industry invariably necessitates the stock corporation with its thousands of stockholding partners, and the stock exchange where its stocks—which are only the certificates of such partnerships—can be readily bought and sold. Upon the ability of the stock exchanges—and in this country, particularly upon the New York Stock Exchange—to render stocks and bonds immediately marketable, has long depended and will always depend, the rate of progress and growth in American industry.

Business Forecasting

The experienced manufacturer, moreover, who bases his decisions upon fact rather than fancy, must have constant recourse to the statistics of trade and industry. Among the most valuable of such statistics are the current prices for the various classes of stocks listed on the Exchange, for, as has already been pointed out,[14] these prices act as a barometer to general business conditions. Some keen student has said that the stock market tells the truth in periods of popular delirium—and a study of financial and economic conditions in the past verifies this statement. The huge advantage of such a service in the world of business, where prices and the forces of supply and demand change so constantly and so swiftly, goes without saying.

The Stock Exchange and Modern Banking

A more frequently misunderstood contact of the Stock Exchange is that existing between it and the bankers. Almost all bankers are in one way or another investors or dealers in securities, and in consequence almost every variety of bank depends in considerable measure upon the operation of the Stock Exchange. This fact was realized by the bankers themselves with particular force during the critical autumn of 1914, when the Exchange was compelled to keep its doors closed for several months, thereby halting the normal process of purchasing, selling, and distributing securities, and temporarily "freezing" many bank loans based on security collateral.

The precise contact of the given banker with the Exchange depends, of course, upon the particular type of banking in which he is engaged. We have seen that the savings bank is interested in securities as an investor. The investment banker, on the other hand, is chiefly an underwriter and dealer in securities.[15] Without a central organized market through which to distribute the larger new issues and render the larger old issues always negotiable, his business would revert rapidly to conditions prevailing in the security market a century ago. The common commercial bank also has a contact with the Exchange of its own. For one thing, it usually holds listed securities as a considerable part of its surplus, owing to their

[14] See Chapter XIV, page 386. [15] See Chapter XVI, page 440.

instant salability on the Exchange. For another, it often makes both time and call loans on security collateral.

The economic function of such loans [16] as well as their advantage to the commercial banker [17] has been touched upon in previous chapters. Nor is this mutually beneficial connection between commercial banking and the Stock Exchange confined simply to the large banks and financial institutions of Wall Street. The so-called "out-of-town banks"—an elastic New York expression which covers anything from the great banks of Boston, Chicago, or Philadelphia to thousands of small banks in all parts of the nation—also are interested in and to a degree dependent upon the Stock Exchange, if not directly, then by proxy,[18] since they are accustomed either to loan part of their surplus funds on security collateral or else send them to their metropolitan correspondents largely for a similar purpose.

There is consequently a close and necessary connection between banks and stock exchanges, and the fact that in every financial center in the world the latter are located close to the former arises from this inevitable link, and their common interest from the inherent nature of their kindred business in credit instruments of one sort or another.[19] Banking would be vastly more hazardous without a Stock Exchange, while the Exchange could not accomplish its vital work of rendering its listings always negotiable, without the employment of credit extended by bankers.

Finally, many of our banks owe to the Stock Exchange a debt, partially historic and partly current, for its services in distributing their own bank stocks and rendering them, like other corporate securities, readily purchasable and salable. The man who wishes to start a large bank or to increase considerably the size and capitalization of a bank already estab-

---

[16] See Chapter XVI, page 486.

[17] See Chapter VIII, page 200.

[18] *Ibid.*, page 177.

[19] See Appendix, Chapter VIII (c).

lished, is in this respect in the same position as the large-scale manufacturer, and he solves his problem in the same way with the aid of the share certificate and the Stock Exchange.

Services to the Organized Commodity Markets

Still another class of business institutions to which the New York Stock Exchange is of no small benefit includes the other organized markets of the country, not only the great commodity exchanges but also the smaller stock exchanges in various parts of the country. Many members of the national New York Stock Exchange are also members of the comparatively local stock exchanges of Boston, Chicago, Philadelphia, and other American cities,[20] and are often able to extend credit to purchasers of local securities listed there by hypothecating at the banks securities listed on the New York Stock Exchange. The same advantage also exists in the case of firms which are members of the New York Stock Exchange and also of the Chicago Board of Trade, the New York Cotton Exchange, and other commodity exchanges. During past periods of liquidation or credit shortage many a purchase of cotton or wheat made on credit has depended upon collateral loans obtained on securities listed on the Exchange. In this indirect but significant way the Stock Exchange, by keeping its many billion dollars' worth of listed securities readily negotiable, is a bulwark of strength to the conditions of credit which underlie the business of the entire nation.

The Value of Stock Exchanges to Modern Government

Finally, organized security markets are essential today to the operation of our governing machinery itself. We so often forget that governments have in the long run, like corporations or individuals, to strike a balance between expenditure and income, and to make the amount of the one dependent upon the

[20] See Chapter XII, page 298.

actual or potential amount of the other. The proudest government that ever existed cannot flout the immutable and eternal laws of economics and continue to exist. To only a limited extent, therefore, can a government stamp off fiat currency or bonds—beyond this point lies only economic chaos, social disruption, and the disintegration of government.

Many sincere citizens of this and other countries have always had and perhaps will always have the curious idea that in these matters there is no limit to the powers of government, and that by some magical process government officials can indefinitely increase currency or issue any amount of its debt obligations simply by printing them, without regard for such dull and meaningless details as gold redemption, sinking fund requirements, or debt service charges. The many extraordinary economic diseases arising since the war among many European governments—diseases which are largely due to this childlike faith in the unlimited financial powers of government and its ability to disregard the immutable principles both of economics and of common sense—will provide a wealth of laboratory material for the scientific economists of the future.

Marketing the Public Debt

It is, of course, no detriment for a nation to remain moderately in debt year after year—on the contrary such a practice, if sanely limited, is probably on the whole a salutary custom. It was not, however, until the late seventeenth century that statesmen discovered this fact, and also the practical methods whereby this debt could be made interest-bearing, split up into small amounts represented by government bonds, and sold to individual investors. Since that time, however, this practice has been resorted to by practically all civilized governments. As an inevitable result, organized security markets have sprung up all over the world where these evidences of the government debt could be bought and sold, and thus given the negotiability essential to the best investments. It is therefore a fair statement that the chief reason responsible for the creation of almost every great stock exchange in the world, in the first instance at least, was to assist the government in maintaining its credit and the negotiability of its debt. In the case of our own nation, former chapters[21] have already shown how the issuance of the original 6 per cent bonds of the United States government was primarily responsible for the first gathering of the earliest Wall Street stock-brokers under the buttonwood tree.

Furnishing the Sinews of War

A study of the listings of the New York Stock Exchange during the past century reveals many instances when the latter institution extended no small assistance to the United States government by providing a ready market for the purchase and sale of its interest-bearing debt. Following the 6 per cent loan into which the debt incurred during the American Revolution was funded, new forms of the government debt found their dominant market on the Exchange during the Civil and Spanish wars. Still more recently the huge Liberty Loan issues were and still are being distributed there.[22] This latter feat in American government financing reflects great credit upon the United States Treasury Department, when the enormous size of the Liberty issues is remembered. In the successful initial marketing of these issues the Exchange can also take a pardonable pride, since many of the more technical features of the task were accomplished through the co-operation of some of its most experienced members.

The government is also served in an entirely different way by the Stock Exchange. The government is, of course, dependent for its income upon taxation, which in turn depends upon the contemporary condition of business. Since the Ex-

[21] See Chapters I and II.

[22] See Chapter XVI, page 457.

change serves as an indirect but powerful stabilizing force in American credit conditions, it very generally assists in making it easier to levy and collect taxes. During the period of severe war taxation how often has the individual or the corporation been able to obtain cash to pay its taxes only by liquidating its security investments on the Exchange! Along with the federal reserve system the Exchange serves to give American property that convertibility into cash and that value as collateral which is so vital to the necessities of government as well as of business.

In addition to these services, past and present, which the Stock Exchange has rendered the federal government, it has performed a similar service for many states, counties, and municipalities. The excellent investment rating of many state, county, and city bonds depends in part at least upon their negotiability on the stock exchanges. With small issues this matter is not perhaps of primary importance; with large issues, however, it is of great moment.

Organized Markets and the Consumer

But before concluding the present sketch of the benefits conferred by the stock exchanges upon American business and society, not simply their services to the above productive individuals or classes but also those rendered to consumers in general must be considered. For the general consumer, whether he be a bank president or a bootblack, also has a vital interest in the successful operation of the stock exchanges, along with the banks and other essential parts of the modern machinery of credit.

It is well known that low costs for goods can as a rule be obtained only through the process of wholesale production in quantity. But the gradual rise in the standards of living has only too often been attributed by academic writers simply and solely to new mechanical inventions and more efficient methods of production. In reality these elements, vital though they be, are only a part of the story. For in order to attain wholesale production of any commodity or article, large amounts of capital and large corporate industrial units are necessary, as well as the ability to distribute wholesale. The indispensable services to industry rendered by the Stock Exchange in enabling large-scale capital to be accumulated through the sale of corporate stocks and bonds has already been noted.[23] Moreover, with respect to the present-day methods of wholesale distribution, the ability of organized markets to carry a large surplus from production into consumption [24] also permits more extensive production than would otherwise be possible. To all these factors, therefore, must be attributed the gradual cheapening of goods and services in terms of wages and salaries, and the consequent rise in the standard of living.

Consumption the Test of Civilization

The vital economic benefit to the public at large of the present-day machinery of credit (of which stock exchanges are an integral and essential part) can better be realized when it is remembered that, in the last analysis, the real purpose of all our modern machinery of both production and distribution—of all our mills, factories, railroads, warehouses and shops, banks, and stock exchanges—is to feed, clothe, and shelter the world's present and prospective inhabitants, and provide them with the commodities, services, and manufactured articles necessary and desirable to their daily existence.

Growth of Population Under Capitalism and Socialism

The rapid increase in population both in this country and abroad has been in a great measure due to the effectiveness of our credit machinery over the past century and a half. This swift growth in the population of civilized countries is, more-

---

[23] See Chapter XIV, page 383. [24] *Ibid.*, page 384.

over a recent phenomenon and peculiar to the present-day so-called "capitalistic" era of history. In the Middle Ages, and even during the earlier portion of the Renaissance period, the population of Europe was largely stationary, for the quantity production of goods, because of the lack of scientific and mechanical knowledge, the strangling grip of the guilds upon production, and the inability to carry and distribute surplus production, was at that time impossible. Since, therefore, the commodities and goods necessary to human existence were produced in a relatively fixed volume, only a fixed number of human beings were permitted to find shelter, clothing, and food. Children born over and above a fixed rate therefore perished from the lack of these essentials to life. If, under this medieval system of fixed production, speculation and usury were largely held in abeyance, it is nevertheless true that the continual economic slaughter of human beings was necessary to its maintenance. An interesting modern analogy to this grim and (to us) inhuman condition of affairs is furnished by Bolshevist Russia, where the population is shrinking to meet the limited output of goods and foodstuffs permitted by the socialist theory of producing without the speculative carrying of surplus, and other functions performed by the modern machinery of capital.

The Instance of Great Britain

Despite the clamor of the agitator and the economic crank, the "capitalistic order," as they call it, has had a very different record. By the invention of mechanical labor-saving devices and the credit machinery needed to install and operate these devices, a vast energy and flexibility was imparted to the production and distribution of goods. At once more goods became available for human consumption, the individual struggle for existence became easier, and the populations of the civilized nations began to grow. A well-known economic authority [25] has stated that during the single century from 1651 to 1751, when the first feeble indications of the coming period of private capitalism were manifested, the population of Great Britain increased from 6,378,000 to 7,392,000. But during the next century (1751-1851), which witnessed the establishment of steam production, steam distribution, modern banking, and the London Stock Exchange, the population shot upward to 21,185,000, an increase of 13,793,000. Even more astonishing was the increase in population during the next sixty years (1851-1911), by 19,350,000 to a total in 1911 of 40,535,000. Nor do these figures reflect the huge emigration of Englishmen to all parts of the world, which occurred during the same periods. As Hartley Withers has so well remarked [26] upon this very point:

> Merely to enable so large a number of people to be alive is not everything, but it is a great deal. Under Capitalism, all these millions saw the light of the sun, smelt the scent of spring, knew love and friendship, made and laughed at good and bad jokes, ate and digested their meals, made their queer guesses at the secret of life, played games, read books, cherished their hobbies and their prejudices, knew a little, thought they knew much more, and went their way leaving others behind them to take up the thread of life and spin another strip of its mysterious cloth. . . . If life is a good thing—and most of us waste little time in sending for a doctor if we do not feel well—Capitalism has made the enjoyment of that good possible to millions.

Owing to the fact that our own country has been, and indeed still is so largely new and unsettled, figures for the growth of population in the United States are not so conclusive. Yet it is undoubtedly true that under any system where a surplus of goods and securities could not be speculatively carried and

---

[25] Dr. Shadwell, "The History of Industrialism," in the Encyclopedia of Industrialism.

[26] Hartley Withers, The Case for Capitalism, p. 116.

distributed, our country could not possibly have attained its present great population, nor could it have developed either a city or rural life at all comparable to modern conditions in town and country. Thus, many of the agitators who declaim loudest against the present economic scheme of things could not have long drawn the breath of life in this world, had their birth and upbringing occurred under those very economic conditions of which they are the incessant advocates.

The Rising Standard of Living

But there is another side to this profound service rendered to the average human being by scientific invention, quantity production, speculative distribution, and the modern machinery of credit in which the Stock Exchange is so integral a factor. Not only can more people live under these conditions but the standards of living of the average human being have been vastly improved by the flood of goods produced by capitalism. Not only the necessities of life, but comforts and luxuries of whose very existence the most wealthy and powerful men in the past never dreamed, have through our factories, our banks, and our stock exchanges, been placed within the reach of practically everyone. In order to get a more vivid and accurate sense of the significance of this economic tendency, it may not be out of place here to note briefly certain differences between the daily life of a medieval baron on the one hand, and that of a very plain modern citizen—say a haberdasher's clerk—on the other.

The baron, for all his jewels, wore coarse hand-made clothes dyed roughly and in few colors. His palace knew no light except candles and torches and no heat except that of open log fires. His food was extremely monotonous, and all the long winter consisted mainly of salted fish and salted meat, with no vegetables or fruit. Hence, contemporary poets hailed "the sweet spring" with no little enthusiasm. Sugar was a rare oriental luxury; tea and coffee were unknown. Even the commonest spices were distinct luxuries and were laboriously brought into Europe by caravan from Asia and sold at extraordinary prices.

Life in the Middle Ages

The baron bathed rarely and without soap. Even as late as the days of "good Queen Bess" it was deemed advisable when presenting a masque to the noble ladies and gentlemen at court, to have a perfumer walk up and down through the audience, lest the odor of the unwashed flower of England's lords and ladies overcome the pleasant fancies of the dramatist. Glass windows were unknown in the castles of the Middle Ages, and the dark castle halls were hung with flapping arras behind which the assassin often lurked. Owing largely to the prevailing ideas of a "fair price" and the punishment prescribed for charging interest or speculating, starvation among the common people was common and hunger among the nobility not unknown.

There were no sewers, no drains, no medicines except the superstitious concoctions of the age, no surgical instruments except the axe and the dagger, and a constant menace from plague and disease which afflicted lord and vassal without partiality. If the baron traveled, he went on horseback and in armor which, if like Banquo he rode unattended at night, did not always save him from being murdered. His wealth consisted mainly of real estate, his income of rents paid in kind—a pig here, a bushel of wheat there, etc.—and his daily work of fighting his tenants to collect the one and his enemies in protecting the other. His only entertainment, apart from these not altogether pleasurable diversions, was furnished by wandering jugglers, the songs of the occasional minstrel, or the reiterated jests of a court fool. Such an existence, colorful as it may be rendered by Sir Walter Scott, scarcely appeals in a practical way to the American of 1922. And yet the baron was undoubtedly the dominant social, political, and economic figure of his age. What the daily life of the common man in the Middle Ages was, can best be left to the imagination.

Standards of Modern Consumer

And now for our haberdasher's clerk. He dresses in a variety of plain but substantial clothing, and for breakfast, if he is especially hungry, has the choice of imported fruits (be it January or June), coffee from Java or Brazil, eggs from a hundred to a thousand miles away, fresh milk, white bread, and cereals, with pepper from the East Indies and sugar from Cuba included as a matter of course. He rides to work in a trolley, subway, or steam railroad car, a distance of several miles, or perhaps he makes the trip by auto bus. He lunches modestly, perhaps, but according to his fancy. And when the day's work is done he puffs contemplatively on a cigar assembled from Sumatra, Virginia, and Maryland, and summoning his friends by telephone, enjoys the most or least classic music on his phonograph, or sallies forth to attend the motion pictures. He lives a longer, more pleasant, and more intelligent life, despite his modest income and subordinate economic position, than the average medieval baron could picture in his wildest dreams.

The writer by no means wishes to imply that all this vast and tremendous economic transformation which the world has experienced in the past few centuries has been due simply to the creation of stock exchanges. Thousands of inventors, genuine statesmen and political reformers, scientists, pioneers, and adventurers have been necessary to obtain the degree of civilization which the average American enjoys today. Nevertheless, in every detail of the clerk's life described above the Stock Exchange as a source of corporate working capital has given a vast and often unrecognized co-operation in producing and making available for everyone's consumption those articles which in our own luxurious times have come to be considered as necessities.

As the clerk lives through what may seem to him a monotonous day, he nevertheless unconsciously depends upon corporations producing textiles and textile machinery, dyes, ships and foreign trade, railroad service, refined sugar, several varieties of electric transportation service, automobiles, tires, petroleum, tobacco, telephone service, phonographs, and the "silent drama," besides hundreds of other basic products like steel, copper, and coal. If the work done during the past century by the New York Stock Exchange for all these corporations could suddenly be subtracted from the present accumulated results of civilization, the indirect but very real link between the clerk's standard of living and the Exchange would not long seem so fanciful as it is otherwise apt to.

Future Tasks of the Securities Market

Apart from its services as a support and stabilizer of business, the Stock Exchange may not inaptly be compared to the driving wheel of our modern economic structure as it is at present constituted. Its past and present services to society at large require not so much argument and contention as simply a true understanding. What its future services will consist of in detail no man can foresee. But certainly vast enterprises remain yet to be undertaken by the modern stock corporation to which, particularly in its initial and adventurous stage, the Exchange can give huge assistance. In the years to come our present means of communication may with its co-operation undergo further improvements. The wireless telegraph and telephone, the aeroplane, and many other inventions still await that commercializing process in which the Exchange must play its vital part before they can become conveniences of our everyday life. All such future corporate undertakings will call first upon the daring of the stock speculator before they can offer new services to mankind or new investments to the investor. As in our past so also in our future, the industrial and commercial progress of this nation is consequently largely in the hands of her stock speculators, who will bear as stockholders the unavoidable risks of this progress. And in providing a market place where this necessary and vital work can be carried on, the Stock Exchange is destined to play an increasingly significant part in the basic and fundamental economic development of the United States.

The more complete and dispassionate understanding of the machinery of industry, trade, and finance, which year by year the American public is obtaining, should in the end effect a considerable change in public sentiment regarding the Stock Exchange. With this fuller understanding the American public will cease to look with prejudice and suspicion upon its principal securities market, but rather with the same legitimate touch of national pride that it feels for other swiftly created, yet great and efficient, American business organizations and institutions which the historian of the future will inevitably consider as monuments to the daring, enterprise, and progress of our race.

CHAPTER XVIII

THE STOCK EXCHANGE AS AN INTERNATIONAL MARKET

The International Traffic in Securities

At first glance it may seem a far cry indeed from the clamorous floor of the New York Stock Exchange to the distant capitals of Europe, Asia, and South America. In all probability, most American business men would greet with incredulity the bold statement that the banks, warehouses, shops, and factories of these far-away communities have a considerable stake in the swift making of security contracts which takes place about the posts or in the bond crowd there. Nevertheless, even a brief examination into the actual structure of international trade reveals an intimate though often unrecognized relationship between the great New York security market and the foreign demand for American goods, the great ships which steam slowly out of our Atlantic and Pacific harbors each day laden with these goods, and American manufacturers who produce them in all parts of our country. So it is, too, with our farmers, lumberjacks, miners, and other producers of American raw materials. Year in and year out, and usually without their knowledge, the New York Stock Exchange extends no slight assistance to them in the sale of their products overseas.

But before we can come to a right understanding of these international functions of the Exchange we must examine some of the most complicated machinery and the least generally understood operations of the modern financial world. Craving the reader's patience, therefore, at the very outset of this arduous quest, we must first briefly consider the mechanism and economic significance of this international traffic in securities occurring between the world's principal stock exchanges.

We have seen that during the century preceding the recent war many American securities were purchased and held abroad,[1] and that formerly American underwriting syndicates frequently allotted participations to foreign firms in foreign financial centers.[2] This foreign absorption of our security issues naturally led to many of them being listed, not simply on the New York Stock Exchange, but on the London Stock Exchange and the bourses of Paris, Amsterdam, and Berlin as well. Our larger issues of railroad and industrial stocks and bonds, such as United States Steel common and preferred stock,[3] Northern Pacific, or Reading, can particularly be cited as having experienced active trading in several foreign organized security markets. Such securities are sometimes called "international" securities because of the international speculation and investment which developed in them.

Communication Between Modern Markets

This system of listing American securities in more than one exchange led naturally to closer communication and greater dealings between the New York and foreign stock exchanges. For otherwise a given security, listed here and abroad might sell at 100 in London and at 90 in New York, owing to local conditions prevailing in each market. In the beginning carrier pigeons were employed in Europe as a means of rapidly communicating news and orders between stock markets, but the present close contact between them became possible only after the laying of telegraph and cable lines. As a result of this scientific employment of electricity for swift international communication not only have international investment transactions in securities been greatly facilitated, but a special type of specu-

[1] See Chapter II, page 35.

[2] See Chapter XVI, page 441.

[3] See Appendix, Chapter XVIII (a).

lator called an "arbitrageur" has been created who attempts to profit from the occasional price disparities between different markets, and whose chief economic function consists in minimizing and often eliminating such disparities. His operations—which are known as "arbitrage"—differ from those of the ordinary speculator, who buys and sells in the same market at different times, chiefly in the fact that he buys and sells in different markets at practically the same time. As may be imagined, arbitrage may take place within a nation as well as between nations. Thus, arbitrage of one sort or another has often occurred between the New York and Boston Stock Exchanges—for example—in such securities as are listed in both places,[4] although domestic arbitrage based upon continuous quotations from the floor is now forbidden.

Principles of Arbitrage

In its basic features arbitrage, as a matter of fact, is only the unfamiliar financial term for a set of operations common to every trading type of business. The writer once heard of a keen book dealer who purchased for $200 some books from a large corporation in order to resell them at once to another company for $350. With a few appropriate substitutions, this transaction might be cited as one of the simple instances of arbitrage. For if an arbitrageur observed that United States Steel common, let us say, was selling at 90 in London and 91 in New York, he might simultaneously attempt to sell 100 shares short in the latter market, and purchase a similar amount in the former market at these prices. If he succeeded in this operation, he could afterwards deliver the certificate received from London to the lender of the stock in New York, and make a profit on the transaction of $100 minus his expenses. Similarly, if the price was 91 in London and 90 in New York, he would sell in London and buy in New York. We have seen

[4] See Appendix, Chapter XVIII (b).

that contracts for the purchase and sale of securities in the New York Stock Exchange can be made for a delivery as remote as sixty days, although most sales are made regular way for delivery on the following day.[5] Sometimes in arbitrage transactions it is deemed preferable to sell for such a future delivery rather than to "sell short." Like other speculators, of course, the arbitrageur risks his money in buying and selling property in order to profit through helping to establish more correct and accurate prices.

In practice, of course, arbitraging in securities is a difficult and highly complex business, as the remarks of a former governor of the Exchange go to show:

> Because of its complexity and its risks, arbitraging is not a business that appeals to beginners on the floor. One must have reliable colleagues on the foreign Exchanges who are constantly watchful and alert, and who are moreover possessed of sufficient capital to finance large transactions. In addition, there are labyrinthine difficulties to surmount in the way of commissions, interest charges, insurance of securities in transit, fluctuations in the money markets abroad and at home, cable tolls, letters of confirmation, rates of foreign exchange, settlement days, contangoes and many other matters. Unless a man has had a long experience in the difficult art of arbitraging, he had better shun it or prepare for trouble.[6]

Into these and other subtleties and technicalities it is not particularly to our present purpose to inquire. It is sufficient to have instanced the basic principles upon which arbitrage operations rest.

Former Arbitrage on the New York Stock Exchange

Formerly this arbitrage business between New York and foreign centers had its appropriate machinery on the Stock Exchange floor. Against the south wall of the board room was

---

[5] See Chapter IX, page 204.

[6] Van Antwerp, p. 284.

the "arbitrage rail," behind which were pneumatic tubes connecting the floor with the cable offices in the basement of the building. As an added convenience, most of the so-called "international stocks" were located at the row of stocks posts nearest the rail. By posting themselves near this rail, therefore, the members of the Exchange who did an arbitrage business could receive and deliver messages and orders from and to the foreign stock exchanges with astonishing speed. According to the same authority cited above,[7] "the arbitrageur may buy in New York and sell in London and receive a confirmation, all in three minutes."

These excerpts were written in 1913 and were of course descriptive of pre-war conditions. Few features of Wall Street life so irresistibly appeal to the imagination as this extraordinary business, conducted in the various world markets over the flashing cables with a speed vastly more rapid than the roll of the earth from darkness into darkness. By such means the New York and London markets particularly were normally kept in the closest touch with each other, as another chronicler of the pre-war securities markets[8] has testified:

> The difference in time between London and New York is four minutes and one second less than five hours. As the New York Stock Exchange opens at 10 A.M., it is then four minutes of three o'clock in the afternoon in London, and by two minutes after three the full New York opening prices are known in London, only the six minutes being required to make the sales in New York, to gather the quotations, to put them into the hands of the telegraph operator, to transmit them to London and to publish them there.
>
> The hour of closing business in the London Exchange is at three o'clock, but the trading goes on until four and on the curb much later. The London two o'clock quotations are received in Wall Street shortly after 9 A.M. London can trade by cable in American stocks during all the time the New York

[7] Van Antwerp, p. 284.

[8] Pratt, p. 159.

Stock Exchange is open, as when it closes it is only eight o'clock in London. The London orders executed in New York are often large. They have amounted to as many as 100,000 shares and over in one day, and they are sometimes an important factor in the market.

Relations Between London and New York

The same author [9] also describes the other side of the picture—how London prices were received in Wall Street:

> The first question anybody puts to anybody else, on arrival at his Wall Street office at 9:30 or so in the morning, is, "How's London?" The London quotations are the first real lead on our market. They to some extent indicate what will be the popular view of the news which has developed over night. There are times when the London view is immaterial. It is even often entirely at variance with that taken in this market. But when stocks are really active it is always important, and the London quotations are indispensable to any forecast of our day's trading.
>
> A few minutes before 2 P.M. London time, the quotations for American stocks in the London market are obtained for transmission to New York. It takes, perhaps, eight minutes to collect these prices and transmit them in code form. The presses in New York are waiting. The code is rapidly translated. The equivalent is calculated at the ruling rate of demand sterling, and in twenty minutes from the receipt of the cable the quotations are being read in the brokers' offices.
>
> London deals in American stocks at a fixed rate of $5.00 for the pound sterling. The reason for this is that the rate of exchange is constantly changing. If the real quotation were taken for transactions there would be a continual dispute as to what the rate was at the time the bargain was made. A fixed figure makes no difference to the trader in London who buys and sells at the same conventional rate. We, however, cannot afford to give more than the rate of exchange for the sovereign. Therefore, to get the difference between the London price and what the price of the stock would actually be

[9] *Ibid.*, p. 160.

here, we deduct the rate of exchange, say, $4.87½, from the conventional $5.00. It is obvious that if a stock is 50 in London it is 48.75; or 48¾, at the parity here.

There are difficulties in connection with the collection of prices in London which people used to New York Stock Exchange methods do not appreciate. Actual sales are not recorded there. The prices at which a few transactions have been made are marked on the official list, but there is no means of telling whether the market has dealt in 5,000 shares or 500,000 during the day. The London ticker only quotes bid-and-asked prices, and never records the price at which any particular transaction was done.

Changes from the Former Arbitrage System

But this arbitrage business caused constant infringements upon the commission law, upon whose importance to the Stock Exchange comment has previously been made.[10] For as a rule it was carried on by "joint account" between a member of the New York Stock Exchange here and some non-member abroad, with the result that the Exchange member received less than the minimum commission. By a resolution of the Governing Committee in 1911, such joint accounts were forbidden.[11] This resolution was subsequently rescinded in 1920, but certain restrictions were placed upon joint account arbitrage which were designed to rid it of its objectionable features.[12] By the terms of these restrictions, the old system of the arbitrage rail was not re-established, and thereafter arbitrage operations have been centered in the offices of the Exchange members instead of in the Board room. The reason for the considerable interval between the prohibition of joint account arbitrage and its restricted revival is to be found in the extraordinary conditions which arose during and after the war. Severe laws were passed abroad forbidding the import of securities because of the consequent export of capital which it caused. In addition,

[10] See Chapter XIII, page 345.

[11] See Constitution, p. 80.

[12] *Ibid.*, Resolution of Nov. 3, 1920.

trading "for the account," as it is called, was likewise suspended for a term of years on the British and continental exchanges. Moreover, the cables were heavily burdened and under severe censorship. Not until two years after the armistice, therefore, were these and other war measures and conditions sufficiently composed to justify the attempt to return to the more normal and efficient pre-war methods of arbitrage.

Functions of International Security Trading

Previous to the war this international traffic in securities had performed certain economic functions which may next be briefly outlined. For one thing, by the gradual passage of our securities from the New York Stock Exchange to the London and other foreign securities exchanges, no small amount of European capital was furnished to America during the century preceding 1914 to develop our railroad system and exploit our natural resources. Without these extensive investments and speculations by Europeans in our securities, the swift economic development experienced by this country during the same period would have been utterly impossible. Reciprocally, of course, the same correlated functioning of the New York and foreign stock exchanges furnished Europe with good investment and profitable speculative securities at a time when the rapidly increasing wealth of that continent could not find sufficient securities of its own in which to invest. As we shall presently see, this European absorption of our stocks and bonds helped Europe to balance her trade with the United States, and consequently to import more physical goods from us than she exported to us—no small benefit to the American farmer and manufacturer as well as to Europe herself.

Benefit of a Broader Market

Moreover, the fact that our securities were listed and traded in abroad as well as in New York made a broader market for them, and tended to make them easier to buy and sell, and at fairer prices.[13] We have seen that similar results were obtained for the Stock Exchange by the extension of its members' branch offices all over the country.[14] One great factor tending toward the elimination of the manipulation of prices was provided by the opposition on foreign stock exchanges to it, transmitted to the New York market by arbitrageurs. This all comes back to the fact previously mentioned [15] that the bigger and broader a market is the more difficult it is for anyone to distort its prices even temporarily by manipulative tactics.

Securities as a Medium of International Exchange

But perhaps most important of all, this close connection between the New York and European securities exchanges made international securities, owing to their instant negotiability here and abroad, practically a medium of exchange like gold or bank credit.[16] As one well-known authority on finance and economics [17] has put it:

> Securities form one of the greatest and the most important parts of the modern mechanism of exchange. They are, in many cases, as good as money, and in some cases are better than money. If a large shipment of money has to be made from New York to London, it is much more economical to ship securities of the same amount than to ship kegs of gold.

This essential though little realized fact, that the international securities on the stock exchanges afford an acceptable substitute for gold as a medium of payment between nations, is of enormous importance with respect to America's whole foreign trade. It therefore deserves detailed explanation here, even though such an explanation lead us into the thorny and

[13] See Chapter XIV, page 374.
[14] See Chapter XIV, page 376.
[15] See Chapter XVI, page 456.
[16] See Appendix, Chapter XVIII (c).
[17] Charles A. Conant, Wall Street and the Country.

seemingly irrelevant jungle of foreign exchange, visible and invisible trade balances, and kindred topics. This task is not made any the easier because of the current extraordinary conditions in international trade and finance which have resulted from the war. Yet these considerations, however abstruse, cannot be disregarded by anyone who would understand the wider significance and economic services rendered by the New York Stock Exchange.

Composition of the International Balance of Trade

Abandoning for the moment our study of the latter institution, therefore, let us consider a few of the general and fundamental principles governing international trade. First of all, we must rid ourselves of the short-sighted but prevalent notion that only physical goods are bought and sold among nations. To be true, our monthly government reports of the foreign exports and imports of the United States include only the physical merchandise and raw materials which are loaded or unloaded as ship cargoes, and which pass inspection of our customs officials at our various ports. This part of our total sales to and purchases from foreign countries is known as our "visible" trade, and the statistics upon it collected by our various customs houses are consolidated in the monthly foreign trade report of United States exports and imports issued by the Department of Commerce in Washington.

The "Invisible Trade"

Yet this buying and selling of physical (and therefore visible) goods between nations constitutes only a portion, albeit the principal and most fundamental portion, of our total international traffic. For as a nation we also are buyers and sellers in what is called in contradistinction the "invisible" trade in what, for want of a better term, are known as "services." This elastic term of "services" covers a multitude of different transactions. If an American exporting firm hires a British vessel or a Canadian railroad to carry its goods into Great Britain or Canada, it is importing transportation service, and must export money out of the country to pay for it. If either cargo is insured in the course of transit by a foreign insurance company, this service too constitutes an American import. When a foreign immigrant here sends money back to the "old country," America may likewise be said, in the economic sense, to be importing the service of his hands and brains from the country whither his funds are sent. When, furthermore, the American ventures abroad, whether to study in the Sorbonne, to admire cathedral towns in Normandy, or simply to enjoy a vacation in any European capital, the grim laws of economics score his expenditures down as another American import—whether of learning, artistic appreciation, or mere pleasure. Gold is also, of course, bought and sold between nations, and is naturally a visible import or export, although because of its special significance to currencies and credits the yellow metal is not included in the ordinary tale of visible imports or exports, along with such less romantic goods as soft coal, machinery, or wheat, but separate statistics are kept of its "arrivals" and "departures," to and from our ports. The same practice is also followed in the case of silver—the other financial metal.

And so this list might be enumerated, to include the thousand-and-one different cases where an international bargain of some kind has been struck. Two other classes of services, however, are of sufficient importance to deserve consideration here—bank credit and securities.[18] Just as securities

[18] In enumerating the various items which constitute a nation's invisible trade, an initial question of definition exists. Contrary to the prevailing custom, securities and bank capital in the last analysis should probably not be included in the so-called "international trade balances" at all, since they do not represent consumable goods or services, but rather income-bearing loans tendered as long- or short-term payments for past or future goods and services. Certainly, a nation is a debtor or creditor nation according to whether it imports or exports a balance of securities and bank credit. Yet, for the sake of simplicity and clarity, the author has deemed it advisable in the ensuing account of international trade and finance conventionally to include securities and bank credit as services in the invisible trade.

can be shifted from one country to another through stock exchanges, so bank credit can be exported and imported by steamer or even by cable. Both represent capital, which must therefore be included as a final but important item in the total exports and imports of any nation. To revert again to the language of economics, when a Frenchman sells his bonds or stocks through this machinery to an American, America may in consequence be said to export its capital to France, and we in turn import the receipt for this exported capital of ours in the form of French stock or bond certificates. So, too, bank credit can be shifted between nations by international banking operations.

The Actual Balance of Trade

But one feature of all this bewildering purchase and sale of goods and services carried on by every modern nation should be clearly noted. In the long run the total exports of every nation must balance its total imports. No nation can regularly and indefinitely buy more than it sells, or sell more than it buys, from or to the rest of the world. This fact may seem in direct contradiction to the facts presented by our past pre-war foreign trade reports. Even before the war the United States regularly showed greater exports than imports in its trade returns, and many people, who gave the matter only a careless consideration, were wont to think that this country profited by the amount of our excess exports. Such a fallacious view, of course, left out of all reckoning our invisible trade, wherein we were steadily importing more services from other nations than we exported. Strictly speaking, then, there is normally no such thing as a permanent "favorable balance" in a nation's total foreign trade with the world. There may be a relatively permanent favorable balance in the visible or in the invisible trade, but total exports must in the long run balance, or be made to balance, total imports.

The Pre-War American Trade Balance

Every nation, according to its age, temperament, situation, and resources, differs from every other nation in the respective proportions to which the many items in its visible and invisible trade enter into its total exports and total imports. For purposes of illustration, the foreign trade of this country as it existed prior to 1914 may be contrasted with that of Great Britain. We regularly exported more raw materials and manufactured goods than we imported. But our excess visible exports were balanced by our excess invisible imports. Despite our large foreign trade, the American flag was hardly ever seen prior to 1914 on the seven seas, and we were consequently forced to pay huge annual sums to British and other foreign shipping companies in freight charges on our foreign trade. The insurance of these goods—another American invisible import of those days—was carried mainly by foreign insurance companies. Our immigrants remitted huge sums each year to Europe, and our tourists abroad spent as much again. Moreover, as we have seen,[19] America was steadily importing capital by selling her securities abroad, and in addition was remitting vast sums annually in interest and dividends on our bonds and stocks held abroad. We were in consequence really a debtor nation then, and wise old Europe as she received dividends from us, and clipped coupons from American bonds, could well afford to agree with us when we told her how prosperous we were and how much money we were making.

The International Trade Position of Great Britain

The situation with Great Britain, however, was just the reverse. The British regularly imported more goods than they exported—a fact which some unsophisticated critics thought alarming. But in the invisible trade Britain exported vastly more services than she imported. Hers was the greatest

[19] See Chapter II, page 35.

merchant marine on the seas, the vast insurance business carried on by Lloyd's was internationally famous, and her preeminent banking center and stock exchange at London exported capital to the far corners of the earth. So successful was Great Britain on her total foreign trade that she was compelled to import, roughly, a billion dollars of foreign securities each year to balance her total exports and imports. And the flood of dividends and bond interest which returned to London each year left no doubt as to the fact that she was the world's greatest creditor nation.

Significance of the Rate of Exchange

At this point the reader, if unacquainted with the economics of international trade, might well ask how it happens that each nation's total trade should be brought to balance as to its exports and imports. Trade is free, and individuals in all countries can buy and sell such goods and services as they please. When the Chicago merchant buys a French bond, or the Detroit manufacturer sells an automobile in the Argentine, neither has the slightest thought or anxiety as to the effect of his transactions upon our total trade balance. So it is with almost everyone both here and abroad. Few indeed even understand what trade balances really are. What, then, brings about this continual balance between each nation's exports and imports? The answer to this question is, of course, found in the current rate of exchange between the currencies of the various nations. With a few exceptions, all the currencies of the leading nations before 1914 were based on gold, and there was consequently a theoretical exchange rate between them known as the "par of exchange," which depended upon the exact amount of gold in the respective standard gold coins of the different nations. But in practice this "par" rate was only a theoretical point about which the actual or current rate fluctuated.

The Market for Foreign Exchange

The current rate of exchange arises from the conditions of supply and demand attending the purchase and sale of bills which are drawn in foreign currencies to make payments for the international traffic in goods and services. When, for example, an American firm ships wheat to an English firm, it usually obtains payment for the shipment by drawing a draft against the latter in pounds sterling and selling it, at the current rate of exchange, for American dollars. Similarly, if the American firm hires a British shipping company to transport the wheat to, say, Liverpool, the British company may elect to draw a dollar draft there against the American shipper and sell it, at the current rate for exchange, for pounds sterling. But while this is going on American buyers of English goods are seeking in New York, and British buyers of American goods are seeking in London, means of making their international payments. This they can do, with the assistance of a dealer in foreign exchange, by purchasing the drafts on the appropriate foreign country, which have been drawn by creditors of their own nationality, as shown above. For this reason there is a constant supply of and demand for sterling drafts in New York, and for dollar drafts in London. The rate of exchange between dollars and pounds depends upon this double supply and demand for bills drawn in the two foreign currencies in the two centers. If more sterling bills, for example, are offered than demanded in New York, the rate for sterling here tends to decline from the mint par rate of exchange between pounds and dollars, and, of course, dollars rise in proportion above the mint par rate. Similarly, if more dollar drafts are demanded than offered in London, dollars will tend to buy more pounds and pounds fewer dollars so long as this condition remains. The same rate of exchange is maintained in both London and New York through constant arbitraging between the two centers by foreign exchange dealers all over the world.

Effect of Supply and Demand on the Rate

But this common current rate of exchange may vary considerably from the par rate, since there may arise an inequality between the total demand and total supply for the two currencies in their relationship to each other. The par rate of exchange between pounds and dollars is £1 = $4.86. But owing to inequalities in the total trade balance the current exchange rate may become £1 = $4.82, or £1 = $4.90. Such a disparity between the par rate and current rate of exchange is immediately due, as we have seen, to an unequal condition arising in the supply and demand for bills drawn in pounds and dollars in New York and London. But the supply and demand for such bills is, in turn, caused by the conditions of the total visible and invisible trade of England and the United States in their relationship to each other, apart from the extent to which transactions with a third country or countries may and usually do complicate the problem. If England is buying more from us than she is selling to us, the rate of exchange between pounds and dollars will inevitably shift; pounds will buy less dollars and dollars will buy more pounds. Thus the rate of exchange serves as an invaluable index to the conditions of trade between nations, and gives fair warning whenever a nation buys more than it sells or sells more than it buys from other nations. Even in normal times (that is, prior to July, 1914) such temporary disparities between the total exports and imports of every nation are frequent and inevitable, and they are at once reflected by a rise or fall in the current exchange rate.

Naturally there can be no normal and healthy trade relationship between nations so long as their current exchange rates are far away from the par rate. This fact is only too well borne out by the difficult experience which all nations are having today, in attempting to carry on international trade while the exchange rates shift so widely and so constantly.[20] We must

[20] See Appendix Chapter IV (d).

next discover by what means a distorted current exchange rate can be brought back in harmony again with the par rate, as such methods of restoring the Exchange rate is of vital importance to any nation's trade.

Since current exchange rates between nations on a gold basis result from the balance, or lack of balance, between the particular nation's total exports and imports, and since it is true that a surplus of total exports over total imports tends to raise its exchange rate above par, while a surplus of total imports over total exports tends to depress its exchange rate below par, it is obvious that a balance between the given nation's total exports and total imports must be attained before its current exchange rate will be identical with its par exchange rate.

Righting the Balance of Trade

There are, of course, as many different ways of restoring the balance between a nation's total exports and total imports as there are separate items which it can buy or sell from or to other nations. If, for example, pounds are below their par rate with dollars, England must increase her total exports to us or to other countries, or decrease her total imports from us or from other countries, or both, before sterling will sell at its par of $4.86 per pound. The same situation, stated in terms of its American phase, is that America must decrease her total exports to England or other countries, or increase her total imports from England or from other countries, or both, before the current rate for sterling will approximate its par rate with dollars. This righting of the unequal balance in Anglo-American trade can be effected by appropriate purchase or sale of merchandise and services, gold, securities, or bank credit, which are the five main classifications of the several items of international trade, visible and invisible.

The fundamental sale of goods and services between nations changes only gradually and cannot be made to vary in amount with every capricious shift in the exchange rate, rapidly enough to restore it readily and quickly to par again. The shifting of gold between nations can be more quickly effected, and is frequently employed to readjust a distorted trade balance. Yet serious limitations are placed upon the extent to which gold can be employed for this purpose. For one thing, the shipment of gold is attended not only by some delay, but also with considerable expense, such as cooperage, cartage, freight, insurance charges, and abrasion in transit. Furthermore, the currency and bank credit of the exporting and importing nations are normally based upon gold, and in consequence any considerable export of it results in the deflation and inflation of both in the exporting and importing nations respectively. If this is allowed to continue, it will be followed by the evils ordinarily produced by the sudden deflation and inflation of credit and currency. In any case, the amount of gold available for export between nations, as well as the rate of the world's production of gold, is entirely too small to serve as a ready and sufficient corrective to the tremendous requirements of international trade today.

International Shifting of Bank Credit

Failing these two methods, there remains the expedient of shifting capital between the two nations to restore the balance in trade, and preventing a possibly disastrous drain on the gold resources of the debtor nation. This can be done very swiftly indeed, either by the use of bank credit or of securities, and it is daily resorted to between nations in normal times to keep exchange approximately at par. If, for example, sterling declines from its par with dollars, American bankers will export capital to Britain in the form of bank credit. Swift and efficient as this method is, and indispensable as it is up to a certain point, nevertheless there are severe limitations upon its employment.

To begin with, it is of only temporary usefulness, for bank

credit except in special circumstances cannot safely be tied up in foreign countries for long periods. Moreover, as in the case with exporting gold, the extent to which bank credit can be employed to balance trade accounts is limited. For if the banks attempted to transfer their credit abroad in unlimited quantities, the practice would soon produce a shortage of credit at home, and not only curtail the accommodation needed by domestic borrowers but also produce violent and convulsive movements in the domestic money rates which would gravely hamper the manufacturer and the merchant at home.[21] All of these three means of readjusting foreign trade balances and maintaining stable exchange rates, therefore, while of course they are all constantly and beneficially employed, could not, either separately or together, accomplish these necessary ends smoothly and efficiently.

Securities as a Factor in the Balance of Trade

In consequence, the fourth and final method—that of exporting capital by importing securities, and vice versa, through the organized securities markets—must constantly be employed to avoid the many harmful economic results of an overexport of gold or bank credit. The international purchase and sale of listed securities therefore contributes in a very vital manner to the maintenance of balanced trade and exchange rates, and also acts as a stabilizing force upon the production rate of goods and services, the buying power of currency, and the rate for domestic as well as foreign loans. Of course, securities which are not listed on an exchange, either here or abroad, are also bought and sold internationally, but not in considerable amounts, owing to the sometimes insuperable difficulties met in readily marketing them. Incidentally it should also be observed that no small part of the task of restoring the gold standard in the badly inflated European currencies of today must in the

[21] See Appendix, Chapter XVIII (d).

future fall upon the Stock Exchange, because of the indispensable part it plays and must play in our international traffic in securities.

Incentive Provided by the Exchange Rate

But in such salutary shifts in exports and imports, however they may be brought about, the current rate for foreign exchange not only serves as an index to reveal their necessity, but also provides an incentive of profit for their correct application. Let us suppose, by way of example, that prior to 1914 France's total exports to us slightly exceeded our exports to her. At once, the exchange rate between francs and dollars would change; francs would buy more dollars, and dollars would buy fewer francs. This would make the purchase by Americans of French goods just that more expensive, and would automatically tend to halt our further imports from France. But at the same time, American goods and services would become proportionately cheaper to Frenchmen, and our exports to France would tend to increase. Of a sudden, too, the export of American gold to France and of French bank credit thither would also become profitable. And as if by magic, our securities would suddenly become bargains for Frenchmen, a fact which the arbitrageurs of France would not be slow to recognize. As a result, our total exports to France would soon equal our total imports from her, the balance of trade would be restored, and dollars and francs would become exchangeable at approximately par again. Thus, in a practical way, the existence of organized securities markets provide under ordinary circumstances a ready means and an automatic incentive for the maintenance of exchange rates close to the par rate.

Owing to the abnormal conditions in trade and finance which have resulted from the war, the foregoing principles which operate to stabilize international trade in normal times may seem rather academic and theoretical today. The war, indeed, has caused a profound economic convulsion among all the great nations. Civilization has been shaken to its depths; the war's wreckage may not be repaired for at least a generation; and its debts may not be liquidated perhaps for several generations. It has provided the severest test imposed thus far of the permanency and ability to endure, of our present economic scheme of things. We must, therefore, next swiftly review a few of the profound economic changes wrought by the great conflict in the United States, and in consequence in the New York Stock Exchange.

The Stock Exchange at the Outbreak of the Great War

When out of an almost clear sky the war suddenly descended upon the nations of Europe, America was still heavily a debtor nation. For years our surplus visible exports had been matched by our surplus invisible imports. Europe, and England in particular, held billions of dollars' worth of our choicest securities, which enjoyed an active market on the New York Stock Exchange. Thus, at the outbreak of the war the latter securities market was suddenly threatened with an avalanche of selling orders from Europe, representing a liquidation of billions of these foreign-held American stocks and bonds. This untoward event was only prevented by the prompt closing of the Stock Exchange.[22] As the president of the Exchange during that trying period has graphically explained the matter:[23]

> . . . the fundamental reason for closing the Exchange was that America, when the war broke out, was in debt to Europe, and that Europe was sure to enforce the immediate payment of that debt in order to put herself in funds to prosecute this greatest of all wars. To use an illustration popular in Wall Street at the time, there was to be an unexpected run on Uncle Sam's Bank and the Stock Exchange was the paying

---

[22] See Appendix, Chapter XVIII (e).

[23] Noble, p. 65.

teller's window through which the money was to be drawn out, so the window was closed to gain time.

Once the initial shock was spent, however, the Stock Exchange was reopened gradually and skilfully. Trading in all securities was again permitted by the following December 15, and at once the Exchange became vitally serviceable to the nation under the new and unprecedented conditions imposed by the war.

Reversal of Our International Trade Balance

Obviously, Europe could not maintain her previous volume of exports to us, for her factories, her ships, and her capital were restricted to war production. On the other hand, the Allies soon began to purchase here enormous quantities of all sorts of raw materials and manufactured goods needed to conduct the war. The result was, of course, that our total exports soon threatened vastly to exceed our total imports. It was vitally important for the Allies to prevent such a condition in our trade, lest dollar exchange soar in terms of francs and pounds, and their purchases of war material here prove impossibly expensive. In consequence, Europe soon began to ship us large quantities of gold to offset our impending surplus of exports. But there was not sufficient gold at their disposal to balance the account in this way, and accordingly the vast European pre-war holdings of our securities began to be sold through the Stock Exchange to American speculators and investors, to pay for the foodstuffs and munitions which we were steadily furnishing to France and England.

Thus it was through the ready market provided by the Stock Exchange that Europe's former mortgage upon our leading railroad and industrial corporations amounting to billions of dollars was gradually liquidated and paid off, and the large sums which it had previously been necessary for us to send abroad to cover dividends and interest coupons due on

Europe's pre-war investment in our corporate shares and obligations, dwindled in proportion. The United States in the next few years not only ceased to be a debtor but became a creditor nation, although these huge amounts of securities were so smoothly and efficiently handled on the great organized securities exchange in New York that this profoundly significant fact attracted little attention at the time except in the technical financial press.

But the Stock Exchange did not simply make possible the transfer of our long lost stocks and bonds from Europe to our shores. With its aid, the Allies also distributed large external loans to American investors, the colossal Anglo-French 5 per cent loan of $500,000,000 being the most notable example. It was largely through the instrumentality and the efficient operation of the Stock Exchange, therefore, that after over a century of international indebtedness America became a creditor nation, and that we were enabled to sell and Europe to purchase our huge foreign exports of goods and foodstuffs in 1915 and 1916. This extraordinary trade, so beneficial to us and so vital to the success of the Allied arms, could not have been maintained without the steady and smooth operation of the Stock Exchange.[24]

The Stock Exchange During the War

Equally important from the national standpoint were the services of the Stock Exchange after the United States entered the war. Indeed, by the critical spring of 1917, the liquid resources of Europe in the shape of gold and salable securities were seriously depleted, and it had become increasingly difficult for the Allies to make payment to us for the vast demands which their fighting forces had placed on our fields and factories. Accordingly, when America entered the conflict, the tremendous and still little appreciated task of financing the war

[24] See Appendix, Chapter XVIII (f).

against the Kaiser was largely shifted from London to Washington, and consequently much of its real burden was likewise transferred from Threadneedle Street to Wall Street. The Allied currencies were accordingly "pegged" near their par rate with dollars, so as to make possible the continual shipment of our goods abroad. But instead of floating in our market new foreign loans which would have interfered with the sale of our own war bonds, the United States successfully floated the gigantic Liberty loans. Almost half of the many billions received from their sale was devoted to advances made to our Allies practically on open-book account by the United States Treasury, to finance their purchases of materials here. The skilful marketing of the huge Liberty issues on the Stock Exchange, the hearty co-operation of the latter organization with the government in this vital operation, and the gradual distribution still being effected there among American investors, have already been commented upon.[25] What the Stock Exchange had done for the smaller issues of American corporations or of foreign governments, it did, and is still doing, with conspicuous success in the case of the unprecedentedly great Liberty loan issues. If money is in truth the "sinews of war," then the Stock Exchange can indeed feel that its indispensable part in the work of marketing billions after billions of the Liberty issues among permanent investors has contributed in no small degree to the successful termination of the great "war against autocracy."

The Postarmistice Stock Market

The wide fluctuations of prices upon the Stock Exchange since the armistice, including as they have the bull market of 1919 and the severe relapse of prices during 1920, have to a

---

[25] On the work of the New York Stock Exchange in placing the Liberty loans with American investors, consult the statement and testimony of Governor Benjamin Strong of the New York Federal Reserve Bank, before the "Agricultural Inquiry" Commission (Washington, August, 1921), p. 687.

considerable extent obscured the quieter but more consistent part played by the Exchange in America's international economic and trade position. Furthermore, the armistice is still too recent for the international services performed for the nation by the Exchange to have reached the conclusion even of their initial phases. At this writing our visible and invisible trade are alike in a state of flux, and the writer would be a prophet indeed could he see the outcome of the economic forces now at work within them. Nevertheless, both to complete an admittedly scanty sketch of what the Exchange has done for America since the historic catastrophe of 1914, and to illustrate by current examples some further services performed for trade and industry in their international phases by organized securities markets, a few concluding features of the stock market during recent years are called for. This postarmistice history of finance verily bristles with exceptional happenings, with unprecedented conditions, with the paradoxical and the unexpected. And yet, after all, through this chaos in foreign exchange, in foreign trade, and in social and political experiment as well, the laws of economics are still visibly at work, immutable and unswerving as fate, shaping the world of tomorrow.

The Collapse in Foreign Exchange

Early in March, 1919, the Allied governments, realizing the impossibility of maintaining longer the "pegged" rates for exchange, ceased to "support the market" for pounds, francs, lire, and other European currencies in terms of the dollar. A violent and unparalleled collapse of European exchange rates on New York succeeded, followed by violent financial and economic retchings which were reflected in the wild fluctuations of British, French, Italian, and other currencies. Meanwhile Europe, in the first difficult days of her reconstruction, so desperately needed our goods that despite their depreciated exchange rates, our huge surplus of exports was for the time being maintained and even increased. As yet, Europe has not been able adequately to make payment to us for our huge exports to her, and thus balance both her own trade and ours. She has sent large quantities of gold to our shores; our bankers have made large advances of bank credit on her account; moreover, through the Stock Exchange and the over-the-counter market, considerable amounts of old American securities have been liquidated in New York and sold to Americans, as well as new foreign external loans placed with our investors. So far as America's foreign trade goes, therefore, the question of the future will be how Europe can pay us for our surplus of exports to her. In all probability payment will ultimately be made, not in any single and novel fashion, but in the many different ways which are permitted in modern trade. Not the least of these, we may at any rate conclude, is the placing of European securities with the American speculator and investor, largely through the indispensable machinery which the Stock Exchange provides.

Economic Functions of Securities in International Trade

Such, then, is in its barest outlines the theory of the function of organized securities markets in foreign trade, and such is the record of the Stock Exchange during the epoch-making period since 1914. And now for the moral; for out of this welter of abstruse economic theory and wild economic upheaval there are a few obvious and practical lessons to be drawn, which possess a profound significance both to the Stock Exchange and the United States.

First of all, we must look upon the purchase and sale of securities between nations as an indispensable means of balancing every nation's total exports and imports, and thereby not only restoring its exchange rates to par, but also powerfully tending to stabilize domestic credit and currency conditions, the price of goods and services at home in terms of currency, domestic and foreign interest rates, and the fundamental costs of production and the domestic level of prices.[26]

Again, the acquisition of a national income derived from holdings of foreign securities is of great value to any nation, for it is thereby enabled to purchase just that additional amount of goods from its debtor nations. England's prominent international trade position before the war and even today, was and is largely founded on this fact. Such income, too, is not a mere temporary affair, since securities, unlike commodities, are not soon consumed, but remain to draw dividends and bond interest after them year after year from the debtor to the creditor country. It may be, as some well-known authorities prophesy,[27] that the imports of the United States will in time come to exceed our visible exports for the first time in many years; yet this excess of visible imports need not alarm us, for they will be balanced by the income from abroad upon our holdings of foreign securities and other factors. Indeed, whether a country is really a debtor or creditor nation depends upon whether it pays or receives an excess of these dividends and interest coupons on securities.

Advantage of Foreign Security Holdings

In the third place, a nation which holds the listed securities of other nations can at any time instantly obtain credit and purchase goods abroad at will. In a minor way, this is of great convenience to foreign exchange dealers, who can transmit instant funds to foreign centers, not only by cable transfers of bank credit, but also by buying a security on the home exchange and simultaneously selling a similar amount of it short or for future delivery on an exchange abroad, and thus obtaining funds in the foreign center. But in a larger and more fundamental way this ability of a nation to liquidate its foreign

[26] See Appendix, Chapter XVIII (g).

[27] F. A. Vanderlip and J. H. Williams, The Future of Our Foreign Trade, 1920.

securities in their home markets is of the greatest significance to its financial welfare and stability, particularly, of course, in times of war. Certainly, if in 1914 Great Britain had not possessed literally billions of dollars in negotiable American securities, it might well have proved impossible for her to make the vast purchases of foodstuffs and munitions here which were so vital to victory.

Benefits to the Debtor Nations

Nor is the purchaser the only gainer by the international traffic in securities. Debtor nations, by selling their stocks and bonds in foreign nations, are enabled to obtain the funds necessary to lay their railroads, sink their mine shafts, increase their agricultural production, and develop their industries. The vast benefits to the United States arising from the absorption of our securities abroad have already been cited.[28] The same general principle holds true also of the Argentine in still more recent years. By investing extensively in the Argentine railroads, the British not only derived very satisfactory dividends and were assured of adequate supplies of wheat and beef, but their exports to Argentine were likewise augmented by orders for steel rails and all manner of railroad equipment. Americans are today beginning to realize that foreign trade follows foreign investments.

One final point remains. All the above-mentioned benefits which result from the international purchasing and selling of securities mainly depend upon the existence of organized securities markets in which the securities thus transferred from country to country can be readily sold. The world's stock exchanges as truly furnish warehousing facilities and points of arrival and departure for much of the invisible trade, as the great ports and storehouses do for the visible trade. Without exchanges, the flow of securities from nation to nation would

[28] See Chapter II.

be seriously interrupted. Apart from their vast domestic, economic services, stock exchanges would still amply justify their existence simply for the invaluable services which they perform in behalf of a nation's foreign trade. And true as this is in times of war and national peril, it is even more profoundly true in times of peace.

America's Economic Maturity

It must be apparent to even the casual student of international finance and trade that today the United States is entering into the period of its economic maturity. Employing the same metaphor, it might be said that from the early colonial days till the middle of the last century our country was still in its economic infancy. Our nation's early manhood was spent from 1850 to 1914 in perfecting our means of transportation, founding our national industries, and creating the bulk of our modern credit machinery. But in the few amazing years since 1914 we have, as regards our international economic position, experienced by far the swiftest development of which history holds any record. In less than a decade, America has attained an international economic and financial pre-eminence which a full century of normal growth and development might well have failed to bring about. But this pre-eminence, flattering as it may be to our national self-esteem, brings with it a vast and heavy responsibility which we cannot evade or shirk. Nowhere in America is this new and unaccustomed burden more pressing than in Wall Street today. New York has become the money and credit center of the world. Even if its present supremacy is destined later to disappear, yet in the future it will undoubtedly share the financial leadership with London. Meanwhile, new tasks are being imposed on our banks and stock exchanges. It would seem that if only for the sake of America's own economic stability and prosperity, Wall Street must shortly finance not only war-shattered

Europe, but perhaps the new economic areas of South America, Asia, and Africa as well.

Future International Rôle of the New York Stock Exchange

In the vast international vistas of commerce and finance which destiny is thus opening before our people, the New York Stock Exchange has a vital rôle to play in behalf of our national future. Its free and open market must function not only as our principal domestic securities exchange, but also as a world market comparable in scope and power to our new world position. We must look upon it as an indispensable part of the national business machinery in times of peace, and if the occasion shall arise, as a huge bulwark of economic and financial strength in times of war. We are justified in feeling a sense of national pride in its rapid growth and swift efficiency, since it so well embodies both the level-headed sagacity and the progressive and daring enterprise of our people.

America today enters this future period of international commercial and financial pre-eminence with a confidence for the future grounded firmly in the achievements of the past. And yet, in the coming years, our vision must be comparable in breadth and depth to the task which fate has set for us. The philosopher, Edmund Burke—that true friend of American political destinies—once declared, "Great empires and little minds go ill together." If this is true of the governmental problems of empires, it is a hundred times truer of the present and future "empires of business." The United States has reached its economic maturity. We have ceased, once and for all, to be a parochial nation on the fringes of modern civilization, nor can we longer judge our economic problems simply with the outlook and the philosophy of the country villager. We should, with regard to the future of this country, have something of the spirit and viewpoint of the British poet who said concerning his own people:

We've sailed wherever ships can sail
We've founded many a mighty state,
God grant our greatness may not stale
Through craven fear of being great.

As Americans, therefore, we must, in our judgment of our economic problems, present and future, clear our minds of sectional prejudices, of political opportunism, and of economic fallacy. We must not allow those business organizations and institutions which perform genuine services to the United States, to become the target of demagogic abuse, nor the victim of rashly conceived and nationally dangerous legal experiments. A great responsibility to the people of this country today rests upon the members and governors of the New York Stock Exchange. In the difficult and necessary tasks which will fall upon them in the future, their hands must be upheld by a wise and patriotic public opinion.

APPENDIX

CHAPTER I

(a) The continual growth of the British national debt through recurrent warfare is shown in the following table, taken from "The Political Economy of War," by F. W. Hirst, and from "National Debt Return" (1920), Cmd. 429:

Date	Total Debt	Historical Events	
1689	£ 664,000	Revolution—Parliament obtained financial control.	
1697	21,515,000	War of League of Augsburg added....	£ 20,851,000— 8 years
1702	16,394,000	Peace reduced debt by.............	5,121,000— 5 years
1713	52,145,000	War of Spanish Succession added.....	35,751,000—11 years
1739	47,954,000	Peace reduced debt by.............	4,190,000—26 years
1748	79,293,000	War of Jenkins' Ears added.........	31,339,000— 9 years
1756	74,332,000	Peace reduced debt by.............	4,961,000— 8 years
1763	138,865,000	Seven Years' War added...........	64,533,000— 7 years
1775	128,584,000	Peace reduced debt by.............	10,281,000—12 years
1783	249,851,000	American War added..............	121,267,000— 8 years
1793	244,118,000	Peace reduced debt by.............	5,733,000—10 years
1816	885,000,000	Napoleonic Wars added............	640,882,000—23 years
1854	803,000,000	Peace reduced debt by.............	82,000,000—38 years
1857	836,000,000	Crimean War added................	33,000,000— 3 years
1899	635,000,000	Peace reduced debt by.............	201,000,000—42 years
1903	798,000,000	Boer War added...................	163,000,000— 4 years
1914	706,000,000	Peace reduced debt by.............	92,000,000—11 years
1919	7,481,000,000	War 1914–1918 added.............	6,775,000,000— 4 years

(b) "We have entirely lost the idea that any undertaking likely to pay, and seen to be likely, can perish for want of money; yet no idea was more familiar to our ancestors, or is more common now in most countries. A citizen of London in Queen Elizabeth's time could not have imagined our state of mind. He would have thought it was of no use inventing railways (if he could have understood what a railway meant), for you would not have been able to collect the capital with which to make them. At this moment, in colonies and all rude countries, there is no large sum of transferable money, and there is no fund from which you can borrow and out of which you can make immense works. Taking the world as a whole—either now or in the past—it is certain that in poor states there is no spare money for new and great undertakings, and that in most rich states the money is too scattered, and clings too close to the hands of the owners, to be often obtainable in large quantities for new purposes. A place like Lombard Street, where in all but the rarest times money can always be obtained upon good securities or upon decent prospects of probable gain, is a luxury which no country has ever enjoyed with even comparable equality before." (Walter Bagehot, Lombard Street, 1878.)

(c) If the old stock in the railroad company cited sells at 115 on the Exchange, while the subscription price to holders of a "right" for new stock is 100, the value of the right is determined in the following manner: Each purchaser or holder of 10 shares of old stock at 115 can acquire another share, or 11 shares altogether, with an additional $100. Thus his 11 shares will be worth $1,250, or $113.63 apiece. But since the old stock is selling at $115 per share, the value of a right would amount to the difference between these figures, or to $1.37 per right. If such rights were listed upon the Exchange, they would be quoted at about 1⅜.

CHAPTER II

(a) "From 1792 to 1801 the number of banks increased from 3 to 23, with a total capital of $33,550,000. A few fire and marine insurance companies had also been organized. The supply of securities available for investment and speculation made therefore quite a stock market. The following advertisement, which appeared in the first issue of the *Evening Post,* November 16, 1801, gives an idea of the dimensions of this market:

PRICES OF STOCKS

6 per cent Funded Debt	98¾ per cent
3 per cent	56½ *a* 57
8 per cent Loan	112½
6 per cent Navy Loan	par

BANK STOCK

United States Bank	143 *a* 143½ per cent
New York (dividend off)	131½
Manhattan	132

INSURANCE SHARES

New York Insurance Company	128 per cent
Columbian	137 *a* 138
United	118 *a* 119

(Pratt, p. 6.)

(b) During the past century the Exchange has successively occupied the old Tontine Coffee House which stood at Wall and Water Streets (1817-1827); the Merchants' Exchange Building formerly at Wall and Hanover Streets (1827-1835 and 1842-1854); a building at 43 Wall Street (1835-1842); the old Corn Exchange Bank Building (1854-1856); the Lord's Court Building at 25 William Street (1856-1865); the old Stock Exchange Building on the present site at 10-12 Broad Street (1865-1901); the Produce Exchange Building (1901-1903); and since 1903 the present Stock Exchange Building fronting on Broad, Wall, and New Streets. To this building an extensive twenty-two story addition was begun in 1920, and should be completed in 1922.

(c) The approximate par value of all securities listed on the New York Stock Exchange as of October 13, 1921, is as follows:

BONDS

Government:		
*Old United States Government Issues	$ 872,010,030.00	
*United States Liberty Victory Loans	19,148,996,350.00	
United States, State and Municipal	772,050,400.00	
*United States Insular Possessions	10,500,000.00	
Foreign Countries and Cities	2,992,261,800.00	
Total Government Bonds		$23,795,818,580.00
Corporate:		
Railroad Companies	$ 9,679,995,200.00	
Telephone and Telegraph Companies	507,966,600.00	
Coal and Iron Companies	135,625,700.00	
Manufacturing Companies	1,293,611,300.00	
Gas and Electric Companies	451,420,400.00	
Street Railway Companies	1,135,974,100.00	
Miscellaneous Companies	573,128,800.00	
Total Corporate Bonds		13,777,722,100.00
Total Bonds Listed		$37,573,540,680.00

* Statement of the public debt of the United States, June 30, 1921.

STOCKS WITH PAR VALUE

Railroad Companies	$ 6,719,178,900.00	
Oil Companies	796,844,075.00	
Mining Companies	1,136,766,000.00	
Street Railway Companies	666,040,100.00	
Express Companies	63,967,300.00	
Coal and Iron Companies.....	170,971,200.00	
Gas and Electric Companies...	478,932,058.00	
Telephone and Telegraph Companies	669,090,700.00	
Manufacturing Companies	6,746,239,995.00	
Banks and Trust Companies..	251,339,200.00	
Miscellaneous Companies	764,935,481.00	
Total Stocks		$18,464,305,009.00
Total Bonds		37,573,540,680.00
Total Stocks and Bonds..................		$56,037,845,689.00

In addition to the above there were listed 15,067,509 shares of oil companies, 1,135,088 shares of mining companies, 10,299,508 shares of manufacturing and industrial companies, and 4,212,529 shares in miscellaneous companies—or a total of 30,714,634 shares—which were without par value and hence not included in the above tables. At an estimated value of $30 per share, these no-par value stocks would be worth $920,000,000. Thus (granted that all the above securities were selling at par, which is of course an extremely theoretical case) the aggregate actual or market value of all securities on the New York Stock Exchange would total (in round figures) $60,000,000,000.

The total number of issues listed on the New York Stock Exchange, at five-year periods since 1900, are given in the following classified tables:

TOTAL STOCK ISSUES LISTED

Year	Banks and Trust Cos.	Railroad	Industrial	Miscellaneous	Total
1900	70	177	46	69	362
1905	55	178	56	82	371
1910	53	175	98	100	426
1915	41	177	173	125	516
1920	34	173	302	173	682

Total Bond Issues Listed

Year	U. S. Government	U. S. State County & City	Foreign Government	Railroad	Utility and Industrial	Total
1900	6	69	1	637	82	795
1905	6	64	5	722	110	907
1910	9	63	10	776	165	1,023
1915	10	72	14	749	151	996
1920	20	78	26	709	283	1,116
1921*	27	97	37	700	250	1,111

* Incomplete for the year.

(d) Dealings in Stocks and Bonds

Annual total of reported sales on the New York Stock Exchange.

Year	Stocks (Number of Shares)	Bonds (Par Value)
1889	72,014,699	$ 493,459,625
1890	71,826,685	409,325,120
1891	99,031,689	888,650,000
1892	86,726,410	352,741,950
1893	77,984,965	301,303,777
1894	49,275,736	352,741,950
1895	66,440,576	519,142,100
1896	56,663,023	394,329,000
1897	77,470,963	544,569,939
1898	112,160,166	922,514,410
1899	175,073,855	336,451,120
1900	138,312,266	578,359,230
1901	265,577,354	999,404,920
1902	188,321,181	891,305,150
1903	100,748,366	684,200,850
1904	186,429,384	1,036,810,569
1905	263,040,993	1,018,090,420
1906	283,707,955	676,392,500
1907	195,445,321	527,166,350
1908	196,821,875	1,084,454,020
1909	214,425,978	1,314,656,200
1910	163,882,956	634,091,000
1911	126,515,906	889,567,100
1912	131,051,116	674,215,000
1913	83,083,585	501,155,920
1914	47,899,573	461,898,100
1915	173,378,655	956,077,700

Year	Stocks (Number of Shares)	Bonds (Par Value)
1916	232,842,807	1,161,625,250
1917	184,536,371	1,052,346,950
1918	143,378,095	2,093,257,500
1919	307,889,450	3,763,217,764
1920	223,931,439½	3,955,036,900

(*The Annalist*, Jan. 3, 1921, p. 35.)

CHAPTER III

(a) "Bids or offers shall not be made at a less variation than ⅛ of one dollar of the value of stocks, and ⅛ of 1 per cent of the par value of bonds, provided, however, that fractional bids and offers of less than ⅛ of 1 per cent of the par value of Foreign and Domestic Government Bonds and Notes, State, County and Municipal Securities, and Short Time Bonds and Notes of Corporations, may be made, if so determined by the Committee of Arrangements with the approval of the Governing Committee." (Constitution, Art XXIII, Sec. 5.)

(b) In case, however, one buying member had simply cried, "Take it," while another buyer had simultaneously made a definite bid for the stock by saying, "I'll give 95 for a hundred (shares)," it is a rule of the Stock Exchange that the bidder shall have the preference and get the selling member's stock. Similarly, after 50—say—has been bid for a stock, if simultaneously one seller cries, "Sold," while another says, "I'll sell a hundred (shares) for 50," the member offering the stock is accorded the sale.

(c) "The Stock Exchange uses every possible precaution to protect its members in making contracts on its 'floor,' and that such action has been well taken is proven by the confidence shown: as evidenced by the fact, that a man's word in the Stock Exchange is his bond, and nowhere in the world is so vast an amount of business carried on without the use of the written pledge or document, and with such small proportionate loss; and this same protection is extended to their clients. Negotiability imparts value to securities, and the New York Stock Exchange promotes negotiability." (Duncan MacGregor in the *Financial Barometer.*)

(d) "It has long been known that investors and speculators in America enjoy vastly more safety in their market operations through these various avenues of publicity than do investors and speculators abroad. There are no tickers worthy of the name across the water, and the daily list of business done, as published in our newspapers, with bid and asked prices and total transactions in detail, is unheard of among all the Bourses in Europe. The eminent French economist, Paul Leroy-Beaulieu, speaks very earnestly of the superiority of our New York Stock Exchange system in this matter, he says the need for a similar method in France is 'very urgent,' that the information thus spread broadcast is 'very instructive,' that the pledge of publicity is 'better assured in the United States than in any other country of the world,' and that an immediate reform along these lines is 'absolutely necessary' in Paris in the interest of the public."* (Van Antwerp, p. 163.)

CHAPTER IV

(a) "English trade is carried on upon borrowed capital to an extent of which few foreigners have any idea, and none of our ancestors could have conceived. In every district, small traders have arisen, who 'discount their bills' largely, and with the capital so borrowed, harass and press upon, if they do not eradicate, the old capitalist. The new trader has obviously an immense advantage in the struggle of trade. If a merchant has £50,000 all his own—to gain 10 per cent on it he must make £5,000 a year, and must charge for his goods accordingly, but if another has only £40,000 by discounts (no extreme instance in our modern trade), he has the same capital of £50,000 to use and can sell much cheaper. If the rate at which he borrows be 5 per cent, he will have to pay £2,000 a year; and after paying his interest, obtain £3,000 a year, or 30 per cent on his own £10,000. As most merchants are content with much less than 30 per cent, he will be able, if he wishes, to forego some of that profit, lower the price of the commodity and drive the old-fashioned trader—the man who trades on his own capital—out of the market. In modern English business, owing to the certainty of obtaining loans on discounts of bills or otherwise at a moderate rate of interest, there is a steady bounty on trading with borrowed capital, and a constant discouragement to confine yourself solely or mainly to your own capital." (Walter Bagehot, Lombard Street, 1878.)

---

* *L'Economiste Français*, Paris, Oct. 5.

(b) An interesting modern instance of selling without the use of money at all, has recently been afforded by the Austrian textile companies. During the war Austrian currency was inflated to such an extent that the krone became practically worthless in foreign countries. The Austrian manufacturers were consequently unable to obtain the needed raw materials from outside nations until they persuaded the latter to extend credit for them not in terms of the depreciated Austrian krone but in terms of the goods they proposed to manufacture. In other words, the Austrian textile manufacturer would turn into cloth every bale of cotton furnished him by an English exporting house; he would then pay the latter with a part of the goods thus manufactured, and earn his other expenses and his profit by retaining the rest of the goods. In such a transaction no money would be involved, since the Austrian obtained the cotton by promising to pay for it later with manufactured goods. This unusual and primitive yet perfectly feasible method of doing business serves to illustrate how fundamental the operations of owing someone goods and paying with goods really is.

(c) The broker's ability to loan or pledge securities carried in his customers' marginal accounts, even after the customers' consent has been obtained, has long been considerably restricted by the ethics of the brokerage business. Recently, these customary limitations have been officially formulated in a resolution of the Governing Committee of the Stock Exchange as follows:

"Referring to the second paragraph of the resolution of the Governing Committee passed Feb. 13, 1913, which reads as follows: 'That the improper use of a customer's securities by a member or his firm is an act not in accordance with just and equitable principles of trade, and the offending member shall be subject to the penalties provided in Section 6 of Article XVII, of the Constitution.'

"Resolved, that an agreement between a Stock Exchange house and a customer authorizing the Stock Exchange house to pledge securities carried for the account of the customer, either alone or with other securities, either for the amount due thereon or for a greater amount, or to lend such securities, does not justify the Stock Exchange house in pledging or loaning more of such securities than is fair and reasonable in view of the obligations of the customer to the broker.

"Resolved, that no form of general agreement between a Stock Exchange house and a customer warrants the Stock Exchange house in using securities carried for the customer for delivery on sales made by the Stock Exchange house for its own account, or for any account in which the house or any general or special partner therein is directly or indirectly interested."

(d) The fluctuations in the value of money become most apparent when the money side of a sale is shifted from the currency of one nation to that of another, at the prevailing rates for the foreign exchange involved. When in the spring of 1920 the German mark rose for a time from 1½ to 2½ cents, many German exporters who had purchased goods on credit from German producers for foreign delivery and who had, consciously or unconsciously, gone short of money in so doing, suffered severe losses.

To take an imaginary but quite typical instance, a German export house, let us say, had purchased a consignment of potash from a German company for 400,000 marks, paying 100,000 marks (or a 25-point margin) down on the transaction. This potash the German exporters agreed to sell to an American firm in New York for $7,500—the equivalent of 500,000 marks at the rate of exchange (1 mark = 1½ cents) then prevailing. The German exporters naturally expected a profit of 100,000 marks in the sale. But, as has been pointed out, the German exporters were forced to go short of money at the same time they bought the potash on margin. During the time elapsing between the receipt of the potash by the German exporters and its delivery by them in New York the value of the potash does not change, but the value of the German mark rises from 1½ to 2½ cents. Observe the result. The $7,500 paid by the American house is exchanged at 2½ cents per mark for only 300,000 marks, instead of 500,000 marks expected under the old rate of 1½ cents. In consequence of this rise in marks, of which the German exporters had gone short, the latter not only do not make their expected profit of 100,000 marks, but in addition lose their margin of 100,000 marks and are barely able to pay the German producers the 300,000 marks still owed to them.

(e) "The legislation of the State of New York on the subject of short selling is significant. In 1812 the legislature passed a law declaring all contracts for the sale of stocks and bonds void unless the seller at the time was the actual owner or assignee thereof or authorized by such owner or assignee to sell the same. In 1858 this act was repealed by a statute now in force, which reads as follows:

"'An agreement for the purchase, sale, transfer, or delivery of a certificate or other evidence of debt, issued by the United States, or by any State, municipal or other corporation, or any share or interest in the stock of any bank, corporation, or joint stock association incorporated or organized under the laws of the United States, or of any State, is not void, or voidable because the vendor, at the time of making such contract, is not the owner or possessor of the certificate or certificates or other evidence of debt, share, or interest.'" (Regulation of the Stock Exchange, p. 801.)

CHAPTER V

(a) Recent comparative rates of taxation upon speculative transactions in securities in the United States and foreign nations are as follows, the unit of taxation being 100 shares:

Selling Price	U. S. Federal Plus State	English	French	Dutch
$ 10	$4	$0.24	$0.20	$ 1.00
50	4	0.72	1.00	5.00
100	4	0.96	2.00	10.00

The English, French, and Dutch taxes are computed on the money value of transactions. United States federal and state taxes are both computed at 2 cents per share of par value $100, regardless of price, except in the case of the federal tax on no-par value stock, which is 2 cents on every $100 of the selling price.

The French tax cited in the table is that imposed on transactions "for the account," corresponding to the speculative or margin transactions of our traders. The French tax on cash or investment transactions is three times as great as the tax on speculative transactions.

The Dutch similarly foster substantial and active markets by removing the tax altogether from transactions for brokers' own accounts. The tax applies to commission business only.

The English also recognize the importance of not restricting markets for securities by what amounts to a discriminatory tax. As will be seen from the table, the tax cited, which applies to the vast majority of their transactions, corresponding to our speculative transactions, is relatively light, while the British tax on registered shares in transfer, which comprise but a small fraction of total transactions, is at the rate of 1 per cent.

The British "dealer," however, enjoys a special exemption from this latter 1 per cent duty. It applies to him only in the rare event that he carries stock over a two months' period. The activities of the dealers practically make the market on the London Exchange, and the Chancellor of the Exchequer, in order to preserve the freedom of the market, made this special exemption in their favor, relieving them from a duty which could be borne by the investor who bought to hold, but which would be absolutely prohibitive to the activities of the dealer or speculator whose quick turnover at small profits maintains the market in the fluid condition essential to financing national enterprises.

(b) "That any member of the Exchange who, while acting as a broker, either as a 'Specialist' or otherwise, shall buy or sell directly or indirectly for his own account, for account of a partner, or for any account in which he has an interest, the securities, the order for the purchase or sale of which has been accepted by him for execution, shall be deemed guilty of conduct or proceeding inconsistent with just and equitable principles of trade, and shall be subject to the penalties provided in Article XVII, Section 6, of the Constitution." (Constitution, p. 85.)

(c) The following sequence of events is typical as a cause of misunderstandings arising from the use of orders "on stop." Commission broker A—let us say—obtains an order from his customer, Jones, to sell 100 shares of an inactive stock at the market. When A arrives at the post where the given stock is traded in, it is quoted "63 bid, 68 asked." A says to the specialist B, "I have a market order to sell." B replies, "I want 200 at 63. I'll stop 100 with you," (i.e., if a sale is publicly made at 63, A and B will conclude a private sale of 100 shares at that price). A moment later broker C enters the crowd and offers 200 shares for sale. B says to him, "I am bidding for 100 (the remaining 100 of his original 200 shares to buy). I also have a market order to sell, so that no matter what you offer your stock at, I must offer it 1/8 lower."

Under the circumstances C says, "I will sell you 100 at 63," to which B agrees. On this sale the order on stop between A and B is also executed. Thus, A sells his stock at 63, and B purchases his

200 shares at that price. But since the order on stop is a private transaction it is not printed on the tape and only C's sale of 100 to B is regarded as "100 shares at 63." The market then becomes stronger and C's order for the remaining 100 to sell is canceled. Soon D comes into the crowd and concludes a sale with E at 64.

Meanwhile, A's customer, Jones, watches the tape. He sees the quotation 100 at 63 (made on C's sale to B), and not understanding that orders on stop are not recorded there, takes it for his own. If the market had continued to decline, he would consider himself fortunate to have received 63 for his stock. But when he sees the next sale at 64 he becomes suspicious. He concludes that the specialist B must have himself bought his 100 shares from A at 63 and later sold them at 64. And thus, although the specialist really did nothing of the kind, Jones becomes very indignant with him and considers that he has been cheated.

CHAPTER VIII

(a) The rediscount by the federal reserve banks of security collateral loans, except those based upon bonds or notes of the United States government, is at present forbidden by the following section of the Federal Reserve Act:

"Upon the endorsement of any of its member banks, which shall be deemed a waiver of demand, notice and protest by such bank as to its own endorsement exclusively, any Federal Reserve bank may discount notes, drafts, and bills of exchange arising out of actual commercial transactions; that is, notes, drafts, and bills of exchange issued or drawn for agricultural, industrial, or commercial purposes, or the proceeds of which have been used, or are to be used, for such purposes, the Federal Reserve Board to have the right to determine or define the character of the paper thus eligible for discount within the meaning of this Act. Nothing in this Act contained shall be construed to prohibit such notes, drafts, and bills of exchange, secured by staple agricultural products or other goods, wares or merchandise from being eligible for such discount; but such definition shall not include notes, drafts or bills covering merely investments or issued or drawn for the purpose of carrying or trading in stocks, bonds, or other investment securities, except bonds and notes of the Government of the United States. (Or bonds of the War Finance Corporation. See act approved April 5, 1918, Appendix p. 70.) Notes, drafts and bills admitted to discount under the terms of this paragraph must have a maturity at the time of discount of not more than ninety days, exclusive of days of grace: *Provided,* that notes, drafts and bills drawn or issued for agricultural purposes or based on livestock and having a maturity not exceeding six months, exclusive of days of grace, may be discounted in an amount to be limited to a percentage of the assets of the Federal Reserve bank, to be ascertained and fixed by the Federal Reserve Board.

"Any Federal Reserve bank may discount acceptances of the kinds hereinafter described, which have a maturity at the time of discount of not more than three months' sight, exclusive of days of grace, and which are endorsed by at least one member bank.

"Any Federal Reserve bank may make advances to its member banks on their promissory notes for a period of not exceeding fifteen days at rates to be established by such Federal Reserve banks, subject to the review and determination of the Federal Reserve Board, provided such promissory notes are secured by such notes, drafts, bills of exchange or bankers' acceptance as are eligible for rediscount or for purchase by Federal Reserve banks under the provisions of this Act, or by the deposit or pledge of bonds or notes of the United States. (Or by bonds of the War Finance Corporation. See Sec. 13, War Finance Corporation Act. Approved April 5, 1918. Appendix 70." (The Federal Reserve Act, as approved April 13, 1920, Section 13, pp. 27–29.)

(b) Without entering into an exhaustive examination of the leading central and rediscounting banks of the world in respect to their rediscounting of security collateral loans, it will be sufficient to outline the practice of the two leading banks of Europe—the Bank of England and the Bank of France—in this regard.

The Bank of England—long recognized as the central credit institution of the whole modern world—has long freely rediscounted loans secured by security collateral. From available statistics it is impossible to determine what proportion of the bank's total rediscounts its holdings of loans on securities constitute. But in general this proportion, whatever it is, has been left to the authorities of the Bank to determine, rather than made subject to some inflexible and arbitrary proportion established by law. But one feature of British practice regarding loans on securities, or as they are called, "Lombard Loans," should be noted. For this class of loans a special rediscount rate is established, which is not only higher than the market rate for those loans but is also slightly higher than the better known official Bank rate applicable to commercial and mercantile loans. By this means all rediscounting of loans at the Bank penalizes the original lending institution and favors commercial loans as against loans on securities, which are so often speculative in their nature. Yet there is no attempt to bar from the rediscount privilege the latter class of loans, which are clearly recognized as performing an indispensable economic function for the entire financial and mercantile community of Great Britain, and indeed of the world.

Essentially identical is the current practice of the Bank of France, which for almost a century has been regularly rediscounting loans on security collateral.*

With the evolution of railroad and other corporations, loans not only upon the obligations of the French government but also upon French railroad securities and city of Paris bonds were permitted.† At first the same rediscount rate was employed for both these loans and the larger amounts of commercial loans, but later a separate rediscount rate for loans on securities was established and maintained slightly higher than the official rate for commercial loans in order to favor commercial over security distribution.‡ As a parallel to America's experience in 1917-1921 with loans upon United States government obligations rediscounted at the federal reserve banks, it is interesting to note that the Bank of France's rediscount rate upon security loans in the crisis of 1870-1871 was similarly lowered below the market rate for these loans and also below the Bank's rediscount rate for commercial loans. The result then (as with us in recent years) was to lodge large amounts of loans on government securities with the central bank and thus lead to a large note issue and inflation of prices.§ This expedient, contrary as it was to sound economic policy, nevertheless permitted the Bank of France in a national emergency very vitally to assist the government in financing the Franco-Prussian War. But this abnormal position of the rates was rapidly corrected afterwards, and the rediscount rate on security loans was again established above the market rate and the Bank's rediscount rate for commercial loans.

The current normal practice of the Bank of France is to discount only first-class paper with three signatures, or with two signatures

* National Monetary Commission, Vol. XV, p. 84.

† *Ibid.*, p. 86. ‡ *Ibid.*, p. 132. § *Ibid.*, pp. 139-140.

with collateral security. But no obligation or restriction concerning loans is forced upon the Bank, and all is left to the discretion of the Committee of the Bank. As indicated by the rediscount rates established, commercial loans made for general business are favored as against the more speculative loans on securities, yet no restriction is placed against loaning on notes secured by collateral.

In this connection the greater safety of the American as compared with the British or French loan on security collateral should be noted. No continuous ticker service is maintained either by the London Stock Exchange or the Paris Bourse. Lenders there are in consequence denied the advantage, enjoyed by the American lender upon securities listed on the New York Stock Exchange, of knowing the value of their collateral hour by hour, or if need be, minute by minute. Also, owing to the vastly more extensive domestic wire connections of the American Stock Exchange, its power to absorb securities in a crisis and in consequence its ability to render its listed securities at all times liquid and negotiable, is probably greater than in the case of the Stock Exchanges of London and Paris today.

A final point regarding the Bank of France should also be noted. In France, owing to popular ignorance of the check and the almost universal use of the bank note as a circulating medium, rediscounted loans in the Bank of France result to a larger extent in the issue of bank notes than in the creation of deposits. Yet in the normal times preceding the war it was never charged that the rediscounting of security collateral loans inflated the currency, except in those periods of national danger when the Bank was compelled owing to the imperative needs of the nation, to rediscount loans on government securities in large amounts and at uneconomic rates.

The best banking practice of Europe, which admittedly is the most skilful and experienced practice in the world, therefore, favors the rediscount of loans on securities at a special rediscount rate above the market rate for these loans and above the "official" rediscount rate for commercial borrowings.

(c) "The different ways in which the money and the stock markets meet are concisely but comprehensively summed up by Professor Jacob H. Hollander as follows:

"(1) Stock Exchange securities are used as collateral to secure mercantile discounts and personal loans in the insufficiency of commercial or personal credit.

"(2) In the interval between original sale and ultimate absorption by investors newly issued corporate securities are used by underwriting syndicates and syndicate participants to secure bank advances.

"(3) Banking institutions invest in Stock Exchange securities such part of their resources as are not employed in loans and discounts in consideration of interest return and an anticipation, semi-speculatively, of appreciation in market value.

"(4) Bond houses and stock brokers engaged in the sale of investment securities obtain bank loans as working capital upon unsold holdings.

"(5) Speculative purchases of Stock Exchange securities are financed partly by time loans, but in the main by demand loans obtained from banking institutions and secured by such securities as collateral." (Pratt, pp. 272-273.)

(d) The establishment of the federal reserve bank system brought about important changes in the market for call loans by creating new conditions in the supply of the various classes of loanable funds.* The excess funds of American banks, whence call loans originate, have since the reserve system was established found additional outlets, with the result that the supply of money available for lending on call has been seriously diminished both in actual amount and in proportion to the needs of the stock market. The new factors which have brought about this change in the call money market will be briefly enumerated:

1. *Commercial Paper.* It will be remembered that the federal reserve banks cannot under the present law rediscount loans based upon any security collateral other than the obligations of the United States government. The effect of this legal discrimination against the collateral of even the oldest and soundest American corporation securities has been to deny to loans secured by them the advantage of rediscount at the reserve banks. That this distrust against the collateral loan is artificial and unnecessary is shown not merely by the fact that the older central and rediscounting banks abroad draw no such line against the collateral loan, but also by the inherently liquid and negotiable character of securities listed on the New York Stock Exchange in contrast to the sometimes unsalable character of other

* See Sixth Annual Report of the Federal Reserve Bank of New York, p. 15.

collateral. This latter contrast was vividly illustrated in 1920-1921 by the widespread "freezing" of commercial paper. There were no frozen security collateral loans during this same period. But, however uneconomic and inequitable, this discrimination against security collaterals has unduly curtailed the excess banking funds formerly loaned upon them, since it has favored the purchase with such excess funds of rediscountable commercial paper in the open market.

2. *Acceptances.* Since and largely owing to the establishment of the federal reserve system, a broad market has grown up for bills or acceptances. These obligations, in addition to other sound and attractive features, have been purchased in large amounts by the reserve banks and have become a proper investment for the surplus banking funds of member banks.

3. *Treasury Certificates.* These short-term evidences of the United States government's floating debt, bearing a high rate of interest and possessing other attractive characteristics, have since the armistice comprised still another means of investing surplus banking funds, in competition with the call loan market.

4. Since the institution of the reserve system the custom has grown for member banks to borrow heavily from their reserve banks. In consequence, when the member banks accumulate surplus funds, they use them largely in paying off their loans at reserve banks, instead of investing them in commercial paper, acceptances, treasury certificates, or call loans.

5. Finally, a former source of supply for call funds has been practically eliminated as a result of the war, by the present impossibility of attracting funds from abroad, into the American call loan market. Formerly, such foreign funds constituted a considerable and stabilizing factor there. Owing, however, to the present position of the United States as a creditor instead of debtor nation, it is altogether improbable that foreign funds will in the near future prove available for lending on call in New York in any appreciable amounts.

The diminution of the supply of surplus banking funds available for making call loans, coupled with the strong demand for such loans during the large turnover in the stock market in 1919 and 1920, naturally imposed a heavy strain upon the whole call loan market, which has been hard put to obtain sufficient excess funds to sustain the great securities market on the New York Stock Exchange. Demand has frequently outrun supply, and as a result bidders for call money have sometimes run up the interest rate upon call loans to the high figures mentioned above.

(e) The world shortage of credit subsequent to the war is vividly illustrated by the accompanying table of rediscount rates (as of October 22, 1920) in the leading financial centers:

Center	Date of Change	Current Rate
Amsterdam	July 1, 1915	4½%
Athens	May 15, 1920	6½
Bengal	July 1, 1920	5
Berlin	Dec. 23, 1914	5
Bombay	July 29, 1920	5
Brussels	Apr. 29, 1920	5½
Christiania	June 25, 1920	7
Copenhagen	Apr. 16, 1920	7
Helsingfors	Mar. 22, 1920	8
Lisbon	June 23, 1913	5½
London	Apr. 15, 1920	7
Madras	July 20, 1920	6
Madrid	Nov. 20, 1919	5
Paris	Apr. 8, 1920	6
Prague	May 12, 1920	6
Rome	May 11, 1920	6
Stockholm	Sept. 16, 1920	7½
Switzerland	Aug. 22, 1919	5
Tokio	Nov. 18, 1919	8
Vienna	Apr. 12, 1915	5
Warsaw	Apr. 12, 1915	6

(*The Street*, Oct. 25, 1920, p. 509.)

(f) The following table, compiled from the more exhaustive statistics contained in Senate Document 262, 66th Congress, 2nd Session, pp. 13-26, illustrates the range of fluctuation and average yearly rates of call money during recent years compared with commercial paper:

	Call Rate		Average Call Rate	Commercial Paper Rate	
Year	High	Low	For Year	High	Low
1906	60	1½	6.42	......	......
1907	125	1	6.38	......	......
1908	20	¾	2.05	......	......
1909	7	1	2.73	......	......

Year	Call Rate High	Call Rate Low	Average Call Rate For Year	Commercial Paper Rate High	Commercial Paper Rate Low
1910	14	1	2.99	......	......
1911	6	1	2.602	......	......
1912	20	1½	3.713	......	......
1913	10	1	3.23	......	......
1914	10	1½	3.766	......	......
1915	3	1	1.959	4	2¾
1916	15	1½	2.592	4½	2¾
1917	10	1½	3.397	6	3½
1918	6	2	5.27	6	5¼
1919	30	2	6.516	6	5

(g) "The only financial center in this country in which there is maintained a call money market of national importance is New York City, and while the rates charged there on call loans are frequently in excess of the legal rates allowed for commercial paper, they are not usurious under the laws of the State of New York, which specifically exempt collateral call loans from the 6 per cent limitation which lenders must observe on other loans on pain of incurring the penalty prescribed for usury. Section 115 of the banking law (L. 1914, ch. 369; Consol L., ch. 2) provides that upon advances of money repayable on demand to an amount not less than $5,000 made upon warehouse receipts, bills of lading, certificates of stock, etc., or other negotiable instruments, as collateral, any bank may receive and collect as compensation any sum which may be agreed upon by the parties to such transaction. The section reads:

> SECTION 115. *Interest on Collateral Demand Loans of not Less Than Five Thousand Dollars.* Upon advances of money repayable on demand to an amount not less than five thousand dollars made upon warehouse receipts, bills of lading, certificates of stock, certificates of deposit, bills of exchange, bonds or other negotiable instruments, pledged as collateral security for such repayment, any bank may receive or contract to receive and collect as compensation for making such advances any sum which may be agreed upon by the parties to such transaction.

"Section 201 of the banking law, identical in language with section 115 above quoted, makes the same provision in the case of collateral loans by trust companies. In the general business law (L. 1909, ch.

25; Consol L., ch. 20) there is the following general provision of a like character:

> SEC. 379. *Interest Permitted on Advances on Collateral Security.* In any case hereafter in which advances of money, repayable on demand, to any amount not less than five thousand dollars, are made upon warehouse receipts, bills of lading, certificates of stock, certificates of deposit, bills of exchange, bonds or other negotiable instruments pledged as collateral security for such repayment, it shall be lawful to receive or to contract to receive and collect, as compensation for making such advances, any sum to be agreed upon in writing, by the parties to such transaction.

"The national-bank act provides that national banks may receive and charge on any loan or discount interest at the rate allowed by the law of the State, territory or district where the bank is located. The applicable provision reads:

> 422, SEC. 3197. *Limitation Upon Rate of Interest Which May Be Taken.* Any association may take, receive, reserve and charge on any loan or discount made, or upon any note, bill of exchange, or other evidences of debt, interest at the rate allowed by the laws of the State, Territory or District where the bank is located, and no more except that where by the laws of any State a different rate is limited for banks of issue organized under State laws, the rate so limited shall be allowed for associations organized or existing in any such State under this title. When no rate is fixed by the laws of the State or Territory or District, the bank may take, receive, reserve or charge a rate not exceeding seven per centum, and such interest may be taken in advance, reckoning the day for which the note, bill, or other evidence of debt has to run. And the purchase, discount, or sale of a bona fide bill of exchange, payable at another place than the place of such purchase discount, or sale, at not more than the current rate of exchange for sight drafts in addition to the interest, shall not be considered as taking or receiving a greater rate of interest.

"It will be observed that the effect of the foregoing provisions is to authorize in the State of New York on collateral loans of not less than $5,000 rates of interest which may be in excess of those permitted for loans of other character, and that such higher rates are not prohibited as usurious. . . .

"In the matter of the supply or attraction of funds to the call-money market, there is generally a definite and well understood obligation on the part of the banks to accommodate first their own commercial clients, so that it is only the excess of loanable funds which they may have from time to time that is available for the collateral call-money market or for the purchase of commercial paper in the open market. This excess of loanable funds available for employment in the securities market varies, therefore, according to the commercial requirements of the country. It has long been recognized that for assurance of a sufficient amount of money to finance the volume of business in securities, reliance cannot be placed on a rate of interest limited to the rates which obtain or are permitted in commercial transactions whose prior claim on banking accommodations is universally conceded." (Rates of Interest on Collateral Call Loans, Sen. Doc. 262, 66th Congress, 2nd Session, pp. 4-6.)

(h) "It is the universal custom of the banks to satisfy first the commercial needs of their customers. They feel an obligation to customers but none to those who borrow in the open market on securities. Besides, as the resources of the banks mainly come from the commercial customers, their own self-interest compels a preference in favor of their commercial borrowers, since failure to grant them reasonable accommodation would induce them to withdraw their deposits and so reduce the ability of the banks to do business. Although the money of the banks and trust companies comprises by far the greater proportion of the money loaned on the securities market, an examination of the prevailing rates on commercial paper at times when the call-money market is particularly strained indicates that there is little causal relation between the rates for call money and those on commercial loans." Rates of Interest on Collateral Call Loans. (Sen. Doc. 262, 66th Congress, 2nd Session, pp. 9-10.)

(i) "The reports of all national banks of the United States as of June 30, 1920, as recently analyzed, show an enormous expansion in their holdings of mercantile paper and of discounts made on the strength of one or more indorsements, and in loans made upon warehouse receipts, etc., and a marked reduction in money loaned on bonds and stocks. . . .

"How was this withdrawal of funds from stock exchange use conducted? There are two ways of reducing the volume of loans: One is by peremptory action, refusing to renew, requiring debtors to repay forthwith; the other is by raising the interest rate. The former is a violent method liable to cause serious disturbance. The latter gives the borrower time to adopt a policy and make new arrangements. It was in the public interest that less capital should be employed in the call market and it was necessary that borrowers should adapt their affairs to this policy, but it was advantageous to them to be allowed to borrow from day to day even on high rates until they had adjusted themselves to the change. If they paid 25 per cent, they paid one three hundred and sixty-fifth of 25 per cent for one day, and were under no obligation to borrow for a day longer than they wanted to.

"A reduction of the amount of money available inevitably causes a rise of rates unless the demand falls off. The borrowers themselves advance the rates by bidding to attract funds to take the place of what has been withdrawn.

"A conference of farmers in session at Washington is reported to have passed a resolution condemning the New York banks for lending at such high rates because the effect was to attract money from the country where it was needed for loans to farmers. They did not understand that it was the withdrawal of funds for that purpose which made the high rates, or that if the New York banks had refused to lend at the rates named, the rates would have gone still higher and the temptation to country bankers have been thereby increased." (George E. Roberts in *National City Bulletin,* quoted in "Agricultural Inquiry," Washington, 1921, p. 540.)

(j) In Europe, as S. F. Streit has pointed out in a pamphlet entitled "Term Settlements," "the call money market is not based on Stock Exchange collateral but the bulk of the call loans is made on acceptances and special governmental obligations. . . . The brokers know what their money requirements will be for the ensuing account a day or two in advance of the final settlement day of the current account. They are thus enabled to make their banking arrangements with the least disturbance; the discount market in the final analysis (rather than the call money market) acting as the regulator of excess demand or supply of Stock Exchange money."

CHAPTER IX

(a) "Of course, a few hours elapse between the certification and the receipt of the broker's checks, and in this brief interval it would be possible for a dishonest man to abuse the privilege extended to him,

(c) Stock Clearing Corporation

Clearance Statistics from May 1, 1920, to April 30, 1921.

Night Clearing Branch

1920		Shares Cleared One Side (Excluding Balances)	Total Value One Side (Excluding Balances)	Share Balances One Side	Value Share Balances One Side	Cash Balances One Side	Number Securities Cleared	Reported Sales of Cleared Stocks	Per Cent Deliveries on Stock Balances to Total Deliveries	Total Sales All Stocks	Per Cent Clearance Volume to Total Volume	Bank Certification Obviated
May	Stocks	19,861,600	$1,456,800,000	8,884,600	$609,726,000	$5,768,100	141–142	14,999,700	44.73	16,711,900	89.75	$847,074,000
	Liberty Bonds	2,842,900	250,700,000	1,694,700	149,500,000	429,700	6	....	.....	....	.....	101,200,000
June	Stocks	11,735,300	791,200,000	5,794,800	381,432,400	2,873,100	141–171	8,469,700	55.61	9,690,500	87.40	409,767,600
	Liberty Bonds	2,334,400	209,000,000	1,251,600	109,700,000	279,900	6	....	.....	....	.....	99,300,000
July	Stocks	14,431,800	753,000,000	7,607,000	480,474,800	3,693,300	171–175	11,012,300	52.62	12,381,500	88.94	272,525,200
	Liberty Bonds	1,677,500	150,250,000	997,200	87,000,000	137,700	6	....	.....	....	.....	63,250,000
August	Stocks	16,271,800	1,004,200,000	8,280,800	466,356,900	4,267,800	174	12,676,100	50.89	14,217,200	89.16	537,843,100
	Liberty Bonds	1,376,400	108,250,000	789,700	72,800,000	152,100	6	....	.....	....	.....	45,450,000
September	Stocks	16,252,100	965,350,000	8,491,800	485,154,900	3,168,500	174–178	12,436,200	52.28	15,290,700	81.33	480,193,100
	Liberty Bonds	1,606,650	143,700,000	958,600	84,600,000	296,800	6	....	.....	....	.....	59,100,000
October	Stocks	16,001,100	1,023,150,000	8,575,500	500,470,000	2,908,600	185–188	12,290,000	52.94	14,021,500	87.65	522,679,200
	Liberty Bonds	1,957,950	173,050,000	1,169,000	106,000,000	245,400	6	....	.....	....	.....	67,050,000
November	Stocks	27,634,100	1,829,250,000	13,162,600	741,155,600	6,783,500	189–190	20,766,600	47.52	22,578,200	91.97	1,088,094,400
	Liberty Bonds	1,926,950	185,550,000	1,200,000	108,100,000	267,200	6	....	.....	....	.....	77,400,000
December	Stocks	30,355,200	1,593,350,000	14,724,100	677,559,200	6,198,300	188–192	22,021,700	48.95	23,897,600	92.15	915,790,800
1921	Liberty Bonds	4,308,950	375,800,000	2,504,100	223,700,000	480,900	6	....	.....	....	.....	152,100,000
January	Stocks	21,419,400	1,209,500,000	10,105,800	486,174,000	6,144,200	192–209	15,731,800	48.65	17,283,000	91.26	723,326,000
	Liberty Bonds	1,985,5 8	178,000,000	1,204,150	108,000,000	238,900	6	....	.....	....	.....	70,000,000
February	Stocks	13,268,500	752,000,000	6,864,900	318,693,200	3,004,400	209	9,419,500	51.74	10,413,100	90.46	433,306,800
	Liberty Bonds	1,530,550	136,000,000	533,980	48,799,050	199,800	6	....	.....	....	.....	87,200,950
March	Stocks	20,852,500	1,156,442,400	9,372,800	439,300,400	4,028,676	209	14,527,800	44.95	15,954,800	91.05	717,142,000
	Liberty Bonds	1,610,290	142,512,790	1,090,550	100,216,930	240,500	6	....	.....	....	.....	42,295,860
April	Stocks	19,023,100	1,125,606,000	8,425,000	415,745,100	3,512,900	210–220	13,369,300	44.29	14,448,800	92.53	709,860,900
	Liberty Bonds	1,372,979	122,117,240	988,160	85,228,540	247,300	6	....	.....	....	.....	36,888,700
Totals	Stocks	227,106,500	13,659,848,400	110,289,700	6,002,242,500	52,351,376	141–220	167,720,700	48.56	186,843,800	89.76	7,657,603,100
	Liberty Bonds	24,531,077	2,174,930,030	14,381,740	1,283,644,520	3,216,200	6	....	.....	....	.....	901,235,510
Grand Total		251,637,577	$15,834,778,430	124,671,440	$7,285,887,020	$55,567,576	147–226	167,720,700	48.56	186,843,800	89.76	$8,558,838,610

Stock Clearing Corporation

Clearance Statistics from May 1, 1920, to April 30, 1921

Day Clearing Branch

1920	Shares Delivered (One Side)	Value of Shares (One Side)	Checks (Amount Deposited)	Per Cent Checks Deposited	Certification Obviated	Per Cent Obviated	Number of Deliveries	Number of Checks Drawn	Per Cent Number Checks Drawn	Reduction in Number of Checks Drawn	Per Cent Reduction Number of Checks Drawn
May	8,884,600	$609,726,000	$235,768,500	38.6	$373,957,500	61.4	43,495	4,200	9.6	39,295	90.4
June	5,794,800	381,432,400	165,238,400	43.3	216,194,000	56.7	31,182	3,816	12.2	27,366	87.8
July	7,607,000	480,474,800	189,889,300	39.5	290,585,500	60.5	38,641	3,981	10.4	34,660	89.6
August	8,280,800	466,356,900	184,506,800	39.5	281,850,100	60.5	43,569	3,807	8.7	39,762	91.3
September	8,491,800	485,154,900	174,762,500	36.0	310,392,400	64.0	45,214	3,494	7.7	41,720	92.3
October	8,575,500	500,470,000	180,286,100	36.0	320,183,900	64.0	45,920	3,464	7.5	42,456	92.5
November	13,162,600	741,155,600	273,519,200	36.9	467,636,400	63.1	64,425	3,856	5.9	60,569	94.1
December	14,724,100	677,559,200	250,626,200	36.9	426,933,000	63.1	72,154	4,266	5.9	67,888	94.1
1921											
January	10,105,800	486,174,000	174,399,900	35.8	311,774,100	64.2	54,780	3,725	6.8	51,055	93.2
February Stocks	6,864,900	318,693,200	144,518,083	39.2	222,974,167	60.8	39,355	3,434	8.7	35,921	91.3
Bonds	533,980	48,799,050									
March... Stocks	9,372,800	439,300,400	222,059,226	41.1	317,458,104	58.9	55,980	4,210	7.5	51,770	92.5
Bonds	1,090,550	100,216,930									
April.... Stocks	8,425,000	415,745,100	203,837,836	40.6	297,135,803	59.4	51,110	3,965	7.7	47,145	92.3
Bonds	988,160	85,228,540									
Totals. Stocks	110,289,700	$6,002,242,500	$2,399,412,045	38.5	$3,837,074,974	61.5	585,825	46,218	7.8	539,607	92.8
Bonds	2,612,690	234,244,520									
Grand Total	112,902,390	$6,236,487,020	$2,399,412,045	38.5	$3,837,074,974	61.5	585,825	46,218	7.8	539,607	92.8

but the fact that such a thing does not happen affords tenable grounds for the belief that it will not happen. The bank does not deal with an individual, but with a firm, and it knows that the firm has a membership in the Stock Exchange, with a cash balance on deposit in the bank that extends the accommodation. Any banker will bear witness that the business is quite satisfactory and that it involves no loss. . . . If the merchant discounts his paper for thirty, sixty, or ninety days, why prevent a similar accommodation to stock brokers for an hour or two? Both are engaged in a strictly legitimate business upon which the welfare of the community in greater or less degree depends, and the fundamental purpose of a bank is to promote and encourage such business. That is what banks are for, and bank officers are supposed to know something about how, when and where accommodations may be extended with safety to all concerned." (Van Antwerp, pp. 114-115.)

(b) The Hughes Commission, in its report in 1909, advocated the retention of the clearing house sheets. In this connection, it said: "In view of the value of these sheets as proving the transactions and the prices, they should be preserved by the Exchange for at least six years, and should be at the disposal of the courts, in case of any dispute."

The Exchange authorities at first demurred to this suggestion, since "clearing house sheets are not legal evidence, being merely copies of records; the actual records of a firm's business are kept in its books, and both the State and the Stock Exchange require that these shall be kept in accordance with the recommendations of the Hughes Commission." More recently, in order to avoid misunderstanding, the Exchange has made it a practice to retain the clearing sheets for a period of years.

(c) See pages 561 and 562.

CHAPTER X

(a) "The result of the operation of the Stock Clearing Corporation fully demonstrates that it has accomplished the purposes for which it was organized. In the Bulletin of the Agent of the Federal Reserve Bank of New York for September, 1920, the statement was made that the bank clearings at New York had a noticeable decline, and that while a large part of it was owing to reduction in general stock market activity, they went on and said further:

"'But a novel factor in the reduction arises from the perfected method of clearing stocks and paying for them put in operation by the New York Stock Exchange late in April. According to this plan, which applies to stocks admitted to clearings by the Stock Clearing Corporation representing ninety per cent of the total transactions, only balances between brokers are settled, whereas formerly settlement was made in full.'

"They then published a table, which was furnished by the Stock Clearing Corporation, showing that in those four months—from the 1st of May to August 31st—the value of the securities delivered was $2,171,000,000, and the actual amount of checks used to settle that was $872,595,000, or an obviation of check clearing or certification of $1,298,000,000, which made a saving of 153,865 checks that otherwise would have had to be drawn and certified if the Stock Clearing Corporation were not in existence.

"Those were four months of inactive stock markets. Taking the two months of November and December, 1920, which were active, the Stock Clearing Corporation saved in those two months $894,569,000 of certification and a saving of 128,457 checks, against $1,298,000,000 and 153,865 checks in four months; and this saving in certification and in the number of checks cleared was accomplished without the clearing of loans (which started March 22, 1921) which in actual volume of saving of demands on the banks when in full operation, will equal about as much again." (S. F. Streit, "Function of the Stock Clearing Corporation," Acceptance Bulletin, May 1921, p. 10.)

CHAPTER XII

(a) "That the taking or carrying of a speculative account, or the making of a speculative transaction in which a clerk of the Exchange, or of a member of the Exchange, or of a bank, trust company, banker, insurance company, or of a broker dealing in stocks, bonds, or other securities, is directly or indirectly interested, unless the written consent of the employer has been first obtained, shall be deemed an act detrimental to the interest and welfare of the Exchange." (Constitution, p. 88.)

(b) The New York State Law covering the point reads as follows:

"The people of the State of New York, represented in senate and assembly, do enact as follows:

"Section 1. Article 86 of Chapter 88 of the laws of 1909, entitled 'An act providing for the punishment of crime' constituting chapter 40 of the consolidated laws is hereby amended by adding at the end thereof a new section, to be section 957, to read as follows:

"'Section 957. *Delivery to customers of memoranda of transactions by brokers*—A person engaged in the business of purchasing or selling as brokers stocks, bonds, and other evidences of debt of corporations, companies, or associations shall deliver to each customer on whose behalf a purchase or sale of such securities is made by him a statement or memorandum of such purchase or sale, a description of the securities purchased or sold, the name of the person, firm, or corporation from whom such securities were purchased or to which the same were sold, and the day, and the hours between which the transaction took place. A broker who refuses to deliver such statement or memorandum to a customer within 24 hours after a written demand therefor, or who delivers a statement or memorandum which is false in any material respect, is guilty of a misdemeanor, punishable by a fine of not more than $500, or imprisonment for not more than one year, or both.'" (Regulation of the Stock Exchange, p. 714.)

For many years previous to the passage of the above law, it was customary for Stock Exchange houses to report on their "confirmations" the names of the other firms or members from whom or to whom their purchases and sales were made.

(c) Commissions charged on transactions effected on the Exchange by its members are subject to the following regulations in the Constitution of the Exchange:

Article XXXIV

Commissions

"Sec. 2. Commissions shall be calculated on the basis hereinafter specified:

"(a) *On railroad, public utility, industrial, and all other bonds not herein specifically provided for, having more than five years to run:*

"(a1) On business for parties not members of the Exchange, including joint account transactions in which a non-member is interested; transactions for partners not members of the Exchange;

and for firms of which the Exchange member or members are special partners only,—the commission shall be not less than $1.50 per $1,000 par value.

"(a2) On business for members of the Exchange when a principal is given up the commission shall be not less than 37½c per $1,000 par value.

"(a3) On business for members of the Exchange when a principal is not given up the commission shall be not less than 50c per $1,000 par value.

"(b) *On securities of the United States, Porto Rico and the Philippine Islands, and of States, Territories and Municipalities therein:**

"(b1) On business for parties not members of the Exchange, including joint account transactions in which a non-member is interested; transactions for partners not members of the Exchange; and for firms of which the Exchange member or members are special partners only, the commission shall be not less than 62½c per $1,000 par value.

"(b2) On business for members of the Exchange when a principal is given up the commission shall be not less than 20c per $1,000 par value.

"(b3) On business for members of the Exchange when a principal is not given up the commission shall be not less than 31¼c per $1,000 par value.

"(c) *On stocks:*

"(c1) On business for parties not members of the Exchange, including joint account transactions in which a non-member is interested; transactions for partners not members of the Exchange; and for firms of which the Exchange member or members are special partners only, the commission shall be not less than the following:

On stocks selling below $10 per share............7½c per share
On stocks selling at $10 per share and above, but
under $125 per share..........................15c per share
On stocks selling at $125 per share and over........20c per share

provided, however, that the minimum commission on an individual transaction shall be not less than one dollar.

---

* Ruling Committee on Quotations and Commissions, September 22, 1920—above commission applies to Victory Liberty Loans 3¾ and 4¾ per cent Notes, due 1922–1923.

"(c2) On business for members of the Exchange when a principal is given up the commission shall be not less than the following:

On stocks selling below $10 per share............1¼c per share
On stocks selling at $10 per share and above, but
under $125 per share.......................2½c per share
On stocks selling at $125 per share and over........3c per share

Except that when the amount dealt in is less than 100 shares, the commission shall be not less than:

On stocks selling below $10 per share..............1c per share
On stocks selling at $10 per share and over..........2c per share

"(c3) On business for members of the Exchange when a principal is not given up the commission shall be not less than the following:

On stocks selling below $10 per share............1¾c per share
On stocks selling at $10 per share and above, but
under $125 per share.......................3¾c per share
On stocks selling at $125 per share and over........5c per share

"(d) In transactions where orders are received from a non-member, wherein the broker filling the order is directed to give up another broker or clearing house, the responsibility of collecting the full commission, as specified in Sub-divisions (a1), (b1) and (c1), hereof, shall rest with the broker or clearing house settling the transaction.

"(e) In transactions where orders are received from a member, on which a clearing firm is given up by said member or by his order, the responsibility of collecting the full commission, as specified in Sub-divisions (a3), (b3) and (c3), hereof, shall rest with said clearing firm; and it shall be the duty of the broker who executes such orders to report such transactions to the clearing firm and render to them and collect his bill therefor at the rate specified in Sub-divisions (a2), (b2) and (c2), hereof; and also that where a broker executes an order for a member and clears the security himself, he must charge the rates specified in Sub-divisions (a3), (b3) and (c3), hereof.

"(f) Whenever a non-member of this Exchange shall cause to be executed in any market outside of the United States any order or orders, for the purchase or sale of securities listed on this Exchange (except as provided in Sub-division (h) hereof), and said purchase or sale shall be accepted by a member or firm who are members of this Exchange, for the account of said non-member, the commission as specified in Sub-divisions (a1), (b1) and (c1), hereof, shall be charged said non-member in addition to any commission charged by the party or parties making the transaction.

"(g) When securities are received or delivered on a privilege for a non-member, the commission as specified in Sub-divisions (a1), (b1) and (c1), hereof, must be charged whether said securities are received or delivered upon the day of expiration of said privilege or prior thereto.

"(h) On Subscription Rights;* Bonds or Notes of Foreign Countries having five years or less to run; Notes of Corporations having five years or less to run; Bonds having five years or less to run; such rates to members or non-members as may be mutually agreed upon; provided, however, that the Committee on Quotations and Commissions with the approval of the Governing Committee may hereafter determine special rates on any or all of the abovementioned securities."

(d) "That any agreement or arrangement entered into between a member or his firm, and his or their customer, whereby special and unusual rates of interest are stipulated for, or money-advances upon unusual terms are made a condition, in connection with the conducting of an account, with intent to give special or unusual advantages to such customer, for the purposes of securing business, shall be deemed to be a violation of Article XXXIV, of the Constitution, commonly known as the Commission Law," (Constitution, pp. 92-93.)

(e) "There is a tendency on the part of the public to consider Wall Street and the New York Stock Exchange as one and the same thing. This is an error arising from their location. We have taken pains to ascertain what proportion of the business transacted on the Exchange is furnished by New York City. The only reliable sources of information are the books of the commission houses. An investigation was made of the transactions on the Exchange for a given day, when the sales were 1,500,000 shares. The returns showed that on

* See also Resolution of Governing Committee, June 8, 1921, as to commission on **rights**.

that day 52 per cent of the total transactions on the Exchange apparently originated in New York City, and 48 per cent in other localities." (Hughes Report, 1909.)

CHAPTER XIII

(a) "Membership in the Exchange is an asset of large value. The price of seats varies, like the price of stocks, although not so volatile. The price is, however, a fair indication of the activity of the stock market in any given year. There are a few old members who joined as far back as the sixties, who paid only $500 for their seats. In 1871 seats were sold as low as $2,750. In the boom year of 1882 the price reached $32,500. Two years later, in the panic, the price fell to $20,000. The next year, however, it reached $34,000, and this remained the highest price for many years. In the panic of 1893 memberships were quoted at $15,250, and in 1896 as low as $14,000. Thereafter, there was a rapid advance, until in the last week of 1901, sales were made at $80,000. At this price the total value of Stock Exchange seats amounted to $88,000,000. In 1902 the price fell to $60,000, and later advanced to $70,000. In 1909 seats sold as high as $96,000, and in January, 1920, to a new high of $115,000. In 1913 they sold down to $37,000. To the price of the seat must be added the initiation fee. The number of membership transfers varies from 40 to 100 a year." (Pratt, p. 139.)

(b) Concerning the legal bearing of an expulsion of a member from the Exchange, John G. Milburn, counsel for the New York Stock Exchange, testified before the Committee on Banking and Currency of the United States Senate as follows:

"What then is the remedy of the member who has been tried and expelled? He may bring a suit in court, claiming that he has been illegally expelled. He can have all the proceedings before the board of governors produced in court. . . .

"On the trial of his suit there is produced in court all the proceedings before the board of governors, including the testimony taken and any documentary evidence, and the settled law is that to sustain the action of the governers it must appear, first, that the written charges alleged a specific violation of a rule; second, that the member had a hearing; third, that there was evidence to sustain the determination of the board of governors; and fourth, that the board of governors acted in good faith. These are the requirements formulated in numerous decisions of the courts, including the highest court of the State. If it were found that any one of these requirements had not been observed, the expulsion would be held to be illegal and a restoration to membership would follow. . . .

"There have been numerous cases of this kind during all the years past, and the board of governors has been sustained in every case. That is a very remarkable record of ability, fairplay and justice." (Regulation of the Stock Exchange, p. 350.)

(c) The single instance where the action of the Governing Committee has been in any important degree modified by the courts occurred in 1882 in the Hutchinson case. At that time seats on the Stock Exchange were nothing like as valuable as today, being worth only a few thousand dollars, and their status as a property right was not legally established. In consequence, when the Governing Committee expelled Hutchinson from the Stock Exchange his seat was declared confiscated by way of fine. But the courts, although completely upholding the main action of expulsion, declared that a Stock Exchange seat constituted a property right, and therefore upon its owner's expulsion from the Exchange did not escheat to the Exchange.

(d) "We have been strongly urged to recommend that the Exchange be incorporated in order to bring it more completely under the authority and supervision of the State and the process of the courts. Under existing conditions, being a voluntary organization, it has almost unlimited power over the conduct of its members, and it can subject them to instant discipline for wrongdoing, which it could not exercise in a summary manner if it were an incorporated body. We think that such power residing in a properly chosen committee is distinctly advantageous. The submission of such questions to the courts would involve delays and technical obstacles which would impair discipline without securing any greater amount of substantial justice. While this committee is not exactly in accord on this point, no member is yet prepared to advocate the incorporation of the Exchange and a majority of us advise against it, upon the ground that the advantages to be gained by incorporation may be accomplished by rules of the Exchange and by statutes aimed directly at the evils which need correction." (Hughes Report [see Van Antwerp, p. 427].)

CHAPTER XV

(a) Many people mistakenly attempt to differentiate between speculation and gambling by stating that speculation is the result of careful study and intelligent judgment, while gambling proceeds from a careless and unintelligent taking of risks. But a moment's reflection will show that this distinction is a fallacy. For according to this view, a man who bet $100 on a given prize-fighter, after a careful and thorough study of him and his prospective opponent, would be a speculator. On the other hand, one would be compelled to classify as gamblers the millions of Americans who in 1918 purchased Liberty bonds, either outright or on credit, without investigating the taxing resources of the United States government. Both such instances are, of course, absurd, and thus the degree of thought employed before risks are taken cannot distinguish the two processes. The fact is that both successful poker-players and successful stock speculators usually study the quite different risks which they assume, while both unsuccessful gamblers and unsuccessful speculators are usually those who have not. But success or lack of success cannot constitute the difference between speculation and gambling.

A similar confusion of thought has sometimes led the courts to declare that the distinguishing mark between the two lay in the intent of the individual, entirely apart from whether commodities were or were not purchased or sold. Such a construction of the matter is even more absurd from the economic standpoint. A man may think a calf is a horse, but that does not make it one. Similarly, a man in a bucket-shop, might think he was speculating, but his intent would not save him from being unknowingly but none the less definitely a gambler. For the bucket-shop keeper would pretend to execute his orders, when he really had not executed them at all. Conversely, a man might, through misunderstanding, quite honestly think he was gambling when he purchased stock on margin, but even his intention to gamble would not make the transaction a gambling wager at all but a speculation, if the stock was honestly purchased for him by his broker. In other words, the true economic distinction between speculation and gambling lies in the objective act of purchasing or selling property on the one hand, or simply placing a wager on the other. Whatever the customer may or may not think about the matter is utterly immaterial. As a matter of fact, few individuals are able to define the difference between speculation and gambling: Since this is so, of what significance is their "intent," to do the one or the other? Thus, arguing about speculation and gambling from the standpoint of intent signifies an ignorance of the real economic value of both processes, and results in obscuring with cloudy legal metaphysics the perfectly simple economic test of whether or not property was bought or sold.

Still another source of mental confusion regarding gambling and speculation arises from a complete misunderstanding of the methods employed in clearing transactions in the organized exchanges. Some critics of the Stock Exchange, indeed, make the specious claim that transactions there in which the trader purchases and sells the same day are gambling, because, forsooth, he does not actually receive or deliver the stock certificates thus bought and sold.

Let us examine this claim in the light of what the Stock Clearing Corporation actually does. It will be remembered that instead of exchanging securities and money at the post when a sale is made, a contract is made calling for the delivery of the security and the payment of money in the future. Mechanically, it would be impossible to settle such contracts immediately, nor would it be desirable even if it were possible. Therefore the Exchange has established a daily settlement, and ruled that all such contracts must be settled by 2:15 on the next full business day. The speed with which settlement follows the making of exchange contracts varies widely in different Stock Exchanges; contrasting with the daily settlement on the New York Stock Exchange is the fortnightly settlement on the London Stock Exchange. Nevertheless, all contracts are made the same way on the floor of the former exchange, call for the assumption of the same risk on the part of buyers and of sellers, and are all equally enforceable.

A trader in the New York Stock Exchange may make a contract to buy stock at 11 A.M., and another contract to sell it again, either at a loss or a profit, at 2 P.M. In such a case the Stock Clearing Corporation would settle this intermediate contract for him, without compelling him to waste time, labor, and the use of banking accommodation in receiving and delivering the stock himself. But far from relieving him from the need of complying with his contracts, the Stock Clearing Corporation really acts as an agent to enforce the settlement of such contracts.

If on the other hand, the same trader buys stock on Monday and sells it again Wednesday, he must receive it Tuesday, since in this case his transaction is slower than the clearance system. But shall we say that the first example is gambling simply because physical delivery is obviated owing to the transaction's being completed more swiftly than the settlement system? If the trader buys a stock Monday at 11 o'clock, will he be a gambler if he sells it again at 2 P.M. the same day, and a speculator if he waits until Wednesday to sell it? Or would he be a gambler if he bought and sold in London, under the fortnightly settlement system, at an interval of a week apart? Such insinuations against intermediate contracts settled by the Stock Clearing Corporation simply show a lack of knowledge regarding the clearance systems of modern organized markets. It would be equally unfair and inaccurate to assert that when bank A owed bank B $10,000 and bank B owed bank A $5,000, and when through the bank clearing house A settled with B by a single check for $5,000, that bank A was not honoring its checks because it owed $10,000 and only paid out $5,000!

(b) Professor H. C. Emery, probably the greatest living American authority upon the economics of speculation, defines speculation, etc., in the following terms:

"In the first place, it is well to recognize what we mean by speculation. The simplest definition is that speculation consists in buying and selling commodities or securities with an idea of making profits out of fluctuating values. Why do such fluctuations occur? Simply because the conditions of supply and demand are always changing. It is the exception rather than the rule for any article of commerce or any piece of property to maintain a perfectly stable price. Since the demand of society is constantly changing, values must constantly fluctuate, and, as long as values fluctuate, speculation must take place. It is not conceivable that, in a system of buying and selling such as we have, values could go up and down without somebody being benefited or injured, or without men consciously attempting to secure the benefit or avoid the injury by their purchases and sales. Speculation has always existed wherever buying and selling has existed—ever since the days when Joseph cornered the grain supply of Egypt as reported in the book of Genesis. As long as private ownership of property is allowed and the value of property varies, speculation will continue. . . .

"Some people speak as if all dealing in securities should be of a pure investment nature. They fail to realize, however, that investments themselves become speculative in proportion as speculation pure and simple is abolished. Investment means primarily the purchase of income-yielding property in order to get an annual income, rather than to make profits from the fluctuations in capital value; but since capital value does fluctuate, investment involves the risk of loss, and . . . this risk of loss to the conservative investor is made very much less when he has an active speculative market for the disposal of his property.

"Still another distinction that must be made is that between speculation and gambling. In the broadest sense, of course, there is a gambling element, not only in all bets, but in all our activities. If gambling means simply the taking of unreasonable risks, almost every act of our lives might be accused of having a gambling element by those whose opinions as to what risks are worth while differed from ours. . . . Every transaction of buying and selling necessarily involves a risk. Betting on merely incidental results of particular contests is the assumption of a risk which did not exist before the bet was made. It would seem as if a fair distinction of this kind might be made, speculation being defined as the assumption of inevitable business risks of fluctuating values; gambling as the assumption of purely artificial risks in connection with some fortuitous events." (Prof. H. C. Emery, "Should Speculation be Regulated by Law," Regulation of the Stock Exchange, pp. 830-832.)

(c) Probably the most famous investment security in the world is the British consol. Certainly, before the war there was no security which apparently possessed less speculative features. Yet even in this case a constant element of risk, and hence of speculative possibilities, existed. Mr. Van Antwerp (p. 45) writing in 1913 before the World War could be foreseen by even the wisest British or American financiers, pointed out this fact:

"British Consols are low today, and there is, of course, no safer investment, but the investor who buys them is influenced by the fact that a long period of peace seems ahead, with reduced expenditures for armament, and hence with diminished borrowings by the Government leading to a substantial recovery in the price of these solid securities. Such a man is 'speculating' on England's abstention from war, on its limitation of military and naval expenditures, and on the probable effect of these matters on Consols."

In the period from 1903 to 1912, consols had not sold lower than 72½. Yet the investor in them at this figure was assuming no slight speculative risk, as Mr. Van Antwerp very keenly stated. In the year 1921, British consols sold around 48, thus showing a 33 per cent shrinkage in price since 1912. This instance vividly illustrates the inseparable union existing between investment and speculation.

(d) "In the spring of 1920, when grain and cotton were being withheld at their sources, partly for speculation and partly owing to inadequate transportation, the out-of-town banks showed double the increase in loans, compared with New York during the year preceding.

800 Reporting Banks	April 9, 1920	May 9, 1919	Per Cent Increase
New York City........	$4,781,000,000	$4,146,000,000	15.3
Rest of Country........	9,445,700,000	7,296,000,000	29.4
Federal Reserve Banks:			
New York City........	932,000,000	806,000,000	15.6
Rest of Country........	1,896,000,000	1,344,000,000	41.1

(Pratt, pp. 316-317.)

(e) "In November, 1919, when the 73 New York City banks reporting had $557,000,000 of loans, and the district's reserve was down to 40, as against 46.8 for the whole system, prompt liquidation of speculative accounts within the next few months reduced loans to $357,000,000 or by $200,000,000. Yet during the 15 months from the Armistice of November 11, 1918, to March, 1920, the rest of the country had expanded its loans by the colossal sum of $5,200,000,000. The whole country was speculating unduly on inflated credits, in which Wall Street, as shown by its stationary loans, had for the later months especially taken little part." (Pratt, p. 297.)

(f) The antecedent part played by liquidation of securities upon the Stock Exchange in a general period of liquidation was stated forcefully by Governor Benjamin Strong of the New York Federal Reserve Bank, in his statement and testimony before the Agricultural Inquiry Commission [(p. 629); see "Bibliography" under "Strong"], as follows: "I wish to call the commission's attention to the important fact . . . that the peak, in volume, of loans on the New York Stock Exchange was in the first part of November, 1919. . . . From that point it is almost a precipitate decline down to the present time, whereas the volume of all loans by all reporting banks during that period increased, and did not reach their peak until October or November of 1920, nearly a year later. If any inferences are justified from this chart [cf. p. 626], they would be, I think, two: one that, as is commonly regarded to be the case, financial markets anticipate movements more promptly than other markets, and, second, that the liquidation in the New York stock market started a year earlier than the liquidation throughout the country; and the effect of it was actually to release credit for purposes such as agricultural and industrial and commercial uses. [See also charts on pp. 644 and 645 and statistics on pp. 646 and 647.]"

(g) "Both the writer and the reformer must reckon more than they have yet done with the fact that speculation in the last half century has developed as a natural economic institution in response to the new conditions of industry and commerce. It is the result of steam transportation and the telegraph on the one hand, and of vast industrial undertakings on the other. The attitude of those who would try to crush it out by legislation, without disturbing any other economic conditions, is entirely unreasonable." (H. C. Emery, Speculation on the Stock and Produce Exchanges of the United States, New York, 1896.)

CHAPTER XVI

(a) "A Committee on Stock List to consist of five members. It shall receive and consider all applications for placing securities upon the list of the Exchange, and make report and recommendation thereon to the Governing Committee, giving full statement concerning organization, capitalization, resources and indebtedness.

"It shall have power to place upon the list, without report and recommendation to the Governing Committee, any obligations of the Government of the United States or of any State or City thereof, or of any foreign State or City, also temporary receipts issued by any corporation or firm for part or full payment of subscription to bonds, stocks and other obligations; and it shall have power to direct that any such securities or temporary receipts be taken from the list, and further dealings therein prohibited.

"It shall have charge of the arrangement and revision of the list of securities." (Constitution, Art. XI, Sec. I, II,)

(b) Requirements for Original Listing
Stock

For form of certificates eligible to be listed under this classification, and list of papers to be furnished, see pages, 4, 6, 7 and 8.

Every application for an original listing of capital stock shall recite:

A Title of corporation.

B (1) State authorizing incorporation; (2) (a) date, (b) duration, (c) rights.

C (1) Business; (2) special rights or privileges granted directors by charter or by-laws.

D (1) Whether capital stock is full paid; (2) non-assessable; and (3) liability attaching to shareholders.

E (1) Issues (by classes), dividend rate and par value; (2) total amount of each, authorized and issued; (3) increases and authority therefor, including (*a*) action by stockholders, (*b*) by directors and (*c*) by public authorities, etc.; (4) amount unissued, (*a*) options or contracts on same, (*b*) specific reservation for conversion.

F If preferred stock; (1) whether cumulative or non-cumulative; (2) preferences, including (*a*) voting power; (b) dividends; (*c*) distribution of assets on dissolution or merger; (*d*) redemption; (*e*) convertibility.

G Voting power of obligations of debt.

H (1) Purpose of issue; (2) application of proceeds; (3) amount issued for securities, contracts, property; description and disposition; (4) additional property to be acquired, with particulars, as required by paragraph *M*.

I (1) History of corporation; (2) of predecessor companies, or firms, with location and stock issues; (*b*) conditions leading to new organization.

J Tabulated list of constituent, subsidiary, owned or controlled companies showing (*a*) date of organization; (*b*) where incorporated; (*c*) duration of charter; (*d*) business and (*e*) capital stock issues (by classes), par value, amount authorized, issued, owned by parent company.

K (1) Mortgage, and (2) other indebtedness, (*a*) date, (*b*) maturity, (*c*) interest rate, (*d*) redemption by sinking fund or otherwise, (*e*) amount authorized, and (*f*) amount issued; (3) similar information regarding mortgage and all indebtedness of constituent, subsidiary, owned, or controlled companies.

L Other liabilities, joint and several, (1) guaranties, (2) leases, (3) traffic agreements, (4) trackage agreements, (5) rentals, (6) car trusts, etc., (7) similar description of other easements; (8) terms of each, and provision for payment; (9) similar information as to constituent, subsidiary, owned or controlled companies.

M (1) Description, location, nature and acreage of property, (*a*) owned in fee; (*b*) controlled; (*c*) leased; (2) railroads, mileage completed, operated and contemplated; (3) equipment; (4) character of buildings and construction; (5) tabulated list of franchises showing (*a*) where granted, (*b*) date, (*c*) duration, (*d*) purpose; (6) timber, fuel or mining lands, water rights; (7) similar information as to constituent, subsidiary, owned or controlled companies.

N Policy as to depreciation.

O (1) Character and amount of annual output for preceding five years; (2) estimated output (character and amount) for current year; (3) number of employees.

P (1) Dividends paid; (2) by predecessor, and constituent, subsidiary, owned or controlled companies.

Q Financial statements; (1) earnings for preceding five years, if available; (2) income account of recent date for at least one year, if available; (3) balance sheet of same date; (4) similar accountings for predecessor, constituent, subsidiary, owned or controlled companies; (5) corporations consolidated within one year previous to date of application, income account and balance sheet of all companies merged and balance sheet of applying corporation; (6) if in hands of receiver within one year previous to date of application, (*a*) income account and balance sheet of receiver at time of discharge, and (*b*) balance sheet of company at close of receivership.

R Agreements contained on page 5.

S Fiscal year.

T Names of (1) officers; (2) directors (classified) with addresses; (3) transfer agents and (4) registrars, with addresses.

U Location of principal and other offices of corporation.

V Place and date of annual meeting.

In addition to the above, applications from corporations which own or operate mines must recite:

A Patented and unpatented claims, by numbers.

B (1) Geological description of country; (2) location and description of mineral and other lands; (3) ore bodies; (4) average value of ore; (5) character; and (6) methods of treatment.

C History of workings, (1) results obtained; (2) production each year.

D (1) Ore reserves compared with previous years showing separately as to character and metal content; (2) estimate of engineer as to probable life of mines; (3) probabilities by further exploration.

E (1) Provisions for smelting and concentration; (2) cost of (*a*) mining, (*b*) milling and smelting, (*c*) transportation; and (3) proximity of property to railway or other common carrier.

F Properties in process of development; income account if available, guaranties for working capital and for completion of development.

G Total expenditures for preceding five years for acquisition of new property, development, proportion charged to operations each year.

H (1) Policy as to depletion; (2) acquisition of new property; (3) new construction and development.

I Annual reports for preceding five years, showing number of tons of ore treated, average assay, yield, percentage of extraction, recovery per ton of ore.

In addition to the above, applications from corporations which own or operate oil and gas wells must recite:

A (1) Brief history of oil fields; (2) character and gravity of oil.

B (1) Total area of oil land (developed and undeveloped), (*a*) owned, (*b*) leased, (*c*) controlled, (*d*) proven, (*e*) under exploitation, (*f*) royalties.

C (1) Number of wells (oil or gas) on each property, (*a*) in operation, (*b*) drilling, (*c*) contemplated; (2) average depth of wells drilled (*a*) shallowest, (*b*) deepest, (*c*) probable life; (3) whether oil sands are dipping.

D (1) Gross daily production—initial and present; (2) annual gross production from each property for past five years, if available; (3) estimated output for current year.

E (1) Storage, capacity and location; (2) (*a*) amount of oil stored, (*b*) character, (*c*) value; (3) pipe line, (*a*) gauge, (*b*) capacity, (*c*) mileage.

F (1) Refineries, (*a*) capacity, (*b*) acreage, (*c*) employees, (*d*) products and by-products.

G Properties in process of development, income account if available, guaranties for working capital and for completion of development.

H Total expenditures for preceding five years for acquisition of new property, well drilling and development, proportion charged to operations each year.

I (1) Policy as to depletion; (2) acquisition; and (3) development of new properties.

(*Note: For requirements as to voting trust or stock trust certificates, or certificates of deposit, see Page* 3.)

Bonds

For form of securities eligible to be listed under this classification, and for list of papers to be furnished, see pages 4, 6, 7.

An application for an original listing of bonds shall recite all information required for listing stock, *and*

A (1) Amount, denominations and numbers; (2) full title; (3) amount authorized and outstanding, authority therefor, including (*a*) action by stockholders, (*b*) directors, and (*c*) public authorities, etc.; (4) whether bonds are coupon (registerable as to principal) or registered, interchangeable or exchangeable; (5) exchangeability or convertibility into other securities, and terms.

B Names and addresses of trustees.

C (1) Date of issue and maturity; (2) interest rate; (3) places at, and dates for payment of interest and principal; (4) where registerable or transferable; (5) kind and standard of money, and options; (6) tax exemption; (7) whether redeemable or purchasable in whole or part, showing (*a*) dates, (*b*) price, (*c*) duration of published notice.

D Provisions for declaration of principal due and payable in event of default of payment of interest, or other defaults, and waiver; percentage of outstanding bonds controlling trustee.

E Purpose of issue and application of proceeds, similar to that called for by Paragraph *H* of the Requirements for Listing Stock; provisions as to additional issue.

F Disposition of bonds refunded, redeemed or purchased for sinking fund, and mortgage securing same.

G Mortgage or indenture provisions for (1) serial issues; (2) values in United States gold coin; (3) issuance in foreign languages and (4) that the English version governs; (5) terms of exchangeability of bonds payable in foreign places for bonds payable in United States or vice versa.

H (1) Security—Mortgage, indenture of trust, or other agreement; and, (2) liens; (*a*) properties covered, (*b*) mileage of railway lines, (*c*) buildings, (*d*) equipment, (*e*) securities, (*f*) rights, (*g*) privileges, (*h*) titles, (*i*) franchises, (*j*) leases, etc.; (3) other liens covering same or any part of same properties, (4) guaranty and terms.

I Any unusual additions or limitations.

Requirements for Listing of Additional Amounts

For list of papers to be furnished, see page 4.

Refer to previous applications and last application by number and date; and recite:

A Title of corporation and name of State authorizing incorporation.

B (1) Securities applied for; (2) amounts authorized; (3) authority for issue, including (*a*) action by stockholders, (*b*) by directors and (*c*) by public authorities, etc.

C (1) Purposes of issue; (2) application of proceeds; (3) amount, description and disposition of securities exchanged for new issues; (4) additional property acquired or to be acquired, with particulars as required by paragraph *M* of the Requirements for Listing Stock.

D (1) Dividends; (2) also by constituent, subsidiary, owned or controlled companies, since previous application.

E Changes, if any, in (1) charter, (2) by-laws, or (3) capitalization.

F Details as to property acquired and property disposed of, since last application.

G (1) Character and amount of output since last application; (2) estimated output (character and amount) for current year; (3) number of employees.

H Income account and balance sheet of recent date, also for constituent, subsidiary owned, or controlled companies, or a consolidated income account and a consolidated balance sheet.

I Names of officials, location of offices, place and date of annual meeting, fiscal year, as covered by Paragraphs *S,T,U,V*, of Requirements for Listing Stock.

(*Note*: *"When a corporation purposes to increase its authorized capital stock, thirty days' notice of such proposed increase must be officially given to the Exchange, before such increase may be admitted to dealings."*)

(*Note*: *"When the capital stock of a corporation is increased through conversion of convertible bonds already listed, the issuing corporation shall give immediate notice to the Exchange and the Committee on Stock List may, thereupon, authorize the registration of such shares and add them to the list."*)

Requirements for Listing of Certificates of Deposit, Voting Trust or Stock Trust Certificates, Etc.

For form of certificates eligible to be listed under this classification, and for list of papers to be furnished, see pages 4,6,7 and 8.

Every application for the listing of certificates of deposit, voting trust or stock trust certificates, etc., shall recite:

A (1) Name of applicant; (2) amount applied for; (3) additional amounts to be listed; (4) depositary, (5) security deposited; (6) whether listed; (7) registrar.

Applications for each class of deposited securities shall be separate and certificates issued of distinctive colors.

B (1) Date of agreement; (2) names of committee, or voting trustees; (3) terms of trust; (4) powers and duties of committee, trustees, or depositary.

C Reasons for deposit.

D (1) Duration of trust or deposit; (2) extensions or limitations; (3) final date of deposits; (4) provision for deposits without penalty for approximately thirty days after listing, or if no time limit for deposit of securities without penalty, is fixed, an agreement that approximately thirty days' notice of such limitation of time shall be published and given to the Stock Exchange; (5) date of presentation of plan; (6) provisions for dissent and withdrawal; (7) percentage necessary to adoption; (8) pro rata charges; (9) provisions for return of securities (or equivalent); (10) provision for payment of interest, dividends, etc.

E Agreement to deliver definitive securities at termination of Voting Trust or Voting Trust to be extended.

F Agreement to have definitive securities listed.

(*Note*: *Applications to list voting trust or stock trust certificates and certificates of deposit for securities not a delivery on the Stock Exchange, must, in addition, comply with the Requirements for Listing Stock.*)

Papers to be Filed with Applications

In addition to application for listing, the following papers must be filed:

For Stocks:

1 Ten copies of charter, with amendments to date, one copy attested by proper public authority.

2 Ten copies of by-laws, with amendments to date, one copy attested by an executive officer of corporation.

3 Ten copies of leases, franchises, easements and special agreements, one copy of each attested by an executive officer of corporation.

4 One copy of resolutions of stockholders and directors and copy of proper public authority authorizing issue, each attested by an executive officer of corporation.

5 One copy of resolutions of stockholders or directors, and copy of proper public authority, authorizing issue of stock on conversion for other securities, attested by an executive officer of corporation.

6 One copy of resolutions of stockholders or directors directing specific reservation of authorized stock for conversion, attested by an executive officer of corporation.

7 One copy of resolutions of stockholders, board of directors or executive committee, attested by an executive officer of corporation, authorizing, by name, official to appear for listing securities (form may be had on application).

8 Opinion of counsel (not an officer or director of the corporation) as to legality of (*a*) organization, (*b*) authorization, (*c*) issue, and (*d*) validity of securities. *The Committee will not accept the opinion of an officer or director of an applying corporation nor of a firm in which the officer or director is a member, as counsel on any legal question affecting the corporation; nor will it accept the opinion of an officer or director of a guarantor corporation, nor of a firm in*

which the officer or director is a member, on any legal question affecting the issuance of guaranteed securities.

9 Detailed distribution of securities and five copies (form may be had on application).

10 One copy of resolution appointing transfer agent and registrar, attested by an executive officer of corporation.

11 Certificate of registrar of amount of securities registered at date of application.

12 Report of qualified engineer covering actual physical condition of property at recent date.

13 Map of property and contemplated extensions.

14 Specimens of all securities to be listed.

15 Questionnaire.

For Bonds:

16 All papers required for listing stocks and also ten copies of the mortgage or indenture, one copy (*a*) certified to by trustee, (*b*) with copies of all certificates of proper recording.

17 Trustees' certificate required on Page 6.

18 One copy of resolutions of stockholders or directors, and copy of proper public authority, authorizing issue of stock in conversion of bonds, attested by an executive officer of corporation.

19 One copy of resolution of stockholders or directors directing specific reservation of authorized stock for conversion, attested by an executive officer of corporation.

20 Certificate of disposition of securities redeemed or refunded.

21 Certificate as to collateral deposited.

22 Certified copy of release or satisfaction of underlying mortgages.

For Securities of Reorganized Corporations:

1 All papers required above for listing stocks and bonds. *Opinion of counsel shall state that proceedings have been in conformity with legal requirements, that title to property is vested in new corporation and is free and clear from all liens and incumbrances, except as distinctly specified; and also as to equities of securities of predecessor corporation.*

2 Certified order of court confirming sale on foreclosure or other authority for reorganization.

3 Certified copy of plan of reorganization.

4 Income account; balance sheet at close of receivership, if available.

5 Balance sheet at date of organization.

For additional amounts:

1 Nos. 4, 5, 6, 7, 8, 9, 11, of papers required for original listings.

2 Nos. 1, 2, 3, 10, 12, of said papers for stock, *if any changes have occurred therein since last listing.*

3 Nos. 15, 16, 17, 18, 19, 20, 21, of said papers for bonds, *if any changes have occurred therein since last listing.*

4 Certified copy of proper public authority for increase.

For Certificates of Deposit, Voting Trust, etc.:

1 Papers required above for listing stocks or bonds.

2 Certified copies of any legal proceedings and court orders.

3 Ten copies of deposit or trust agreement, one certified to by proper authority.

4 Ten copies of circulars, issued by trustees or committee, one certified to by proper authority.

5 Amounts deposited.

6 Detailed distribution (form may be had on application).

Agreements

To be made part of all applications:

1 Not to dispose of its stock interest in any constituent, subsidiary, owned or controlled company, to allow any of said constituent, subsidiary, owned or controlled companies to dispose of stock interests in other companies unless for retirement and cancellation, except under existing authority or on direct authorization of stockholders of the company holding the said companies.

2 To publish at least once in each year and submit to the stockholders, at least fifteen days in advance of the annual meeting of the corporation, a statement of its physical and financial condition, an income account covering the previous fiscal year, and a balance sheet showing assets and liabilities at the end of the year; also annually an income account and balance sheet of all constituent, subsidiary, owned or controlled companies; or a consolidated income account and a consolidated balance sheet.

3 To maintain, in accordance with the rules of the Stock Exchange, a transfer office or agency in the Borough of Manhattan,

City of New York, where all listed securities shall be directly transferable, and the principal of all listed securities with interest or dividends thereon shall be payable; also a registry office in the Borough of Manhattan, City of New York, other than its transfer office or agency in said city, where all listed securities shall be registered.

4 Not to make any change in listed securities, of a transfer agency or of a registrar of its stock, or of a trustee of its bonds or other securities, without the approval of the Committee on Stock List, and not to select as a trustee an officer or director of the company.

5 To notify the Stock Exchange in the event of the issuance of any rights or subscriptions to or allotments of its securities and afford the holders of listed securities a proper period within which to record their interests after authorization, and that all rights, subscriptions or allotments shall be transferable, payable and deliverable in the Borough of Manhattan, City of New York.

6 To notify the Stock Exchange of the issuance of additional amounts of listed securities, and make immediate application for the listing thereof.

7 To publish promptly to holders of bonds and stocks any action in respect to interest on bonds, dividends on shares, or allotment of rights for subscription to securities, notices thereof to be sent to the Stock Exchange, and to give to the Stock Exchange at least ten days' notice in advance of the closing of the transfer books or extensions, or the taking of a record of holders for any purpose.

8 To redeem preferred stock in accordance with the requirements of the Stock Exchange.

9 To notify the Stock Exchange if deposited collateral is changed or removed.

10 To have on hand at all times a sufficient supply of certificates to meet the demands for transfer.

The Committee recommends a date be fixed as record for dividends, allotment of rights and stockholders' meetings, without closing the transfer books.

Notice of rights, allotments, subscription privileges, etc., to bondholders and shareholders, should be as of a date after authorization.

Forms for warrants may be had on application.

Trustees of Mortgages

The Committee recommends that a trust company or other financial corporation be appointed trustee of mortgages, indentures, and deeds of trust; and when a State law requires the appointment of an individual as trustee, a trust company or other financial corporation be appointed as co-trustee.

Each mortgage, indenture, or deed of trust should be represented by a separate trustee.

The Committee will not accept as trustee:

(*a*) An officer or director of the issuing corporation;

(*b*) A corporation in which an officer of the issuing corporation is an executive officer.

The trustee shall present a certificate accepting the trust and certifying (1) securities are issued under the terms of the mortgage or indenture, giving the numbers and amount certified; (2) collateral is deposited; (3) disposition of prior obligations. For additional issues of bonds, the trustee must certify that (1) increase is in conformity with terms of mortgage or indenture; (2) additional collateral deposited; and (4) disposition of prior obligations.

The company and trustee shall notify the Stock Exchange of the holding, cancellation, or retirement of securities, by redemption, through the operation of sinking fund or otherwise.

The trustee must notify the Stock Exchange if deposited collateral is changed or removed, and furnish a list of collateral substituted.

A change of trustee shall not be made without the approval of the Committee.

Transfer and Registry

Every corporation whose securities are listed upon the Stock Exchange must, in accordance with the rules of the Exchange, maintain (*a*) a transfer office and (*b*) a registry office, both in the Borough of Manhattan, City of New York. The transfer agency and registrar *shall not be identical,* and both must be acceptable to the Committee. A company cannot act as registrar of its own stock.

Where a stock is transferred at the company's office, the transfer agent or transfer clerk shall be appointed by specific authority of the board of directors to *countersign* certificates, in said capacity, and shall be other than an officer who is authorized to sign certificates of stock.

The entire amount of the capital stock of a corporation listed upon the Stock Exchange *must be directly transferable* at the transfer office of the corporation in the Borough of Manhattan, City of New York.

When a corporation makes transfer of its shares in other cities, certificates shall be interchangeable, and *identical in color and form, with the New York Certificates,* except as to names of transfer agent and registrar; and the combined amounts of stocks registered in all cities shall not exceed the amount authorized to be listed.

Interchangeable certificates must bear a legend reciting the right of transfer in New York and other cities.

The registrar must file with the Secretary of the Stock Exchange an agreement to comply with the requirements in regard to registration and *not to register any listed stock, or any increase thereof, until authorized by the Committee.*

Certifications of registry must be dated and signed by an authorized officer of the registrar.

A change in the form of a security, of a transfer agency, or of a registrar, shall not be made without the approval of the Committee.

Forms of Certificates, Engraving, Etc.

General Requirements

(See Specific Requirements below.)

All securities for which listing upon the Exchange is requested, except as otherwise herein stated, must be engraved and printed in a manner satisfactory to the Committee from at least two steel plates by an engraving company whose work the Committee is authorized by the Governing Committee to pass upon; the name of the engraving company must appear upon the face of all securities and also upon the face of coupons and the title panel of each bond. Securities must bear a vignette upon their face.

Said plates shall be: (1) *A border and tint plate* from which should be made a printing in color underlying important portions of the face printing; (2) *A face plate* containing the vignettes and descriptive or promissory portion of the document, which should be printed in black or in black mixed with a color. The combined effect of the impression from these plates must be as effectual security as possible against counterfeiting.

The printing of securities should be in distinctive colors, to make classes and denominations readily distinguishable.

All certificates, except as otherwise stated herein, must provide for transfer and for registration with dates; when a corporation makes transfers of its shares in other cities, certificates shall be identical in color and form, with the New York certificates, except as to names of transfer agent and registrar; interchangeable certificates must bear a legend reciting the right of transfer in New York and other cities.

The Committee recommends that the text of securities shall provide for transfer, in person or by duly authorized attorney, upon surrender of the security properly endorsed.

A change in the form of a security, transfer agency, registrar, or trustee of bonds, shall not be made without the approval of the Committee.

The Committee will object to any security upon which an impress is made by a hand stamp, except for a date or power of substitution.

Bonds

(In addition to the General Requirements above outlined, the following apply specifically to bonds.)

All bonds must be fully engraved and printed in a manner satisfactory to the Committee; face of bonds and coupons must bear a vignette.

The text of bonds should recite conditions of issuance, terms of redemption, by sinking fund or otherwise, convertibility default, interchangeability or exchangeability of coupon and registered bonds, and conversion into other securities.

Bonds, in the text and on the reverse must recite payment of principal and interest and transfer and registration in the Borough of Manhattan, City of New York. Coupons must recite payment of interest in the Borough of Manhattan, City of New York.

Registered bonds must carry a power of assignment in such form as the Committee may approve.

The Committee recommends that registered bonds be made interchangeable with coupon bonds.

Registered bonds interchangeable with coupon bonds and coupon bonds exchangeable for fully registered bonds shall bear a legend reciting the fact.

Coupon bonds issued in denominations of less than $1,000 should provide for exchangeability into coupon bonds of $1,000, the smaller bonds to bear a legend reciting such privilege.

Registered bonds made such by detaching coupon sheets are not eligible for listing.

Forms of Legends for Bonds

For a coupon bond of a thousand dollars exchangeable for coupon bonds of smaller denominations:

"The holder of this bond may, at his option, on surrender and cancellation and on payment of charges, as provided in the indenture, receive in exchange coupon bonds of this issue for an amount aggregating $1,000 in denominations of $............. of numbers not contemporaneously outstanding."

For coupon bonds of smaller denominations exchangeable for a $500 or a $1,000 coupon bond:

"The holder of this bond may, at his option, on surrender and cancellation of this bond and others of the same issue aggregating $500 or $1,000 and on payment of charges, as provided in the indenture, receive in exchange a coupon bond of this issue of a number not contemporaneously outstanding, for the amount aggregated."

For registered bond(s) issued for coupon bond(s) of denomination(s) of less than $1,000:

"This bond is issued in exchange for coupon bond(s) of this issue numbered............in denominations of $..........not contemporaneously outstanding, aggregating the face value hereof and coupon bond(s) of this issue bearing the said number(s) and of the same denomination(s) will be issued in exchange for this bond upon surrender, cancellation and payment of charges provided in the indenture."

For registered bond(s) issued for $1,000 coupon bond(s):

"This bond is issued in exchange for coupon bond(s) of this issue numbered............for $1,000 (each), not contemporaneously outstanding, and coupon bond(s) of this issue bearing the said number(s) will be issued in exchange for this bond upon surrender, cancellation and payment of charges provided in the indenture."

Stock

(In addition to the above General Requirements, the following apply specifically to stock certificates.)

The border and tint plate for one-hundred share certificates of stock shall have *said denomination engraved thereon in words and figures; the plates for smaller amounts shall bear some engraved device whereby the exact denomination of the certificate may be distinctly designated by perforation;* also conspicuously upon the face *"Certificate for less than one hundred shares."*

Certificates for every class of stock shall recite preferences of all classes.

Certificates of stock should recite (1) ownership; (2) par value; (3) whether shares are *full* paid and (4) non-assessable; (5) preference as to dividends; (6) distribution of assets upon dissolution or merger; (7) terms of redemption; (8) convertibility; (9) voting power, or (10) other privilege; and (11) must bear the following legend:

This certificate is not valid until countersigned by the transfer agent, and registered by the registrar.

The following form is required upon the reverse of a certificate of stock:

For value received........hereby sell, assign and transfer unto ....
....
.... shares
of the *capital stock represented by the within certificate and do hereby irrevocably constitute and appoint
.... attorney
to transfer the said stock on the books of the within named company with full power of substitution in the premises.
Dated........................19......
....
In presence of
....

Notice: The signature to this assignment must correspond with the name as written upon the face of the certificate in every particular without alteration or enlargement, or any change whatever.

* On certificates without nominal or par value the word "capital" may be omitted.

Certificates of Deposit, Voting, Trust Certificates, etc.

In addition to the General Requirements above outlined, certificates of deposit and voting trust certificates must conform in every particular to the Specific Requirements as to stock certificates, except that the descriptive portion of a certificate of deposit may be typed, satisfactorily to the Committee.

Temporary Securities or Subscription Receipts

Temporary securities or subscription receipts must conform to the General Requirements above outlined and to the Specific Requirements as to stock certificates, except that the text may be typed satisfactorily to the Committee.

REMOVALS OR SUSPENSIONS IN DEALINGS OF LISTED SECURITIES

Whenever it shall appear that the outstanding amount of any security listed upon the Stock Exchange has become so reduced as to make inadvisable further dealings therein, the Committee may direct that such security be removed from the list and further dealings therein prohibited.

"The Governing Committee may suspend dealings in the securities of any corporation previously admitted to quotation upon the Exchange, or it may summarily remove any securities from the list."

E. V. D. Cox, Secretary. Robert Gibson, Chairman.

(c) "When a new stock is put on the exchange, or any great exchange like the New York Stock Exchange, there is one thing that is very necessary, and that is that its price shall be steady. When you have no active market in a stock, when you are building up an active market in a new stock, the first thing a banking house does, what it wants to do, and what it must do, whether it makes a profit or loss out of it, is to steady the price of the stock. If people come in to buy 6,000 or 7,000 shares of stock, and there is not much around if they do not sell the stock it will be bid away up, and have a big advance. On the other hand, if somebody comes in to sell 6,000 or 7,000 shares, and there are no large buying orders in there, the price of the stock is going to be a great deal lower than it would be otherwise. If you put in buying orders on a scale down and selling orders on a scale up, the effect of that is to steady the price of the stock. Its fluctuation is not as violent or as wide as it would be otherwise." (Money Trust Investigation, pp. 1282-1283, testimony of Mr. Henry; quoted in Regulation of the Stock Exchange, p. 542.)

(d) "Stocks in a liquidating market pass from what are described as weak hands to strong hands; stocks pass from the hands of those who buy them and carry them with borrowed money to those who buy them and pay for them. . . . The best evidence, Congressmen, of such a movement, I believe, is found in the stock books of corporations whose stocks are dealt in on the exchange, where, in a period of liquidation, what is known as the odd-lot buyer appears in the market;

then, with stock like that of the Steel Corporation and General Motors and others, you will find the number of stockholders increases tremendously in a declining market. Figures have recently been published in New York market reviews showing the changes in the number of stockholders in those two companies. And what happens is that the public, in a declining market, see that stocks are selling at a bargain and come in with the cash, buy the stock, and take it out of the stock loan account." (Statement and testimony of Governor Benjamin Strong of the New York Federal Reserve Bank before the Agricultural Inquiry Commission [Washington, August, 1921], p. 630.)

(e) Distribution of United States Steel Common and Preferred Stocks, 1910-1920

Showing drift of shares from speculators (brokers' names) to investors (individual names)

Date of Quarterly Statement	Common Stock		Preferred Stock	
	Brokers	Individuals	Brokers	Individuals
December 31, 1909	66.41%	33.59%	17.57%	82.43%
March 31, 1910	63.94	36.06	16.79	83.21
June 30, 1910	61.54	38.46	15.62	84.38
September 30, 1910	57.86	42.14	14.98	85.02
December 31, 1910	58.32	41.68	14.59	85.41
March 31, 1911	58.36	41.64	14.59	85.41
June 30, 1911	58.29	41.71	14.39	85.61
September 30, 1911	55.41	44.59	14.13	85.87
December 31, 1911	55.26	44.74	14.67	85.33
March 31, 1912	54.54	45.46	14.39	85.61
June 30, 1912	56.27	43.73	13.90	86.10
September 30, 1912	57.58	42.42	13.67	86.33
December 31, 1912	57.36	42.64	13.49	86.51
March 31, 1913	54.71	45.29	13.75	86.25
June 30, 1913	51.07	48.93	12.71	87.29
September 30, 1913	50.80	49.20	12.41	87.59
December 31, 1913	49.34	50.66	12.39	87.61
March 31, 1914	49.86	50.14	12.64	87.36
June 30, 1914	48.90	51.10	12.49	87.51
September 30, 1914	45.01	54.99	11.90	88.10
December 31, 1914	43.15	56.85	11.82	88.18

Date of Quarterly Statement	Common Stock		Preferred Stock	
	Brokers	Individuals	Brokers	Individuals
March 31, 1915	42.33	57.67	11.59	88.41
June 30, 1915	44.42	55.58	11.70	88.30
September 30, 1915	46.94	53.06	11.69	88.31
December 31, 1915	49.80	50.20	11.15	88.85
March 31, 1916	53.87	46.13	11.02	88.98
June 30, 1916	52.75	47.25	10.73	89.27
September 30, 1916	55.67	44.33	12.13	87.87
December 31, 1916	58.04	41.96	12.74	87.26
March 31, 1917	53.16	46.84	11.39	88.61
June 30, 1917	55.15	44.85	10.94	89.06
September 30, 1917	52.66	47.34	10.16	89.84
December 31, 1917	46.53	53.47	9.61	90.39
March 31, 1918	44.51	55.49	9.37	90.63
June 30, 1918	43.78	56.22	9.17	90.83
September 30, 1918	43.88	56.12	9.18	90.82
December 31, 1918	40.71	58.29	9.11	90.89
March 31, 1919	38.91	61.09	9.00	91.00
June 30, 1919	42.53	57.47	9.03	90.97
September 30, 1919	41.52	58.48	8.78	91.22
December 31, 1919	39.65	60.35	8.29	91.71
March 31, 1920	33.46	66.54	7.88	92.12
June 30, 1920	32.09	67.91	7.68	92.32
September 30, 1920	30.69	69.31	7.42	92.58
December 31, 1920	25.17	74.83	7.53	92.47

(f) The following statistical tables show the constantly widening public distribution of the common stock of three large American corporations—a public utility, an industrial, and a railroad, as of the earliest period in the years indicated:

	American Telephone and Telegraph Company		United States Steel		Pennsylvania Railroad	
	Number of Shareholders	Average Number of Shares Held	Number of Shareholders	Average Number of Shares Held	Number of Shareholders	Average Number of Shares Held
1910	35,823	72	22,033	230.70	65,283	126.41
1914	55,983	62	47,221	107.64	91,571	109.04
1917	70,555	56	42,564	119.42	100,138	99.82
1920	120,460	37	104,376	48.69	133,068	75.04

CHAPTER XVIII

(a) International Speculative and Investment Distribution of United States Steel Common and Preferred Stock

	Preferred Stock (3,602,811 Shares)				Common Stock (5,083,025 Shares)			
	June 30, 1920		Sept. 30, 1920		June 30, 1920		Sept. 30, 1920	
New York	Shares	Ratio	Shares	Ratio	Shares	Ratio	Shares	Ratio
Brokers.....	227,113	6.30	221,599	6.15	1,313,269	25.83	1,259,328	24.77
Investors....	1,480,167	41.08	1,481,340	41.11	1,277,423	25.13	1,275,906	25.10
England								
Brokers.....	14,884	.....	13,530	.....	143,866	2.83	143,172	2.81
Investors....	19,208	.....	18,601	.....	19,694	.....	17,664	.....
France								
Brokers.....	500	.....	500	.....	11,200	.....	3,050	.....
Investors....	18,111	.....	17,609	.....	11,441	.....	10,399	.....
Holland								
Brokers.....	19,800	.....	16,830	.....	110,400	2.17	102,300	2.01
Investors....	2,019	.....	2,019	.....	838	.....	845	.....
Brokers and Investors								
Domestic....	3,478,465	96.54	3,484,599	96.72	4,740,458	93.26	4,759,587	93.64
Foreign.....	124,346	3.46	118,212	3.28	342,567	6.74	323,438	6.36
Domestic and Foreign								
Brokers.....	278,743	7.68	266,596	7.42	1,631,406	32.09	1,560,125	30.69
Investors....	3,326,068	92.32	3,336,215	92.58	3,451,619	67.91	3,522,900	69.31

(b) "Whereas, the so-called arbitrage business or trading between this Exchange and that of any other city in the United States, based upon quotations from the floor of this Exchange, has resulted in practically ignoring the commission law; therefore

"Resolved, that in the judgment of this Committee the sending of continuous quotations, or quotations at frequent intervals by members of this Exchange, from the floor of the Exchange, is detrimental to the interest and welfare of the Exchange, and that any member engaging in such business or trading, shall be proceeded against under Section 8 of Article XVII of the Constitution." (Constitution, p. 80.)

(c) "Negotiable securities which are quoted upon the exchanges rank next to banking credits as a medium of exchange because they are more readily convertible into money or credits than any specific commodity. Their value in this respect was recognized at least a century ago in the London market. It was declared by Thornton, in 1807, that stocks, by being at all times a salable and ready-made article, are, to a certain degree, held by persons in London on the same principle as bills, and serve, therefore, in some measure, like bills, if we consider these as a discountable article, to spare the use of bank notes. Such securities partake of the exchangeable character of money because they are not themselves specific commodities of limited consumption, but are titles to the earnings of corporations or pledges for periodical payments of sums of money in the form of dividends or interest. They come nearer than any other article to performing the function of money, in commanding all commodities, because they are desired for their power to earn money, rather than for their power to satisfy any special want." (Charles A. Conant, Principles of Money and Banking.)

(d) "There is one point I think I am justified in referring to, and that is the influence of the exchange on the international money market. If we had no general market like the stock exchange, and no great mass of listed securities which are known abroad as well as at home, the movements in the international money market would be much more violent and acute than they now are. Today the ordinary merchant, or the manufacturer on a large scale, can go about his business serenely conscious that he will get his money at from 4 to 6 per cent at the outside, and he does not concern himself to see whether we are exporting gold or not. But if we had no general securities market by which we could borrow on securities in Europe and sell drafts to meet demands, you would have a most violent and convulsive movement of the foreign exchanges, which would react upon the whole money market. You would have large exports of gold, because there was no other way of meeting obligations or getting credits abroad. We have had, as you know, violent fluctuations, in fact, by reason of the defects in our currency system, but they would be multiplied many fold if we could not establish foreign credits. As you know, there is a class of persons who make it a business of seeking a profit of a small fraction of 1 per cent when securities are a little higher here than they are in Paris or a little lower in London than they are in New York. Their operations tend to keep uniform, comparatively uniform, the supply of credit and they influence the foreign exchange market, and thereby travel toward the same stabilizing tendency as short-selling and the general functions of the exchange itself." (Regulation of the Stock Exchange, p. 189, testimony of Charles A. Conant.)

(e) "To close America's chief securities market, and thereby render its $40,000,000,000 of listed securities almost non-negotiable, was a momentous step. Not since 1873 had the Stock Exchange suspended except for a few hours. Even the panics of 1907 and 1893 had not halted its operations. Yet to have attempted to maintain trading in New York, and thus invite the tremendous selling orders in which the whole world with its billions of American securities would undoubtedly have participated, would have been sheer folly. On the other hand, it was almost equally important that the maximum amount of liquidation comparable with national safety should be permitted to run its course there, in order that the reopening of the New York market might be effected the more speedily and the more safely. The able manner in which the governing committee of the New York Stock Exchange rose to meet this difficult dilemma has been dramatically related by H. G. S. Noble, then president of the Exchange. A few minutes before the usual opening hour of 10 A.M. the governors voted by a large majority to close the Exchange until further notice. Subsequent events wholly confirmed the complete wisdom of this step. If, as has been so frequently asserted, the war was eventually won by the individual initiative of the American soldier, sailor and business executive, it is equally certain that our then debtor nation owed its avoidance of a panic to the ability of the governors of the Stock Exchange to meet on their own responsibility an unparalleled crisis with an expert knowledge of its possible consequences and of the exact minute at which to terminate dealings on the floor." (Brigham in the *Boston Evening Transcript,* Oct. 20, 1920.)

(f) In the last few years many prices marked "S 30" (seller thirty days) have appeared on the tape and in the daily financial reports. Such transactions are usually assumed to be sales by European holders of our securities back to American purchasers, through the machinery of the Stock Exchange, for it usually requires a European seller thirty days to liquidate any securities in our markets, owing both to the fortnightly term settlement system in vogue on European stock exchanges and the time required to send the certificate across the Atlantic. These "seller 30" transactions in recent years on the New York Stock Exchange were the outward and manifest sign of the gradual lifting of the vast mortgage previously held by European investors on our leading railroad systems and industrial establishments.

(g) "Japan passed through a severe crisis in 1901, and part of the year before, because of the barrenness of her stock market. She had had been engaged in great enterprises, but the stimulus given her industrial interests did not prove immediately profitable. Her people had begun importing great quantities of foreign goods, including too many luxuries, and the result was that she had large debts to pay abroad. If she had had a good security market, these debts would have been settled by the transfer of securities; but having only a few securities, and those of doubtful value, to throw upon the London market, she was compelled to settle at a sacrifice the demands upon her for money. She was compelled to sell goods for any price that could be obtained. . . .

"France was saved from one of the greatest crises of history by the large holdings of securities among her people during the Franco-Prussian War. When Germany demanded an indemnity of five thousand millions of francs ($1,000,000,000), it was in the belief that its payment would throw a paralysis upon French industry and enterprise which would prostrate them for a generation. But what happened? When the French Government appealed to the people, saying, 'We need five thousand millions of francs to pay off this indebtedness,' the whole matter was adjusted through the securities market, and in a few years the Bank of France resumed the payment of gold for its notes, Frenchmen subscribed liberally for the securities of the new loans to pay off Germany, and in order to obtain the necessary funds, they directed their broker to sell in London, Berlin, Vienna, Brussels and New York the old securities which they held. Five thousand million francs were thus taken from the capital of France, but she was so rich that she was able to submit to it without disaster. She was rich because she had piled up these securities, with which she was able to part without suffering. . . .

"France, by the possession of a flexible stock exchange and a great mass of the securities negotiable upon such exchanges, was saved from the convulsion which must have prostrated her entire industrial system if it had been necessary for her to find money to discharge the demands of the conqueror." (Charles A. Conant, Wall Street and the Country.)

BIBLIOGRAPHY

THE SUBJECT IN GENERAL[1]

America

Anderson, Benjamin M. (See under Chapter VIII.)

Atwood, Albert. (See under Chapter XV.)

——Exchanges and Speculation. New York, 1917.

Black, William H. The Real Wall Street (dictionary). New York, 1910.

Blackmar, Frank. Economics. New York, 1907.

Boyle, James E. Speculation and the Chicago Board of Trade. New York, 1920.

Brace, H. H. (See under Chapter XV.)

Browne, Scribner. (See under Chapter XV.)

Burton, Theodore E. (See under Chapter XV.)

Callaway and English. (See under Chapter XII.)

Cannon, J. G. (See under Chapter IX.)

Chamberlain, Lawrence, (See under Chapter VII.)

Clark, Albert B. (See under Chapter XV.)

Clark, John B. (See under Chapter XVI.)

Clews, Henry. (See under Chapter II.)

Conant, Charles A. Principles of Money and Banking. New York, 1905.

——(See under Chapters XV, XVII, and XVIII.)

Conway, Thomas. (See under Chapter XV.)

Crump, Arthur. (See under Chapter XV.)

Davenport, Herbert J. Outlines of Economic Theory. New York, 1896.

Davis, A. McF. (See under Chapter XV.)

Dewey, D. R. Financial History of the United States. New York, 1903.

Dewey, T. H. (See under Chapter XV.)

Dos Passos, John R. Treatise on the Law of Stock Brokers and Stock Exchanges. New York, 1905.

Dow, Charles H. (See under Chapter XV.)

Eames, Francis L. (See under Chapter II.)

Emery, Henry C. (See under Chapter XV.)

[1] Chapter references are to "Readings by Chapters of this Book," pp. 605–613.

England, M. T. (See under Chapter XV.)
Fayant, Frank. (See under Chapter XV.)
Federal Reserve Bank. (See under Chapter VIII.)
Fisher, Irving. The Nature of Capital and Income. New York, 1906.
Gerstenberg, Charles W. (See under Chapter I.)
Gibson, George R. The Stock Exchanges of London, Paris and New York. 1889.
Gibson, Thomas. (See under Chapter XV.)
Glenn, Garrard. (See under Chapter XII.)
Goldman, Samuel. Handbook of Stock Exchange Laws. New York, 1914.
Greenwood, W. J. American and Foreign Stock Exchange Methods. New York, 1921.
Hadley, Arthur T. (See under Chapters I and XV.)
Hall, Henry. (See under Chapter XVII.)
Hamon, Henry. (See under Chapter II.)
Hepburn, A. Barton. (See under Chapter VIII.)
Hickernell, W. F. (See under Chapters XIV and XV.)
Hill, Frederick T. (See under Chapter II.)
Hirst, F. W. (See under Great Britain.)
Hollander, Jacob H. (See under Chapter VIII.)
Holt, B. W., and Williams, A. (See under Chapter XIV.)
Huebner, Solomon S. The Stock Exchange Business: a Course of Study with References. New York, 1918. (See under Chapter XIV.)
Hughes Commission. Report of the Governor's Committee on Speculation in Securities and Commodities. New York, 1909.
Investment Banker's Association. The Stock Exchange Business: a Course of Study with References. New York, 1918.
Jones, Edwin D. (See under Chapter XV.)
King, M. The New York Stock Exchange. New York, 1904.
Lange, F. A. The History of Materialism. Boston, 1879-1881.
McVey, Frank L. Modern Industrialism. New York, 1904.
Mackay, Charles. (See under Chapter XV.)
Martin, Harrison S. The New York Stock Exchange. New York, 1919.
Mason, Frank H. (See under Chapter XV.)
Medbery, James K. (See under Chapter II.)
Milburn, John G. (See under Chapters VIII, XIII, and XV.)
Mitchell, Wesley C. (See under Chapter XV.)

Moulton, The Financial Organization of Society. Chicago, 1920.

Nelson, S. A. (See under Chapter XV.)

New York Stock Exchange, Constitution of the New York Stock Exchange and Resolutions adopted by the Governing Committee. New York, 1918. (Regulation of the Stock Exchange, as of February, 1914, pp. 685-710.)

Noble, H. G. S. (See under Chapters II, IV, VI, and XVIII.)

Norton, Eliot. (See under Chapters III and IV.)

Norton, J. P. (See under Chapter VIII.)

Noyes, Alexander D. (See under Chapter IX.)

—— Thirty Years of American Finance. New York, 1898.

Parker, William. (See under France.)

Persons, W. M. (See under Chapter XIV.)

Pomroy, H. K. (See under Chapter XVI.)

Pratt, Sereno S. The Work of Wall Street. 3d edition. New York, 1921.

Prendergast, William A. Credit and Its Uses. New York, 1906.

Richter, F. E. (See under Chapter X.)

Rollins, Montgomery. (See under Chapter VII.)

Sager, Hiram N. (See under Chapter XVII.)

Schiff, Jacob H. (See under Chapter XVI.)

Seager, Henry R. Introduction to Economics. New York, 1904.

Selden, George C. (See under Chapter XV.)

Seligman, Edwin R. (See under Chapter XV.)

Sexsmith, Thomas L. (See under Chapter XV.)

Smith, Howard I. Financial Dictionary. New York, 1908.

Smitley, Robert L. (See under Chapter XII.)

Stafford, William Y. (See under Chapter XV.)

Stedman, E. C. (See under Chapter II.)

Stevens, Albert C. (See under Chapter XV.)

Stock Clearing Corporation, The, (publications). (See under Chapters IX, X, and XI.)

Streit, Samuel F. (See under Chapters IX and X.)

Strong, Benjamin. (See under Chapter VIII.)

Sumner, W. G. (See under Chapter VII.)

Taussig, F. W. Principles of Economics. New York, 1911.

Taylor, Walter F. (See under Chapters VIII and XV.)

United States Government. Money Trust Investigation (investigation of financial and monetary conditions in United States under H. R. Nos. 429, 504, 62nd Congress, 2nd session). Washington, 1912.

—— Pujo Report (report of the committee appointed pursuant to H. R. 429 and 504 to investigate the concentration of control of money and credit).

—— Regulation of the Stock Exchange (hearings before the Committee on Banking and Currency, United States Senate, 63rd Congress, 2nd session on S. 3895). Washington, 1914.

Van Antwerp, William C. The Stock Exchange from Within. New York, 1914.

White, Horace. (See under Chapters VIII and XII.)

Withers, Hartley. (See under Great Britain and Chapter VIII.)

France

Boissiere, G. La Compagnie des Agents de Change et la Marche Officiel à la Bourse de Paris. Paris, 1908.

Courtois, fils, Alphonse. Traite des opérations de Bourse et de Change, Paris, 1901.

Georges-Levy, Raphael. Melanges Financiers, Paris, 1894.

Gide, Charles. Principles d'Economie Politique. Paris, 1889.

Greenwood, W. J. (See under America.)

Hamburger, A. Le Guide Pratique de la Bourse. Paris, 1902.

Leroy-Beaulieu, Anatole. (See under Chapter XV.)

Leroy-Beaulieu, Paul. Nouveau Dictionnaire d'Economie Politique. Paris, 1892.

—— Traite de la Science des Finances. Paris, 1898.

—— Traite Théorique et Pratique d'Economie Politique. Paris, 1896.

Liesse, Andre. (See under Chapter VIII.)

Neymarck, Alfred. French Savings and Their Influence upon the Bank of France and upon French Banks. (National Monetary Commission Report, Vol. XV.) Washington, 1909.

Parker, William. The Paris Bourse and French Finance. New York, 1920.

Patron, Maurice. (See under Chapter VIII.)

Proud'hon, P. J. Manuel du Speculateur à la Bourse. Paris, 1857.

Say, Jean Baptiste. Traite d'Economie Politique. Paris, 1803.

Sayous, Andre E. Etude Economique et Juridique sur les Bourses Allemandes de Valeurs et de Commerce. Paris, 1898-1901.

Vidal, E. History and Methods of the Paris Bourse (in National Monetary Commission Report, Vol. XV). Washington, 1909.

Germany

Bender. Der Verkehr mit Staatspapieren. Göttingen, 1830.

Bruckner. Der Differenz handel an der Börse. Berlin, 1894.

Cohn, Gustav. Grundlagen der Nationalokonomie. Stuttgart, 1885-1898. (See under Chapter XV.)
—— The Science of Finance. Stuttgart, 1885-1898.
—— Ueber das Börsenspiel. Berlin, 1875.
Eberstadt, Rudolph. Der Deutsche Kapitalmarket. Leipzig, 1901.
Endermann, Adolph. Das Börsengesetz (Conrad's Jahrbuch). Berlin, 1894.
Friend, Emil. (See under Chapter XV.)
Germany (Government). Bericht der Börsen-Enquête-Kommission. Berlin, 1894.
—— Zur Vorschlage der Börsen-Enquête-Kommission. Berlin, 1894.
Gibson, George R. (See under America.)
Goldbaum, F. (See under Chapter XV.)
Greenwood, W. J. (See under America.)
Knipper, Chr. (See under Chapter XV.)
Koch, R., editor. German Imperial Banking Laws, together with the German Stock Exchange Regulations (the National Monetary Commission Report, Senate Doc. 574). Washington, 1910.
Lexis, Dr. D. (See under Chapter XV.)
Loeb, Ernst. (See under Chapter XV.)
Michaelis, Otto. (See under Chapter XV.)
Pfleger and Geschwindt. (See under Chapter XV.)
Plochmann, G. (See under Chapter XV.)
Reichsbank, The. (See under Chapter VIII.)
Sayous, Andre. (See under France.)
Struck, E. Die Effektenbörse. Leipzig, 1881.

Great Britain

Anderson, A. History of Commerce. London, 1764.
Ashley, W. J. Introduction to English Economic History and Theory. London, 1892.
Bagehot, Walter. Economic Studies. London, 1879.
——Lombard Street. London, 1873.
Bisschop, W. R. (See under Chapter I.)
Branson. The Stock Exchange and Its Machinery. London, 1913.
British Government, London Stock Exchange: Report of the Commissioners. Parliamentary Blue Books: C 8850, 1898; Cd. 1756, 1904; Cd. 3280, 1907; Cd. 3683, 1907.
British Government. Report of the Royal Commission. Parliamentary Blue Book, London, 1878.

Broadhurst, B. E. S. Law and Practice of the Stock Exchange. London, 1897.

Bronson. (See Schwabe.)

Castelli. Theory of Options. London, 1877.

Cautley, H. S. Law and Usages of the Stock Exchange. London, 1901.

Cordingley. Guide to the Stock Exchange. London, 1910.

Crump, Arthur. The Theory of Stock Exchange Speculation. London, 1887.

Cunningham, William. An Essay on Western Civilization in its Economic Aspects. London, 1898-1900.

—— Growth of English Industry and Commerce. Cambridge, 1882.

Duguid, Charles. The History of the Stock Exchange. London, 1901.

Ellis, Arthur. (See under Chapter XV.)

Gibson, George R. (See under America.)

Greenwood, W. J. (See under America.)

Hirst, F. W. The Stock Exchange. New York, 1911.

Hobson, John A. The Evolution of Modern Capitalism. London, 1894.

Ingall, G. D., and G. Withers. The Stock Exchange. London, 1904.

Jevons, W. Stanley. The Theory of Political Economy. p. 92. London, 1907.

——(See under Chapter XVIII.)

Lavington, F. The English Capital Market. London, 1921.

MacLeod, Henry D. Theory and Principles of Banking. London, 1866.

Marshall, Alfred. Principles of Economics. London, 1890.

Mill, John Stuart. Principles of Political Economy. London, 1848.

Poley, A. P. History, Law and Practice of the Stock Exchange. London, 1907.

Rogers, James E. T. Industrial and Commercial History of England. London, 1892.

Schwabe and Bronson. Treatise on the Laws of the Stock Exchange. London, 1913.

Spicer, Ernest E. (See under Chapter XVII.)

Stutfield, G. H. The Law Relating to Betting, Time-Bargaining and Gaming. London, 1886.

Tooke, Thomas. (See under Chapter XIV.)

Usher, Roland. Industrial History of England. New York, 1920.

Withers, G. (See under Ingall, G. D.)

Withers, Hartley. The Case for Capitalism. New York, 1920.

——(See under Chapter XVIII.)

Young, Thomas E. Plain Guide to Investment and Finance. London, 1921.

READINGS BY CHAPTERS OF THIS BOOK

Chapter I—The Evolution of Securities

Adams, John, Jr. Stocks and Their Features—Division and Classification (Annals of the American Academy, Vol. XXXV, pp. 525-544). Philadelphia, May, 1910.

Bisschop, W. R. Rise of the London Money Market, 1640-1826. London, 1910.

Burgunder, B. B. The Declaration and Yield of Stockholders' Rights (Annals of the American Academy, Vol. XXXV, pp. 554-578.) Philadelphia, May, 1910.

Conyngton, Thomas. Corporate Organization and Management, New York, 1919.

Gerstenberg, Charles W. Materials of Corporate Finance. New York, 1915.

Giffen, Robert. Stock Exchange Securities. London, 1879.

Hadley, Arthur T. Report of the Railroad Securities Commission (H. R. Doc. No. 256). Washington, 1911.

Lyon, Hastings. Corporation Finance. New York, 1916.

Mead, Edward S. Corporation Finance. New York, 1920.

——Trust Finance. New York, 1901.

Moody, John. How to Analyze Railroad Reports. New York, 1912.

Pratt, Sereno S. The Work of Wall Street, 3d ed. pp. 105-125. New York, 1921.

Stetson, J. F. L. and others. Legal Phases of Corporate Financing, Reorganization and Regulation. New York, 1917.

Sullivan, John J. American Corporations, 1910.

Withers, Hartley. Stocks and Shares. London, 1910.

Wood, W. A. Modern Business Corporations. Indianapolis, 1917.

Chapter II—The Rise of the New York Stock Exchange

Barrett, Walter. The Old Merchants of New York. New York, 1885.

Clews, Henry. Fifty Years in Wall Street. New York, 1908.

Eames, Francis L. The New York Stock Exchange. New York, 1894.

Hamon, Henry. New York Stock Exchange Manual. New York, 1865.

Hemming, H. G. History of the New York Stock Exchange. New York, 1905.

Hill, Frederick T. The Story of a Street. New York, 1908.

Lippincott, Isaac. The Economic Development of the United States. New York, 1921.

Medbery, James K. Men and Mysteries of Wall Street. Boston, 1870.

Noble, H. G. S. The New York Stock Exchange in the Crisis of 1914. New York, 1915.

Pratt, Sereno S. The Work of Wall Street. 3d ed. pp. 1-35, 49-77, 134-163. New York, 1921.

Stedman, E. C., and others. History of the New York Stock Exchange. New York, 1904.

Villard, O. G. Early History of Wall Street. New York, 1897.

Chapter III—A Typical Investment Transaction

Leroy-Beaulieu, Paul. L'Economiste Français. Paris, October 5, 1912.

Norton, Eliot. A Simple Purchase and Sale through a Stockbroker. (Harvard Law Review, Vol. VIII, No. 8.) Cambridge, June, 1894.

Chapter IV—Credit Transactions in Securities

Noble, H. G. S. Testimony (Regulation of the Stock Exchange). pp. 160-164. Washington, 1914.

Norton, Eliot. On Short Sales of Securities through a Stockbroker. New York, 1907.

Chapter V—The Floor Trader and the Specialist

Van Antwerp, William C. The Stock Exchange from Within. p. 285. New York, 1914.

Chapter VI—The Odd-Lot Business

Noble, H. G. S. Testimony (Regulation of the Stock Exchange). pp. 164-169. Washington, 1914.

Chapter VII—The Bond Market

Chamberlain, Lawrence. Principles of Bond Investment. New York, 1911.

—— The Work of the Bond House. New York, 1912.

Rollins, Montgomery. Convertible Securities. Boston, 1913.

Sumner, W. G. Specimens of Investment Securities for Class-room Use, New York, 1901.

Chapter VIII—The Security Collateral Loan Market

Anderson, Benjamin M. (See under Hepburn.)

Federal Reserve Bank. Rates of Interest on Collateral Call Loans (Senate Document No. 262, 66th Congress, 2nd session). Washington, 1920.

Griesel, J. H. Testimony (Money Trust Investigation. Vol. I, p. 742). Washington, 1912.

Hepburn, A. Barton, and Anderson, B. M. The Gold and Rediscount Policy of the Federal Reserve Banks (pamphlet). The Chase Economic Bulletin, Vol. I, No. 5. New York, 1921.

Hollander, Jacob H. Bank Loans and Stock Exchange Speculation (National Monetary Commission Report, 61st Congress, 2nd session, Senate document 589, p. 27). Washington, 1911.

Liesse, Andre. Evolution of Credit and Banks in France (National Monetary Commission Report, Vol. XV, pp. 84, 86, 132, 139, 140). Washington, 1909.

Milburn, John G., and Taylor, Walter F. Brief of counsel on behalf of the New York Stock Exchange (Regulation of the Stock Exchange, pp. 550-554). Washington, 1914.

Norton, J. P. Statistical Studies in the New York Money Market. New York, 1902.

Patron, Maurice. The Bank of France in Its Relation to National and International Credit (National Monetary Commission Report, Vol. XV). Washington, 1909.

Pratt, Sereno S. The Work of Wall Street. 3d ed. pp. 257-297, 405-410. New York, 1921.

Reichsbank, The. The Reichsbank 1876-1900 (National Monetary Commission Report, Vol. X, pp.173-202). Washington, 1910.

Strong, Benjamin. Statement and Testimony (pp. 450-814) in Agricultural Inquiry (hearing before the Joint Commission of Agricultural Inquiry, 67th Congress, 1st session, under Senate Concurrent Resolution 4, Part 13). Washington, 1921.

Taylor, Walter F. (See under Milburn, John G.)

Turner, Charles W. Testimony (Money Trust Investigation. Vol. I, p. 752). Washington, 1912.

White, Horace. The Stock Exchange and the Money Market (Annals of the American Academy, Vol. XXXVI, pp. 563-573). Philadelphia, November, 1910.

Withers, Hartley. The English Banking System (National Monetary Commission Report, Vol. VIII, pp. 111-149). Washington, 1910.

Chapter IX—The Night Clearing Branch

Cannon, James G. Clearing Houses (National Monetary Commission Report). Washington, 1910.

Committee on Clearing Houses. Report of Committee on Clearing Houses of the New York Stock Exchange (pamphlet). New York, 1892.

Noyes, Alexander D. Stock Exchange Clearing Houses (Political Science Quarterly, Vol. VIII, p. 252.)

Pratt, Sereno S. The Work of Wall Street, 3d ed., pp. 164-181. New York, 1921.

Stock Clearing Corporation, The. By-laws and Rules of the Stock Clearing Corporation (pamphlet). New York, 1921.

—— The Stock Clearing Corporation (pamphlet). New York, 1920.

Streit, Samuel F. Term Settlements: a Study of Clearing and Settling Security Contracts on Foreign Stock Exchanges (pamphlet). American Acceptance Council publications. New York, 1920.

Todman, Frederick S. Wall Street Accounting. New York, 1921.

Chapter X—The Day Clearing Branch

Richter, F. E. The Stock Clearing Corporation (Quarterly Journal of Economics, Vol. 34, pp. 538-544). Cambridge, Mass., May, 1920.

Stock Clearing Corporation, The. (See publications listed under Chapter IX.)

Streit, Samuel F. Function of the Stock Clearing Corporation (Acceptance Bulletin). New York, May, 1921.

Chapter XI—The Clearance of Loans

Stock Clearing Corporation, The. Bankers' Agreement. New York, 1921.

Chapter XII—The Commission House

Callaway and English, Stock Brokers' Accounts. London, 1901.

Commerce and Finance, Wire House Number. New York, June 22, 1921.

Glenn, Garrard. Rights of the Customer of an Insolvent Broker (Columbia Law Review). New York, May, 1912.

Pratt, Sereno S. The Work of Wall Street, 3d ed., pp. 214-230. New York, 1921.

Smitley, Robert L. Handling a Brokerage Account. New York, 1920.

—— You and Your Broker. New York, 1920.

Todman, Frederick S. Wall Street Accounting. New York, 1921.

White, Horace. The Hughes Investigation (Journal of Political Economy, Vol. XVII, pp. 528-540). Chicago, October, 1909.

Chapter XIII—The Government of the Stock Exchange

Conant, Charles A. The Regulation of the Stock Exchange (Atlantic Monthly, Vol. CII, pp. 307-314). Boston, September, 1908.

Milburn, John G. Statement (Regulation of the Stock Exchange, pp. 345-383). Washington, 1914.

New York Stock Exchange. Constitution of the New York Stock Exchange and Resolutions adopted by the Governing Committee. New York, 1918.

United States Government. Money Trust Investigation. Washington, 1912.

—— Regulation of the Stock Exchange. Washington, 1914.

Chapter XIV—Organized Markets and Their Economic Functions

Boyle, James E. (See under General List.)

Hallam, H. The Middle Ages. New York, 1862.

Hickernell, W. F. Forces which make Prices (pamphlet). New York, 1920.

Holt, B. W., and Williams, A. Market Information. New York, 1920.

Huebner, Grover G. Agricultural Commerce. New York, 1919.

Huebner, Solomon S. The Scope and Functions of the Stock Market (Annals of the American Academy, Vol. XXXV, pp. 483-505). Philadelphia, May, 1910.

Mudgett, Bruce D. Current Sources of Information in Produce Markets (Annals of the American Academy, Vol. XXXVIII, pp. 442-443). Philadelphia, September, 1911.

Murray, Nat. C. The Crop Reporting System (Annals of the American Academy, Vol. XXXVIII, pp. 409-421). Philadelphia, September, 1911.

Persons, W. M. Measuring and Forecasting General Business Conditions (pamphlet). New York, 1920.

Tooke, Thomas. A History of Prices (Part II, p. 46). London, 1840.

Usher, Roland. (See under Great Britain.)

Chapter XV—The Dangers and Benefits of Stock Speculation

Atwood, Albert. (See under Conway, Thomas.)

Brace, H. H. The Value of Organized Speculation. New York, 1913.

Browne, Scribner. How to Read the Financial Page. New York, 1920.

Burton, Theodore. Financial Crises and Periods of Industrial and Commercial Depression. New York, 1907.

Clark, Albert B. The Utility of Speculation in Modern Commerce (Political Science Quarterly). New York, September, 1892.

Clark, John B. Insurance and Business Profits (Quarterly Journal of Economics). Cambridge, October, 1892.

Cohn, Gustav. Beitrage zur Deutschen Bōrsenreform. Leipzig, 1895.

—— Die Bōrse und die Spekulation. Berlin, 1868.

Conant, Charles W. The Uses of Speculation (Forum). New York, August, 1901.

Conway, Thomas, and Atwood, Albert. Investment and Speculation. New York, 1911.

Crump, Arthur. The Theory of Stock Speculation (Annals of the American Academy). Philadelphia, May, 1910.

Davis, A. McF. A Search for the Beginnings of Stock Speculation (Publications of the Colonial Society of Massachusetts). Cambridge, Mass., 1906.

Dewey, T. H. Contracts for Future Delivery and Commercial Wagers. New York, 1886.

—— Legislation against Speculation and Gambling in the Forms of Trade. New York, 1905.

Dow, Charles H. The A.B.C. of Stock Speculation. New York, 1900.

Ellis, Arthur. Rationale of Market Fluctuations. London, 1876.

Emery, Henry C. Bibliography upon German legislation in the stock exchange (Regulation of the Stock Exchange, p. 830). Washington, 1914.

—— Should Speculation be regulated by Law? Lessons from German experience (Regulation of the Stock Exchange, pp. 830-838). Washington, 1914.

—— Speculation on the Stock and Produce Exchanges of the United States (Columbia University Studies in History, Economics and Law). New York, 1896.

—— Ten Years' Regulation of the Stock Exchange in Germany (Yale Review). New Haven, May, 1908.

—— Testimony (Regulation of the Stock Exchange, pp. 324-344). Washington, 1914.

—— The Place of the Speculator in the Theory of Distribution (paper before the American Economic Association). 1899.

England, M. T. Speculation in Relation to the World's Prosperity. (University of Nebraska Studies). 1897-1902.

Fayant, Frank. Some Thoughts on Speculation (pamphlet). New York, 1909.

Friend, Emil. Stock Exchange Regulation in Germany (Journal of Political Economy, Vol. XVI, pp. 369-374). Chicago, June, 1908.

Gibson, Thomas. Cycles of Speculation. New York, 1907.

—— Elements of Speculation. New York, 1913.

—— Pitfalls of Speculation. New York, 1909.

Goldbaum, F. Auflosung und Wieder Nerstellung der Berliner Produktenborse (Schmoller's Jahrbuch). 1900 and 1901.

Hadley, Arthur T. Economics (Chapter IV). New York, 1896.

Hawley, Fred B. The Risk Theory of Profits (Quarterly Journal of Economics). Cambridge, Mass., July, 1897.

Hickernell, W. F. Business Cycles. New York, 1920.

Jones, Edwin D. Economic Crises. New York, 1900.

Knipper, Chr. Der Berliner Effektenhandel unter dem Einflusse des Borsengesetzes (Schmoller's Forschungen, Vol. 20). 1902.

Leroy-Beaulieu, Anatole. La Regence de l'argent (Revue des Deux Mondes, p. 894). Paris, February 25, 1897.

Lexis, Dr. D. Speculation (Schonberg, Handbuch der Politischen Oekonomie). Tübingen, 1896-1898.

Loeb, Ernst. The German Exchange Act of 1896 (Quarterly Journal of Economics). Cambridge, Mass., July, 1897.

Mackay, Charles. Extraordinary and Popular Delusions. London.

Mason, Frank H. Working of the German Law against Speculation in Grain (U. S. Consular Reports). Dec., 1900.

Michaelis, Otto. Die Wirthschaftliche Ralle des Spekulationshandels (Volkswirthschaftliche Schriften). Berlin, 1874.

Milburn, John G., and Taylor, Walter F. Brief of counsel on behalf of the New York Stock Exchange (Regulation of the Stock Exchange, pp. 529-554). Washington, 1914.

Mill, John Stuart. Principles of Political Economy. London, 1848.

Mitchell, Wesley C. Business Cycles (Publications of the University of California). Berkeley, Cal., 1913.

Nelson, S. A. The A.B.C. of Stock Speculation. New York, 1904.

Pfleger and Geschwindt. Bōrsenreform in Deutschland (Munchener Volkswirthschaftliche Studien).

Plochmann, G. The German Bourse Law (North American Review, pp. 742-748). New York, May, 1908.

Pratt, Sereno S. The Work of Wall Street, 3d ed., pp. 78-91. New York, 1921.

Selden, George C. The Psychology of the Stockmarket. New York, 1912.

Seligman, Edwin R. A. Principles of Economics. New York, 1905.
Sexsmith, Thomas L. The Technical Position of the Market. New York, 1920.
Stafford, William Y. Safe Methods of Stock Speculation. New York, 1911.
Stevens, Albert C. The Utility of Speculation (Political Science Quarterly). New York, Sept., 1892.
Taylor, Walter F. (See under Milburn, John G.).
U. S. Commissioner of Corporations. Report on Cotton Exchanges. Washington, 1908.
U. S. Industrial Commission. Report on the Distribution of Farm Products, Vol. VI. Washington, 1900-1902.

Chapter XVI—The Distribution of Securities

Clark, John B. The Distribution of Wealth. New York, 1899.
Pomroy, Henry K. Testimony (Regulation of the Stock Exchange, pp. 198-209). Washington, 1914.
—— Testimony (Money Trust Investigation, Vol. I, pp. 488, *et seq.*). Washington, 1912.
Pratt, Sereno S. The Work of Wall Street, 3d ed., pp. 126-133; 349-357. New York, 1921.
Schiff, Jacob H. Testimony (Money Trust Investigation, Vol. III, p. 1661). Washington, 1912.
Williams, W. D. The Committee on Stock List (pamphlet). New York, 1920.

Chapter XVII—The Stock Exchange and American Business

Conant, Charles A. Wall Street and the Country. New York, 1904.
Hall, Henry. The Imaginary Terrors of Wall Street (Moody's Magazine). New York, March, 1909.
Sager, Hiram N. Prosperity and the Exchange (Harper's Weekly, Vol. LII, pp. 10-12). New York, April 4, 1908.
Spicer, Ernest E. The Stockmarket in Relation to Trade and Commerce. London, 1920.

Chapter XVIII—The Stock Exchange as an International Market

Conant, Charles A. Testimony (Regulation of the Stock Exchange, pp. 189, *et seq.*). Washington, 1914.
——The World's Wealth in Negotiable Securities (Atlantic Monthly, Vol. CI, pp. 97-104). Boston, Jan., 1908.
Escher, Franklin. Foreign Exchange. New York, 1910.

Gonzales, Vincente. Foreign Exchange. New York, 1920.
Jevons, W. S. Money and the Mechanism of Exchange. London, 1876.
Noble, H. G. S. The New York Stock Exchange in the Crisis of 1914. New York, 1915.
Pratt, Sereno S. The Work of Wall Street, 3d ed., pp. 329-348; 395-404; 411-429. New York, 1921.
Vanderlip, Frank A. and Williams, John H. The Future of our Foreign Trade (Review of Economic Statistics, Harvard University). Cambridge, Mass., April, 1920.
Withers, Hartley. International Finance. New York, 1916.
York, Thomas. Foreign Exchange. New York, 1920.
—— International Dealings in Securities (Administration, Vol. II, pp. 519-532). New York, Oct., 1921.

INDEX

Arabic numerals refer to pages, roman to appendices.

C

D

www.ingramcontent.com/pod-product-compliance
Lightning Source LLC
LaVergne TN
LVHW010515100826
845148LV00001B/15

* 9 7 8 1 4 2 5 5 7 4 0 1 7 *